Introduction to Programming Using

java™

An Object-Oriented Approach

DAVID M. ARNOW • GERALD WEISS

Brooklyn College of City University of New York

ADDISON-WESLEY

An imprint of Addison Wesley Longman, Inc.

Reading, Massachusetts • Menlo Park, California • New York
Harlow, England • Don Mills, Ontario • Sydney • Mexico City
Madrid • Amsterdam

Senior Acquisitions Editor: Susan Hartman
Senior Production Editor: Amy Rose
Compositor: Michael and Sigrid Wile
Text Designer: Melinda Grosser for *silk*
Cover Designer: Diana Coe

Library of Congress Cataloging-in-Publication Data
Arnow, David M.
    Introduction to programming using Java : an object-oriented
approach / David M. Arnow, Gerald Weiss. – Java 2 update
    p.   cm.
    ISBN 0-201-61272-0
    1. Java (Computer programming language)   2. Object-oriented
programming (Computer science) I. Weiss, Gerald. II. Title.
    QA76.73.J38 A77 2000
    005.13'3—dc21   99-28546
                                                CIP

Access the latest information about Addison-Wesley titles from our World Wide Web site: http://www.awlonline.com

This book was typeset in FrameMaker 5.5 on a Power Macintosh G3. The fonts used were Franklin Gothic, ITC Giovanni, and Violation. It was printed on #50 Rolland, a recycled paper.

Cover image © H. Kuwajima/Photonica

1 2 3 4 5 6 7 8 9 10-MA-02010099

To my wife, Fern, my parents, Joseph and Lorraine,
and my children, Yocheved, Zvi, and Shlomo.

Gerald Weiss

To my wife, Barbara, my parents, Aron and Tessa,
and my children, Kera, Alena, and Joanna.

David M. Arnow

Preface

This book is intended as the primary text of an introductory course in programming. It assumes no programming background. The material covered is sufficient for a one- or two-semester sequence that would then be followed by a traditional CS2 (data structures) course.

To the Student

Java is the most recent arrival on the programming language landscape. It is a language that literally appeared at the right place, at the right time. Its popularity is partly due to the hyperbolic expectations surrounding anything related to the Internet, but is also due to several more legitimate factors:

- It borrows many features from other popular languages, most notably C and C++. This familiarity makes it attractive to users of those languages.
- It allows even the novice programmer to produce programs with fairly sophisticated user interfaces, that is, buttons, list boxes, scroll bars, and so on.
- It runs on many machines—PCs, Macintoshes, Sun workstations.
- It provides some fairly sophisticated facilities, making it attractive to many areas of programming.
- Extreme expectations notwithstanding, it does provide convenient access to the Internet.

This book is an introduction to the art of computer programming in Java. It uses this popular language for the above reasons and also because of the following factors:

- Java is an object-oriented language. Object orientation is a somewhat recent approach to programming that has captured the interest of a large segment of the computer science community. Many feel that programming in an object-oriented language is an improvement over working in a more traditional language such as C or Pascal. Over the course of this text we will explain what makes a language object-oriented.

- Java is a relatively *simple* object-oriented language, at least compared to some of the other ones such as C++. Although much of the complexity of C++ is in areas beyond the scope of our book, there are occasional pitfalls into which the beginning student can wander. Many of these *gotchas* cannot occur in Java.
- Programming in Java can be fun. As we pointed out above, even a relative newcomer can use the facilities provided by Java to write a program with a neat look to it.

Despite all the hooplah and fun, and despite the fact that you'll learn to use Java along the way, we have a very specific purpose, to get you to begin to think like a programmer. That means learning to analyze a problem, break it up into its component parts, and devise a solution. It also means practicing a lot. Programming is not learned simply from a book—you have to write lots of computer code. You won't be an expert by the end of our book, but if you pay careful attention and work at the programming exercises, you'll be on your way.

To the Instructor

In this text, we use the Java programming language to introduce students to programming. Our primary focus is on the process of developing software solutions to problems. This process cannot be achieved in the abstract but requires a description of much of the Java language and some of its class library, as well as a discussion of a number of programming techniques and algorithms. The preface elaborates on how we achieve these goals.

A FAQ (frequently asked questions) section follows the preface and covers many of the topics in a question-answer form.

Paradigm

Any introduction to programming must take a stand on the issue of paradigm choice. Our language platform is Java, so it is not surprising that our choice is object-oriented programming (OOP). However, although it is pretty clear what procedural and functional programming entail at the CS1 level, there are a variety of competing visions of what OOP at this level signifies. We concentrate on:

- Defining and using classes
- Issues of behavior and responsibility
- Using composition, rather than inheritance

A typical problem in this text is solved by identifying a primary object in the problem, describing its behavior, and then defining a class to provide that behavior. Usually a small number (often just one) of independent subsidiary classes are defined in the solution process. The solution is completed by writing a small imperative driver, in the form of a main method, for the primary object.

In the early 1990s there was some confusion regarding the relationships between OOP, procedural programming, and imperative programming. By now, it is generally well-understood that even though OOP and procedural programming are distinct paradigms, imperative programming is equally a part of both. Certainly, as soon as assignment enters the picture, one is doing imperative programming, and sending messages that change object state may be viewed as imperative programming as well. Thus, this text teaches both OOP and imperative programming from the start. However, just as the procedures-early approach, long popular in procedural CS1 classes, introduces the mechanics and use of procedure invocation prior to imperative devices such as conditionals and loops, so here do we introduce the mechanics and use of message sending, object creation, and class definition before the `if` and `while` statements. The rationales in both cases are identical; it is preferable to introduce the paradigm first and develop the imperative devices in that context.

In procedural programming, the way to get a task done is to find a procedure that does it and then to invoke the procedure. If no such procedure exists, the programmer has to write one. In OOP, the way to get a task done is to find or create an object of a class whose behavior includes carrying out the task and sending the object a message. If no such class exists, the programmer has to write one.

The last sentence sums up our approach to OOP in this text.

Process

Our primary focus is the process of developing software solutions to problems. To this end, we introduce informal but methodical approaches to four areas:

- Developing a class specification from a problem statement
- Implementing a class given a class specification
- Constructing loops
- Constructing recursive methods

The first two of these approaches are introduced in a rudimentary way in Chapter 4, are fleshed out in Chapter 5, and used consistently thereafter throughout the book. The other two approaches are introduced with iteration and recursion, in Chapters 9 and 11, respectively. They, too, are used consistently thereafter, wherever iteration or recursion appear.

The consistent reuse of these methodical approaches is necessary so that students realize that methodology is not just something to which one pays lip service but that it can really be used to guide the development of solutions to problems.

The emphasis on process means that two common fixtures of introductory texts are rarely seen in this book: dissection of code and incremental modification of code (although the latter does appear in some exercises). Dissection of code requires at the outset the presentation of a complete class implementation without development. It is followed by a careful analysis of the code. This approach is helpful in explaining how code works, but does not explain the process of developing code.

Many of the topics and their order in the text have been determined by our commitment to process. For example, before presenting the approach to class specification and definition, the student must be quite familiar with the idea of classes as repositories of behavior and the use of composition of classes. To that end, Chapter 3 discusses some of Java's predefined classes. We choose the input/output classes for this purpose for the following two reasons:

- There aren't many other useful predefined classes that students can use at this point.
- We are able to show how each models a particular view of input or output and provides a behavior appropriate to that view.

Chapter 3 also shows how composition of these classes can be used to provide interactive, file and network input/output. To the casual observer, Chapter 3 appears to be an unusually detailed introduction to input and output. In fact, input/output is merely the vehicle for laying the foundation for the subsequent development of class specification and implementation.

Language

As we elaborate on the process of program development, we introduce the features of the Java language. To prevent the discussion of the details of those features from digressing too far from the process of developing code, we often defer such discussions to special sections called Java Interludes. In these sections, we fill in the details of features introduced in the course of code development. We also use these sections to introduce language features that do not appear elsewhere but with which a CS1 student should have familiarity. Nevertheless, several features of the Java language are not covered—bit operations, package organization, concurrency synchronization, and inner classes.

GUI Programming

Java's support for graphical user interface (GUI) programming is one of the reasons for its appeal in CS education—both to instructors and students. We have chosen to treat this topic in a series of GUI Supplements, that is, special sections that appear at the end of nearly every chapter in the text. The main body of each chapter is entirely independent of these supplements. Each supplement introduces a new set of GUI tools and/or techniques in a context that reinforces the material introduced in the main body of its chapter.

The advantage of this organization is that it permits instructors to omit GUI programming altogether or introduce it at any time. It also isolates the main body of the text from changes to the class library, primarily in the Abstract Window Toolkit (AWT) portion of the class hierarchy.

We have chosen to work exclusively with applets rather than applications in the GUI Supplements for several reasons:

- It is easy to transform an applet into an application; the reverse is more difficult and in some cases impossible.
- The execution context of applets is more involved and therefore more worthy of a discussion in the text.
- Students love creating "cool" web pages and displaying their applets in them.

Broad coverage of the AWT is beyond the scope of this text. Our approach therefore is to address the following critical issues:

- Applet basics (Chapters 2 and 3)
- Layout—placement of components (Chapter 4)
- Event handling (Chapters 6 and 8)
- Precision in text and graphics (Chapters 5, 11, and 12)
- Threads (Chapters 9 and 10)

Along the way many useful AWT classes and methods are encountered.

Flexibility

Every CS department has its own culture and its own goals for CS1. Even instructors who completely share our approach to OOP in CS1 may want to reorder or even omit some of the topics in this text. Accordingly, we have made every effort to make the introduction of many topics mutually independent. At the same time, we do want the topics in the book to build on each other. It's worth mentioning a few ways in which we resolved this tension.

Inheritance   Inheritance is the subject of Chapter 13. However, an instructor who wishes to introduce this topic earlier in the course can go directly from Chapter 6 to Chapter 13 and work with the first two thirds of that chapter. The last third of the chapter addresses polymorphism and interfaces and uses material from Chapters 9 and 10.

Recursion   Recursion is the subject of Chapter 11. However, an instructor who wishes to introduce recursion earlier in the course can go directly from Chapter 6 (conditionals) to Chapter 11 and work with the first third of the chapter, which does not involve arrays and vectors. On the other hand, an instructor who wishes to omit the topic of recursion can do so—only one of the examples in Chapter 12 depends on it.

Exceptions   Exceptions are the subject of Chapter 14. However, the first half of the chapter is approachable directly after Chapter 6, the second half after Chapter 9. And, of course, the GUI Supplements offer the instructors a great deal of flexibility with respect to the topic of graphic and event-driven programming.

The dependency diagram summarizes these relationships.

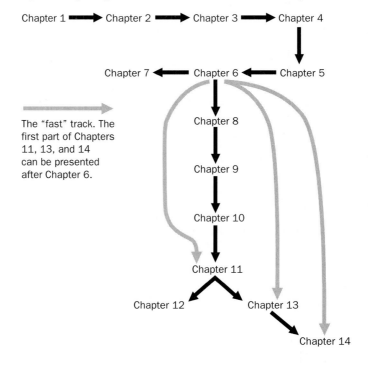

The "fast" track. The first part of Chapters 11, 13, and 14 can be presented after Chapter 6.

An Annotated Overview of the Chapters—The Non-GUI Parts

Chapter 1: Jumping Into Java   Here we introduce the concept of programming as a means of creating models of situations. Our primary goal is to introduce the reader to ideas of classes, objects, and message passing as they are realized in Java. In addition, we present and explain an example of a program and discuss the mechanics of writing and running Java programs.

Chapter 2: Using Objects   In this chapter, the focus is on the mechanics of using objects by sending them messages and all that this entails. We elaborate on the three key ideas presented in Chapter 1—classes, objects, and message passing—and introduce additional OOP and imperative essentials: methods, arguments, return values, signature, prototype, overloading, reference variables, declarations, and assignment. The `String` and `PrintStream` classes are used to illustrate these ideas.

Chapter 3: Using Classes   The chapter begins by showing how to use a class's constructor to create objects. We continue to emphasize the theme of class as a repository for behavior. This idea is reinforced through an exploration of some of Java's input and output classes. This way, we change the CS1-unfriendly, cumbersome

```
BufferedReader br = new BufferedReader(
                      new InputStreamReader(
                         new FileInputStream(
                            new File("infile"))));
```

from a liability to an advantage, as we explain the different behavior modeled by the `File`, `FileInputStream`, `InputStreamReader`, and `Buffered-Reader` classes. Of course, amid all these input and output classes, we can't help making several useful points about I/O (buffers, flushing, reading from web pages), but the essence of the chapter is behavior, not I/O.

Chapter 4: Defining Classes   By this time, the student is quite clear about the first principle of OOP: If anything needs to be done, find an object that can do it and send it a message. Now we show the reader how to define new classes. This definition requires quite a bit in the way of mechanics: class definition structure, method and constructor definition structure, declaration, scope and use of parameters, local variables, instance variables, the `return` statement, the keyword `this`, and static methods. Amid all these necessary language details we try to maintain a focus on the concepts of behavior, interface, and state. Along the way we introduce an embryonic version of the methodical approach to class definition that is presented in the next chapter.

Despite the embryonic character of the approach, once we get through this chapter in our courses, we breathe our first sigh of relief. At this point we can give assignments that involve the definition of new classes. We are now doing OOP.

Chapter 5: The Class Design Process; Method Implementation and Numerical Processing   Ironically, the chapter with the worst title is perhaps the most important chapter in the text. It is here that we introduce a methodical approach to class definition that we use consistently through the rest of the text. In order to have a richer set of classes to develop in the way of examples, and because in any case it is a necessary topic, we introduce for the first time primitive data types—numerical types in particular—their variables, declaration, and associated operations. These are contrasted with the now familiar reference types. The text's theme of programs as models continues in the explanation of floating point numbers as modeling measurable quantities.

Chapter 6: Controlling Behavior—Conditional Execution   This chapter adds to the imperative repertoire of the student by introducing the conditional in its various forms and the `boolean` primitive data type. Equally important is the development of additional classes using the approach introduced in Chapter 5.

Chapter 7: Verifying Object Behavior   This chapter is an overview of the need for and techniques for testing. It introduces the concept of test drivers and module testing. Additionally, it provides the reader with a starting point for the selection and construction of test cases.

Chapter 8: Working with Multiple Objects   Here we introduce a limited form of iteration and the notions of a collection and its enumeration. The `while` loop is introduced and its mechanics are explained but, pending further discussion in the next chapter, its use is confined to two loop patterns:

```
read                        obtain enumeration
while (not eof) {           while (enumeration not empty) {
    process                     get element from enumeration
    read                        process
}                           }
```

The collection we use is the vector class. This provides several advantages:

- The complexity of indexing is deferred until the student can get a handle on the processing of multiple objects.
- No new syntax is required. The vector is just another object and is managed by sending messages to it.

Despite the limitations, once we get through this chapter in our courses, we breathe a second sigh of relief. At this point we can give assignments that are much more reminiscent of "real" applications, as distinct from utility classes.

Chapter 9: Iteration   This is an in-depth chapter on an all-important CS1 imperative programming issue: the construction of loops. A survey of CS1 texts and courses reveals three approaches:

- The null approach—just imitate the code in the book
- Providing a set of loop patterns
- Some kind of methodical development technique, usually a watered-down formal method

In this chapter, we combine the last two of these. We present a methodical technique and then apply it to quite a few typical problems, identifying the results as loop patterns that we can refer to later.

Chapter 10: Organizing Objects   Here we introduce indexing, arrays, and several associated algorithms. Our approach is a gradual one. The student is already familiar with Vectors as objects. So we successively present vector methods such as elementAt, insertElementAt, removeElementAt, and setElementAt, allowing the new index concept and its uses to be introduced without any new syntax. When arrays are introduced, the student is well-versed in working with indices, having encountered sequential and binary search, selection sort, and several self-organizing list algorithms along the way. The only new topics introduced by the use of an array vis-a-vis a vector are the subscript notation and capacity issues.

Chapter 11: Recursion   In this treatment of recursion, we focus on its use as a programming tool. We start with extremely simple problems that some might consider inappropriately easy for recursion. These problems provide a context for developing an approach to constructing recursive solutions. We then take an obligatory detour and discuss how recursion is implemented, but we end that discussion with a stern admonition for the student to focus on how recursion is used and to ignore the implementation issue. We then move to two problems whose complexity cry out for recursion—generating permutations and the classical Towers of Hanoi problem—and end with a comparison of recursion and iteration.

When we get through this chapter in our courses we breathe a third sigh of relief. At this point, we have covered assignment, variables, expressions, numeric and logical and string types, interactive and file I/O, control structures, functions (methods), structures (classes), arrays, several algorithms, recursion, testing and debugging—all the traditional material of CS1. And of course we've done more: classes, objects, messages, plus any material from the GUI supplements that have been included. There are no more sighs of relief save the sigh when the final grades of the course are turned in to the registrar.

Chapter 12: Examples   We present three large—by CS1 standards—examples: a Logo-like turtle, a Web-surveying application, and a simple strategy game. These examples serve as a means to reinforce the techniques of class design and of loop and recursion construction that we presented earlier in the text. In addition, these examples, though not truly large scale, are nevertheless valuable to the CS1 student, giving her or him a glimpse of the complexity and techniques of writing "real" programs.

These examples are not needed for any of the remaining chapters, and only one of them—the web surveyor—requires recursion.

Chapter 13: Extending Class Behavior   Our approach to inheritance is to emphasize the extending of the behavior of a superclass by a subclass. This is the way in which inheritance is most commonly used, especially by the beginning programmer—taking an existing class and adding state and behavior to produce a richer class. We do this in the context of those classes, both pre- and programmer-defined, introduced in Chapters 3–6 for the following reasons:

- The classes that we extended are already familiar to the student.
- The instructor may introduce inheritance earlier in the course, for example, immediately after Chapter 6, if it is so desired.

Extension of state, protected instance variables, overriding, and polymorphism are easily motivated in this context.

The instructor covering the GUI supplements may wish to cover at least the beginning of Chapter 13 somewhat early to give the student some appreciation of how inheritance allows even the beginner to implement complex windowed applications.

We also present an introduction to another use of inheritance: factoring out the common behavior/state of several logically related classes, producing a superclass and a class hierarchy. Again we emphasize the concept of behavior and modeling in which the various layers of the hierarchy model different abstractions of the objects.

Finally, interfaces are presented as a means of forcing a class to conform to a specified protocol.

Chapter 14: Exceptions   Another theme running through the text is that of responsibility-driven programming. Classes should be responsible for as much of their behavior as possible. The other side of the coin is the idea that classes should not be responsible for behavior that is not logically theirs. We present exception handling in this light—as a way for a method to signal an exceptional, not necessarily erroneous, situation to an invoker of that method. Though some knowledge of inheritance is necessary to fully appreciate the structure of an exception hierarchy, the first part of this chapter may be covered at a relatively early stage (after Chapter 6) in order to clarify the throws clause code present in many of the methods signatures.

Appendices   The appendices include:

- A glossary of all the defined terms in the text (containing chapter terminology lists and terms from the GUI Supplements)
- A description of how to write and run Java programs in a Solaris, Windows95/NT, or MacOS environment

- An abbreviated reference manual for all the classes and methods used in the text
- A set of exercises for the GUI supplements

A Summary of the GUI supplements

The following list summarizes the content areas of the GUI supplements.

Chapter 1:   A brief definition of GUI.

Chapter 2:   A brief description of HyperText Markup Language or HTML; document-structure tags, format and typeface control tags, link tags.

Chapter 3:   A first applet: A hello-world paint method, linking an applet in a web page, color, font, and drawing simple shapes.

Chapter 4:   Components (buttons) and containers (panels), layout managers, and border and flow layouts. Setting up a calculator applet.

Chapter 5:   Precision in drawing text providing a nice application of numerical types. Canvases.

Chapter 6:   Event-handling and the JDK 1.1 event model. Completing the calculator applet.

Chapter 8:   Check boxes, lists, and text fields. A visual interactive set object.

Chapter 9:   Threads—a simple controllable clock applet.

Chapter 10: The Game of Life—separation of model, view, and control. More practice with threads.

Chapter 11: Towers of Hanoi animation—separation of model, view, and control. More experience with detailed drawing calculations and more practice with threads.

Chapter 12: Interactive GUI Mancala game. Mouse tracking and a lot more practice in precise graphical calculations.

Chapter 13: The GUI Supplement in the previous chapters introduced the basics of GUI programming: events, components, containers, layout, graphics, and threads. We finish up these supplements with an overview of the AWT class hierarchy, in the context of the topics of inheritance and polymorphism presented in the main body of the chapter. Each of the major AWT classes and interfaces is presented in terms of their modeling behavior, and the manner in which they interact with the AWT's event model.

Chapter 14: Not a GUI supplement at all, but a network programming supplement. A discussion of IP, TCP, sockets, client-server programming, and the relevant Java classes. Simple web and mail clients.

Supplementary Materials

The book's official World Wide Web page, `http://www.awl.com/cseng/titles/0-201-31184-4/`, provides links to the following supplementary materials:

- Source code. This link will download all the completed classes and methods that appear in the text. This material can also be accessed by FTP from: `ftp://ftp.aw.com/cseng/authors/arnow`
- Instructor's Manual. This link provides information on how to obtain this document, which is available only to instructors. In contains solutions to the exercises, additional questions, and problems that are suitable for homework, quizzes, or exams, as well as suggestions on teaching.
- Errors. We have worked hard to avoid these and hope there are few. This link provides a list of those errors that have been discovered.

Contact Us

We welcome questions, comments, suggestions, and corrections. Our email addresses are:

`arnow@sci.brooklyn.cuny.edu`
`weiss@sci.brooklyn.cuny.edu`

To All

Typefaces in Code Examples

It would be useful now to identify the typefaces of the four elements that appear in code examples.

First there is the code itself:

```
class PrefaceExample {
    public static void main(String[] arg) {
      System.out.println("just an example");
    }
}
```

We often add comments to the code, notations that start with `//` or are surrounded by `/*` and `*/`. These are intended to be notations that would actually be part of the code. The second line of the following code is an example of a comment:

```
class PrefaceExample {
    // Just print a short exemplary statement on the display.
    public static void main(String[] arg) {
      System.out.println("just an example");
    }
}
```

As we develop computer code, we will often make a notation that "holds the place" and represents code that is yet to be written. An example of such a placeholder (or pseudocode) appears in the fifth line of the following code:

```
class PrefaceExample {
    // Just print a short exemplary statement on the display.
    public static void main(String[] arg) {
        System.out.println("just an example");
        Additional output statements go here.
    }
}
```

Finally, explanatory remarks that would not normally be part of the code but serve to aid our presentation are placed in shaded screens around the code, often with arrows:

```
class PrefaceExample {
    // Just print a short exemplary statement on the display.   ◀────  A comment
    public static void main(String[] arg) {                            A class with a
        System.out.println("just an example");                         main method
        Additional output statements go here.
    }
}
```

Acknowledgments

As everyone who reads the acknowledgments section of prefaces knows, textbooks are really the result of the collaboration and support of many people. The support we received from Addison Wesley Longman was first rate. We are grateful to Acquisitions Editor Susan Hartman (for her continued confidence in the project), her assistant Julie Dunn (for the great reviewer summaries and taking care of so many logistical details), editor/reviewer Jerry Ralya (who greatly helped to bring out the best we had to offer), Production Editor Amy Willcutt (who managed to keep a dozen different threads running on a very tight schedule), Production Assistant Brooke Albright, copyeditor Roberta Lewis (hers was truly a Herculean labor!), and the compositor Mike Wile and his wife Sigrid Wile (for integrating an ocean of copyedits into the text). We are also grateful to the marketing and sales staff that worked with us: Vice President Bob Woodbury, Sales Manager Michael Hirsch, Marketing Manager Tom Ziolkowski, and Sales Representative Chris Kelly. Their encouragement and insights were most valuable. In addition, there are many others—marketing folk, book designers, cover designers, artists and production staff—whose names we don't know but who have our gratitude. Also essential to this effort were a host of reviewers: Jan Bergandy, University of Massachusetts-Dartmouth; Robert H. Dependahl, Jr., Santa Barbara City College; Eileen Kraemer, Washington University in St. Louis; Ronald L. McCarty, Penn State Erie; David

D. Riley, University of Wisconsin-La Crosse; Jim Roberts, Carnegie Mellon University; Dale Skrien, Colby College; and Ken Slonneger, University of Iowa.

These reviewers made many valuable suggestions and challenged us to refine and at times rethink our approach. The diversity of views, all of which had merit, was an education in itself. We had sought out Addison Wesley Longman because we sensed a great seriousness in their textbook publishing and a great deal of author support. The company surpassed our expectations many times over.

We also benefited greatly from early readings by our colleagues at Brooklyn College: Dayton Clark, Chaya Gurwitz, Steve Jervis, Jacqueline Jones, Keith Harrow, Aaron Tenenbaum, Carol Tretkoff, Paula Whitlock, Stathis Zachos, as well as by our colleague, Douglas Troeger, from our sister school, City College. In addition, thanks to Dale Shaffer of Lander University, Scott Rhodes of Metamorphic Computing and Donald and David Koosis, Anatoliy Goroshnik, and Stas Zeitlin of ISC for the many discussions, suggestions, and comments.

We also acknowledge the Brooklyn College students in our introductory CS classes who worked with various stages of the manuscript as their textbook and whose reactions and comments resulted in many improvements. The original impetus to consider Java in CS1 at Brooklyn College was motivated in part by an NSF grant to introduce "distributed programming across the CS undergraduate curriculum."

The customary place for acknowledgments to the family of the author is at the end. We are not ready to violate tradition, but the thanks we owe to our families for their support, encouragement, involvement, and love belongs not just at the end but at the beginning, the middle, and the end of the acknowledgments because that's where they were with us: all along, at every stage. During the course of the project, our wives and children put up with absences, late nights, early mornings, obsessive muttering about "GUI Supplements," unwashed dishes, late dinners, hasty drives to the Manhattan FedEx office, lots of take-out, and monopolization of the family computer, not to mention bouts of discouragement and worry. In spite of this, they gave us all the love and support one could dream of and we will never forget this. Thank you,

Barbara	Fern
Kera	Yocheved
Alena	Zvi
Joanna	Shlomo

David M. Arnow   **Gerald Weiss**

Preface to the Java 2 Version

If there were a perfect language for introducing programming and computer science and for use as a platform in CS 1, one of its characteristics would be stability. In this regard, the bad news is that Java continues to evolve. The good news, however, is that since the release of Java 1.1, the evolution has not greatly affected matters that are of concern to the beginner. With the release of Java 2 and the steady improvement of Java development and learning environments, CS instructors who have been cautious in adopting Java on stability grounds could take another look. Those of us who have been using Java in CS 1 may spend less time worrying about language version and more time about pedagogy.

Despite its incremental character, the release of Java 2 does require some changes in the examples of code in this text book and at the same time offers some new opportunities. An example of a Java 2-required change can be seen in the run-time type of the return value of the URLConnection's getContent method—formerly a BufferedInputStream, now a FilteredInputStream. The opportunities presented by Java 2 are described below.

Swing

The inclusion of the javax.swing package in the standard Java 2 distribution provides the opportunity to strongly demonstrate the distinction between library and language. It also illustrates how object-oriented programming makes possible levels of abstraction that give both power and flexibility. Accordingly, we have added a second GUI Supplement to Chapter 13 that introduces Swing, illustrates its use, and makes these important points. We cannot overemphasize the fact that the inclusion of this supplement is not to provide a glitzier-than-AWT GUI. Rather, by considering Swing alongside the

AWT the student should come to understand that the classes contained in these packages simply contain different behaviors of the same genre.

Chapter 3, Input/Output, and the AWIO Package

We believe that it is important to give students additional experience with classes, objects, constructors, composition, cascading, and the concept of a class as a model before they go about the business of writing class definitions in Chapter 4. In Chapter 3, the only classes readily available for a rich and involved discussion of these vital topics are those in java.io. Chapter 3 is not [ital for not] an I/O chapter. It is a chapter on working with classes prior to learning how to define them. We therefore encourage instructors not to skip Chapter 3.

Neverthless, for the sake of those instructors who may have alternative approaches to preparing students for Chapter 4 and who therefore wish to bypass Chapter 3, we have provided a very simple i/o package, AWIO, which is presented in Appendix E. Sections 3.1, 3.2, and 3.3 should still be covered, but the remainder of Chapter 3 (sections 3.4-3.7) may be replaced by Appendix E.

The Great PrintStream Constructor Deprecation Controversy

In Java 1.1, the PrintStream constructor was deprecated in favor of PrintWriter despite the fact that System.out and System.err referred to PrintStream objects. We made the conscientious decision, however, to continue to employ the PrintStream constructor. As we explained to countless (well, four or five) instructors who sent e-mail inquiring about this choice that this decision resulted from the combination of the following three points:

(a) System.out and System.err are PrintStream objects.

(b) We want our students to design objects with methods that can receive as arguments both references such as System.out as well as references to output objects constructed from FileOutputStreams and the like.

(c) If we were to stick with PrintWriter, avoid constructing PrintStreams, and simultaneously take (a) and (b) into account, we would have been forced to write some type-checking code or to employ overloading, with a textual duplication of every method with a PrintWriter or PrintStream parameter. Both approaches are, we think, inappropriate for the beginner (and debatable in any case).

The price we pay for this choice is that there will be compiler warning concerning "deprecated methods" in every example that creates a PrintStream object. The fault lies in the persistence of System.out and System.err as Print-Streams. (Alternatively, had PrintStream and PrintWriter both implemented an interface that included print/println as methods, we might have avoided this problem, but at the price of an early discussion of polymorphism.)

Most faculty, we believe, found this a satisfactory explanation. At the heart of all this discussion is the conflict between the laudable goal of a Unicode-based system that supports the linguistic diversity of our planet and the fact that most of the computing infrastructure remains 8-bit byte-oriented and ASCII.

With the release of Java 2, this conflict has been recognized and the Print-Stream constructor has been "rehabilitated": it no longer is deprecated.

David M. Arnow   **Gerald Weiss**

Frequently Asked Questions

Why another CS1 textbook?

Java offers new possibilities in CS1 instruction—a well-designed OOP language, uniquely associated with the Internet and supportive of GUI and network programming at a level that is accessible to the CS1 student.

Why are integers, arithmetic, and conditionals introduced after class design?

We have to cover both OOP and imperative programming. By doing the latter in the context of OOP, the student receives a consistent view of problem solving in an OO environment.

Why applets and not applications in GUIs?

An instructor who wants to do applications instead of applets can easily supply boilerplate that converts our applets to applications. Also, students like to display their own work on web pages.

Why separate the GUIs from the text?

This arrangement permits instructors to start (and stop or even ignore) the GUI topics independently of the rest of the text.

Why two chapters on looping?

The first chapter that mentions looping (Chapter 8, Multiple Objects) introduces the `while` statement and the `Vector` class in a minimal way and uses them together to introduce the student to handling multiple objects. The primary chapter on iteration then follows (Chapter 9, Iteration).

Why recursion so late?

Although recursion appears rather late—at the end of a series of chapters that introduce imperative programming techniques such as iteration and indexing—instructors can introduce it early, right after the conditional.

Why all that I/O in Chapter 3? Why network I/O in Chapter 3?

The I/O classes are a set of related classes, each modeling a different view of an input source or output target. They provide a concrete setting for a discussion of classes as repositories of behavior appropriate to a particular abstraction. This approach gives the student experience with object creation and message sending, including composition and cascading. After we have introduced all those I/O classes, the introduction of network I/O via the URL and URLConnection classes is simple and irresistible. The students love it!

Why is I/O so difficult?

It really isn't. Programmers can, if they choose, encapsulate their preferred abstraction in a class once and for all and use that class. We show how this encapsulation is possible in Chapter 4.

Why a chapter on testing?

We all know that our students should test their programs more carefully. We hope that by focusing on this issue squarely, early in the course, students will understand why testing is important and see how to go about it.

Why not more extensive class library coverage?

This is a CS1 text. Although we do present a number of Java's predefined classes and methods, our primary goal is to introduce the student to the programming process, not to give an exhaustive review of the Java library.

Why inheritance so late?

Our view is that in CS1 the key to object-oriented programming is to present it as behavior-centered, responsibility-driven programming. This can be accomplished with composition. However, it is possible to do the first two-thirds of Chapter 13 right after Chapter 6. Doing so for the sake of giving the student a better understanding of the AWT used in the GUI supplements is a perfectly reasonable approach.

Why exception handling? Why so late?

A full discussion of exception handling requires inheritance. In addition, exception handling would be a digression from the main thrust of the text: the process of class development. The price we pay is the occasional annoying throws-Exception clauses, which we treat as boilerplate until Chapter 14. Instructors may elect to cover the first half of that chapter after Chapter 6, at which point it is accessible to the student.

Why Java Interludes?

Our focus is process—the process of developing classes, loops, recursive methods. The discussions that develop this concept necessarily introduce elements of the Java language. However, we don't want to get so bogged down in language details that the process of class development is obscured. We defer discussion of language details to special sections called Java Interludes.

Where is good, old-fashioned, still widely used, procedural programming?

It's not there. However, in our own classes we have found that students readily pick up procedural programming after learning Java. Just ask them to imagine Java without classes. With a little thought, they will tell you that this implies that there are no objects and no messages and that all methods must be static. You can then tell them that the way to get something done in C is not to find or define a class but rather to find or define a function. From there on it's smooth sailing, really!

Why aren't loops earlier, so students can write "real" programs?
It is possible to create classes that are both useful and closely related to "real" classes without loops. We want the students to develop class definitions as early as possible. Introducing loops before Chapter 4 would delay this development.

What about bit operations, packages, native methods, synchronization, etc., etc.?
Specific topics were omitted either because they were too advanced for CS1 and/or did not fit well with the main goals of the text and could be treated effectively in a later course.

Why the big deal about loop construction techniques in Chapter 9?
Loops *are* a big deal. Students and programmers in general make mistakes. Students benefit from having a clearly stated, consistently followed methodology. We start with simple loops—ones that could be constructed in an ad hoc fashion—because it is easier to develop an approach with simple examples than difficult ones. Because students need repetition to assimilate such an approach, we reinforce it in subsequent chapters as well.

Why not just list the N kinds of loops?
First of all, given any set of N kinds of loops, one can find another, $(N + 1)$st kind. Secondly, students sometimes have trouble matching a problem to a loop pattern. However, we do use and encourage identification of loop patterns when appropriate.

Why vectors before arrays?
In a word: gradualism. Vectors provide collections of multiple objects without indexing. Indexing can then be introduced in the context of familiar message-sending, with no new syntax. Furthermore, the rich set of Vector methods allows the beginner to reorder a collection of objects without getting bogged down in data-movement details. When the time comes to introduce arrays, just about the only thing left is syntax.

Why don't you use notation-X, OOP methodology Y, or design tool Z?
While design methodologies are invaluable for developing larger software systems, our sense is that their introduction in a CS1 course would be too distracting. Such a course must above all teach the students programming. Formal design at such an early stage is too abstract for a student who does not have a grasp of concrete implementation. However, we do feel it is necessary to give the student direction as to how to proceed in class development. We present a fixed procedure for class design, one that is simple

enough for a CS1 student to employ. The procedure provides a solid foundation for formal design methods.

Where are algorithms in this course?

Here and about. Summing, counting, and Newton's method are in Chapter 9. Chapter 10 has sequential and binary search, self-organizing lists, and selection sort. Chapter 11 has permutations and Towers of Hanoi. Other instances of algorithmic thinking appear in Chapter 12.

Why an examples chapter?

Students need at least a glimpse of problems that go beyond the toy problems of CS1.

Contents

3   ⚫ Using Classes 57

4 Defining Classes 89

5 The Class Design Process; Method Implementation and Numerical Processing 141

6 🌑 Controlling Behavior—Conditional Execution 189

7 🌑 Verifying Object Behavior 245

10   Organizing Objects   379

11   Recursion   461

12   Examples   515

chapter 1

Jumping Into Java

1.1   Computers and Programs

Because this is an introduction to computer programming and computer science, you might expect to be given a straightforward definition of a computer. However, a good definition of a computer is not the starting point of the study of computer science—it is, perhaps, a midpoint. For now, we will live with our everyday notions of computers: They are the machines that compute taxes, help us write term papers, monitor airplanes, control car engines, help find the gene sequences in living things, and amuse us with various games.

In this book, therefore, our focus will be on **programs**—texts that can make a computer do a task. Programs are written in a specialized language, called a **programming language.** The content of a program is called **code.** When a computer carries out or runs a program we say that it **executes** the code. Our goal is to teach you how to read and write programs using the Java programming language.

Java is a newcomer among the hundreds of programming languages. Because it was developed recently, its design reflects much of the wisdom acquired over the last few decades concerning program development and programming language design. This acquired wisdom is reflected in Java's design as an *object-oriented* language.

To get an idea of what Java code looks like, let's take a quick look at a small Java program:

```java
import java.io.*;
class Program1 {
    public static void main(String[] arg) {
        System.out.println("Welcome To Java!");
    }
}
```

This program displays the greeting "Welcome To Java!" on the computer's screen. If you look closely, you will see this greeting embedded in the fourth line of the program. There is clearly a relationship between this code and a real event—the display of text on the screen.

In this chapter, we will explore this relationship and show you how to use objects in Java to write your first Java program.

▮ 1.2 ▮   Programs and Models

Nearly all programs model something. What does it mean to model? A **model** is a simplified representation. It includes features that are considered important to its user while neglecting others. For example, when our first program displays "Welcome To Java!" our interest is only in the characters that are displayed, not their color, the brightness of the screen or any other attribute of the screen. A child's plastic car model may show the exterior details and the wheels, but leave out the engine and transmission entirely. A more sophisticated version might include a working engine and realistic interior details. Of course, the more realistic and detailed the model, the greater the effort and expense in its creation.

People have constructed models long before there were computers. Consider the following example:

The service dispatcher for the Brooklyn Edison Gas company keeps track of 43 repairpeople in the Brooklyn area. She does this using a large map and numbered pushpins: pushpin #1 represents repairperson #1, pushpin #2 represents repairperson #2, and so forth. The pins are pushed into the map and represent the most recent location of a particular vehicle. When a repairperson calls in a new position, the pin representing that individual is moved.

The dispatcher also must keep track of customer service requests. When a call for service comes in, the dispatcher places a thumbtack at the customer's location. When service is completed, the thumbtack is removed.

Even though the pushpins are clearly not repairpeople, the dispatcher refers to them as if they were, both in her mind and when talking about them with coworkers. Yet if she came to work one day and discovered that the pushpins were replaced by numbered carpet tacks, she would have no problem referring to the carpet tacks as "repairpeople."

The model is not a complete representation. For example, the thumbtacks on the map don't indicate the kind of problem the customers have. In spite of such apparent lapses, models are acceptable and useful if they *abstract* the important details (the ones that matter) and thereby get the job done.

Although there is a logical correspondence between elements of the model and what they represent, models are physically quite different from the things they represent. There is no way that anyone could look at the dispatcher's map out of context and know what the pins mean. One might guess they were locations of robberies in the last month, or particularly bad potholes, or especially nice restaurants. The meaning of the pins is not inherent in the map but is given by the dispatcher.

Models can also represent an imaginary or hypothetical world, such as "the city of the future." Furthermore, not all models are something physical that you can touch. A model may exist only on paper, or even just in someone's mind—a mental model.

For example, someone planning on financing her college education might hypothetically assume that she will find a certain amount of part-time work during the semester, full-time work in the summer, government loans, school financial aid, and so on. Writing these down and adding them up (in the hope that they will equal or exceed tuition) is an act of modeling. The numbers written down represent hypothetical amounts of money.

Every model, whether representing the real world or a hypothetical one, shares the following characteristics:

- Elements of the model represent other, more complex things; for example, pins can be used to represent repairpeople.
- These model elements exhibit consistent *behavior*; for example, pins indicate position and can be moved.
- The model elements can be grouped into different categories based on their common behaviors; for example, the thumbtacks appear and disappear. Once placed on the map, they are not moved until they are taken off the map. In contrast, the pushpins stay on the map all the time but can be moved about. (This reflects the reality that the repairpeople travel but customer locations either need service or they don't.)
- Actions external to a model element cause the behavior of the model element; for example, a hand moves the pin.

In the preceding example, the model elements are physical objects (pushpins, thumbtacks), the external actions came from a person, and even the behavior was in part carried out by a person. In programming, we dispense with these physical means and instead represent model elements and behavior within a program. At first, we will work with models much simpler than those described in the example. However, as we acquire more tools in the coming chapters, we will be able to build increasingly complex models in our programs.

▊ 1.3 ▊   Objects, Behavior, and Classes

Model elements in Java programs are called **objects.** Objects that share a common behavior can be grouped into distinct categories called classes. In this section, we begin our exploration of these fundamental ideas.

1.3.1   Objects

Let's consider how objects would be used in a Java model of the repair service compared with the model the dispatcher uses of pushpins and thumbtacks.

Dispatcher model	Java model
The service dispatcher models each of her 43 repairpeople with a pushpin.	In Java, the repairpersons would be modeled by 43 Repairperson objects.
The dispatcher models her customers with thumbtacks.	In Java, customers would be modeled by Customer objects.
When a call from a customer comes in, the dispatcher pushes a thumbtack into the board.	In Java, a Customer object would be created.

1.3.2   Behavior

Although they represent distinct repairpeople, Repairperson objects behave similarly; they change their position, they service customers. We say that Repairperson objects share a **common behavior,** meaning they do the same kinds of things. Customer objects also share a common behavior; they do not change their position, they are created when a call comes in, and they eventually disappear from the model (once the service has been completed). We are not surprised that Repairperson objects share a common behavior that differs from the common behavior shared by Customer objects. The two kinds of objects model distinct categories of things (repairpeople and customers).

In the dispatcher's office, the behavior of the pushpins and thumbtacks is determined by her understanding of how real repairpeople and customers behave. In Java, the behavior of an object is determined by a section of code called a class.

1.3.3   Classes

A category of model elements is called a **class** in Java. Defining a class is a matter of writing a section of code that specifies how objects of that class behave or act.

Once a class has been defined, objects of that class can be created. Every object belongs to exactly one class and is said to be an **instance** of that class.

If we were modeling the service dispatcher office in Java, there would be a Repairperson class. It would define the behavior of Repairperson objects and allow us to create Repairperson objects, each an instance of the Repairperson class. There would also be a Customer class. It would define the behavior of Customer objects and allow us to create new Customer objects as calls from customers came in.

Programming in Java amounts to nothing more or less than writing the definitions of classes and using those classes to create objects.

1.3.4 Predefined Objects and Classes

Fortunately, you don't have to constantly reinvent the wheel. Java comes with some classes and objects already defined. In addition, you can use classes and objects that you or other programmers have created and made available. In this way, program code can be reused to create increasingly powerful programs.

In this chapter, we will work with one of these predefined objects. This will help you begin to learn how to use objects.

EXERCISES

1. Consider the following situation. A proofreader for a publisher checks a manuscript for spelling errors. The manuscript is in English but also contains some words in French, German, and Latin. The proofreader uses four dictionaries, one for each of these languages and looks up each word in the manuscript. Identify the relevant classes and objects here.

2. Consider a chess player, playing the great game. To model this activity, what would the relevant classes and objects be? (If you don't know chess, pick another favorite, for example, checkers or othello.)   •

▬▬ 1.4 ▬▬ Our First Object: A Monitor

A program's purpose is to provide information. Most of the programs that you'll write will display information on a *monitor*; that is, it will show information on a computer screen. In this section we'll learn how to use one of Java's predefined objects to control a monitor.

Monitors play two roles. For people, monitors are devices to read information from. For programs, monitors are devices to display information on. These two roles are pictured in Figure 1.1.

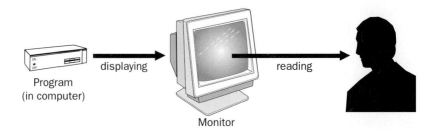

FIGURE 1.1   The roles of a monitor.

First, let us consider how people might use a monitor. To be concrete, imagine two electrical engineers, Erika and Errol, at a desk with a small monitor and a big monitor. Suppose too that Errol is closer to the controls of both. If Erika wants the brightness of the larger one increased, she'll say to Errol, "Turn up the big one's brightness." Consider the separate pieces of information in this command:

- The big one's
- Brightness should be turned
- Up

Errol carries out the request by turning a knob. In doing so, Errol acts as a mere conveyer of the command from Erika to the monitor itself. Using Java terminology, we say that Erika uses a *reference* ("the big one") to identify an *object* (the larger monitor) and send a *message* to it. The message specifies a *behavior* (change brightness) along with *further details* (up or down). Figure 1.2 illustrates how Erika sends a message to the monitor.

Now let's consider how a Java program might use a monitor. To be concrete, imagine a program that displays the greeting: "Welcome Erika and Errol" on the monitor.

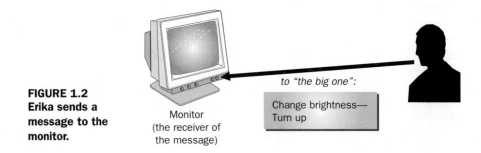

**FIGURE 1.2
Erika sends a
message to the
monitor.**

In Java, the computer's monitor is represented by a predefined object. The object is an instance of the `PrintStream` class. `PrintStream` is one of Java's predefined classes. It does not model all the features of the monitor. For example, a `PrintStream` object cannot control monitor brightness. But it does permit the display of a line containing some particular group of **characters** (letters, digits, punctuation marks, spaces, and so on).

For Erika, "the big one" referred to the monitor of interest. In a Java program, the phrase `System.out` refers to the predefined `PrintStream` object that represents the monitor. We say that `System.out` is a *reference* to that object.

A **reference** in Java is any phrase that is used to refer to an object. Figure 1.3 shows the `System.out` reference in use.

To display the greeting, the Java program sends a message to the `System.out` object. The message specifies a desired behavior that the `PrintStream` class provides, in this case, printing a line (or `println` as it is called) in the `PrintStream` class. Along with the name `println`, further details must be provided, namely the characters we want displayed, "Welcome Erika and Errol."

A **message** in Java is a request for some desired behavior from an object. For Java we looked at the message to the monitor to print a greeting. For Erika we looked at turning up the brightness. Now let's compare the analogous tasks.

- To refer to a monitor,
  - Erika: ". . . the big one. . . ."
  - Java: `System.out` . . .
- To indicate what is needed:
  - Erika: "Turn . . . brightness."
  - Java: . . . `println` . . .
- To convey the necessary details:
  - Erika: " . . . up . . . ."
  - Java: . . . `("Welcome Erika and Errol")`

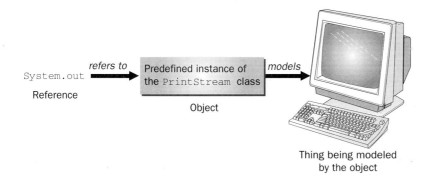

FIGURE 1.3   **An example of a reference.** Here the reference `System.out` refers to a predefined `PrintStream` object that models a monitor.

You can see that Java's actions are analogous to a person's. Both refer to a monitor, indicate what's needed, and both give the necessary details.

1. For each of the following common appliances, list the behaviors one might evoke in a message and indicate in each case what, if any, additional details are needed: dryer, washing machine, video player.

2. Consider the statement, "Tell the personnel department to hire Connie." What words refer to the object receiving the message? What words specify the desired action? What words provide a necessary detail?   •

1.5   Sending a Message to the `System.out` Object

A message in Java is composed of the following:

- The name of the desired behavior (for example, `println`)
- Any further details (for example, `"Welcome Erika and Errol"`) surrounded by parentheses

So to make the monitor greet our two engineers, we must send it this message:

```
println("Welcome Erika and Errol")
```

This Java message is shown in Figure 1.4.

To send a message, we must specify the **receiver,** that is, the object that is the recipient of the message. In Java we write a phrase consisting of:

- A reference to the receiver object (for example, `System.out`)
- A period
- The message we want to send

So to send our `println` message to the monitor object we must write the following:

```
System.out.println("Welcome Erika and Errol")
```

Form: *behavior (details)*

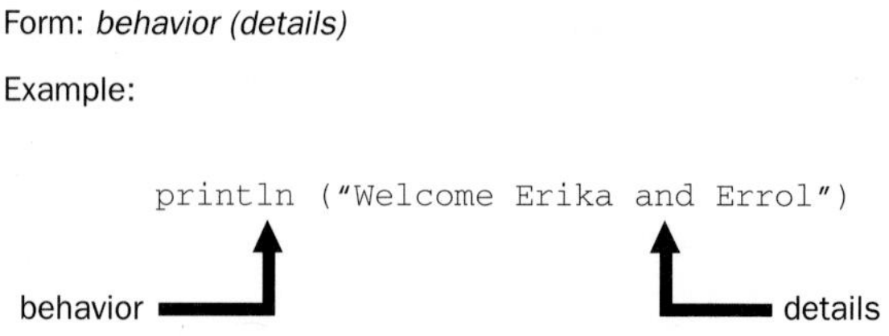

FIGURE 1.4
Messages in Java. A message contains the behavior desired, with further details in parentheses.

Example:

```
println ("Welcome Erika and Errol")
```

behavior ⟶   ⟶ details

Form: *reference • message*
Example:

FIGURE 1.5   Messages in Java. The reference.message form is used to send a message to a receiver.

Figure 1.5 illustrates the parts of this Java message.

When this statement is executed, the `System.out` object receives the `println("Welcome Erika and Errol!")` message and in response prints the greeting on the screen. In this example, pictured in Figure 1.6, `System.out` is a reference to the receiver of the `println` message.

1.5.1   Java statements

Sending a message to an object is an action that the programmer specifies and that the computer carries out when the program runs. In Java, all actions are specified in **statements**.

To make a Java phrase that sends a message to an object a complete Java statement, we add a semicolon to the end.

```
System.out.println("Welcome Erika and Errol");
```

just as we add a period to complete the end of a sentence in English. (See Figure 1.7.)

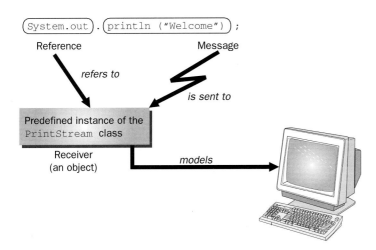

FIGURE 1.6   The role of the receiver in sending a message.

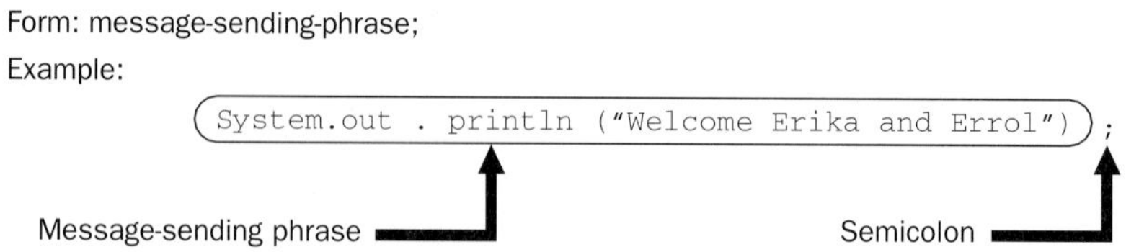

Form: message-sending-phrase;

Example:

System.out . println ("Welcome Erika and Errol") ;

FIGURE 1.7   A statement that sends a message.

Message-sending phrase ▬

Semicolon ▬

EXERCISES

1. Write a Java statement that makes the monitor display your full name.

2. Consider the statement that you wrote in the above exercise. Identify the following elements: the reference, the message, the name of the behavior.

1.6   A Java Program

Much of the joy of programming comes from seeing our programs in action. Even a program that just prints an announcement is an important first step, and it *is* modeling something—a human being making an announcement. Suppose we want to write a program that displays the words "This is my first Java program" on the screen and right below that displays "but it won't be my last." The following ideas provide you with a guide for writing the program described.

- There is a predefined object (referred to by System.out) whose behavior includes displaying characters on the screen.
- The way to get the behavior is to send a message.
- The first part of the message must be the name of the method that provides the behavior (println).
- The rest of the message must consist of arguments containing information the object needs to do the job (the line to be displayed).

Since there are two lines to be displayed, we must send two messages to the System.out object. This recognition leads to the following kernel of a Java program, consisting of a pair of statements:

```
System.out.println("This is my first Java program");
System.out.println("but it won't be my last.");
```

To make this a valid Java program, we must choose a name for it, and then surround it with some additional notation. Names in Java are called **identifiers**. An identifier is a sequence of letters, digits, or underscores. The first character must be a letter. A good name for this program is Program1. Using that name and adding the required notation, we can write our Java program as:

```
import java.io.*;
class Program1 {
    public static void main(String[] arg) {
        System.out.println("This is my first Java program");
        System.out.println("but it won't be my last.");
    }
}
```

For the rest of this chapter and also Chapter 2, the first three lines

```
import java.io.*;
class program-name {
        public static void main(String[] arg) {
```

and the last two lines

```
        }
}
```

will be the beginning and end of each program that we write.

The appendices describe the steps you must take on a particular computer to type in and run this program. If you have a computer close at hand and wish to do so, you could skip ahead to that section now in order to find out how to run this program.

1. Write a program that prints out your name and your complete address.

2. Write a program that prints out a message that is obviously false.

3. Write a program that does absolutely nothing.

EXERCISES

Identifiers, Statement Order, Format, and Comments

The purpose of this book is to teach programming. Lest that all-important goal suffer from distractions involving the details of the Java language, we will frequently omit some details and variations from our discussion. To fill in the gaps and to review and summarize, we will periodically have Java Interlude sections such as this one that look solely at the language itself.

JAVA RULES

Just as English has a set of rules that tells us what's an acceptable sentence, Java has a set of rules that tells us what's an acceptable program. We call code legal if it does not violate these rules.

IDENTIFIERS

A class or a behavior must have a name—an **identifier.** Be careful: Java recognizes the distinction between uppercase and lowercase letters. That means that `system` and `System` are different identifiers! If you write `system` when you mean `System`, your program will not work.

KEYWORDS

Keywords are special words with predefined meanings in the Java language. Words like `import`, `class`, `public`, `static`, and `void` are all keywords. `PrintStream` is not a keyword—it is the name of a predefined class.

THE ORDER OF JAVA STATEMENTS

The order of statements matters because they are executed by the computer in the order of appearance. So

```
System.out.println("One two three");
System.out.println("Four five six");
```

yields a different order of messages and therefore a different display on the screen than:

```
System.out.println("Four five six");
System.out.println("One two three");
```

PROGRAM FORMAT AND COMMENTS

The Java program that we wrote in the last section was written in a particular format. The statements of the programs were indented using the TAB key several times. Each statement appeared on one line, and one line never contains more than one statement.

The rules of Java are very flexible with respect to format. The chief format rule is that two adjacent identifiers or keywords must be separated by at least one space. Thus we could not legally write:

```
classProgram1 ...
```

instead of `class Program1`.

But one could legally have written the example program as:

```
import  java.io.*;  class  Program1  {  public  static  void
main(String[]
arg) { System.out.println(
"This is my first Java program"); System.out.println(
"but it won't be my last."); } }
```

Though legal, this code is very difficult to read. One of our goals when we write code is to make it readable. Readability is important because programs have to be periodically updated and also *debugged* (examined for errors and corrected) by people who are often not the ones who originally wrote them. At this point, it is too early to provide a detailed list of explicit formatting rules. However, here is a start:

- Write one statement per line. If the statement is too long to fit on a line, break it up at some reasonable point and indent by one tab past the beginning of the statement.
- Use the TAB key, not the space bar, to indent. This will make it easier to have nicely aligned left margins.
- In general, imitate the style used in this textbook.

As we present additional features of the Java language, we will show you how to format them.

COMMENTS

Java allows the programmer to write comments in the code. Comments are notes that are ignored by the computer, but that appear in the program in order to clarify it to the reader. There are two ways of writing comments in Java, as surrounded comments or line comments.

SURROUNDED COMMENTS

Any text that starts with /* and ends with */ is a comment. The /* and */ do not have to be on the same line. Thus,

```
/*
 * This program prints out several greetings
 */
```

is a legal comment.

LINE COMMENTS

Once // appears on a line, all text on the rest of the line is a comment. Thus,

```
// This program prints out several greetings.
```

is also a legal comment.

Because comments are ignored by the computer, you can put them anywhere in your program.

As with program format, though the rules for comment placement are quite liberal, there are certain conventions. Here are a few guidelines:

- There should be a comment before the line that starts with the keyword class, indicating the purpose and behavior of the code.
- Comments should not explain how Java works. Assume that the reader of the program understands Java. Rather, comments should give insights not readily apparent from the code.
- Comments should not appear in the middle of a statement.

As an example of the use of comments, here is a program that prints several greetings:

```java
import java.io.*;
/*
 *  Program1: Announces my first Java program experience and my intent to continue
 */
class Program1 {
    public static void main(String[] arg) {
        System.out.println("This is my first Java program");
        System.out.println(" but it won't be my last.");
    }
}
```

EXERCISES

1. For each program you wrote at the end of Section 1.6, add an appropriate comment in the program

2. Look at the program below. Determine if it is a legal Java program. Will it run correctly? Is there anything wrong with it?

```java
import java.io.*;
/*
 *  MyName: Displays my name to the user
 */
class MyName {
        public static void main(String[] arg) {
        System.out.println("718-951-5861");
        }
}
```

1.7 Mechanics

Writing down a Java program on a piece of paper will not by itself make the computer do anything. First, the program has to be made accessible to the computer. Second, the program must be translated into a form that the computer can execute. Finally, the computer must be directed to execute, that is, carry out, the instructions of the translated program.

Fortunately, these three steps are quite easy to undertake, in part because there are programs that carry out each of these steps in a nearly automatic fashion. The precise details of these programs vary from one computer system to another. In this section we will describe the general steps. Details for some specific systems (including Windows95, Solaris, and Macintosh) are provided in the appendices.

1.7.1 Accessibility

A program written on paper with pen is not accessible to a computer. To make a program accessible we need to create a file containing the program. A **file** is simply a collection of information that has a name and that can be stored on the disk of a computer system. Most computer application software (word-processors, drawing programs, spreadsheets, etc.) involves the creation of files. A user writes a letter in a word-processor and wants to save it, so she directs the word-processor software to save it in a file. To write a program and save it in a file we need an application program called an *editor*. An editor is similar to a word-processor in that it allows the user to type in text that will be saved in a file. Where it differs is that it lacks text-formatting, typeface control, and other word-processing-oriented features (such as spell-check). Furthermore, a good editor program will have some features that help in writing programs (for example, displaying comments in a different color to readily differentiate them from program text).

So, step 1 involves starting an editor program, typing in the program, and saving the resulting changes in a file. Try this using the first Java program developed in this chapter:

```
import java.io.*;
class Program1 {
/*
 * Program1: Announces my first Java program experience and my intent to continue
 */
  public static void main(String[] arg) {
      System.out.println("This is my first Java program");
      System.out.println("but it won't be my last.");
  }
}
```

Java has strict rules regarding the name of the file in which you save your Java program. The file name must be of the form X.java where X is the name of the program. So this program would have to be stored in file named:

```
Program1.java
```

1.7.2   Preparing for Execution: Translation

Even after the Java program has been stored in a file in the computer system, the computer cannot immediately carry out its instructions. That is because computers can only carry out instructions of languages that are much more primitive than Java. These languages are called *machine languages.* Each different kind of computer has its own unique machine language. Though simple, machine languages are so inconvenient for writing programs that they are almost never used. Instead, we use *high-level languages,* such as Java and C++, to write our programs. A bridge is needed between the high-level languages and the machine languages. Two such bridges are compilers and interpreters.

We can use a program called a **compiler** to translate the program from the high-level language to machine language. The compiler accepts a file that contains a high-level language program as input and produces a file containing a machine language program that is equivalent to the input.

Another approach is to use a program called an **interpreter.** An interpreter also uses the high-level language program as input, but instead of translating the whole program, it carries out the instructions of the program directly.

So, if a compiler encountered a program in a high-level language that contained instructions to print the numbers from 0 to 99, it would produce a machine-language program that contained instructions to print the numbers. On the other hand, if an interpreter encountered such a program, it would directly print the numbers from 0 to 99.

1.7.3   Execution

Once a program has been translated into machine code, you have to tell the computer to execute the program. On some computers, all you have to do is point to an icon on the screen that represents the file containing the machine code, and double-click the mouse; on other computers, you have to type the name of the file containing the machine code, and hit the RETURN key. The details of how this is handled depends on a program called the *operating system.* Every computer system has such a program. Its chief task is to load translated programs into memory, and set things up so that the computer will carry out the instructions in these programs.

Java involves a combination of the two approaches—compiling and interpreting. Java programs are translated using a Java compiler. However, the Java

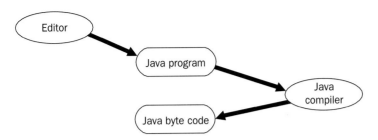

FIGURE 1.8 **Creating an executable Java program.**

compiler translates the program not to true machine language but rather to an idealized form of machine language called Java Byte Code. Suppose you have a file called X.java that contains Java code. When you invoke the Java compiler on this file, the result is called X.class and contains Java Byte Code. Since this byte code file does not contain real machine code, it cannot be directly executed by any computer. Rather, a Java interpreter is used. Note, however, that the Java interpreter does not interpret the Java program (that is, the statements in X.java)—rather it interprets the byte code file (X.class) produced from the Java program. Figures 1.8 and 1.9 illustrate the processes of creating an executable program and then executing it.

There are two advantages to this scheme. First, by translating the Java program to Java Byte Code instead of real machine code, the resulting translation is not bound to any particular machine—it can be executed on any machine that has a Java interpreter. Second, because the Java interpreter has to interpret only the simpler byte code rather than the more complicated Java program, it is relatively easy to write Java interpreters and they can be embedded in other programs, notably Web browsers such as Netscape Navigator and Internet Explorer (more about all these later). This makes it possible for people to

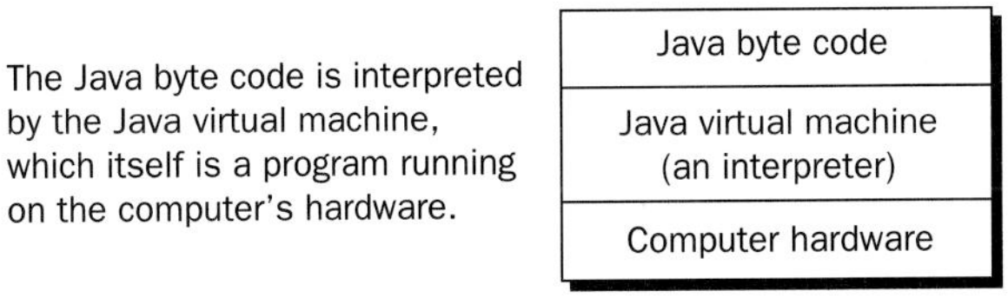

The Java byte code is interpreted by the Java virtual machine, which itself is a program running on the computer's hardware.

Java byte code
Java virtual machine (an interpreter)
Computer hardware

FIGURE 1.9 **Executing a Java program.** The Java Byte Code is interpreted by the Java virtual machine, which itself is a program running on the computer's hardware.

write Java programs, put their translations (byte code files) into their Web pages and for these programs to be carried out by computers of all varieties.

In order to start writing and running Java programs, ask your instructor, system administrator, help desk, or friend:

- What editor do I use? How do I invoke it?
- How do I invoke the Java compiler? How do I tell it what Java program file (`.java` file) to compile?
- How do I invoke the Java interpreter? How do I tell it what Java byte code file (`.class` file) to interpret?

The appendices answer these questions for a few systems. However, if you are using a different system, or one that has been customized in some way, the answers will be different.

1.8   Time

In the previous section, we identified three activities that are done by programmers: writing the program, compiling the program, and running the program. Different issues arise in each of these phases, and it helps to refer to the time period in which each activity takes place: program-writing time, *compile-time*, and *execution-time* (also called *run-time*).

Some aspects of programming occur at one time but not another. Consider comments in a program. They are added to the program at program-writing time. They are ignored by the compiler at compile-time, and do not even exist at execution-time.

Or consider the errors that may occur during programming. They may be made by the programmer at program-writing time. They may be detected at compile-time or execution-time. For example, suppose we mistakenly wrote our first program as:

```
import java.io.*;
class Program1 {
   public static void main(String[] arg) {
      Sistem.out.println("This is my first Java program");
      Sistem.out.println("but it won't be my last.");
   }
}
```

We would be informed of the mistake (`Sistem` instead of `System`) at compile-time. That is, when we invoke the compiler to translate this Java program into byte codes, the compiler will detect the error, print an error message, and refuse to complete the translation (no `.class` file will be produced).

On the other hand, suppose the purpose had been to write additional Java programs. If we mistakenly wrote:

```
import java.io.*;
class Program1 {
    public static void main(String[] arg) {
        System.out.println("This is my first Java program");
        System.out.println("but it will be my last.");
    }
}
```

the Java compiler would not detect the error of printing `will be my last` instead of `won't be my last`. How could it know our intentions? The compiler will produce a `.class` file, and it won't be until execution-time, when we run the program, that we will have a chance to notice the error. Unlike a compile-time error, however, there will be no obvious indication in the output that an error has occurred. Rather, one must be familiar with the program's purpose, be aware of the expected output, and see that the expected result was not produced.

SUMMARY

Programs are texts that make a computer carry out a task. Java is a programming language that can be used to construct such texts. From another perspective, programs can be viewed as models. In Java, the basic model elements are called objects. Objects are grouped together in categories on the basis of common behavior. These categories are called classes. In this chapter, you have seen a Java program that displays a greeting on a computer screen by sending a message to an object that models a computer screen. This object is an instance of a class called `PrintStream`, a class that models output pathways. `PrintStream` is one of many predefined classes that Java provides. Later in this text, you will learn to define your own classes.

To send a message in a Java program, we specify the receiver object and the message itself. The receiver is specified using a reference—a phrase that refers to an object. For example, `System.out` is a reference to the object that models a monitor. The message is specified by the name of the desired behavior (`println`, for example) and additional information in parentheses.

At the heart of the Java programs that we considered here is a sequence of Java statements—phrases that send messages, written with semicolons after them.

Once a Java program has been written it needs to be translated by the Java compiler into Java Byte Code before it can execute on the computer. The instructions in the translated program can then be interpreted—carried out— by the Java interpreter.

STUDY AID: TERMINOLOGY REVIEW

behavior Any action that an object may take in response to a message.

character A distinct elementary symbol, often corresponding to a single keyboard keystroke; letters, digits, punctuation marks, space, and tab are all examples of characters.

class A category of objects that share the same behavior.

code A section of text written in some programming language such as Java.

common behavior The behavior shared by objects in the same class. It is this behavior that defines the class.

compiler A program that translates code written in a high-level programming language into machine language.

execute To carry out instructions of program code.

file A collection of information that has a name and that can be stored on a disk of a computer system.

identifier A sequence of characters which may be used as a name in a Java program. An identifier typically consists of an alphabetic characters(A–Z, a–z) followed by zero or more alphanumeric characters (A–Z, a–z, 0–9).

instance A particular object of a class.

interpreter A program that directly carries out the statements of a high-level programming language.

Java The name of one of the most recent and popular programming languages; also the one used in this text.

keyword A word with a special, predefined meaning in Java language.

message The mechanism by which an object's behavior is invoked. A message consists of the name of the behavior along with further details.

model A representation of something. Models are usually simpler than the object they are representing; they only contain those aspects relevant to the user of the model.

object An entity in Java that models something; a member of a class.

program A Java text that can be compiled and executed.

programming language A specialized language for writing programs.

receiver An object to which a message is sent.

reference   A value or expression that refers to an object, thereby allowing us to send messages to the object.

statement   A sentence of the Java programming language. A statement represents an action to be carried out.

QUESTIONS FOR REVIEW

1. Can an *object* belong to more than one class?

2. What is a *message* composed of?

3. What is the importance of proper *indentation*? What about program *comments*?

4. Describe the development process of a program from its creation through its execution.

5. What are the advantages of Java Byte Code?

FURTHER EXERCISES

1. Write a program that prints out the first two lines of itself.

2. In the previous exercise, you wrote a program that reproduces itself partially. Have you ever heard of programs that do that entirely? What are they called? Moving beyond the world of programming, what sorts of things in the real world reproduce themselves? What do you make of this common attribute?

Introduction

The interest in Java displayed by the computer world has centered upon the ability of Java programs to be run across the Internet. An essential element of this capability is the fact that Java makes it relatively easy to write programs that employ fancy **graphical user interfaces,** that is, interfaces that use graphic elements such as buttons, menus, scrollable windows, and graphical drawings to communicate with end users.

We will introduce you to this aspect of Java in supplementary sections at the end of each chapter. The examples will draw often upon material covered in the chapter proper, but will incorporate it into a program with a graphical user interface (**GUI**) suitable for inclusion on the World Wide Web.

chapter 2

Using Objects

2.1　Introduction

Chapter 1 presented some fundamental Java concepts that enabled us to create our first program. In that program, we sent a message to a predefined object of the `PrintStream` class in order to print an announcement on the screen.

In this chapter we will continue our exploration of the use of Java's predefined objects. As we proceed, we'll acquire some additional tools and techniques that will be useful in working with all objects.

2.2　Using `PrintStream` Objects

In the last chapter we sent messages of the form

```
println("something to display")
```

to the `PrintStream` object that `System.out` refers to. When `println` is used, the next character that is displayed appears at the beginning of the next line.

Another kind of message we can send to a `PrintStream` object is of the form:

```
print("something to display")
```

When `print` is used, the next character that is displayed appears on the same line. Thus

```
System.out.print("JA");
System.out.print("VA");
```

causes the monitor to display:

```
JAVA
```

while

```
System.out.println("JA");
System.out.println("VA");
```

causes the monitor to display:

```
JA
VA
```

Repeatedly invoking `print` builds a single line of output. Invoking `println` guarantees that the next character displayed will appear on a new line.

`PrintStream` provides a second version of the `println` method, one that requires no additional information. Invoking *that* `println` method, as in:

```
System.out.println();
```

simply causes the `PrintStream` object referred to by `System.out` to display subsequent output on the next line.

EXERCISES

1. Write two different sequences (each containing three statements) that display a single line, "Malice towards none, charity for all," on the monitor.

2. Write the words "System Unavailable" on separate lines, double spaced. •

java interlude

References, Methods, and Messages

A reference in Java is any phrase that refers to an object. By this we mean a reference can be used to send a message to the object. Strictly speaking,

System.out is not an object, but a reference to one. However, rather than writing the cumbersome phrase, "the object to which System.out refers," we shall often simply write "the System.out object." This usage is acceptable provided we remember that System.out is a reference to the object, not the object itself.

As we saw earlier, it is the **behavior** of objects that distinguishes those in one class from those in another class. In Java, class behavior is specified by methods. A **method** is a section of Java code within a class that provides a particular behavior. Associated with the method is an identifier that names the method: the **method-name**.

A class's methods determines the kind of messages that can be sent to objects of that class. You already know three of the PrintStream class's methods:

- println, with additional information
- println, with no additional information
- print, with additional information

The additional information items that are sometimes provided in a message are called the **arguments**. The print and one of the println methods of PrintStream each require one argument.

With these terms in mind, we can give a more precise form for a message:

methodname (*arguments*)

Some methods, as we shall see, require more than one argument.

WHEN A MESSAGE IS SENT

Java statements are ordinarily executed by the computer in the order they occur in. However, when a **message** is sent to an object (the receiver), the execution of the sending code is suspended until the receiver gets the message and acts on it. The receiver then executes the method indicated in the message. We call this process *invoking the method*. Eventually, the receiver finishes executing its method. At that point, the execution of the sending code is resumed. We say in that case that the method (of the receiver) *returns* to the sending code.

IDENTIFIERS, AGAIN

Java has certain conventions for selecting names. The first letter of a class name should be uppercase (as in PrintStream). The first letter of a method name should be lower case (as in print and println). All other letters should be lowercase except where needed to make it easy to see multiple words within an identifier—that's why we wrote PrintStream instead of Printstream.

EXERCISES

1. For each Java statement below, identify the reference, the method-name, and the arguments (or indicate if there are none).

```
System.out.print("Ad Astra Per Aspera");
car54.ask("Where are you?");
smart.get();
x.y("a","b");
```

2. What is meant by the term *invoking a method?*

2.3   The `String` Class

Another class that Java predefines is named `String`. It models a sequence of characters (letters, digits, punctuation marks, spaces, or special symbols). Such sequences are commonplace (license plate numbers, names, a line in a love letter, an entire essay).

In Java, any group of characters in double quotes, like

```
"Welcome Erika and Errol"
```

is a reference to a `String` object that models precisely that character sequence. Thus, `"Welcome To Java"` is a reference to a `String` object modeling the characters `W`, `e`, `l`, and so on. We have already seen this kind of a reference; it is the argument we send in `println` and `print` messages to `System.out`, as shown in Figure 2.1.

`String` references of this kind are called **`String` Constants**. (See Figure 2.2.)

What can we do with a reference to a `String` object? We have already seen one use—as an argument to a message:

```
System.out.println("Welcome To Java Programming!");
```

References are also used to send messages to the objects they refer to. We use `System.out`, a reference to a `PrintStream` object, in this way when we

FIGURE 2.1   A `String` object is referenced within quotes.

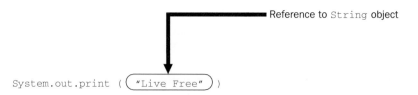

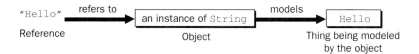

FIGURE 2.2 `String` **constants: References to String objects.** `"Hello"`, a `String` constant, is a reference. It refers to a `String` object that models the character sequence H e l l o.

send `println` messages to that object. Sending messages to objects is how we evoke their behavior.

We can send `print` and `println` messages to `PrintStream` objects. What kind of messages can we send to `String` objects? That question is the same as the following two questions:

- What behavior does the `String` class provide?
- What methods do the `String` class provide?

One of the methods `String` provides is called `toUpperCase`. The `toUpperCase` method requires no arguments. To send a `toUpperCase` message to the `String` object that `"ibm"` refers to, we follow the form:

   reference . *methodname* (*arguments*)

and write:

   `"ibm".toUpperCase()`

The receiver of the `toUpperCase` message is the `String` object to which the `String` constant `"ibm"` refers. Figure 2.3 illustrates the process of sending a `toUpperCase` message.

You might think that this method changes the *receiver*, making it all uppercase. However, the designers of the `String` class decided that a `String`

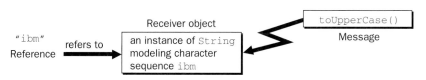

FIGURE 2.3   Sending a `toUpperCase` **message.** The `"ibm".toUpperCase()` message is sent to the String referred to by `"ibm"`.

method should never change the `String` itself, but rather produce a new `String` object with the desired change. So, the `toUpperCase` method creates a new object, one that is also an instance of the `String` class. This object has the same characters as the original except that all the letters are uppercase.

A new object is useless unless there is a way to reference it. So besides creating a new all-uppercase `String` object, `toUpperCase` provides a reference to this object. In Java lingo we say that `toUpperCase` **returns** a reference to the new object. Alternatively, we say the **return value** of `toUpperCase` is a reference to a `String` object. In the Java language, when a method such as `toUpperCase` returns a reference, the phrase that sent the message becomes that reference after the method has completed executing and control returns to the sender of the message.

That means that

```
"ibm".toUpperCase()
```

not only sends a `toUpperCase` message to the `"ibm"` object, but is also a reference to the result of that message, that is, it is a reference to the newly created `"IBM"` object. See Figure 2.4 for an illustration of a returned reference.

What can we do, then, with an expression like `"ibm".toUpperCase()` if it represents a reference to a `String` object? Remember, we can take two actions with references. We can

- Send messages to the object the reference refers to
- Send the reference itself as an argument in a message to another object

For example, since the `println` method of `PrintStream` requires a `String` reference as an argument, we could write:

```
System.out.println("ibm".toUpperCase());
```

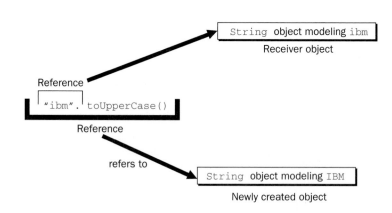

FIGURE 2.4   A returned reference to a new object. The entire expression `"ibm".toUpperCase()` is the reference returned by `toUpperCase`.

We would thus send the reference returned by `toUpperCase` to the `println` method as an argument. In effect, we are sending a reference to the `String` `"IBM"` to `println`.

1. Which of the following are references? For those that are, identify the class of the object that is referred to and briefly describe the object.

```
System.out
System.out.println("hello, world");
"hello, world"
"hello, world".toUpperCase()
toUpperCase()
```

●

2.4 Methods, Arguments, and Return Values

We have so far encountered three methods: (1) `print` and (2) `println`, provided by the `PrintStream` class, and (3) `toUpperCase`, provided by the `String` class. The `print` and `println` methods do not return a reference to an object, but the `toUpperCase` method does. The latter does not receive any arguments, whereas the `print` and `println` methods both receive a reference to a `String` object, a reference such as `"hello, world"`.

As we proceed, we will learn many more methods from these and other classes in Java. Becoming familiar with a method means knowing what it returns and what it receives as an argument. Here are the characteristics of the four methods encountered so far:

Class	Method	Return value	Arguments received
PrintStream	println	none	none
PrintStream	println	none	reference to a String object
PrintStream	print	none	reference to a String object
String	toUpperCase	reference to a String object	none

The **signature** of a method consists of its name and a description of its arguments. The **prototype** of a method consists of a description of its return value along with its *signature*. The preceding table gives us information about the prototypes (and therefore the signatures) of four methods.

2.5   Reference Variables

A **variable** is an identifier that can be given a value, as in the letter x in "let x be 5." It is called a variable because it can contain different values at different times, that is, its value can vary. A **reference variable** is a variable whose value is a reference.

Reference variables allow us to save a reference for a later or repeated use. For example, suppose we had an identifier `line` that had somehow been given the following reference value:

```
"xxxxxxxxxxxxxxxxxxxxxxxxxxxxxxxxxxxxxxxx"
```

Such a variable is called a *String reference variable,* because the reference it is given is a reference to a `String` object.

If we wanted to print three lines of x's, we could write:

```
System.out.println(line);
System.out.println(line);
System.out.println(line);
```

When the argument is evaluated, the value of the variable replaces the variable. It is as if we had written:

```
System.out.println("xxxxxxxxxxxxxxxxxxxxxxxxxxxxxxxxxxxxxxxx");
System.out.println("xxxxxxxxxxxxxxxxxxxxxxxxxxxxxxxxxxxxxxxx");
System.out.println("xxxxxxxxxxxxxxxxxxxxxxxxxxxxxxxxxxxxxxxx");
```

If at various places in our program we needed to print a line of x's of this sort, it is easier to use `line` than to type the same number of x's out each time.

If we wanted a line of uppercase X's, we could write:

```
System.out.println(line.toUpperCase());
```

Again, the value of the variable, a reference to a `String` of x's, replaces `line`. The `toUpperCase` message is sent to the `String` of x's, creating a `String` of X's. It is as if we had written:

```
System.out.println(
    "xxxxxxxxxxxxxxxxxxxxxxxxxxxxxxxxxxxxxxxx".toUpperCase());
```

2.5.1   Declaring Reference Variables and Saving References

To introduce a reference variable in a Java program, we write the class of the object to be referenced followed by the name (an identifier of our choice) of the reference variable:

```
String        greeting;  // Will refer to a String modeling a greeting.
PrintStream   output;    // Will refer to the same PrintStream object that
                            System.out does.
```

These statements (note the required semicolon!) are called declarations. A **declaration** is a statement that introduces a variable in a program. It supplies an identifier that will be the name of the variable and a type, such as `String` or `PrintStream`, that establishes what kind of value the variable can possess. The first declaration establishes that `greeting` is a variable that can contain a reference to a `String` object, and the second establishes that `output` is a variable that can contain a reference to a `PrintStream` object. We say that we have *declared* `greeting` as a `String` reference variable and `output` as a `PrintStream` reference variable. Until a variable is declared in a program, you can't use it. Any attempt to do so will result in a compile-time error.

To give a variable a value, we use an **assignment** statement:

```
greeting = "Hello";
```

This statement *assigns* to `greeting` the reference `"Hello"` so that they both refer to the same object. We could then write

```
System.out.println(greeting);
```

instead of

```
System.out.println("Hello");
```

Figure 2.5 illustrates the result of executing `greeting = "Hello";`.

The general form of the assignment statement is:

variable = value ;

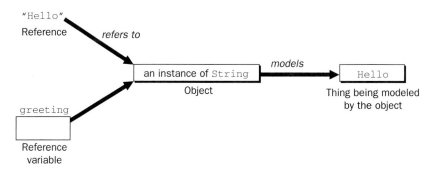

FIGURE 2.5   `String` reference variables and `String` objects. The `String` constant `"Hello"` and the variable `greeting` refer to the same object. Therefore, `"Hello"` and `greeting` can be used interchangeably to send messages to this object or to refer to it in an argument.

The *value* is *assigned* to (saved in) the *variable*. The value must have the same type as the variable.

To make `output` refer to the same `PrintStream` object as `System.out`, we may write:

```
output = System.out;
```

We could then write

```
output.println("Hello");
```

instead of

```
System.out.println("Hello");
```

You may find it quite convenient to use a reference variable to hold a returned reference from a message. For example, we might have:

```
String  bigGreeting;
bigGreeting = greeting.toUpperCase();
```

This code makes `bigGreeting` refer to the new `String` object returned by the receiver of the `greeting.toUpperCase()` message. If we need to use the reference to the new `String` repeatedly, we can write

```
System.out.println(bigGreeting);
System.out.println(bigGreeting);
System.out.println(bigGreeting);
```

instead of repeatedly sending `toUpperCase()` messages to `greeting`:

```
System.out.println(greeting.toUpperCase());
System.out.println(greeting.toUpperCase());
System.out.println(greeting.toUpperCase());
```

EXERCISES

1. Write declarations of three `String` reference variables that are intended for use as references to your first name, your last name, and your full name. Choose appropriate identifiers for these variables.

2. Write code that arranges for the three variables of the previous exercise to refer to `String` objects representing your first, your last, and your full name.

3. Declare another `String` reference variable and save in it a reference to an all-uppercase version of your last name. Use the `toUpperCase` method and one of the variables that you have used in the previous two exercises. •

Variables and Assignment

VARIABLES

A variable is an identifier that can have a value. One kind of value—the only kind we've seen so far—is a reference to an object. To create a variable, we must *declare* it by indicating the type of value it may contain, followed by the identifier that names the variable. The form of a declaration statement is:

> *type*   *identifier;*

Alternatively, if there is more than one identifier of the same type to declare, we can use this form:

> *type*   *identifier1, identifier2, ...;*

The convention for naming variables is the same as for method: Start with a lowercase letter. If the variable is intended to be a reference variable, then we must write, in place of `type`, the name of the class of the object. For example,

```
String s;
```

makes the identifier `s` the name of a reference variable, one that can contain a reference to a `String` object. Strictly speaking `s` is not a variable—it is the *name* of a variable. The variable itself is actually a small portion of the computer's internal memory. However, most of the time we will not make that distinction and we will speak of "`s`, the variable", meaning the variable that is named `s`.

ASSIGNMENT

Variables are given values by assignment. Until a variable is assigned a value, it cannot be used for any purpose. An assignment statement has the form

> *variable = value;*

We often speak of the `variable` as the *left-hand side* of the assignment, and the `value` as the *right-hand side*. The variable must have already been declared, and the value must be consistent with the variable's declared type. For example, given the declarations

```
String       s;
PrintStream  p;
```

these assignment statement are legal:

```
s = "Hello";
p = System.out;
```

but these are not:

```
s = System.out; // Wrong! Can't assign a PrintStream reference to a String variable
p = "Hello";      // Wrong! Can't assign a String reference to a PrintStream variable
```

Consider the assignment

```
t =  "Red tape holds up bridge";
```

The variable t now contains a reference to the same String object that "Red tape holds up bridge" refers to. This assignment doesn't keep us from subsequently making t refer to some other object of the String class, for that is what it means to be a variable: its value varies.

ASSIGNMENT IS NOT EQUALITY

Consider the assignment

```
t =  "Springtime";
```

This statement does not assert that t already refers to the String object "Springtime" or that t will always be associated with this object. Instead, the statement is an *imperative,* a direct order to the computer to make the value of the variable t be a reference to the String object referred to by the String constant at that point in the program. One thing, and only one thing, is certain in connection with this statement. Immediately after it is executed by the computer, the variable t refers to the same String object referred to by "Springtime". However, it is entirely possible that the very next statement in the program could change the value of t again. Consider the sequence

```
t = "Springtime";
t = "Wintertime";
```

Although it is unlikely that this sequence of statements would be useful, it is perfectly legal. It illustrates the way in which a variable contains a value. These two statements will be executed by the computer in the order in which they appear. After the first statement above is executed, the value of t is a reference to the String object "Springtime". Any previous value contained in t is lost. Immediately after the first assignment, the second statement is executed,

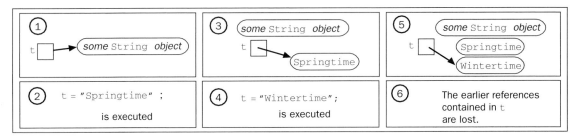

FIGURE 2.6   The references in t change.

after which t refers to the String object "Wintertime". Now, the reference to the String object "Springtime" is gone. (See Figure 2.6.) Variables *remember* (contain) only one thing at a time, the last value they were assigned. In particular, reference variables refer to only one object at a time.

REFERENCE VARIABLES AND OBJECTS

A reference variable refers to just one object at a time, but several reference variables may simultaneously refer to the same object:

```
String        s, t;
s = "Springtime";
t = s;
```

Here the first assignment makes s refer to the same object that the String constant "Springtime" refers to. The second assignment makes t refer to the same object that s refers to. In the end, two variables, s and t, are referring to the same object. This process is illustrated in Figure 2.7.

A SUBTLE BUT IMPORTANT POINT: TWO ROLES FOR VARIABLES

Memory involves two different actions:

- Saving information for possible future use, like memorizing a fact for a test
- Retrieving information for immediate use, like remembering the fact during the test

The role that a variable plays—saving or retrieving—depends on whether it is on the left or right side of the = in an assignment statement.

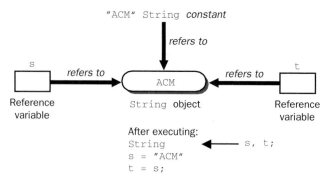

FIGURE 2.7 Two reference variables and a String constant referring to the same object.

Consider the following code:

```
String  s;
String  t;
s = "Inventory";   Here s has the role of variable and "Inventory" the role of value.
t = s;             Here t has the role of variable and s the role of value.
```

In the first assignment statement, the value "Inventory" is *saved* in s, which appears on the left side of the =. In the second assignment statement, s is on the right side of the = and its value is retrieved and assigned to t. On the left side, s is a variable whose old value is discarded and is assigned a new value; on the right side, s provides a value. Thus there are two roles for a variable, depending on the position of the variable in the assignment statement.

VARIABLES ARE INDEPENDENT

Consider again the above code. The last assignment,

```
t = s;
```

guarantees only that after it is executed, t will have the same value as s. If we then change s by assigning a new value to it:

```
s = "Payroll";
```

the value of t does not change. The assignment of s to t did not set up a permanent equality relationship between s and t, it just copied the value of s to t at the time of executing the assignment. Variables are independent of each other—their values can vary independently.

STATEMENTS

So far we have encountered three kinds of Java statements:

- Declarations.
- Assignment statements.
- Message-sending statements.

An example of the last kind of statement can be seen in the following `println` message to the `System.out` object:

```
System.out.println("Bonjour, tout le monde");
```

The right-hand side of an assignment statement can be a value that comes from invoking a method on an object that results in a value, as in the following statement:

```
bigGreeting = greeting.toUpperCase();
```

VARIATIONS

The computer executes the statements in Java in the order that they appear. Order can be very important. If you want to fry an egg, it is not good to put the egg in the pan first, heat it for three minutes and then crack it. However, some variations in the order of statements are possible. Consider the following program:

```
import java.io.*;
class Program2 {
    public static void main(String[] arg) {
        String  greeting;
        String  bigGreeting;
        greeting = "Yo, World";
        bigGreeting = greeting.toUpperCase();
        System.out.println(greeting);
        System.out.println(bigGreeting);
    }
}
```

The program prints out `"Yo, World"` (the `String` object that `greeting` refers to) and then prints out the uppercase version `"YO, WORLD"` (referred to by `bigGreeting`).

Alternatively, we could have written:

```
import java.io.*;
class Program2 {
    public static void main(String[] arg)   {
        String  greeting;
        greeting = "Yo, World";
        String  bigGreeting;
```

Declarations can come anywhere provided they precede any appearance of the variable.

```
            bigGreeting = greeting.toUpperCase();
            System.out.println(greeting);
            System.out.println(bigGreeting);
        }
    }
```

or:

```
import java.io.*;
class Program2 {
    public static void main(String[] arg) {
        String  greeting = "Yo, World";
        String  bigGreeting = greeting.toUpperCase();
        System.out.println(greeting);
        System.out.println(bigGreeting);
    }
}
```

Declarations can include assignments to the variable. (These are called initializations.)

2.6 Using `String` Methods

We have already encountered the `toUpperCase` method of the `String` class. The table below gives information about its prototype and the prototypes of some other methods of the `String` class:

Prototype information for some `String` methods

Method	Returns	Arguments
toUpperCase	reference to a String object	none
toLowerCase	reference to a String object	none
length	a number (like 5 or 17)	none
trim	reference to a String object	none
concat	reference to a String object	reference to a String object
substring	reference to a String object	a number (like 5, 0, or 27)
substring	reference to a String object	two numbers

The `length` method returns the number of characters in the receiver `String` object.

All of the other methods return a reference to a newly created `String` object, one that is based on the receiver `String` object and the arguments. For example, the `toUpperCase` and `toLowerCase` methods return references to new `String` objects that are uppercase only or lowercase only versions of the receiving `String`.

The trim method creates a copy of the receiving String, but removes spaces and tabs from the beginning and end.

The concat method creates a new String consisting of the characters of the receiving String object followed by those of the String object referred to by the argument, as in the following statements:

```
String   s, t, u;
s = "ham";
t = "burger";
u = s.concat(t);
```

As a result of the last assignment, u refers to "hamburger". We say that "ham" and "burger" have been *concatenated* (joined). Figure 2.8 presents a diagram of the process of receiving a concat message.

The substring method creates a new String consisting of a subset of the characters in the receiving String object. It does so by assuming the positions are numbered 0, 1, 2 starting from the left. Java considers a substring at position 3, say, to include the character at position 3 (which is the fourth character since we're numbering from 0) all the way to the end of the String. These positions are illustrated in Figure 2.9.

In the one-argument version of substring, the argument specifies the position of the first character that will be part of the new String—and all succeeding characters are included. Here is an example; the process of receiving a substring message with one argument is illustrated in Figure 2.10.

```
String   s, t;
s = "hamburger";
t = s.substring(3);
```

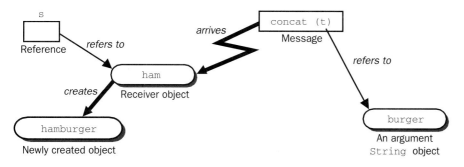

FIGURE 2.8 Receiving a concat message. When given a concat message, the receiver object produces a new String, consisting of its characters concatenated with the characters of the argument String.

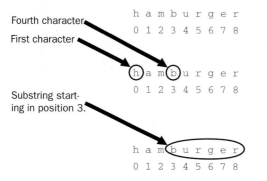

Fourth character

First character

h a m b u r g e r
0 1 2 3 4 5 6 7 8

The positions of the characters in a string are numbered, starting with 0.

h a m b u r g e r
0 1 2 3 4 5 6 7 8

The first character is in position 0. The fourth character is in position 3.

Substring start-ing in position 3.

h a m b u r g e r
0 1 2 3 4 5 6 7 8

The substring starting in position 3 is considered to be the character in that position along with all subsequent characters.

FIGURE 2.9 `String` **positions and substrings.**

Now t refers to `"burger"`, because 3 is the position of "b" in the receiving `String` object shown in Figure 2.9, and all the succeeding characters are part of the new `String`.

In the two-argument version of `substring`, the first integer argument specifies, as before, the position of the first character that is to be part of the new `String`. All succeeding characters up to but *not* including the character whose position is given by the second argument are incorporated into the new `String` object. The role of the two integers is shown in Figure 2.11.

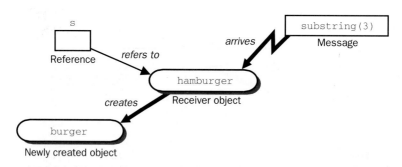

s

Reference

refers to

arrives

substring(3)

Message

hamburger

Receiver object

creates

burger

Newly created object

FIGURE 2.10 Receiving a `substring` message. Given a `substring` message with one argument, the receiver object produces a new `String`, starting with the character in the position indicated by the argument and going to the end.

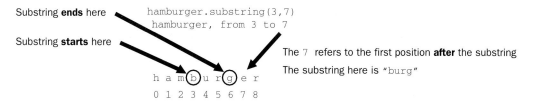

Substring **ends** here

Substring **starts** here

```
hamburger.substring(3,7)
hamburger, from 3 to 7
```

The 7 refers to the first position **after** the substring

The substring here is "burg"

```
h a m b u r g e r
0 1 2 3 4 5 6 7 8
```

FIGURE 2.11 Substrings specified by two integers. The first integer specifies the position of the first character in the substring. The second integer specifies the position after the last character of the substring.

For example, consider the role of 3 and 7 in the statements following:

```
String   s, t;
s = "hamburger";
t = s.substring(3,7);
```

As a result of the last assignment, t refers to "burg", because 3 is the position of "b" in the receiving String and all the succeeding characters, up to but not including position 7 ("e"), are part of the new String.

EXAMPLE **Finding the middle character of a String.** Let's write a program that displays the middle character of "antidisestablishmentarianism", which at one time was the longest word in the English language. A word can be modeled as a String. We can sketch our program using the usual boilerplate, along with a declaration of and assignment to a String variable to represent our long word this way:

```
import java.io.*;
class Program2 {
   public static void main(String[] arg) {
      String  word = "antidisestablishmentarianism";
      ... rest of program goes here ...
   }
}
```

The middle character of a String is itself a sequence of characters (a single character in this case) and can thus be modeled as a String. We can use a String reference variable, middle, to refer to it:

```
String  middle;
```

Sending a `substring` message to `word` could create a `String` composed of just that middle character. All we need to do is specify the starting position of the substring. This position must be the middle of the `String`, and the first position after the substring, which will be one position beyond that:

```
middle = word.substring(the middle position of word,
            the position after that);
```

To find the middle of `word` we must determine its length. The `length` method of `String` provides us with this information. Given the length of a `String`, its middle can be found by dividing by two:

```
word.length()/2
```

The position after the middle can be found by dividing the length by two and adding one:

```
1+word.length()/2
```

We can use these two expressions as arguments to the `substring` method:

```
middle = word.substring(word.length()/2, 1+word.length()/2);
```

The completed program is as follows:

```java
import java.io.*;
class Program2 {
    public static void main(String[] arg) {
        String  word = "antidisestablishmentarianism";
        String  middle;
        middle = word.substring(word.length()/2,
                1+word.length()/2);
        System.out.println(middle);
    }
}
```

Running this program yields the output:

```
s
```

⬤ **EXAMPLE   Initials of a name.** Let's practice with another problem: Given a first, middle, and last name, print the initials. In particular, let's write a program that prints out the initials of `"John Fitzgerald Kennedy"`, where the three names are modeled as distinct `String` objects. We can sketch our program using the usual boilerplate, along with declarations of and assignments to three `String` variables used to represent, for convenience, the first, middle, and last names of the former president by writing the following:

```
import java.io.*;
class Program2 {
    public static void main(String[] arg) {
        String  first = "John";
        String  middle = "Fitzgerald";
        String  last = "Kennedy";
        ... rest of program goes here ...
    }
}
```

The initials can be modeled using a `String`,

```
String  initials;
```

and can be constructed from three other `String` objects: the first initial of the first, middle, and last names. For convenience, let's use `String` reference variables for these as well:

```
String  firstInit, middleInit, lastInit;
```

An initial of a name is the first character (position 0, according to Java's scheme for numbering characters in `Strings`). If we send a `substring` message to the name, indicating to start with position 0 and not include position 1, the resulting `String` will consist of just the first character. We can pick up each initial this way:

```
firstInit = first.substring(0,1);
middleInit = middle.substring(0,1);
lastInit = last.substring(0,1);
```

All that remains is to concatenate the three initials into a `String` object, a reference to which is assigned to `initials`. We do this by making `initials` refer to the `String` object that results from concatenating `firstInit` with `middleInit` and then concatenating that object with `lastInit`. The reference that results, stored in `initials`, can be used as an argument in a `println` message.

```
initials = firstInit.concat(middleInit);
initials = initials.concat(lastInit);
System.out.println(initials);
```

The entire program to print out the initials we are seeking is as follows:

```
import java.io.*;
class Program2 {
    public static void main(String[] arg) {
        String  first = "John";
        String  middle = "Fitzgerald";
        String  last = "Kennedy";
        String  initials;
```

```
        String  firstInit, middleInit, lastInit;
        firstInit = first.substring(0,1);
        middleInit = middle.substring(0,1);
        lastInit = last.substring(0,1);
        initials = firstInit.concat(middleInit);
        initials = initials.concat(lastInit);
        System.out.println(initials);
    }
}
```

Smart and Helpful Objects

Wait a minute! What kind of a string does the `String` class model, anyway? Whoever heard of getting a substring from a string by "sending the string a message" to do so? After, all when we want to find a substring within a string, we do it ourselves, the strings do *not* do it for us.

The answer to this objection is this. In Java, we have the freedom to design our classes any way we choose. The wisest choice is one that makes the object a helpful one, one that can, upon request, carry out any useful operation related to that object. By providing methods such as `toUpperCase` and `substring`, the Java class designers are following that principle.

EXERCISES

1. Suppose you had a reference variable, x, containing a reference to a `String` object that you knew contained exactly three distinct characters (like `"abc"` or `"9=3"`). Write Java code that displays every permutation of this `String`. For instance, if the `String` were `"abc"`, the output would be:

   ```
   abc
   acb
   bac
   bca
   cab
   cba
   ```

   Your code will use the reference variable x, some of the `String` methods you have learned, and both the `print` and `println` methods of `System.out`.

2. Write a Java program that starts by creating a three-character `String` object such as `"abc"` and then, using the code you wrote in the previous exercise, displays every permutation of these characters. ●

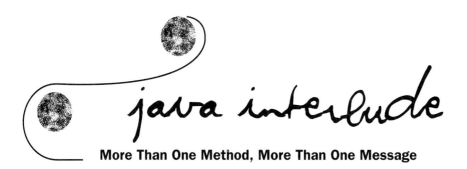

More Than One Method, More Than One Message

OVERLOADING METHODS

The `String` class has more than one method by the name of `substring`. The methods are distinguished from each other by the arguments they require; that is, they have different **signatures**. One requires one integer as an argument, the other requires two integers as arguments. The methods are distinct and model different, though related, behaviors. Methods of the same name but different signatures in the same class are said to be **overloaded**. The practice of designing classes with such methods is called **overloading**.

CASCADING

Consider the fragment of code:

```
initials = firstInit.concat(middleInit);   Now initials is "JF"
initials = initials.concat(lastInit);       Now initials is "JFK"
```

The value we assign to `initials` in the first line, `"JF"`, is a reference to an object that is just an intermediate step in building the `String` `"JFK"`. It is used just once—in the second line, where we send a `concat` message to it—and is replaced by `"JFK"`, as shown in Figure 2.12.

In some sense, the first assignment is a waste: The value given to `initials` is changed immediately in the next line. We can avoid this by directly using the reference returned by `firstInit.concat(middleInit)` to send a `concat` message to the `"JF"` `String` object:

```
initials = firstInit.concat(middleInit).concat(lastInit);
```

The following list tells how the right-hand side is executed.

- A `concat` message (with `middleInit` as argument) is sent to `firstInit`.
- The `firstInit` object returns a reference to a new `String` object (`"JF"`).

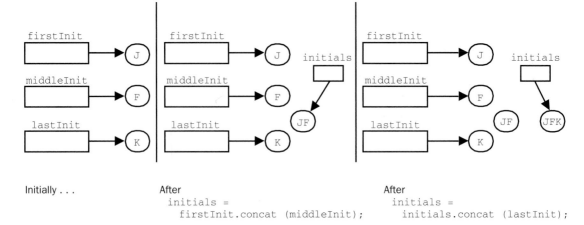

FIGURE 2.12   Repeated assignment.

- Another `concat` message (with `lastInit`) is sent to the new `String` object whose reference was just returned.
- A reference to yet another new `String` object is returned.

This sequence is called **cascading.** It is the process of sending a message to an object to create a new object, which in turn is sent a message to create another new object, which in turn is sent a message to create yet another new object, and so on. (See Figure 2.13.)

COMPOSITION

Alternatively, for the same task of printing out the first, middle, and last initials, we could have written

```
initials = firstInit.concat(middleInit.concat(lastInit));
```

The following list tells how the right-hand side expression is executed.

- A `concat` message (with `lastInit` as argument) is sent to `middleInit`.
- The `middleInit` object returns a reference to a new `String` object (consisting of the middle and last initials).
- The reference to this new object is sent as an argument in another `concat` message.
- A reference to yet another new `String` object is returned.

This sequence is called **composition.** It is the process of sending a message to an object to create a new object whose reference is used *as an argument* in a message. In turn, this may yield a reference to another new object, which then could be used as an argument in yet another message, and so on.

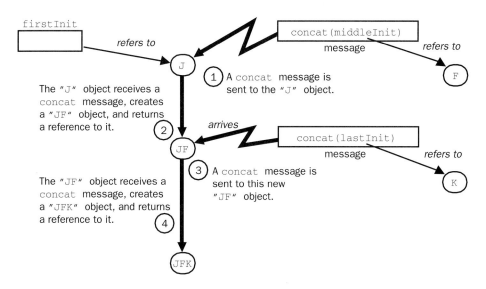

FIGURE 2.13   Cascading. In *cascading*, a message is sent to the object returned by a message and, in turn, a message is sent to the object returned by that message.

In cascading, the results of messages are used as receivers of additional messages; in composition, the results of messages are used as arguments in additional messages. Taken to an extreme, cascading and composition can rapidly lead to unreadable and error-prone code. Used judiciously, they lead to terse, elegant code.

Figure 2.14 shows composition.

A concat message whose argument is the return value from the "F" object is sent to the "J" object that firstInit refers to.

STRINGS ARE IMMUTABLE

Once created, String objects are never changed. Concatenation, trimming, or taking a substring never affects the receiver object. Rather, they create a new String object. The String class did not have to be designed this way—the designers of Java chose to make Strings unchangeable, that is, *immutable*.

EMPTY STRINGS

A String object that has an empty sequence of characters is called an empty String. "" is a reference to such a String. The empty String returns 0 as its length: "".length() equals 0.

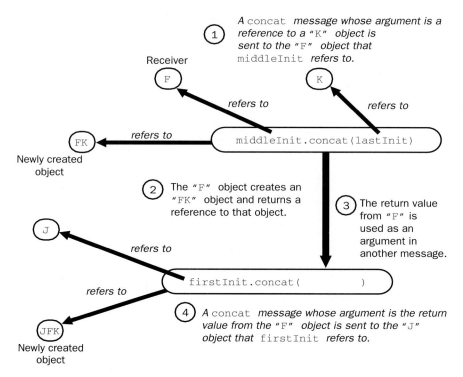

FIGURE 2.14   Composition. In *composition*, the return value of one message becomes the argument of another message.

1. Can you think of any methods of the `PrintStream` class that are *overloaded*?

2. Rewrite the following code fragment using composition and cascading as described previously:

```
s = "how";
s = s.concat(" now");
s = s.concat(" brown");
s = s.concat(" cow?");
```

SUMMARY

In this chapter we used some of Java's predefined objects to write a few simple programs. Behavior of objects is implemented by the methods their class provides. Messages consist of method names and a parenthesized list of additional information called arguments. Each method is characterized by its signature: its name and the number and type of arguments that it expects to receive. A class may provide more than one method of the same name, so long as their signatures are distinct. This is called overloading.

When a message is sent to an object, the sender is suspended while the object executes the method that was invoked. Some methods return a reference value to the sender of the message. This is called a return value. The type of a method's return value together with its signature is called the method's prototype. When a method does not return a value we say its return type is `void`.

Values may be assigned to variables. These are identifiers that may be associated with a value. A variable may have only one value at a time. Assignment to a variable is destructive in the sense that any previous value will no longer be associated with the variable.

Variables are established in a program by declarations—statements that indicate the type of the variable and its name (identifier). Only values that are compatible with the declared type of the variable may be assigned to it.

The reference values returned by method invocations may be assigned to variables or they may be used to specify receivers of additional messages—this process is called cascading. Alternatively, the return value may be used as an argument in a message to a different object—this process is called composition.

In this chapter we also made the further acquaintance of two of Java's predefined classes, `PrintStream` and `String`. We encountered three of `PrintStream`'s methods: `print`, `println` with a `String` argument, and `println` without an argument. We also encountered a half-dozen `String` methods: `toUpperCase`, `toLowerCase`, `concat`, `substring`, `trim`, and `length`.

STUDY AID: TERMINOLOGY REVIEW

argument   Information provided in a message in addition to the method-name.

assignment   The association of a value with a variable; the new value replaces any previous value associated with the variable.

assignment statement   A statement that results in an assignment; the statement consists of the name of the variable being assigned, the assignment operator =, and an expression that gives the value that is assigned to the variable.

behavior   Any action that the object may take; any change it may undergo or characteristic it may reveal.

cascading   A technique in which the result of one method invocation is used as the *receiver* of a second method invocation.

composition   A technique in which the result of one method invocation is used as an *argument* in a second method invocation.

declaration   A Java statement that introduces a variable into Java program. A declaration of a reference variable specifies the name (identifier) of the variable and the class of object to which it may refer.

message   The mechanism by which a method is invoked. A message consists of a method name followed by a (possibly empty) argument list.

method   A self-contained section of code belonging to a class that defines a specific behavior for that class. It is referred to in a message by its method-name.

method-name   The identifier associated with a method.

overloading   The practice of having a class provide different—though highly related—methods of the same name; the methods are distinguished by the types of arguments they receive, that is, their signatures.

prototype   A method's name along with a description of its return type and arguments.

reference variable   An identifier that may be assigned a reference to an object of a particular class.

return   The action of the receiver of a message providing a value that is given to the sender; the value replaces the phrase that sent the message.

return value   The value given back to the sender by the receiver of a message.

signature   A method's name along with a description of its arguments.

String constant   A sequence of characters embedded in double quotes, e.g, `"Hello"`. The constant is a reference to the `String` object consisting of the characters between the quotes, in our case, the characters `Hello`.

QUESTIONS FOR REVIEW

1. What is the purpose of a *declaration*?

2. What is a *message* composed of?

3. Can a *reference variable* refer to more than one object at the same time? At different times?

4. Can more than one *reference variable* refer to the same object?

5. What does the *assignment statement* do?

6. Give two examples of *overloading*.

FURTHER EXERCISES

1. Suppose you are given the following code:

```
String  first = "someone's first name ";
String  last  = "someone's last name ";
```

where each `String` starts with some unknown number of spaces followed by a first or last name. Write a fragment of code that creates a `String` containing the initials of the first and last name and print it out.

2. Given the following code:

```
String  x = "Studebakers of yesteryear";
String  y = "banana freak";
System.out.println(x.substring(0,4)
      .concat(x.substring(15,16)).concat(y.substring(0,1))
      .concat(y.substring(8)));
```

a. What is printed out?
b. Draw a diagram, showing every object that is created at some point in the execution of this code. Label each object with the phrase of the above code that refers to it. Show, using arrows, the order in which the objects are created.

Web Pages and HTML

Browsing the World Wide Web   If you have never "surfed the Web," that is used at web browser application such as Netscape to access World Wide Web sites, you should *stop reading at this point and make arrangements to do so*. It is not difficult, and having the concrete experience of at least one session with Netscape or the equivalent is necessary for the rest of this section to have much meaning for you. So, *if you haven't done so before, go surf the web. We'll wait for you right here.*

Web Pages   Welcome back, we hope you enjoyed your web-surfing experience. In it, you observed that your screen jumped from one page to another as you clicked on various pieces of text and graphics. These *web pages* are the basic unit of information on the World Wide Web. Their significance to our endeavor is this: To place a Java program on the Internet, it must be embedded in a web page. In Chapter 3 we will see how to do just that, but first we must learn some basics in web page construction. That is our task here.

HTML: HyperText Markup Language   A web page is defined by a file containing a mixture of two constructions:

- Ordinary text (just words, like this very line).
- Special notations called *tags*, which control the appearance of the text (**boldface** vs. regular font, for example), bring in pictures, set up *links* to other web pages, and so forth.

The set of rules that govern the construction and use of tags is called HyperText Markup Language, or HTML. We can say therefore that a web page is defined by an HTML file.

HTML Tags   An HTML tag consists of

- An open angle bracket, <
- A tag word
- Possibly some additional information, depending on the tag
- A close angle bracket >

An example of an HTML tag is:

```
<B>
```

Note the open and close angle brackets, the tag word B. In this tag there is no other information provided beyond the tag word. The meaning of this tag is to make the following text in **boldface.** So if our HTML file contained the fragment

```
learning the Java language is a <B> worthy endeavor
```

the resulting web page would contain something that looked like

learning the Java language is a **worthy endeavor**

Once the `<B>` tag appears in an HTML file, all succeeding text will be in boldface until a `</B>` tag appears. The `/B` is a closing tag word. Most tag words are associated with closing tag words that signify when the tag's effect is to end. For example, suppose we wanted the above fragment to boldface only "worthy" and not "worthy endeavor." Then our HTML file should include the fragment

```
learning the Java language is a <B> worthy </B> endeavor
```

Here is an assortment of HTML tags useful for controlling text appearance:

```
<B>...</B>
<I>....</I>
<CENTER>....</CENTER>
<FONT COLOR=RED>....</FONT>  (or BLUE or YELLOW etc.)
<SMALL>...</SMALL>
<BIG>...</BIG>
```

Note that this is an example of a tag that contains additional information, i.e., COLOR=RED.

Each of these modifies the text that appears between the tag and its corresponding closing tag. Caution: Do not leave out the closing tags—the effect on the web page may be worse than merely boldfacing the rest of your page.

HTML File Structure   HTML files should be structured in the following way:

```
<HTML>
<HEAD>
    <TITLE>
            Place the title of your web page here.
    </TITLE>
</HEAD>
<BODY>
            Write the content of your web page here: text, fancy tags,
                and so on.
</BODY>
</HTML>
```

You will note the introduction of four new tags and their associated closings: HTML, HEAD, TITLE, BODY. The text that appears within <TITLE>...</TITLE> becomes the window title of the web browser document window. The HTML that appears within <BODY>...</BODY> is the content of the web page.

HTML Text Formatting   Web browsers ignore spaces, tabs, and new lines in HTML documents. Faced with this text:

```
If it makes you happy
It can't be so bad
If it makes you happy
Then why... are you so sad?
```

a web browser will display something like

> If it makes you happy It can't be so bad If it makes you happy Then why... are you so sad?

To force line breaks where we want them, we must use the <BR> tag. Its presence forces a new line:

```
If it makes you happy <BR>
It can't be so bad <BR>
If it makes you happy <BR>
Then why... are you so sad? <BR>
```

The BR tag has no closing tag because it has its effect only at the point where it appears—it forces a new line.

A Sample HTML File   Here is a simple web page file that illustrates some of the above and that can serve as a model for your own explorations of HTML:

```
<HTML>
<HEAD>
    <TITLE>
        Abraham Lincoln's Home Page
    </TITLE>
</HEAD>
<BODY>
    <CENTER><B>Abraham Lincoln's Home Page</B></CENTER>
    <BR><BR>
    <B>Address</B><BR>
        1600 Pennsylvania Avenue<BR>
        Washington D.C.<BR>
    <BR><BR>
    <B>Needs</B><BR>
        One capable general<BR>
    <BR><BR>
    <B>Statement</B><BR>
    Four score and seven years ago our forefathers
    brought forth upon this continent a new nation,
    conceived in liberty and dedicated to the proposition
    that all men are created equal.
</BODY>
</HTML>
```

The Advantages of Hypertext[1]   So far, all we have seen is a markup language—rules for controlling the format and appearance of text. There is nothing "hyper" about it. What does Hyper mean anyway, in the sense of hyper-

---

[1]Tim Berners-Lee, the inventor of the World Wide Web, is credited with originating HTML. Isn't it amazing? You can actually point to someone who invented this language. It's like being able to identify the person who invented sliced bread.

text? Ordinary text is linear in the sense that one could imagine stringing out all the words in a normal document in a single line. The essence of linearity here is that there is one and only one order for the words—given any two words in an ordinary text, one can say which one comes first.

In hypertext, this linear organization vanishes to some extent. If you recall your web browsing experience, you remember going from one web page to another based on the text or image you chose to click on. If you had made different choices, the order in which the web pages appeared would have been different. This is what is meant by hypertext—nothing more and nothing less.

OK, having taken some of the hype out of hypertext, let's see how to put hypertext into our web pages.

The way you achieve any effect when designing a web page (other than when providing literal text) is with a tag. The way to put in a link to another web page is with the `<A>` tag. Its format is:

```
<A HREF=name-of-another-html-file>
    Here is the text that will be underlined.
</A>
```

The browser will display the text that occurs between the `<A>` and closing `</A>` tags in a color and style that distinguish it from surrounding text. If the user clicks on that distinguished text, the browser will jump to display the other HTML file, the one specified in the `<A>` tag.

Lincoln's home page file might thus be modified:

```
<HTML>
<HEAD>
    ...
</HEAD>
<BODY>
    ...
    Check out my <A HREF=secondInaug.html> Second Inaugural
    Address</A> for some more moving words.
</BODY>
</HTML>
```

When the user clicks on "Second Inaugural Address", the browser will jump to the file `secondInaug.html`.

Active Content   HTML is a fantastic tool that makes it possible to organize information in new and useful ways and present this information to a truly worldwide audience. However, it has a number of limitations. One of these is its passive character. Once downloaded onto the web browser's display area, it can only present the information that it carries. It can't interact with the user and, based on that interaction, produce new information. In other words, HTML does not compute (hence it is *not* a programming language). Using HTML, you cannot put up a web page that invites a customer to input specifications of an order and respond with a suggested model number, price, and anticipated delivery date. All you can do with HTML is present a list of models, prices, and similar information. The customer is expected to pore over them to make a decision.

This limitation is solved by all sorts of extensions to the original text-describing HTML. One of these extensions is the **Java applet.** A Java applet is a Java program that is referred to in a web page and is downloaded by the browser along with the web page. Once downloaded into the browser, it starts executing. It can invite the user to type in input, or click and drag on graphical icons. It can respond to these actions and display images or text.

In the GUI supplement in later chapters, you will learn how to write this kind of Java application. In the meantime, try playing around with HTML, making some cool web pages.

chapter 3

Using Classes

3.1   Introduction

In Chapter 2, we learned how to use objects. This was a matter of using references to objects in order to send messages to them. Most of the objects we used were Java's *predefined objects*. However, the set of predefined objects is quite small—String constants, System.out, and a couple of other similar objects. To accomplish anything useful, we will need to create objects ourselves. In this chapter we will learn how to use Java's predefined classes to do just that.

A class always models something. The predefined classes that we have chosen as examples in this chapter model disk files, Internet sites, and various modes of input and output. We will start the discussion with a familiar class: String. This will lead us, by the end of the chapter, to writing programs whose reach extends out to the Internet.

3.2   Creating Objects

3.2.1   Creating Objects with Constructors

Every class has one or more methods that are used to create the object. These methods are called **constructors** (because they construct the object). The name of a constructor method is *always* the same as its class. So the `String` class has a constructor method called `String`.

Like all methods, constructors may or may not require arguments. The `String` constructor takes a reference to an existing `String` object as an argument as follows:

```
String("hello world")
```

This message requests that the newly constructed `String` represent the characters h e l l o   w o r l d. That is, the new object will be a copy of the one referred to by the argument.

Messages must be sent to an object. But in the case of constructors, we don't yet have an object—we are trying to create one. There is no object to receive this message. In Java, we use the keyword `new` to arrange for the creation of an object that can receive this message and to invoke the constructor method as follows:

```
new String("hello world")
```

This creates a `String` object and sends it the message `String("hello world")`. Since a constructor's only purpose is to aid in the construction of an object, it can only be invoked with the `new` keyword during object creation. The constructor returns a reference to the newly created object. Therefore, the following is a reference to the `String` object it creates:

```
new String("hello world")
```

The `new` keyword denotes an **operation** to be performed. An operation is an action that results in a value. The value of the `new` operation is a reference to the newly created object. An **operator,** such as `new`, is a symbol or keyword that represents an operation.

3.2.2 Reference Variables to the Rescue

The `new` operator gives us a reference to a newly created object, but unless we save that reference for future use, we will not be able to continue sending messages to the object. At this point the reference variables, introduced in the previous chapter as a convenience, become essential. By declaring a reference variable and assigning it the result of the `new` operation, we can continue to use the reference to the newly created object, as follows:

```
String    s, upper, lower;
s = new String("Hello");
upper = s.toUpperCase();
```

```
lower = s.toLowerCase();
System.out.println(s);
```

In this code, the reference returned by the new operation is used three times: twice to specify a receiver of a message and once as an argument in a message.

1. Write a fragment of code that uses the new operator to construct a String object that models the title of the textbook, *Introduction to Programming Using Java.* Print the title both in all CAPITALS and in all lowercase letters by sending toUpperCase and toLowerCase messages to the newly created object.

2. Is the following a legal Java statement? Explain why or why not. If it is legal, what does it do?

```
System.out.println(new String("second exercise"));
```

3. Is the following a legal Java statement? Explain why or why not. If it is legal, what does it do?

```
String s = new String("third exercise").toUpperCase();
```

Origins of Objects

OVERLOADING, AGAIN

The String constructor is intentionally overloaded so that when given no arguments, it produces an empty String, as follows:

```
String  empty = new String();   the same as ""
```

WHERE DO OBJECTS COME FROM?

Sometimes we get new `String` objects by using the `new` operator. Other times we get them by invoking methods that return references to `String` objects that they themselves created using `new`. We have already seen the following six methods that return references to newly created `String` objects:

`String` Methods That Return References to Newly Created `String` Objects

Method	Arguments
toUpperCase	none
toLowerCase	none
trim	none
concat	reference to a `String` object
substring	a number
substring	two numbers

Remember that although the last two methods have the same name, `substring`, they are different methods because they have different signatures; that is, they receive different sets of arguments.

We will encounter many other methods in other classes that also return references to newly created `String`s.

3.3   Disk Files

So far, all the output generated by our examples has gone to "standard output," which is usually the monitor. But you are certainly aware that computer systems store data in files on disks and that we might want to write output to a data file on a disk rather than to the screen. One advantage of storing data in files on a disk is *persistence*: Screen information lasts as long as it is on the screen and may be easily lost—data stored in a file last much longer. Another advantage of disk files is their capacity: Much more data can be stored in a disk file than can be displayed on the screen or even printed conveniently on a printer.

Disk files have the following two attributes:

- Contents (data)
- A file name

The *data* in a disk file can be any information: a letter, a shopping list, current price list of auto parts—anything. The rules for choosing file names vary from one system to another. Typically they are similar to but a bit more liberal than the rules governing identifiers. For example, they can start with nonletters and can contain periods.

Given these attributes, it is not surprising that the most common disk file operations include the following:

- Creating a file and providing it with contents (writing to a file)
- Deleting a file (removing the name and the contents)
- Renaming a file (changing the name but keeping the contents)
- Overwriting a file (keeping the name but changing the contents)
- Obtaining the contents of the file (reading from the file)

3.3.1   The `File` Class

Java provides a predefined class for modeling disk files, called `File`. The constructor for `File` accepts the file's name (a `String` reference) as its argument, as follows:

```
new File(filename)
```

An example of this follows:

```
File    f1, f2;
f1 = new File("letterToJoanna");
f2 = new File("letterToMatthew");
```

These statements create two `File` objects that refer to files named `letterToJoanna` and `letterToMatthew`.

When a `File` object (as above) is created, it does not create a corresponding file (that is, a file with the same name). That is, if `letterToJoanna` did not exist as a file on the disk, the construction

```
f1 = new File("letterToJoanna");
```

would not create it. Keep in mind that a `File` object in a Java program merely represents a possible file and does not guarantee that it exists. However, if the corresponding file does exist already, the `File` object provides two methods that model some of the file operations we listed earlier.

First, we can delete a file, using the `delete` method. To remove a file named `junk`, we can write the following:

```
File    f;
f = new File("junk");
f.delete();
```

Second, we can rename a file. Suppose we have a file named `junk` and we want to change its name to `garbage`. We create two `File` objects, one representing `junk` the other representing `garbage`, as follows:

```
File    f1, f2;
f1 = new File("junk");
f2 = new File("garbage");
```

and then we use the `renameTo` method, as follows:

```
f1.renameTo(f2);
```

Although useful, these methods have not given us the means to create a file that does not exist (and provide it with contents, that is, store output in it) nor have they given us means to read from or write to a file. The table below summarizes the two `File` methods we have learned.

Some **File** methods

Method	Returns	Arguments	Action
delete	nothing	none	deletes the file
renameTo	nothing	ref. to a `File` object	renames the file

EXERCISES

1. Write a program that removes the files named `"trash"` and `"refuse"`.

2. Write a program that takes a file called `"trash"` and renames it `"recyclables"`.

3.4   Writing Output to Files

We create a new file, or overwrite an existing one in the same way in Java. Both require a pathway (or *stream*) for output from the program to provide the newly created or existing file with content.

3.4.1 The `FileOutputStream` Class

Java provides a predefined class for modeling a stream of output that goes to a file; it is called `FileOutputStream`. The constructor for `FileOutputStream` accepts a reference to a `File` object as its argument, as follows:

```
new FileOutputStream(file)
```

An example of this follows:

```
File    f = new File("Americas.Most.Wanted")
FileOutputStream    fs = new FileOutputStream(f)
```

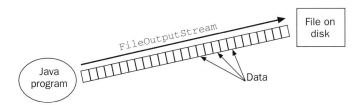

FIGURE 3.1
FileOutputStream.
FileOutputStream models output as
a sequence of tiny units of uninterpreted
data. Methods like println, which
"know" about lines, are not provided.

This code opens the disk file Americas.Most.Wanted so that it can receive
output; it creates the file if it doesn't already exist. The reference to the new
FileOutputStream object is returned and stored in fs. As soon as the
FileOutputStream is constructed, the file is created if it did not exist
before or its contents are removed if the file already exists. (See Figure 3.1.)

It models the stream of data as a sequence of tiny units of data called
bytes, but it does not recognize their organization into large units, such as
lines or strings. Therefore, it does not provide any convenient methods for
output—certainly nothing like println or print. The class gives us the data
pathway to the file, but it does not give us the methods we want. The next section discusses how we can get around this problem.

3.4.2 Using PrintStream Objects

Let's recall how output has been handled until now. We have always sent
either a println or a print message to the System.out object. As we
learned in Section 1.4, System.out is a reference to an instance of the
PrintStream class, which provides the println and print methods. If we
could get a reference to a PrintStream object that represents a file instead of
the screen, we could send println messages to that object, and the output
would presumably go into the file. Here's an example of what we have in
mind:

```
String      s;
PrintStream p;
s = new String("Hello, File");
p = new ...
```

We haven't learned how to make a new
PrintStream yet, but we will shortly.
Just assume here that p now refers to a
PrintStream going to a disk data file.

```
System.out.println(s);
p.println(s);
```

Tell the PrintStream referred to by System.out to print s.
Tell the PrintStream referred to by p to print s.

NOTE: We have now printed "Hello, File" to both
System.out and the disk data file to which the PrintStream reference p refers.

But how do we create a new PrintStream object, one that is associated
with a disk file and not the monitor?

3.4.3 Creating `PrintStream` Objects

The constructor for `PrintStream` accepts a reference to a `FileOutput-Stream` object as its argument, as follows:

```
new PrintStream(fileoutputstream)
```

This associates the `PrintStream` object with the output stream modeled by the `FileOutputStream` object. Invoking `print` and `println` methods on the new `PrintStream` object results in the output going into the disk file, as shown in the following example:

```
File            diskFile = new File("data.out");
FileOutputStream  diskFileStream =
                          new FileOutputStream(diskFile);
PrintStream       target  = new PrintStream(diskFileStream);
target.println("Hello Disk File");
```

This causes the `String` `"Hello  Disk  File"` to be written to the file `data.out` as its contents. If `data.out` does not already exist, it is created. If `data.out` already exists, the new contents replace the old ones.

3.4.4 Creating or Overwriting a File

To summarize, to write content to a file we do the following:

- Create a `File` object to represent the file and then use it to
- Create a `FileOutputStream` object to represent the output pathway to the file (passing the `File` reference to the `FileOutputStream` constructor). Use this `FileOutputStream` object to
- Create a `PrintStream` object to provide a convenient output pathway to the file (passing the `FileOutputStream` reference to the `Print-Stream` constructor).
- Use the `print` or `println` methods of `PrintStream` as needed to write content to the file.

Typically, our `File` and `FileOutputStream` variables are only used to create a `PrintStream` object. We can dispense with these variables using the following composition:

```
PrintStream    target = new PrintStream(
                    new FileOutputStream(
                        new File("data.out")));
```

Note that although we have dispensed with the `File` and `FileOutput-Stream` variables, we have not dispensed with `File` and `File-OutputStream` objects—both are created here and are used in the creation of the `PrintStream` object.

EXAMPLE **Maintaining a Backup of Screen Output.** Suppose we want our program to maintain a disk file copy (named `backup`, say) of the screen output that it generates. Let's assume this is an improvement of `Program1`. We write the program as before but add the code needed to create a new file `backup` with an associated `PrintStream`. Then, whatever we write to `System.out`, we also write to this `PrintStream` object, as follows:

```
import java.io.*;
class Program1Backup {
    public static void main(String[] arg) throws Exception {
        PrintStream        backup;
        FileOutputStream   backupFileStream;
        File               backupFile;
        backupFile = new File("backup");
        backupFileStream = new FileOutputStream(backupFile);
        backup = new PrintStream(backupFileStream);
        System.out.println("This is my first Java program");
        backup.println("This is my first Java program");
        System.out.println("... but it won't be my last.");
        backup.println("... but it won't be my last.");
    }
}
```

3.4.5 What Can go Wrong?

As our programs further interact with their computing environment—creating new files, for example—there are more opportunities for them to fail through no fault of their own. For example, the program above is perfectly correct, but if someone runs it in a directory where he or she doesn't have permission to create files, the program will fail. Java requires that the programmer acknowledge potential failures of this kind by adding the phrase `throws Exception` to the boilerplate, as we have done above. If the phrase is omitted the compiler will issue an error. The phrase means that it is conceivable that an unrecoverable error might occur because of a problem in the computing environment, and as a result the program might terminate abruptly. We will learn more about this issue and exceptions in general in Chapter 14.

3.4.6 Why Did They Design It That Way?

Often we will encounter what seem to be peculiar design decisions in the Java class libraries. Most of the time, there is good reason for the design decision. Consider `FileOutputStream`—why doesn't it provide `print` and `println` methods? The reason is that there are many ways a `FileOutput-Stream` object can be used. Our interest is in simple usage, such as printing

`String` objects with `println`. However, there are other ways to do output. Rather than model them all, `FileOutputStream` models just the stream of output going to the file and little else. For additional capabilities, we must turn to other classes, such as `PrintStream`, which build upon this behavior.

EXERCISES

1. Write a program that writes your name and your complete address to a file called `MyAddress`.

2. Write a program that writes a message that is patently false to two files, called `lie1` and `lie2`.

3. Write a program that creates an empty file that is named `nothing`.

4. Write a program that creates a file called `Program1.java` and writes into it the contents of our first program (`Program1` from Chapter 1).   •

3.5 Input: An Overview

We have not yet considered how to use information coming from a keyboard or stored in a file, that is, *input*, to create objects. (See Figure 3.2.) This has forced us to place all information into the programs themselves. If we could get information, such as `String`s, from input, our programs could be more general. For example, instead of writing a program that changes a file's name from `ford` to `lincoln` by specifying the names, we could write a program

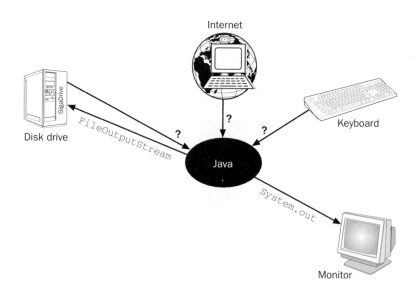

FIGURE 3.2 Where's the input? We can output to disk and monitor, but what about input to our Java programs?

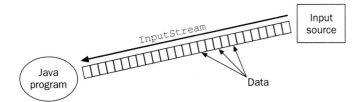

FIGURE 3.3 `InputStreams`. *InputStreams*, such as `File-InputStream`, model input as a sequence of tiny units of uninterrupted data.

that reads two `String`s from the keyboard (what the user types) and treats them as the old and new names of a file that is renamed. We'll learn how to read input in this and the next two sections.

In the preceding section, we saw that writing output to a file involves several stages, as follows:

- Create a `File` object
- Create a `FileOutputStream` object
- Create a `PrintStream` object

Input—whether coming from the keyboard, from a file, or from a network connection—requires a similar sequence of stages, as follows:

- STAGE 1: *Construct an object that models some sort of input stream, either a* `FileInputStream` *object or a* `BufferedInputStream` *object.*

   The `FileInputStream` object models a stream of input coming from a file (analogous to the stream of output going to a file modeled by `FileOutputStream`). (See Figure 3.3.) The `BufferedInputStream` class models a stream of input coming from a keyboard or a network connection.

- STAGE 2: *Use the InputStream object (either a* `FileInputStream` *or a* `BufferedInputStream`) *to construct an* `InputStreamReader` *object.*

   The `InputStreamReader` object models the stream of input specifically as a stream of characters (suitable for forming `String`s). (See Figure 3.4.) However, it does not recognize ends of lines or any other boundaries between strings in input—it can't tell where one string in input ends and the next one begins.

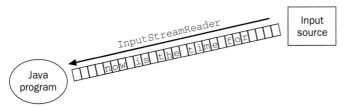

FIGURE 3.4 `InputStreamReader`. `InputStreamReader`s model input as a sequence of characters, suitable for putting together `String`s. They do not, however, recognize boundaries (like ends of lines) between strings in the input.

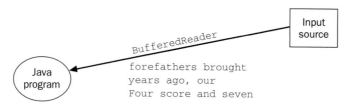

FIGURE 3.5 `BufferedReader.` `BufferedReader`s can be used to model input as a sequence of distinct lines, each capable of being represented as a `String`.

- STAGE 3: *Use the* `InputStreamReader` *object to construct a* `BufferedReader` *object.*

    The `BufferedReader` object adds the capability we are looking for. It provides a method, `readLine`, that reads an entire line, creates a `String` object, and returns a reference to the newly created `String` object. (See Figure 3.5.)

    To summarize, to arrange to do input, we do the following:

- Create an `FileInputStream` or `BufferedInputStream` object which we use to
- Create an `InputStreamReader` object which we use to
- Create a `BufferedReader` object

3.6 Input: The Keyboard

As our first source of input, we turn to the keyboard. Java provides a predefined `BufferedInputStream` object to represent the stream of input that comes from the keyboard. `System.in` is a reference to this object.

Unlike `System.out`, which refers to a `PrintStream` object and therefore can be used right away to write `String`s to the monitor, `System.in`, a reference to a `BufferedInputStream` object, cannot be readily used to read `String`s. Instead,

        `System.in`

must be used as an argument to construct

        an `InputStreamReader` object,

which then must be used as an argument to construct

        a `BufferedReader` object,

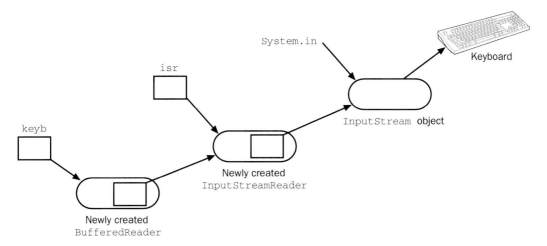

FIGURE 3.6   A `BufferedReader` for the keyboard. The `BufferedReader` is constructed with a reference to an `InputStreamReader` that was constructed with a reference to an InputStream, such as the one that `System.in` refers to.

which then can be sent `readLine` messages to read lines as `Strings`. (See Figure 3.6.)

Each successive construction yields an object that comes closer to doing what we need. One way to accomplish the above is to declare the reference variables that we will need to refer to the objects being created, as follows:

```
                              // System.in models a keyboard that reads a stream
                                   of bytes
InputStreamReader   isr;   // models a keyboard that reads a stream of
                                   characters
BufferedReader      keyb;  // models a keyboard that reads lines as Strings
```

Then we construct the objects step by step, as follows:

```
isr = new InputStreamReader(System.in);
keyb = new BufferedReader(isr);
```

Once we have a `BufferedReader` object, we can use its ability to read a line from some source of input and create a `String` object, whose characters are those that appeared in the input line. The method that models this behavior is called `readLine`. Because it creates an object, it returns a reference to that object, just as the `String` methods `toUpperCase` and `substring` return references to the new `String` objects that they create. Therefore, the following is a reference to a `String`:

```
keyb.readLine()
```

The `String` is returned by `BufferedReader` when it reads the next line of input from the keyboard in response to the `readLine` message.

To use the `String` object that `keyb` creates, we declare a `String` reference variable, as follows:

```
String          inputLine;        // Models a line of input
```

We use it to save the `String` reference that the `BufferedReader` returns, as follows:

```
inputLine = keyb.readLine();
```

Let's use these new tools to write a program that reads a single noun from the keyboard and displays its plural on the screen. We don't yet have the tools to come close to doing this correctly, so we will assume that merely adding an s to a word correctly results in the plural form (thereby ignoring words like fox and baby).

We write a comment defining the meaning of the program followed by the usual first two lines of boilerplate notation and then the above four pieces of code, as follows:

```
import java.io.*;
/*
 * Program4: Displays the plural form of the word typed on the keyboard.
 *             Uses the naive and wrong(!) approach of just adding s.
 */
class Program4 {
   public static void main(String[] arg) throws Exception {
      InputStreamReader   isr;            // Models a keyboard that reads
                                          //   a stream of characters
      BufferedReader         keyb;        // Models a keyboard that reads
                                          //   lines as Strings
      String                 inputLine;   // Models a line of input.
      isr = new InputStreamReader(System.in);
      keyb = new BufferedReader(isr);
      inputLine = keyb.readLine();

            Rest of the program goes here ...

   }
}
```

All that remains is to arrange to display the `String` as intended. We will send a `print` (not a `println`) message to `System.out` with the word read from input as an argument. We send `print` instead of `println` because we want the s to appear on the same line as the word, not on the succeeding line. Then we will send a `println` message with s as an argument in order to display the s and complete the line, as follows:

```
System.out.print(inputLine);
System.out.println("s");
```

Here is the complete program:

```
import java.io.*;
/*
  * Program4: Displays the plural form of the word typed on the keyboard.
  *           Uses the naive and wrong(!) approach of just adding s.
*/
class Program4 {
    public static void main(String[] arg) throws Exception {
        InputStreamReader isr;          // Models a keyboard that reads in a
                                        //    stream of characters
        BufferedReader    keyboard;     // Models a keyboard that reads in
                                        //    lines as Strings
        String            inputLine;    // Models a line of input
        isr = new InputStreamReader(System.in);
        keyboard = new BufferedReader(isr);
        inputLine = keyboard.readLine();
        System.out.print(inputLine);
        System.out.println("s");
    }
}
```

EXERCISES

1. Rewrite `Program4` so that it does not have an `InputStreamReader` variable (`isr`) and instead uses the composition of `InputStream-Reader` and `BufferedReader` to create a `BufferedReader` for the keyboard.

2. Write a program that reads two `String`s from the keyboard. The first is the name of a file that is to be opened up for writing output to. The second is a `String` that is to be written to the file. If the user types in

```
mynumber
867-5304
```

the phone number 867-5304 is written to a file named `"mynumber"`.   •

3.7   Interactive Input/Output

Keyboards are only one source of input for programs. Other sources include data files on disk and even other programs that are running on the computer. We will explore all of these other sources as we proceed in this book.

One characteristic distinguishing keyboard input is that it directly involves a human being, often termed an **enduser** (of the program). In practice, endusers are almost never the authors of the programs that they use.

Millions of people use WordPerfect—only a handful of them had a role in writing that program.

Because endusers (or users for short) are not the authors of the programs they use, they cannot be expected to automatically know what to type on the keyboard and when to type it. A program that expects input from a keyboard must, in order to be useful, provide that information to the users as it runs. It must display messages such as `"Please enter your PIN # now"` and `"Sorry, that choice is not correct—please make your selection again."` These **prompts** tell the user what to type on the keyboard. The flow of data between users and programs is referred to as **interactive** input and output.

Consider `Program4` from the previous section. The program includes the following line:

```
inputLine = keyboard.readLine();
```

It expects the user to type in a word that is to be made plural. But how will the user know that this is expected of him or her? The `readLine` method waits silently for the user to type in a line—it cannot offer any guidance. The solution is to display a prompt, such as, `"Type in a word to be pluralized, please"` just before the `readLine` message is sent to `keyboard`. We know how to display such a string to the user: We must send a `print` message to `System.out` prior to reading in the line, as follows:

```
System.out.println(
            "Type in a word to be pluralized, please ");
inputLine = keyboard.readLine();
```

Unfortunately, the prompt might not be displayed until after the line is read—defeating the whole purpose of having a prompt in the first place. The reason for this lies in the details of the behavior of `PrintStream`, the class that `System.out` is an instance of.

A `PrintStream` object receives `print` and `println` messages and will eventually display the `String`s requested. However, the key word here is *eventually*. `PrintStream` behaves much as you do when you write several letters for mailing. You do not write a letter, go off to the mailbox and mail it, and come home to write another. You write a batch (all you had planned to) and then mail them together, saving multiple trips to the mailbox.

`PrintStream` takes the same approach, and for similar reasons. It is costly (relatively speaking) in computer time to transfer a `String` from a program to an output device such as a screen. It is more efficient to do the transfer all at once or at least in large batches. So, `PrintStream` collects the `String`s it is to display in a holding area in memory. Such a holding area is called a **buffer.** `PrintStream` does not display the `String`s in its buffer until the program completes or the buffer gets full. If the output is going to a file, this is fine—the file definitely does not mind waiting for its output from `PrintStream`.

On the other hand, for issuing prompts, this approach is a disaster. It means that we could write a line of code that asks `System.out` (an instance of `PrintStream`) to display a `String`, but the `String` wouldn't be displayed until the program completes—after the user has typed in his or her input.

It turns out that most implementations of Java recognize this problem and arrange for output held in a `System.out` buffer to be displayed when keyboard input is requested. That's good, but not good enough. At the time of this writing, this approach is optional for implementations of Java and one might still encounter implementations in which `System.out`'s buffer is not displayed.

There is a fix. `PrintStream` provides another method, which forces it to write out all the `String`s in the buffer. The method is called `flush` and requires no arguments. An example of its use is as follows:

```
System.out.flush();
```

This forces `PrintStream System.out` to display all the output it had been keeping in its buffer. To guarantee that the prompt appears right away, we must write the following:

```
System.out.println(
          "Type in a word to be pluralized, please ");
System.out.flush();
inputLine = keyboard.readLine();
```

A general form for interactive input and output is as follows:

```
System.out.println(prompt goes here);
System.out.flush();
string reference variable = keyboard.readLine();
```

possibly compute something (using, for example, concatenation)

```
System.out.println(output string goes here);
```

There can be variations on this prompt-flush-compute-output paradigm. For example, the prompt may be generated by several `println` messages. The `flush` method only has to be invoked after the last of these and before the `readLine` method.

EXERCISES

1. Write a program that prompts the user for a `String` to be printed three times, reads the `String`, and prints it out three times.

2. Most computer systems provide a utility or other means for removing a file. Write a program that does this. It should prompt the user for the name of a file to delete. After the user types in the file name, the program deletes it.

3. Write a program that changes the name of a file. It prompts the user for the original name of the file and then for the new name of the file. After the user types in both names, the program renames the file accordingly.

3.8   Input: Disk Files

Obtaining input from a disk file is only slightly more involved than obtaining it from a keyboard. Our starting point must always be to find some sort of *InputStream* object, that is, either a `BufferedInputStream` (such as `System.in`) or a `FileInputStream`. It is the latter that we need for modeling the flow of input from a file to a program.

Once we have a reference to a `FileInputStream` object, we can use it exactly as we used `System.in`. That is, we use it to construct an `Input-StreamReader`, which in turn is used to construct a `BufferedReader` object that can deliver lines of input to us as `String` objects.

Constructing a `FileInputStream` object is much like constructing a `FileOutputStream` object. First, we create a `File` object and then use it to create a `FileInputStream` object, as follows:

```
File    f = new File("Americas.Most.Wanted");
FileInputStream  fs = new FileInputStream(f);
```
From file name to FileInputStream

At this point, we have our *InputStream* object, which is referred to by `fs`. The latter plays the same role as `System.in`, and we can proceed as follows, as we did for the keyboard:

```
InputStreamReader   isr;
BufferedReader        fileInput;
isr = new InputStreamReader(fs);
fileInput = new BufferedReader(isr);
```
From FileInputStream to BufferedReader

The object that `fileInput` references is a `BufferedReader`, just like the one `keyboard` referenced in Section 3.6. (See Figure 3.7.) We can send `readLine` messages to this object to read successive lines from the file, as follows:

```
String     line;
line = fileInput.readLine();
System.out.println(line);
line = fileInput.readLine();
System.out.println(line);
```
Using the BufferedReader

EXAMPLE   Making a Copy of a File. Let's write a program that reads, interactively from the keyboard, the name of a file that contains two lines. The program creates a copy of the file whose name is the original name with `.copy` added to it. We write it using sections of code (annotated below) based on the various examples we have seen so far in this chapter. (See Figure 3.8.)

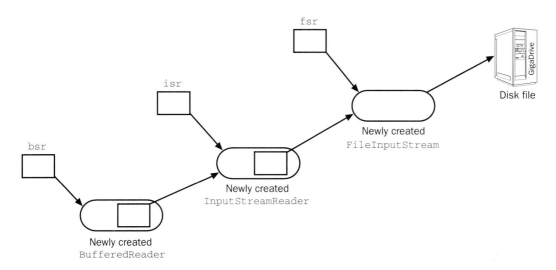

FIGURE 3.7   A `BufferedReader` for a file. The `BufferedReader` is constructed with a reference to an `InputStreamReader` that was constructed with a reference to a `FileInputStream` object.

Here is the program:

```
import java.io.*;
class CopyFile {
    public static void main(String[] arg) throws Exception {
    InputStreamReader    isrKeyboard;
    BufferedReader       keyboard;              For modeling the keyboard

    String               fileNameOrig;
    File                 fOrig;
    FileInputStream      fisOrig;               For modeling the file input
    InputStreamReader    isrOrig;
    BufferedReader       rdrOrig;

    String               fileNameCopy;
    File                 fCopy;                 For modeling the output going to
    FileOutputStream     fosCopy;               file
    PrintStream          psCopy;
    String               s;

    isrKeyboard = new InputStreamReader(System.in);   Access keyboard
    keyboard = new BufferedReader(isrKeyboard);

    System.out.print("name of file to copy: ");
    System.out.flush();                                Read file name from keyboard
    fileNameOrig = keyboard.readLine();                and create name of backup file
    fileNameCopy = fileNameOrig.concat(".copy");
```

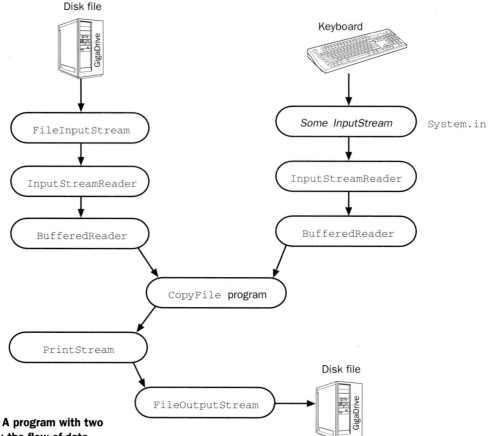

FIGURE 3.8 A program with two input sources: the flow of data.

```
fOrig = new File(fileNameOrig);
fisOrig = new FileInputStream(fOrig);
isrOrig = new InputStreamReader(fisOrig);
rdrOrig = new BufferedReader(isrOrig);

fCopy = new File(fileNameCopy);
fosCopy = new FileOutputStream(fCopy);
psCopy = new PrintStream(fosCopy);

s = rdrOrig.readLine();
psCopy.println(s);
s = rdrOrig.readLine();
psCopy.println(s);
    }
  }
```

Access original file

Arrange to write to backup file

Read two lines from original and write to backup

1. Assume that there is a file called `"singer"`, which contains the name of a famous singer, and there is another file called `"actress"`, which contains the name of a famous actress. In both cases, the information is on one line. Write a program called `EnquirerPredictor` that reads these files and produces a file called `"predictions98"`. The new file contains a prediction that the given singer and actress will marry.

2. Write a program called `GreetingMaker` that reads a single line from a file called `"greeting"` and produces a file called `"Greeting.java"` that contains a simple Java program that will, when compiled and executed, print to standard output the given line (from `"greeting"`). To represent a double quote in a `String` constant use the two character combination `\"`.

3. Rewrite the `CopyFile` program using composition to eliminate some of the variables and shorten the program text.   •

3.9   Network Computing: An Introduction

In this section you will learn how to write programs that read publicly available information from the Internet—available sites range from the White House in Washington D.C. to the web site of my favorite radio station in New York City.

3.9.1   Network Concepts

Before jumping into Java code, a quick overview of some basic network concepts are in order.

A **computer network** is a group of *computers* that can directly exchange information with each other. This is usually accomplished by connecting the computers with a wire of some kind.

The **Internet** is a group of *computer networks* that allows a computer on one network to exchange information with a computer on any of the other networks. The networks are connected to each other by means of special telephone lines or satellite relays. You can get on the Internet by getting a connection to one of those networks that are part of the Internet and installing the necessary software on your computer. You can then communicate with every machine on the Internet because of the following:

- Each computer on the Net (as we call the Internet for short) has a unique **Internet address.**
- The software on the computers on the Net can forward information to the correct computer, provided that information comes with a proper Internet address.

The Internet addresses of machines on the Net are `Strings` like `"www.whitehouse.gov"` or `"home.netscape.com"` or `"machine1.somestateu.edu"`.

Information on the Internet is organized into units called **network resources.** These resources may be pictures, audio segments, videos, plain text, and so on. Usually, a resource is simply a file stored on some machine that is on the Net. Each resource is available from a particular machine on the Internet. Each resource is uniquely identified by what is called an **URL,** pronounced "earl," which stands for Universal Resource Locator.

What's especially nice about URLs is that they are not just arbitrary unique identifiers (like social security numbers), but they have several parts, each of which has a meaning, as follows:

Part	Example	Purpose
protocol	http	identifies the kind of software that is needed to access the data
internet address	`www.yahoo.com`	identifies the computer with the resource
file name	`index.html`	identifies the file on the computer holding the resource

These pieces are put together to form an URL the following way:

```
protocol://internet address/file name
```

A `://` separates the protocol from the machine address, and a `/` separates the internet address from the file name. For example, the URL

```
http://www.yahoo.com/index.html
```

means: use World Wide Web software (*protocol:* `http`) to contact the `www.yahoo.com` (the Internet address of the computer that has this resource) to access `index.html` (the file name for the resource). (See Figure 3.9.)

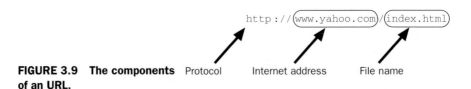

FIGURE 3.9 The components of an URL.

3.9.2 Network input

Reading input from World Wide Web resources in a Java program is as simple as reading input from a disk file. Again, the key is to obtain an `InputStream` —in this case a `FilterInputStream`—that provides the fundamental behavior of modeling a stream of input (in this case from a Web site).

The Java class library provides a class, `URL`, to model URLs. The `URL` class provides a constructor that takes a `String` argument (the URL as we would write it) as follows:

```
URL    u = new URL("http://www.yahoo.com/");
```

It also provides a method, `openStream`, that takes no arguments but returns a `FilterInputStream`, as follows:

```
FilterInputStream      ins = u.openStream();
```

This method does quite a bit of work behind the scenes: It sets up communication software on your side, initiates contact with the remote machine, waits for a response, sets up the connection, and then constructs an `FilterInputStream` object to model the connection, returning a reference to this object.

Once we have a `FilterInputStream` like this, we are in business: We can easily construct a `BufferedReader` object (as we did for file and keyboard) and then read from the remote resource, as follows (see Figure 3.10):

```
InputStreamReader   isr = new InputStreamReader(ins);
BufferedReader   remote = new BufferedReader(isr);
... remote.readLine() ...
```

EXAMPLE   Here is a program that reads and prints out the first five lines of the White House's web page:

```
import  java.net.*;
import  java.io.*;
class WHWWW {
    public static void main(String[] arg) {
        URL    u = new URL("http://www.whitehouse.gov/");
        FilterInputStream  ins = u.openStream();
        InputStreamReader  isr = new InputStreamReader(ins);
        BufferedReader  whiteHouse = new BufferedReader(isr);
```

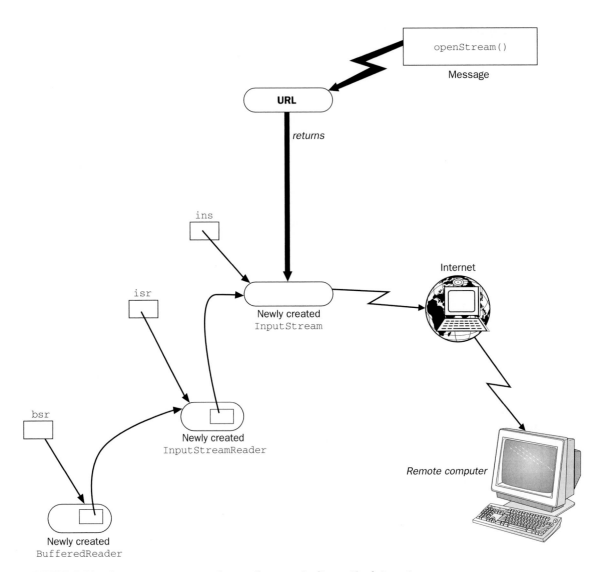

FIGURE 3.10 A `BufferedReader` for reading a web site on the internet.

```
            System.out.println(whiteHouse.readLine());
            System.out.println(whiteHouse.readLine());
            System.out.println(whiteHouse.readLine());
            System.out.println(whiteHouse.readLine());
            System.out.println(whiteHouse.readLine());
        }
    }
```

1. Write a program that prompts for and reads a `String`. The program should then construct an URL for `http://www.X.com/`, where X is the `String` read in, and arrange to print the first five lines of the resource at that site. If the user types in "ibm," the first five lines from `http://www.ibm.com/` will be printed.

2. At the time of this writing, the current value of the Dow Jones Industrial Average can be found in the thirty-fourth line of the following URL: `http://quotes.yahoo.com/`. Write a program that prints that line and only that line.

SUMMARY

In this chapter we have learned to create new objects, instances of Java's pre-defined classes. This requires the `new` operator followed by a message to the newly created object that invokes its constructor. The constructor is a special method, used in the creation of an object. The name of the constructor is always the same as the name of its class. Like other methods, constructors may require arguments.

We were also introduced to some of the classes that Java provides to support input and output. We learned how each of these classes provides just the behavior needed to model a particular input or output service. To create the object with the behavior that we wanted we had to create a sequence of objects, each used in the creation of the next. This could be done with multiple assignments or by composition of constructors with the `new` operator.

For example, to create a `BufferedReader` object that would allow lines to be read from a disk file, we had to create a `File` object, use the `File` object to create a `FileInputStream` object, use that object to create an `InputStreamReader` object that finally could be passed to the `BufferedReader` constructor.

We also explored the particulars of interactive input and output and learned about the buffering that is used by `PrintStream`, with the resulting need for a flush method. We were introduced to classes that model URLs and network connections to URLs; these allowed us to create objects that model URLs and the behavior of Internet connections.

STUDY AID: TERMINOLOGY REVIEW

buffer   A place to store information temporarily, prior to further processing.

computer network   A collection of computers, connected by wires, that can exchange data with each other.

constructor   A method that is invoked when an object is created. The name of the constructor method is the same as the corresponding class name.

end-user   A person who is using a program, usually not the author of the code.

file   A named collection of data on the disk.

flush   The forced output of characters saved in a buffer.

input   Information from outside the program that is provided to the program.

interactive   An arrangement of bidirectional and alternating data flow between user and program.

Internet   A rapidly growing, very widely used global network of networks.

Internet address   A `String`, such as `www.aw.com`, that identifies a machine on the Internet.

network resource   A resource, usually a file, that is available to users on machines other than the one on which the file is stored.

operation   An action in Java that results in a value.

operator   A symbol or keyword representing an operation (e.g., the identifier `new` represents the operation that creates an object).

output   Information that the program provides to the outside world.

prompt   A `String` that is written to the screen to tell an end-user what kind of input should be entered next.

URL   A unique identification of a network resource, including the Internet address of the machine on which the resource is stored, the file name of the resource, and the protocol (such as HyperText Transfer Protocol, or HTTP) that should be used to access the resource.

QUESTIONS FOR REVIEW

1. What does the `new` operator do?

2. When is a *constructor* invoked? How is it invoked? What is its purpose?

3. How can a Java program create or remove a file?

4. Why does the phrase "throws Exception" appear now in our code?

5. How do you read a line of text from a keyboard? From a file? From an Internet file?

FURTHER EXERCISES

1. Rewrite the program in Exercise 2 in Section 2.6 so that it prompts for and reads a three-character string, and prints all permutations of the string's characters.

2. Write a program that takes a file named `"ford"` renames it `"lincoln"` and then creates a file called `"ford"` that contains the single line `"get a horse"`.

3. Write a program that models a psychiatrist by asking the user (patient) what the problem is. Upon getting the user's response, the program asks "Why do you say '...whatever the response was...'?" When the user answers this question, the program responds: "That's very interesting, we can talk more about that next session." Sample session (user input in bold):

```
What are you thinking of today?
I'm depressed.
Why do you say 'I'm depressed'?
I didn't say you're depressed, I said I'm depressed.
That's very interesting, we can talk more about that
next session.
```

4. (A challenge.) How big is the `PrintStream` buffer? Write a program that allows you to estimate its size accurately.

Applets

Introduction to Writing Programs In the Supplement section of Chapter 2, you learned to write simple web page files using HyperText Markup Language (HTML). This section marks the first of our forays into writing *Graphical User Interface* (GUI) programs for the Internet's World Wide Web.

An **applet** is a Java program that is embedded in a web page. It is one way of providing the kind of active content that we mentioned in the last chapter. Unlike HTML, an applet does not merely display information—it can get input and compute as well.

Applets use the GUI facilities that are provided with Java. These are not part of the language proper; they belong to a package of predefined classes known as the **abstract window toolkit (AWT).** Thus, most of the code in the following sections will employ language constructs that will be familiar to us once we get past the first several chapters of this book. We may not understand exactly how a piece of code fits into the big picture, but we will at least understand what it does at the statement level.

However, there will be some "magic" (i.e., portions of code whose purpose or even basic meaning cannot be discussed until later—this will obviously occur more frequently in the beginning and less as we progress). Our attitude toward this is *do as we do* (i.e., play with the code presented in the following sections and build upon them). For example, in the following sample piece of code, you will see the method invocation:

```
g.drawString("This is everyone's first applet.",20,20);
```

Modifying (playing with) the arguments will give you a sense of how coordinates (20,20) work and how this method behaves. We will provide examples and some explanation, but you will have to experiment and learn to read existing documentation.

The **Java Application Programming Interface (API)** is a description of the classes and methods distributed with Java. This documentation can be accessed via the World Wide Web (ask your instructor or administrator for details). All the classes and methods used in these sections are documented in the Java API. In addition, other related methods of interest (e.g., changing colors, fonts) will often be documented nearby. You should feel free to experiment with such methods. You may crash your program, but that too is part of the learning process.

Reading documentation is an essential skill any computer scientist must acquire. It is also often a multipass effort, sometimes because the documentation is not particularly well written, other times because the reader does not have the full prerequisite background. Do not be discouraged if you cannot make much sense out of the API at first. Frequent contact with it will make you familiar with its "geography," and you will eventually feel quite at home.

In summary, the following sections are a break in approach from the main parts of the chapter. They are intended to be fun, as well as instructive. Remember, though, that these sections are more like the bumper car ride in an amusement park than driving in the city, and things may get quite bumpy at times.

Our First Applet   Let's start with the following example, which is perhaps the most frequently written Java program:

```
import java.awt.*;                        // Our first applet
import java.applet.*;
public class FirstApplet extends Applet {
    public void paint(Graphics g) {
        g.drawString("This is everyone's first applet.",
                    20,20);
    }
}
```

The following is the applet version of the program we encountered on the first page of Chapter 1:

```
import java.io.*;
class Program1 {
    public static void main(String[] arg) {
```

There is almost a line-by-line correspondence between the two, as shown below:

- The applet requires predefined classes from both the AWT and the applet packages.
- The two lines after the `import` and the two lines that end the applet correspond to their counterparts in `Program1` (given in Chapter 1).
- In an applet, we have no `PrintStream` object available; one way to display text is to send a `drawString` message to a `Graphics` object, instead of using `println`.

A `Graphics` object models the drawing behavior of a portion of a computer screen; that is, it will respond to messages requesting that rectangles be drawn, background colors be set, current font information be returned, etc. One of these methods, `drawString`, allows a `String` to be displayed at a particular position on the screen. The first argument to this method specifies the `String`; the next two arguments specify the horizontal and vertical coordinates (x and y, respectively) of the starting position of the `String` on the screen (i.e., the location at which the first character in the `String` is displayed).

Embedding an applet in a web page means arranging for it to be downloaded as part of a web page and executed by the web browser. To embed the `FirstApplet` applet, you must do the following:

- Compile `FirstApplet.java`, yielding `FirstApplet.class`.
- Include the following HTML code in your web page:

```
<APPLET CODE="FirstApplet.class" WIDTH=300 HEIGHT=60>
        </APPLET>
```

(The class file must be in the same directory or folder as your HTML code and, depending on the system, the access permissions may have to be changed—you may have to consult your instructor, system administrator, or help desk for details.)

A complete HTML file for this applet might be as follows:

```
<HTML>
<HEAD>
    <TITLE>Hw1</TITLE>
</HEAD>
<BODY>
    <HR>
        <APPLET CODE="FirstApplet.class" WIDTH=300
                        HEIGHT=60></APPLET>
    <HR>
    <A HREF="FirstApplet.java">The source.</A>
</BODY>
</HTML>
```

This HTML file also provides the source code for the applet (using the A tag), and so we assume that the source code, `FirstApplet.java`, is in the same directory as the HTML file.

When this web page is accessed, the web browser will detect the `APPLET` tag and download the `FirstApplet.class` file. The web browser creates a `Graphics` object and associates it with part of the screen. The size of the screen portion associated with the `Graphics` object is determined in part by the `WIDTH` and `HEIGHT` specifications in the `APPLET` tag. At some point, the browser starts the applet executing, and, like `main` in the programs in the chapter, `paint` executes. In the above example, it simply invokes the `drawString` method of this `Graphic` object, and the `String` "This is everyone's first applet." appears on the screen.

Variations The AWT provides a `Color` and a `Font` class that enable the programmer to define and use new colors and fonts for the applet's display. Colors are described using three integers that specify the amount of red, green, and blue, each on a scale from 0 to 255. Fonts are specified by naming a font family (expressed as a `String`: "TimesRoman" or "Helvetica", for example), a font style (`Font.PLAIN`, `Font.BOLD`, or `Font.ITALIC`), and a number specifying point size (12 is typical). To change the color to purple, we create a `Color` object that represents purple and then send a `setColor` message to the `Graphics` object before we draw our message. The code is as follows:

```
import java.awt.*;                    // Our first applet (a variation)
import java.applet.*;
public class FirstApplet extends Applet {
   public void paint(Graphics g) {
```

```
Color   c;
c = new Color(180,10,120);   // Lots of red and blue but not too
                             // much or it will be too light; there is
                             // almost to no green.
g.setColor(c);               // Make the color purple.
g.drawString("This is everyone's first
            applet.",20,20);
   }
}
```

To change the font we similarly insert the following:

```
Font    f;
f = new Font("Helvetica", Font.ITALIC, 18);
g.setFont(f);
```

Besides drawing `Strings` and setting the font and color, `Graphics` provides the following simple geometric object drawing methods:

- `fillOval`: arguments are four numbers specifying *x,y* coordinates and width, height.
- `fillRect`: similar arguments.
- `drawOval`: similar arguments.
- `drawRect`: similar arguments.
- `drawLine`: arguments are four integers specifying *x,y* coordinates of start and end of line.

For example:

```
import java.awt.*;     // Our first applet (a variation)
import java.applet.*;
public class FirstApplet extends Applet {
   public void paint(Graphics g) {
      Color   c = new Color(20,120,160); Can you guess the color?
      g.setColor(c);
      g.fillOval(20,20,60,30);
   }
```

chapter 4

Defining Classes

4.1   Introduction

"Why did they design it that way?" we asked at one point in the previous chapter. At the time we were referring to the design of `FileOutputStream` and the question was motivated by the nuisance of having to go from `File` to `FileOutputStream` to `PrintStream` in order to write to a file. We have encountered other nuisances as well. Setting up to read a Web site (`URL` to `URLConnection` to `BufferedInputStream` to `InputStreamReader` to `BufferedReader`) made the file output setup seem simple in comparison. But perhaps the worst was interactive input and output. It was too bad that there was no method that would issue a prompt and read a response, but having to flush `System.out` every time we wrote a prompt was really objectionable.

    Are we as programmers therefore condemned to cumbersome compositions each time we want to read a Web site or write to a file? Must we frequently flush output in interactive applications? Do we have to accept the inadequate (for our purposes) behavior of existing classes because some other programmers chose to design it that way? No, we can define our own classes to provide the behavior that we require.

4.2   Class Definitions

Our First Class Definition: Constructors and Methods   Before learning how to develop class definitions, let's take a quick look at a three very simple ones first. We start with the following:

```
class Laugher1 {
    public Laugher1() {
    }
    public void laugh() {
        System.out.println("haha");
    }
}
```

This defines a class called `Laugher1`. It provides a single method, `laugh`, that simply prints `"haha"`. Using this definition, we can, for example, create a `Laugher1` object, as follows:

```
Laugher1    x;
x = new Laugher1();
```

and send it the following `laugh` message:

```
x.laugh();
```

The phrase

```
class Laugher1 {
```

indicates that this is the beginning of the definition of a class named `Laugher1`. The `}` on the last line signifies the end of the definition. These lines are called **delimiters** because they set the limits (beginning and end) of the class definition within the program text. Between these two delimiters is the definition of a **constructor**

```
public Laugher1() {
}
```

and the definition of a **method**

```
public void laugh() {
    System.out.println("haha");
}
```

The definition of the `laugh` method consists of a **prototype**

```
public void laugh()
```

and a method body

```
    {
System.out.println("haha");
}
```

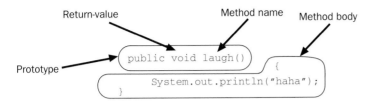

FIGURE 4.1 **Structure of a simple method definition.**

The prototype starts with the keyword **public.** Following this is the **return-type**—the type of value that the method returns. The keyword void is used for methods, such as laugh, that return no values. Following the return-type is the method's name and a pair of parentheses.

The method body contains statements that are executed when it is invoked. The method body tells us what this method does when invoked: It prints "haha". When the closing brace } is reached, the method terminates. The sender of the laugh message can then resume execution. (See Figure 4.1.)

The form of a constructor definition is identical to that of a method except that constructors are not given a return-type—they are always invoked in conjunction with new, which itself returns a reference to the newly created object. The constructor for Laugher1 does nothing at all. (See Figure 4.2.)

4.2.1 A Second Class Definition: Parameters and Overloading

Suppose we want the sender of the laugh message to decide whether the "laugh syllable" should be ha or ho or hee, etc. This is additional information, and so the sender of the message would have to provide it as an **argument,** as follows:

```
x.laugh("ha");
```

or

```
x.laugh("yuk");
```

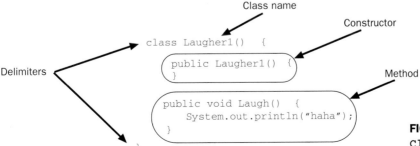

FIGURE 4.2 **Structure of a** Class **definition.**

To use this information, it must be accessible in the method. **Parameters** are variables that are declared in the method's prototype and that are initialized with the values of the arguments when the method is invoked.

Because our new version of `laugh` is sent a `String` argument, its prototype must be as follows:

```
public void laugh(String syllable)
```

The method body can be the following:

```
    {
    String  laughSound;
    laughSound = syllable.concat(syllable);
    System.out.println(laughSound);
}
```

The method body declares a variable `laughSound` that is initialized to the `String` that `syllable` refers to concatenated with itself. So if the method is invoked as follows,

```
x.laugh("ho")
```

`syllable` will refer to `"ho"` and `laughSound` will refer to `"hoho"`. (See Figure 4.3.)

Our second class then is:

```
class Laugher2 {
    public Laugher2() {
    }
    public void laugh() {
        System.out.println("haha");
    }
```

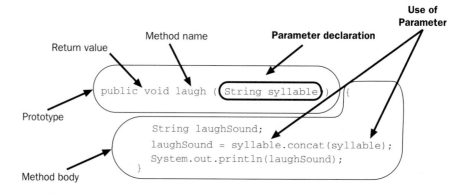

FIGURE 4.3
Structure of a
method definition:
Parameters

```
    public void laugh(String syllable) {
        String  laughSound;
        laughSound = syllable.concat(syllable);
        System.out.println(laughSound);
    }
}
```

By providing two methods of the same name but with different *signatures*,

```
laugh()
laugh(String syllable)
```

we are *overloading* the method-name `laugh`. As a result, a user of this class can write the following to get `"haha"` printed by default:

```
x.laugh();
```

And the user must write the following to get `"yukyuk"` printed:

```
x.laugh("yuk");
```

Because we can print `"haha"` out without explicitly specifying the laugh syllables, we say that `"ha"` is the default laugh syllable. A **default** is a behavior or value that is used if no explicit behavior or value is provided. Of course, we can always write the following:

```
x.laugh("ha");
```

4.2.2   A Third Class Definition: Instance Variables

Finally, suppose we wanted to give the creator of a `Laugher` object the option of specifying the default laugh syllable so that it would not have to always be `"ha"`. This is additional information that would have to be supplied to the constructor as an argument when the object is created. For example, the following would display `"heeeheee"` and then `"hoho"`:

```
Laugher3   x;
x = new Laugher3("ho");
x.laugh("heee");
x.laugh();
```

How can a class definition support this? The constructor now gets a `String` argument, so its signature must include a declaration of a `String` parameter, as follows:

```
Laugher3(String s)
```

Although it is the constructor that gets the default syllable `String` as an argument, it is the `laugh()` method (with no arguments) that needs access to it. Unfortunately, methods cannot access variables, including parameters, of other methods. How can `laugh()` get access to this `String`?

The answer is to declare a `String` variable inside the class definition but outside any of the methods. Such a variable is called an **instance variable** because it belongs to the entire object (instance) and not to any one particular method. Instance variables may be accessed by *all* the methods in the class. (See Figure 4.4.) Declarations of instance variables have the same form as the declarations we have encountered so far, except that we start the declaration with the keyword **private.**

The constructor's job is to save the information it received as an argument by copying its parameter's value to the instance variable, as follows:

```
public Laugher3(String s) {
    defaultSyllable = s;
}
```

Now the `laugh()` method can use the information saved in `default-Syllable`, as follows:

```
public void laugh() {
    String  laughSound;
    laughSound = defaultSyllable.concat(defaultSyllable);
    System.out.println(laughSound);
}
```

Our complete third class definition follows:

```
class Laugher3 {
    public Laugher3(String s) {
```

```
class Laugher3 {
    public Laugher3 ( String s ) {
    }
    public void Laugh () {
    }
    . . .
    private String defaultSyllable;
}
```

Instance variable declaration

Note that `defaultSyllable` may be used in any method body.

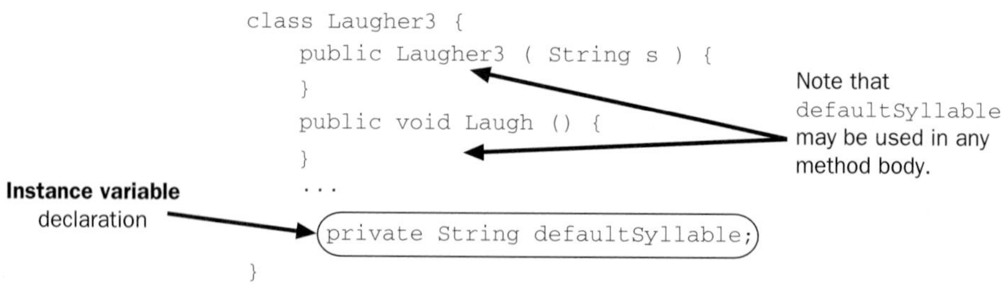

FIGURE 4.4   Accessing an instance variable.

```
            defaultSyllable = s;
        }
        public void laugh() {
            String  laughSound;
            laughSound = defaultSyllable.concat(defaultSyllable);
            System.out.println(laughSound);
        }
        public void laugh(String syllable) {
            String  laughSound;
            laughSound = syllable.concat(syllable);
            System.out.println(laughSound);
        }
        private String defaultSyllable;
    }
```

4.2.3   Using a Class Definition

All the classes we have used so far have been predefined ones that are provided by the Java distribution itself. Now we have our own, Laugher3. How do we use it?

First, we create a file, Laugher3.java, containing our class definition. At the beginning of the file, however, we add the following because the Laugher3 class uses PrintStream objects:

```
import java.io.*;
```

Second, we compile our Laugher3.java file. If there are no errors, this produces Laugher3.class.

Once these steps are taken, we can write programs using the Laugher3 class. Here is an example:

```
import java.io.*;
class LaughALittle {
    public static void main(String[] arg) {
        System.out.println("Live and laugh!!!");
        Laugher3    x,y;
        x = new Laugher3("yuk");
        y = new Laugher3("harr");
        x.laugh();
        x.laugh("hee");
        y.laugh();
    }
}
```

The `LaughALittle` program can be compiled and run in the usual way.

1. Add a pair of overloaded `bigLaugh` methods to the `Laugher3` class that are identical to the `laugh` methods except that their output is all in uppercase letters.

2. Write a class definition for a class named `NextToNothing`. It has a constructor that takes no arguments and doesn't do anything. It has a method named `nothing` that takes no arguments and doesn't do anything. Write a program that creates a `NextToNothing` object and sends it a `nothing` message.

3. Add a constructor to `Laugher3` that doesn't take any arguments—it just sets the instance variable to `"ha"`. Why is such an overloaded constructor useful?   •

4.3   Designing Classes: Specifying an `InteractiveIO` Class

In the previous section our approach to class design was extremely casual. We started with one overly simple class. Then we added a little of this, followed by a little of that. Such an approach was useful for explaining what a class definition is, but it is unworkable when it comes to designing classes of any significance. It would be like building a house a room at a time. A more systematic approach is needed.

To illustrate our approach to class design, we start with the problem of interactive **input** and **output**—writing and flushing output to the monitor as well as prompting the user for and reading in `String`s typed from the keyboard. The first phase of class design involves the following steps:

- Decide on the behavior that the class will provide; because the behavior of an object is provided through its methods, this step and the next result in a decision about what methods to provide.
- Determine the way the class will be used (its *interface*); this means determining the *prototypes* of the methods.
- Write a *sample program* using the class; this provides a way to check that our design makes sense so far.
- Write a *skeleton* of the class definition, that is, the class boilerplate along with the prototypes and empty method bodies.

4.3.1 Determining the Behavior

If we had a class called `InteractiveIO`, we would want the following *behavior*:

- Write a message to the monitor (with the assurance that it is displayed immediately)
- Prompt for and read a `String` from the keyboard

Also, the user should be able to create an `InteractiveIO` object without reference to `System.in` or `System.out`.

4.3.2 Interface and Prototypes

Once we have a good idea of the behavior we want our class to offer, we can take the next step in class definition: determining the interface of the class. The **interface** of a class is the way in which one can use an object of that particular class. Guided by our discussion of `InteractiveIO`'s desired behavior, we would like the ability to do the following:

- *Declare a* `InteractiveIO` *reference variable as follows:*

  ```
  InteractiveIO    interIO;
  ```

  This is easy. Once we have a name for a class, we can use it to declare reference variables.

- *Instantiate (create) a new* `InteractiveIO` *object, without making references to* `System.in` *and* `System.out` *or using composition as follows:*

  ```
  interIO = new InteractiveIO();
  ```

  We must design the class with a constructor that requires no arguments.

- *Send the object a message to write a* `String` *to the monitor as follows:*

  ```
  interIO.write("Please answer each question");
  ```

  We must design the class to provide a method (we call it `write`) to do this.

- *Prompt for and read a* `String` *from the keyboard, returning a reference to the* `String` *as follows:*

  ```
  String  s;
  s = interIO.promptAndRead("What is your first name? ");
  ```

  We must design the class to provide a method (we call it `promptAndRead`) to do this.

We gave meaningful names to the methods and followed the standard Java capitalization conventions: `write` and `promptAndRead`. The name of the constructor, `InteractiveIO`, was not our choice—the constructor name is always the same as the class name itself—which *was* our choice.

Our constructor was given no arguments, so its prototype is as follows:

```
public InteractiveIO()
```

Because it is a constructor, we don't specify return-type.

Our `write` method needn't return anything, so its return-type is `void`. We intend to give it a `String` argument in the messages that invoke it. It has a `String` parameter and its prototype is as follows:

```
public void write(String s)
```

The `promptAndRead` method returns a reference to a `String` that was read. So its return-type is `String`. Its prototype is as follows because it too is invoked with a `String` argument:

```
public String promptAndRead(String s)
```

4.3.3   A Sample Program that Uses the Class

Writing a sample program serves two purposes. First, it helps clarify how our new class, `InteractiveIO`, is to be used. Second, it is a check to make sure that the interface that we developed above is really satisfactory. It would be a shame to go further with the definition of the class only to find out at the end that it was not quite what we wanted after all.

The simplest example of the use of this class would be a program that prompts for the word, reads it, and writes it back. If our `InteractiveIO` class does all we claim, we can just write the following:

```
import java.io.*;
class TryInteractiveIO {
    public static void main(String[] arg) throws Exception {
        InteractiveIO  interIO;
        String      line;
        interIO = new InteractiveIO();
        line = interIO.promptAndRead(
                            "Please type in a word: ");
        interIO.write(line);
    }
}
```

We see that `InteractiveIO` can get the job done, and it beats having to always flush output and to create `BufferedReader` objects by composition. `InteractiveIO` does all that dirty work for us.

4.3.4   Class Definition Skeleton

Using our prototypes, we can write a skeleton of the `InteractiveIO` class as follows:

```
class InteractiveIO {
    public InteractiveIO() {  ◄──────  The constructor—no return-type
        statements
    }

    // Write s to the monitor.
    public void write(String s) {
        statements
    }

    // Write s to the monitor, read a string from the keyboard, and return a reference to it.
    public String promptAndRead(String s) {
        statements
    }

    instance variables, if we need them
}
```

In front of each method prototype, we write a comment that states what the method is supposed to do. This completes our specification of the `InteractiveIO` class.

EXERCISES

1. Consider the code below. Identify the method-name, the parameters, the return-type, the body, the prototype, and the signature.

```
public void printTwice(String x) {
    System.out.println(x);
    System.out.println(x);
}
```

2. Consider a `DoubleSpacer` class. It would work the same way that `PrintStream` works, except it would add an empty line to the output after each line (to double space the output). Follow the steps outlined above to produce a skeleton of a class definition for `DoubleSpacer`.

███ 4.4 ███ Implementing the `InteractiveIO` Class

The **implementation** of a class is a matter of writing its method bodies and declaring any instance variables that are needed. It is worth remembering the following:

- You can start working on any of the methods.
- You can stop working on one method before you've completed it and go to work on another method.

Start with the method that seems easiest to write. We have three methods to complete: `promptAndRead`, `write`, and the constructor, `InteractiveIO`. The `write` method looks the easiest. We know how to write a `String` s to the monitor, as follows:

```
System.out.print(s);
```

We remember that we are supposed to make sure that all output is immediately displayed. We also know how to do this, as follows:

```
System.out.flush();
```

Putting it together, we have our method definition, as follows:

```
// Write s to the monitor
public void write(String s) {
    System.out.print(s);
    System.out.flush();
}
```

One method down, two to go. Let's tackle `promptAndRead` next. In Chapter 3 we developed the following code to write s to the monitor and to read a line from the keyboard:

```
System.out.print(s);
System.out.flush();
BufferedReader  br;
br = new BufferedReader(new InputStreamReader(System.in));
String  line;
line = br.readLine();
```

The `promptAndRead` method can't stop here—it has to return the reference that `line` now contains. Java provides a special statement, the **return** statement, to return a value for a method as follows:

```
return value;
```

When the `return` statement is executed, the method terminates and the sender resumes execution. (Recall from Chapter 2 that the sender of a message suspends execution until the method returns.) In addition, the value indicated in the `return` statement is returned to the sender of the message.

In `promptAndRead`, the value that is to be returned is the reference to the newly read `String`, `line`. Therefore, we have to add the following to the above statements:

```
return line;
```

The complete definition of the `promptAndRead` method follows:

```
// Write s to the monitor, read a string from the keyboard, and return a reference to it.
public String promptAndRead(String s) throws Exception {
    System.out.print(s);
    System.out.flush();
    BufferedReader  br;
    br = new BufferedReader(
                        new InputStreamReader(System.in));
    String  line;
    line = br.readLine();
    return line;
}
```

Finally, we turn to the constructor. Our interface indicated that it receives no arguments. Furthermore, as far as we can see, the two methods `promptAndRead` and `write` don't require any information from an instance variable. Therefore, we don't need any instance variables, and our constructor is as simple as the one in `Laugher1`. The complete class definition for `InteractiveIO` follows:

```
class InteractiveIO {
    public InteractiveIO() {   The constructor—nothing to do, so it is empty.
    }

    // Write s to the monitor.
    public void write(String s) {
        System.out.print(s);
        System.out.flush();
    }

    // Write s to the monitor, read a string from the keyboard, and return a reference to it.
    public String promptAndRead(String s) throws Exception {
        System.out.print(s);
        System.out.flush();
        BufferedReader  br;
        br = new BufferedReader(
                            new InputStreamReader(System.in));
        String  line;
        line = br.readLine();
        return line;
```

```
    }
```

No instance variables needed, apparently.

```
}
```

4.5   Improve the Implementation but Don't Touch the Interface!

We have a class definition of InteractiveIO, but we will not rest here. Like any kind of writing, code, even if it "works," can often be improved. In the case of our InteractiveIO class, the chief improvement results from recognizing that it is silly to construct new InputStreamReader and BufferedReader objects each time we read a single line. It would be better to create them once at the outset and then just use the same Buffered-Reader to keep reading from the keyboard.

There is one method that is always invoked once and only once at the outset, when the object is created: the constructor. So it is quite logical to move

```
br = new BufferedReader(new InputStreamReader(System.in));
```

into the constructor, as follows:

```
class InteractiveIO {
    public InteractiveIO() throws Exception  {    ◄── The constructor
        br = new BufferedReader(
                        new InputStreamReader(System.in));
    }
    ...
    public String promptAndRead(String s) throws Exception {
        System.out.print(s);
        System.out.flush();
        BufferedReader br;

        String  line;
        ...
    }
}
```

However, now it seems we face a problem: Where should the declaration of the BufferedReader reference variable be placed? Both the constructor and promptAndRead need access to it; therefore, it must be declared outside of either method; that is, it must be an instance variable.

Accordingly, we move the declaration of br out of promptAndRead to the end of the class definition:

```
class InteractiveIO {
    public InteractiveIO() throws Exception  {    ◄── The constructor
```

```
        br = new BufferedReader(
                        new InputStreamReader(System.in))'
    }
    ...
    public String promptAndRead(String s) throws Exception {
        System.out.print(s);
        System.out.flush();

        String  line;
        line = br.readLine();
        return line;
    }
    private BufferedReader br; // now an instance variable
}
```

We can make a couple of other minor improvements to our class as well. First, there is no need to store the `String` reference returned by `readLine` in `line` when we just return that value in the next statement. We can return it directly. Thus,

```
String  line;
line = br.readLine();
return line;
```

may be replaced with the shorter and equally clear

```
return br.readLine();
```

Second, `promptAndRead` and `write` share some common behavior: They both send a `String` in a `println` message to `System.out` and then send a `flush` message. We can add a method—let's call it `writeAnd-Flush`—to the class whose sole purpose is to provide this common behavior, as follows:

```
private void writeAndFlush(String s) {
    System.out.print(s);
    System.out.flush();
}
```

Now both `promptAndRead` and `write` can be rewritten: Their first two lines can be replaced by an invocation of `writeAndFlush`. As we know very well by now, methods are invoked by sending messages to an object. What object should receive the `writeAndFlush` message that `promptAndRead` and `write` send? The answer is that the very same object that `promptAndRead` and `write` belong to should receive the message. Java provides the keyword **this** so that a method can reference the object it belongs to. Therefore, `promptAndRead` can send a `writeAndFlush` message to the object if we write the following:

```
this.writeAndFlush(s);
```

With these improvements, our class definition is as follows:

```
class InteractiveIO {
    public InteractiveIO() throws Exception {  ◄─ The constructor
        br = new BufferedReader(new
                                  InputStreamReader(System.in));
    }

    // Write s to the monitor.
    public void write(String s) {
        this.writeAndFlush(s);
    }

    // Write s to the monitor, read a string from the keyboard, and return a
    // reference to it.
    public String promptAndRead(String s) throws Exception {
        this.writeAndFlush(s);
        return br.readLine();
    }

    // Write s to the monitor, display it immediately.
    private void writeAndFlush(String s) {
        System.out.print(s);
        System.out.flush();
    }

    private BufferedReader  br;
}
```

The `writeAndFlush` method has only one purpose: to help the other methods in the class do their job. It is therefore called a *helper* method. We shall see shortly why its prototype starts with `private` rather than `public`.

Our improvements have not changed the interface and behavior of our class one bit. The change is just in the speed of execution and the elegance of the code.

EXERCISES

1. Improve the `Laugher3` class by writing a helper method called `laughItUp`. Once this method is written, the two overloaded `laugh` methods should just be calls to `laughItUp` with different arguments.

2. Is the helper method `writeAndFlush` really necessary? Could we have simplified `promptAndRead` without it? How?

3. Add a `writeln` method to `InteractiveIO` that gets a `String` argument, prints it, and guarantees, as `println` does, that the next character of output will appear on a new line.

4. Add a second, overloaded, `writeln` method to `InteractiveIO` that gets no argument but guarantees that the next character of output will appear on a new line.   ●

Variables, Declarations, and the `return` Statement

We have covered quite a bit of ground in the last three sections, and it is time to turn briefly away from the process of class definition and consider some points about the Java language.

DECLARATION ORDER

As you have seen, a class in Java is defined by declaring a set of variables and methods. Objects, that is, particular instances of a class, are characterized by this set.

The particular order of the variable and method declarations within the braces ({...}) of the class is irrelevant. Any order is legal. However, we will adopt the convention of always placing method declarations at the beginning of the class, followed by variable declarations.

THE RETURN STATEMENT

The sender of the message cannot proceed until the method *returns*. This is accomplished either by executing the Java `return` statement, or if the method's return-type is `void`, reaching the closing brace of the method.

A `void` method may alternatively have an explicit `return` statement—with no return-value—as follows:

```
public void write(String s) {
    System.out.print(s);
    System.out.flush();
    return;
}
```

In the case of `void` methods, the return serves merely to stop the execution of the method and allows its invoker to proceed. For methods that return values (such as `promptAndRead` in the `InteractiveIO` class), the `return` statement does more—it specifies the value that is returned. Because of this additional role, in a method that returns a value, the `return` statement is mandatory; it does not suffice to reach the closing brace.

Methods can only return one value for a given invocation. For example, it's impossible to write a method that returns two `Strings`, say `"Flower"` and `"Power"`. One could concatenate the `Strings` in some way (making `"Flower Power"` or `"PowerFlower"`) and return the result, but then we are back to returning a single value.

ACCESS CONTROL: `public` VS. `private`

A class definition consists of method definitions and instance variable declarations. **Access** to a method or variable is the ability to use it. By using the keywords `public` or `private` we allow or prevent code outside the class from accessing these methods and variables. When we use the keyword `public`, we make the method or variable accessible to all code outside the class. When we use the keyword `private`, we prevent the method or variable from being accessed outside of the class. This is called **access control.**

How do we decide whether to use `public` or `private`? In this text we will use the following simple but very effective rule:

> If we must make it accessible outside the class, we make it `public`; otherwise, we make it `private`.

The methods that appear in the interface should be `public` because we want them to be accessible (that is, used in messages) from code outside the class.

The helper methods do not appear in the interface. They are present only for the sake of easing the implementation of the methods that do appear in the interface. There is no need to make them `public`, so we make them `private`. Likewise, the instance variables are there only for the sake of implementing the `public` methods, so these we make `private` as well.

VARIABLES AND THEIR LIFETIMES

In the `InteractiveIO` class definition above, we encountered variables declared in the following three different contexts:

- As *parameters* (in parentheses next to a method-name in the method definition)
- As *local variables* (declared somewhere within the braces of a method body)
- As *instance variables* (declared within the braces of a class definition but not within any method).

Parameters are variables that are automatically created when the method is invoked, and they disappear when the method terminates. Their *lifetime* is the same that of the method invocation. They get their initial values from the arguments that were part of the message that invoked the method. The arguments must correspond in number and, on a one-to-one basis, in type with the parameters.

Given a method with prototype,

```
void f(String s1, PrintStream p)
```

here are some valid and invalid messages:

```
f("hello", System.out)            Valid: Arguments match parameters in number and type
f("hello")                        Invalid: Too few arguments
f("hello", "goodbye")             Invalid: First argument/parameter type mismatch
f("hello", System.out, "bye")     Invalid: Too many arguments
```

Local variables have similar lifetimes as parameters—they are automatically created when the method is invoked and are automatically destroyed when the method returns. Unlike parameters, they must be initialized (given initial values) in the method itself.

Parameters and local variables have something else in common—they are not visible outside the method in which they are defined. Given a method with a local variable or parameter s, no other method can refer to s. Because of this common characteristic, we often consider parameters to be a special kind of local variable. If three methods each have a local variable s, in essence, there are three different variables s. Consider the following:

```
String getGenre() {
    String  s = "classic rock/".concat(getFormat());
    return s;
}

String getFormat() {
    String  s;
    s = "no commercials";
    return s;
}
```

The assignments to s in getFormat will not affect the local reference variable s in getGenre. Even if we had left out the declaration of String s in getFormat, the reference variable s in getGenre could not be modified—it will continue to refer to the same object.

Since local variables and parameters are not visible outside the methods in which they're declared, they are not accessible outside these methods either. That is why the keywords public and private don't apply to them.

Instance variables have the same lifetime as the object to which they belong. An instance variable is created when its object is created, and it vanishes when that object vanishes. They can be accessed by any method in the class. Access to instance variables in code outside the class is determined by their `private` or `public` declaration—we will always use `private` in this text.

OBJECTS AND THEIR LIFETIMES

An object lasts as long as some reference variable, somewhere, refers to it. When no such variable exists any more, the object is automatically destroyed by Java. Thus, while object creation in Java is a matter of the programmer explicitly requesting it with the `new` operator, object destruction is a quiet affair. No announcements, just a hidden occurrence when the last reference to an object is itself destroyed. The upshot is that when it comes to objects, you don't have to worry. Once you create them, as long as you have some reference to them, they won't go away.

A USEFUL PRONOUN: `this`

We have seen that the keyword **this** can be used to allow an object to refer to itself—that's how `promptAndRead` sent a message to the object it was a part of. Another use for this keyword is when a local variable in a method has the same name (say *s*) as an instance variable in the class, and as a result the method can't refer to the instance variable using *s*—it would refer to the local variable, as follows:

```
class {
   ...
   public void m1() {
       String s;          ◄─────────  local variable
       ...

       s refers to the local variable, not the instance variable

       ...
   }
   ...
   private String s; ◄─────────  instance variable
}
```

Of course we could program around this. We could change the local variable name to `t`. However, since the keyword `this` always refers to the currently executing object, we can use it to unambiguously indicate that an identifier should be treated as an instance variable: we simply **prepend** `"this."` to the identifier, as shown below:

```
class {
   ...
   public void m1() {
```

```
      String s;
   ...
```
s refers to the local variable, not the instance variable
but this.s refers to the instance variable, not the local variable
```
   ...
   }
   ...
   private String s;
}
```

4.6   Specifying a `Name` Class

The `InteractiveIO` class definition was motivated by a desire to make a class that would be more convenient for interactive use than `PrintStream` and `BufferedReader`. Often, however, our starting point is not existing Java classes but real-world problems that we would like to solve by modeling in some way.

The ready-made classes that Java provides us with, such as `String` and `BufferedReader`, by themselves do not come close to modeling the behaviors of the elements of our world. Consider an item as simple as a person's name. We might be tempted to model it as a `String`, but we would find that `String`'s behavior does not directly provide the behavior we would want from a `Name`. Rather, we will have to build our own `Name` class. We follow the approach we used in developing `InteractiveIO`.

4.6.1   Determining the Behavior

Given a `Name` object, we would like to do the following:

- Get the initials as a `String` object
- Get the name as a `String` object in last name, first name order
- Get the name as a `String` object in first name, last name order
- Add or replace a title (such as Sir or Ms. or Mr.)

This behavior is just one possibility. Another designer might have chosen a different set of behavior.

4.6.2   Interface

We would like to be able to do the following:

- *Declare a `Name` reference variable, as follows:*

  ```
  Name pres;
  ```

  This is easy. Once we have a name for a class, we can use it to declare reference variables.

- *Instantiate a new* `Name` *object, based on first and last names, as follows:*

  ```
  pres = new Name ("Calvin","Coolidge");
  ```

  We must design the class with a constructor that takes two `String` arguments: a first and a last name.

- *Send the object a message to get the initials as a* `String` *object, as follows:*

  ```
  String  s0;
  s0 = pres.getInitials();
  ```

  We must design the class to provide a method (let's call it `getInitials`) to do this.

- *Send the object a message to get the full name as a* `String` *object in last, first form, as follows:*

  ```
  String  s1;
  s1 = pres.getLastFirst();
  ```

  We must design the class to provide a method (let's call it `getLast-First`) to do this.

- *Send the object a message to get the full name as a* `String` *object in first, last form, preceded by an optional title, as follows:*

  ```
  String  s2;
  first = pres.getFirstLast();
  ```

  We must design the class to provide a method (let's call it `getFirst-Last`) to do this.

- *Send the object a message to add a title or replace an existing title, as follows:*

  ```
  pres.setTitle("President");
  ```

  We must design the class to provide a method (let's call it `setTitle`) to do this.

Notice that the arguments to the constructor do not include a title. This is our choice (as designers of this class). Our rationale is that not everyone has a title. Furthermore, a title, unlike a first or last name, is not a permanent aspect of a name. We thus provide a `setTitle` method to permit the addition or modification of a title.

The constructor example above (`new Name("Calvin","Collidge")`) informs us that the constructor prototype will be as follows:

```
Name(String first, String last)
```

The `setTitle` method requires one `String` parameter and returns nothing. Its prototype is as follows:

```
void setTitle(String newTitle)
```

The methods whose names start with `get` all return references to `Strings`, but none of them are given arguments, so they don't need parameters. Their prototypes are as follows:

```
String getInitials()
String getLastFirst()
String getFirstLast()
```

4.6.3   A Sample Program that Uses the Class

Consider the following task: *Write a program that prompts for and reads three strings (a first name, a last name, and a title). The program writes all three strings on the same line, followed by the name in last, first format, the initials, and then the name in first, last format, each on separate lines.*

We will also assume the availability of the `InteractiveIO` class—we did all that work; we might as well reap its benefits.

We start by declaring reference variables for the different objects that we know we will need (a `Name`, several `Strings`, and an `InteractiveIO` object for input) and will put them in the usual boilerplate, as follows:

```
import java.io.*;
class IllustrateName {
    public static void main(String arg[]) throws Exception {
        Name    n;                        // The name we are modeling
        String  first, last, title;
        InteractiveIO    io;              // Models our interactive setup
```

We then add code to create the `InteractiveIO` and use it to read a first and a last name and a title (all `Strings`), with suitable prompts, as follows:

```
io = new InteractiveIO();
first = io.promptAndRead("First name, please: ");
last  = io.promptAndRead("Last name, please: ");
title = io.promptAndRead("Title, please: ");
```

Then we get to the point of this exercise: We use the `String` objects to create a new `Name` object and then send it the `setTitle` message. Next we print the results of sending `getInitials`, `getLastFirst`, and `getFirstLast` messages. The program is completed as follows:

```
n = new Name(first,last);
n.setTitle(title);
io.write(first);
io.write(last);
io.writeln(title);          See Exercise 3 in Section 4.5—writeln
io.writeln(n.getFirstLast());
```

```
            io.writeln(n.getInitials());
            io.writeln(n.getLastFirst());
        }
    }
```

4.6.4   Class Definition Skeleton

Confident that our design for Name is workable, we use the prototypes we wrote above to write a skeleton of the Name class definition, as follows:

```
class Name {

    public Name(String first, String last) {
        Java statements
    }

    public String getInitials() {
        Java statements
    }

    public String getLastFirst() {
        Java statements
    }

    public String getFirstLast() {
        Java statements
    }

    public void setTitle(String newTitle) {
        Java statements
    }

    Instance variables if needed
}
```

EXERCISES

1. Consider an Address class. Take the first steps in defining such a class by determining its interface, as was done with Name in this section. Then write a sample program illustrating the use of such a class. Given the interface you worked out for the Address class, sketch out a skeleton of the Address class definition.

2. Write a program that reads three sets of firstname/lastname pairs and for each pair creates a Name object and prints the initials on a separate line.

3. Suppose our plan for the Name class included a method that would simply print the Name object to the System.out PrintStream object. Choose a name for such a method and add an example of its use to IllustrateName above.

4. Consider a `LongName` class, one that is like the `Name` class but which takes into account middle names. Take the first steps in defining such a class by determining its interface, as was done with `Name` in this section. (You may want to use some of the methods of the `Name` class but provide additional ones as well.) Then write a sample program illustrating the use of such a class. Given the interface you worked out for the `LongName` class, sketch out a skeleton of the `LongName` class definition.

5. Suppose we added to the `Name` class a method, `print`, that printed the `Name` object using `System.out`. What would the return-type be? What would the arguments be? Write a prototype for this method.

6. (A challenge.) We will eventually encounter (and create) `PrintStream` objects other than `System.out`. Suppose our plan for the `Name` class included a method that could be told to output the name to a particular `PrintStream`. Sketch (as we have done above) the use of such a method. Add to `IllustrateName`, above, an example of the use of this method to output to `System.out`.

7. (A challenge) Suppose we added to the `Name` class a method called `readIn`, whose job it would be to read the first and last names and return a `Name` object. What would the return-type of this method be?   •

4.7   Implementing the `Name` Class

As we search for an easy method to implement, we discover that each method must have access to information that other methods will also need. For example, both `getLastFirst` and `getFirstLast` need the first and last name strings. Both will need `String` reference variables as follows:

```
String      firstName;   // Will refer to the first name of this Name
String      lastName;    // Will refer to the last name of this Name
```

The reason why these declarations cannot be placed inside either of the methods (that is, why `firstName` and `lastName` cannot be local variables) are as follows:

*   Local variables cannot be used outside that method—so if we place these declarations within one method (like `getLastFirst`), we would not be able to use the variables in `getFirstLast`
*   Local variables declared within a method exist only while the method is active—but the first and last names of a `Name` object must be a permanent part of the object

Therefore, these must be declarations of instance variables. Similarly the title, needed by both `setTitle` and `getFirstLast`, must be an instance variable. We then have the following:

```
class Name {
    public Name(String first, String last) {
        Java statements
    }
    public String getInitials() {
        Java statements
    }
    public String getLastFirst() {
        Java statements
    }
    public String getFirstLast() {
        Java statements
    }
    public void setTitle(String newTitle) {
        Java statements
    }
    private String firstName;    // Will refer to the first name of this Name
    private String lastName;     // Will refer to the last name of this Name
    private String title;        // Will refer to the title part of this Name
}
```

Declaring an instance variable does not by itself give the variable a useful value. How are the three instance variables to get values? To answer that question, we must ask another: How is information provided to the `Name` object?

The specifications for the `Name` constructor indicate that the first and last names are `String`s sent as arguments when a `Name` object is created, as follows:

```
public Name(String first, String last) {
        Java statements
    }
```

When the constructor is invoked, its parameters, `first` and `last`, refer to the two `String` arguments.

It is the job of the constructor method to make the instance variable `firstName` refer to the same `String` object that parameter `first` refers to, and likewise for `lastName` with respect to last, as follows:

```
firstName = first;
lastName = last;
```

What about `title`? The specifications imply that until `setTitle` is invoked, there is no title in the `Name`. This is certainly in accordance with our intuitive understanding of names and titles. What value can be given to the instance variable title to reflect this? There are several possibilities, but the one that will shortly turn out to be most convenient is to make `title` refer to an empty `String`, as follows:

```
title = "";
```

Putting these statements together, we complete our constructor as follows:

```
public Name(String first, String last) {
    firstName = first;
    lastName = last;
    title = "";
}
```

Because the constructor is *always* the first method that is invoked, we can be confident that `firstName`, `lastName`, and `title` will all have meaningful values whenever any of the other methods are invoked.

The Job of a Constructor: The purpose of a constructor is to guarantee that the object starts its life with a sensible set of values in its instance variables.

A properly written constructor means that as we write the statements for `getInitials`, `getLastFirst`, etc., we can be sure that `firstName` is a reference to a `String` object representing the first name, `lastName` is a reference to a `String` object representing the last name, and `title` is a reference to a `String` object representing the title.

The `setTitle` method assigns its parameter to the corresponding instance variable as follows:

```
public void setTitle(String newTitle) {
    title = newTitle;
}
```

The other methods return references to `String` objects, so each of them will use a `return` statement. In each case, the return value is obtained by concatenating the instance variables in a particular order and returning the resulting reference.

Let's see how this might work in the `getLastFirst` method. Our task is to create a `String` object consisting of the last name followed by a comma followed by a space followed by the first name. A cascade of `concat` method invocations does the trick nicely:

```
lastName.concat(", ").concat(firstName);
```

This results in the value that we are supposed to return (i.e., if our `Name` was created with arguments `"Mary"` `"Smith"`, the resulting `String` would be `"Smith, Mary"`). Thus, `getLastFirst` can be written as follows:

```
public String getLastFirst() {
    return lastName.concat(", ").concat(firstName);
}
```

By analogy, we can write the `getFirstLast` method, keeping in mind that the title is meant to be part of the newly constructed `String` and that although there is no requirement for a comma, there must be a space between the title and first and last names, as follows:

```
public String getFirstLast() {
    return title.concat(" ").concat(firstName).concat(" ").
              concat(lastName);
}
```

The `getInitials` method is similar, too, except that we need to use the following `substring` method that we encountered in Chapter 2:

```
x.substring(0,1)
```

Here x is a reference to a `String`. The `substring` method, you recall, returns the first character of the `String`. Using that method to get the initials of the `firstName` and `lastName`, we may write `getInitials` as follows:

```
public String getInitials() {
    String  s;
    s = firstName.substring(0,1);
    s = s.concat(".");
    s = s.concat(firstName.substring(0,1));
    s = s.concat(".");
    return s;
}
```

Here we chose not to use cascading because of the number of methods that needed to be invoked. To do so would result in the following unreadable mess:

```
return firstName.substring(0,1).concat(".").
            concat(firstName.substring(0,1)).concat(".");
```

Putting this all together, we have the following complete definition of the Name class:

```
class Name {
    public Name(String first, String last) {
        firstName = first;
        lastName = last;
        title = "";
    }
    public String getInitials() {
        String  s;
        s = firstName.substring(0,1);
        s = s.concat(".");
        s = s.concat(lastName.substring(0,1));
        s = s.concat(".");
```

```
            return s;
    }
    public String getLastFirst() {
        return lastName.concat(", ").concat(firstName);
    }
    public String getFirstLast() {
        return title.concat(" ").concat(firstName).
                    concat(" ").concat(lastName);
    }
    public void setTitle(String newTitle) {
        title = newTitle;
    }
    private String firstName;    // Will refer to the first name of this Name
    private String lastName;     // Will refer to the last name of this Name
    private String title;        // Will refer to the title part of this Name
}
```

EXERCISES

1. Rewrite the `Name` class methods using parameter names that match those of the instance variables and use `this` as a means of referring to instance variables.

2. Working from the skeleton of the `Address` class that you wrote in Exercise 1 in the previous section, complete the class definition of the `Address`.

3. Working from the prototype of the `print` method that you wrote in Exercise 5 in the previous section, complete the definition of that method for the `Name` class.

4. Working from the skeleton of the `LongName` class that you wrote in Exercise 4 in the previous section, complete the class definition of the `LongName`.

5. Consider a `Dog` class that models a dog in a primitive way. It allows one to create a `Dog` object by specifying a sound that the dog makes (e.g., `"Woof"`, `"Bowwow"`, etc.). The behavior of such an object is simple. It provides three methods: `bark`, `barkLoud`, and `barkSoft`. Each of these displays the dog's sound on the monitor in different ways. The bark method displays the sound as it was specified originally (e.g., `"Woof"`). The `barkLoud` method displays the sound in all capitals (e.g., `"WOOF"`), and the `barkSoft` method displays the sound in all lowercase letters (e.g., `"woof"`).

   a. Write a program that uses this class to create three `Dog` objects, a beagle (that howls), a pitbull (that growls), and a retriever (that barks in a husky way). Then have these three objects converse as you see fit.

   b. Next, implement the `Dog` class.

4.8 State and Behavior

In the case of the `InteractiveIO` class, it would be unlikely to have more than one object of that class in a program (after all, there is usually only one keyboard and monitor to work with). However, in the case of `Name`, it is quite likely that a program using this class would have multiple instances, one per name. Each such instance will share the same methods but possess its own set of the three *instance variables:* `firstName`, `lastName`, and `title`. This makes sense because each different `Name` object must keep track of its own first name, last name, and title.

Consider the following program

```
import java.io.*;
class Program4 {
    public static void main(String arg[]) throws Exception {
        Name            n1, n2;              // The names we are modeling
        InteractiveIO   io = new InteractiveIO();
        n1 = new Name("Tom","Petty");
        n2 = new Name("Alanis","Morrisette");
        io.writeln(n1.getLastFirst());
        io.writeln(n2.getLastFirst());
    }
}
```

This is a program that involves two different `Name` objects, each referred to by a different `Name` reference variable. Both objects belong to class `Name` and therefore share the same behavior; that is, the same methods can be invoked on these objects. Yet upon receiving a `getLastFirst` message, they return different values. This is because each object of class `Name` contains its own copy of the instance variables, and these will contain different values. For example, the object to which n1 refers has a value of "Tom" for its `firstName`, whereas n2's `firstName` has a value "Alanis." The values of the instance variables of an object constitute its **state**. Although n1 and n2 both respond to the `getLastFirst` message identically, *the results are different because their states are different.*

EXERCISES

1. First consider the following code:

```
String  s1, s2, s3, s4, s5;
s1 = new String("ALP");
s2 = new String("HCE");
s3 = new String("ALP");
s4 = s2;
```

Now, for each of the following pairs, indicate whether the two reference variables refer to the same object, different objects but with identical states, or different objects with different states:

a. `s1,s2`
b. `s1,s3`
c. `s1,s4`
d. `s2,s4`

2. Consider the following code:

```
Name n1 = new Name("Ulysses", "Grant");
Name n2 = new Name("Ulysses", "Grant");
Name n3;
Name n4 = new Name("Ulysses", "Grant");
n3 = n1;
n4.setTitle("General");
```

Which among n1, n2, and n3

a. Refer to the same object?
b. Refer to different objects that have the same state?
c. Refer to different objects that have different states?

4.9   Outputting Objects: Revisiting the Name Class

In our original design, the `Name` class itself did not read `Name` objects nor did it print them out. The **responsibility** for input and output rested entirely with the *user* of the class. `Program3`, for example, read `String` objects that it used to send to the `Name` constructor to create a new `Name` object, and then it received `String` objects of various sorts (for example, the initials or the name in last, first format) from the `Name` object and then printed them out. `Program3` handled all the input and output.

Sometimes it is desirable to enable a class to take responsibility for its own input and output. When this is needed is a class design issue and one that we won't address now. Instead, we'll focus on the mechanics of how we can provide this capability to a class, and we will use the `Name` class as our context.

We start with output. In the case of output, we can assume that a `Name` object already has been created—otherwise, there would be nothing to output. We need the ability to send a message to this object instructing it to write itself out, as follows:

```
Name    someName;
someName = new Name(...);
```

...
Send message to someName *indicating that it should be output*

To do this, we design a `print` method for `Name` that performs output. What should the behavior of this `print` method be? In particular,

- In what form should the `Name` be output? (First Last? Last, First? How should the title be displayed?)
- Where should the output go?

The first question is harder to answer. Many choices are possible and there is no such thing as a right answer. Of course, one could write a different method for each potentially desirable choice, but method clutter has its own disadvantages. We will arbitrarily decide to write the `Name` out in Title First Last format.

We might take the same approach to the second question and arbitrarily decree that the output should go to standard output or to some particular file. However, if we are going to the trouble of adding a method to the `Name` class, we ought to make it as broadly useful as possible and not limit it to a single output target. This means that the method should not take the responsibility of choosing the output target—the responsibility for that choice should be left up to the invoker (that is, the user) of the method. Therefore, the invoker will have to provide information to let the method know where to target the output. How can this be done?

All along, we have done output by sending `println` or a `print` messages to a `PrintStream` object. As designers of the `Name` class, we may insist that the output target be a `PrintStream` object. With this choice, we could demand that the invoker of the `print` method for `Name` pass a reference to a `PrintStream` object—the target of the output—as an argument. The prototype of `print` method then is as follows:

```
void print(PrintStream target)
```

This means that the invoker could pass `System.out` as an argument because `System.out` is a reference to a `PrintStream` object. Alternatively, the invoker could pass a reference to a different `PrintStream` object if desired. The possibilities become intriguing: For example, we can use this method to write a `Name` out both to the screen and to a data file:

```
Name                n;
PrintStream         p;
n = new Name("Alvin","Karpis");
n.setTitle("Public Enemy Number One");
p = new PrintStream(
        new FileOutputStream("Americas.Most.Wanted"));

n.print(System.out);     Tell n to write itself to the PrintStream referred to by
                         System.out.

n.print(p);              Tell n to write itself to the PrintStream referred to by p.
```

NOTE: we have now printed "Public Enemy Number One Alvin Karpis" to both standard output and the disk data file ("Americas.Most.Wanted") to which the `PrintStream` *reference p refers.*

4.9.1 Implementing the `print` Method

Implementing the `print` method turns out to be quite straightforward. If we were writing the `Name` object to `System.out`, we would write the following:

```
System.out.print(this.title);
System.out.print(" ");
System.out.print(this.firstName);
System.out.print(" ");
System.out.print(this.lastName);
```

However, now we wish to use the `PrintStream` that the user sent as an argument. This is the parameter `target`, and so we write (showing the complete method here) the following:

```
void print(PrintStream target) {
    target.print(this.title);
    target.print(" ");
    target.print(this.firstName);
    target.print(" ");
    target.print(this.lastName);
}
```

EXERCISES

1. Implement a class named `LoggedSysOut`. The constructor for the class takes a single argument: a reference to a `String` object that is the name of a file to be used to create a new `PrintStream` to a disk. The class provides two methods, `print` and `println`, both of which receive `String` arguments. These methods take their `String` arguments and send them off as arguments in a `println` (or `print`) message to both `System.out` and the `PrintStream` object that the constructor created from the file name argument it received.

2. Create another overloaded `laugh` method for `Laugher3`. It should allow the sender of the message to determine the destination of the laugh output.

4.10 Inputting Objects: Another Visit to the `Name` Class

We now turn to input: We want the ability to send a message asking that a `Name` object be created from input. Immediately we run into a problem of sorts. Messages are sent to objects. But we don't have an object to send a message to. We are sending a message in order to create an object. We actually don't want to send a message to a `Name` object; we would like to send a message to the `Name` class (if that were possible) and ask it to create the `Name` object for us.

In Java, this is accomplished with a special kind of method: a **class method,** also known as a **static method.** These methods are defined in the same way as other methods are, except that the keyword `static` appears before their return-type. Class methods are never associated with an object of their class. As a result,

- Class methods must be invoked independently of any instance of the class; so, they are invoked by using the class name as the receiver of the message.
- Class methods may not access any instance variables (because the receiver is not an object, there are no instance variables).

As in the case of our `print` method, we must address the following two questions:

- In what format will the data for the `Name` be?
- Where will the input come from?

We will require that the first name appears on a line by itself in the input and the last name appears on a line immediately afterward. As was the case for output format, this is an arbitrary choice.

We design our method so that the responsibility for the input source rests with the invoker of the method. Accordingly, we require that a reference to a `BufferedReader` object be passed as an argument to `read`.

First, we write the prototype for `read`. It must be `static` and return a `Name` reference, and it receives a `BufferedReader`, as follows:

```
public static Name read(BufferedReader br)
```

This allows a user of the `Name` class to read a `Name` from both a file (called `name.list` in the example) and the keyboard and write them to standard output, as follows:

```
Name                n;
FileInputStream     f;
BufferedReader      brFile, brKey;
brKey = new BufferedReader(
                    new InputStreamReader(System.in));
f = new FileInputStream(new File("name.list"));
brFile = new BufferedReader(new InputStreamReader (f));
n = Name.read(brKey);
n.print(System.out);
n = Name.read(brFile);
n.print(System.out);
```

Now that we have the prototype for the method and an understanding of how it will be used, we can write its body. The method reads two lines from the `BufferedReader`, constructs the new `Name`, and returns the resulting reference, as follows:

```
public static Name read(BufferedReader br) throws Exception {
    String  first, last;
    first = br.readLine();
    last = br.readLine();
    return new Name(first,last);
}
```

4.10.1   Interactive Input

You may recall from the last chapter that when input is coming from a keyboard, it is advisable to provide some kind of prompt for the human user. Where should the responsibility for displaying a prompt line be placed: within the `Name` class or in the code that is using the `Name` class? There is no right or wrong answer to this question. Here, and in many of the other classes that we build in this text, we will put responsibility on the class, not on the user of the class. To that end, we present a second version of `read` for `Name`, one that will issue prompts for the first and last names. We call it `readi` (the i standing for interactive) and use our `InteractiveIO` class as the parameter. The code is as follows:

```
public static Name readi(InteractiveIO io) throws Exception {
    String first, last;
    first = io.promptAndRead("First name: ");
    last = io.promptAndRead("Last name: ");
    return new Name(first,last);
}
```

4.10.2   The Revised `Name` Class and Its Use

With the additional methods introduced in the previous section and this, the revised `Name` class now is as follows:

```
class Name {

    public Name(String first, String last) throws Exception {
        firstName = first;
        lastName = last;
        title = new String("");
    }

    public String getInitials() {
        String  s;
        s = firstName.substring(0,1);
        s = s.concat(".");
        s = s.concat(lastName.substring(0,1));
        s = s.concat(".");
```

```java
        return s;
    }

    public String getLastFirst() {
        String  s;
        s = lastName.concat(", ");
        s = s.concat(firstName);
        return s;
    }

    public String getFirstLast() {
        String  s;
        s = title.concat(" ");
        s = s.concat(firstName);
        s = s.concat(" ");
        s = s.concat(lastName);
        return s;
    }

    public void setTitle(String newTitle) {
        title = newTitle;
    }

    public void print(PrintStream target) {
        target.print(this.title);
        target.print(" ");
        target.print(this.firstName);
        target.print(" ");
        target.print(this.lastName);
    }

    public static Name read(BufferedReader br)
                                        throws Exception {
        String  first, last;
        first = br.readLine();
        last = br.readLine();
        return new Name(first,last);
    }

    public static Name readi(InteractiveIO io)
                                        throws Exception {
        String  first, last;
        first = io.promptAndRead("First name: ");
        last = io.promptAndRead("Last name: ");
        return new Name(first,last);
    }

    private String firstName;    // Will refer to the first name of this Name.
    private String lastName;     // Will refer to the last name of this Name.
    private String title;        // Will refer to the title part of this Name.
}
```

Here is an example program that uses the new version of the Name class to read a name and print it out, after adding the title "His Honor, the Mayor":

```
class MakeMayor {
    public static void main(String[] arg) throws Exception {
        Name   mayor;
        mayor = Name.read(new BufferedReader(
                        new InputStreamReader(System.in)));
        mayor.setTitle("His Honor, the Mayor");
        mayor.print(System.out);
    }
}
```

1. Add read, readi, and print methods to the other classes you have developed in earlier exercises: Address, LongName, Dog.

EXERCISE

4.11   Our First Program Revisited

Look back at any of the programs from the preceding chapters, for example, our very first one, which follows:

```
import java.io.*;
class Program1 {
    public static void main(String[] arg)   {
        System.out.println("This is my first Java program");
        System.out.println("... but it won't be my last.");
    }
}
```

You will now recognize that programs, such as Program1, themselves are classes. Every class that can exist as a program must, as we mentioned in Chapter 1, have a main method. We are now in a position to explain some more of the boilerplate. We see that the main method is static; that is, it is not associated with an instance of the Program1 class. This is for a good reason. Execution of the program has to begin somewhere. In a sense, it is the Java interpreter that invokes the main method. But it does so at the outset of program execution, before any objects from our code could have been created. In general, it is the task of the main method to start the process of creating objects and invoking their methods (which in turn may create additional objects and lead to additional method invocations).

We can also understand the use of the keyword `public`. It is there to make it possible for `main` to be invoked by something outside the class that we have written—namely, the Java interpreter.

SUMMARY

A class definition consists of a group of method definitions and declarations of instance variables enclosed in the class definition delimiters. A method definition consists of the prototype of the method followed by the method body--a sequence of Java statements enclosed in braces. The prototype consists of the return type of the method possibly `void`), the name of the method, and a parenthesized list of parameter declarations. The definition of a constructor is the same as a method definition except that it lacks a return type.

Methods and instance variables are labeled `public` or `private` to either permit or prevent access from code outside the class. As a rule, instance variables and helper methods--methods whose only purpose is to help implement other methods--are `private`. Methods that are part of the interface of the class, that is, that define the behavior of the class are `public`.

We have encountered three kinds of variables. Parameters are variables declared within a method prototype. They are initialized with the values given by the arguments of the invoking message. Local variables are variables declared within a method. They must be initialized explicitly by the programmer. Both local variables and parameters are created when each time the method is invoked and destroyed each time the method returns. Both local variables and parameters are only visible to the method in which they are declared; as a result, different methods may declare local variables and parameters of the same name. Instance variables are declared outside of method bodies. They are created when the object is created and last throughout its lifetime. Instance variables are used to store information that must be preserved between message invocations. The values of the instance variables determine the state of the object.

Static methods are methods that are not associated with any particular object. Instead, they are associated with the class as a whole. One use we have seen for a static method is to read data from an input source to create an object and return a reference to it.

STUDY AID: TERMINOLOGY REVIEW

access   The ability to use a method or variable.

access control   The ability to allow or prevent access to a method or variable.

argument Information provided in a message in addition to the method-name and ultimately made available to the method via a parameter; one of the two ways that methods get needed information.

behavior Any action that the object may take, any change it may undergo, or any characteristic it may reveal as a result of a method being invoked.

class method A method that is not associated with any particular object of a class but rather the class itself. As a result, it can be invoked without reference to an object. Such a method is also called a *static* method.

constructor A method that is invoked when an object is created. The name of the constructor method is the same as the corresponding class name. The purpose of the constructor is to guarantee a reasonable and consistent state at the time of object creation.

default A behavior or value that is used if no explicit behavior or value is provided.

implement Provide the code that realizes a design.

implementation The specific code that realizes a class.

initialized Given a first value.

instance variable A variable that is declared within a class but outside of any method; its purpose is to store information needed by methods to be preserved in between invocations. Each object has its own set of instance variables that have their own unique values—it is these values that distinguish one object from another. The entire set of the instance variables of an object define its state.

local variable A variable that is declared within a method; it exists only during the invocation of the method and is used as a temporary convenient holder of information.

method A self-contained section of code belonging to a class that achieves a specific behavior for that class. A method consists of a return type, method-name, and parameter list, all of which form the method's signature, and the section of code that is called the body of the method.

parameter A variable that is declared in the parentheses of a method signature and whose purpose is to store the value of the corresponding argument; naturally, the type of the argument and the parameter must match in some sense.

prepend Place in front of, place before.

private A keyword modifier in a method definition or instance variable declaration that *prevents* access to a method or variable from any code outside the class.

prototype   Part of a method definition that consists of return-type, method-name, and argument list in parentheses.

public   A keyword modifier in a method definition or instance variable declaration that *allows* access to a method or variable from any code outside the class.

reference   A value whose sole significance is that it refers to an object and hence can be used to send messages to that object.

responsibility   The characteristic of being obligated to provide a certain behavior or carry out a certain task.

return   A verb keyword that allows a method to terminate its own execution and allows the sender of the message to resume execution; additionally, the return statement allows the method to send some information back to the receiver.

return-type   The first part of the prototype; it specifies what kind of information will be returned by the method.

state   The collection of values of the instance variables of an object at any given time.

static method   See "class method."

this   A pronoun keyword that refers to the current object; this allows for convenient reference to the objects instance variables, particularly when the parameters have the same name.

QUESTIONS FOR REVIEW

1. Describe the stages of designing a class such as Name.

2. What is the principal task of a constructor method?

3. What are instance variables? Why are they necessary? Why can't they be declared within methods?

4. What sources of information are available to a method?

5. How can a method convey information to the sender?

6. What is a static method? Why can't a static method access instance variables?

FURTHER EXERCISES

1. Implement a class called `FileCopier3`. The constructor takes a single argument, a `String` argument specifying the name of a file that contains at least three lines. The only other argument is a method called `copyTo`. This method also takes a `String` argument, one that specifies the name of a file to be written to. The `copyTo` method writes the first three lines of the file it was instantiated with to the file given by the argument.

2. Implement a `RepoMan` class. Its constructor is given a reference to a `Name` object and a `String` object. The `Name` is the name of some hapless soul who has fallen behind on car payments. The `String` is a dollar and cents amount, such as $3879.95. The class provides one method (other than the constructor), `sendWarning`, that takes no arguments. This method writes the following to `System.out`:

   ```
   Dear name,
   We know you don't want to be a deadbeat, but if you
   don't pay up the amount you owe (amount) we will find
   your car and repossess it. You can run, but your car
   can't hide.
   Sincerely,
   The Friendliness-First Auto Credit Corporation
   ```

   The underlined parts are substituted with the given `Name` (in first last format) and the given dollar amount.

   Write a program that reads two name/dollar amount pairs, creates two `RepoMan` objects, and prints two such warning letters.

Applets, Painting, and Creating Controls

Let's revisit our first applet:

```java
import java.awt.*;       // Our first applet
import java.applet.*;
public class FirstApplet extends Applet {
   public void paint(Graphics g) {
```

```
         g.drawString("This is everyone's first applet.",
               20,20);
     }
  }
```

We can understand its structure much better now that we have learned about class definitions. We observe the following:

- We have defined a class called `FirstApplet`.
- `FirstApplet` apparently contains a single method, `paint`.
- The `paint` method has a single parameter g, a reference to an object of the `Graphics` class.

Understanding the behavior of this class hinges on the following:

- Class `FirstApplet` is an applet. This is a result of the phrase `extends Applet`.
- The behavior of a `Graphics` object, in particular the `drawString` method.

At some point, the browser will use the class definition of `FirstApplet` to create a `FirstApplet` object. Eventually, the browser will invoke the `paint` method, just as the Java interpreter invokes the `main` method of a program. Before doing so, the browser creates a `Graphics` object. A reference to this object is passed to `paint`.

Extends   Let us return to a pair of words that appeared in the definition of our first applet class:

```
public class FirstApplet (extends Applet) {
```

It is far too early in our exploration of Java to explain these words in full detail but we can make a few remarks about their impact on the class, `FirstApplet`, that we are defining. In particular, there is a predefined class called `Applet` and as a result of this clause, `extends Applet`, our `FirstApplet` class possesses all of `Applet`'s methods without our having to write so much as an open brace. These methods provide basic behavior for applets. Any time we want to customize that behavior, we can do so by defining our own method to replace one of those that are predefined in `Applet`. `FirstApplet` does this. It provides its own method, `paint`, to draw the desired `String` on the Web page.

Our Second Applet: Toward Interaction   Our first applet merely displays a string on a web page—no big deal, we can do that with HyperText Markup Language (HTML) and not bother with Java. Recall that the purpose of Java in the Web is to provide active content—that is, web pages that can dynamically interact with users (web surfers) and compute things in response to that inter-

FIGURE 4.5   An applet with two buttons.

action. To do this, there has to be a means for communication between the program and the web user.

The Java class libraries provide an assortment of such communication means, all of them part of a graphical user interface. In other words, Java provides menus, text choices, buttons, checkboxes, and an assortment of various graphical devices all aimed at providing different means of communication between an applet and the user. In this section we will begin—just begin—our exploration of these.

We start by proposing that we write an applet that takes a poll for a marketing company: Do web users think Certs is a breath mint or a candy mint? The applet will have a simple appearance: just two buttons, each labeled as shown in Figure 4.5.

To write such an applet, we must learn the following two things:

- How to make the applet create buttons and place them on the screen
- How to make the applet respond to buttons being clicked by the user

We will address only the first item in this chapter, leaving the second item for Chapter 6.

The Life Cycle of Applets   Before we start throwing buttons around, however, we need to learn a bit more about the *life cycle* of applets. When an applet is first loaded into the browser, the browser invokes its `init` method. This always happens! You may be startled, because our first applet, `FirstApplet`, did not have such a method. Remember, though—the `FirstApplet` class possesses all the methods of the `Applet` class, except for the one that it replaced with its own (`paint`). The `paint` method is invoked whenever the system detects the need for the applet to be displayed anew on the screen (for example, at the outset when it is first loaded, or later if something covered it up on the screen and then was moved). The `init` method on the other hand is called just once— when the applet is first loaded into the browser. Its intended role is suggested by its name: *init*, that is, doing the initial setup for the applet.

It is in the `init` method that we must set up the controls such as buttons that we want our applet to have, as follows:

```
public void init() {
    carry out necessary setup here
}
```

Our First GUI Component   The Java AWT provides a class, `Button`, to model the buttons in a graphical user interface. The `Button` constructor takes as an argument a `String` that will serve as a label in the button itself. So our `init` will contain the following:

```
Button breath, candy;
breath = new Button("Certs is a BREATH mint.");
candy = new Button("Certs is a CANDY mint.");
```

Creating the buttons is only part of what we must do. We must also accomplish the following:

- The buttons should appear in the applet.
- The applet should be able to respond to clicks in the buttons.

The `add` method, one of the methods that our applet possesses, handles both of these. So our next code follows:

```
add(breath);
add(candy);
```

Putting this all together, our second applet becomes

```
import java.awt.*;
import java.applet.*;

public class Certs extends Applet {
    public void init() {
        Button breath, candy;
        breath = new Button("Certs is a BREATH mint.");
        candy = new Button("Certs is a CANDY mint.");
        add(breath);
        add(candy);
    }
}
```

It doesn't do much. It just creates and displays two buttons. We will have to wait until Chapter 6 to learn how to respond to clicks on buttons.

Our Third Applet: Introducing Layout   In the `Certs` applet we did not care about the placement of the buttons. The fact that they appeared vertically resulted from the width given to the applet by the following HTML line:

```
<APPLET code="Certs.class" WIDTH=150 HEIGHT=60></APPLET>
```

```
         0.000                        0.000    C   =   /

     C   =   /   *                 *   7   8   9   -   4

     7   8   9   -                 5   6   +   1   2   3

     4   5   6   +                     0   .
                                   =
     1   2   3
                 =
         0   .
```

Our goal: calculator with   To avoid: losing control over
reasonably placed buttons   the placement of buttons

FIGURE 4.6   Two calculator layouts.

Had we specified a width of 300, say, the two buttons would have appeared horizontally—on the same line. Sometimes the placement of graphic controls such as buttons doesn't matter, but often it does. In our next example, a simple calculator applet, the placement of the buttons that serve as the keys of the calculator is critical. (See Fig. 4.6.)

We will have our hands full just managing the layout. Implementing the actions that result from clicking on the calculator keys will have to wait until the GUI supplement in Chapter 6.

`Applet` is an example of a *container* class in Java—a class whose objects can graphically contain controls or other containers. By contrast, `Button`s are not containers; you can't put anything into a `Button`. To put something into a container object, you send it an `add` message, with an argument that specifies the item being added. This is exactly what we did when we added the buttons in the `Certs` applet above.

Container objects such as `Applet`s rely on `LayoutManager` objects to guide the placement of their contents. These objects are instances of one of several different `LayoutManager` classes, `FlowLayout` and `BorderLayout` being the ones we will explore here. (The relationship of these classes to each other is analogous to the relationship of the InputStream classes, `BufferedInputStream` and `FileInputStream`.)

Programmers can control the way `Applet`s or other container objects place their contents by creating a `LayoutManager` object of their choice and sending it as an argument to a `setLayout` message to the container, as shown in the following code:

```
public class MyApplet extends Applet {
    public void init() {
        setLayout(new FlowLayout());   sends a setLayout message to itself
        ...
    }
}
```

If we used `FlowLayout` for our Calculator applet.

FIGURE 4.7 The result of using `FlowLayout` for our `Calculator` applet.

The `FlowLayout` manager causes the controls to be placed one after the other in the order in which they were added to the container. The controls start in the upper left corner and proceed to the right. Depending on the particular container, they may or may not "wrap around" to the space below when they reach the right end of the container. If we used a `FlowLayout` for our `Calculator` applet, its appearance would be unacceptable. (See Fig. 4.7.)

The `BorderLayout` manager views the container as divided into five regions: north, south, east, west, and center. It allows the programmer to assign `Buttons` (or other controls) to these regions. The controls assigned to the north and south are stretched out horizontally to cover the top and bottom borders of the container, the controls assigned to east and west are stretched vertically to fill the sides between the north and south controls, and the control in the center gets what's left. Obviously we can't rely on `BorderLayout`—we have 19 controls, not 5. If we put the 7, 8, 9, –, and 4 to positions north, west, center, east, and south, it would look quite silly. One can, however, choose to use fewer than five positions, a technique that we will put to good use below. (See Fig. 4.8.)

There are other layout manager classes available in Java, but their use is beyond the scope of this text. We are not stuck, however. Java provides a tool—the `Panel` class—that, when combined with the layout managers described above, allows us to accomplish our goal.

FIGURE 4.8 Two results of using `BorderLayout`.

Using `BorderLayout` with:
   north: 7
   south: 4
   east: 8
   west: -
   center: 9

Using `BorderLayout` with:
   north: 7
   south: 8
(only 2, not 5 controls)

The `Panel` class is the simplest container class one can imagine—just about the only thing you can do with a `Panel` object is assign it a layout manager and start adding objects. The trick to using `Panels` is to divide one's applet region into different `Panels`, each containing a handful of the applet's controls. This makes it easier to lay out the controls; just a few are given to each `Panel`. The `Panels` themselves can be contained in other `Panels` and or in the applet itself.

Our `Panel` strategy is shown in Fig. 4.9.

The first three rows of keys on the calculator are `Panels` containing four `Buttons` in a row—perfect for a `FlowLayout` layout manager. The 1 and 2 keys are placed in a `Panel` using `BorderLayout` and occupy west and east. This `Panel` is itself placed in another `Panel` along with the 0 key. By using `BorderLayout` again with 1 and 2 in north and 0 in south, we get the effect of stretching out the 0 key as desired.

In order for this strategy to work, we must guarantee that our `Buttons` have the same basic size (unless stretched by a `BorderLayout`). We do this by labeling each `Button` with a single character and using a fixed-width font (i.e., all letters are the same width, even, for example, l and W).

The `Label` object, which we use to display the result of a calculation, and the `Panel` objects that contain the `Buttons` are added to the applet in `FlowLayout` fashion.

To prevent the `Panels` of the applet from marching off horizontally in unfavorable ways, we can force the applet to assume a certain size by using the `resize` method. The arguments to this method are the desired width and height of the calculator. We compute these by examining the components of the applet itself. For example, `row1` is a variable that holds a reference to the `Panel` object that contains the first row of `Buttons`. The width of that row, plus a little bit of elbow room, is the width we desire for the applet itself; the code follows:

```
row1.getSize().width
```

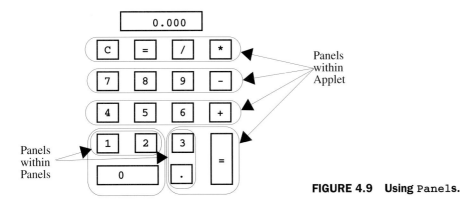

Panels within Applet

Panels within Panels

FIGURE 4.9   Using `Panels`.

The height of a row is the same as the height of a button. There are five rows of buttons, plus the text field, and there is spacing between the rows. Multiplying button height by 8, as follows, easily accomodates the height of the applet:

```
8*d1.getSize().height
```

Once the applet is resized,

```
setSize(row1.getSize().width,8*d1.getSize().height);
```

all its components must be laid out again. This is accomplished by invoking the applet's `validate` method.

This calculation, unfortunately, cannot be done within `init`—at that point the sizes for the `Panels`, `Buttons`, and so on, have not yet been computed by the system. So we carry out this calculation and the `resize` operation in the `paint` method.

The code for the applet is given below—its length is primarily a direct result of the fact that there are 19 buttons plus one `Label`. The code is made somewhat simpler by using the following helper methods:

- `makeButton`—given a label for the button and a `Color`, create a `Button`, set its color, set its font to `Courier` and a fixed-width, and return a reference to it.
- `makeButtons`—call `makeButton` with different arguments 19 times in order to create all the `Buttons`.
- `makePanel`—given a reference to some layout manager and a `Color`, create a `Panel` with the given layout manager and `Color` and return a reference to it.

Now `init` can place the various components in their containers, as follows, in the manner sketched above:

```java
import java.awt.*;
import java.applet.Applet;

public class Calculator extends Applet {

    private Button makeButton(String label, Color color) {
        Button b = new Button(label);
        b.setBackground(color);
        b.setFont(new Font("Courier", Font.BOLD, 10));
        return b;
    }

    private Panel makePanel(LayoutManager lm, Color c) {
        Panel p = new Panel();
```

```
        p.setLayout(lm);
        p.setBackground(c);
        return p;
    }

    private void makeButtons() {
        Color lightRed = new Color(255,100,100);
        Color lightBlue = new Color(100,100,255);
        Color yellow = new Color(255,255,0);

        c = makeButton("C",lightRed);
        eq = makeButton("=",lightBlue);
        div = makeButton("/",lightBlue);
        times = makeButton("*",lightBlue);
        d7 = makeButton("7",yellow);
        d8 = makeButton("8",yellow);
        d9 = makeButton("9",yellow);
        minus = makeButton("-",lightBlue);
        d4 = makeButton("4",yellow);
        d5 = makeButton("5",yellow);
        d6 = makeButton("6",yellow);
        plus = makeButton("+",lightBlue);
        d1 = makeButton("1",yellow);
        d2 = makeButton("2",yellow);
        d3 = makeButton("3",yellow);
        d0 = makeButton("0",yellow);
        dp = makeButton(".",yellow);
        eq2 = makeButton("=",lightBlue);
    }

    public void init() {
        background = new Color(200,255,255);
        this.setLayout(new FlowLayout(
                    FlowLayout.CENTER,4,1));

        result = new Label("0.00000 ",Label.RIGHT);
        result.setBackground(new Color(255,255,255));
        add(result);
        makeButtons();

        row1 = makePanel(new FlowLayout(FlowLayout.LEFT,4,2),
                    background);
        row1.add(c);
        row1.add(eq);
        row1.add(div);
        row1.add(times);
```

```
            row2 = makePanel(new FlowLayout(FlowLayout.LEFT,4,2),
                             background);
            row2.add(d7);
            row2.add(d8);
            row2.add(d9);
            row2.add(minus);

            row3 = makePanel(new FlowLayout(FlowLayout.LEFT,4,2),
                             background);
            row3.add(d4);
            row3.add(d5);
            row3.add(d6);
            row3.add(plus);

            add(row1);
            add(row2);
            add(row3);

            p12 = makePanel(new BorderLayout(2,2),background);
            p12.add("West",d1);
            p12.add("East",d2);

            p120 = makePanel(new BorderLayout(2,2),background);
            p120.add("North",p12);
            p120.add("South",d0);

            p3p = makePanel(new BorderLayout(2,2),background);
            p3p.add("North",d3);
            p3p.add("South",dp);

            p3peq = makePanel(new BorderLayout(2,2),background);
            p3peq.add("West",p3p);
            p3peq.add("East",eq2);

            add(p120);
            add(p3peq);

            setBackground(background);
        }
    public void paint(Graphics g) {
        setsize(row1.getSize().width,8*d1.getSize().height);
        validate();
    }

    private Panel row1, row2, row3, p12, p120, p3p, p3peq;

    private Button c, eq, div, times,
                   d7, d8, d9, minus,
                   d4, d5, d6, plus,
                   d1, d2, d3,
                   d0,     dp, eq2;
```

FIGURE 4.10   The final calculator result.

```
    private Color background;
    private Label result;
}
```

Figure 4.10 shows the results of this code.

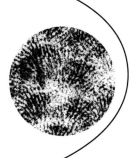

chapter 5

The Class Design Process; Method Implementation and Numerical Processing

5.1 Introduction

In Chapter 4, we focused on the definition of classes and methods, instance variables, prototypes, arguments, and method invocation. This chapter concentrates on the following:

- The process of developing class definitions by elaborating on the approach introduced in Chapter 4.
- A broadening of the kind of behavior that methods provide. We do this here by introducing numerical processing.

We start with the approach to the class definition process that we will continue to use throughout the rest of the book.

5.2   Designing Classes—An Overview

We first require a *statement of the problem*, which describes the object or system to be modeled. Without a clear understanding of the problem, a correct solution is not possible. Next, we sketch a *sample scenario*, that illustrates how a solution might be used.

The first step in the actual class design is to *find the primary objects*. If programming is an attempt to model something, we should first determine the key elements of the model. A good starting point is to collect all the nouns in the problem statement and to choose those that are the most important.

We then *determine the desired behavior* for each of the primary objects. This step will produce our basic set of required methods for the classes that these objects will belong to. If several classes need to be designed, we proceed one class at a time.

Determining the interface is next. We determine the prototype of each method: its arguments and return type. A good aid is to try to write sample code that uses the object and see how the method invocations naturally occur.

Once the interface has been defined, we direct our effort toward the class internals. We *define the instance variables* and then *implement the methods*. We will often conclude with a *discussion* of the solution.

5.3   Numeric Processing—The `int` Data Type

With the intense interest in graphics, windowing environments, and the Internet, we may forget the original purposes of the computer. The machine was so named because of its ability to perform *numeric* computations. Its first uses in the 1940s were military related: code breaking, ballistic calculations, and simulations of nuclear reactions—all essentially numerical calculations. When it was introduced into industry in the 1950s, the computer's primary functions were financial calculation and recordkeeping; character-based data (i.e., strings such as names and addresses) appeared only as descriptive elements. With the introduction of the PC, nonnumeric tasks became more prevalent: word processors and games, for example. Even so, the first astonishingly successful application of the PC was the Visicalc spreadsheet program, which was in essence a numerical calculator of unprecedented flexibility.

In today's highly graphical environments, numerical calculations play an ever-important role: drawing graphical shapes, such as circles, spirals, and arcs, determining the width of a line of characters in a proportional font, and plotting the path of the mouse across a window—all require numeric processing of some sort. Finally, although today's software applications are diverse and graphical in nature, there remains a need for those traditional, numerical applications as well: Employees still get paid, students still get graded, and customers still get billed.

Java does not offer predefined classes to provide numeric processing. Instead, it gives us a built-in data type, `int`, that models the behavior of integers. This data type provides the basic arithmetic operations such as +, −, *, and /, which may be used to construct standard arithmetic expressions such as the following:

```
x+(y/z)
```

and

```
rate*hours
```

Printing of integers is provided by the (overloaded) `print` and `println` methods of `PrintStream`, which accept an `int` as an argument:

```
System.out.println(rate*hours);
```

On the whole, the use of `int` corresponds closely to our intuitive notion of arithmetic expressions using integers.

Unlike class objects, primitive data types have no methods or instance variables—an integer value is the only thing associated with a variable of type `int`. This value may be assigned when the `int` variable is declared:

```
int  i  =  7;
```

or through an assignment statement:

```
i  =  3*y;
```

No constructor is needed (or allowed—there are no methods associated with an `int`), and no `new` is required.

The Java interlude that follows the next section presents a more detailed discussion of `int` and primitive data types in general. Right now we have the essence of what we need to get started, so let's use `int` in an application.

5.4 Collecting Tolls: An Example

This example develops classes and software using the procedure outlined in the introductory section.

5.4.1 Statement of the Problem

The Department of Highways of a particular county is installing a toll collection system on one of its major roads. Trucks pulling up to a tollbooth are required to pay a toll of $5 per axle plus $10 per half-ton of the truck's total weight. A display in the booth shows the toll receipts and the number of truck arrivals since the last collection.

5.4.2 A Sample Scenario

To aid in our design, let us imagine how such a toll collection system might work. A toll agent sits in a tollbooth that is equipped with a computer screen and a bar-code reader. When a truck arrives at the booth, the agent scans a bar code on the windshield of the truck; it contains information about the truck, including its number of axles. The weight of the truck is obtained by scanning a bar code contained on the bill of lading presented by the driver. The truck information and toll due are then displayed on the computer screen:

```
Truck arrival - Axles: 5 Total weight: 12500 Toll due: $145
```

When a button on the side of the screen is pressed, the booth's totals are displayed:

```
Totals since last collection - Receipts: $205 Trucks: 2
```

When the cash drawer is removed from its cradle, the following is displayed on the screen. The totals are displayed and then reset to zero:

```
*** Collecting receipts ***
Totals since last collection - Receipts: $523 Trucks: 5
```

5.4.3 Finding the Primary Objects

The objects of a problem, that is, the *things* that we are going to model, can be discovered by looking for the relevant noun phrases in the problem statement. In our example, these are *trucks, tollbooth, axle, weight,* and *receipts.* Of these, toll-booth and truck seem to be the most important. Axles and weight are properties of a truck, and receipts are secondary to the tollbooth. Therefore, we choose truck and tollbooth as our primary objects and introduce the classes `Truck` and `TollBooth`:

```
class Truck {
    Class definition will go here.
    ...
}
class TollBooth {
    Class definition will go here.
    ...
}
```

We now will design the two classes. The order does not matter at this stage, so we will do `Truck` first.

5.4.4   Determining the Desired Behavior—Class `Truck`

Tolls depend on the number of axles and the weight of a truck. Tollbooths need to get both of these from a truck. Our `Truck` class should have methods to provide this information. We will also have a constructor to allow us to create trucks:

- `Truck` (constructor)
- `getAxles`
- `getTotalWeight`

Although we are concentrating on designing the `Truck` class now, we are not operating in a vacuum—we are taking into account the behavior that the tollbooth requires of a truck. In fact, for our purposes, the *only* behavior required of the truck is that needed by the tollbooth. Everything else—the shipping company, destination, and so on—can be ignored.

5.4.5   Defining the Interface—Class `Truck`

The interface of the `Truck` class consists of the signature of each `Truck` method. It determines the way other classes communicate with a `Truck` object.

A good starting point in defining an interface is to write some typical code that uses an object of the class being designed. Let us write a simple fragment of code that creates a `Truck` object that models a three-axle, 4000-pound truck and then asks for the same information that a tollbooth requires: the number of axles and the total weight.

When creating the `Truck` object, we need to specify its number of axles and weight so that it can eventually supply that information to the tollbooth for toll calculation:

```
Truck truck1 = new Truck(3, 4000);    // 3 axles, 4000 lb total weight
```

Querying the `Truck` for its axles and total weight is straightforward:

```
truck1.getAxles()
```

and

```
truck1.getTotalWeight()
```

No information need be supplied to either method, so no arguments are present.

Because the toll calculation will be performing arithmetic on the number of axles ($5 per axle) and the truck's total weight ($10 per half-ton), the above methods should each return `int`.

This sample code provides us with the following interface for the `Truck` class:

```
class  Truck {
    //   Methods
    public  Truck(int  axles,  int  totalWeight)  {...}
    public  int  getAxles()  {...}
    public  int  getTotalWeight()  {...}
    // Instance  Variables
    ...
}
```

5.4.6 Defining the Instance Variables—Class `Truck`

The information about the truck's axles and its total weight must be maintained within the `Truck` object so it can provide this information when queried. We therefore add instance variables to our `Truck` class that correspond to the number of axles and total weight. The same argument as before determines that they be declared `int`:

```
class  Truck {
    //  Methods
    public  Truck(int  axles,  int  totalWeight)  {...}
    public  int  getAxles()  {...}
    public  int  getTotalWeight()  {...}
    //  Instance  Variables
    private  int  axles;
    private  int  totalWeight;
}
```

5.4.7 Implementing the Methods—Class `Truck`

The methods `getAxles` and `getTotalWeight` are queries that simply return the values of `axles` and `totalWeight`, respectively, to the caller. These variables will get their values from the constructor, `Truck`, which must assign its parameters to the corresponding instance variables. The finished class definition follows:

```
class  Truck  {
    //   Methods
    public  Truck(int axles,  int  totalWeight)  {
            this.axles  =  axles;
            this.totalWeight  =  totalWeight;
    }
    public  int  getAxles()  {return axles;}
    public  int  getTotalWeight()  {return totalWeight;}
    //  Instance  Variables
```

```
    private  int  axles;
    private  int  totalWeight;
}
```

We now turn our attention to the `TollBooth` class.

5.4.8 Determining the Desired Behavior—Class `TollBooth`

The chief behavior required of the tollbooth is the ability to *calculate the toll due*. We also want to be able to *display the data* for the total receipts and number of trucks since the last receipt collection. This implies that these totals are reset by the tollbooth *on receipt collection;* that is, there is tollbooth behavior associated with this event. Together with a constructor, this leads to the following behavior set:

- `TollBooth` (constructor)
- `calculateToll`
- `displayData`
- `onReceiptCollection`

5.4.9 Defining the Interface—Class `TollBooth`

Let's start by writing some sample usage code that creates a `TollBooth` object, uses it to compute the toll of a `Truck` object, displays the booth's totals, and notifies the `TollBooth` object that receipts are being collected. No information is needed to create a `TollBooth`:

```
TollBooth  booth  =  new  TollBooth();
```

Each time a toll is calculated, it is for a different truck. The `Truck` must therefore be supplied as an argument:

```
booth.calculateToll(truck1);
```

We can look at the totals maintained by the `TollBooth`:

```
booth.displayData();
```

Finally, collecting the booth receipts requires no additional information because the `TollBooth` object should keep track of its own receipts and totals:

```
booth.onReceiptCollection();
```

None of these methods return any information. They just make the `TollBooth` object do things. This leads to the following interface for the `TollBooth` class:

```
class  TollBooth  {
    //   Methods
```

```
public   TollBooth()   {...}
public   void   calculateToll(Truck   truck)   {...}
public   void   onReceiptCollection()   {...}
public   void   displayData()   {...}
//   Instance  Variables
...
}
```

5.4.10   Defining the Instance Variables—Class `TollBooth`

The tollbooth must maintain the total receipts and number of trucks since the last collection. We will use `int` instance variables to represent these values because we will do arithmetic with them—each truck passing through causes the total number of trucks to increase by 1 and the total receipts to be increased by the toll collected:

```
class   TollBooth   {
    //   Methods
    As  above
    //   Instance  Variables
    private   int   receiptsSinceCollection;
    private   int   trucksSinceCollection;
}
```

5.4.11   Implementing the Methods—Class `TollBooth`

The `TollBooth` class has richer behavior than the `Truck` class and is thus somewhat more involved.

The constructor, `TollBooth`, sets the total variables `receiptsSince-Collection` and `trucksSinceCollection` to zero because at the outset there are no receipts and no trucks have come by:

```
public   TollBooth()   {
    trucksSinceCollection   =   0;   // Clear out totals
    receiptsSinceCollection = 0;
}
```

Displaying the booth's totals simply prints those values to `System.out`:

```
public void displayData() {
    System.out.print(
        "Totals   since   last   collection   -   Receipts:   ");
    System.out.print(receiptsSinceCollection);
    System.out.print("  Trucks:   ");
    System.out.println(trucksSinceCollection);
}
```

To model collecting the receipts from the tollbooth, we first display the totals maintained by the booth (as we did in our scenario) and then reset them to zero because receipts and truck totals are maintained only since the most recent collection. This corresponds to a supervisor emptying the cash box in the booth and resetting the meters. Because we have already written a method, `displayData`, that displays the totals, we invoke that method rather than rewriting the code:

```
public  void  onReceiptCollection()  {
   System.out.println("***  Collecting receipts ***");
   displayData();
   trucksSinceCollection  =  0;            // Clear out totals
   receiptsSinceCollection  =  0;
}
```

Finally, we must implement the `calculateToll` method. In order to determine the toll due, the booth must know the number of axles and weight of the `Truck`, which are passed as an argument. These values may be determined by sending the `getAxles` and `getTotalWeight` methods to the `Truck` object. We included those two methods in the required behavior of a `Truck` precisely because of the tollbooth.

Once the values have been obtained, the toll due may be calculated by the following formula:

tollDue = 5 * axles + 10 * (totalWeight / 1000)

This reflects the specification of the toll calculation in the problem statement.

Once the amount due has been determined, it is printed, and the booth's totals are updated. The resulting method follows:

```
public  void  calculateToll(Truck  truck)  {
    int  axles  =  truck.getAxles();
    int  totalWeight  =  truck.getTotalWeight();
    int  tollDue  =  5*axles+10*(totalWeight/1000);
                                    // Toll calculation
    System.out.print("Truck  arrival  -  axles:  ");
    System.out.print(axles);
    System.out.print(" total  weight:  ");
    System.out.print(totalWeight);
    System.out.print(" Toll  due:  ");
    System.out.println(tollDue);
    trucksSinceCollection  =  trucksSinceCollection+1;
    receiptsSinceCollection  =  receiptsSinceCollection+
                                         tollDue;
}
```

5.4.12   Using the Class

This software is intended to be embedded in a working automated toll system as described in the scenario. Prior to investing in the hardware, it is a good idea to first test our classes using software alone. We can do this by creating an application class that mimics the hardware. This has the following benefits:

- It provides us with an initial program that tests the classes.
- By writing a complete program, we make sure the interface is consistent— all arguments make sense in the context of their methods and no arguments are superfluous or missing.

Our sample usage code for the classes provides a good starting point:

```
class  TestTollBooth  {
  public   static   void   main(String   []   args)   {
    //   Create the tollbooth
    TollBooth  booth   =   new   TollBooth();
    //   Now for some trucks
    Truck   truck1   =   new   Truck(5, 12500);
    Truck   truck2   =   new   Truck(2, 5000);
    Truck   truck3   =   new   Truck(6, 17000);
    //   Let's start collecting tolls!
    booth.calculateToll(truck1);
    booth.displayData();
    booth.calculateToll(truck2);
    //   Time to collect the receipts
    booth.onReceiptCollection();
    //   Here comes another truck
    booth.calculateToll(truck3);
    booth.displayData();
  }
}
```

The `TestTollBooth` class acts as an *application class*—it provides a `main` method. `TestTollBooth` uses the `TollBooth` and `Truck` classes to create a working toll application. The only methods in the system not invoked by this class are the `getAxles` and `getTotalWeight` methods of class `Truck`; however, those methods are used by the `calculateToll` method. Thus the `main` method of `TestTollBooth` invokes, directly or indirectly, the complete set of methods of the two classes.

5.4.13   The Complete Solution

Here is the implementation of the toll collection system in its entirety:

```
class  TestTollBooth  {
      public  static  void  main(String  []  args)  {
            //   Create the tollbooth
            TollBooth  booth  =  new  TollBooth();
            //   Now for some trucks
            Truck  truck1  =  new  Truck(5, 12500);
            Truck  truck2  =  new  Truck(2, 5000);
            Truck  truck3  =  new  Truck(6, 17000);
            //   Let's start collecting tolls!
            booth.calculateToll(truck1);
            booth.displayData();
            booth.calculateToll(truck2);
            //   Time to collect the receipts
            booth.onReceiptCollection();
            //   Here comes another truck
            booth.calculateToll(truck3);
            booth.displayData();
      }
}
class  TollBooth  {
   //   Methods
   public  TollBooth()  {
      trucksSinceCollection  =  0;  // Clear out totals
      receiptsSinceCollection  =  0;
   }
   public  void  calculateToll(Truck  truck)  {
      int  axles  =  truck.getAxles();
      int  totalWeight  =  truck.getTotalWeight();
      int  tollDue  =  5*axles+10*(totalWeight/1000);
                              // Toll calculation
      System.out.print("Truck  arrival  -  Axles:  ");
      System.out.print(axles);
      System.out.print("  Total  weight:  ");
      System.out.print(totalWeight);
      System.out.print("  Toll  due:  ");
      System.out.println(tollDue);
      trucksSinceCollection  =  trucksSinceCollection+1;
      receiptsSinceCollection  =  receiptsSinceCollection+
                                           tollDue;
   }
   public  void  onReceiptCollection()  {
            System.out.println(
               "***  Collecting  receipts  ***");
            displayData();
            trucksSinceCollection  =  0;  // Clear out totals.
            receiptsSinceCollection  =  0;
   }
   public  void  displayData()  {
      System.out.print(
         "Totals  since  last  collection-Receipts:  ");
      System.out.print(receiptsSinceCollection);
      System.out.print("  Trucks:  ");
```

```
            System.out.println(trucksSinceCollection);
        }
        //   Instance Variables
        private int   receiptsSinceCollection;
        private int   trucksSinceCollection;
    }
    class   Truck   {
        //   Methods
        Truck(int   axles,   int   totalWeight)   {
            this.axles   =   axles;
            this.totalWeight   =   totalWeight;
        }
        public int   getAxles()   {return   axles;}
        public int   getTotalWeight()   {return   totalWeight;}
        //   Instance Variables
        private int   axles;
        private int   totalWeight;
    }
```

5.4.14   Discussion

Our first task of finding the primary objects uncovered two classes: tollbooths and trucks. We first defined the truck class completely and then attacked the tollbooth. We could just as easily have reversed the order—tollbooth first and then the truck.

We did point out, however, during our definition of Truck that we could not completely ignore the tollbooth—trucks only had to provide the behavior required by tollbooths. If there is more than one primary object in a system, we rarely define them completely independently of each other.

A High-Tech Version of the Toll System   Our initial scenario required a human toll collector to scan the bar codes that contained the truck's axles and weight. Let's imagine a fully automatic version of our toll system: as a truck enters the toll gate, it triggers a photocell, which causes the calculateToll method to be invoked. Instead of the toll collector querying the truck (using its bar codes) for its axles and weight (which in real life might not be such a great idea—we want to make sure we get an honest answer), sensors and a scale in the roadway count the number of axles passing over it and determine the weight of the truck. The result of the toll calculation is displayed on a monitor at the collection station. Supervisors can also press a button at this station that causes the invocation of the displayData method, which displays the station totals. When the cash box is opened, a sensor invokes the onReceiptCollection method, which displays and resets the station's totals. (See Figure 5.1.)

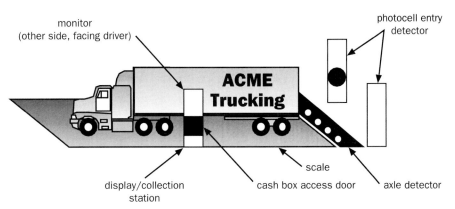

monitor
(other side, facing driver)

photocell entry
detector

**ACME
Trucking**

display/collection
station

scale

cash box access door

axle detector

**FIGURE 5.1 An
automatic imple-
mentation of our
toll system.**

1. Add a name to the `TollBooth` class. When a `TollBooth` is created, a nice descriptive message, including the name, should be sent to `System.out`.

2. Add "lifetime" totals to the tollbooth that track the total number of trucks and receipts collected since the booth was placed into operation.

3. Try developing this application by defining the `TollBooth` class first instead of the `Truck` class.

4. Carefully examine the automatic tollbooth presented in the discussion. Does it correspond exactly to our specifications? (Hint: Do the various classes and objects still have the same responsibilities in the automatic system as in the original one?) •

java interlude

Primitive Data Types, `int`, Expressions, and Operators

PRIMITIVE DATA TYPES

The basic data type of the computer's hardware is the integer. Instead of providing an integer class, Java furnishes us with direct access to this data type, which it calls `int`—`int` is a keyword of the language, rather than a class name. Because this data type is implemented using the underlying machine, rather than via a class definition, it is highly efficient. We call such a data type a *primitive data type.*

This direct support of primitive data types results in some changes in the way we use them. First, `int`s are not objects (they are not defined by classes), so you can't send them messages. Instead, we manipulate `int`s using the standard arithmetic operator symbols (`+`, `−`, `*`, `/`, and `%` for remainder) rather than method names such as `add` or `subtract`. This is actually beneficial, given our familiarity with these symbols. For example,

```
x/(y+1)
```

is more readable than using the hypothetical method invocations:

```
x.divide(y.add(1));
```

which is what we would have to write if integers were defined as a class and manipulated by methods.

Reference variables and primitive data type variables are declared the same way:

```
String  s1,s2;
int     i1,i2;
```

An `int` is a relatively simple entity compared to an object that belongs to a class. The `int`'s internal state is just its value, in contrast to a class instance, which may have a number of instance variables. There is no need for a constructor call for `int` values. Instead, the `int` variable is directly assigned and reassigned values:

```
int  i  =  12;
i = 25;
i = i+1;
```

A reference value is always associated with an object. Integer values on the other hand are simple and not associated with objects. (See Figure 5.2.)

FIGURE 5.2   Reference and primitive data type variables.

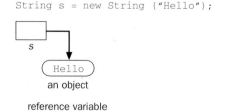

```
String s = new String ("Hello");
```

s

Hello
an object

reference variable

```
int i = 3;
```

3
i

primitive data type variable

TABLE 5.1   Differences between objects and primitive data values

	Reference variable	Primitive data variable
Type defined by	Class definition	Language
Value created by	new	See note below
Value initialized by	Constructor	See note below
Variable initialized by	Assignment of reference value	Assignment of primitive data value
Variable contains	Reference to object	Primitive value
Used with	Messages	Operator symbols
Can appear as a receiver	Yes	No

Note: As we mentioned above, objects are created and initialized, but the primitive values, such as the number 2, are already available through the underlying hardware.

Like reference variables, primitive data type variables require initialization before use.

The above differences apply to primitive data types in general, not just `int`, and are summarized in Table 5.1.

Although primitive data types cannot appear as receivers, they can be used as arguments and return values, as we have seen in the constructor method of the class `Truck`, and as return types, as seen in `getAxles` and `getTotal-Weight`.

THE BASIC ARITHMETIC OPERATORS

Some of the Java arithmetic operators that can be used with `int` are listed in Table 5.2.

Because we are dealing with integers (whole numbers) only, / means integer division. The quotient is an integer and the remainder is ignored. This means that `17/3` is 5, and the remainder, 2, is discarded. If you need the remainder, you write `17%3`.

TABLE 5.2   Basic arithmetic operators

+	Addition
−	Subtraction
*	Multiplication
/	Division
%	Remainder

OPERATORS, OPERANDS, AND EXPRESSIONS

We first encountered the term *operator* in Chapter 3 when we introduced the use of the `new` operator. We mentioned that operators are actions that result in values. The values that operators act upon are known as the operator's *operands*. In

```
x/y
```

the operator is `/` and the operands are `x` and `y`.

An operator and its operands form a phrase known in Java as an *expression* that is itself a value (the result of an operation). Because expressions are values, we can use them as operands to other operators to build yet larger expressions. For example, given the following `int` declarations:

```
int x, y, z, w;
```

we can form the following expressions:

```
x+y
z/w
```

(Note the lack of semicolons—these are expressions, not statements.) These expressions can be combined into yet larger expressions:

```
(x+y)-(z/w)
```

In this expression, the operands of `+` are `x` and `y`, the operands of `/` are `z` and `w`, and the operands of `-` are the expressions `(x+y)` and `(z/w)`.

LITERALS AND CONSTANTS

Integer constants can get into the act as well:

```
2*(x+y)-(z/73)
```

The operands `x` and `y` are `int` variables. Variables represent locations that contain integer values that can change over time. The operands `2`, `-1`, and `0` are called *literals* because their names (e.g., `2`) are literal representations of their values, which can never be changed.

In addition to literal values, Java provides another form of constant value. Our toll system called for a charge of $5 per axle and $10 per half-ton. The implementation of our toll-due formula was

```
                                // Toll calculation
int  tollDue  =  5*axles+10*(totalWeight/1000);
```

Although this is perfectly correct, there are two basic objections to it:

- Code is meant to be read by others. The reader does not necessarily know the meaning of literals like 5 and 10 here; the reader may think that the 1000 suggests some kind of metric conversion.
- If the politicians raise the tolls and 5 must be replaced by 6, for example, we do not want to search our method implementations for the formula. Also, if the toll charge appears in several places, it is possible to overlook one occurrence, thereby introducing an error in our class.

The values 5 and 10 in the above formula are sometimes referred to as *magic numbers* because they seem to come from nowhere. A better approach is to assign them descriptive names. If we simply use instance variables, we might inadvertently change their values. To avoid this, Java provides the ability to declare variables that are constant in nature. That is, once initialized with a value, they cannot be assigned another value:

```
static  final  int
     DuePerAxle   =  5,
     DuePerHalfTon   =  10,
     TonInPounds   =  2000,
     HalfTonInPounds   =  TonInPounds/2;
```

The keyword **final** states that the variable's value is *final*—it will never change again. We have already seen the static keyword; it states that this variable belongs to the class, not each individual instance.

The toll-due formula may now be rewritten as follows:

```
int  tollDue   =  DuePerAxle*axles+DuePerHalfTon*
                    (totalWeight/HalfTonInPounds);
```

PRECEDENCE

There is a potential for ambiguity in expressions with more than one operator. An expression is *ambiguous* if there is more than one way of interpreting it. Consider the expression 5+3*2. This might be interpreted to mean either 16 (if we do the addition 5+3 first and then multiply by 2) or 11 (if we do the multiplication 3*2 first and then add the result to 5).

Java, along with most programming languages and mathematics itself, uses *precedence rules* to resolve such ambiguities. For example, multiplication and division have higher precedence than addition and subtraction and are therefore done first. In the case of 5+3*2, this forces the second interpretation (* before +) and the result is 11. As usual, parentheses can be used to override precedence. If, in 5+3*2, we want the addition to be performed first, we must write (5+3)*2. If you were thinking that there was no problem at all, obviously the multiplication is performed first, it's precisely because these precedence rules have become second nature for you.

Parentheses can also be used for clarity or when a programmer is uncertain of the precedence rules. As you learn more of the Java language, you will encounter many more operators. As the number of operators grows, so does the number of precedence rules. It is perfectly acceptable to use parentheses to guarantee the desired interpretation. Thus, one may write `5+(3*2)` instead of `5+3*2`. The precedence rules are just shortcuts that allow us to use fewer parentheses.

COMPOUND ASSIGNMENT OPERATORS

Assignments involving arithmetic expressions often take the following form:

```
x = x op some-value
```

where *op* is an arithmetic operator. For example,

```
yearToDate = yearToDate + currentWages;
```

or

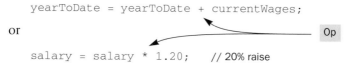

```
salary = salary * 1.20;     // 20% raise
```

This pattern occurs so often that Java provides special operators to handle such assignments. The above statements can be rewritten as

```
yearToDate += currentWages;
```

and

```
salary *= 1.20;                 // 20% raise
```

These operators are known as *compound assignment operators*. The effect is to view the variable on the left-hand side of the assignment as both an operand to the arithmetic operator and as the target of the assignment. Each of the above arithmetic operators has a corresponding compound assignment operator, as shown in Table 5.3.

We strongly advocate the use of these operators, and we will always write `x += 3` instead of `x=x+3`. This is not because we are lazy typists. It is a matter of minimizing the likelihood of error. If our purpose is to add 3 to x, `x = x + 3` is more error prone than `x += 3` because we could mistype the second x (hit c instead, for example). This is especially true for long identifiers. If the mistyped identifier is not a variable name, the compiler will catch the error. However, if it is a name of a variable (for example, `customerName1` instead of `customerName2`), we could introduce an error that is murderously difficult to track down.

TABLE 5.3   Related binary and compound assignment operators

Operator	Compound assignment	Effect
+	+=	Add and assign
−	−=	Subtract and assign
*	*=	Multiply and assign
/	/=	Divide and assign
%	%=	Take remainder and assign

One characteristic of operators is that they produce values. This is true of compound assignment operators as well. Therefore they can be embedded in larger expressions:

```
x = y+(z += w);
```

The result of an assignment operator is the value assigned to the left-hand side. In the above example, the value of the expression z += w would be $z + w$ because that is the value assigned to z by the compound assignment +=.

In this book we will not embed assignment operators in larger expressions, nor do we recommend doing so. The proper use such expressions is often misunderstood, and their misapplication can result in code that is hard to understand, frequently incorrect, and difficult to debug.

Interestingly, our familiar assignment symbol, =, is also an *assignment operator* and therefore also produces a value (the value assigned to the left-hand side) just as the compound assignment operators do. We will use this fact in one way only: in a multiple assignment, as in

```
x = y = z = 0;
```

Here, z is assigned the value 0. The value of *that* operation is 0, which is assigned to y. The value of *that* operation is then also 0, which in turn is assigned to x.

INCREMENT/DECREMENT

The most common arithmetic operations in a program are adding and subtracting 1:

```
x = x + 1;        // Also written as x += 1;
```

and

```
x = x - 1;        // x -= 1;
```

As before, Java provides us with special operators for these assignments. The above two statements may be rewritten as

```
x++;
```

and

```
x--;
```

The first is called an *increment operator* because its effect is to increment (increase) its operand by 1. The second is called a *decrement operator* because it decrements (decreases) its operand by 1. (There are two other increment/decrement operators: `++x` and `--x`. For our purposes they have the same effect as the pair presented in the text.)

Because the operand is itself modified (as opposed to producing a result by being added to 1), the following are illegal:

```
6++;          ◄───────────── No good—Can't modify a literal!
```

and:

```
(x + y)++;    ◄───────────── No good—Can't modify an expression!
```

Like the assignment operators, the increment and decrement operators result in a value and can appear as operands of larger expressions, and as in the case of assignment operators, we strongly caution against doing so.

STRING OBJECTS AND THE + OPERATOR

`String` concatenation is so common an operation that the Java designers felt impelled to represent it with a simple operator symbol in order to provide the same convenience that is associated with arithmetic operations. Thus, the expression

```
string1 + string2
```

is a Java shorthand for

```
string1.concat(string2)
```

Furthermore, the operator +, when used with a `String` operand, is defined to allow primitive data types, such as `int`, to appear as the other operand. When they do, they are automatically converted to their `String` representation.

EXERCISES

1. Write expressions for each of the following:

   - The average of the `int` variables a and b
   - The circumference of a circle with radius r.
   - Increase the value of the `int` variable i by 10.

2. Give three different ways of adding 1 to an `int` variable in Java.

3. Associated with a student is a name and a midterm and final average. The averages each consist of a grade between 0 and 100. Create a `student` class that allows you to create a student instance from data contained in an input file and that contains a method that returns the student's term average (midterm and final each count for half the grade).

4. Create a `Circle` class that can be queried for its circumference and area.

5. Create a `Rectangle` class that can be queried for its perimeter and area.

6. Create a `Square` class that can be queried for its perimeter and area.

7. Experiment with integer arithmetic. Create a class with a `main` method that contains various interesting expressions and see what the behavior is. For example, try dividing 0 by a number. Or see what happens if you multiple two large numbers. Does Java limit the size of the integer constant that it allows you to enter?

int **Methods and** int **Input**

WHERE DO int METHODS LIVE?

The set of `int` operators that the Java language provides is small. If we need to compute the absolute value of an `int` or raise one `int` to the power of another, we must use a method. But `int`s are not objects and thus can't be the receiver of a method. What can we do about this?

In Chapter 4 we introduced you to `static` methods. Such methods were necessary whenever no object was available to act as the receiver. This was the case under the following circumstances:

- When reading in data from a `BufferedReader` and then using that data to create an object. There was no object to invoke a method upon—it was precisely the creation of the object that we were trying to achieve. We thus declared `read` (and `readi`) to be `static` methods.
- The `main` method was declared `static` because at the outset of program execution, there were no objects to invoke methods upon.

We now present a third situation that calls for a `static` method:

- If the value to be manipulated is a primitive type rather than an instance of a class, we use a `static` method for precisely the reason that there is no receiver.

Java supplies several classes consisting of `static` methods that manipulate primitive types. For example, there is the `Math` class, which contains various mathematically oriented methods, including the `abs` method:

```
class Math {
    ...
    static  int abs(int a) {...}   // Returns the absolute integer value of a
    ...
}
```

Remembering that `static` methods are invoked by including the class name in the position of the message where the receiver normally goes, `abs` can then be passed the integer whose absolute value is to be obtained:

```
int i = -2;
int j = Math.abs(i);            After this statement, j contains 2.
```

Although `static` methods could be placed in any class (as they are not associated with any receiving object), we apply some common sense guidelines as to where to put them. Classes such as `Math` usually contain logically related methods, in this case methods that are mathematical in nature: logarithmic and trigonometric functions, and so on. Input methods, which create an object from input data, are best placed in the class of the object that they create. The `main` method, which is where a Java application's execution begins, is usually placed in its own class, whose sole purpose is to act as a placeholder for that method. Sometimes, though, it is added to the class of *the* primary object of the application. For example, it might have been reasonable to have placed the `main` method of the tollbooth application in the `Toll-Booth` class.

`int` INPUT

We need the ability to read an `int` value into a variable. This is accomplished using the composition of two methods: The first reads in a `String` object from the stream, and the second transforms the characters of that `String` into a number, as follows:

- Read a line from the data file into a `String` object, using `readLine`. For example, reading in a line containing 465 results in the `String`; object `"465"` (note this is still a `String`; it is not yet an `int`).
- Convert (transform) the `String` value (`"465"`) into the `int` value 465 using the `static` **parseInt** method of the predefined class **Integer**.

The word *parse* means to break up a portion of text into its component parts. In our case, we are breaking up the `String` object, which consists of a sequence of digits, and reconstructing it into an `int`. The above two steps translate into

```
String s = br.readLine();          Need s only briefly.
int i = Integer.parseInt(s);       Converts s to int.
```

or more succinctly,

```
int  i  =  Integer.parseInt(br.readLine());
```

Note that the line read in *must* be capable of being turned into an integer value; otherwise the Java interpreter produces a error. Thus, input such as

```
2
75
-1
```

are fine, but an error will occur for

```
Hello
57 40
12o
```

(the last line contains a lowercase o rather than a zero).

We can now write a `read` method for our `Truck` class:

```
static public Truck read(
                   BufferedReader br) throws Exception {
    int axles      = Integer.parseInt(br.readLine());
    int totalWeight = Integer.parseInt(br.readLine());
    return new Truck(axles, totalWeight);
}
```

EXERCISES

1. Add the `read` method to the `Truck` class.

2. Modify the `read` method presented in this section so that it is interactive (i.e., it prompts the user).

3. Modify the `Student` class from the Exercise 3 in the previous section so that it contains a `read` method.

4. More experimentation: Try entering nonnumeric values when the resulting input will be sent to `parseInt`. What happens?   •

5.5 Other Integer Types

The `int` type models the set of integers ranging from approximately –2 billion to 2 billion. Today, in commerce, administration, engineering, and science, 2 billion is often a small number. Numbers greater than 2 billion are needed to specify the federal deficit, the annual sales revenue of a major corporation, and hours of TV that U.S. residents watch.

Java provides a numeric primitive data type, `long`, that models the set of integers ranging from approximately –8 quintillion to 8 quintillion. A quintillion is a million times greater than a trillion. In commerce and administration, there are no relevant quantities that get anywhere near this large.

The `long` type is identical to the `int` type (in terms of values, operators, and behavior) except that `long` literals can be used to represent values whose magnitude exceeds 2 billion:

```
long    x = 2000L,  y = 1000L,  z = 1000000000L;
y   *=  x;  ◄────────────────── y is now 2 million—could have used an int for y.
y   =   y*1000L; ◄───────────── y is now 2 billion—still could have used an int for y.
y   +=  z; ◄─────────────────── y is now 3 billion—good thing we used an int for y.
y   *=  x; ◄─────────────────── y is now 6 trillion—small change for a long.
```

One minor difference between `int` and `long` is that `long` literals have an L appended to them.

5.5.1   Why Have an `int` at All?

Why shouldn't everyone just use `long`? The reason is twofold. First, `int`s require only 32 bits of memory, whereas `long`s require 64 bits. So, when a program uses a large number of numeric variables, using `long`s increases its memory requirements. Sometimes we know with certainty that `int` will be adequate. In those cases we should use `int` and save the space.

There is an even more important reason, although it is one that is likely to decrease in relevance in the future. Many computers today are only 32-bit machines; therefore, they cannot carry out 64-bit arithmetic—the kind that involves `long`s—with anywhere near the efficiency with which they process `int`s (using 32-bit arithmetic). This factor is becoming less important as companies continue to introduce new 64-bit computers, such as DEC's Alpha and Sun's Ultrasparc.

5.5.2   Mixed Type Arithmetic

Java allows `int` values to be assigned to `long` variables because there is no chance of information being lost: if *n* is an integer whose magnitude is less than 2 billion, it certainly is an integer whose magnitude is less than 8 quintillion. Thus, we can write

```
long    x, y z;
int     j=55, k;
x  =   98; ◄──────────── Assign an int literal to a long variable: OK
y  =   j; ◄───────────── Assign an int variable's value to a long variable: OK
z  =   2*j; ◄─────────── Assign an int expression's value to a long variable: OK
```

However, one cannot write

```
j  =  y;     ◄─────  Illegal: can't assign a long to an int, even if the long value is within the int's range
k  =  32L;   ◄─────  Illegal: can't assign a long to an int, even if the long value is within the int's range
```

If we *must* assign a `long` value to an `int` and are certain that it will fit the `int`'s range, we may write

```
j  =  (int) y;    ◄─────  Acceptable
k  =  (int) 32L;  ◄─────  Acceptable
```

Preceding the expression with the conversion type (`int`) in parentheses tells the Java compiler that the `long` value is small enough to fit in an `int`. This notation is called **casting,** and we often say we are *casting a `long` to an int.*

5.5.3 Other Integer Types: `short` and `byte`

Java provides two other integer types as well, `short` and `byte`. These represent even smaller ranges of integers and, accordingly, require less memory. A `short` models the set of integers from –32768 to 32767 and requires 16 bits of memory, half that needed by an `int`. A `byte` models the set of integers from –128 to 127 and requires 8 bits of memory, half that needed by a `short`.

The mixed arithmetic rules involving `short` and `byte` are based on the same principle as `long` and `int`: If information might be lost as a result of an assignment, an explicit *cast* is required.

5.6   Modeling the Numbers of Measurement

Integers are the numbers of counting. There is the implicit understanding that one could, in principle, count whatever is being quantified to obtain an integer value. For example, if there are five sections of calculus offered and each section has a maximum of 30 students, we multiply to get the maximum number of students taking calculus—150. We understand, however, that if the maximum number of students did enroll in calculus, we could count the students in all the sections and arrive at that same number. Furthermore, as long as counting is carried out accurately, precision is not an issue. The only reason for saying that the number of students in a university is "around 16,000" is that one has chosen not to count carefully.

In measurement we often obtain numbers that are not integers but that have fractional parts (six and one-half, or 3.14159, for example). For the numbers of measurement, *precision* always is an issue. We can measure the length of a desk and come up with 64 inches. But is it really 64 inches? If a more careful measurement yields 66 inches, then the first measurement was wrong. But if a more careful measurement yields 64.3 inches, we recognize that the first was not wrong, just not as precise as the second. The first measurement had a precision of two digits, while the second had a precision of three.

Precision issues affect calculations based on measurement. Suppose the length of a photograph is measured as 6.4 inches and its width is measured as 3.3 inches. Its area, we might say, is 6.4*3.3 or 21.12 square inches. Yet this is not a reasonable claim. We only measured the linear dimensions with a precision of two digits, so how could the calculated area have four digits of precision? In fact it doesn't. If, for example, a more precise measurement indicates that the dimensions are 6.41 by 3.32, then the resulting area calculation is 21.28... and we see that our original area calculation was incorrect.

Scientists and engineers avoid this problem by recognizing that when we are multiplying two measured values, the precision of the result can't be better than that of the least precise of the measured values. So in our area calculation, the scientifically correct value is not 21.12 square inches, but 21 square inches.

Actually, the rules governing precision in scientific measurement and calculations are more complex than we described above, and they take into account other operations such as addition, division, subtraction, and so on as well.

Keep in mind, however, that most of the numbers used in scientific and engineering applications have a different behavior than integers or even than the set of real numbers from mathematics. In the integer world, 64*33 is 2112, but in the numbers of measurement it is 2100 because assigning nonzero values to the tens and ones place would imply a precision we can't claim, given that 64 and 33 only have two digits of precision themselves. Similarly, in the world of real numbers, 0.064*0.033 is 0.002112, but in the numbers of measurement it is just 0.0021.

5.6.1   The `float` and `double` Primitive Data Types

In the world of computer science, numbers that have this behavior are called **floating-point** numbers. The term derives from the way computer hardware handles operations involving these values and the way these values are represented in memory.

Java provides two primitive data types for modeling floating-point behavior: **float** and **double**. The `float` data type models floating-point numbers with approximately seven digits of precision, `double` with 15 digits of precision. The range for both of these greatly exceeds that of **int**, which only represents integers between –2 billion and 2 billion (approximately). The largest value a `float` can have is:

    34028235000000000000000000000000000000

or

$$3.4028235 \times 10^{38}$$

or, as we would write it in Java:

    3.4028235E38f

How big is that? Bigger than the number of atoms in the Pacific Ocean.
    The smallest (in magnitude) value a `float` can have is:

    0.00000000000000000000000000000000000000000000014012985

or

$$1.4012985 \times 10^{-45}$$

or, as we would write it in Java:

    1.4012985E-45f

The range for `double`s is even huger, ranging from $2.2250738585072014 \times 10^{-308}$ to $1.79769313486231570e^{+308}$.
    A `float` and an `int` take up the same memory. So how can the `float` represent numbers from

    –34028235000000000000000000000000000000

    to

    34028235000000000000000000000000000000

when an `int` can only represent numbers from –2147483648 to 2147483647? It's simple: the `float` can't represent *all* the numbers in that huge range, only those with seven or eight digits of precision. For example, a `float` can't even represent 1,234,567,089, which is a perfectly good `int` value! The closest it can come to this value is 1234567000.

5.6.2   Printing `float` and `double`; `float` and `double` Literals

As was the case with `int`, the `println` and `print` methods of `Print-Stream` are overloaded to accept and then display `float`s and `double`s.
    Rather than print gigantic `String`s such as

    34028235000000000000000000000000000000

the format for printing `floats` and `doubles` borrows from scientific notation:

$$3.4028235 \times 10^{38}$$

Since superscripts are traditionally not easy to print, the power of 10 is represented by the letter E followed by the value of the exponent:

```
3.4028235E38
```

Literals of type `float` and `double` are can be written using the scientific notation style. The decimal point, the fraction, the exponent may all be omitted. To distinguish `float` from `double`, `float` literals must have a trailing f, as, for example, `3.14159f`. To distinguish them from `int` literals, `double` literals with no decimal point or exponent (i.e., those that look like `int` literals) must have a trailing d, as, for example, `98d`.

5.6.3   Using `float` and `double`

Despite their profound differences with integer types, the syntax for using `float` and `double` are comfortingly similar to `int`. Consider the following code that computes the area of a circle whose radius is 12:

```
double   area, radius;
radius  =  12.0;
area  =  3.14159*radius*radius;
```

The familiar int operators + – * / (not % though!) along with their assignment operator counterparts += –= *= /= are used. The general meanings are the same, but the behavior is different.

For example,

```
int       j = 1222333444;
float     x = 1222333444.0f;

System.out.println("j =" +j);
System.out.println("x =" +x);
j += 1;
x += 1.0;
System.out.println("j =" +j);
System.out.println("x =" +x);
```

displays

```
j = 1222333444
x = 1.22233344E9
j = 1222333445
x = 1.22233344E9
```

The increment to j changed its value as expected; the increment to x did not because only the most significant seven digits or so are maintained in a `float`.

5.6.4 Reading `float` and `double` Values

There are no `parseDouble` or `parseFloat` methods in the predefined `Double` and `Float` classes. As a result, reading `doubles` and `floats` from input is a bit more cumbersome that reading `ints`. Given a reference, s, to a `String` object containing a string representation of a `double` (i.e., something like `5.3e2`) we first create a `Double` object (an object, not a primitive data value!) by invoking the static `valueOf` method of the `Double` class, passing it the `String` reference:

```
Double  d  =  Double.valueOf(s);
```

To get the `double` value we send the object a `doubleValue` message:

```
double  x  =  d.doubleValue();
```

This can, of course, be combined into one line:

```
double  x  =  Double.valueOf(s).doubleValue();
```

So, to read a `double` value from a `BufferedReader br` into a `double` variable x, we do the following:

```
s  =  br.readLine();
x  =  Double.valueOf(s).doubleValue();
```

5.6.5 When to use `float` and `double`

By now it should be quite clear that `float` and `double` were designed for a very specific purpose: to model numbers related to measurement. When you encounter scientific or engineering problems that demand this data type, the need will be obvious.

You will find that `double` is frequently used in contexts that have nothing to do with measurement. It is used for the following reasons:

- `double` supports fractions (digits past the decimal point).
- `double` has a great enough precision (around 15 digits) so that as long as the values stay within the 100 trillion range, no additions will be lost (as we saw happened with `float` earlier).

Thus, you may find that some programmers will represent dollar quantities—things that are ultimately counted, not measured—with `doubles`, making the calculation of cents or other fractional parts easier. Although this practice is generally harmless in the short run, consider what would happen if the global concern you're writing software for decides to use it in a country whose currency exchanges at a 10,000 to 1 ratio. All of a sudden the margin for safety in the `double`'s precision seems a lot smaller!

On the other hand, you will find that `doubles` (and `floats`) are quite legitimately used in graphical calculations. That's because graphics involves geometry (a word meaning "*measurement* of the earth").

A useful rule of thumb is this: Floating-point arithmetic is acceptable when you are satisfied to compute a result just within a certain precision.

5.6.6   Mixed Type Arithmetic

The rules governing assignment between `doubles` and `floats` follows the same principle as `long` and `int`: If it is certain that no information may be lost, the assignment is legal. Thus, `float` may be assigned to `double`, but the reverse requires a cast.

When you are mixing integer types and floating point types, the general rule is that integer types may be assigned to floating-point types, but the reverse requires a cast. Be warned, however, that assigning a `long` to a `float` or `double` can result in information being lost. The idea is that `float` or `double` can represent numbers at least as large as the largest `long` but without the same degree of precision.

5.6.7   The `Integer, Double, Float, Long, Short,` and `Byte` Class

For each primitive data type, Java provides a corresponding class: Interger, Long, Short, Byte, Double, Float, and so on. These classes contain static methods that operate upon the associated primitive data type.

EXERCISES

1. Recode the `Employee` class, allowing noninteger values for hours worked. What data type would you use?

2. Suppose the `Employee` class had to allow payrates that are not whole dollar amounts. Would `double` or `float` be an appropriate representation? Why?

SUMMARY

Programming an application in Java is largely an exercise of using existing classes and defining new classes to fill in the gaps. A procedure that aids in the discovery of the relevant objects of an application and the design of any new classes is thus a valuable tool for the programmer. This chapter presents the following procedure:

- Determine the primary objects of the application by examining the nouns of the problem statement.
- Decide upon the desired behavior of the classes corresponding to these objects. This provides the basic set of methods available to the user of the class.

- Define the interface. The prototypes of the methods are defined, including the nature of additional information provided as arguments.
- Instance variables are introduced to maintain the state of the class.
- The method bodies are implemented.

Method implementation requires a broad set of tools and techniques to provide rich behavior within method bodies. In particular, numeric processing plays a very important role in modern-day computing. This chapter introduced Java's numeric types: integers and floating point types of various ranges and precisions: `int`, `short`, `byte`, `long`, `float`, `double`. These types belong to the larger set of Java types, known as primitive data types. Such types are not defined through class definitions but rather utilize the underlying hardware facilities. As they do not belong to classes and are not objects, primitive data types cannot act as receivers, and have no associated methods. Instead they appear as operands of operators to form expressions. To supplement the basic arithmetic operations, methods, such as absolute value, may be defined to accept a primitive data type as an argument, and operate upon it in some fashion. These methods, which have no receiver, are known as static methods.

STUDY AID: TERMINOLOGY REVIEW

byte   A primitive data type modeling whole numbers (integers).

constant   A variable whose value may not be changed after initialization.

double   A primitive data type modeling floating point numbers.

expression   A sequence of operands and operators producing a value.

float   A primitive data type modeling floating point numbers.

floating-point number   A number that models measurement with a fixed precision.

int   A primitive data type modeling whole numbers (integers).

literal   A value whose name is a literal representation of itself, e.g., 2.

long   A primitive data type modeling whole numbers (integers).

operand   A value participating in an operation.

operator   An action resulting in a value.

primitive data type   A data type provided as part of the language definition rather than through a class definition. No class or methods are associated with the data type.

short   A primitive data type modeling whole numbers (integers).

static final   The Java keywords used to declare a constant.

QUESTIONS FOR REVIEW

1. Why does Java have primitive data types?

2. How does a primitive data type differ from a class?

3. What are the basic operations for `int`?

4. Why are methods that manipulate primitive data types typically static methods?

5. How does one read in an integer in Java?

FURTHER EXERCISES

1. Create a class that models an employee. Creating an `Employee` object entails providing the name and hourly rate of the worker. The `Employee` object should possess a method that receives the number of hours worked as an argument and returns the earned wages.

2. Add a read method to the `Employee` class.

3. What data type did you use to define the hourly rate of the employee? What about the hours worked?

4. Write a function that accepts a temperature represented in Celsius and returns the equivalent Fahrenheit value. Should this method be declared `static`? Should the temperatures be represented as integer or floating point type?

5. Write similar functions for converting Fahrenheit to the Kelvin scale, and from Kelvin to Celsius. Create a class `TempConverter` to hold these methods. Can you think of a simple way to code the remaining functions such as Celsius to Kelvin?

6. In an earlier exercise you associated a name and a midterm and final average with a `student` class. (See Exercise 3 following the Java Interlude on primitive data types, `int`, expressions, and operators.) Redo the `student` class; this time the student's final and midterm averages are accompanied with a weight represented by a `double` between 0 and 1. A value of 0.25, for example, indicates that the accompanying mark counts for 25%, or one-quarter of the average. You may assume the two weights add up to 1.

7. Add a car class to the tollbooth example. Cars are charged a flat fee of $3. Overload the `TollBooth` class's `calculateToll` with a method that accepts a car argument and returns the above charge. Make sure you use constants.

Drawing Text

In many computer systems, the display devices, such as the monitor or printer, operate in what is known as *text mode*. Output in this mode is restricted to text characters (alphabetic, digits, and punctuation) and possibly some very simple symbols. The sizing, positioning, and actual drawing of the individual characters are handled directly by a portion of the display hardware known as a *character generator*. Communication with the display device is controlled through a piece of software, known as a *device driver*, specifically designed for that particular device.

In the case of a video monitor, the character display is usually restricted to a single typeface, with the possible addition of underlining and/or italicizing. The display surface (the screen on a monitor) is divided into a uniform grid, with each position displaying a single character. (See Figure 5.3.)

Printers may provide a larger but still somewhat limited number of fonts and sizes, but not graphics or images. Initially monitors could not display the fonts used for printing; therefore word processors could not show the user

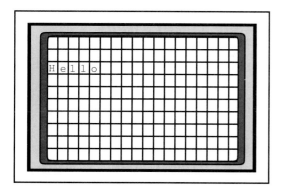

FIGURE 5.3 A monitor in character display mode.
When in character display mode, the monitor treats the screen as a grid in which each position can contain exactly one character.

what the final output would look like—they were not WYSIWYG (an acronym for 'what you see is what you get').

Printing text to `System.out` models this text mode. When we write

```
System.out.print("Hello ");
System.out.println("world");
System.out.print("I'm ready to go");
```

we need not concern ourselves with where the text will be displayed—the positioning of the characters is taken care of for us. When the `println("world")` is invoked, the argument is displayed immediately following the last character position of the previous `print` method. Using `println` rather than `print` results in the text cursor being positioned at the beginning of the next line, a position that is likewise determined for us.

This style of output is fine (even wonderful) for beginning programmers—it relieves them of the tedious burden of positioning text and allows them to concentrate on more important things, such as getting their basic classes to work. However, a reduction in responsibility is usually accompanied by a reduction in flexibility. The user cannot specify what font, size, or color the text should use. Nor can the text be positioned—it is restricted to a left-to-right, top-to-bottom flow, just like a typewriter.

As computers became more powerful, display technology more sophisticated, and users more demanding, more and more systems began to operate in what is known as *graphics mode*. The display surface is broken up into a grid of dots rather than character positions. On a monitor these dots are called *pixels*, for picture elements. (See Figure 5.4.)

When in graphics mode, the individual pixels (picture elements) can be accessed, allowing for the display of arbitrary shapes and figures.

In this mode, graphical shapes, such as lines or rectangles, may be displayed by essentially connecting the dots. A particular pixel position may be referred to by its *x* (horizontal) and *y* (vertical) *coordinates*, with the point (0,0)

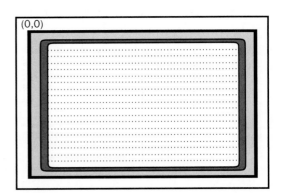

FIGURE 5.4   A monitor in graphics mode.

FIGURE 5.5 Using guesswork to draw text.

occupying the upper left corner. Lines may be drawn by specifying their end-points, and rectangles, by specifying their upper left corners, height and width.

Text may also be displayed in graphics mode by actually drawing the shapes of the characters. That is why we speak of *printing* to System.out, but we *draw* text in an applet. Once we are drawing the character, we can do so in any font or size—we are no longer restricted to the characters provided by the hardware device. We can also position the characters anywhere on the display by specifying a starting point, as we saw in the drawString method.

This is the other side of the coin from text mode. Increased flexibility also entails increased responsibility. If we wish to write Hello to the screen, and then world, we must determine the proper position to place the second string so that the result is smooth and continuous. Simply guessing or approximating produces choppy or even overlapping output. (See Figure 5.5.)

In graphics mode, text must be positioned like any other graphics. Attempting to determine the proper position through guesswork or estimation produces choppy or overlapping text.

Figure 5.5 was produced by the following applet. The first guess was too far, the second, too close.

```
import java.applet.*;
import java.awt.*;
public class TextApplet0 extends Applet {
    public void paint(Graphics g) {
        g.drawString("Hello",20,20);
        g.drawString("world",60,20);
        // I'm guessing horizontal (x), but vertical (y) is same
        g.drawString("Hello",20,60);
        // Another guess
        g.drawString("world",40,60);
    }
}
```

Through trial and error we would eventually arrive at a suitable spacing. However, that is just for this pair of words—what about the next piece of text we wish to display? When we want to go to the next line (the equivalent of `println`), how far do we move in the vertical position? If we go to a different character size, the size of the words change, and thus the spacings are different.

We see that working with text in applets is vastly different from the simple mechanics of the `print` method. This GUI supplement shows you the basics of how to work with text in a graphic environment. The techniques rely heavily upon numeric processing, which is why we are presenting it at the end of this chapter.

Fonts   Even before there were computers, printers employed different character styles to *emphasize* text, **highlight** text, even create a mood. An artist would create a style, known as a *font,* in which each character was designed to reflect the theme of the style. The resulting characters would then be cast in lead and could then be used to print the pages of a book. To allow printers to refer to them, a font is assigned a name; some popular ones are **Helvetica**, Times Roman, and `Courier`. A font can be a work of art in the truest sense—you may have noticed the end pages of a book in which the font and its designer are acknowledged.

The font could be cast in various *sizes,* usually expressed in terms of *points,* with one point being 1/72 inch. The font could also be cast in different *styles:* **bold,** *italic,* or plain. The combination of a font, size, and style is referred to as a *typeface.*

In *fixed-width* fonts, all characters are of equal width; in *proportional fonts* the widths of the characters vary, for example an i would be narrower than an m, as shown:

im

Once computers got into the act, the number of fonts began to explode. Programs were written that allowed anyone to design a font. Rather than being cast in lead, the resulting design is saved in a font file. This file can then be loaded by a program and used for the display of text.

Fonts are modeled in Java by objects of the `Font` class. To be precise, these objects actually model typefaces: They represent a particular font, style, and size. To create a new font object, the name of the font, the style, and the size are supplied to the constructor:

```
Font  f  =  new  Font("TimesRoman",  Font.PLAIN,  12);
```

The first parameter is a `String` containing the name of the font. The standard fonts available in Java are `Helvetica`, `TimesRoman`, `Courier`, `Dialog`, and `Symbol`. The second parameter is an integer constant representing the font style; the `Font` class provides the constants `PLAIN`, `BOLD`, and

`ITALIC`. The third parameter is the size expressed in points; as a rule of thumb, book type is printed in the range of 10 to 12 point type.

Fonts are used to draw text, which is a graphical operation and thus is maintained by the `Graphics` class. An object corresponding to the current font may be obtained from a `Graphics` object with the `getFont` method:

```
Font getFont();  Class Graphics
```

We can also set the current font for the `Graphics` object with the `set-Font` method:

```
void setFont(Font f);  Class Graphics
```

Once we have a `Font` object, we can query it for the name, size, and style, using the `getName`, `getSize`, and `getStyle` methods of class `Font`. We can also get a description of the font as a `String` object using the `toString` method of the `Font` class. For example,

```
Font  f  =  new Font("Helvetica",  Font.BOLD,  12);
System.out.print(f.toString);
```

produces

```
java.awt.font[family=Helvetica,name=Helvetica,
                         style=bold,size=12]
```

Fonts with similar characteristics, such as fixed width or serifed, are grouped into *families*. If a font is unavailable, using one from the same family will provide a somewhat reasonable substitution. We will not be working with font families in our applets.

Taking a Font's Measure—Class `FontMetrics`   In order to properly position text, we must know the height and width of the various text `String`s we are displaying. This becomes especially true when we are working with proportional fonts in which the characters have varying widths. Without height and width information, we cannot determine how far a text `String` extends along the line or down the screen. (See Figure 5.6.)

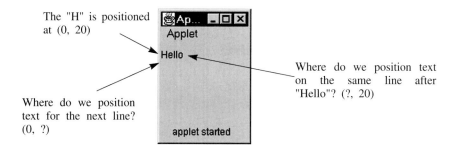

The "H" is positioned at (0, 20)

Where do we position text for the next line? (0, ?)

Where do we position text on the same line after "Hello"? (?, 20)

FIGURE 5.6   The need for font height and width information.

Without information regarding a font's height or the width of a string displayed in that font, we are unable to properly position text either after or below the string.

Text on the same line has the same y coordinate, but what is the proper x coordinate of the position following the text we displayed? Similarly, what y coordinate should we use to position text on the next line? When drawing text, there really is no next character or line—it's simply where we position the next piece of text. All of this becomes even more complex in the presence of multiple fonts and sizes.

What we require is information regarding the dimensions of a font. This information is known as the font's *metrics* and is maintained in an object of the `FontMetrics` class. The dimensions of the characters of a particular typeface (font + size + style) are not simply a function of the font—they also depend upon the device we are drawing the text upon. The `Graphics` object associated with a GUI component, such as an applet or panel, is responsible for the graphics operations performed upon that component. We therefore query the `Graphics` object for the `FontMetrics` object of the current font:

```
g.getFontMetrics();   Class Graphics
```

The `FontMetrics` class contains two highly useful methods: one to determine the width of a text fragment in the current typeface and the other to determine the height of a line of text, again in the current typeface:

```
int  stringWidth(String  s);      // Returns width of s
int  getHeight();                 // Returns height of typeface
```

The `getHeight` methods returns a value that includes spacing between two lines of text. (See Figure 5.7.)

In addition to string width and font height, there are other font-related measurements obtainable from `FontMetrics`, several of which are necessary to achieve high-quality text positioning. We will only use width and height—they are more than sufficient for our example.

This height, including line spacing, is returned by `getHeight`

This width is returned by `stringWidth("Hello world")`

Hello world
On the next line

FIGURE 5.7   Obtaining height and width information.

Text Drawing 101   We now have all the essential components for drawing text:

- The `Graphics` object associated with the component upon which we wish to draw
- The `Font` currently associated with the `Graphics` object
- The associated `FontMetrics` objects

Let us now develop an applet that displays text in various typefaces. We will display one line per typeface. Drawing two text fragments per line, will give us practice with `stringWidth`. The applet displays the current font and then the standard fonts in several sizes and styles. (See Figure 5.8.)

An Overview   We have no GUI components to create or any other sort of initialization, so we have no need for an `init` method. We do require a `paint` method, however, which draws the text on the applet:

```
import   java.applet.*;
import   java.awt.*;
public   class   TextApplet   extends   Applet   {
         public   void   paint(Graphics   g)   {
             ...
         }
}
```

We will use two helper methods. The `paintTypeface` method does most of our work: It sets the font, determines string widths, does the actual text drawing, and spaces to the next line. To accomplish this, it is passed the `Graphics` object to use for the drawing and the font to be used:

```
private   void   paintTypeface(Graphics   g,   Font   f)
```

The `paintFont` method's primary responsibility is to invoke `paint-Typeface` with a variety of sizes and styles of a particular font. In addition, it will perform a line space so that the various fonts displayed are neatly separated. `paintFont` is passed the `Graphics` object (mainly to be able to pass it on to `paintTypeface`), a font, and a starting point size:

```
private   void   paintFont(Graphics   g,   String   fontName,
                   int   startSize)
```

In order to keep track of the vertical position so that we know where to begin the next line, we maintain an instance variable, `startY`, which contains the y coordinate of the next line to be drawn. We will begin all our lines $x = 0$.

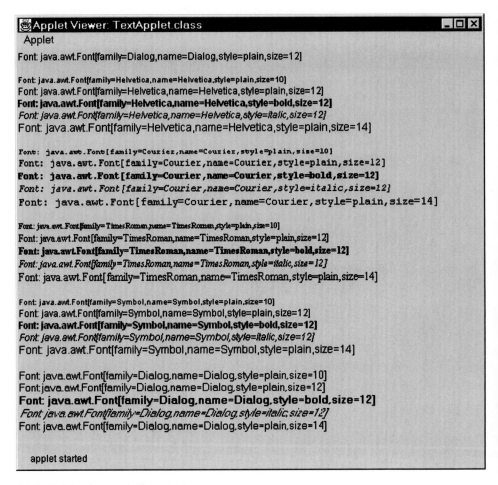

FIGURE 5.8 Our applet's output.

The Method Implementations Our `paint` method first passes the current typeface (font, style, and size) to `paintTypeface`. It then passes the standard fonts, one at a time, together with a point size, to `paintFont`:

```
public void paint(Graphics g) {
    startY = 0;

    // Display current font
    Font f = g.getFont();
    paintTypeface(g, f);

    startY += g.getFontMetrics().getHeight();  // Blank line
```

```
    //   Display  the  standard  fonts
    paintFont(g,  "Helvetica",  12);
    paintFont(g,  "Courier",  12);
    paintFont(g,  "TimesRoman",  12);
    paintFont(g,  "Symbol",  12);
    paintFont(g,  "Dialog",  12);
}
```

The statement

```
startY  +=  g.getFontMetrics().getHeight();  // Blank line
```

causes a blank line to be displayed. It obtains the current `FontMetrics` object and then queries it for the current height. What is *really* happening is that we are moving our vertical position holder, `startY`, downward by the height of the font. Because subsequent displaying will use the new value, we have effectively caused a blank line to appear on the display.

The `paintFont` method creates various `Font` objects and passes them onto `paintTypeface`. The typefaces include the various styles using the passed size, as well as larger and smaller sizes:

```
private  void  paintFont(Graphics  g,  String  fontName,
                             int  startSize)  {
    Font  f;
    f  =  new  Font(fontName,  Font.PLAIN,  startSize-2);
    paintTypeface(g,  f);
    f  =  new  Font(fontName,  Font.PLAIN,  startSize);
    paintTypeface(g,  f);
    f  =  new  Font(fontName,  Font.BOLD,  startSize);
    paintTypeface(g,  f);
    f  =  new  Font(fontName,  Font.ITALIC,  startSize);
    paintTypeface(g,  f);
    f  =  new  Font(fontName,  Font.PLAIN,  startSize+2);
    paintTypeface(g,  f);

    startY  +=  g.getFontMetrics().getHeight();  Blank line
}
```

Again, a blank line is displayed to separate this output from that of the next invocation.

We finally get to the workhorse method: `paintTypeface`. We first set the current font to the one passed in as an argument. We then retrieve the `FontMetrics` object associated with the newly set font. We can now begin the actual task of drawing. Positioning ourselves at the left edge and spacing down a line from the previous output, we print out our first piece of text, the `String` constant `"Font:    "`. We then obtain the width of that `String` using the `stringWidth` method and use the resulting value to position our-

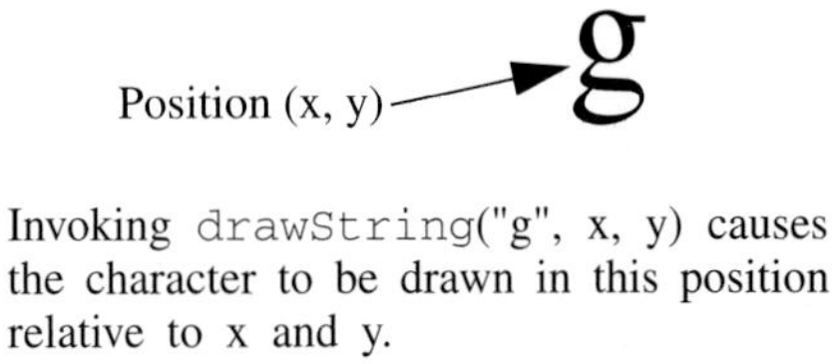

Position (x, y) ➤ *g*

FIGURE 5.9   The location of the point specified in the drawString method

Invoking drawString("g", x, y) causes the character to be drawn in this position relative to x and y.

selves beyond the String. We finally draw our second String, a description of the current font, which we obtain from the toString method of class Font:

```
private void paintTypeface(Graphics g, Font f) {
    FontMetrics fm;
    String str1 = "Font:  ";   Precedes the font description
    g.setFont(f);
    fm = g.getFontMetrics();
    int startX = 0;                    // Start at left edge.
    startY += fm.getHeight();          // Go to next line.
    g.drawString(str1, 0, startY);
    startX += fm.stringWidth(str1);   // Space over.
    g.drawString(f.toString(), startX, startY);
}
```

When drawing text, the position specified in the drawString method actually corresponds to a position approximately in the middle of the left edge of the character, not the upper left hand corner as you may have expected. The arrow in Figure 5.9 shows the position.

The position specified in the drawString method is somewhere in the middle of the left edge of the character—not the top or bottom left corner as you might have expected.

Invoking drawString("g", x, y) causes the character to be drawn in the position shown. This seemingly strange positioning has to do with those aspects of the font metrics that we chose to ignore. There is, however, a practical consequence to what we did. Displaying text at position (0,0) will cause the upper half of the first line to be truncated. We therefore had paintTypeface space down a line *before* displaying any text. This is not perfect but was fine for our applet.

The Complete Implementation   Putting it all together, we have the following code:

```
import java.applet.*;
import java.awt.*;
public class TextApplet extends Applet {
    public void paint(Graphics g) {
```

```
       startY  =  0;
        //  Display current font.
       Font  f  =  g.getFont();
       paintTypeface(g,  f);


       startY  +=  g.getFontMetrics().getHeight();  [Blank line]


        //  Display the standard fonts.
       paintFont(g,  "Helvetica",  12);
       paintFont(g,  "Courier",  12);
       paintFont(g,  "TimesRoman",  12);
       paintFont(g,  "Symbol",  12);
       paintFont(g,  "Dialog",  12);
   }


private  void  paintFont(Graphics g,  String fontName,
           int  startSize)  {
  Font  f;
  f  =  new  Font(fontName,  Font.PLAIN,  startSize-2);
  paintTypeface(g,  f);
  f  =  new  Font(fontName,  Font.PLAIN,  startSize);
  paintTypeface(g,  f);
  f  =  new  Font(fontName,  Font.BOLD,  startSize);
  paintTypeface(g,  f);
  f  =  new  Font(fontName,  Font.ITALIC,  startSize);
  paintTypeface(g,  f);
  f  =  new  Font(fontName,  Font.PLAIN,  startSize+2);
  paintTypeface(g,  f);

  startY  +=  g.getFontMetrics().getHeight();       [Blank line]
  }


private  void  paintTypeface(Graphics  g,  Font  f)  {
     FontMetrics  fm;
     String  str1  =  "Font:  ";
     g.setFont(f);
     fm  =  g.getFontMetrics();
     int  startX  =  0;                         // Start at left edge.
     startY  +=  fm.getHeight();                // Go to next line.
     g.drawString(str1,  0,  startY);
     startX  +=  fm.stringWidth(str1);  // Space over.
     g.drawString(f.toString(),  startX,  startY);  .
  }
private int  startY  =  0;
}
```

Mixing Graphics with GUI Components   Applets and panels are examples of what Java calls *container* components—other components may be placed within them, using a layout manager and the `add` method.

User interface components, such as buttons, text fields, and panels, are maintained as objects distinct from the container component on which they are placed. Their primary responsibility is to provide a mechanism for the user to interact with the program, and therefore each component has its own specific behavior provided by the corresponding class: `Button` for buttons, `Panel` for panels, and so on. These components may be placed within a container, but they maintain their own identity.

In contrast, text and the graphic shapes such as lines, rectangles, and ovals have no existence independent of the component they are drawn upon. For example, they cannot be given their own background color—they use the color of the component they are drawn upon. We can change that color, using the `setBackground` method of the `Graphics` class but then the background color of the whole component would change as well, not just the text string or shape.

In summary, components are created and placed upon their containers using a layout manager. Graphical shapes (including text), on the other hand, are drawn directly upon the display surface—the layout manager knows nothing of them.

When a component is created, it has its own display surface, and when it is placed into position by the layout manager, it hides the portion of the display surface directly beneath it. If there is text in that area, it will be hidden by the component.

If we draw text on an applet and then add GUI components to it, the layout manager, which knows nothing of the text, will position the components without regard to the underlying text. Using our `TextApplet` as a starting point, let us add an `init` method that creates and adds several buttons to the applet:

```
public  class  TextApplet2  extends  Applet  {
        public  void  init()  {
                add(new  Button("Previous"));
                add(new Button("Next"));
                add(new Button("Cancel"));
        }
        ...    // The rest is the same as TextApplet.
}
```

Running the resulting applet produces a display in which the text and buttons clash. (See Figure 5.10.)

The `Canvas` Component   To prevent the clash shown in Figure 5.10, we must isolate the shapes and text from the GUI components. We accomplish this using the `Canvas` component, whose behavior models a drawing canvas—we can draw our text and shapes upon it. Since a `Canvas` is a compo-

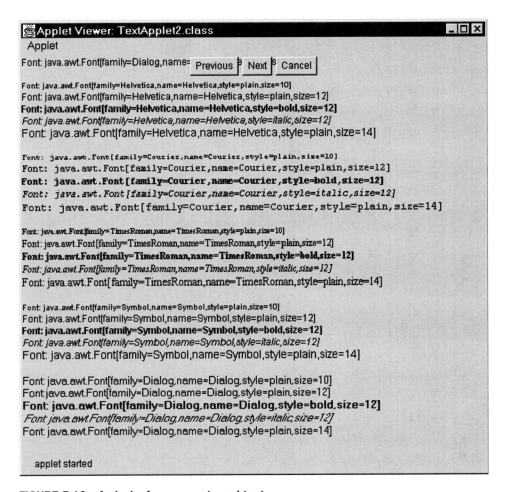

FIGURE 5.10   A clash of components and text.

nent, it may be added to the panel and will be known to the layout manager. When the buttons are added, the layout manager will prevent them from overlapping the `Canvas`, preserving our display.

Each time we created a new applet, we defined a new applet class. In a similar fashion, each time we wish to draw a new type of canvas, we define a new canvas class. In our case, we will have a class, `TextCanvas`, whose responsibility is the display of our text.

The primary restructuring of our applet involves taking all the text-related code and placing it into our new `TextCanvas` class. When an applet is repainted, the components are automatically repainted as well. Thus the `paint` method of `TextCanvas` will be invoked under the same circumstances as `TextApplet`'s `paint` method.

All our `TextApplet3` applet needs to do now is create the canvas and buttons. The buttons are placed into a `Panel` (using `FlowLayout`, the default layout manager for panels), which is in turn added to the applet, together with the `TextCanvas` component using a `BorderLayout`. Here is the complete implementation:

```java
import   java.applet.*;
import   java.awt.*;

public  class  TextApplet3  extends  Applet  {
        public  void  init()  {
                setLayout(new  BorderLayout());
                add("Center",  new  TextCanvas());
                Panel  p  =  new  Panel();
                add("South",   p);
                p.add(new  Button("Previous"));
                p.add(new  Button("Next"));
                p.add(new  Button("Cancel"));
        }
}

class  TextCanvas  extends  Canvas  {
   public  void  paint(Graphics  g)   {
                startY  =  0;
                Font  f  =  g.getFont();
                paintTypeface(g,   f);
                startY  +=  g.getFontMetrics().getHeight();
                paintFont(g,   "Helvetica",   12);
                paintFont(g,   "Courier",   12);
                paintFont(g,   "TimesRoman",   12);
                paintFont(g,   "Symbol",   12);
                paintFont(g,   "Dialog",   12);
   }

   private  void  paintFont(Graphics  g,  String  fontName,
                           int  startSize)  {
      Font  f;
      f  =  new  Font(fontName,   Font.PLAIN,   startSize-2);
      paintTypeface(g,   f);
      f  =  new  Font(fontName,   Font.PLAIN,   startSize);
      paintTypeface(g,   f);
      f  =  new  Font(fontName,   Font.BOLD,   startSize);
      paintTypeface(g,   f);
      f  =  new  Font(fontName,   Font.ITALIC,   startSize);
      paintTypeface(g,   f);
      f  =  new  Font(fontName,   Font.PLAIN,   startSize+2);
      paintTypeface(g,   f);
      startY  +=  g.getFontMetrics().getHeight();
   }

   private  void  paintTypeface(Graphics  g,  Font  f)  {
      FontMetrics  fm;
      String  str1  =  "Font:  ";
```

```
        int  startX;
        g.setFont(f);
        fm  =  g.getFontMetrics();
        startX  =  0;
        startY  +=  fm.getHeight();
        g.drawString(str1,  0,  startY);
        startX  +=  fm.stringWidth(str1);
        g.drawString(f.toString(),  startX,  startY);
    }

    private int  startY  =  0;
}
```

The result of running this is shown in Figure 5.11.

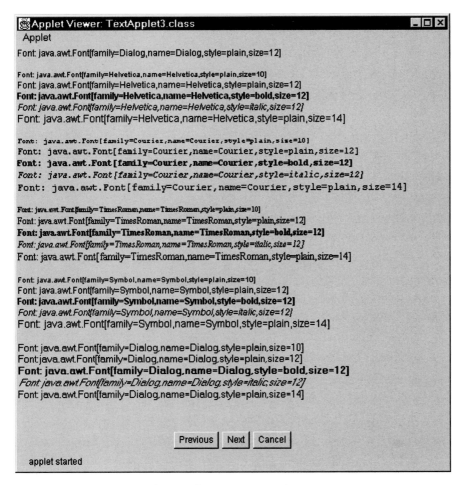

FIGURE 5.11   A correct display of components and text.

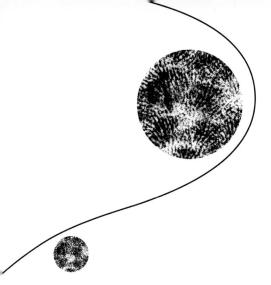

chapter 6

Controlling Behavior— Conditional Execution

6.1 Introduction

Until now, the bodies of our methods, which is where computation actually takes place, have been simple, consisting solely of assignment statements and the invocation of other methods. Because of their simplicity, our methods are not flexible. For example, we have no way of writing a method that takes one action or another depending on circumstances. This chapter introduces *conditional execution*—the ability to execute some code contingent upon some condition. This will enable us to write more flexible methods and define classes that are more sophisticated models.

6.2   Conditional Execution—The `if` Statement

In order for our methods to be flexible they must be able to respond differently to different situations. This requires the ability to test a value and carry out some action depending on the result of the test.

Java provides a mechanism, called a **conditional,** that gives us this ability. The simplest Java conditional (and in fact that of most programming languages) is the **if statement.** This statement allows us to test a condition and perform one of two statements depending upon the outcome of the test.

Suppose the requirements of the toll system in Chapter 5 stated that all vehicles with two axles should be charged a flat rate of $4; all other vehicles should be charged $5 per axle. Our `calculateToll` method must then distinguish between trucks with two axles and all others. This can be accomplished by testing the value returned by the call to the `getAxles` method. Here is the if statement that does this:

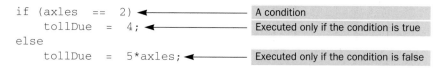

Line 1 of the above presents the *condition*, that is, the test we are performing. Here, we are testing whether the number of axles is equal to 2.

Line 2 is the statement that is executed if the condition is true (we sometime call this the *true portion*). In our particular case, if `axles` equals 2, the value of `tollDue` becomes 4.

Line 3 consists of the keyword `else`. It's sole purpose is to introduce the *false portion,* which is the statement (line 4 here) that is executed if the condition proves false.

Note that if the condition is true, the false portion is not executed, and similarly if the condition is false, the true portion is not executed. The two alternatives of the `if` statement are thus said to be *mutually exclusive.*

Let us now use the conditional in a complete example. Following that we will explore the `if` statement in more depth in a Java Interlude.

6.3   Employee Payroll: An Example

The point of this example is to introduce the `if` statement and provide more practice designing classes.

Statement of the Problem Model a payroll system that deals with employees earning an hourly rate. The system should be able to calculate an employee's payroll based on the hourly rate and hours worked and print out the employee's name, hours, and calculated wage. Employees working more than 40 hours receive overtime pay consisting of $1\frac{1}{2}$ times their normal rate of pay for the additional hours. To prevent overtime abuse, at the time of pay calculation, if an employee has worked 30 or more hours of overtime in the past two weeks, a warning message is issued.

A Sample Scenario Here is a possible session of the system to be designed. A user is prompted for an employee's name and hourly rate, and then the payroll for the employee is calculated for three weeks. The per week salary is then printed.

```
Enter employee name: Gerald Weiss
Enter employee rate/hour: 20

Enter Gerald Weiss's hours for week 1: 30
Gerald Weiss earned $600 for week 1
Enter Gerald Weiss's hours for week 2: 50
Gerald Weiss earned $1100 for week 2
Enter Gerald Weiss's hours for week 3: 60
Gerald Weiss earned $1400 for week 3
*** Gerald Weiss has worked 30 hours of overtime in the
    last 2 weeks
```

Finding the Primary Object The nouns in our case are *employees, hours, name, rate,* and *wage.* Of these, the most significant is *employee.* The others all are subsidiary to an employee in that they describe various attributes of an employee. To model an employee's behavior, we introduce a class, which we name `Employee`:

```
class  Employee  {
    Class definition will go here.
    ...
}
```

Determining the Desired Behavior We now turn to the desired behavior of class `Employee`. We do this by returning to the statement of the problem and the sample scenario, this time with our primary object in mind, and determine its responsibilities. The result is our initial set of behaviors (or methods) for the class.

The statement of the problem requires that we be able to calculate the pay of an employee. We name the method that realizes this behavior `calcPay`.

We also want to be able to query the `Employee` object for its name (the statement of the problem requires us to print it together with the earned wage). Let's call this method `getName`.

We know that we will have a constructor, `Employee`, although we do not know the nature of its arguments.

Examining the scenario provides us with the same plan. We see that we will be constructing an employee. The calculation of the employee's payroll, the printing of the employee's name with the pay, and the issuing of the warning message are also clearly seen.

We now have the following behaviors (methods):

- `Employee`—constructor for an `Employee` object
- `calcPay`—calculates the pay of an `Employee` object
- `getName`—queries the `Employee` object for its name

Defining the Interface To help us as we define the interface, we will write some sample usage code that creates an object that models an employee named Rudy Crew, who is paid $10 per hour. The code will compute his pay for 30 hours of work, printing that value out along with his name. Declaring a reference to an `Employee` instance is straightforward:

```
Employee e;
```

The `Employee` Constructor Creating a new `Employee` instance entails invoking its constructor and providing any data necessary to create the object. A real employee has many characteristics: pay rate, social security number, name, and so on. We must strive to abstract only the necessary information.

With this in mind, let us return to the statement of the problem and the scenario and determine what information we must maintain regarding an employee. The name must be supplied when we create the `Employee` instance because we want to be able to query an `Employee` object for its name. Likewise, the hourly rate must be provided because it is needed to calculate pay. The hours worked, however, vary over successive pay periods. They cannot be supplied to the constructor. The only pieces of information we need to supply when we create the `Employee` instance are the name and hourly rate, which we pass to the constructor:

```
e = new Employee("Rudy Crew", 10);    // Name, pay rate
```

The first argument (name) to `Employee` is a `String` corresponding to the employee's name; the second is an `int` containing the hourly rate.

The Other Methods   To calculate pay for 30 hours work, we invoke the `calcPay` method. The pay calculation requires the number of hours worked, so we pass 30 as an argument:

```
e.calcPay(30);
```

The result of a pay calculation is the number of dollars to pay the worker. This is an `int`, and we can save that value in an `int` variable:

```
int  pay;
pay = e.calcPay(30);
```

To get the employee's name for printing, we invoke the `getName` method. No argument is needed because the object should keep track of its own name, which, unlike the number of hours worked, does not change every week:

```
System.out.print(e.getName());
```

The complete sample usage code is as follows:

```
Employee e;
e = new Employee("Rudy Crew", 10);     // Name, pay rate
int  pay;
pay = e.calcPay(30);
System.out.print(e.getName());
System.out.print(" earned ");
System.out.println(pay);
```

The prototype for `calcPay` then is

```
public int calcPay(int hours) {...}
```

The prototype for `getName` is just

```
public String getName() {...}
```

We have now completed the interface to our `Employee` class:.

```
class Employee {

        public Employee(String name, int rate) {...}
        public int calcPay(int hours) {...}
        public String getName() {...}
        Instance variables to be supplied.

}
```

We have defined the external aspects of the class and we are now ready to begin working on the class internals.

6.3.1 Defining the Instance Variables

The `Employee` object is being constructed with a name (represented as a `String`) and has a method, `getName`, that must return that name. It must therefore maintain this information as part of its state. Similarly, the rate, also supplied at object creation, and subsequently used in `calcPay`, must be maintained as part of the object:

```
class Employee {
    // Methods
    ...
    // Instance variables
    private String name;
    private int rate;
    ...
}
```

In contrast, the number of hours worked is passed to `calcPay` as an argument. This value need not be maintained within the object because it is supplied each time it is required.

Our specifications also call for issuing a warning message if an employee has worked more than 30 hours of overtime in the past two weeks. This requires the object to "remember" the number of overtime hours the employee worked during the last period, introducing yet another instance variable:

```
class Employee {
    // Methods
    ...
    // Instance variables
    private String name;
    private int rate;
    private int lastWeeksOvertime;
}
```

6.3.2 Implementing the Methods

The `Employee` Constructor The constructor assigns its parameters to the corresponding instance variables so that these values may be used by the object later in other methods. It also clears the `lastPeriodsOvertime` instance variable (because a newly added employee has never been paid, the previous overtime hours should be 0).

```
public Employee(String name, int rate) {
    this.name = name;
    this.rate = rate;
    this.lastWeeksOvertime = 0;
}
```

The `calcPay` method If no overtime is involved, multiplying the hours worked by the hourly rate gives us the pay:

```
pay = hours*this.rate;    // No overtime
```

What would an appropriate expression be for the calculation of the pay for an employee *with* overtime? The first 40 hours are not overtime and thus would be paid at the employee's normal rate:

```
40 * rate
```

The remaining number of hours, `hours-40`, would then be paid at $1\frac{1}{2}$ times the employee's normal rate, `rate+(rate/2)`:

```
(hours-40)*(rate+rate/2)
```

The total pay of the employee is the sum of the overtime and nonovertime portions:

```
pay = 40*rate+(hours-40)*(rate+rate/2);   // With overtime
```

Which of these two statements is used to compute the pay depends on whether the number of hours worked is less than or equals 40. This can be arranged with an `if` statement:

```
if (hours<=40)
   pay  =  hours*rate;    // No overtime
else
   pay  =  40*rate+(hours-40)*(rate+rate/2);    // With overtime
```

We also need to issue a warning message if the employee has worked too much overtime in the past two weeks. The `lastWeeksOvertime` instance variable provides us with the previous week's overtime. We introduce a local variable `currentOvertime` to contain this week's overtime hours.

If there was no overtime this week, the current overtime hours equal zero:

```
currentOvertime  =  0;
```

Otherwise, we have to take this week's overtime (`hours-40`) into account in the calculation:

```
currentOvertime  =  hours-40;
```

Again, we use an `if` statement to determine which of these two statements is to be used:

```
int currentOvertime;
if  (hours<=40)
   currentOvertime  =  0;
else
   currentOvertime  =  hours-40;
```

We print the warning out only if the sum of the current and last week's overtime hours is 30 or more. If it is less than 30, we don't print anything—so in this case, no `else` is required:

```
if (currentOvertime+lastWeeksOvertime>=30)  {
      System.out.print(name);
      System.out.print(
         " has worked 30 or more hours overtime");
}
```

Finally, the current amount of overtime becomes the previous overtime hours for the next pay period:

```
lastWeeksOvertime  =  currentOvertime;
```

Putting this all together, we get the following implementation of `calcPay`:

```
public int  calcPay(int hours)  {
    int  pay;
    if (hours<=40)     // Test for no overtime.
        pay  =  hours*rate;
    else
        pay  =  40*rate+(hours-40)*(rate+rate/2);
    int  currentOvertime;
    if  (hours<=40)
        currentOvertime  =  0;
    else
        currentOvertime  =  hours-40;
        if (currentOvertime+lastWeeksOvertime>=30)  {
        System.out.print(name);
        System.out.print(
           " has worked 30 or more hours overtime");
    }
    lastWeeksOvertime  =  currentOvertime;
    return pay;
}
```

The `getName` Method   `getName` simply returns the value of the `name` instance variable:

```
public String getName() {
        return this.name;
}
```

Simplifying `calcPay`   The `calcPay` method contained two fragments of code that we developed independently of each other: calculation of the pay and the possible issuing of a warning message. In performing their tasks, each fragment tests for `hours<=40`. We can combine these two tests into a single one, merging the true and false parts to produce a somewhat cleaner piece of code:

```
public  int  calcPay(int  hours)  {
    int  pay;
    int  currentOvertime;
    if  (hours<=40)  {          Test for no overtime.
        pay  =  hours*rate;
        currentOvertime  =  0;
    }
    else{
        pay  =  40*rate+(hours-40)*(rate+rate/2);
        currentOvertime  =  hours-40;
    }
    if  (currentOvertime+lastWeeksOvertime>=30)  {
        System.out.print(name);
        System.out.print(
           "  has worked 30 or more hours overtime");
    }
    lastWeeksOvertime  =  currentOvertime;
    return pay;
}
```

6.3.3 The Complete Implementation

Putting it all together, we get the following code:

```
class  Employee  {
   // Methods
   public Employee(String name, int rate) {
       this.name = name;
       this.rate = rate;
       this.lastWeeksOvertime  =  0;
   }
   public int  calcPay(int  hours)  {
       int  pay;
       int  currentOvertime;
       if (hours<=40)  {  // Test for no overtime.
           pay  =  hours*rate;
           currentOvertime  =  0;
       }
       else{
           pay  =  40*rate+(hours-40)*(rate+rate/2);
           currentOvertime  =  hours-40;
       }
```

```
            if  (currentOvertime+lastWeeksOvertime>=30)  {
                System.out.print(name);
                System.out.print(
                    " has worked 30 or more hours overtime");
            }
            lastWeeksOvertime  =  currentOvertime;
            return pay;
        }
        public String getName() {
            return this.name;
        }
        //  Instance variables
        private String name;
        private int rate;
        private int lastWeeksOvertime;
    }
```

6.3.4   Using the Class

Our sample usage code for the class provides a good starting point for a sample application:

```
class Payroll {
    public static void main(String a[]) throws IOException {
        Employee e;
        e = new Employee("Rudy Crew", 10);    // Name, pay rate
        int  pay;
        pay = e.calcPay(30);
        System.out.print(e.getName());
        System.out.print(" earned ");
        System.out.println(pay);
    }
}
```

6.3.5   Discussion

In the *determining the primary objects* step, we stated that the employee was the primary object and the name, rate, and hours were subordinate to it. Let us examine the consequence of these relationships. By the time we were done, the name and rate were instance variables of the `Employee` object. In some sense, we could say that an `Employee` object possesses a name property and a rate property. We thus speak of a **has-a** relationship and say that `Employee` has-a name and a rate. The *X* has-a *Y* relationship is usually expressed in Java by having the class of *X* contain an instance variable representing *Y*.

The hours worked is also related to an employee but not in the same "permanent" sense of name and rate. Although we would hope that the employee's rate is not truly permanent, it is a value that remains the same for a relatively long period of time compared with the hours worked, which change at each pay period. It is for this reason that hours was made an argument to calcPay rather than an instance variable.

Our overview of the design associated the sample scenario with the determination of behavior and the sample usage code with the definition of the interface. Of the steps of the procedure, these two are the most closely related. Often, sample usage code can help determine *what* you want to do (the actual behavior), in addition to *how* you wish to invoke that behavior (the interface). Similarly, the sample scenario can help determine the interface by clarifying the role different types of information play in the class. We saw this with the hours value. The sample scenario indicated that hours was not an integral part of the class, but rather a value used to calculate a week's pay.

EXERCISES

1. Write an application class (i.e., a class with a main method) that performs the scenario presented at the beginning of Section 6.3. That is, the user should be prompted for an employee's name and rate. Following that, three weeks of hours are to be prompted for and the pay of each week and the cumulative pay should be printed.

2. Modify the Employee class to allow the pay rate of an employee to be retrieved. In which steps of our class development procedure do changes occur because of this modification?

3. Modify the Employee class to provide the ability to give an employee a pay raise. The raise should be reflected as a number between 1 and 100, which reflects the percentage of raise. For example, a raise of 5 indicates a 5 percent raise for the employee. Furthermore, when the employee is given a raise, a message should be sent to System.out.

4. The conditional tested whether the hours worked were less than or equal to 40. The true portion was thus the nonovertime case, and the false portion was the overtime case. Rewrite the if statement so that the true portion becomes the overtime case and the false portion is the nonovertime case.

5. What is wrong with using the condition (hours<40) rather than (hours<=40) to determine the overtime? •

The `if` Statement

The `if` statement has two general forms. The first provides two alternative execution paths—one for a true outcome, the other for a false one:

```
if (condition)
        statement1
else
        statement2
```

The second form of the `if` statement allows us to omit the false portion if no action is necessary when the condition is false:

```
if (condition)
        statement
```

In this form, *statement* is executed if *condition* is true; otherwise *statement* is skipped and no action is performed.

Note that

- The condition of the `if` statement must be surrounded by parentheses.
- If *condition* is true, *statement1* (the true portion) is executed; otherwise *statement2* (the false portion) is executed.
- The *statement* portions (both true and false) are restricted to a single statement. If we wish to execute more than one statement as a result of *condition* being true or false, we surround the statements with braces {} (like the body of a method or class) to create a **compound statement**, which is considered a single statement:

```
if (x > y) {
    System.out.print(x);
    System.out.print(" is greater than ");
    System.out.println(y);
}
else    {
    System.out.print(x);
    System.out.print(" is not greater than ");
    System.out.println(y);
}
```

compound
statements

CONDITIONS

The condition must be an expression that evaluates to true or false. For the moment we'll restrict ourselves to conditions that are comparisons of two numerical values. These comparisons use the familiar relational operators shown in Table 6.1.

MORE COMPLEX `if` STATEMENTS

The `if` statement provides a clean mechanism for selecting one of two actions based on the test of a single true or false condition. Things, however, often get a little more involved. In particular, we must consider a situation that resolves to more than two alternatives. For example, in our `Employee` class, we might wish to use different pay formulas for employees who worked 40 hours or less, more than 40 hours (overtime), and more than 60 hours (double overtime, say). In this situation, there are three alternative actions.

MULTIWAY TESTS

Let us first consider the situation where there is more than a simple pair of alternatives. We often refer to these as *multiway tests*. We will use *no overtime/ overtime/double overtime* as a guiding example. First, let's assume that we have an `hours` variable that we wish to test (think of all this occurring in `calcPay`). Suppose we wish to print out what category the employee falls into based upon the hours worked:

```
if (hours <= 40)
    System.out.println("No overtime");
else if (hours <= 60)
    System.out.println("Overtime");
else                                    // Hours > 60
    System.out.println("Double overtime");
```

TABLE 6.1   Java's relational operators

Operator	Meaning
<	Less than
>	Greater than
==	Equal (note the pair of equal signs)
<=	Less than or equal
>=	Greater than or equal
!=	Not equal

Although this code sequence may have seemed obvious to you, let us examine it just a bit. The first `if` distinguishes the *no overtime* case from everything else. Its true part can therefore print out "`No overtime`" for `hours<=40`. The false part then distinguishes two further alternatives: `40<=hours<=60`, and `hours>60`. We distinguish between these by a second `if` statement. The result is three distinct cases. Note the indentation that we used.

This style of code fragment, a sequence of conditionals taking the form

```
if (...)
    ...
else if (...)
    ...
else
    ...
```

is often called a **cascaded if/else.** Of the various forms we will be presenting it is considered the cleanest and most understandable.

An alternate indentation style is

```
if (hours <= 40)
    System.out.println("No overtime");
else
    if (hours <= 60)
        System.out.println("Overtime");
    else                                        // Hours > 60
        System.out.println("Double overtime");
```

This style emphasizes that the second `if` is contained within the first `else`. We usually avoid this form for the following reasons:

- Situations requiring multiple embedded conditionals such as the above occur quite frequently. The second style causes the code to march across the page, producing code that is unreadable and making it difficult to distinguish what code is of the same indentation level:

```
if (...)
    ...
else
    if (...)
        ...
    else
        if (...)
            ...
        else
            if (...)
                ...
```

- The second conditional being embedded within the else of the first is merely a consequence of the `if` statement providing only two alternatives. There is really nothing "second class" about the second conditional. All we are really doing is testing the value of `hours` against several ranges. Leaving the indentation at the same level and placing the `if` on the same line as the containing `else` emphasizes this.

Ifs within `ifs`   Consider the following permutation of our overtime test:

```
if (hours <= 60)
          if (hours>40)
             System.out.println("Overtime");
          else
             System.out.println("No overtime");
      else
             System.out.println("Double-overtime");
```

The above is an example of a **nested if,** so named because one `if` is nested within another. Only if the condition of the outer `if` is true will the inner `if` be tested.

Let us now decide that we only wish to print out the special cases of over-time and double overtime—the normal case of 40 hours or less requires no special attention. Although we still have three alternatives, we will only be taking action for two of them, retaining our logic,

```
if (hours<=60)
    if (hours>40)
        System.out.println("Overtime");
else                          Note the indentation.
        System.out.println("Double-overtime");
```

Because we are not taking any action for the no overtime case, the `else` corresponding to the `hours>40` is no longer necessary. Our indentation reflects this—the remaining `else` is lined up with the `if` it is meant to match. However, the rules for matching an `else` to an `if` will match the `else` to the most recent unmatched if, namely `hours>40`. This situation is often called the **dangling-else** problem (because the `else` is dangling from the wrong `if`).

We can resolve this problem in a fairly simple manner. Recall that if we require more than one statement be executed within the `if`, they must be enclosed in braces (`{}`). There is nothing that prevents us from doing this even if we have only one statement. We can therefore write the above correctly as

```
if (hours<=60) {
    if (hours>40)
        System.out.println("Overtime");
} else                                  // Note the indentation.
        System.out.println("Double-overtime");
```

Note that braces now explicitly delimit (mark off) the beginning and end of the statements belonging to the first `if`.

Most conditions can be designed using either cascaded or nested `if`s. However, dangling `else`s can only arise when code contains nested `if`s—they cannot arise from the cascaded `if` style. Furthermore, the logic of a cascaded `if` is easier to understand than that of a nested `if`. As a guideline, if your logic results in a dangling `else`, or even a nested `if`, it is likely that you can improve the readability of your code by restructuring it using cascaded `if`s.

THE SWITCH STATEMENT

The cascaded `if/else` often takes on the following form:

```
if (x==value1)
    statement1
else if (x==value2)
    statement2
else if (x==value3)
    statement3
else
    statement4
```

That is, it tests the same expression (in this case a single variable, `x`) against a series of values. Java provides a simpler construct, the **switch** statement, which eliminates a lot of the extra syntax (those `else-if`s) and factors out the common expression. Here is an example of it:

```
switch (x)  {
case value1:    statement1
                break;
case value2:    statement2
                break;
case value3:    statement3
                break;
default:        statement4
                break;
}
```

The above is known as a `switch` statement because it allows the flow of execution to "switch" among many different cases. The various cases consist of the keyword `case` followed by a value, a colon, and a series of statements.

The expression is evaluated and compared with the various `cases`. When a match is found, the corresponding statement is executed. If no match is found, the statement associated with `default` is executed.

The case values must be constants or literals. Associated with each case is a sequence of one or more statements—unlike the conditional, compound statements are not necessary for grouping.

The default case is optional. If it is not present and no match is found, no action is taken.

Each case should be terminated with a break. The compiler will not enforce this. If a break is omitted, execution will continue with the statements of the next cases until the next break or the end of the switch. Usually this is a disaster.

As an example, suppose we have a method that is passed an integer value from 1 to 7 that represents the day of the week. The method is to print and return a String corresponding to the name of the day; the code is as follows:

```java
public String  dayName(int  d)  {
    String  dname;
    switch(d)  {
    case  1:  dname  =  "Sunday";
              break;
    case  2:  dname  =  "Monday";
              break;
    case  3:  dname  =  "Tuesday";
              break;
    case  4:  dname  =  "Wednesday";
              break;
    case  5:  dname  =  "Thursday";
              break;
    case  6:  dname  =  "Friday";
              break;
    case  7:  dname  =  "Saturday";
              break;
    default:  dname  =  "Unknown  day";
              break;
    }
    System.out.println(dname);
    return  dname;
}
```

Execution of this switch statement causes the expression d to be compared against the various case values. The matching case assigns the corresponding day's name to the dname String variable. If the value of d is not in the range 1 through 7, the String "Unknown day" is assigned to dname.

EXERCISES

1. Return to the Employee class and add double time to calcPay; that is, hours worked beyond 60 are paid at twice the normal rate (overtime is in effect as well).

2. Modify the `Student` class from Exercise 3 in the Java Interlude in Chapter 5 on primitive data types so that it contains a method that returns students' letter grades based upon their term averages (the midterm and final each count for half the grade). Use the standard (i.e., 90 and above = A, 80 and above = B, etc.) cutoffs for the letter grades.

3. Using the previous exercise, make the final exam count twice as much as the midterm.

6.4   Input Methods Revisited: Testing for End of Input

Many of the methods we have encountered returned references as their return values: `toUpperCase`, `substring`, and the various `read` methods we have written. Although most of the time a reference to an actual object is returned, occasionally we would like to return some indication that no object can be returned. This could happen in the `read` method if no data remain in the file—no data mean no object can be constructed.

6.4.1   The `null` Value

The keyword `null` is used in precisely such a situation. Unlike all other references, which refer to objects, `null` refers to *no object*. In addition, `null` may be assigned to reference variables of *any* class, and a reference variable can be tested to see if it contains `null`:

```
String   s;
s  =  null;
if  (s  ==  null)    True
    ...
```

6.4.2   Using `null` in `read` Methods

The `readLine` method reads in a line of data from a `DataInputStream` and returns a reference to a `String` object that is created from that line. In the event that there are no more data in the file (a condition known as *end-of-file*), `readLine` returns a `null` rather than a `String` object.

We wish to return `null` as the return value of our `read` methods as well when there are no data to be read in. Let us modify the `read` method of the `Employee` class to include this feature.

Here is the `read` method for class `Employee` that was presented as an exercise at the end of Chapter 5:

```
public static Employee read(BufferedReader br) throws
                                          Exception {
        String name = br.readLine();
        int rate = Integer.parseInt(br.readLine());
        return new Employee(name, rate);
}
```

We make the following modification to this method: If the result of the `readLine` method that returns the `String` corresponding to the employee's name returns a `null`, indicating end-of-file, we will return `null` as the value of our method:

```
public static  Employee  read(BufferedReader br)  throws
                                          Exception  {
    String  name  =  br.readLine();
    if  (name  ==  null)
        return  null;
    int  rate  =  Integer.parseInt(br.readLine());
    return  new  Employee(name,  rate);
}
```

With the introduction of this ability to indicate that no object has been created, we have completed our presentation of input methods.

EXERCISES

1. Modify the `read` method of the `TollBooth` class developed in Section 5.4 so that it returns a `null` when there is no data to be read in to create the object.

2. In the `Employee read` method, should we test the `readLine` that returns the rate for a `null` return value? What would such a value indicate?

6.5   Type `boolean` and Boolean-Valued Expressions

Arithmetic expressions like `5+13` result in integer values. Conditions like `5>3` result in **boolean** values. Like `int`, `boolean` is a primitive data type. The `boolean` type models the behavior of a truth value, and so it has exactly two possible values: **true** or **false**. You can declare variables of type `boolean`, assign `boolean` values to `boolean` variables, construct `boolean` expressions, pass `boolean` values as arguments, and return `boolean` values from methods. But most significantly, you can use any `boolean` value in a condition.

Because we can return `boolean` values from methods and then use these values in conditions, we can write predicate methods for our classes. A **predicate** method is one that returns a `boolean`, and therefore it can be used as a condition in an `if` statement. For example, the `String` class contains a predicate method, `equals`, that tests to see if the receiver and its argument are identical. We can write

```
if  (s1.equals(s2))   s1 and s2 are both of type String.
    System.out.println("s1 has the same characters as s2");
```

Testing for equality is useful for many objects. As a quick exercise, let's develop a method, `equals`, for the `Name` class of Chapter 4. This method accepts a `Name` object as its argument and determines whether or not it is equal to the receiver:

```
class  Name  {
    ...
    public boolean  equals(Name  n)  {
        ...
    }
}
```

This method should compare the first name, last name, and title instance variables of the two objects and return `false` if there is any mismatch. To compare these `String` objects, we make use the `String` class's `equals` method.

To compare the first names, we can access the receiver's copy of the first name instance variable either as `first` or `this.first`. But how do we access the corresponding value for the object referenced by the parameter n?

Just as the pronoun `this` can be used to access the current object's instance variables, so can any reference to an object be used to reference its instance variables. Here, n, our parameter, is a reference to a `Name` object. The instance variables of that object can then be referenced using `n.first`, `n.last`, and `n.title`. The `equals` method of `Name` can now be written as follows:

```
public boolean  equals(Name  n)  {
    if  (this.first.equals(n.first)  ==  false)
        return  false;
    if  (this.last.equals(n.last)==false)
        return  false;
    if  (this.title.equals(n.title)==false)
```

Same as
`if(first.equals(n.first) ==`
`                false)`

```
            return  false;
        return  true;
    }
```

Now let's develop a class that contains several predicate methods and works with `boolean`s.

6.6 ■ A Time Class

This is an example of a utility class and the use of type `boolean` and boolean-valued expressions. It is also an example of a clever internal representation.

6.6.1   Statement of the Problem

Construct a class that allows us to manipulate time values. We will restrict ourselves to a 24-hour period, thus requiring hours and minutes only.

6.6.2   A Sample Scenario

A time class is not something an enduser would use directly. Rather it would be used by other classes. Such a class is called a *utility* or *helper* class. Our scenario consists of thinking of how we might wish to use time within our software.

Given a starting time and an interval, our software might need to determine the time at which the interval expires. It might also compare two times and print out those times.

6.6.3   Determining the Primary Objects

The nouns of our problem are *time-of-day, hours,* and *minutes.* Hours and minutes are subsidiary to the concept of time (they are used to represent a time value rather than having a separate meaning of their own). We will call the primary class of such objects `Time`.

6.6.4   Determining the Behavior

In our scenario, we identified a useful set of operations upon time values. These become our class's behavior (set of methods):

- `Time`—constructor
- `addDuration`—given a duration, determine the ending time

- `isBefore`—determine if the receiver occurs before (less than) a second time
- `isAfter`—determine if the receiver occurs after (greater than) a second time
- `print`—print a time to a `PrintStream`

6.6.5   Defining the interface

Let us write some sample code that uses the `Time` class:

```
Time    t1  =  new  Time(10,15,  "am");
Time    t2  =  new  Time(3,10,   "pm");
Time    t3  =  t2.addDuration(30);        Adds 30 minutes
t3.print(System.out);                     Prints 3:40 pm
System.out.println();
Time    t4  =  t2.addDuration(3,30);      Adds 3 hours and 30 minutes
t4.print(System.out);                     Prints  6:40 pm
System.out.println();
Time    earlier;
Time    later;
if   (t3.isBefore(t4))   {                Look: a predicate method.
    earlier = t3;
    later = t4;
}
else   {
    earlier = t4;
    later = t3;
}
earlier.print(System.out);
System.out.print("  is   earlier   than");
later.print(System.out);
System.out.println();
```

Note that `addDuration` is overloaded to allow a duration to be specified either in minutes only or in hours and minutes.

We want to be able to use the `isBefore` (and similarly the `isAfter`) methods as conditions within an `if` statement. For this to be possible, these methods must be predicates; that is, they must return `boolean` values.

We now use the above to fill in the interface of our class definition:

```
class Time {
    public Time(int  hours,  int  minutes)  {...}
    public Time addDuration(int  minutes) {...}
    public Time addDuration(int  hours,  int  minutes)
        {...}
    public boolean isBefore(Time t) {...}
```

```
    public boolean  isAfter(Time t) {...}
    public void print(PrintStream ps) {...}
}
```

6.6.6   Determining the Instance Variables

The obvious representation for a time, given our specification, is to have three instance variables: hours, minutes, and a value indicating am or pm. However, what is obvious is not always best. Instead, we decide to represent the time inside the class by the total number of minutes since 12:00 am. Thus the time 3:20 am, which is 3 hours and 20 minutes after midnight, would be represented by the value 200 (3 hours = 180 minutes + 20 minutes). On the other hand, 3:20 pm, which is 15 hours and 20 minutes after midnight, is represented as 920 minutes (15 hours = 900 minutes + 20 minutes). Therefore, just one instance variable, the total number of minutes since midnight, is required:

```
Class Time {
            //  Methods
            as above
            //  Instance variables
            private int totalMinutes;
}
```

6.6.7   Implementing the Methods

Our implementation choice greatly simplifies the various methods; for example, comparing total minutes is simpler than comparing hours and minutes.

The Predicate Methods   The task of isBefore is to return true if the receiver Time object is earlier than the Time object passed as an argument. This can be determined by comparing the totalMinutes instance variable of the two objects:

```
public boolean isBefore(Time t) {
    if (totalMinutes < t.totalMinutes)
        return true;
    else
        return false;
}
```

Similarly for the isAfter method, we write

```
public boolean isAfter(Time t) {
    if (totalMinutes > t.totalMinutes)
        return true;
    else
```

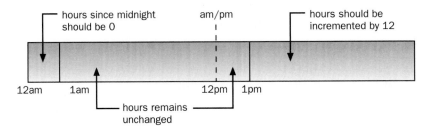

FIGURE 6.1   Breaking the day up into sections. Different sections of the day require different processing to convert them to our internal representation.

```
        return  false;
}
```

The `Time` Constructor   The constructor does most of the work for the class in that it converts our external notion of a time value, hours and minutes and am or pm, into the representation used internally by the class. The value of the hours parameter must be converted to a value that is the number of hours since midnight. Figure 6.1 shows how the conversion must be done for different periods of the day.

There are four cases:

- The first hour of the day (the midnight hour 12:00 am to 12:59 am)
- The remaining morning hours: 1:00 am through 11:59 am
- The noon hour, 12:00 pm through 12:59 pm
- The remaining afternoon hours: 1:00 pm through 11:59 pm

We first distinguish between the am and pm cases:

```
if  (amOrPm.equals("am"))
    am case
else
    pm case
```

Only the midnight hour of the am case requires action: hours must be set to 0. Similarly only the 1:00-pm through 11:59-pm period of the pm case requires action: hours must be incremented by 12. This results in the nested `if` shown in the following constructor:

```
public  Time(int  hours,  int  minutes,  String  amOrPm)  {
    if  (amOrPm.equals("am"))  {
        if  (hours==12)
            hours  =  0;
    }
    else                        // pm
        if  (hours!=12)
```

```
        hours  +=  12;
        totalMinutes = hours * 60 + minutes;
}
```

Although we have discouraged the use of nested `ifs`, we don't have a choice in this case, given the tools that we have available. The Java Interlude that follows will remedy this.

The Print Method   In contrast to the constructor, this method involves moving from the internal representation, total minutes, to a representation suitable for printing. We first calculate the hours:

```
int hours = this.totalMinutes / 60;
```

We now check to see whether the time is during the afternoon hours, setting a local `boolean` variable `isAfternoon`. If it is afternoon, we must subtract 12 from `hours` to obtain the correct 12-hour value. If it isn't, we still have to check for `hours` equal to 0 (which represents the first hour of the day) and adjust it accordingly:

```
if(hours >= 12){
    isAfternoon = true;
    hours -= 12;
} else  {
    isAfternoon = false;
    if (hours  ==  0)
        hours  =  12;   // In the 12 am hour
}
```

The result, together with the minutes (whose calculation is still the remainder of the total minutes when divided by 60), is then printed, together with a trailing `am` or `pm` depending on the value of the `isAfternoon` variable.

The completed method is as follows:

```
public void  print(PrintStream  ps){
    int  hours  =  totalMinutes / 60;
    boolean  isAfternoon;
    if(hours >= 12){
        isAfternoon = true;
        if (hours != 12) hours -= 12;
    } else  {
        isAfternoon = false;
        if  (hours  ==  0)
            hours  =  12;   // In the 12 am hour
    }
    ps.print(hours);
    ps.print(":");
```

```
        ps.print(totalMinutes%60);
        if(isAfternoon)
            ps.print(" pm");
        else
            ps.print(" am");
    }
```

The `addDuration` Methods Let us first address the single parameter version:

```
public Time  addDuration(int  minutes)  {
    ...
}
```

Adding the `minutes` argument to the receiver's `totalMinutes` instance variable produces the total number of minutes of the time at the end of the interval. We would like to return a newly created `Time` object as the result of this method; however, our present constructor requires hours, minutes, and am or pm as its arguments, not total minutes. We therefore introduce an overloaded constructor that accepts a single argument consisting of the total number of minutes of the time value we are creating; it does nothing more than assign its argument to the `totalMinutes` instance variable:

```
private Time(int  minutes)  {   Used by addDuration
    this.minutes  =  minutes;
}
```

Unlike our other methods, which arise from an analysis of the desired behavior of our class, the introduction of this constructor is solely the result of trying to implement the `addDuration` method. We can therefore think of it as a *helper* method and thus as `private`.

Once we have this constructor, the single-argument `addDuration` method becomes

```
public Time  addDuration(int  minutes)  {
    return  new  Time(totalMinutes+minutes);.
}
```

The two-argument `addDuration` is almost as straightforward:

```
public Time  addDuration(int  hours,  int  minutes)  {
        return  new  Time(hours * 60 + minutes +
                          this.totalMinutes);
}
```

The Final Class The code for the final class follows:

```
import  java.io.*;
class  Time  {
```

```java
    public Time(int  hours,  int  minutes,  String  amOrPm)
    {
        if  (amOrPm.equals("am"))  {
            if  (hours == 12)
                hours  =  0;
        } else  // pm
            if  (hours != 12)
                hours  +=  12;
        totalMinutes = hours * 60 + minutes;
    }
    private Time(int  minutes)  {   Used by addDuration
        this.totalMinutes  =  minutes;
    }
    public Time  addDuration(int  minutes)  {
        return  new  Time(minutes + this.totalMinutes);
    }
    public Time  addDuration(int  hours,  int  minutes)  {
        return  new  Time(hours * 60 + minutes +
                        this.totalMinutes);
    }
    public boolean  isBefore(Time  t){
        return  totalMinutes  <  t.totalMinutes;
    }
    public boolean  isAfter(Time  t){
        return  totalMinutes  >  t.totalMinutes;
    }
    public void  print(PrintStream  ps){
        int  hours  =  totalMinutes / 60;
        boolean  isAfternoon;
        if(hours >= 12){
            isAfternoon=true;
            hours -= 12;
        }
        else  {
            isAfternoon = false;
            if  (hours  ==  0)
                hours  =  12;
        }
        ps.print(hours);
        ps.print(":");
        ps.print(totalMinutes%60);
        if(isAfternoon)
            ps.print(" pm");
        else
            ps.print(" am");
    }
    private int  totalMinutes;
}
```

6.6.8 Using the Class

We can produce a `main` method from our sample code in the defining the interface section:

```
class  TimeUser  {
    public  static  void  main(String  []  args)  {
        Time    t1 = new   Time(10,15,   "am");
        Time    t2 = new   Time(3,10,   "pm");
        Time    t3 = t2.addDuration(30);   // Adds  30  minutes
        t3.print(System.out);   // Prints 3:40 pm
        System.out.println();
        Time    t4 = t2.addDuration(3,30);
                                    // Adds 3 hours and 30 minutes
        t4.print(System.out);          // Prints 6:40 pm
        System.out.println();
        Time    earlier;
            Timelater;
        if  (t3.isBefore(t4))    { Look: a predicate method!
            earlier = t3;
            later = t4;
        }
        else  {
            earlier = t4;
            later = t3;
        }
        earlier.print(System.out);
        System.out.print(" is earlier than");
        later.print(System.out);
        System.out.println();
    }
}
```

6.6.9 Discussion: Choice of Representation

Up until this example, there was a close correspondence between the instance variables (i.e., internal states) of a class and the arguments to the constructor for the class. Because those arguments were to be supplied by the user, this in turn corresponded with the user's perspective on the object. The `Time` class is our first experience with a class for which the internal and external representations were quite different:

- Internal: minutes only
- External: hours, minutes, and am or pm

This difference was created to simplify the implementation of the class's behavior (i.e., its methods).

The translation from the external representation to the internal one is performed by the constructor. The translation in the other direction, internal to external, is accomplished by our `print` method. Although it is true that we may be able to produce an internal representation that simplifies many of the methods, moving between the outside world and the internal representation often involves some effort. In our case, we had to test for various cases. This translation effort must be weighed against the benefit of the simplification produced when deciding upon a representation.

Regardless of our choice of representation, it is important to remember that *the user sees no difference in the class.* From the user's perspective, the class simply provides a specified behavior, which is accessed through its interface. How that behavior is implemented is of no concern to the user.

EXERCISES

1. Implement the `Time` class using three instance variables, one for hours, a second for minutes, and the third to indicate am or pm. Does the user of the class see any difference?

2. Modify the `Time` class so that seconds are also maintained.

3. Implement a date class whose constructor accepts an eight-character `String` in the form: mm/dd/yy. The constructor checks to make sure the date is correct (i.e., the month is between 1 and 12, the month/day pair is possible—April 31, for example—is incorrect—and so on). (Hint: use substrings and `parseInt`.) Do some research to see if you can find out the *real* rules for when a year is a leap year. If the date is correct, break it up into its parts. Have the class also have a `boolean` instance variable that is set to `true` by the constructor if the date is valid and to `false` otherwise. You should have a method that returns whether the object contains a valid date (by examining that instance variable). Allow the user of the class to specific whether the date is to be printed in American (mm/dd/yy) or European (dd/mm/yy) format. Finally, provide a print method.

4. Create an application class that provides the scenario presented at the beginning of the problem. To accomplish this, you will need to break up the time input by the user into hours and minutes. (Hint: use the `String` method `indexOf` to find the `:`. We discuss this and other `String` methods in the GUI Supplement at the end of the chapter.) Assume correct user input.

5. Make the following useful additions to the `Time` class:

    *   Allow the user to retrieve the hours or minutes values of the object.
    *   Allow to user to determine whether the object represents an afternoon or morning time value.

boolean, **Compound Conditionals, and Logical Operators**

THE `boolean` PRIMITIVE DATA TYPE

The behavior modeling true and false is provided through the `boolean` primitive data type. It possesses two literal values: `true` and `false` (remember, a literal is a constant value of a data type whose name is a literal representation of its value, for example, `3` or `false`). These two values have their expected behavior:

```
if (true)    statement1 is executed.
        statement1
else
        statement2
```

and

```
if (false)    statement2 is executed.
        statement1
else
        statement2
```

We can also declare `boolean` variables:

```
boolean isFreezing;
```

set them:

```
if (temp < 32)
        isFreezing = true;
else
        isFreezing = false;
```

and, finally, use them:

```
if (isFreezing)
        System.out.println("Brrrrrr!");
```

As you can see, names for `boolean` variables are chosen to reflect their use as a condition: `isFreezing`, `hasVacation`, `containsCoupon`, etc.

`boolean` variables can also be used as return types:

```
public boolean previouslyWorkedOvertime(Time t)
        if (previousOvertimeHours  >  40)
            return true;
        else
            return false;
}
```

`boolean` EXPRESSIONS

The condition `temp  <  32` is an expression that contains the relational operator, `<`, and its two operands, `temp` and `32`. The result of the operation is a `boolean` value (i.e., `true` or `false`), and therefore we say that this is a **boolean expression**. Such expressions are also called *logical expressions.*

Since `temp < 32` results in a `boolean` that can be assigned to `isFreezing`, we can dispense with the `if` statement entirely and simply write

```
isFreezing = temp < 32;
```

Similarly, we could have written

```
public boolean previouslyWorkedOvertime(Time t)
    return previousOvertimeHours  >  40;
}
```

Assigning the result of a boolean-valued expression to a `boolean` variable is a standard idiom in Java that is used often. Loosely speaking, an idiom of a programming language is a technique or approach that displays familiarity with the language, just as an idiom of a spoken language such as English shows familiarity with *that* language. A job interviewer, for example, might gauge job candidates' fluency in a language by seeing which idioms they know.

We can now provide a precise definition for what constitutes a valid condition: Any expression of type `boolean` is valid as the condition of an `if` statement.

LOGICAL OPERATORS AND COMPOUND CONDITIONS

Let us return to the analysis that led up to our `Time` constructor. (See Figure 6.1.)

If we only consider the conversion of the hours parameter that must occur, we see that there are actually only three, not four, distinct cases:

- The first hour of the day: am *and* hours is 12.
- The hours from 1:00 pm to 11:59 pm: pm *and* hours is not 12.
- The other hours (from 1:00 am to 12:59 pm).

Java provides an operator, `&&`, that represents *and*. Using this operator, which we call the *logical and* operator, we can express the condition for the first case as a single **compound condition**:

```
amOrPm.equals("am")  &&  hours == 12
```

The logical and operator accepts two `boolean` values and produces a `boolean` result. The `&&` operator evaluates to `true` only if *both* operands are true. Writing the condition for the second case using the logical and operator, we have

```
amOrPm.equals("pm")  &&  hours != 12
```

Now we can rewrite the `Time` constructor using a cascaded `if` rather than a nested one:

```
public Time(int  hours,  int  minutes,  String  amOrPm)  {
    if  (amOrPm.equals("am")  &&  hours == 12)
          hours  =  0;
    else  if  (amOrPm.equals("pm")  &&  hours != 12)
          hours  += 12;
}
```

The third case requires no action and therefore no final `else` appears in the cascaded `if`.

The `&&` operator is one of several operators known as logical operators. These operators accept `boolean` expressions and combine them to form larger `boolean` expressions. There is also a *logical or* operator, `||`, that also accepts two `boolean` operands:

```
operand1  ||  operand2
```

The *logical or* evaluates to `true` if *either or both* of its two operands are true, and evaluates to `false` otherwise. The following predicate accepts a day and returns true if it's a weekend day and `false` otherwise:

```
public boolean  isWeekend(String  day)  {
    if  (day.equals("Sunday")  ||  day.equals("Saturday"))
        return  true;
    else
        return  false;
}
```

Finally there is the *logical not* (or *negation*), !, which accepts a single logical operand:

> ! *operand*

The ! operator evaluates to `false` if its operand is true and vice versa. For example, the following predicate accepts a day and returns `true` if it is a weekday and `false` otherwise:

```
public boolean isWeekday(String day) {
    return !isWeekend(day);
}
```

LARGER LOGICAL EXPRESSIONS; PRECEDENCE

Just as with arithmetic expressions, logical expressions can be further combined. Let us consider an implementation of the `Time` class, which uses the "obvious" representation of both `hours` (since midnight) and `minutes` instance variables:

```
class Time {
        ...
        // Instance variables
        private int hours, minutes;
}
```

In this representation, 3:10 am is represented as `hours == 3, minutes == 15`, while 4:45 pm is `hours == 16, minutes == 45`. We will not present the entire implementation but will rather focus on the `isBefore` comparison method.

To compare two `Times` in this representation, we first compare the `hours` instance variables. Whichever is less is the earlier time. If the `hours` are equal, we compare the `minutes`. Again whichever is less is the earlier time. If both `hours` and `minutes` prove equal, the times are equal. Placing this in the context of the `isBefore` method gives us

```
public boolean isBefore(Time t) {
        if (this.hours < t.hours)
            return true;
        else if (this.hours == t.hours &&
                this.minutes < t.minutes)
            return true;
        else
            return false;
    }
```

Only if neither condition evaluates to `true` do we return a `false`.

The above two `if` statements may be merged into one by combining the conditions into a larger logical expression:

```
if (this.hours < t.hours ||
        (this.hours = t.hours && this.minutes < t.minutes))
    return true;
```

There are several points about this to keep in mind:

- The parenthesis around the `&&` expression is not necessary. The precedence of the logical operations are `!`, `&&`, `||` (highest first). Thus even without the parentheses, the `&&` would be performed first. However, to keep things clean, we always use parentheses with large logical expressions. The precedence of these operators is not nearly as familiar as those of the arithmetic operators, so we like to spell things out completely.
- The indentation is our personal style. There are many other; the important thing is to be consistent. Find a style and stick with it.

LOGICAL OPERATORS AND THE `if` STATEMENT TYPES

Note that the logical and operator is a substitute for a nested `if`; that is, the following are equivalent:

```
if (condition1)
    if (condition2)
        statement
```

and

```
if (condition1 && condition2)
    statement
```

In general, the compound condition is easier to read than the corresponding nested `if`.

There is a similar relationship between the logical or

```
if (condition1 || condition2)
    statement
```

and the cascaded `if/else`:

```
if (condition1)
    statement
else if (condition2)
    statement          Same statement as 2 lines back
```

Note the need to repeat the statement for the corresponding cascaded `if/else`. Also, the `else` must be present; otherwise *statement* would be executed twice (once in each `if`) if both conditions were true. Unlike the logical and nested `if`, the logical or cascaded `if`/`else` are not properly viewed as substitutes for each other.

REVISITING THE `equals` METHOD OF THE `Name` CLASS

As a last example of compound conditionals, let us rewrite the `equals` method of the `Name` class. Recall that if *any* of the three instance variables do not match, the `Name` objects are not equal. We can now write this as

```
public boolean  equals(Name  n)  {
    if  (!this.first.equals(n.first)  ||
         !this.last.equals(n.last)  ||
         !this.title.equals(n.title))
       return  false;
    else
       return  true;
}
```

Alternatively, we could think of the `Name` objects as being equal only if *all* the instance variables matched. We could thus equivalently write

```
public boolean  equals(Name  n)  {
    return  this.first.equals(n.first) &&
            this.last.equals(n.last) &&
            this.title.equals(n.title);
}
```

EXERCISES

1. Redo the `Time` class developed in Section 6.6 using compound conditionals.

2. Redo Exercise 6.6.1 (a `Time` class implemented with hours, minutes, and seconds instance variables) using compound conditionals.

3. The `compareTo` method of class `String` accepts a `String` object as its parameter. The method returns:

   • a negative value if the receiver `String` is less than the parameter `String`.
   • 0 if they're equal.
   • a positive value if the receiver `String` is greater than the parameter `String`.

   Write a `compareTo` method for the `Name` class. To do this you must first decide upon what it means for one `Name` object to be less than another. •

SUMMARY

Conditional statements perform one of several alternative actions as a result of some condition in a program. They allow the programmer to control the flow of execution. The `if` statement provides for a single action to be executed when a condition proves true, the `if/else` gives two alternatives, one for true, the other for false, while the `switch` statement allows a multiway test on the value of a single expression. More complex conditionals may be formed by cascading and/or nesting `if/else` statements.

Having a conditional available allows us to code input methods for objects that operate in a similar fashion to the `readLine` method for `String` objects—returning `null` upon end of input.

Conditions are expressions of the `boolean` primitive data type, which models true/false values. In addition, `boolean` expressions are created from `boolean` variables and the literal values `true` and `false`. `boolean` expressions may also be created using the relational operators (<, >, ==, !=, <=, >=). They may also be combined into larger `boolean` expressions using the logical operators &&, ||, and !.

Several examples employing conditionals and `boolean` expressions were developed in this chapter using the design procedure presented in Chapter 5.

STUDY AID: TERMINOLOGY REVIEW

boolean   A primitive data type modeling true and false values.

boolean expression   An expression evaluating to a boolean value.

cascaded `if/else`   A sequence of `if/else` statements in which the else portion of one `if` statement consists of another `if` statement.

compound condition   A condition (boolean expression) containing one or more logical operators.

compound statement   One or more statements surrounded by braces and thereby treated as a single statement.

conditional   A statement that allows selective execution of code depending upon some true or false condition.

dangling `else`   A problem occurring in a nested `if`, in which the single `else` is associated with the wrong `if`.

false   The literal of type `boolean` representing a false value.

has-a   A relationship between an object and some value such that the value is part of the object's state. This is usually expressed in Java by the object possessing an instance variable corresponding to the value.

if statement   The `if` statement conditionally executes a statement based upon the value of a `boolean` condition. The true-part is executed if the condition is `true`, the else-part, if present, is executed if the condition is `false`.

logical operator   An operator that combines boolean expressions into larger boolean expressions.

nested `if/else`   An `if/else` or `if` statement appearing as the true portion of another `if` or `if/else` statement.

predicate   A method whose return value is `boolean`.

relational operator   An operator that compares two values, producing a boolean expression as the result.

switch statement   A multiway conditional. The switch allows selective execution of multiple cases based upon the value of an expression.

true   The literal of type `boolean` representing a true value.

QUESTIONS FOR REVIEW

1. What are the two forms of the `if` statement?

2. What is the purpose of type `boolean`? What are its two constants?

3. What are the relational operators?

4. What is a compound condition?

5. What are the logical operators?

6. What is a cascaded `if/else`? A nested `if`?

7. What is the `dangling-else` problem?

FURTHER EXERCISES

1. Write a method, `max`, that accepts two integers and returns the larger of the two. Why should this method be `static`? If you were on the Java design team, where might you place such a method?

2. Add a method, `calcTax`, to the `Employee` class. The method should accept an amount earned and return the tax to be deducted according to the following table:

Less than 100	5%
Between 100 and 500	10%
Greater than 500	15%

This method should be `static`. Why?

3. Can you spot a potential problem with way the tax table in Exercise 2 is specified?

4. Write a method `max` that accepts three integers and returns the largest. Can you write this without using nested `if`s?

5. Modify the `Student` class (from Exercise 2 on page 206) to check that the two exam weights sum to 1, and, if not, print out an error message.

GUI *supplement 1*

Responding to Controls: Event-Handling

This chapter provided us with a wealth of material to work with: integers, booleans, and conditionals. We can now begin to actually do something with some of the controls introduced in the last chapter's supplement. Let us take the payroll example and place it into an applet so that we can perform our payroll calculation from the comfort of a browser.

First, let us design our applet's interface. We want to be able to enter a name and rate (in order to create an `Employee` instance) and an hours-worked value (to serve as an argument to `calcPay`). We will also need a place to display the result and some way to tell the applet that we have entered our data and wish the calculation to proceed.

Let us see what sort of controls we need:

- Three data entry fields for the name, hours, and rate. For these we can use `TextField` controls, which allow the entry of a single line of text. Unfortunately, there is no way to specify that the entry is to be exclusively numeric (which is what we need for the rate and hours fields); we'll have to take care of that ourselves.

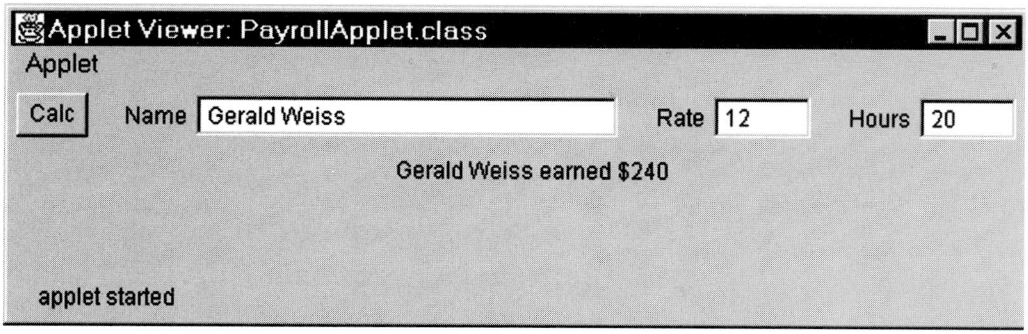

FIGURE 6.2   **Our payroll program as an applet.**

- Several labels, one to identify each of the data entry fields (otherwise we won't know what their function is) and one to hold the result. We can use the `Label` control for this. A `Label` is nothing more than a piece of text (`String`) and is read-only (i.e., it is not an entry field).
- One button. Clicking this button will indicate that the data has been entered and the calculation of the payroll value is to proceed.

Figure 6.2 shows how we envision our applet.

We can begin to create our applet class, which we will call `PayrollApplet`. Recall the basic structure of an applet-based class:

```
import java.awt.*;
import java.applet.*;
public class PayrollApplet extends Applet {
    public void init() {
        ...
    }
    ...
}
```

In `init` we create the controls and place them on the applet:

```
import java.awt.*;
import java.applet.*;
public class PayrollApplet extends Applet {
    public void init() {
        // We have a good reason not to have declarations yet.
        calcButton = new Button("Calc");
        add(calcButton);
        add(new Label("Name"));
        nameField = new TextField(30);
        add(nameField);
        add(new Label("Rate"));
        rateField = new TextField(5);
```

```
        add(rateField);
        add(new Label("Hours"));
        hoursField = new TextField(5);
        add(hoursField);
        resultLabel = new Label("Result goes here");
        add(resultLabel);
    }
    Other methods
    // Instance Variables
    private Button calcButton;
    private TextField nameField;
    private TextField rateField;
    private TextField hoursField;
    private Label resultLabel;
}
```

The constructor for `TextField` accepts the width of the field in characters (i.e., the maximum number of characters that may be typed into the field). Although we may encounter a name greater than 30 characters, or a rate greater than 5, we're not going to worry about it.

We are going to want to subsequently refer to the `name`, `rate`, and `hours` `TextField` controls, so we assign the references returned by the constructors to variables. The same holds true for the `resultLabel` control because we are going to place the result of our payroll calculation there. We will also need to refer to `calcButton` (although we haven't gotten to that yet). On the other hand, the other label fields (e.g., the `new Label("Name")`) are there only to provide descriptive titles for the entry fields—we won't be referring to them again. Therefore, we need not assign their reference to a variable; it's sufficient to create them and send the new reference directly to the applet's `add` method.

The constructor for the `Label` control accepts as its argument the text to be placed in the label. `Label` also has a constructor that accepts no arguments—it creates a label without any text. Although our result label initially has no value, and thus logically should have been created using the argument-less constructor, we decided to provide some sample text so you could see the label when the applet first begins.

We declare the controls as instance variables because more than one method will have to reference them.

We can compile this class, add the appropriate HTML (HyperText Markup Language) (left as an exercise; use 550 as your width and 100 as your height), and run the applet. The result is a very pretty but rather useless applet. You can even type values into the text fields, but because clicking on the button does nothing, we can't perform the calculation.

Handling Events In order to respond to the button, the applet must somehow be *notified* when it is clicked on and then take some action. In our example, when the calculate button is clicked on, we wish to create an `Employee` object, calculate its payroll, and display the result in the applet.

Clicking on a button on the interface is an example of an *event*. Think of an event as something the user does in the graphic interface to get the program's attention: clicking on a button, moving or clicking the mouse, closing a window.

When an event occurs, there are three objects of interest:

- The object causing the event, for example, the button (when it is clicked). This object is called the *event source.*
- An object representing the event. For example, the event associated with clicking a button is represented by an `ActionEvent` object—so called because clicking a button usually indicates the user's desire for some action.
- The object that should respond to the event, for example, our `PayrollApplet` object. This object is called the *listener.*

In our example, the only event of interest is clicking the calculate button. When that button is clicked, the three objects of interest are

- The object referenced by `calcButton`—the event source.
- An `ActionEvent` object to represent the click of the calculate button.
- Our `PayrollApplet` object, which should respond to the click by calculating and displaying the payroll. It, therefore, is the listener.

When an event occurs, the source creates the corresponding event object. It then notifies the listener that the event has occurred by sending it a message particular to that event, passing the event object as an argument. This can work only if

- The source knows which particular object is the listener.
- The listener object provides the needed method.

In our example, when the button is clicked, the `calcButton` object, the event source, creates an `ActionEvent` object. It then sends an `actionPerformed` message to the `PayrollApplet` listener, with the `ActionEvent` object as an argument. This can work only if

- The `calcButton` is aware that the `PayrollApplet` is a listener.
- The `PayrollApplet` object provides a method called `actionPerformed` that accepts an `ActionEvent` argument. (See Figure 6.3.)

In order for `calcButton` to know that `PayrollApplet` is the listener, we send it an `addActionListener` message, passing a reference to the

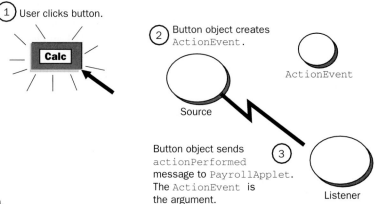

FIGURE 6.3   Event notification.

PayrollApplet object as an argument. We do this in the PayrollApplet init method after creating the calcButton object:

```
calcButton.addActionListener(this);
```

Remember: this refers to the object executing this code (the PayrollApplet object).

We must also implement an actionPerformed method in PayrollApplet:

```
public void actionPerformed(ActionEvent ae) {
    code to handle the event
}
```

When this method is invoked, we know that the button is clicked, so we create an Employee object using the values of the nameField and rateField controls. The value of a TextField may be queried via the getText method, which returns a String containing the field's contents:

```
String name = nameField.getText();
int rate = Integer.parseInt(rateField.getText());
Employee e = new Employee(name, rate);
```

If the value in rateField cannot be converted to int, an error will occur because the parseInt will fail.

Now that the Employee object has been created, we can obtain the value of the hoursField control and use it an argument to calcPay:

```
int hours = Integer.parseInt(hoursField.getText());
int pay = e.calcPay(hours);
```

Having calculated the employee's pay, we now wish to display that value in the resultLabel. This can be accomplished by invoking the setText method of the `Label` class. This method expects a `String` object as its argument, which we build from the employee's name, pay, and some descriptive text:

```
resultLabel.setText(e.getName()+" earned $"+pay);
```

The result is a complete `actionPerformed` method:

```
public  void  actionPerformed(ActionEvent  ae)  {
    String name = nameField.getText();
    int rate = Integer.parseInt(rateField.getText());
    Employee e = new Employee(name, rate);
    int hours = Integer.parseInt(hoursField.getText());
    int pay = e.calcPay(hours);
    resultLabel.setText(e.getName()+" earned $"+pay);
    doLayout();
}
```

This completes our definition of the `Payroll` applet. The final class is

```
import java.awt.*;
import java.applet.*;
import java.awt.event.*;

public class PayrollApplet extends Applet implements
                            ActionListener {
    public void init() {
        calcButton = new Button("Calc");
        add(calcButton);
        calcButton.addActionListener(this);

        add(new Label("Name"));
        nameField = new TextField(30);
        add(nameField);

        add(new Label("Rate"));

        rateField = new TextField(5);
        add(rateField);

        add(new Label("Hours"));
        hoursField = new TextField(5);
        add(hoursField);

        resultLabel = new Label("Result goes here");
        add(resultLabel);
    }

    public void actionPerformed(ActionEvent event) {
        String name = nameField.getText();
        int rate = Integer.parseInt(rateField.getText());
        Employee e = new Employee(name, rate);
```

```
        int hours = Integer.parseInt(hoursField.getText());
        int pay = e.calcPay(hours);
        String result =
          e.getName() + " earned $" +
                                  (Integer.toString(pay));
        resultLabel.setText(result);
        doLayout();
    }

    private Button calcButton;
    private TextField nameField;
    private TextField rateField;
    private TextField hoursField;
    private Label resultLabel;
}
```

Event-Driven Programming   When our applet is created, its `init` method is invoked. In `init`, the controls are created and placed onto the applet and any other initialization is performed. After executing all the code in `init`, we return to the browser. Our applet does not become active again until an event takes place. It is the user's clicking on the Calc button that generates this event.

More sophisticated applets have numerous interface components (our calculator has 19 buttons). These buttons may be clicked on in any order at any time. It is the `actionPerformed` method that responds to each event with the appropriate action. We say that the events *drive* the applet and call this style of programming *event-driven programming*.

GUI *supplement 2*

Bringing the Calculator to Life

In Chapter 4's GUI supplement, we developed a layout for a calculator applet, shown in Figure 6.4.

Now that we know how to handle events, let us complete the applet.

Handling Events from Multiple Sources   We would now like to process the button click events. Unlike the payroll applet, this applet has many buttons, not just one. Again, the applet object will act as the listener, but there must be a way for it to distinguish which button was clicked on when `action-Performed` is invoked.

FIGURE 6.4   Our calculator's layout.
Our calculator applet as developed in
Chapter 4.

The `ActionEvent` object that is passed to `actionPerformed` provides this information. The `ActionEvent` class provides a method called `getActionCommand` that returns an object that contains information specific to the source of the event. In the case of a clicked on button, `getActionCommand` returns a `String` object that corresponds to the label of the button.

We can use this to identify the individual buttons:

```
public void actionPerformed(ActionEvent ae) {
    String s = ae.getActionCommand();
    if (s.equals("+"))
        handle the plus operation
    ...
    else if (s.equals("1"))
        handle the one case
    ...
}
```

As we see, setting up the cases for each of the buttons is easy, although tedious; figuring out what to do once we know which button has been clicked on is an entirely different matter. We have to analyze what happens when each of the buttons is clicked.

The Processing Logic   The first thing we should realize is that the processing for each of the buttons `d0` through `d9` is basically the same—add the digit to the display; the only difference is what is actually displayed. Similarly, the `plus`, `minus`, `times`, and `div` buttons are processed in a similar manner—they perform the operation; again the only real difference is which operation is used.

We can thus group the buttons into several categories:

- Digit buttons
- Operator buttons
- The C (clear) button
- The . (decimal)
- The = (equals) button

We must also analyze what action should be taken for each of these categories.

When a digit is clicked, it should be added to the rear of the displayed value. This is true if the previous key clicked was also a digit or the decimal point. If the previous key clicked was the C button, the = button, or an operator button, the clicked digit is the first digit of a new operand, and the display should be cleared and set to this digit alone.

If the decimal button is clicked, a decimal point should be added to the display, but only if we have not already done so for this operand.

Clicking the clear button should reset the calculator to its original state when the applet began.

When an operator button is pressed on a calculator, the corresponding operation cannot be performed until the *next* operand is input. However, the operator does signify the *end* of the previous operand. Furthermore, assuming there was a previous operator, *that* operator may be applied to the two previous operands. For example, suppose the user clicks the following button sequence:

```
123 + 23 *
```

When the + is first entered, the addition cannot be performed yet—we don't have the second operand, namely, 23. When the * is entered, we know that the previous operand, 23, has been completed and the addition may be performed. At this point the multiplication cannot be performed because we don't know *its* second operand.

Once an operation has been performed, its result becomes the new display and also the first operand for the next operator. In addition, as we mentioned in the context of the digit buttons, pressing an operator key signals that the next digit entered is the beginning of a new operand.

Pressing the equals button has a similar effect. The previous operator can be evaluated and the result displayed. Again, subsequent digits form a new operand. The only difference between this button and one of the four operators is that the equals button does not perform another operation. Because the equals button is so similar to the operator buttons, we will handle it together with them.

The above discussion leads to the following methods:

- `handleDigit`—processes digits
- `handleOperator`—processes operators and equals

- `handleDecimal`—processes decimal point
- `handleClear`—processes clear button

Rather than have `actionPerformed` test for each individual case, we can be clever and group the cases into the above categories. We do this with the `indexOf` method of class `String`, which tests to see if one `String` object appears in another. We declare a constant `String`:

```
static final String digits = "0123456789";
```

Given the variable `s`, which contains a reference to the button text, the expression

```
digits.indexOf(s)
```

returns the location in `digits` of the first occurrence of `s`. If the `String` referenced by `s` does not occur in `digits`, `-1` (an invalid location for a `String`) is returned. This tells us whether `s` was created from the text of digit `Button`.

We can use a similar constant, `operators`:

```
static final String operators = "+-*/=";
```

and have the expression

```
operators.indexOf(s)
```

test whether the button clicked was an operator.

We will pass the `String` `s` to `handleDigit` and `handleOperator` to allow them to identify the actual button pressed. These methods, therefore, each have a `String` parameter. The `handleClear` and `handleDecimal` methods don't need any information—in each case there is only one button that would cause them to be invoked.

Here is the code for our `actionPerformed` method:

```
public void actionPerformed(ActionEvent e) {
    String s = (String)e.getActionCommand();

    if (digits.indexOf(s) != -1)
        handleDigit(s);
    else if (s.equals("."))
        handleDecimal();
    else if (operators.indexOf(s) != -1)
        handleOperator(s);
    else if (s.equals("C"))
        handleClear();
}
```

The Instance Variables and their Initialization   Before we write the other methods, let us determine the state that must be maintained by our calculator: That will provide us with our instance variables.

We must keep track of the last operator entered because we cannot apply it until its second operand is entered.

The entry of an operator signals the end of the previous operand; we must keep track of that so that the next digit entered becomes the first digit of the next operand and not the trailing digit of the previous one.

Pressing an operator key only makes sense if at least one operand has been entered, so we must keep track of that as well. After the operator has been clicked, we must wait for the next operand to be entered—however, we must hold onto the first operand.

Pressing the decimal key should be legal only if we have not already done so for this operand.

The above leads to the introduction of a `double` instance variable, three `boolean` instance variables, and one `String` instance variable:

```
double   opd1;                              // First operand
boolean  sawDecimal,  newOpd,  sawAnOpd;
String   lastOptr;                          // Last operator
```

These variables have the following initial values:

```
sawDecimal - false
newOpd - true
sawAnOpd - false
lastOptr - " "
```

The `opd1` variable need not be initialized—it will get its value when the user enters it.

In addition, these variables should be reset to these values when the clear button is clicked—the effect of that button is to completely clear out the calculator's operation. We therefore introduce a method, `clearCalc`, to perform this initialization:

```
private void clearCalc() {
    sawDecimal = false;
    newOpd = true;
    sawAnOpd = false;
    lastOptr = " ";
    result.setText(initialString);
}
```

This method also displays the initial value in the result label, using the constant

```
static final String initialString = "0.00000";
```

The Other Methods   We must now implement the methods that process our four button categories. Our previous analysis of the actions taken by each of the categories will help us here.

The `handleClear` method is nothing more than an invocation of `clearCalc`:

```
private void handleClear() {
    clearCalc();
}
```

We also add an invocation of `clearCalc` to the end of our `init` method to initialize the calculator the first time through.

The `handleDigit` method receives a `String` that corresponds to the text of the button pressed: "0", "1", ..., "9". If this is the beginning of a new operand (`newOpd` evaluates to `true`), we reset the display to contain the digit alone and set `newOpd` to `false`. Otherwise, we get the label text and concatenate the new digit onto the end. We must also set `sawAnOpd` to `true` to signal that an operand has been entered:

```
private void handleDigit(String s) {
    if (newOpd) {
        result.setText(s);
        newOpd = false;
    }
    else
        result.setText(result.getText()+s);
    sawAnOpd = true;
}
```

The method `handleDecimal` checks to see if a decimal point has already been entered. If one has not been entered, `handleDecimal` operates in a similar manner to `handleDigit`: If this is the beginning of a new operand, it resets the display to "0" (calculators always place a 0 in front of a leading decimal point), and `newOpd` is set to `false`. If this is not a new operand, the decimal point is concatenated to the end of the display. Once the point has been added, `sawDecimal` is set to `true` to prevent another decimal point from being added:

```
private void handleDecimal() {
    if (!sawDecimal) {
        if (newOpd) {
            result.setText("0.");
            newOpd = false;
        }
        else
            result.setText(result.getText()+".");
        sawDecimal = true;
    }
}
```

The `handleOperator` method receives the text of the clicked-on operator button. However, it is not *this* operation that is performed, but rather the previous one (if it exists). The operations must be performed on numbers. However, the operands are obtained from the display as `Strings`, through the `getText` method. To make things nice and clean, we introduce a helper method, `getDisplay`, that returns a `double` corresponding to the value displayed in the result label:

```
private double getDisplay() {
    return Double.valueOf(result.getText()).doubleValue();
}
```

Unlike `parseInt`, which converts a `String` into an `int`, there is no `parseDouble`. Instead we first convert the `String` using the `valueOf` method of the `Double` class, the wrapper class for `double`. This returns a reference to a `Double` object. From this we extract the `double` value using the `doubleValue` method.

We can now write `handleOperator`. If no operand has been seen yet, we ignore the operator click and return. Otherwise, we perform the appropriate operation depending upon the *last* operator, contained in `lastOptr`. In each case, the result becomes the new operand to remember for the next operation. For example, given

```
1 + 2 * 5
```

when we evaluate the +, the result, 3, becomes the first operand to the *.

If the last operator was an = or the current operator is the first to be entered (and thus `lastOptr` equals " "), the operand is simply the value already in the display.

Once the new value has been obtained, it is set as the new result value. The operator just entered becomes the last operator, and we signal that a new operand is to be entered and no decimal points have been entered:

```
private void handleOperator(String s) {
    if (!sawAnOpd)
        return;
    if (lastOptr.equals("+"))
        opd1 += getDisplay();
    else if (lastOptr.equals("-"))
        opd1 -= getDisplay();
    else if (lastOptr.equals("*"))
        opd1 *= getDisplay();
    else if (lastOptr.equals("/"))
        opd1 /= getDisplay();
    else
        opd1 = getDisplay();
    result.setText(opd1+"");        concatenation with "" converts opd1
    lastOptr = s;                    to a String
    sawDecimal = false;
    newOpd = true;
}
```

The Complete Applet   Here is the completed applet, including our layout code from Chapter 4. Notice that we did not pay any attention to the layout during the course of developing the event-handling logic. In this case, where the buttons were made no difference to us.

```java
import java.awt.*;
import java.awt.event.*;
import java.applet.Applet;

public class Calculator extends Applet implements
                        ActionListener {
    public void init() {
        backgroundColor = new Color(200,255,255);
        this.setLayout(new FlowLayout(FlowLayout.
                    CENTER,4,1));

        result = new Label(initialString, Label.RIGHT);
        result.setBackground(new Color(255,255,255));
        add(result);
        makeButtons();

        row1 = makePanel(new FlowLayout(FlowLayout.LEFT,
                    4,2),backgroundColor);
        row1.add(c);
        row1.add(eq);
        row1.add(div);
        row1.add(times);

        row2 = makePanel(new FlowLayout(FlowLayout.LEFT,
                    4,2),backgroundColor);
        row2.add(d7);
        row2.add(d8);
        row2.add(d9);
        row2.add(minus);
        row3 = makePanel(new FlowLayout(FlowLayout.LEFT,
                    4,2),backgroundColor);

        row3.add(d4);
        row3.add(d5);
        row3.add(d6);
        row3.add(plus);

        add(row1);
        add(row2);
        add(row3);
        p12 = makePanel(new BorderLayout(2,2),
                    backgroundColor);
        p12.add("West",d1);
        p12.add("East",d2);
```

```
                    p120 = makePanel(new BorderLayout(2,2),
                                  backgroundColor);
                    p120.add("North",p12);
                    p120.add("South",d0);

                    p3p = makePanel(new BorderLayout(2,2),
                                  backgroundColor);
                    p3p.add("North",d3);
                    p3p.add("South",dp);

                    p3peq = makePanel(new BorderLayout(2,2),
                                   backgroundColor);
                    p3peq.add("West",p3p);
                    p3peq.add("East",eq2);

                    add(p120);
                    add(p3peq);

                    setBackground(backgroundColor);

                    c.addActionListener(this);
                    eq.addActionListener(this);
                    eq2.addActionListener(this);
                    div.addActionListener(this);
                    times.addActionListener(this);
                    minus.addActionListener(this);
                    plus.addActionListener(this);
                    d0.addActionListener(this);
                    d1.addActionListener(this);
                    d2.addActionListener(this);
                    d3.addActionListener(this);
                    d4.addActionListener(this);
                    d5.addActionListener(this);
                    d6.addActionListener(this);
                    d7.addActionListener(this);
                    d8.addActionListener(this);
                    d9.addActionListener(this);

                    clearCalc();

               }

          public void start() {
               appletWidth =  8 * 4 + row1.getSize().width;
               appletHeight =  8 * (2 + d1.getSize().height);
          }

          public void paint(Graphics g) {
               setSize(appletWidth,appletHeight);
               validate();
          }
```

```java
public void actionPerformed(ActionEvent e) {
    String s = (String)e.getActionCommand();

    if (digits.indexOf(s) != -1)
        handleDigit(s);
    else if (s.equals("."))
        handleDecimal();
    else if (operators.indexOf(s) != -1)
        handleOperator(s);
    else if (s.equals("C"))
        handleClear();
}

private void handleDigit(String s) {
    if (newOpd) {
        result.setText(s);
        newOpd = false;
    }
    else
        result.setText(result.getText()+s);
    sawAnOpd = true;
}

private void handleClear() {
    clearCalc();
}

private void clearCalc() {
    sawDecimal = false;
    newOpd = true;
    sawAnOpd = false;
    lastOptr = "";
    result.setText(initialString);
}

private void handleOperator(String s) {
    if (!sawAnOpd)
        return;

    if (lastOptr.equals("+"))
        opd1 += getDisplay();
    else if (lastOptr.equals("-"))
        opd1 -= getDisplay();
    else if (lastOptr.equals("*"))
        opd1 *= getDisplay();
    else if (lastOptr.equals("/"))
        opd1 /= getDisplay();
    else
        opd1 = getDisplay();
```

```
            result.setText(opd1 + "");
```
concatenation of opd1 with "" converts opd1 to String
```
            lastOptr = s;
            sawDecimal = false;
            newOpd = true;
    }

    private void handleDecimal() {
        if (!sawDecimal) {
            if (newOpd) {
                result.setText("0.");
                newOpd = false;
            }
            else
                result.setText(result.getText() + ".");
            sawDecimal = true;
        }
    }

    private double getDisplay() {
        return Double.valueOf(result.getText()).
                            doubleValue();
    }

    private Button makeButton(String label, Color color,
                            Font font) {
        Button b = new Button(label);
        b.setBackground(color);
        b.setFont(font);
        return b;
    }

    private Panel makePanel(LayoutManager lm, Color c) {
        Panel p = new Panel();
        p.setLayout(lm);
        p.setBackground(c);
        return p;
    }

    private void makeButtons() {
        Font    f = new Font("Courier", Font.BOLD, 10);
        Color   lightRed = new Color(255,100,100);
        Color   lightBlue = new Color(100,100,255);
        Color   yellow = new Color(255,255,0);

        c = makeButton("C",lightRed,f);
        eq = makeButton("=",lightBlue,f);
        div = makeButton("/",lightBlue,f);
        times = makeButton("*",lightBlue,f);
        d7 = makeButton("7",yellow,f);
        d8 = makeButton("8",yellow,f);
```

```
        d9 = makeButton("9",yellow,f);
        minus = makeButton("-",lightBlue,f);
        d4 = makeButton("4",yellow,f);
        d5 = makeButton("5",yellow,f);
        d6 = makeButton("6",yellow,f);
        plus = makeButton("+",lightBlue,f);
        d1 = makeButton("1",yellow,f);
        d2 = makeButton("2",yellow,f);
        d3 = makeButton("3",yellow,f);
        d0 = makeButton("0",yellow,f);
        dp = makeButton(".",yellow,f);
        eq2 = makeButton("=",lightBlue,f);
    }

    static final String initialString = "0.00000";
    static final String digits = "0123456789";
    static final String operators = "+-*/=";
    private String lastOptr;
    private String Filler = "        ";
    private boolean sawDecimal, newOpd, sawAnOpd;
    private double opd1;

    private Panel  row1, row2, row3, p12, p120, p3p, p3peq;
    private int    appletWidth, appletHeight;

    private Button c, eq, div, times,
                   d7, d8, d9, minus,
                   d4, d5, d6, plus,
                   d1, d2, d3,
                   d0,     dp, eq2;

    private Color  backgroundColor;
    private Label  result;
}
```

Summary

In Chapter 4 we developed the display layout for a calculator. Now that we
have discussed numeric types of the conditional, we are able to implement the
actual processing logic for the calculator. What is interesting to note, however,
is that the "layout-only" applet as presented in Chapter 4 was a full applet in
that it compiled cleanly and could even be executed—it just couldn't respond
to buttons, perform the operations, or do anything remotely useful. Our chapter, on the other hand, focused solely on those very tasks. What we thus see is
a clear and clean separation of the part of the applet that is responsible for the
display and input from the portion that does the actual processing required by
the application. You will see this separation in several of the other applets we
develop in this text.

chapter 7

Verifying Object Behavior

7.1 ▮ Introduction

All applied sciences possess the concept of a *testing phase:* determining whether a hypothesis, product, or design is correct and behaves in the expected manner. Pharmaceutical companies test new drugs first on laboratory animals, and then possibly on a select segment of the population prior to a general marketing of the product. Aircraft manufacturers test new designs of planes endlessly, first on computer, then in physical mock-ups, and finally in full prototypes.

Testing is a crucial part of the software cycle. It is too often overlooked by students who have unique time and effort constraints. Yet it is precisely those students who, as the programmers of the future, will bear the responsibility for creating code that is safe to operate. Code with errors can have disastrous consequences. A computerized stock trading program that malfunctions could cause the loss of millions of dollars if trade is interrupted for even the shortest period of time. The computer that monitors the heart rate of an intensive care patient and triggers an alarm in the event of heart failure cannot afford to malfunction.

It is the goal of this chapter to impress upon you the importance of testing. From the outset, therefore, let us state: *testing is not an afterthought or something that you do* after *you've finished developing the program*. Rather, it is an integral part of the program development process, for which time and effort must be allocated. Any thought to the contrary will guarantee the failure of your programming effort.

Beginners sometimes think that once their code has compiled with no errors, they are almost finished. Nothing could be further from the truth. If you were able to develop a class using the steps outlined in the previous chapters for developing code, it should be a fairly straightforward matter of removing any compilation errors. The class is, however, not ready to be released. It must first be tested to ensure that it behaves in the expected manner. In an industrial setting, a set of tests known as a **test suite** is usually created, and we speak of *running the code against the test suite.*

Testing is an attempt to minimize the errors in our programs. However, as a famous computer scientist, Edsgar Djikstra, once said, "testing merely confirms the presence of errors, never their absence." That is, if during testing an error is discovered, we determine its cause and fix it. However, if no errors arise during the testing phase, there is no guarantee that the code has no errors, merely that our tests have not exposed any.

Errors come in all varieties. Sometimes they are trivial to fix, sometimes they take days to discover and then correct, and sometimes they force us to go back to the drawing board and redo some of our design. We really hate having to do that—that's one reason for having a careful approach to class design.

Testing is more than simply running a few arbitrarily chosen cases. It involves careful thought and a good knowledge of both the application and the software solution. With improperly designed testing, the most obvious errors can and will remain in your programs. Consider the following class, which contains an (admittedly stupid) erroneous method:

```java
class DoubleTrouble {
    public DoubleTrouble(int value) {
        this.value = value;
    }
    // doubleIt returns the value instance variable multiplied by 2.
    public int doubleIt() {
        this.value += 2;        Ooops! Adding 2, not doubling
        return this.value;
    }
    private int value;
}
```

together with a fragment of code that is supposed to test it:

```java
DoubleTrouble t = new DoubleTrouble(2);
System.out.println(t.doubleIt());   Prints 4, looks OK.
```

Executing this test fragment produces the correct result, even though the method is completely wrong. The moral of this story is that it is rather easy for a small set of test cases to falsely validate the code.

7.2 Categories of Errors

Although errors arise in a number of ways, they fall into one of three basic categories. Errors that occur during the translation of the source (e.g., during compilation) are, appropriately enough, known as *compilation errors*. Errors that cause a program to abruptly terminate during execution without completing its task are called *run-time* errors. In a Java program this is usually accompanied by an announcement of an "Exception" followed by a small torrent of error messages. Finally there are errors that don't cause any explicit error but rather cause the program to produce an incorrect result. This kind of an error is known as a *logic error*. Run-time and logic errors are commonly referred to as *bugs*.

7.2.1 Compilation-time Errors—Syntax and Semantics

As the name implies, compilation errors occur at compile or program translation time. Such errors range from the trivial omission of a semicolon to the use of an uninitialized variable.

Let us examine several examples of compilation errors, beginning with the missing semicolon:

```
x = 5      No semicolon
```

Roughly speaking, this mistake corresponds to leaving out a period or comma in a sentence. We thus further categorize this as a *syntax error,* the word *syntax* meaning sentence structure or grammar. In other words, leaving out a semicolon is a grammatical error as far as the Java compiler is concerned—the statement has not been formed correctly. We may understand the intent of the statement (just as we understand the grammatically incorrect sentence, The boy have a toy.), but the compiler still generates the error message.

Other examples of syntax errors include

- Omitting a comma between arguments in an argument list—f(a b)
- Badly parenthesized expressions—(3 + 5, or 3 + 5)
- Other badly formed expressions—3 + % 5

Syntax errors are usually easy to fix—they are often caused by typing mistakes. Upon occasion, however, the compiler does get tripped up by a syntax error and has a difficult time getting back on track. This in turn can cause it to generate (or *cascade*) numerous additional spurious error messages (i.e., messages that are caused by the compiler's "confusion" rather than any real errors in the subsequent source). If during compilation you see an error message that is followed by a slew of additional messages (beginning with the same or next statement as the first error), none of which seem to make sense, try fixing the first error—many of the others will often disappear as well.

Another kind of error, using an uninitialized variable, does not arise as a result of a badly formed statement:

```
int i;
i++;    i was never assigned an initial value.
```

Although the structure of each of the statements is correct, there is a mistake in the meaning, or *semantics,* of the code. The above fragment makes no sense: The value of i cannot be meaningfully incremented if it has no meaningful value in the first place.

Other examples of semantic errors are

- Forgetting to declare a variable—it makes no sense to assign to or from a variable that has not been declared to exist.
- Assigning a String constant to an int variable—the assignment makes no sense.

The majority of semantic errors (including the last error above) fall into a category known as *type errors.* These are errors resulting from an attempt to use a variable in a manner that is incompatible with its type. For example, String values may not be assigned to int variables. Other examples of type errors include

- Using a class object in an arithmetic expression—it makes no sense to apply an arithmetic operator to an instance of a class.
- Invoking a message upon an object whose class does not possess such a method—it makes no sense to ask the object to do something for which it was not defined.
- Sending a message to a primitive data type—message sending is incompatible with such types.
- Assigning a double to an int—the resulting possible loss of precision is too dangerous for the compiler to allow without any complaint.

Unlike syntax errors, the intended meaning behind a semantic error is not always clear. For example, given the error

```
int i = "Hello";
```

what was the intent of the programmer? Because of this, semantic errors are usually somewhat more difficult to correct than syntax errors. They reflect some mistake in your understanding of the meaning of a particular construct or variable or of the relationships between variables. That the compiler detects such errors and prevents us from running our code until they have been eliminated is extremely important. A semantically incorrect construct by definition is one that makes no sense, and executing such a construct would surely result in incorrect results.

7.2.2 Run-time Errors

The second general category of errors arises during the execution of the Java code. These are errors that could not be detected during translation time. An example of such an error is

```
int w, x;
x = Integer.parseInt(...);
w = 10 / x;
```

Suppose the value 0 is read into x. The third statement then results in a division by 0, which is illegal (mathematically as well as in Java) and results in the program terminating abruptly with an error message from the Java interpreter such as

```
java.lang.ArithmeticException:  divide  by  zero
      at Test.main(TrivialApplication.java:10)
```

Run-time errors are usually the most difficult to correct. Unlike compile-time errors, it is not always clear what the true source of the error is. As an extremely simple example, suppose the above code were instead

```
int w, x, y, z;
x = Integer.parseInt(...);
y = Integer.parseInt(...);
z = Integer.parseInt(...);
...
```
Code that manipulates x, y, and z using if statements
```
...
w = 10 / ((x - y) * z);
```

A division by zero error here can arise from either x being equal to y or z being zero. Before you can fix the error you first have to determine how it arose. Even once the nature of the error is known, it is not always clear how to remedy the situation. For example, in the division by zero example, what are we supposed to do when a zero value for z occurs?

The process of fixing such errors or **bugs** is called debugging, and often is the most time-consuming aspect of the software development process. But even before we can fix such errors, we must be made aware of their existence. This can only be done properly through a thorough testing of the code.

7.2.3 Logic Errors

Even worse than run-time errors are those errors that do not reveal themselves in any obvious fashion. They often arise as a result of not correctly implementing the requirements of the software. In our context, this would mean not following the statement of the problem correctly. The example at the beginning of our chapter was just such a situation. If the statement of the problem calls for a method that doubles the instance variable and instead we produce a method that adds 2 to the variable, the only way we will detect such a mistake is through the execution of test cases and an examination of the results. No run-time error will occur to notify us that something is wrong.

These last two categories, run-time and logic errors, are the subject of the rest of this chapter. Unlike compile-time errors, which are revealed and eliminated in the safety and comfort of our development environment, run-time and logic errors can occur at any in time and seem to mostly reveal themselves once the code has been released to the general user population. Although one can never be sure that no errors exist, we must still test our code to the utmost to minimize the existence of such errors.

1. List some more syntax and semantic errors.

2. Would you rather have an error discovered at compile time or run-time? Explain your answer.   •

7.3   Test Drivers

An application like `Payroll` in Chapter 6 can and should be tested by repeatedly giving it various combinations of input and comparing the actual results with the expected results. What about utility classes, such as `Time` or `InteractiveIO`? These classes exist primarily for use by other classes. One can't execute these classes until they are actually incorporated into a larger program. Giving in to the temptation to minimize the testing of such a class until it is actually necessary is unwise for several reasons:

- Testing is part of the development phase of software. After software is released, there is less opportunity to do thorough testing because the programmers are under great pressure to fix bugs discovered by customers.
- When you use a utility class, you need a high degree of confidence in its correctness. If you discover an error in the behavior of your code, finding the error is substantially more difficult if you have to worry about both the correctness of the utility classes *and* that of the newly created code.
- Creating the test cases is best when the class is fresh in your mind. Testing in a production environment, that is, where the code will actually be used (in contrast to assignments in a programming class in school), is usually done in stages: first by the creator of the code, then by some other member of the group, and finally by some dedicated test group within the company. Although the others will test only the external behavior of the

class and how it *integrates* or fits with the rest of the software being designed, you as the designer can test other aspects of the class as well, for example, the values of instance variables.

Therefore, all code, even utility classes, should be thoroughly tested before actual use. The question of how to test a class whose usefulness is limited to being incorporated into larger programs then arises. The answer is to create a **test driver** for the class, that is, a method whose sole purpose is to test the class. For convenience, this method can be incorporated into the class that it is testing:

```
class Employee {
        ...
        public static void testDriver() {
            Employee e = new Employee("Gerald Weiss", 25);
            int hours = 36;
            System.out.print("Employee name: ");
            System.out.println(e.getName());
            System.out.print("Rate: ");
            System.out.println(e.rate);
            System.out.print("Hours: ");
            System.out.println(hours);
            System.out.print("Pay: ");
            System.out.println(e.calcPay(hours));
        }
}
```

This way, a class can carry around its own test driver.

The test driver method is `static` because it is not invoked with a receiver. Rather we invoke the method as follows:

```
Employee.testDriver();
```

Thus, a program that tests the `Employee` class is just

```
class testEmployee {
    public static void main(String[] a) {
        Employee.testDriver();
    }
}
```

The driver itself merely invokes the methods of the class and prints out the results; you, or whoever is using the test driver, must check that the results are correct.

7.3.1   Some Advantages of Test Drivers

Testing is not particularly glamorous or enjoyable. You want to produce good software; testing makes it work. Like anything unglamorous and unenjoyable (taking out the trash, for example), the trick is to make it as convenient as possible. Writing a test driver helps us in the following ways:

- A test driver at least partially automates the testing of your class.
- A test driver eliminates the need for you to remember which tests you originally ran the class against. This makes it easier to retest the class after fixing a bug just in case your "fix" messed something else up. This process is known as *regression testing*.
- A class with a test driver benefits other programmers who use it because if the programmers discover bugs in their program, they can run the driver to confirm the class's correctness—and then look elsewhere for the problem.

EXERCISES

1. Add a test driver to each of the classes you have written.

2. We suggested that the test driver for a class be placed into the class itself so that it is carried along with the class definition. Can you think of another reason to have the test driver be a part of the class. (Hint: think of `public` and `private`.)

7.4 Automatic Testing

Even with a test driver, we still have the problem of determining whether the class successfully passed the test. In the example above, we had the input data as well as the results printed, thus allowing us to perform the necessary calculations and determine whether the payroll was correctly computed. This approach has the following drawbacks:

- If the calculation is a relatively simple one, as is the case for our payroll example, it is easy to calculate the proper answer and compare it against the one displayed by the test driver. However, if the calculation is even moderately complex (such as calculating the interest on a student loan over 10 years), recalculating the value each time the code is to be retested is not desirable.
- A good test driver typically performs many tests upon the class. As discussed earlier, each method representing some external behavior must be tested. Any special cases must be also be tested. The verification of even simple calculations becomes difficult when there are many.

One solution is to calculate the correct answers once, embed them in the test driver, and print out those values as well as those computed by the class:

```
public static void testDriver() {
        Employee e = new Employee("Gerald Weiss", 25);
```

```
        int hours = 36;
        int correctAnswer = 900;    I used my calculator to get this value.
        System.out.print("Employee name: ");
        System.out.println(e.getName());
        System.out.print("Rate: ");
        System.out.println(e.rate);
        System.out.print("Hours: ");
        System.out.println(hours);
        System.out.print("Pay (computed): ");
        System.out.println(e.calcPay(hours));
        System.out.print("Pay (correct): ");
        System.out.println(correctAnswer);
    }
```

This way both the correct and computed values are printed, eliminating the need to constantly recalculate the results each time we run the test. However, this doesn't solve our second problem, the difficulty of comparing all the computed and calculated results for a large number of tests. To solve this problem, we can have the computer check the computed values with the correct ones for us and notify us only when there is a problem:

```
public static void testDriver() {
        Employee e = new Employee("Gerald Weiss", 25);
        int hours = 36;
        int correctAnswer = 900;    I used my calculator to get this value.
        System.out.print("Employee name: ");
        System.out.println(e.getName());
        System.out.print("Rate: ");
        System.out.println(e.rate);
        System.out.print("Hours: ");
        System.out.println(hours);
        int computedPay = e.calcPay();
        System.out.print("Pay (computed): ");
        System.out.println(computedPay);
        if (computedPay != correctAnswer) {          Check computed answer
           System.out.print(                         against my calculation
              "*** Error - computed pay does not ");
           System.out.print("match correct answer of ");
           System.out.println(correctAnswer);
           System.out.println("Test failed!");
        } else
           System.out.println(
                        "Test completed successfully!");
    }
```

This method now does all the work except for the original calculation of the correct answer. It performs the test *and* checks the answer for us.

The testing approach in which a test driver checks the results for correctness is often known as **automatic testing.** That is not to say that the test driver determines the test automatically—that can only be done by someone knowledgeable of the class. In fact, the ability to create a proper test suite is quite a talent and is a bit of an art in itself. Rather, when we speak of an automatic test, we mean that the test driver checks the correctness of the results, and the human tester is only informed when something is amiss.

7.4.1 Test Drivers Made Easier

It is quite cumbersome to repeatedly write a sequence of the form

```
if (theCorrectAnswer != theComputedAnswer) {
           a series of System.out.print statements
                      displaying the error.
}
```

For the reader of the test driver, this is a fairly large distraction in the logical flow.

To facilitate the writing of an automatic test driver, we would like a method that performs the above test and subsequent action. In addition, it would be great to find out the chain of method invocations (and line numbers) that led to the error. We can obtain this using the `static dumpStack` method of the predefined class `Thread`:

```
class TestHelper {
    public static void verify(boolean testCondition, String
                              message) {
        if (!testCondition) {
            System.out.print("*** Error - test failure: ");
            System.out.println(message);
            Thread.dumpStack();
        }
    }
}
```

Because `verify` depends solely upon its arguments, it has no need for a receiver object and should therefore be declared `static`. Furthermore, this method will be used by many test drivers of various classes, so we place it in its own class, `TestHelper`. For example, executing the following simple program

```
public class Test {
    public static void main(String args[]) {
        int x = 5, y = 0;
        TestHelper.verify(x==y,"Just a test");
    }
}
```

Here's an invocation of verify that causes a test failure.

yields

```
*** Error - test failure: Just a test
java.lang.Exception: Stack trace
    at java.lang.Thread.dumpStack(Thread.java:534)
    at TestHelper.verify(TrivialApplication.java:20)
    at Test.main(TrivialApplication.java:9)
```

Reading from the bottom upward, we see that at line 9 in `main`, we invoked `verify`. It was that invocation that detected the failure of the test condition and invoked `dumpStack`.

Returning to our test driver, the fragment

```
if (computedPay != correctAnswer) {
    System.out.print("*** Error - computed pay does not ");
    System.out.print("match correct answer of ");
    System.out.println(correctAnswer);
    System.out.println("Test failed!");
}
```

could then be replaced by the less verbose (and more readable)

```
TestHelper.verify(computedPay ==
               correctAnswer, "calcPay test");
```

The easier it is to write a test, the more likely it is for the programmer to do so; a method such as `verify` can be a very handy tool in the creation of a test driver.

EXERCISES

1. Implement the `TestHelper` class and use it to automate as much as possible the test drivers of Exercise 1 in Section 7.3. •

7.5 What to Test and How to Test It

By now you should be convinced that testing is both useful and crucial to the development of successful software. Furthermore, we can attempt to alleviate some of the problems inherent in testing: laziness, boredom, manual checking of results, and so on, through the use of test drivers and, whenever possible, the automation of the tests themselves. What we haven't yet discussed are the following questions:

- What constitutes a good and thorough test?
- What values should be used for the various tests?

Let us now address these issues. Be cautioned, however, that we are merely touching the surface of testing techniques. And once again, don't forget

Djikstra's statement regarding testing. In general, you can never be absolutely certain there are no errors in your code.

7.5.1   What Constitutes a Good and Thorough Test?

As we've said, you can never test too much. However, since we are usually unable to perform an exhaustive test, how do we determine the point at which we've sufficiently tested our code? We will present several standard testing guidelines to help you.

All Behavior Must Be Tested   Recall the `Employee` class of Chapter 6. It contained the following methods:

- `Employee` (constructor)
- `getName`
- `calcPay`

Our initial temptation might be to test only the `calcPay` method; after all, that method is what the class is all about. Ignoring the other methods, however, is just asking for trouble. An incorrect constructor, for example, one that incorrectly initializes the `rate` instance variable, would prove disastrous. Similarly, if the `getName` method was incorrect, the name on the check that would be eventually printed would be wrong.

If a method is invoked by a user of the class, it *must* be directly tested in the test suite. If the method is not used by the outside, but rather exists as a helper method called by other methods of the class, if possible that method should also be tested.

Try to Find a Logical Test Order   Many tests are independent of each other. For example, it does not really matter in which order we test `calcPay` with overtime and nonovertime hour values. On the other hand, it makes more sense to test the constructor prior to testing `calcPay`; after all, if the former doesn't work, the second will definitely produce an incorrect result. Often the methods of a class can be ordered on the basis of how *primitive* they are, that is, how much their implementation depends upon other methods in the class. The more primitive the method, the less it uses other methods of the class. Because all (non-`static`) methods of a class ultimately depend upon the constructor properly initializing the object, its proper operation is vital to the correct operation of the class.

The more primitive the method, the earlier it should be tested in the test suite. If we are testing a method that uses other methods of the class, any debugging is made easier if we have already tested those methods.

In addition, we would like to be able to print out the value of our object for the purpose of debugging. We would like to have confidence in any methods that print the object, and those should therefore also be tested early in the suite.

Make Sure Each Statement Has Been Executed At Least Once   Every-statement testing is a useful approach, and when there are conditionals, it is quite an important approach. This technique requires that every statement in the code has been executed at least once during the test. The idea is that an untested statement is an incorrect statement. Look at the following code from the `calcPay` method of the `Employee` class:

```
if (hours <= 40)
    pay = hours * rate;
else
    pay = hours*rate + (hours - 40) * (rate / 2);
```

If no test of `calcPay` involves overtime, (with overtime the condition of the `if` statement evaluates to `false`), there is an untested statement in the program:

```
pay = hours * rate + (hours - 40) * (rate / 2);
```

Untested statements can be disastrous. Some user of the class will eventually have a situation in which there is overtime. If you have never encountered that case, the user is essentially executing untested code.

Sufficient tests must be used to ensure that at least each alternative of a conditional (one for an `if`, two for an `if-else`) has been executed at least once during some test. Choosing such data can often be challenging, but if you overlook it now, you will be doing it later. After all, the conditional is there for a reason—do not lull yourself into a false sense of security by deciding that case will *never* happen.

There is an alternative to the every-statement testing technique, known as **all-paths testing.** In this approach, not only is every statement tested, but *every sequence of statements in the program is tested as well.* To see the difference between the two techniques, consider the following code, which uses objects of the `Time` class:

```
Time t1, t2, t3, earliest;
...
if (t1.isBefore(t2))
    earliest = t1;           // (1)
else
    earliest = t2;           // (2)
if (t3.isBefore(earliest))
    earliest = t3;           // (3)
```

The every-statement approach requires that each statement be executed at least once. In particular, we are interested in making sure the true and false parts of the `if` statements—the statements labeled (1), (2), and (3)—are each executed at least once during our tests. We can guarantee this with merely two tests. For example, the test data

```
t1:  04:00
t2:  06:30
t3:  02:00
```

causes the execution of (1) and (3); the test data

```
t1:  05:00
t2:  02:00
t3:  12:00
```

forces the execution of (2).

The all-paths approach, however, goes even further. It requires the testing of the following sequences:

- (1) followed by (3)
- (2) followed by (3)
- (1) alone (the condition of the second if evaluates to `false`)
- (2) alone

This is a minimum of four sets of test data to cover all cases.

While all-paths testing is certainly a more comprehensive testing approach than every-statement testing, it quickly becomes overwhelming in size.

7.5.2   What Values Should Be Used for the Various Tests?

The ideal answer to this one is those that uncover all the bugs. Unrealistic as it may be, however, it provides us with a good criteria for selecting test cases.

Look For and Test Special Cases   In addition to testing each alternative of a condition, it is a good idea to test the value, if such a one exists, that lies on the boundary of the conditional. For example, consider the `calcPay` method for the employee-with-overtime example in Chapter 6:

```
public int calcPay(int hours) {
    if (hours <= 40)
        pay = hours * rate;
    else
        pay = 40 * rate +
                (hours - 40) * (rate + rate / 2) ;
    return pay;
}
```

We might have a test for 20 hours (corresponding to the true alternative of the conditional) and one for 50 hours (for the false). In addition, we should test the case of 40 hours, because that is the dividing point for the two categories. We call such cases *boundary conditions* because they are at the boundary between the alternatives of a conditional. Incorrect treatment of the values of boundary conditions is often the origin of logic errors. For example, a careless implementor of `calcPay` might have written

```
if (hours < 40)                          // Note the strict inequality.
        pay = hours * rate;
    ...
```

Someone working exactly 40 hours would now (incorrectly) fall into the overtime alternative. Simply testing the case for 20 hours and 50 hours would not have exposed the error. (Actually, although there is a logic error, the results would still be correct.) Although a similar argument could conceivably be made for *any* value (say 73 hours), the fact that 40 is the cutoff value makes it prone to being incorrectly handled.

Values sometimes require special consideration even if there are no overt conditionals present. One of the most common examples is the division operation. As you know from mathematics, division by zero is undefined, and thus dividing by zero is always an error. In the context of division, we might then think of `int` values as falling into two categories: 0 and everything else. A method that uses the division operator must ensure that it is never applied when the divisor is zero. So, if we are testing this method, we should construct a data set that causes the divisor to be zero and another that causes it to be nonzero. If the division is not prevented in the zero case, the method has an error.

The value `null` is another special case that arises in the context of reference variables. Attempting to send a message using a reference variable whose value is `null` results in a run-time error in Java. Whenever possible, the `null` value should be used as a test case to determine its effect upon the code. If nothing else, you might wish to ask yourself, Can this reference variable ever assume the `null` value and if so, what happens?

Do Not Be Concerned with the Efficiency of the Test   Unlike other applications in which performance time can and usually does play a role, the sole purpose and goal of testing software is to verify behavior. We would rather have a slow but comprehensive test than one that, although lightning fast, performs only a cursory check.

1. Review your test drivers created in the exercises of the previous sections, applying the guidelines presented in this section. Did you miss any cases? Are all statements executed by your tests?

EXERCISES

7.6 Debugging Techniques

No matter how well we design our code, errors will arise. As testing proceeds and the code matures and becomes used more and more, the frequency of discovering errors should decrease. However, those errors that *do* arise after reasonable testing are often quite difficult to pin down. The process of discovering an error is known as **debugging**.

Although specialized tools known as debuggers exist to aid in the tracking down of errors, they are not always available. A universal method of finding bugs, regardless of the computer system or language being used, is to print out values at appropriate points in the program's execution. Finding those *appropriate* points is a skill that improves with practice.

As an example, suppose when implementing the `Employee` class of Chapter 6, we left out the last line in `calcPay`. That line updated the `lastWeeksOvertime` instance variable. As a result, this variable's value will always be zero, as initialized by the constructor, and the previous week's overtime will never be taken into consideration.

```
class Employee {
Methods
    ...
    public int calcPay(int hours) {
        int pay;
        int currentOvertime;
        if (hours <= 40) {   // Test for no overtime
            pay = hours * rate;
            currentOvertime = 0;
        }
        else{
            pay = 40 * rate + (hours - 40) * (rate +
                                        rate / 2);
            currentOvertime = hours - 40;
        }
        if (currentOvertime + lastWeeksOvertime >= 30) {
            System.out.print(name);
            System.out.print(
                " has worked 30 or more hours overtime");
        }
        // lastWeeksOvertime = currentOvertime;
        return pay;
    }
    ...
    private int lastWeeksOvertime;
}
```

Suppose we omitted this line? Oops!

7.6.1 Discovering the Bug

In order to comply with every-statement testing, we must ensure that the condition `currentOvertime + lastWeeksOvertime >= 30` evaluates to `true` for some test. The following code should do that:

```
Employee e = new Employee("James Arnold", 20);
System.out.println(e.calcPay(45)); // 5 hours overtime
System.out.println(e.calcPay(65)); // 25 hours overtime
```

When we run this test we notice that the expected warning message "has worked 30 or more hours overtime" is not issued. This is a bug.

7.6.2 Hunting for the Error

If we examine the code of `calcPay`, we realize that if no message was printed out, somehow the condition `currentOvertime + lastWeeksOvertime >= 30` is not true. If the condition is not true, somehow `currentOvertime + lastWeeksOvertime` is less than 30. How could this be? We specifically invoked `calcPay` so that first there were 5 hours and then 25 hours of overtime. Somehow the value of `currentOvertime` or the value of `lastWeeksOvertime` (or both) is in error.

To see which variable is the culprit, we can print their values just before the condition is tested:

```
public int calcPay(int hours) {
    ...
    System.out.print("currentOvertime = ");
    System.out.println(currentOvertime);
    System.out.print("lastWeeksOvertime = ");
    System.out.println(lastWeeksOvertime);
    if (currentOvertime + lastWeeksOvertime >= 30) {
        System.out.print(name);
        System.out.print(
            " has worked 30 or more hours overtime");
    }
    // lastWeeksOvertime = currentOvertime;   Suppose we omitted this
                                              line? Oops!
    return pay;
}
```

When we repeat the test, we will see that `lastWeeksOvertime` is always 0. Returning to our class definition, we see that the only assignment to `lastWeeksOvertime` is the assignment of 0 in the constructor.

Fixing the error requires a similar analysis of the problem to the one we presented in Section 6.3, when we implemented `calcPay` correctly.

SUMMARY

Code testing is an integral and essential part of the software development process. Code that has not been tested must be assumed to be flawed. Even tested code cannot truly be said to be error-free—at most we are trying to minimize the number of errors and their frequency of occurrence. As we become more and more dependent upon software in our lives, the potential for disaster resulting from poorly tested code becomes more pronounced.

Any application or class definition should have an associated collection of tests known as a test suite. While a test suite cannot guarantee that no errors exist, it does provide some measure of confidence in the software, especially if it contains a comprehensive set of tests.

The test suite itself automatically verifies the success or failure of each test. It relieves the programmer of having to do each verification and makes it possible to run thousands of test cases against the software, a daunting task to the most dedicated programmer. It also allows for convenient regression testing— testing performed after the elimination of a bug to ensure no old bugs have reappeared as a result of the fix. A method that allows the tester to easily specify conditions that *must* hold true, and that provides useful diagnostics when such conditions fail, aids in the testing process.

There are several items to keep in mind when testing:

- Test all behavior.
- Find a logical order for the tests, typically testing simpler methods before more complex ones.
- Ensure each statement has been executed at least once.
- Look for special cases.
- Do not worry about the test's efficiency.

Once a bug has been discovered, it must be tracked down. Printing relevant values is an invaluable aid to hunting down the source of an error.

STUDY AID: TERMINOLOGY REVIEW

all-paths testing   An approach to testing in which every possible sequence of statements is tested at least once.

automatic testing   An approach to testing in which the test suite verifies the correctness of the test results.

bug   A run-time error in a program.

debugging   The process of finding and fixing bugs.

every-statement testing   An approach to testing in which every statement is tested at least once.

test driver   A method (or collection of methods) whose purpose is to test the behavior of one or more utility classes.

test suite   A set of tests.

QUESTIONS FOR REVIEW

1. What is the purpose of testing?

2. What is the purpose of a test driver?

3. Where might a test suite of a class be placed?

FURTHER EXERCISES

1. Write a test driver for the `Name` class of Chapter 4.

2. Write a test driver for the `TollBooth` and `Truck` classes of Chapter 5.

3. Exercise 5 in Section 6.3 presented an incorrect condition for the overtime test. Would the error resulting from using the condition `hours<40` have been caught?

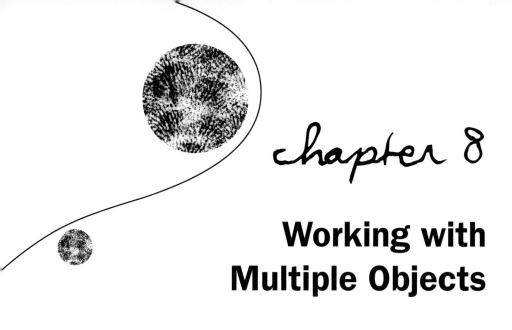

chapter 8

Working with Multiple Objects

8.1 ■ Introduction

Up until now we have written programs that basically dealt with one object of a class at a time: calculating one employee's payroll, calculating the toll for a single truck, etc. However, what we can do for one, we would like to be able to do for many: calculating payroll for a thousand employees; collecting tolls from all vehicles over the course of a day. Once we have determined how to perform a calculation on one object, we should be able to repeat that calculation for as many times as desired.

The ability to repeatedly perform an action is the second of the tools that alter the flow of program execution—the other being the conditional, which we introduced in Chapter 6.

Much of the power of programming comes from this ability. Our payroll calculation is a simple matter of multiplying hours by rate; however, performing that simple calculation for 10,000 employees becomes a tedious, repetitive, and thus error-prone task for several people. Computers, on the other hand, do not get bored and are not subject to the errors that result from repetition and quantity.

We start by considering repetitive processing in the context of multiple instances of a class. This processing includes

- Processing multiple objects created by input
- Maintaining multiple instances
- Processing the multiple objects in some manner (for example, calculating the payroll of all the employees of a company)

8.2   Processing Multiple Objects

We begin with the simple but common case of multiple objects that

- Can be processed independently of each other
- Once processed, are no longer needed

For example, consider a simplified payroll system with many employees. On payday the wages for each employee can be calculated independently. Once payment has been made, the `Employee` object may be discarded. We have the code that processes a single `Employee` object:

```
Employee  e  =  Employee.readIn(br);
int  hours  =  Integer.parseInt(br.readLine());
System.out.print("Employee " + e.getName() +
                  " has earned " + e.calcPay(hours));
```

We now want to be able to repeat this piece of code for each object to be processed. If we have five such objects, we will repeat the process five times, for 1000 objects, 1000 times, and so on:

repeat as necessary

```
Employee  e  =  Employee.readIn(br);
int  hours  =  Integer.parseInt(br.readLine());
System.out.print("Employee " + e.getName() +
                  " has earned " + e.calcPay(hours));
```

The construct we are looking for, one that repeats a sequence of code, is known as a **loop.** If we examine the above, we see that a loop consists of two parts:

- The *body* of the loop, that is, the sequence of code we wish to be able to repeat. In the above example, the body consists of the three boxed statements.
- The code for the looping mechanism itself. Although we wish to repeat the body of the loop, we do want the loop to eventually *terminate,* at which point execution moves to the code after the loop. In the above sample, "repeat as necessary" and the arrow constitute an informal loop construct.

A looping construct must, therefore, specify what constitutes the body of the loop and under what circumstances the loop terminates.

8.2.1   The `while` Statement

Our first loop construct is the **`while` statement.** Its general form is

```
while   (condition)
            body
```

Condition and *body* are the same constructs as those that are present in the `if` statement:

- *Condition* is a boolean-valued expression. It is also called the *loop test*.
- *Body* is a single statement or a compound statement.

The phrase `while (condition)` is called the *loop header*. As in the case of the conditional, the *body* should be indented for clarity.

The execution of the `while` statement proceeds as follows:

- The condition is tested.
- If the condition evaluates to `false`, the loop is *terminated;* execution continues with the statement immediately following the loop (i.e., the statement after the body of the loop).
- On the other hand, if the condition evaluates to `true`, the body of the loop is executed (we often say "the loop is entered") and these steps are repeated.

This repetition proceeds until in step 2 it is discovered that the condition evaluates to `false`.

8.2.2   Back to the Payroll Loop

Let us now use a `while` statement to code the payroll loop introduced at the beginning of the section. First, recall our discussion in Chapter 6 regarding returning `null` as the result of a `read` method for which no data are present in the file. When `read` returns `null`, there is no more employee data and our loop should terminate:

```
(1)   Employee   e   =   Employee.readIn(br);// Read first object.
(2)   while  (e  !=  null)  {                 // Was an object read?
(3)     int  hours  =
              Integer.parseInt(br.readLine()); // Process object.
(4)     System.out.println("Employee " + e.getName() +
            " has earned " + e.calcPay(hours)); // Process object.
(5)     e  =  Employee.readIn(br); // Read next object.
(6)   }
```

The loop proper consists of lines (2) through (6). Line (1) invokes the `readIn` method of `Employee` in order to read the first object. The condition of the `while` tests whether an `Employee` object has been successfully read. If so, the loop is entered and the `Employee` object is processed. Prior to returning to line (2), another `Employee` object is read, and the process repeats.

The first `Employee` object is read *before* the loop body—in line (1). This is to guarantee that the condition `e != null` is meaningful, that is, that `e` has been given a value (either a reference to an `Employee` object or `null`) that can be tested.

Your first intuition might have been to write

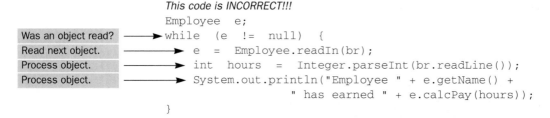

This code is INCORRECT!!!

Was an object read? ⟶	`while (e != null) {`
Read next object. ⟶	`    e = Employee.readIn(br);`
Process object. ⟶	`    int hours = Integer.parseInt(br.readLine());`
Process object. ⟶	`    System.out.println("Employee " + e.getName() +`
	`                       " has earned " + e.calcPay(hours));`
	`}`

```
Employee e;
```

This, however, results in an undefined value for `e` the first time it is used in the condition of the `while`. Fortunately, the Java compiler would issue an error message to that effect, preventing the error from becoming a serious bug.

An equally incorrect loop is

Also INCORRECT!!!

Read first object. ⟶	`Employee e = Employee.readIn(br);`
Was an object read? ⟶	`while (e != null) {`
Process object. ⟶	`    int hours = Integer.parseInt(br.readLine());`
Process object. ⟶	`    System.out.println("Employee " + e.getName() +`
	`        " has earned " + e.calcPay(hours));`
	`}`

In this instance, only the first `Employee` object is read—the loop body does not contain an invocation of the `readIn` method and no additional objects are read. Assuming there are data corresponding to at least one employee in the data file, this loop will never terminate. Such a situation is known as an *infinite loop*. (What happens if the data file contains *no* data?)

In this example, we must read the first object *prior* to the loop body and then read subsequent objects at the very end of the body *immediately before* retesting the `while` condition.

EXERCISES

1. Write a program that uses the `read` method of the `Name` class to read in a series of names. Once read in, each name should be printed.

2. Write a program that reads in a series of `int` values using the technique presented in Section 5.6 for performing integer input. Do you see any difference in structure between this program and the one presented that read employees?   •

8.3 Loop Patterns

Reading in a series of data items and processing them, as we did with `Employee` data in the previous section, is a fairly common task. That loop read a series of `Employee` objects and calculated their payroll. This sort of loop can be easily adapted to handle other types of objects and other types of processing as well. For example, the following reads information about trucks from a file and calculates their tolls:

```
TollBooth  tollBooth  =  new TollBooth("Bridgeport");
Truck   truck;
truck  =  Truck.read(...);     ◄───────────────  Read first.
while  (truck  !=  null)  {    ◄───────────────  Test for termination.
    tollBooth.calculateToll(truck);  ◄────────  Processing
    truck  =  Truck.read(...)    ◄─────────────  Read next.
}
```

This reads `String`s and prints them out:

```
String  s;
s  =  br.readLine();     ◄───────────────────  Read first.
while  (s  !=  null)  {   ◄──────────────────  Test for termination.
    System.out.print(s);  ◄──────────────────  Processing
    s  =  br.readLine();  ◄──────────────────  Read next.
}
```

Consider a loop that reads a series of integers and prints their squares. Recall that our method for reading in integers consists of reading in a line as a `String` object and then using the `parseInt` method to produce the `int` value:

```
int  i;
i  =  parseInt(br.readLine());
```

However, if we want to test for end-of-file, we must check for a `null` value returned from the `readLine` method. Furthermore, this must be done *prior* to invoking `parseInt`—attempting to invoke that method with a `null` argument produces a run-time error. We must break up the two steps of the integer input:

```
int  i;
String  temp;
temp  =  br.readLine();          Read first.
while  (temp  !=  null)  {        Test for termination.
    i  =  Integer.parseInt(temp);  Processing—first convert to int.
    System.out.print(i * i);       Now print square.
    temp  =  br.readLine();        Read next.
}
```

We first read the line into the `String` object, `temp`. This value is used as the controlling condition of the loop. The processing portion in the body of the loop consists of converting the `String` into an integer and then printing out the square. We then read the next `String`.

A variation on this last example is to read integers until a negative value is read. In this situation, there is no need to break up the `readLine` and the subsequent `parseInt`. In fact, to do so would be wrong. The `parseInt`, not the `readLine`, must immediately precede the test because the test is performed on the result of `parseInt`, not on the result of `readLine`:

```
int  i;
i  =  Integer.parseInt(br.readLine());        Read first.
while  (i  >=  0)  {                           Test for termination.
    System.out.print(i * i);                   Print square.
    i  =  Integer.parseInt(br.readLine());     Read next.
}
```

Although the exact type of data, the condition for loop termination, and the actual processing differed from one example to the next, they all had much in common. In all cases, the purpose of the loop was to read and process successive data items. The basic structure of the loop was the same: read first item, test for termination, process, read next item, repeat test, and so on. We can depict this sequence of actions with a generalized sketch of such a loop:

```
//  Loop Pattern: read/process
read first item
while  (a valid item has been read)  {      Test for termination.
    process the item
    read the next item
}
```

We call such a sketch a **loop pattern** because it provides us with a starting point for the construction of a loop whose purpose is to read and process multiple data items. To use this pattern, supply the following:

- The means of reading the item
- The condition that will determine that no valid item has been read
- The code that specifies the processing

Plug this into the pattern and you have a working loop.

We will give names to our various patterns so that we can speak about them. We call our first pattern *read/process* because that is precisely what it does: reads data and processes the objects created from that data. In this chapter we will present several loop patterns that perform other common tasks.

8.4   The Impact of Loops on Testing

We call a code fragment that contains no conditionals or loops *straight-line* because execution moves in a straight line—no statements are skipped or repeated. With the introduction of conditionals, our programs are no longer strictly linear in nature: Different states of the program cause alternative sequences of execution. However, one could test all possible paths of execution by running the program several times and supplying the appropriate data that would cause a particular path to be taken. For example, given the test

```
if (x < 10)
```

we could run the program twice—once making sure x is less than 10 and once with x equal to or greater than 10).

With the introduction of loops, however, such an exhaustive testing approach can no longer be employed for precisely the same reason that loops are so powerful in the first place. The looping construct allows us to repeat a block of code an arbitrary number of times (our `Employee` example, for instance, would loop for as many times as there are entries in the input file). We can thus no longer test every possible scenario (the all-paths approach)— the very nature of an arbitrary loop precludes us from such an exhaustive test.

The other side of the coin is that loops allow us to run our classes through a battery of tests. Recall the concept of automatic testing introduced in Chapter 7. In that technique, the programmer set up test cases that could verify themselves. Assuming such verification could be performed, we could create a loop that might run hundreds or even thousands of test cases without us having to tediously check each and every one.

Regardless of the number of test cases we might run against our software, the existence of loops within the code makes it improbable that we will be able to test *every* case. To have some confidence in our code, we must then be very careful in the construction of loops. In this chapter, we are restricting ourselves to a small number of very specific loop designs. In the next chapter, we will present a more general approach to loop design, one that will provide guidance in the development of correct loops.

However, no matter how good our loop design is, we must still methodically test our loops. The all-paths approach is impossible, but as a minimum, we should test the following cases:

- The loop condition is false the first time, and the loop body is never executed.

- The loop body is executed exactly once.
- The loop body is executed more than once.

EXERCISES

1. Explain how each of the three loop test categories arise. That is, what sort of data must be in the file for each of the cases to occur.

2. Apply the test method outlined above to our payroll loop.

3. How do the three minimal loop test categories approximate *all-paths* testing?

8.5   A Radio Station's Song Library

This is another example of the read/process loop pattern.

8.5.1   Statement of the Problem

WOLD, the local radio station, wants to computerize its song library. A file has been created with entries consisting of a song's title and its composer. We want to provide the disc jockey with the ability to query the library for all songs by a particular artist.

8.5.2   A Sample Scenario

Here's how a disc jockey might interact with the software:

```
Enter the name of the song library file: ClassicRock.lib
File ClassicRock.lib loaded.
Enter artist to search for: Beatles
Songs found by Beatles:
        Back in the USSR
        Paperback Writer
        She Loves You
Enter artist to search for: Mozart
No songs found by Mozart
```

8.5.3   Determining the Primary Objects

The relevant nouns of the problem are *song library*, *song*, *file*, *entry*, *title*, and *artist*. Artist and title are subsidiary to song, which is subsidiary to song library. Entry and file are just the data on disk, representing song and song library, respectively. Our primary class will thus be `SongLibrary`.

8.5.4   Determining the Desired Behavior

We want to be able to create a `SongLibrary` as well as print out all songs composed by a particular artist. Our methods are

- `SongLibrary` (constructor)
- `lookUp`

8.5.5   Defining the Interface

Here is some typical usage code:

```
SongLibrary  classical  =
    new SongLibrary("classical.lib");
SongLibrary  jazz  =  new SongLibrary("jazz.lib");
classical.lookUp("Gould");
classical.lookUp("Marsalas");
jazz.lookUp("Corea");
jazz.lookUp("Marsalas");
```

A `SongLibrary` is associated with a particular input file whose name is given to the constructor. The `lookUp` method accepts a `String` that is the artist and prints the results to `System.out`:

```
class  SongLibrary  {
    public SongLibrary(String  songFileName)  {...}
    public void  lookUp(String  artist)  {...}
}
```

8.5.6   Defining the Instance Variables

Each time `lookUp` is invoked, it will create a new `BufferedReader` that is associated with the disk file specified by the name of the song file. This name, therefore, must be maintained as an instance variable of the `SongLibrary` object:

```
class  SongLibrary  {
    public SongLibrary(String  songFileName)  {...}
    public void  lookUp(String  artist)  {...}
    //   Instance variables
    String  songFileName;
}
```

8.5.7   Implementing the Methods

The constructor is just an assignment of its argument to the `songFileName` instance variable:

```
public SongLibrary(String  songFileName)  {
```

```
        this.songFileName  =  songFileName;
    }
```

The `lookUp` method must create a `BufferedReader` from `songFile-Name`. It then reads songs from the `BufferedReader`, looking for the desired artist. To do this we require a class that models songs; let us call this class `Song`. Given such a class, we might then apply our read/process loop pattern. Let us make the following sketch of the loop that reads in the songs, searching for the desired artist:

```
public void  lookUp(String artist) throws Exception {
    BufferedReader  br  =
            new BufferedReader(
                new InputStreamReader(
                    new FileInputStream(songFileName)));

    //  Using  read/process  loop  pattern
    Song  song  =  Song.read(br);    ◄─────────  First object
    while  (song  !=  null)  {  ◄─────────  Was an object read?
        Check song's artist and print out if match (processing).
        song  =  Song.read(br);  ◄─────────  Read next object.
    }
}
```

As a result of this, we see that we are going to have to develop a `Song` class. Before we do so, however, let us more carefully examine what behavior we want this class to have. To do this, we complete the above sketch of the `lookUp` method:

```
public void  lookUp(String  artist) throws Exception {
    BufferedReader  br =
            new BufferedReader(
                new InputStreamReader(
                    new FileInputStream(songFileName)));

    Song  song  =  Song.read(br);
    while  (song  !=  null)  {                Check song's
        if  (artist.equals(song.getArtist()))    artist and print
            System.out.println(song.getTitle());  out if match.
        song  =  Song.read(br);
    }
}
```

That is, in order to compare the song's artist, we will need a method that returns the song's artist. If the artist matches the one we are looking for, we then need to print out its titles; thus, we also need a method that returns the song's title. Finally, we require a method that creates a `Song` object from input.

Notice that the above code completes the implementation of the `lookUp` method and thus the definition of the `SongLibrary` class. In order to complete our application, we must now define the `Song` class.

8.5.8   Using the Class

We present our sample usage code of the `SongLibrary` class as a complete program:

```
class  WOLD  {
    public  static  void  main(String[]  a)
                                    throws Exception {
        SongLibrary  classical  =
                        new SongLibrary("classical.lib");
        SongLibrary  jazz  =  new  SongLibrary("jazz.lib");
        classical.lookUp("Gould");
        classical.lookUp("Marsalas");
        jazz.lookUp("Corea");
        jazz.lookUp("Marsalas");
    }
}
```

8.5.9   Finding the Primary Object—The `Song` Class

We don't need to find the primary object here because we have already decided on a class to create—Song. We are not, at this point, searching through a statement of the problem. This problem differs from the previous ones in that our class is motivated by very specific requirements, namely, providing the behavior necessary to complete the implementation of `Song-Library`.

8.5.10   Determining the Desired Behavior—The `Song` Class

As discussed above, we require the following methods:

- `read`
- `getTitle`
- `getArtist`

You may have noticed that we haven't mentioned the constructor. Although, our `read` methods have always invoked a constructor as part of their implementation, and we have no reason to suspect that this class will be different, the constructor is not required by the `SongLibrary`. We thus omit it from the list of behaviors required from outside the class.

8.5.11   Defining the Interface—The Song Class

We don't need to imagine "typical usage code"—we have very specific usage code in the lookUp method above that was the actual motivation for our class:

```
public void  lookUp(String artist) throws Exception {
    BufferedReader  br =
            new BufferedReader(
                new InputStreamReader(
                    new FileInputStream(songFileName)));

    Song  song  =  Song.read(br);
    while  (song  !=  null)  {
        if  (artist.equals(song.getName())
            System.out.println(song.getTitle());
        song  =  Song.read(br);
    }
}
```

Again, note there is no need for an explicit constructor call. We expect that a constructor will be invoked from the read method, but that does not make it part of the interface:

```
class  Song  {
    public static  Song  read(BufferedReader  br)  {...}
    public String  getTitle()  {...}
    public String  getArtist()  {...}
}
```

8.5.12   Defining the Instance Variables—The Song Class

The Song class is relatively simple. We require only a song title and an artist. Note that in this case there is no constructor to motivate our instance variables; instead the requirements of the SongLibrary class's methods get-Title and getArtist determine the information that needs to be maintained in Song:

```
class  Song  {
            Methods specified above
            private String  title,  artist;
}
```

8.5.13   Implementing the Methods—The Song Class

The only new aspect here is that it is the implementation of the read method that introduces the need for a constructor:

```
public static  Song  read(BufferedReader  br)
                                        throws Exception {
    String  title  =  br.readLine();
```

```
      if  (title  ==  null)
          return  null;
      String  artist  =  br.readLine();
      return  new Song(title,  artist);
   }
```

It is only at this point that we are actually required to introduce a constructor.

We leave the implementation of the `Song` constructor, and the methods `getTitle` and `getArtist` as an exercise.

8.5.14   Using the Methods—The `Song` Class

The `lookUp` method of `SongLibrary` provided us with a full usage of the `Song` class. We might also want to create a test driver for `Song`. We leave this as an exercise as well.

8.5.15   Discussion

Our solution introduced two classes: `SongLibrary` and `Song`. The `Song` class was not introduced until a need for it arose when the methods for the `SongLibrary` class where implemented. Our tollbooth example in Chapter 5 also required the development of two classes: `Truck` and `Tollbooth`; however, in that example, we made the determination from the outset while determining the primary object.

If you review the statement of the problem for the song library, the need to model a song is present (the noun *song* does appear), so we might indeed have been able to introduce the need for a second class when we determined the primary objects. However, because songs are subsidiary to the song library, we elected to address the issues of the song library first.

Finally, a slight change in `SongLibrary`'s behavior could cause us to discover the need for a `Song` class at a different step in the development process (see Exercise at the end of this section).

8.5.16   The Iterative Nature of the Class Development Procedure

Our class design procedure is an iterative one: During the course of designing a class, we might require some object (as an instance variable, for example) that exhibits a specific behavior. We would then have to either find an existing class that supplies that behavior or, failing that, create a new class. The song library application that we just solved was such an instance. During the implementing the methods step for class `SongLibrary`, we introduced a local variable, `song`, when we wrote the `lookUp` method. This variable was to model the behavior of a song. We didn't really expect there to be an appropriate predefined Java class; the desired behavior after all was fairly specific to this particular application, and the Java classes are more general purpose in nature: `Strings`, output devices, collections, etc. We therefore were required to create a new class, `Song`.

As our applications get more and more sophisticated, this iterative process will often extend to many more steps. A typical commercial system may have hundreds of classes, many of which were created specifically for that system.

1. Complete the implementation of the `Song` class by implementing the `getTitle` and `getArtist` methods.

2. Rework the behavior of the class so that `lookUp` returns the song it found, rather than simply printing out the title. Does this change the point at which the need for a `Song` class is discovered?

8.6   Maintaining Multiple Values

Our manipulation of multiple objects has so far consisted of working with an individual object to completion and only then moving on to the next object. There are times, however, when we must maintain a reference to an object even after we move on to the remaining objects.

8.6.1   Another Look at `SongLibrary`

Although the `SongLibrary` class does provide the necessary behavior of looking up songs by a particular artist, `lookUp` is quite slow (i.e., it takes several seconds before the songs are displayed on the screen). The reason for this is that each time `lookUp` is invoked, the song library file is reopened (by creating the `FileInputStream`) and its entire contents are processed.

Input/output (I/O), the reading or writing of data to or from a file, is a very expensive—that is, slow—task compared to the manipulation of objects stored in memory. This is because memory is an electronic device, and I/O usually involves some form of mechanical device subject to the physical laws of inertia and friction. A faster implementation of the `SongLibrary` class is to read the song library in once (say, during creation of the `SongLibrary` object) and then perform our lookup completely in memory. Because the input file consists of pairs of lines, each pair containing of the data necessary to read a `Song` object, reading in the file involves creating multiple `Song` objects. The number of `Song` objects is, however, unknown—it depends upon the number of song entries in the file. Thus, we cannot simply declare two or five or any other specific number of `Song` instance variables for our `SongLibrary`. Rather, a **collection** of objects must be maintained.

A collection is a group of objects that can be declared as a single entity. The collection itself is an object that may be created and for which a reference variable may be declared. The individual objects in a collection are known as the **elements** of the collection.

8.6.2 Collections of Dependent Objects

In our earlier employee payroll example, the specific employee information being processed during a particular pass through the loop was no longer necessary once that employee's information had been processed. Once the employee's payroll had been calculated, and the information printed and used to update the total, the employee data could be discarded. The next time through the loop, the variable e was reassigned to reference a new Employee object. In terms of our previous discussion, the various Employee objects are independent of each other.

There are times, however, when the objects created during each pass are dependent upon each other and cannot be discarded immediately. Here are some examples:

- Reading in a list of names and printing them in reverse order of appearance. In this situation, we must retain all the names until the last one has been read (because it must be the first printed out).
- If the above seems somewhat artificial, how about reading them in and then printing them out alphabetically. We are faced with the same problem because until the last name has been read, we cannot be sure which name should be printed first.
- Suppose we have a roster file for a college course. Each student registered in the course has the following pair of lines in the file:

  name
  average

  We want to determine which students are performing above and below the average of the class. To do this, we must first calculate the average of the class, a process entailing reading in all the students' grades, summing their averages (i.e., accumulating a total), and then dividing by the number of students (obtained by maintaining a counter). Only after we have done this can we examine *each* student's average to see if it's above or below that of the class. (This example is discussed in Section 8.10.)
- A *concordance* is a list of all the words in a document together with their frequency of occurrence. We would like to create a concordance for a document contained in a file. The list of words encountered must be maintained until the entire document has been read.

These examples seem somewhat more compelling in their need for a collection than the revision of SongLibrary, for which a collection was a matter of efficiency. In these cases it seems that a collection is unavoidable. We now present our first example of a collection in Java.

8.7 Vector—A Simple Collection Class

Working with collections of objects is somewhat different from the type of code we've been writing until now. However, using our standard approach, we can try to come up with a list of the behaviors we would like the collection to exhibit. To do this let us examine in a bit more detail what a collection does for us:

- Create a new collection (i.e., the constructor)
- Add an object to the collection
- Process the objects in a collection

The important point here is that once we have added an object to a collection, we can come back later and process it and all the others in the collection. We can do this as often as is needed.

Java supplies several collection classes, as part of its java.util package. The simplest of these, and the one we are interested in, is the `Vector` class. We can easily create a `Vector` object, add elements to it, and go through the collection processing those elements.

The constructor to the `Vector` class takes no arguments. Thus to declare a `Vector` reference variable and create a new `Vector`, we can write (see also Figure 8.1):

```
Vector  v  =  new  Vector();
```

Let us now read some `String` objects and add them to `v`. This is just another application of the read/process loop pattern. In this case, the processing involved is adding the `String`s to the `Vector`. To add an element to a `Vector` we use the method `addElement`, passing the object to be added as an argument (see also Figure 8.2):

```
String  s;
s  =  br.readLine();
```
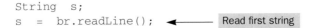

Read first string

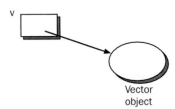

FIGURE 8.1 A `Vector`, just created.

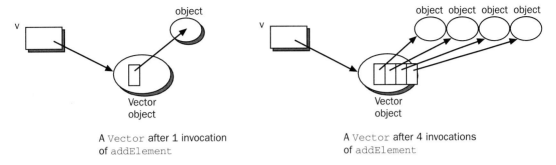

A `Vector` after 1 invocation
of `addElement`

A `Vector` after 4 invocations
of `addElement`

FIGURE 8.2   A `Vector`, after `addElement`.

```
while (s != null) {
    v.addElement(s);        ◄——————  Processing-adds s to v
    s = br.readLine();      ◄——————  Read next string.
}
```

Again, this is just another example of our read/process loop pattern. The reading in of each `String` object is straightforward; the processing portion of the loop is the addition of the object to the collection.

8.8   Moving Through a `Vector`— Enumerations

The process of going through a collection of objects is known as a *traversal* of the collection, and we thus speak of *traversing the collection* and *visiting* (processing) each element. A traversal is a repetitive process (visit *each* of the elements), and thus we should not be surprised that a loop is involved:

```
while  (we still have elements to visit)
        visit the next element
```

In order to visit each of the elements of a `Vector` we need to be able to

• Somehow get to the elements
• Get the next element
• Test whether there are any more elements to be visited

We might expect `Vector` to provide these methods. However, `Vector` is not the only collection class that Java defines, and the above behavior (that is, visiting all the elements) is common to all collections.

Java therefore provides a class **Enumeration,** which models this traversal behavior. (In actuality, `Enumeration` is not exactly a class, but we can view it as such for now.) Each collection class provides a method that creates and returns a reference to an object of class `Enumeration`. It is the `Enumeration` object that provides the methods to get the next element and test for more elements.

In particular, the `Vector` class contains a method, `elements`, that returns a reference to an `Enumeration` object:

```
Enumeration  elements()  {...}  ◄——  Returns an Enumeration for the Vector
```

In turn, `Enumeration` provides the following methods:

```
boolean  hasMoreElements()    // Returns true if there are more
                              // elements to visit; returns false otherwise.
ToBeDetermined nextElement()  // Returns reference to next element.
```

The return type of `nextElement` is a bit problematic; after all it can return a reference to *any* class. This is a marvelous flexibility. It means that today we can make a `Vector` of `Name` objects and retrieve references to them using `nextElement`, and tomorrow we can do the same for `String` objects. But how can `nextElement` return `String` references, `Name` references, and *anything-else* references? So far, all our experience with methods shows that if they return a reference, it is always the same kind of reference.

Collection classes such as `Vector` and utility classes such as `Enumeration` must work with any object class. Java provides a predefined class, called `Object`, that models *any* object. `Name`, `Employee`, and `String` references are also `Object` references. When we pass a `String` reference to the `addElement` method of `Vector`, as far as `addElement` is concerned, we are just passing a reference to an `Object` object. We deliberately use the phrase "an `Object` object" to emphasize that `Object` is a class (as is `String`), and just as there are `String` objects, so are there `Object` objects: in fact, every object—`String`, `Name`, `Employee`, and so on—is an `Object` object. Similarly, as far as the `nextElement` method of `Enumeration` is concerned, it is just returning a reference to an instance of the `Object` class. Hence its prototype is

```
Object  nextElement();
```

Because `nextElement` is declared as returning a reference to an `Object`, it can return references to `String` objects when we use a `Vector` to store `String`s, and it can return references to `Name` objects when we use a `Vector` to store `Name`s—all because a reference to a `Name` object is also a reference to an `Object` object.

We have to pay a small price for this flexibility. This extra work is illustrated in the following snippet of code, which creates a `Name` object, adds it to a `Vector` object (making it an element of the collection), and then gets a reference to that element (the original `Name` object) via an `Enumeration` object:

```
Name n = new Name("Gerald","Weiss");
Vector v = new Vector();
v.addElement(n);      ◄——————  Add a Name reference to the Vector—but to the
                               Vector we are just adding another Object reference.
Enumeration e = v.elements();
Name n2 = (Name) e.nextElement();  ◄———  What is the purpose of (Name)?
```

Because `nextElement` is declared as returning a reference to an `Object` and we are assigning it to `n2`, a `Name` reference variable, we must inform Java that the kind of `Object` reference we are expecting to get from `nextElement` is a `Name` reference. As long as we are sure we put only `Name` references into the `Vector` (using `addElement`), we know we are correct. So the extra work is simply

- Making sure that, for any given `Vector` object, we add only references to one kind of object
- Inserting the phrase (*ClassName*) in front of any invocation of `nextElement`, where *ClassName* is the name of the class of object stored in the `Vector`

The action of informing the system of the true nature of an object reference is known as *casting*. For example, in the statement

```
Name n2 = (Name) e.nextElement();
```

we speak of *casting the next element of e to a Name*.

We can now write the code to **enumerate** (traverse) through a collection. As a first example, let's print the `Strings` of the `Vector` we created above. The following is a sketch of a traversal loop:

```
while  (there are more elements)  {
    x  =  get the next element
    process x
}
```

It now translates to

```
Enumeration  enum  =  v.elements();
while  (enum.hasMoreElements())  {
    String  s  =  (String)enum.nextElement();
    System.out.print(s);
}
```

8.8.1 Another Loop Pattern—Enumerating through a Collection

Enumerating through a collection is the second of our loop patterns. Its general form is

```
// Loop pattern - enumerate
Enumeration  enum  =  get an Enumeration reference from
                          the collection
while  (enum.hasMoreElements())  {
    String  s  =  (String)enum.nextElement();  ◄—  Extracts
                                                    elements

    process the element
}
```

EXERCISES

1. Write code to read a series of `Name` objects into a `Vector` and then enumerate through the `Vector`, printing out the values.

2. Add a `read` method to the `Time` class of Section 6.6. Use it to read a series of `Time` objects into a `Vector`, then enumerate through the `Vector` printing them out.

3. Can we add an `int` value to a `Vector`? What about `double`? •

8.9 Revisiting the `SongLibrary` Class

The point of this example is to use a `Vector`. It is also an example of software refinement—providing a more efficient implementation.

8.9.1 A Better Implementation

As our first application of `Vector`, let's return to the example that led us to collections: the `SongLibrary` class. Recall that rather than having the `lookUp` method read through (i.e., traverse) the file each time, we instead wish to read the file once and maintain it in memory as a collection. If you go back and examine our original development of `SongLibrary`, you'll see that this change becomes relevant only when we reach the defining the instance variables step. Prior to that step, we were defining the behavior and interface to the outside world. These are not and must not be affected by our proposed change. It is the instance variables, however, that must change, as we shall now see.

8.9.2 Defining the Instance Variables

We originally introduced a `String` instance variable that contained the name of the disk file. This was necessary because each time `lookUp` was invoked, we had to create the `BufferedReader` (for subsequent reading) from that name. This is no longer necessary. We will be reading the input file once and after that we no longer need to know the name of the file. We do, however, need an instance variable to maintain the collection. We use a `Vector` and name the variable `songColl`:

```
class  SongLibrary  {
    public SongLibrary(String   songFileName)   {...}
    public void  lookUp(String   artist)   {...}
    //   Instance variables
    private Vector   songColl;
}
```

8.9.3 Implementing the Methods

Our constructor will now be responsible for reading the input file into `songColl`. Notice that this constructor does more than a simple assignment of arguments to constructors—as our classes become more sophisticated, this will occur more frequently.

```
public SongLibrary(String   songFileName) throws Exception {
    songColl   =  new  Vector();
    BufferedReader br =
            new BufferedReader(
                new InputStreamReader(
                    new FileInputStream(songFileName)));
    Song   song  =  Song.read(br);
    while  (song  !=  null)  {  ◀——— read/process loop pattern
        songColl.addElement(song);
        song  =  Song.read(br);
    }
}
```

Once the collection has been created and read, `lookUp` needs only to traverse the collection in its artist search using the *enumerate loop pattern*:

```
public void  lookUp(String   artist)  {
    Enumeration  enum  =  songColl.elements();
    while  (enum.hasMoreElements())  {  ◀—— enumerate loop pattern
        Song  song  =  (Song)enum.nextElement();
        if  (artist.equals(song.getArtist()))
            System.out.println(song.getTitle());
    }
}
```

8.9.4   Discussion

Along with the efficiency gained by this reimplementation, the most important lesson of this example is that the user of the class sees absolutely no change in the class. The behavior is the same, and the interfaces (i.e., the arguments to the methods) are the same. No code changes are needed wherever the `SongLibrary` class is used when we go to this more efficient implementation.

Primitive Types and Collections; Revisiting the Wrapper Classes

Suppose we want to maintain a collection of some primitive data type, say `int`. Although a `Vector` might come to mind, we have to deal with one serious obstacle: A `Vector` accepts an object (`Object`) as its element type, while an `int` is a primitive data type, not an object.

To solve this problem, Java introduces a set of classes, known as *wrapper classes*. There is one per primitive data type: `Integer` corresponds to `int`, `Boolean` to `boolean`, and so on. These classes play two important roles. First, as discussed in Chapter 5, they provide a logical place to keep `static` methods related to the corresponding primitive data type. Thus, the method `parseInt` is logically located in the `Integer` class.

The second function of the wrapper class is to provide the ability to maintain collections of primitive data types such as `int` and `boolean`. For example, to maintain a `Vector` of integer values, we create instances of the `Integer` class to contain the various `int` values we wish to have in the collection. These instances are proper objects and can thus be added to a `Vector`. The basic mechanism is the same for all the wrapper classes. Here's how to do it for integers:

```
Vector  vi  =  new  Vector();
int  i;
i  =  1;
vi.addElement(new  Integer(i));        ◄——  wrap the int value
                                             within an Integer object.
```

```
i  =  2;
vi.addElement(new  Integer(i));
i  =  3;
vi.addElement(new  Integer(i));
Enumeration  e  =  vi.elements();
while  (e.hasMoreElements())  {
    Integer  integer  =  (Integer)e.nextElement();
    System.out.println(integer.intValue());
}
```

'unwrap' the Integer object, retrieving the int value.

The constructor of the `Integer` class accepts an `int` argument that corresponds to the integer value to be wrapped in the new object. The new object can then be added to the `Vector`. We can now enumerate through the `Vector`, retrieving the `Integer` objects and extracting the wrapped value using the `intValue` method of the `Integer` class.

Analogous methods in the `Boolean`, `Double`, `Float`, and `Long` wrapper classes provide a similar capability for wrapping `boolean` values.

8.10 An Example—Determining a Student's Relative Performance

In this section we have more examples of the read/process and enumerate loop patterns.

As another example of using `Vector` and `Enumeration`, we implement one of the applications that motivated the use of collections.

8.10.1 Statement of the Problem

Suppose we have a roster file for a college course. Each student registered in the course has the following pair of lines in the file:

name
average

We want to determine which students are performing above and below the average of the class.

8.10.2 Determining the Primary Object

The nouns are *roster file, student, name,* and *average.* Name and average are subsidiary to student, which is in turn subsidiary to the roster file (the roster consists of a sequence of student data). We will therefore introduce a class, `StudentRoster`, which will be associated with the input file.

As we gain experience in designing and writing classes, we begin to see and exploit similarities when creating new classes. Looking back at `SongLibrary`, we see a similarity to our current application. In both cases, subsidiary objects (songs there, students here) are read from a file, after which operations are performed upon them. Associated with the file is an object (`SongLibrary` and `StudentRoster`, respectively) that will provide the necessary behavior.

8.10.3 Determination of the Behavior

We want to be able to evaluate the students in the roster. In addition we have a constructor, as follows:

- `StudentRoster` (constructor)
- `evaluate` (goes through the roster and evaluates the student)

Notice we haven't yet discussed when the class average will be calculated, when the student information will be read, or whether there will be a collection—none of that is relevant to the user of the class and does not belong in a discussion of the behavior. Rather, it will be introduced when we define instance variables and implement methods.

8.10.4 Defining the Interface

As usual, we write some typical code to help us determine the interface. We are taking our lead from the `SongLibrary` class—creating the roster entails associating it with the appropriate input file. After the object is created, we may invoke its `evaluate` method:

```
StudentRoster roster = new StudentRoster("CS1.f98");
roster.evaluate();
```

Our interface is as follows:

```
class StudentRoster {
    public StudentRoster(String rosterFileName) {...}
    public void evaluate() {...}
}
```

8.10.5 Defining the Instance Variables

In order to evaluate each student, we must first compute the class average. This average can be calculated in the constructor as soon as the student data are available. So that the average can be used later in the `evaluate` method, it is stored in an instance variable.

The information associated with each student is required twice: first to compute the class average in the constructor and then later for the assessment.

This student information must be maintained as an instance variable. Because this information consists of many objects, one per student, a collection is in order:

```
class  StudentRoster  {
    //   Methods
    ...
    //   Instance variables
    private Vector  studentColl;
    private int  classAverage;
}
```

8.10.6 Implementing the Methods

Using `SongLibrary` as a guide, we create the `studentColl` collection and load it up in the constructor. In the course of writing the loop that reads in the input, the need arises for a class, `Student`, that models a student:

```
public StudentRoster(String
                        rosterFileName) throws Exception {
    studentColl  =  new Vector();
    BufferedReader  br =
            new BufferedReader(
                new  InputStreamReader(
                    new FileInputStream(rosterFileName)));
    Student  student  =  Student.read(br);
    while  (student  !=  null)  {  ←——————— read/process loop pattern
        studentColl.addElement(student);
        Any other processing
        student  =  Student.read(br);
    }
}
```

Once again, we have encountered an application of the read/process pattern. This constructor, however, has more to do. It must calculate the class average. To do this, we maintain a total of the individual averages read as well as a count of the number of students. Thus, we initialize an `int` variable, `count`, to zero, reflecting that at the outset no students have been processed. Each time we successfully read a student, we increment this variable. Similarly, we initialize an `int` variable, `total`, to zero, reflecting that at the outset the sum of the averages of the students read is zero—because no students have yet been read. Each time we successfully read a student, we add the student's average to this variable. Once the input has been completely read, we can compute the class average by dividing `total` by `count`. Here is the full constructor:

```
StudentRoster(String
                rosterFileName) throws Exception {   A second look
    studentColl  =  new Vector();
    BufferedReader  br =
            new BufferedReader(
```

```
                     new  InputReaderStream(
                         new FileInputStream(rosterFileName)));
       int   total   =   0;   // accumulated total of averages
       int   count   =   0;   // count of students
       Student   student   =   Student.read(br);
       while  (student  !=  null)  {          read/process loop pattern
           total  +=  student.getAverage();
           count++;
           studentColl.addElement(student);
           student  =  Student.read(br);
       }
       classAverage  =  total  /  count;
   }
```

Besides fleshing out the implementation of `StudentRoster`, this additional code in the constructor provides us with more behavior for the `Student` class that we must write (the method `getAverage`).

We can now write `evaluate`, using the enumerate loop pattern. Processing each student consists of comparing the student's average against the class average and displaying the appropriate results:

```
public void  evaluate()  {
    Enumeration  enum  =  studentColl.elements();
    while  (enum.hasMoreElements())  {          ← enumerate loop pattern
        Student  student  =  (Student)enum.nextElement();
        System.out.print(student.getName());
        System.out.print(" is  performing  ");
        if  (student.getAverage()  >=  classAverage)
            System.out.println("above  average");
        else
            System.out.println("below  average");
    }
}
```

Again, `evaluate` has also introduced further required behavior for `Student` class (method `getName`).

8.10.7   Using the Class

We introduce another class, `Evaluator`, whose sole purpose is to contain a `main` method that will use our `StudentRoster` class. We could have just as easily placed the `main` method in the `StudentRoster` class itself:

```
class  Evaluator  {
    public  static  void main(String[]
                                args) throws Exception {
        StudentRoster  roster  =
                    new StudentRoster("CS1.f98");
```

```
            roster.evaluate();
            roster  =  new StudentRoster("CS2.f98");
            roster.evaluate();
        }
    }
```

We leave the design of the `Student` class as an exercise.

8.10.8 Discussion

Our applications are growing in complexity. As we progress, we should be collecting techniques and design ideas from the classes we create and using these ideas in future class designs. `SongLibrary` and `StudentRoster` were somewhat similar. Having implemented one, we were able to glean ideas from it for the second. In some sense, when we look at classes we have already implemented to get ideas for new classes, we are working with patterns, class patterns rather than the loop patterns we have been discussing.

When we first introduced collections, we presented the `StudentRoster` application as one that seemed to *require* a collection because of the dependent nature of the student objects. However, this is not strictly the case. In our implementation of the methods, we discussed the possibility of `evaluate` traversing the `songColl` collection twice: once to calculate the average and once to evaluate the individual students. Another possibility might have been to eliminate the collection entirely and have `evaluate` read the roster file twice: once to calculate the average and once to evaluate the students. Although this would be highly inefficient, it is no more so than our original `SongLibrary` implementation, which constantly read through the song file every time `lookUp` was invoked. Furthermore, it emphasizes a very interesting point: *files are in essence nothing more than collections sitting on disk.* The primary reason we use collections (when working with files) is for efficiency; it is just too expensive to keep reading in the same file over and over again.

EXERCISES

1. Complete the design and implementation of the `Student` class that is required by `StudentRoster`.

2. Can you think of any reason not to place a `main` method in `Student-Roster` that simply demonstrates the use of the class. (Hint: go back and look at Section 7.3 on test drivers.)

3. Write a program that reads in customer information from a file. The information for each customer is a name, address, and amount purchased over the last three months. Calculate the average purchasing amount for each customer. If particular customers have purchased more than the average,

send those customers letters thanking them for their patronage. Otherwise, send the customers letters notifying them that they will receive 5% off their next purchases (in an attempt to get them to buy more). •

8.11   A Set Class

Now that we have worked with one of Java's predefined collection types, `Vector`, let us create one of our own.

8.11.1   Statement of the Problem

Model the mathematical notion of a set.

8.11.2   Determining the Primary Object

There is no challenge here because we are given a specific class to design. We'll call it `Set`. It should be pointed out that `Set` is a collection class, because by its very nature it maintains a collection (set) of elements.

8.11.3   Determining the Behavior

The statement of the problem did not go into detail about what operations we want the `Set` to support. Left to our own devices, we decide upon the following typical methods:

- `Set` (constructor)
- `contains` (membership test)
- `isEmpty` (test for `null` set)
- `addElement` (adds an element to a `Set`)
- `copy` (makes a copy of a `Set`)
- `size` (number of elements)
- `elements` (returns an `Enumeration` for `Set` traversal)
- `union` (union of two `Set`s)
- `intersection` (intersection of two `Set`s)
- `print` (prints out the set)

A word about the `copy` method's function. Normally, when one writes

```
Set   s1,  s2;
s1  =  new  Set();
...
s2  =  s1;
```

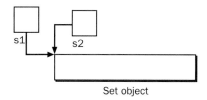

FIGURE 8.3   Two Set reference variables referencing the same Set object. When two Set reference variables reference the same Set object, changes made through one variable affects the other variable as well.

s2 is assigned a reference to the same object that s1 refers to. There is still only one Set object, but there are two references to it. Because there is only one object, any changes made to s1 will affect s2 as well (and vice versa). (See Figure 8.3.)

We want the copy method to create a *new* Set object and copy the elements of the old set into the new. (See Figure 8.4.)

By doing this, future changes to one Set will not affect the other.

Because Set is a collection class, we would like to be able to traverse the elements. We thus will have a method, elements, that returns an Enumeration object for the Set object.

To maintain uniformity with our other collection class, Vector, we employ similar methods names whenever appropriate; thus we use addElement rather than add, etc.

8.11.4   Defining the Interface

Typical usage code is as follows:

```
class  UseSet  {
    public  static  void  main(String[]  args)()  {
        Set  s1  =  new  Set();
        s1.addElement("A");
        s1.addElement("B");
        s1.addElement("C");
        s1.addElement("A");
```

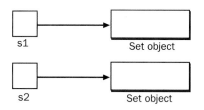

FIGURE 8.4   Two Set reference variables referencing different Set objects. When two Set reference variables reference different Set objects, changes made through one variable do not affect the other object.

```
                    System.out.println(s1.toString());
                    Set  s2  =  new  Set();
                    s2.addElement("B");
                    s2.addElement("C");
                    s2.addElement("D");
                    s2.addElement("D");
                    s2.print(System.out);
                    s1.union(s2).print(System.out);
                    s1.intersection(s2).print(System.out);
            }
    }
```

The above suggests the following interface:

```
    class  Set  {
                    public Set()  {...}
                    public boolean  contains(Object  value)  {...}
                    public boolean  isEmpty()  {...}
                    public void  addElement(Object  value)  {...}
                    public Set  copy()  {...}
                    public int  size()  {...}
                    public Enumeration  elements()  {...}
                    public Set  union(Set  s2)  {...}
                    public Set  intersection(Set  s2)  {...}
                    public void  print(PrintStream  ps)  {...}
            }
```

Object parameter. See text below.

Object parameter. See text below.

The arguments to contains and addElement are references to the generic Object class we spoke of earlier. This is in keeping with that discussion. Because we want to allow Sets whose elements are of an arbitrary type, all that we can say about an element to be inserted into or extracted from a Set is that it is an Object.

8.11.5 Defining the Instance Variables

A Set typically contains an arbitrary number of elements; a collection is thus called for:

```
    class  Set  {
            ...
            private Vector  theElements;
    }
```

Again, our choice for the collection is the Vector class because, so far, that is the only collection class that we've seen. However, once we have completed the definition of the Set class, this lack of choice will no longer exist.

In the future, when building an application that requires a collection, we will have to examine all available collection classes for appropriate behavior.

Recalling our discussion regarding the `nextElement` method of Enumeration, a `Vector` may contain any type object as its element. Because we will be using a `Vector` to store our `Set` elements, this will be true of `Set`s as well. We can thus have a `Set` of `String` objects, one of `Integer` (wrapper class) objects, and so on.

8.11.6 Implementing the Methods

Our `Set` constructor need only create the underlying `Vector` that will contain the elements:

```
public Set()  {
    theElements  =  new  Vector();
}
```

The `size` and `isEmpty` methods simply invoke the corresponding methods on the underlying `Vector` and return the resulting values:

```
public boolean  isEmpty()  {
    return  theElements.isEmpty();
}
public int  size()  {
    return  theElements.size();
}
```

All the above methods are saying is that a `Set` is empty when the underlying `Vector` is empty and that its size is that of the `Vector` as well.

Enumerating through the `Set` object entails enumerating through the underlying `Vector`; thus our `elements` method invokes the `elements` method of `Vector` and returns the resulting `Enumeration`:

```
public Enumeration  elements()  {
        return vector.elements();
}
```

The `copy` method enumerates through the `Vector`, adding each element to a new `Set` object.

```
public  Set  copy()  {
        Set  destSet  =  new  Set();
        Enumeration  enum  =  vector.elements();
        while  (enum.hasMoreElements())  ◄——— enumerate loop pattern
           destSet.addElement(enum.nextElement());
        return  destSet;
    }
```

The `size`, `isEmpty`, and `elements` methods of our `Set` object provide identical behavior to that of the `Vector` class. If the entire class, however, behaved identically to `Vector`, we wouldn't need a second class. The behavior of the `Set` class that is different from a mere `Vector` is exhibited by the `union` and `intersection` methods and its specific behavior for `addElement`.

Although the `addElement` method can also exploit the underlying `Vector`'s `addElement` method, it does so only if the `Set` does not already contain the element to be inserted. We use the yet-to-be-implemented `contains` method to accomplish this (the implementation of `contains` requires some explanation, so we'll leave it for last—for the moment we know how it's supposed to behave):

```
public void  addElement(String  s)  {
        if  (!contains(s))   ◀——— Same as this.contains(s)
            theElements.addElement(s);
}
```

To take the union of two `Set`s (the receiver and the argument), we copy one (resulting in a new `Set` object) and then enumerate through the second, adding its elements to the new copy. It makes no difference which `Set` we start with:

```
public  Set  union(Set  s)  {
    Set  unionSet  =  s.copy();
    Enumeration  enum  =  vector.elements();
    while  (enum.hasMoreElements())  ◀——— enumerate loop pattern
        unionSet.addElement(enum.nextElement());
    return  unionSet;
}
```

To perform the intersection, we create an (initially empty) `Set` object. We then enumerate through one of the two `Set`s (the receiver or argument, again it makes no difference which) and add it to the new `Set` only if the element is contained in the other `Set` as well:

```
public  Set  intersection(Set  s)  {
    Set  interSet  =  new  Set();
    Enumeration  enum  =  this.vector.elements();
    while  (enum.hasMoreElements())  {  ◀— enumerate loop pattern
        Object  elem  =  enum.nextElement();
        if  (s.contains(elem))
            interSet.addElement(elem);
    }
    return  interSet;
}
```

The assignment of the extracted object to the variable, `elem`, is necessary because we need to refer to it twice: once to test it for membership in the second Set and once to insert it into the new Set. All we know about the object being extracted is that it is an Object. Furthermore, all the addElement method is interested in about its argument is that it also is an Object. In this case we therefore do not require any casting to a particular type—it can remain an Object.

Our Set object contains an object if it is an element of the underlying Vector. To determine this, we enumerate through the Vector, looking for the element. However, as we have just said, all we know about the objects we extract from the Vector during the traversal is that they are of class Object. How can we perform a comparison if we don't know the exact class of the object and thus do not know the name of its comparison method?

The solution to this problem lies in the methods of the Object class. Recall that this class represents *all* object types. The designers of this class (that is, the designers of Java itself) provided it with a general equals method for the comparison of objects. Any two objects can be compared for equality using this method. Individual classes, such as String, Integer, and so on, can provide their own version of equals, which replaces the general one from class Object and which takes into consideration the nature of the specific object. For our purposes, all that is important is that there is *some* equals method defined for every object:

```
public  boolean  contains(Object  o)  {
    Enumeration  enum  =  vector.elements();
    while  (enum.hasMoreElements())  {  ◄─  enumerate loop pattern
        Object  elem  =  enum.nextElement();
        if  (elem.equals(o))
            return  true;
    }
    return  false;
}
```

In general, the equals method from the Object class does not perform satisfactorily. This does not present a problem if we limit ourselves to elements of predefined classes, such as String or Integer, because their individual equals methods do a proper comparison. However, this will not be true of classes that we define unless we provide a properly defined equals method. We discuss how to do this in the Java Interlude immediately following the example.

Printing a Set entails traversing the Set and printing the individual elements that are retrieved. Here we have a similar problem to that encountered when implementing contains. All we know about the objects we extract from the Vector during the traversal is that they are of class Object. How can we print such an object comparison, if we don't know the exact class of the object and thus do not know the name of its print method (or even if it has a print method at all)?

Again, the solution is that `Object` provides a general method, `toString`, for all objects. This method is much more general than printing in that it produces a `String` object from the object. This `String` can then be printed if we wish, or it can be manipulated like any other `String` object. This method allows us to print out the contents of the `Set`:

```
public void print(PrintStream ps) {
    Enumeration enum = vector.elements();
    while (enum.hasMoreElements()) {   ◄─ enumerate loop pattern
        ps.print(enum.nextElement().toString());
        ps.print(" ");
    }
}
```

8.11.7 The Final Class Definition

Here is complete implementation of our `Set` class.

```
import java.io.*;
import java.util.*;
class Set {
    public Set() {
        vector = new Vector();
    }
    public boolean isEmpty() {
        return vector.isEmpty();
    }
    public int size() {
        return vector.size();
    }
    public boolean contains(Object o) {
        Enumeration enum = vector.elements();
        while (enum.hasMoreElements()) {
            Object elem = enum.nextElement();
            if (elem.equals(o))
                return true;
        }
        return false;
    }
    public void addElement(Object o) {
        if (!contains(o))
            vector.addElement(o);
    }
    public Object copy() {
        Set destSet = new Set();
        Enumeration enum = vector.elements();
        while (enum.hasMoreElements())
            destSet.addElement(enum.nextElement());
        return destSet;
    }
```

```
public  Set  union(Set  s)  {
    Set  unionSet  =  s.copy();
    Enumeration  enum  =  vector.elements();
    while  (enum.hasMoreElements())
        unionSet.addElement(enum.nextElement());
    return  unionSet;
}
public  Set  intersection(Set  s)  {
    Set  interSet  =  new  Set();
    Enumeration  enum  =  this.vector.elements();
    while  (enum.hasMoreElements())  {
        Object  elem  =  enum.nextElement();
        if  (s.contains(elem))
            interSet.addElement(elem);
    }
    return  interSet;
}
Enumeration  elements()  {
        return  vector.elements();
}
public  void  print(PrintStream  ps)  {
    Enumeration  enum  =  vector.elements();
    while  (enum.hasMoreElements())  {
        ps.print(enum.nextElement().toString());
        ps.print("  ");
    }
}
private Vector  vector;
}
```

8.11.8   Using the Class

We introduce a class `useSet` whose `main` method contains code that uses our `Set` class:

```
class  UseSet  {
    public  static  void  main(String  []  args)()  {
        Set  s1  =  new  Set();
        s1.addElement("A");
        s1.addElement("B");
        s1.addElement("C");
        s1.addElement("A");
        System.out.println(s1.toString());
        Set  s2  =  new  Set();
        s2.addElement("B");
        s2.addElement("C");
        s2.addElement("D");
        s2.addElement("D");
```

```
            s2.print(System.out);
            s1.union(s2).print(System.out);
            s1.intersection(s2).print(System.out);
        }
    }
```

Because we are using `String` elements here, everything will be fine. The exercises discuss the use of other element types.

EXERCISES

1. Write a version of the `UseSet` class that uses integers as the element type. Don't forget that you need to use the `Integer` wrapper class.

2. Try writing a version of the `UseSet` class that uses one of the classes you have defined. In particular, see what happens when you try to insert duplicate elements into the `Set`.

Class `Object` Methods

Since *all* objects are considered as instances of class `Object`, any methods defined for that class must be universally applicable. In particular, we wish to examine two of these `Object` class methods: `equals` and `toString`.

The purpose of the `toString` method is to create a `String` representation of the object for which this method is invoked. Invoking `toString` on an `Integer` object that contains the integer value `275` thus produces the `String "275"`. Invoking `toString` on a `String` object merely produces the same object.

Because the `toString` method provided by the `Object` class knows nothing about the actual class of the object, it produces a `String` with minimal information—essentially the name of the object's actual class. For example, suppose we have the following (relatively useless) class:

```
class  Test  {
    public Test()  {    This class has no behavior or state
    }
}
```

The result of executing `toString` on a `Test` object

```
Test  t;
String  s  =  t.toString();
```

causes the `Object` class `toString` method to be invoked, producing a `String` of the form

```
Test@15368
```

(The `@15368` could be any number; it is tied to the particular object and is meaningless to us.)

If we want `toString` to produce a `String` that is customized to our `Test` class, we have to implement such a method in the class itself. To do this *we have to exactly match the signature of the `toString` as implemented in class `Object`.* This signature can be seen in the prototype

```
public String  toString();
```
The prototype of the toString method as specified in class Object

By adding this method to our class, we are indicating that an invocation of `toString` upon a `Test` object should invoke the version in `Test`, not the one in the `Object` class. This is known as *overloading*, and we will see a lot more of this in later chapters.

```
class  Test  {
    public Test()  {
    }
    public  String  toString()  {
        return  "I  am  a  Test  object";
    }
}
```

Invoking `toString` upon a `Test` object now produces the `String` `"I am a Test object"`. This is not much better, but the class is a trivial one. Let us write a `toString` method for our `Name` class of Chapter 2. We (somewhat arbitrarily) decide that `toString` for `Name` objects should return the title followed by the first name followed by the last name, separated by spaces:

```
class  Name  {
    ...
    public String  toString()  {
        String  result  =  this.title;
        result += " " + firstName + lastName;
        return  result;
    }
    ...
}
```

Now any user of the class who wants to get a custom `String` representation of a `Name` (say, for debugging purposes) can do so by invoking `toString`.

We can also create a `toString` method for our `Set` class. One way of doing this is to enumerate through the `Set`, invoking `toString` on the retrieved objects and concatenating these `Strings` as we go, enclosing the whole thing in a pair of braces:

```
class  Set  {
    ...
    public String  toString()  {
        String  result  =  "{";
        Enumeration  e  =  elements();
        while  (e.hasMoreElements())  {    ◀──── enumerate loop pattern
            result += e.nextElement().toString();
            result += " ";
        }
        result += "}";
        return  result;
    }
}
```

We could alternatively simply invoke the `toString` method of the `Vector` class on the `Set`'s vector instance variable:

```
class  Set  {
    ...
    public String  toString()  {
        return  vector.toString;
    }
    ...
    //   Instance  variable
    private Vector  vector;
}
```

This does, however, produce a `String` enclosed in brackets rather than braces, because the designers of the `Vector` class decided to use those delimiters.

The second `Object` class method of interest is `equals`. The intent of this method is to allow the comparison of two objects for equality. As we saw with `Set`, this function is particularly useful when searching for a particular element of a collection. The signature of this method can be seen in the prototype

The prototype of the equals method as specified in class Object ──▶ `public boolean  equals(Object  o)`

Because this method is defined in class `Object`, all we can say is that we are comparing two objects—the receiver and the argument—and thus the `Object` type for the parameter. Lacking any detailed information regarding the actual class of the two objects, the `Object` class `equals` method merely checks to see if the receiver and argument reference the same exact object. Suppose we have the following two objects of our `Name` class:

```
Name  n1  =  new  Name("John",  "Smith");
Name  n2  =  n1;
```

The invocation

```
n1.equals(n2)
```

results in a true because n1 and n2 reference the exact same object. However, given the two Name objects

```
Name  n1  =  new  Name("John",  "Smith");
Name  n2  =  new  Name("John",  "Smith");
```

the invocation

```
n1.equals(n2)
```

results in false because n1 and n2 refer to different objects. The fact that they contain the same information and would thus be equal from the perspective of the Name class does not matter.

As with toString, if we want to have a customized version of equals, one that works with our understanding of what it means for two Name objects to be equal, we must supply our own version in the Name class itself. The only problem is that the signature must exactly match the one in the Object class that accepts an Object argument. We resolve this by taking the argument and casting it to a Name object. The receiver *is* a Name object (the method is defined in the Name class; thus the receiver must be a Name). We can then access the instance variables to perform our Name-specific equality test:

```
class  Name  {
    ...
    public boolean  equals(Object  o)  {
        Name  n  =  (Name)o;
        return  this.first.equals(n.first)  &&
                this.last.equals(n.last)  &&
                this.title.equals(n.title);
    }
    ...
}
```

SUMMARY

The repetition of a series of statements is one of the most powerful programming constructs. Once a task has been defined for a single object, it may be repeated for hundreds, thousands, or even millions of objects. A loop is a language construct that supports such repetition. It consists of a body—the statements to be repeated—and a termination condition.

One application for a loop is to read in a series of objects belonging to the same class or primitive data type and process them individually. Once an object has been processed, it is no longer needed. We say such objects are independent of each other. Though the exact processing or method of input may vary depending on the nature of the object, the basic structure of the loop in all such cases is the same, and to emphasize this similarity, we introduce the concept of a loop pattern. Such patterns give the programmer a starting point for designing simple loops. The basic structure is provided by the pattern; the programmer must provide the read and processing logic to complete the loop.

Often we must maintain multiple objects, as for example, when we wish to read in a list of numbers and print it in reverse. In this case, we cannot discard each object as it is read in. Since there is an arbitrary number of such objects to be processed, declaring individual variables for each object is impossible. A collection is an object that models a number of related objects. The simplest collection class in Java is the `Vector`. Objects may be added to the `Vector` object using the `addElement` method.

The objects of a `Vector` may be processed by enumerating through them using an object of type `Enumeration`. This object is obtained by invoking the `elements` method of the `Vector` class. The next item in the vector may be retrieved using the `nextElement` method of the `Enumeration` class. The `hasMoreElements` method, also belonging to class `Enumeration`, may be used to determine when there are no more objects left to process.

In order to allow primitive data types to be added to a `Vector` that requires its elements be objects, Java provides wrapper classes `Integer`, `Long`, `Double`, `Byte`, `Short`, `Float`, and `Boolean` for each of the primitive types.

A `Set` class that models the behavior of a mathematical set is developed as an example of an additional collection class.

STUDY AID: TERMINOLOGY REVIEW

collection   A class or language construct that manages one or more objects.

elements   The individual objects contained within a collection.

enumerate   List or go through all members of a collection.

enumeration   A particular class in Java.utils that facilitates enumerating the elements of a collection.

loop   A language construct that repeatedly executes a section of code.

loop pattern   The code structure of a loop that is frequently used.

vector   A particular collection class in Java.utils.

while statement   A particular loop construct in the Java language.

QUESTIONS FOR REVIEW

1. How does a `while` statement work?

2. Why are programs that contain loops difficult to test thoroughly?

3. When is a collection necessary?

4. What is the read/process loop pattern?

FURTHER EXERCISES

1. Add the method `complement(Set  s1,  Set  s2)` to the `Set` class. The complement of two sets is a new set consisting of all elements in the first set but not in the second.

2. Add the method `symmetricComplement(Set  s1,  Set  s2)` to the `Set` class. The symmetric complement of two sets is a new set consisting of all elements in one but not both of the input sets.

3. Create a test driver for the `Set` class. Be sure to address each of the points presented in Section 7.5.

GUI *supplement*

`List, Checkbox,` **and** `CheckboxGroup`

For our GUI example, we write an applet that allows us to play with the `Set` class that we just developed. Our applet will allow us to

- Select which of two sets we wish to modify
- Add elements to a set
- Examine the union or intersection of the two sets
- Clear a set

This will give us a chance to work with some of other user-interface components provided by the AWT (abstract window toolkit). Our interface design is shown in Figure 8.5.

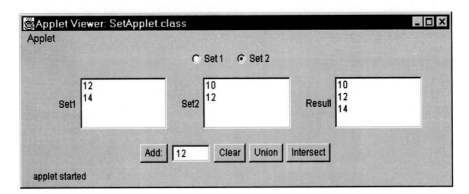

FIGURE 8.5 **An applet that allows us to manipulate `Set` objects.**

Some New GUI Components In addition to the `Buttons`, `Labels`, and `Text-Fields` that we've already seen, we have two new components: `List` and `Checkbox`. A `List` provides for the display of a number of elements—if there are too many to fit within the box proper, a scroll bar is added. Elements may be added to and removed from the `List`. An entry in the `List` may also be selected, but we will not be using that facility here. Our present use of the `List` will be limited to the display of multiple values—the elements of our sets.

The second component is a pair of `Checkbox` components. A `Checkbox` can either be *selected*, in which case a check appears in the box, or *unselected*, and the box remains empty. Because the `Checkbox` can be in one of only two states; *selected* or *unselected*, its state is represented by a `boolean` value: `true` for selected; `false` otherwise.

When a `Checkbox` is selected, an `ItemEvent` is generated. Processing these events is similar to `ActionEvent` handling. An object can act as an `ItemListener` by announcing that fact in the class heading and providing a method called `itemStateChanged`:

```
class SetApplet ... implements ItemListener {
    ...
    public void itemStateChanged(ItemEvent ie) {
        ...
    }
    ...
}
```

The listener must also register itself as such with the source component, in our case the two `Checkbox`es.

An object may act as listener to more than one event type; in fact our applet is going to do exactly that—it will act as an `ActionListener` for handling the `Button`-generated events and an `ItemListener` for handling the `Checkbox`-generated events.

In our example, the two `Checkbox`es indicate which of the two sets we wish to either add an element to or clear. We thus wish exactly one of them to be selected at any point; that is, if we select one, the other should become unselected. (The traditional analogy for this is the set of station buttons on an old-fashioned radio. Only one can be pushed in at a time.) `Checkbox`es that cooperate in this manner are said to be *mutually exclusive*.

This is not the default behavior of `Checkbox`es, they normally act independently of each other, and several of them may be selected simultaneously. To have them act in a mutually exclusive manner, we can use a `CheckboxGroup`. The `CheckboxGroup` class is not a component; rather it represents a relationship among multiple `Checkbox` components, ensuring that *only one* is selected at a time. Methods of this class allow us to query or set the currently selected `Checkbox`.

The Design of Our Interface Our interface has several descriptive `Label`s: `"Result"`, `"Set 1"`, `"Set 2"`. Our two input sets and the set resulting from a union or intersection operation are displayed in `List` components adjacent to those labels. The pair of `Checkbox`es allows us to select which input set is to be the active one, that is, the one to be modified—either by the addition of an element or by being cleared. A `TextField` allows us to enter element values, and several buttons allow us to signal that we wish to add an element, clear a set, or perform a union or intersection.

To begin our implementation, let us set up the basic component structure of the applet. Recall that the components are usually created and inserted into the applet in the `init` method along with any other initialization required for the applet. We also introduce instance variables for the various components.

In addition to the components, we have to create a `CheckboxGroup`. The `setCheckboxGroup` method of the `Checkbox` class is then invoked with the new `CheckboxGroup` instance as an argument for each `Checkbox` that is to be a part of the group. We also have an instance variable for the `CheckboxGroup` object.

We must also set up an initial selection for the `CheckboxGroup`. We do this by invoking the `setSelectedObject` method of `CheckboxGroup`. This method accepts a `Checkbox` as its argument and sets it to be the current selection (deselecting any other).

Finally, we must create our two input `Set` objects, which are also declared as instance variables. Each of these `Set` objects will be associated with a `List` component—`set1` with `set1List` and `set2` with `set2List`. The contents of each set will be displayed in the corresponding list.

Here is our applet so far:

```
import  java.awt.*;
import  java.applet.*;
import  java.util.*;

public  class  SetApplet  extends  Applet
                          implements  ActionListener,
                                      ItemListener {

    public void init() {
        set1 = new Set();
        set2 = new Set();

        // Components

        setLayout(new BorderLayout());

        // Checkboxes
        set1Selector = new Checkbox("Set 1");
        set1Selector.addItemListener(this);
        set2Selector = new Checkbox("Set 2");
        set2Selector.addItemListener(this);
        selectorGroup = new CheckboxGroup();
        set1Selector.setCheckboxGroup(selectorGroup);
        set2Selector.setCheckboxGroup(selectorGroup);
        Panel p = new Panel();
        p.add(set1Selector);
        p.add(set2Selector);
        add("North", p);

        // Lists
        set1List = new List();
        set1List.setBackground(Color.white);
        set2List = new List();
        set2List.setBackground(Color.white);
        resultList = new List();
        resultList.setBackground(Color.white);
        p = new Panel();
        p.add(new Label("Set1"));
        p.add(set1List);
        p.add(new Label("Set2"));
        p.add(set2List);
        p.add(new Label("Result"));
        p.add(resultList);
        add("Center", p);

        // Buttons
        add = new Button("Add:");
        add.addActionListener(this);
        value = new TextField(5);
```

```
            clear = new Button("Clear");
            clear.addActionListener(this);
            union = new Button("Union");
            union.addActionListener(this);
            intersect = new Button("Intersect");
            intersect.addActionListener(this);
            p = new Panel();
            p.add(add);
            p.add(value);
            p.add(clear);
            p.add(union);
            p.add(intersect);
            add("South", p);
            // Set active Checkbox
            selectorGroup.setSelectedCheckbox(set1Selector);
        }

        public void actionPerformed(ActionEvent ae) {
            Button-handling code goes here
        }

        public void itemStateChanged(ItemEvent ie) {
            Checkbox-handling code goes here
        }

        private Button add, union, intersect, clear;
        private List set1List, set2List, activeList,
                     resultList;
        private Checkbox set1Selector, set2Selector;
        private CheckboxGroup selectorGroup;
        private TextField value;
        private Set set1, set2, activeSet;
    }
```

The above layout results in the interface displayed at the beginning of the section. There are several other equally reasonable interface designs—we chose this one in order to present the Checkbox and List components.

The Event-Handling Logic Let us now handle the applet's events. Our applet is acting as both an ActionListener, handling ActionEvents, and an ItemListener, handling ItemEvents. Let us analyze the actions for each event that can occur.

Checkbox **Event Logic** When the user selects a Checkbox, the corresponding Set object (set1 or set2) becomes the active one. That is, subsequent adds or clears are performed upon that Set object (and displayed in the corresponding List component). We introduce a pair of instance variables, activeSet and activeList, which will always contain references to the currently active `Set` object (a reference to either `set1` or `set2`) and the corresponding `List` object (`set1List` or `set2List`). Selecting the `set1Selector` or `set2Selector` `Checkbox` causes the corresponding set/list pair to be assigned to these instance variables.

We use a helper method, `setActive`, to determine which of the boxes was selected and to set the instance variables:

```
private void setActive() {
    List newActiveList;
    if (selectorGroup.getSelectedCheckbox() ==
            set1Selector) {
        activeList = set1List;
        activeSet = set1;
    }
    else {
        activeList = set2List;
        activeSet = set2;
    }
}
```

The `getSelectedCheckbox` method of class `CheckboxGroup` returns the `Checkbox` component that is currently selected. Using that information, we then set the `activeList` and `activeSet` instance variables.

The code for `itemStateChanged` is very simple. The only components that can generate an event that will cause this method to be invoked are the two `Checkbox`es. In both cases, we wish to invoke `setActive`:

```
// Handles item events generated by the Checkboxes
public void itemStateChanged(ItemEvent ie) {
    setActive();
}
```

We must also go back to the `init` method and invoke `setActive` when we set the initial selection of the `CheckboxGroup`. We arbitrarily choose `set1` to be the initially active set.

Another Way to Distinguish among Multiple Event Sources   Our applet, like the `CalculatorApplet` of Chapter 6, contains several buttons. In our calculator we used the `getActionCommand` method to distinguish between the various event sources (buttons) that generated events that invoked `action-Performed`. Although this was perfectly reasonable in that situation where the button texts were simple digits and arithmetic operators, we prefer not to use the button text to identify our buttons in this example. This is because it is quite easy to make a mistake when performing the comparisons. For example, although the test

```
String s = ae.getActionCommand();
if (s.equals("ADD"))
    handle add element to set logic
```

may look correct, the condition will *never* be true because the actual text of the button is Add, not ADD. The potential for mistakes in upper- and lowercase, misspellings, and abbreviations indicates that getActionCommand should be used prudently.

Instead, we turn to the getSource method, which is provided by all event classes. This method returns the component that generated the event—the event source. Given our instance variable, add, which refers to the Add button, we can write:

```
if (ae.getSource() == add)
    handle add element to set logic
```

Now we no longer have to worry about spelling—if we make a mistake in case, the compiler will generate an *undefined variable* error.

Button **Click Logic**   Clicking the Add button causes the value currently in the TextField to be added to the currently active Set and List. Just to make things interesting, our applet works with sets of integers so that we get some practice with the Integer wrapper class. We introduce a helper method, addElement, to add the element to our active set and list. The action code for the Add button then becomes

```
else  if  (ae.getSource()  ==  add)  {
    addElement();
    repaint();
}
```

The addElement method retrieves the value of the text field and converts it to an int, from which it creates an Integer object, which is then added to the active set. We also add the element to the active List component. We do this by passing the element, converted to a String, to the addItem method of the List class:

```
private  void  addElement()  {
    int  i  =  Integer.parseInt(value.getText());
    activeSet.addElement(new  Integer(i));
    activeList.addItem(Integer.toString(i));
}
```

Clicking the Clear button causes the active set to be emptied. The active List component is cleared by invoking its removal method.

```
else if (ae.getSource() == clear) {
    activeSet.removeAllElements();
    activeList.removeAll();
}
```

The Union and Intersection buttons perform the corresponding operations upon set1 and set2, and the resulting set is sent to a helper method, `loadResult`, which moves it into the result `List` component:

```
else  if  (event.target  ==  union)
    loadResult(set1.union(set2));
else  if  (event.target  ==  intersect)
    loadResult(set1.intersection(set2));
```

The `loadResult` method clears out `resultList` and then adds the elements of the `Set` argument to it, using an application of the *enumerate* loop pattern.

```
private void loadResult(Set resultSet) {
    resultList.removeAll();
    Enumeration e = resultSet.elements();
    while (e.hasMoreElements())   ◀──── enumerate loop pattern
        resultList.addItem(e.nextElement().toString());
    repaint();
}
```

The Complete Applet The complete implementation of our set manipulation applet is as follows:

```
import java.awt.*;
import java.awt.event.*;
import java.applet.*;
import java.util.*;
public class SetApplet extends Applet
                    implements ActionListener,
                               ItemListener {

    public void init() {
        set1 = new Set();
        set2 = new Set();

        // Components

        setLayout(new BorderLayout());
        // Checkboxes
        set1Selector = new Checkbox("Set 1");
        set1Selector.addItemListener(this);
        set2Selector = new Checkbox("Set 2");
        set2Selector.addItemListener(this);
        selectorGroup = new CheckboxGroup();
        set1Selector.setCheckboxGroup(selectorGroup);
        set2Selector.setCheckboxGroup(selectorGroup);
        Panel p = new Panel();
        p.add(set1Selector);
        p.add(set2Selector);
        add("North", p);
        // Lists
        set1List = new List();
```

```
          set1List.setBackground(Color.white);
          set2List = new List();
          set2List.setBackground(Color.white);
          resultList = new List();
          resultList.setBackground(Color.white);
          p = new Panel();
          p.add(new Label("Set1"));
          p.add(set1List);
          p.add(new Label("Set2"));
          p.add(set2List);
          p.add(new Label("Result"));
          p.add(resultList);
          add("Center", p);
          // Buttons
          add = new Button("Add:");
          add.addActionListener(this);
          value = new TextField(5);
          clear = new Button("Clear");
          clear.addActionListener(this);
          union = new Button("Union");
          union.addActionListener(this);
          intersect = new Button("Intersect");
          intersect.addActionListener(this);
          p = new Panel();
          p.add(add);
          p.add(value);
          p.add(clear);
          p.add(union);
          p.add(intersect);
          add("South", p);
          // Set active Checkbox
          selectorGroup.setSelectedCheckbox(set1Selector);
          setActive();
     }


     // Handles action events generated by the buttons
        public void actionPerformed(ActionEvent ae) {
            if (ae.getSource() == add) {
               addElement();
               repaint();
            }
            else if (ae.getSource() == union)
               loadResult(set1.union(set2));
            else if (ae.getSource() == intersect)
               loadResult(set1.intersection(set2));
            else if (ae.getSource() == clear) {
               activeSet.removeAllElements();
               activeList.removeAll();
            }
```

```java
        }
    // Handles item events generated by the Checkboxes
    public void itemStateChanged(ItemEvent ie) {
            setActive();
    }
    private void addElement() {
        int i = Integer.parseInt(value.getText());
        activeSet.addElement(new Integer(i));
        activeList.addItem(Integer.toString(i));
    }
    private void setActive() {
        List newActiveList;
        if (selectorGroup.getSelectedCheckbox() ==
                        set1Selector) {
            activeList = set1List;
            activeSet = set1;
        }
        else {
            activeList = set2List;
            activeSet = set2;
        }
    }
    private void loadResult(Set resultSet) {
        resultList.removeAll();
        Enumeration e = resultSet.elements();
        while (e.hasMoreElements())
            resultList.addItem(e.nextElement().toString());
        repaint();
    }
    // Instance Variables
    private Button add, union, intersect, clear;
    private List set1List, set2List, activeList,
                resultList;
    private Checkbox set1Selector, set2Selector;
    private CheckboxGroup selectorGroup;
    private TextField value;
    private Set set1, set2, activeSet;
}
```

chapter 9

Iteration

9.1   Introduction

In Chapter 8 we introduced the `while` statement, which allowed us to implement methods that use **iteration.** Iteration is the repeated, controlled execution of a piece of program text. In that chapter, we provided the following two loop patterns:

- Read/process: constructing and processing objects read from input
- Enumerate: iterating through a collection, that is, applying a piece of code to every object in the collection

Although these patterns are very common, other situations arise that require different patterns or significant variations of the above. However, it is neither possible nor desirable to memorize all possible loop, or iteration, patterns. Therefore, we now introduce an approach that can be fruitfully employed to construct `while` statements when one doesn't know of or can't recall the appropriate loop pattern. This approach for writing loops not only works well for the simple loops that appear in this chapter but for the more complex ones that appear later in this text.

9.2 Designing Loops

Suppose we were defining a class that had several methods that needed to calculate the value of one nonnegative integer raised to the power of another:

$$x^y$$

For example, 5^7 or 23^4. (We exclude 0^0 because that is undefined.) As we have done since Chapter 4, we implement a helper method:

```
private int power(int x, int y) { // y>=0 returns x**y.
    ...
}
```

(The notation x**y is widely used to represent x^y when superscripts are not available.) This method could be invoked by other methods to compute various exponentiations as illustrated by the following code:

```
int     a,b,w,z;
...
z = power(5,7);
w = power(a,b+2);
```

One way to begin to implement the power method, that is, write its body, is to view exponentiation as repeated multiplication and to use *iteration* to explicitly repeat, in a controlled way, code that carries out multiplication.

Our approach to developing this iteration involves several stages. Each stage will be described in general terms and then applied to the problem at hand, exponentiation.

9.2.1 Informal Procedure

We begin by asking ourselves how we, as humans, could solve the problem. At this point we don't worry about specific coding issues such as variables, loops, and assignments. *We are working with our intuition, not with code.*

How do we compute x^y by hand? We recognize that exponentiation is repeated multiplication, that is,

$$x^y == 1*x*x*x*\cdots*x \quad \text{1 multiplied by } x, y \text{ times}$$

The use of 1 in the definition of exponentiation allows us to cover the case when y==0: 1 is multiplied by x *no* times and so x^0==1. An informal procedure immediately presents itself: Start with 1 and multiply it by *x*, then multiply the result by *x*, and continue multiplying subsequent results by *x* until *y* multiplications have been performed. The *last* result is the value to return. The remaining steps of our approach will transform this intuition into working code.

9.2.2 Choosing and Defining Variables

We identify the information items that our informal procedure requires us to keep track of. These items become our variables. We choose names for them, write declarations for them, and most important, we write down precise definitions of their meanings as comments.

In this case, we need to keep track of the *result of the most recent multiplication* (note that we do not need remember all the multiplication results, just the most recent one). We also need to keep track of *the number of multiplications that we have done so far*. So, we need two variables that we call `result` and `count`:

```
int count,   // count==the number of multiplications done.
    result; // result==1*x*x*···*x (count times), that is, result==x**count.
```

Notice that our comments use equality notation (`==`). This style of comment for numerical variables, which means this variable is equal to ..., tends to encourage the kind of precision we seek in our definitions. Furthermore, as you will see, we will make good use of this form of comment to guide our code development.

At this point our comments are not statements of fact but statements of *intent*. So far, both `count` and `result` remain uninitialized, so it is not yet true that $result==x^{count}$. We have to write code that makes this intention a reality.

9.2.3 Skeleton of the Code

We write a skeleton of the code of the method, including the method header, the declarations, and a skeleton of a `while` statement.

Here we write the following code:

```
private int power(int x, int y) {
    int count, // count==the number of multiplications done.
        result; // result==1*x*x*...*x (count times), that is,
                //   result==x**count.
    ...
    while (condition)
        body
    ...
}
```

9.2.4 The `while` Condition

Next comes the crucial question: What do we want to be the case *after* the `while` statement terminates? To answer this question, we must express what it means for our task to be completed in terms of the values of our variables and any input/output that we are doing.

In the case of `power`, our informal procedure calls on us to carry out `y` multiplications. According to our variable definitions (see the declarations), our intention is for `count` to equal the number of multiplications done at any given point. So, it seems that we are be finished when `count` equals `y`.

Let's verify that we are really finished when `count==y`. According to the definition for `result` in the comment, `result==x`^{count}. If and when `count` equals `y`, `result==x`^{y}. This value is exactly what we want to return. So, after the `while` statement, we want `count` to equal `y`. To remind ourselves of this as we write our code, we add a comment to that effect immediately after the `while` statement:

```
private int power(int x, int y) {
        int count, // count==the number of multiplications done.
           result; // result==1*x*x*...*x (count times), that is,
                   //    result==x**count.
        ...
        while (condition)
            body
        // At this point, after the loop terminates, count==y.
        ...
}
```

The condition that controls the `while` statement's execution is called the `while` condition, or **loop condition.** The `while` statement terminates when its loop condition is false. So we can guarantee that a condition *X* will be true *after* the `while` statement by making the `while` loop condition the negation of condition *X*.

In our case, we want `count==y` to be true after the `while` statement. So our `while` condition becomes its negation: `count!=y`. This guarantees that when the `while` statement terminates, `count==y` and hence `result==x`^{y}. We can therefore return `result` immediately after the `while` statement. Our code now is as follows:

```
private int power(int x, int y) {
        int count, // count==the number of multiplications done.
           result; // result==1*x*x*...*x (count times), that is,
                   //    result==x**count.
        ...
        while (count!=y)
            body
        // count==y, result==x**y
        return result;
}
```

9.2.5 Initialization

When execution reaches the `while` statement, the variables that appear in its condition must have values—otherwise the condition will not be meaningful. Parameters receive values from arguments, but local variables must be initialized prior to the `while` statement.

In this case, we must assign `count` a value before the `while` statement. Your intuition might tell you that this value should be 1, or it might tell you 0. Actually, it is possible to do it either way, depending on what code we write later. But that best way of proceeding and the best way of making sure that the code we write now is consistent with the code we write later is to *consult our variable definitions.*

According to these, `count` == the number of multiplications done. Before the `while` statement, no multiplications have been performed. So the initial value of `count` should be 0. Our `power` method so far is

```
private int power(int x, int y) {
        int count, // count==the number of multiplications done.
            result; // result==1*x*x*···*x (count times), that is,
                    //     result==x**count.
        count = 0;
        while (count!=y)
            body
        // count==y, result==x**y
        return result;
}
```

9.2.6 Guaranteeing Termination

Now we turn to the body of the loop. A good way of getting started is to guarantee **loop termination,** that is, to make sure that the loop will *terminate* (we almost never want a loop to be *infinite*—never ending). A loop terminates when its condition is tested and is found to be `false`. So the loop body must contain some code that makes *progress toward termination*, that is, some code that guarantees that the loop condition will eventually become `false`.

In our case, the `while` statement will not terminate until `count` equals `y`. We need to write code in the loop that will eventually make `count` equal to `y`. Our informal procedure and our intuition tells us that we should increment `count` by 1 in the loop body. We can readily see that if we do that, `count` will eventually equal `y` (provided `y` is nonnegative, which is a requirement of the method). Our loop then is

```
while (count!=y) {
    rest of body
    count++;
}
// count==y, result==x**y
```

9.2.7 Completing the Loop Body

We complete the body of the `while` statement. We are guided both by our informal procedure and by the definitions of our variables. In particular, we take into account the effect that the code in the previous step (guaranteeing termination) might have on the equalities that appear in the definitions of the variables.

One of our variable definitions tells us that `count` should be the number of multiplications we have carried out. Thus, every time that we increment `count`, we should have done another multiplication by x in the loop body—this is certainly consistent with our informal procedure too.

Furthermore, the definition of `result` tells us that `result==x`^{count}. If we increment `count`, the equality is broken: The right side is too large by a factor of x. To restore this equality we multiply `result` by x so that `result` can "catch up." The following code completes our loop body:

```
result *= x;
count++;
```

9.2.8 Initialization (Again)

Variables must have values before they are used. Any variables that are used in the loop body must be given appropriate values prior to entering the loop. Guided by our variable definitions and our informal procedure, we write assignment statements needed to initialize variables referred to in the `while` statement body.

The variables used in the loop body here are `result`, x, and `count`. The latter has already been initialized, and x receives its value from the argument to the `power` method, so we have only to initialize `result`. What should its value be, before entering the loop?

To answer this question, we *turn again to the definition* of `result`: `result==x`^{count}. Prior to the loop, `count` is 0, so, according to this definition, prior to the loop `result==x`^{0}, or 1. So we initialize `result` to 1 before the loop, and our code is finished:

```
private int power(int x, int y) {
        int count,    // count==the number of multiplications done.
            result;  // result==1*x*x*···*x (count times), that is,
                     //      result==x**count.
        count = 0;
        result = 1;
        while (count!=y) {
            result *= x;
```

```
        count++;
    }
    // count==y, result==x**y
    return result;
}
```

9.2.9 Discussion

The advantage of this approach is that it allows a programmer to start with an intuitive and informal solution and work toward a complete solution in Java. Furthermore, the approach accommodates some gaps in one's intuition. For example, suppose our intuition had been less clear on the matter of incrementing count. How can we guarantee termination? We could consider different alternatives. For example, most naively we could propose to simply assign count=y. That guarantees that count==y eventually, but it disregards the requirement that count must equal the number of multiplications—how could we possibly do y multiplications at once? Other alternatives could also be ruled out: For example, if we increment count by 2 in the body, count+=2, we have to worry about y being odd and never reaching count==y. We therefore recognize incrementing by 1 as the only viable approach.

EXERCISES

1. Rework the example by modifying the definition of count so that it must be initialized to 1.

2. The condition for termination was count!=y. Compare this with the condition count<y. Is the result the same? Does this change our reasoning about the value of result after the loop terminates? •

9.3 Another Simple Example

Our approach involves the following eight steps:

* Informal procedure
* Choosing and defining variables
* The while sketch
* The while condition
* Initialization
* Guaranteeing termination
* Completing the loop body
* Initialization (again)

Of these eight, the first four should be undertaken in the order shown, but the remaining four can be done in any order that is convenient. Also, if we get stuck, we can always revisit an earlier step. The willingness to rethink is an important quality for programmers. In fact, even if we do not get stuck at any point, we should, when we are finished, go back to step 1 and try to improve the informal procedure in light of our experience developing the loop.

In this section and the exercises that follow, we look at a group of easy problems in order to further illustrate this approach and to make some broader points about computer science.

9.3.1   Multiplication

Suppose there were no multiplication operator. In that case, in order to implement classes such as `Employee` that require multiplication, we would write a helper method, `multiply`, whose arguments are two integers and whose return value is the integer product of its arguments:

```
private int multiply(int x, int y) { // y>=0, returns x*y.
    ...
}
```

To complete this method definition, we take the same approach that we used for exponentiation.

Informal Procedure   We start with the observation that multiplication is repeated addition, that is,

$x+y == 0+x+x+\cdots x$ x added to 0, y times

(The use of 0 in the definition of multiplication allows us to cover the case when $y==0$: x is added to *0 no* times, and so $x*0 == 0$.) So an informal procedure immediately presents itself: Start with zero and add x to it, then add x to the result, then add x to *that* result, and so on, until y additions have been performed. The *last* result is the value to return.

Choosing and Defining Variables   We need to keep track of the result of the most recent addition and the number of additions done so far. Therefore, we need two variables, which we call `result` and `count`:

```
int count,   // count==the number of additions done.
    result;  // result==0+x+x+···+x (count times), that is, result==x*count.
```

In this exercise, we are assuming that there is no `*` operator available. However, in a comment we can use any notation we choose; hence `*` is used in the definition of `result`.

Skeleton of the Code We write

```
private int multiply(int x, int y) {
        int count,  // count==the number of additions done.
            result;  // result==0+x+x+···+x (count times), that is,
                     //     result==x*count.
        ...
        while (condition)
            body
        ...
}
```

The while Condition Our informal procedure calls on us to carry out y additions. According to our variable definitions, it is our intention that count equal the number of additions done so far at any given point. Therefore, it seems that we are finished when count equals y.

Indeed, according to the definition for result in the comment, result==x*count. If and when count equals y, result==x*y. This value is exactly what we want to return. So we want

```
count==y
```

to be true immediately after the while statement. We note this with a comment immediately after the while statement:

```
private int multiply(int x, int y) {
        int count,  // count==the number of additions done.
            result;  // result==0+x+x+···+x (count times), that is,
                     //     result==x*count.
        ...
        while (condition)
            body
        // count==y
        ...
}
```

Our while condition then is count!=y. This will guarantee that when the while statement terminates, count==y and hence result==x*y. We can therefore return result immediately after the while statement. Our code now is

```
private int multiply(int x, int y) {
        int count,  // count==the number of additions done.
            result;  // result==0+x+x+...+x (count times), that is,
                     //     result==x*count.
        ...
        while (count!=y)
            body
```

```
    // count==y, result==x*y
    return result;
}
```

Initialization   According to our variable definitions, `count`== the number of additions done. Before the `while` statement, no additions have been performed. So the initial value of `count` should be `0`:

```
private int multiply(int x, int y) {
    int count,  // count==the number of additions done.
        result;  // result==0+x+x+···+x (count times), that is,
                 //     result==x*count.
    count = 0;
    ...
    while (count!=y)
        body
    // count==y, result==x*y
    return result;
}
```

Guaranteeing Termination   The `while` statement we have written will not terminate until `count` equals `y`. Following our informal procedure and our intuition, we increment `count` by `1` in the loop body. Doing this makes `count` eventually equal to `y`, provided `y` is nonnegative. If `y` is negative, the loop will not terminate. (Addressing this problem is left as an exercise.) Our loop then is

```
while (count!=y) {
    rest of body
    count++;
}
```

Completing the Loop Body   One of our variable definitions tells us that `count` should be the number of additions we have carried out. Thus, each time we increment `count`, we should do another addition of `x` in the loop body. Furthermore, the definition of `result` tells us that `result==x*count`. If we increment `count`, the equality is broken: The right side is too large by `x`. To restore this equality we add `x` to `result` so that `result` can "catch up." The following code completes our loop body:

```
result += x;
count++;
```

Initialization (Again)   The variables used in the loop body here are `result`, `x`, and `count`. The latter has already been initialized, and `x` receives its value from the argument to the `multiply` method, so we have only to initialize result. Its definition is `result==x*count`. Prior to the loop, `count` is 0; therefore, according to this definition, prior to the loop `result==0`. So we initialize `result` to 0 before the loop, and our code is finished:

```
private int multiply(int x, int y) {
        int count,   // count==the number of additions done.
            result;  // result==0+x+x+···+x (count times), that is,
                     //     result==x*count.
        count = 0;
        result = 0;
        while (count!=y) {
            result += x;
            count++;
        }
        // count==y, result==x*y
        return result;
    }
}
```

9.3.2 Discussion

In the exercises that follow, you are asked to apply the above approach to implement methods that add, subtract, and divide. The fact that one can do this demonstrates the power of iteration. All the operations of arithmetic can be implemented merely with increments and decrements of 1, provided iteration is available. The discovery, by logicians in the 1930s, that all computation ultimately requires only iteration and a tiny handful of elementary operations is one of the cornerstones of modern computer science.

EXERCISES

1. Correct the `multiply` method so that it correctly handles negative values in its second argument. (*Hint:* One approach might be to make part of the loop body conditional on the sign of the second argument.)

2. Implement an `add` method that adds two arbitrary integers using only increment and decrement.

3. Implement a `subtract` method that subtracts arbitrary integers using only increment and decrement.

4. Implement a `quotient` method that returns the quotient of two integers; the method may not use the divide (/) or percentage (%) operators.

5. Implement a `remainder` method that returns the remainder of dividing two integers.

6. Implement an integer log-base-2 method. The log (base 2) of an integer is the number of times the integer can be divided by 2 before the integer result becomes 1. For example, the integer log-base-2 of 6 is 2 because 6

can be divided by 2, yielding 3, which can be divided by 2, yielding 1 (integer division).

7. Extend the method of the previous exercise to any positive base. •

9.4 Revisiting the Loop Patterns of Chapter 8

In Chapter 8, we presented two loop patterns. In this section, we apply our systematic approach to derive them.

9.4.1 The Read/Process Pattern: Printing the Payroll

This pattern was introduced in the payroll printing code in Chapter 8. The problem was as follows: given the following input,

- Information that defines employee 1 (name, wage rate)
- Hours worked by employee 1
- Information that defines employee 2 (name, wage rate)
- Hours worked by employee 2
- and so on

print the calculated pay for each employee. Assume the availability of the `Employee` class (from Chapter 6) with methods `readIn`, `getName`, and `calcPay`.

Informal Procedure This task can be accomplished by repeatedly reading the data for the employee, reading the hours worked, computing the resulting pay, and printing it out until there are no more data left.

Choosing and Defining Variables We need two variables. One is a reference to the most recent `Employee` object returned by `Employee.readIn`, which we will use to read employee-defining data, and the other an `int`, the number of hours that correspond to the most recently read `Employee` object. We may call these variables `emp` and `hours`:

```
Employee emp;   // emp refers to the most recently read Employee object
                //    or is null.
int hours;      // hours==the number of hours worked by the most
                //    recently read employee.
```

Note that we have amended the defining comment for `emp` to reflect this new consideration. Revisiting earlier steps in light of further development is normal. It is essential to keep the comment that defines a variable's meaning precise.

Skeleton of the Code   We write

```
Employee     emp;  // emp refers to the most recently read Employee object
                   //    or is null.
int hours;         // hours== the number of hours worked by the most
                   //    recently read employee.

...
while (condition)
    body
...
```

The `while` Condition   Our informal procedure calls on us to continue reading information, processing it, and printing out results until there are no more data left to read. Accordingly, we want to write the following with confidence after our `while` statement:

```
//  No more data to read.
```

How can we express in Java code the condition "no more data to read"? The possibility that there are no more data was considered in the design of the `Employee` class in Chapter 6. When an attempt to read data and construct an `Employee` object fails because there are no more data, the `Employee.readIn` method returns `null`. Thus, `emp` will equal `null` when there are no more data and will not equal `null` when data are available to construct an `Employee` object. So, the above comment can be rewritten (in more Java-like terms) as

```
//  emp==null.
```

Accordingly, the `while` condition is the negation of this, and we now have

```
Employee     emp;  // emp refers to the most recently read Employee object
                   //    or is null.
int hours;         // hours== the number of hours worked by the most
                   //    recently read employee.

...
while (emp!=null)
    body
//  No more data to read, i.e., emp==null.
```

Initialization   Because `emp` is used in the loop condition, it must be initialized prior to the loop. In order for it to refer to the most recently read `Employee` object at that point, we initialize it from `Employee.readIn`:

```
Employee     emp;  // emp refers to the most recently read Employee object
                   //    or is null.
int hours;         // hours== the number of hours worked by the most
                   //    recently read employee.
emp = Employee.readIn(br);
```

```
while (emp!=null)
    body
// No more data to read, i.e., emp==null.
```

Guaranteeing Termination   The loop terminates only when there are no more data to read. To guarantee that this eventually happens, we must continue reading data. With this in mind and following intuition and our informal procedure, we attempt to read data and create a new `Employee` object in the loop body:

```
Employee    emp;  // emp refers to the most recently read Employee object
                  //    or is null.
int hours;        // hours== the number of hours worked by the
                  //    most recently read employee.
emp = Employee.readIn(br);
while (emp!=null) {
    rest of body
    emp = Employee.readIn(br);
    rest of body
}
// No more data to read, i.e., emp==null.
```

At this point, we are stuck. Certainly our intuition may suggest what we do next, but let us pause and consider what our approach tells us—in the absence of intuition.

In the previous examples, whenever we added code to the loop body to guarantee termination, we disturbed one or more of the definitions of our variables. For example, when we incremented `count` by 1 in the multiplication example, it was no longer the case that `result==x*count`—and we were forced to add `x` to `result` to restore this equality.

In other words, in the previous examples, the definitions themselves were enough to drive the development of the `while` statement.

Here, however, they are not enough. The code above does not result in the violation of any of the meanings of the variables, but we can be certain that it does not yet accomplish our objective. The code as it stands just reads through employee data but does not process anything.

Our final condition (no more data to read) is useful only if we know that all the data have been processed at that point, not just thrown away. In fact, our informal procedure explicitly tells us to process the employee data each time they have been read. Implicit in that directive is the understanding that when we test to see if we can terminate the loop (test whether `emp!=null`), we are confident that all the `Employee` objects created prior to the one `emp` refers to have been processed.

This assumption is extremely important and should be stated as a comment prior to the loop:

```
emp = Employee.readIn(br);
// All Employee objects created prior to the one emp refers to have been processed.
while (emp!=null) {
    rest of body
    emp = Employee.readIn(br);
    rest of body
}
// No more data to read, i.e., emp==null.
```

Completing the Loop Body   With this comment in mind (along with our own intuition), we are compelled to process the `Employee` object to which `emp` refers *before* carrying out the `Employee.readIn` in the loop body. After the `Employee.readIn`, however, there is nothing to do but retest the loop condition and continue. The loop's structure is as follows:

```
// All Employee objects created prior to the one emp refers to have been processed.
while (emp!=null) {
    process the object to which emp refers
    emp = Employee.readIn(br);
}
```

Our understanding of what it means to process employee information requires that we prompt for and read the number of hours for the given employee, tell the `Employee` object to compute and return the pay, and print the pay. The following statements accomplish this:

```
System.out.print("Enter hours for "+emp.getName()+": ");
System.out.flush();
hours = Integer.parseInt(br.readLine());
System.out.println(emp.calcPay(hours));
```

Initialization (Again)   In this case, there are no variables used in the loop body that are not initialized. (The `hours` variable is initialized in the loop body itself.) Our final code is

```
Employee    emp; // emp refers to the most recently read Employee object
                 //    or is null.
int hours;       // hours== the number of hours worked by the
                 //    most recently read employee.
emp = Employee.readIn(br);
// All Employee objects created prior to the one emp refers to have been processed.
while (emp!=null) {
    System.out.print("Enter hours for "
                     +emp.getName()+": ");
```

```
        System.out.flush();
        hours = Integer.parseInt(br.readLine());
        System.out.println(emp.calcPay(hours));
        emp = Employee.readIn(br);
    }
```

This code is virtually identical to the code given in Chapter 8.

9.4.2 The Enumerate Pattern: Printing All the Song Titles of a Given Artist

We encountered this pattern in the `SongLibrary` class in Chapter 8. There we wrote a method, `lookup`, that receives a `String` parameter, artist, and has access to an instance variable, `songColl`, that is a `Vector` of `Song` objects. Each of these `Song` objects provides a `getTitle` and a `getArtist` method. To access these objects we use an `Enumeration` object that the `Vector` can provide. The job of `lookup` is to print the title (returned by `getTitle`) of each song whose artist (returned by `getArtist`) matches the parameter.

Informal Procedure We could accomplish this task manually if the `Enumeration` object were a stack of index cards, labeled with artist and song title. We could take one index card after the other, checking to see if the artist matched the one we were interested in. Where there was a match, we would write down the song title that the index card bore.

Choosing and Defining Variables We need a variable to refer to the `Enumeration` object and we also need a variable to refer to the most recent `Song` object that we have taken from the `Enumeration`:

```
Enumeration enum;   // Refers to an Enumeration of songColl
Song        song;   // Refers to the most recent Song object taken from enum
```

Skeleton of the Code Our method so far is as follows:

```
public void lookUp(String artist) {
    Enumeration enum;    // Refers to an Enumeration of songColl
    Song        song;    // Refers to the most recent Song object taken
                         //    from enum
    while (condition)
        body
}
```

The `while` Condition Informally, our task is complete when there are no more index cards; in the program, the corresponding condition is when the `Enumeration` has no more objects to be taken. The negation of this condition—and the condition for the `while` statement here—is that the `Enumeration` object has more objects:

```
while (enum.hasMoreElements())
      body
// !enum.hasMoreElements(), that is, there are no more elements in the enumeration.
```

Initialization   Because `enum` is used in the `while` condition, it must first be initialized:

```
enum = songColl.elements();
```

Guaranteeing Termination   Termination can come only when the `enum` has no more elements. In order to progress to this point, we must send a `nextElement` message to the `Enumeration` object each time the loop body is executed:

```
while (enum.hasMoreElements()) {
        ...
        enum.nextElement();
        ...
}
// !enum.hasMoreElements(), that is, there are no more elements in the enumeration.
```

Completing the Loop Body   According to its definition, `song` is the most recent `Song` object taken from the `Enumeration`. Hence the above invocation of `nextElement` must be completed as

```
Song song = (Song)enum.nextElement();
```

At this point, our code is

```
public void lookUp(String artist) {
    Enumeration enum;      // Refers to an Enumeration of songColl
    Song        song;      // Refers to the most recent Song object taken
                           //    from enum
    enum = songColl.elements();
    while (enum.hasMoreElements()) {
        song = (Song)enum.nextElement();
    }
}
```

And once again, we are stuck: There is nothing in the definition of the variables that demands further code—yet we know that we are not finished. All that the above code will do is deplete the `Enumeration`.

Going back to our informal procedure, we see that we are instructed to check each song for the matching artist and take appropriate action in case of a match. Implicitly, there is an assumption that this has been done for all the songs considered to date. We express this assumption in a comment before the loop. We also add to the loop body the code that outputs the song title if the artist matches. The complete method is as follows:

```
public void lookUp(String artist) {
    Enumeration enum;      // Refers to an Enumeration of songColl
    Song         song;     // Refers to the most recent Song object taken
                           //    from enum
    enum = songColl.elements();
    // All song objects removed from enum so far have had their artist checked for
    //    match to artist and if there was a match, the title was printed out.
    while (enum.hasMoreElements()) {
        song = (Song)enum.nextElement();
        if (artist.equals(song.getArtist()))
            System.out.println(song.getTitle());
    }
}
```

9.5   Variations on the Payroll Loop

In this section we consider a few of the many possible variations on the Payroll loop.

9.5.1   Printing the Payroll and Computing the Total Payout

A minor variation on the above problem is to also compute the total number of employees processed and the total payout. We present the additional considerations that would result during the loop development process below.

Informal Procedure In addition to any other processing of each employee, we have to add the resulting pay to a number (representing the total payout) that we are keeping track of, and we have to increment a number that serves as a count of the employees we process.

Choosing and Defining Variables We therefore require two more variables, both `int`s, to hold this information:

```
int totalPay;   // totalPay== the total paid out so far.
int count;      // count== the number of employees processed so far.
```

Skeleton of the Code The skeleton is the same except for the addition of the above declarations. The `while` condition, initialization of the `while` condition variables, and code to guarantee termination do not change in this variation.

Completing the Loop Body   According to its definition, `count` is the number of employees processed. So, in the loop, after an employee is processed, `count` must be incremented:

```
count++;
```

According to its definition, `totalPay` must equal the total paid out so far. Therefore, as soon as we output the value returned by `emp.calcPay()`, we must add this amount to `totalPay`. Because we need this value twice, once to print and a second time to add to `totalPay`, we declare a variable to hold it:

```
int  pay = emp.calcPay(hours);
```

We then use this variable for printing and adding into `totalPay`:

```
System.out.println(pay);
totalPay += pay;
```

Initialization (Again)   Both `totalPay` and `count` appear in the loop body but are not initialized there. Their initial values are easily inferred from their definitions. Prior to the `while` statement, no employees have been processed and no payments have been made—both variables are initialized to 0. The resulting code follows:

```
int totalPay;      // totalPay== the total paid out so far.
int count;         // count== the number of employees processed so far.
Employee    emp;  // emp refers to the most recently read Employee object.
int hours;         // hours== the number of hours worked by the
                   //     most recently read employee.
count = 0;
totalPay = 0;
emp = Employee.readIn(br);
// All Employee objects created prior to the one emp refers to have been processed.
while (emp!=null) {
    System.out.print("Enter hours for ");
    System.out.print(emp.getName());
    System.out.print(": ");
    hours = Integer.parseInt(br.readLine());
    count++;
    int  pay = emp.calcPay(hours);
    System.out.println(pay);
    totalPay += pay;
    emp = Employee.readIn(br);
}
System.out.print("Total payout: ");
System.out.println(totalPay);
```

9.5.2 Counting Subgroups: Employees Whose Pay Exceeds $500

Here's another variation of the payroll problem: We want, in addition to the other information, the number of employees whose pay exceeded $500. Again, we present only the additional considerations resulting from this requirement, not the full development.

Informal Procedure   In addition to everything else, we must remember the number of employees that we have encountered so far whose pay exceeds $500.

Choosing and Defining Variables   We require another variable to hold our count:

```
int count500;    // count== the number of employees processed so far whose
                 //    pay exceeds $500.
```

Skeleton of the Code   The skeleton is not changed in this variation, except for the addition of the above declarations. The `while` condition, initialization of the `while` condition variables, and code to guarantee termination do not change in this variation.

Completing the Loop Body   According to its definition, `count500` is the number of employees processed whose pay exceeded $500. So, in the loop, after an employee whose pay exceeds $500 is processed, `count500` must be incremented:

```
if (pay>500)
    count500++;
```

Initialization (Again)   Because `count500` appears in the loop body but is not initialized there, it must be initialized before the loop. Prior to the `while` statement, no employees have been processed; therefore the number of employees whose pay exceeds $500 is 0. We therefore initialize `count500` to 0:

```
int totalPay;      // totalPay== the total paid out so far.
int count;         // count== the number of employees processed so far.
int count500;      // count== the number of employees processed so far whose
                   //    pay exceeds $500.
Employee    emp;   // emp refers to the most recently read Employee object.
int hours;         // hours== the number of hours worked by the
                   //    most recently read employee.
count500 = 0;
count = 0;
totalPay = 0;
```

```
emp = Employee.readIn(br);
// All Employee objects created prior to the one emp refers to have been processed.
while (emp!=null) {
    System.out.print("Enter hours for ");
    System.out.print(emp.getName());
    System.out.print(": ");
    hours = Integer.parseInt(br.readLine());
    count++;
    int pay = emp.calcPay(hours);
    if (pay>500)
        count500++;
    System.out.println(pay);
    totalPay += pay;
    emp = Employee.readIn(br);
}
System.out.print("Total payout: ");
System.out.println(totalPay);
System.out.print("Number whose pay exceeds 500: ");
System.out.println(count500);
```

9.5.3 Finding an Extreme: The Employee Who Worked the Most Hours

We consider one last variation of the payroll problem: In addition to the other information, we want to identify the employee who worked the most hours. As we did in the previous examples, we present only the additional considerations resulting from this requirement, not the full development.

Informal Procedure In addition to everything else, we must remember the employee who has worked the most hours of those we've encountered so far. We must also remember the number of hours worked by that employee. As we encounter employees, we can compare their hours with the hours of the one who has worked the most so far. There is a difference, however, between this problem and our earlier ones. Counting employees and computing total pay are tasks that seek a property of the entire group of employees and are meaningful even if the group is empty: In such a case all counts and totals are 0. However, if there are no employees, there is no such thing as an employee who worked the most hours. Furthermore, at the outset of our employee iteration, we are in a similar position—the counts are 0, the totals are 0, but there is no employee who has worked the most.

Choosing and Defining Variables We therefore require two more variables. One variable either refers to an employee (who has worked the most hours among those employees considered) or is **null** (in the case where no employees have yet been considered) and an `int` to hold the number of hours that employee has worked (assuming there is such an employee):

```
Employee    emax;      // emax== the employee with the most number of hours
                       //    worked(so far) or is null if none have been considered
                       //    so far.
int maxhours;          // maxhours== the number of hours worked by employee
                       //    emax.
```

Skeleton of the Code   The skeleton is not changed in this variation, except for the addition of the above declarations. The `while` condition, initialization of the `while` condition variables, and code to guarantee termination do not change in this variation.

Completing the Loop Body   According to its definition, `emax` refers to the employee who worked the most hours (of the employees seen so far). So, after reading another employee and his or her hours, we need to check to see if the new employee's hours exceeds the largest seen so far. However, if `emax` is `null`, we haven't yet considered any employees and the one we just read is the largest so far (in hours). So, if `emax` is `null` or if the new value for `hours` exceeds `maxhours`, we take appropriate action and recognize the newly read employee as the one with the most hours:

```
if (emax==null || hours>maxhours) {
    maxhours = hours;
    emax = emp;
}
```

Initialization (Again)   Because `emax` and `maxhours` both appear in the loop body but are not initialized there, they must be initialized before the loop. Prior to the `while` statement, no employees have been processed, and so `emax` should be made equal to `null`:

```
emax  =  null;
```

At this point there is no meaningful value to assign to `maxhours`. However, because `maxhours` is used in a condition in the loop, Java requires that it be initialized to some value (Java doesn't and can't know that the only time that `maxhours` would be uninitialized is when `emax` is `null` and the condition is thereby true). We therefore choose a dramatically meaningless value to assign to `maxhours` and note this anomaly with a comment:

```
maxhours  =  -999;     // No meaningful value for maxhours at this point.
```

The completed code follows:

```
int totalPay;          // totalPay== the total paid out so far.
int count;             // count== the number of employees processed so far.
```

```
int count500;           // count== the number of employees processed so far
                        //     whose pay exceeds $500.
Employee    emp;        // emp refers to the most recently read Employee object.
int hours;              // hours== the number of hours worked by the
                        //     most recently read employee.
Employee    emax;       // emax== the employee with the most number of hours
                        //     worked(so far) or is null if none have been considered
                        //     so far.
int maxhours;           // maxhours== the number of hours worked by employee
                        //     emax.

count500 = 0;
count = 0;
emax  =  null;
maxhours  =  -999;  // No meaningful value for maxhours at this point.
totalPay = 0;
emp = Employee.readIn(br);
// All Employee objects created prior to the one emp refers to have been processed.
while (emp!=null) {
    System.out.print("Enter hours for ");
    System.out.print(emp.getName());
    System.out.print(": ");
    hours = Integer.parseInt(br.readLine());
    count++;
    int  pay = emp.calcPay(hours);
    if (pay>500)
        count500++;
    if (emax==null || hours>maxhours) {
        maxhours = hours;
        emax = emp;
    }
    System.out.println(pay);
    totalPay += pay;
    emp = Employee.readIn(br);
}
System.out.print("Total payout: ");
System.out.println(totalPay);
System.out.print("Number whose pay exceeds 500: ");
System.out.println(count500);
System.out.print("Employee with the longest hours: ");
System.out.println(emax.getName());
```

EXERCISES

1. Modify the last version of the payroll code so that at the end it prints out the name of the employee who earned the most pay.

2. Modify the last version of the payroll code so that at the end it prints out the total payout to those who made more than $500 and the total payout to those who made less than or equal to $500.   •

■ **9.6** ■ More Loop Patterns: Counters, Accumulators, and Extremes

The loops we have developed in the previous sections exhibit patterns that one frequently sees in programming.

9.6.1 Loop Pattern: The Counter

We often need to count objects. The objects we count might be the elements of a collection for which a particular condition holds. Alternatively, the objects might be values read from an input source. To do this we need a loop that will iterate through the entire group of objects (whether obtaining them from input or an `Enumeration` of a collection such as a `Vector`) and a variable, called a **counter.** The counter equals the number of occurrences encountered at any given point. The counter is an `int` variable and must be initialized to zero. It is incremented, sometimes conditionally, in the loop body:

```
int       countSomething  =  0; // countSomething== the number of
                                //    somethings encountered so far.
...
while (...) {
    ...
    if (the something we're interested in)
        countSomething++;
    ...
}
```

We have used counters to count the number of employees on the payroll and the number of employees paid more than $500.

9.6.2 Loop Pattern: Counting Loops

Sometimes the goal of the `while` loop is synonymous with the counter reaching a particular value. We call this a **counting loop.** We saw this in the arithmetic calculations (exponentiation and multiplication). In that case the loop condition is simply the counter not equaling the goal value:

```
int       countSomething  =  0; // countSomething== the number of
                                //    somethings encountered so far.
...
while (countSomething!=desiredValue) {
    ...
    if (the something we're interested in)
        countSomething++;
    ...
}
```

Often in the case of counting loops, we are counting all objects or values considered, and so the counter is incremented unconditionally (without an `if`). A common example of this is reading input where the number of data items to be read is known in advance. Often that happens when the input consists of a *header* followed by the rest of the data. The **header** is an integer that indicates how much data follow. The input

3
every day
is a
new beginning

is an example of this kind of data organization. The header is 3 and it indicates that three data items follow. Suppose we wished to read these data and write each `String` (after the header) to standard input. We could use the counting loop pattern with the header value in place of `desiredValue`—therefore, we first must read the header and assign it, as an `int`, to an `int` variable:

```
int     klines = 0;  // klines== the number of lines read and printed so far.
int     header;      // header== the number of lines available from input.
header  =  Integer.parseInt(br.readLine());
while (klines!=header) {
    System.out.println(br.readLine());
    klines++;
}
```

Handling input this way is sometimes called the *header method*.

9.6.3   Loop Pattern: The Accumulator

We often wish to apply a binary operation—such as multiplication, addition, or even concatenation—to a group of values or objects, that is, to add, multiply, or concatenate them all together. To do this we need a loop that iterates through the entire group of objects or generates the entire group of values and a variable, called an *accumulator*. The **accumulator** equals the result of applying the binary operation to all the objects or values so far encountered. The accumulator's type is usually determined by the type of the other operand. If a product of `doubles` is being computed, the accumulator is a `double`; if a bunch of `Strings` are being concatenated, the accumulator is a `String` reference variable. Its initial value depends on the operation. If the accumulator is a *sum*, 0 is an appropriate initial value, because 0 is the only number that does not contribute to the result. If the accumulator is a *product*, the appropriate initial value is 1, for similar reasons. If the accumulator is a `String` that results from concatenation, an empty `String` is the appropriate initial value.

In the loop body, the accumulator is assigned a new value, resulting from applying the given operation to it and the next value or object in the group that is being iterated:

```
SomeType accumulator;      // accumulator== the application of operation to
                           //    set of objects or values encountered so far.
...
while (...) {
    ...
    accumulator = apply operation to both accumulator and next object
                      or value
    ...
}
```

We have used accumulators to compute the total payroll for a set of employees as well as to maintain a product of one value that is repeatedly multiplied (to compute the exponential) and to maintain a sum of one value that is repeatedly added (to compute the product).

Accumulators need not be applied to all the values or objects encountered in the iteration. Like counters, they can be applied conditionally. For example, suppose we wanted to concatenate all the lines of input from a `Buffered-Reader`, `br`, that start with the character `":"`:

```
String s = "";
String line;
line = br.readLine();
while (line!=null) {
    if (line.substring(0,1).equals(":"))
        s = s.concat(line);
    line = br.readLine();
}
```

9.6.4   Loop Pattern: Extremes Among Objects

Some loops seek an object that is an *extreme*. An **extreme** object is one that in comparison with other objects in the group under consideration is the most extreme in some sense. Examples are

- A `String` that has more vowels than all the other `String`s
- An employee who worked more hours than every other employee

To find an extreme object, we need a loop to iterate over a group of objects and a variable (such as `emax`) to remember the most extreme object encountered so far. In addition, we need a way of determining whether the current object under consideration is more extreme than the one that was most extreme so far. Sometimes, as in the case of our employee problem (where the `Employee` object had no knowledge of the hours worked by the employee), this requires maintaining an additional variable (such as `maxhours`). At other times—when the object provides more information—that is not necessary. The general pattern is

```
SomeType    extreme;  // extreme== a reference to the object that is most
                      //    extreme among the set of objects encountered so far
                      //    or that is null if no objects have been considered.
extreme = null;
```

if other variables are required to represent the extreme character of the object, initialize them as required by Java (their value is not significant because at this point extreme is null)

```
while (...) {
    ...
    if (extreme==null || current object is more extreme
                                 than extreme)
        extreme = current object
    ...
}
```

As a further example of this pattern, suppose we wanted to print the longest `String` in a `Vector` of references to `String` objects `v`:

```
Enumeration    e = v.elements();
String  s;
String  longest = null;  // The longest String encountered so far or null if no
                         //    String has been encountered.
while (e.hasMoreElements()) {
    s = (String) e.nextElement();
    if (longest==null || s.length()>longest.length())
        longest = s;
}
System.out.println("Longest String is ".concat(longest));
```

9.6.5 Loop Pattern: Extremes Among Primitive Data Values

The construction of a loop that seeks an *extreme* primitive data type value among a set of such values is quite similar to the search for an extreme object, except for one problem. When searching for an extreme object, we had a special value, `null`, that indicated that we had not yet examined any objects in our search for the extreme. Often no such value exists for primitive data types. In this case we need a `boolean` variable, called `foundExtreme`, perhaps, that is `true` once some extreme has been found (upon examining the first value) and until then is `false`. The general pattern is

```
boolean    foundExtreme;    // true if an extreme has been found so far;
                            //    false otherwise.
```

```
SomeType    extreme;          // extreme== the most extreme value
                             //     encountered so far if foundExtreme is
                             //     true; otherwise its value is meaningless.
extreme = some arbitrary and meaningless value;
foundExtreme  =  false;
while (...) {
    ...
    if (!foundExtreme  ||  current value is more extreme
                                  than extreme) {
        extreme = current value
        foundExtreme  =  true;
    }
    ...
}
```

As an example of this pattern, suppose we wanted to print the largest integer read from a `BufferedReader br`:

```
boolean    foundExtreme;
int        largest;
int        x;
foundExtreme  =  false;
largest  =  0;
String  line;
line  =  br.readLine();
while (line!=null) {
    x  =  Integer.parseInt(line);
    if (!foundExtreme  ||  x>largest) {
        largest = x;
        foundExtreme  =  true;
    }
    line = br.readLine();
}
System.out.println("Largest integer is " + largest);
```

9.6.6 Loop Pattern: Extremes Among a Subrange of Primitive Data Values

The problem of not having a special `null` value for primitive data types goes away when we are assured that the range of values under consideration is a *subrange* of the type. For example, we may be looking for the largest integer but we know that none of the integers under consideration are negative. In such a case, we can let one of the "forbidden" values play the role of `null` and we can dispense with the `boolean` variable `foundExtreme`:

```
SomeType    extreme;     // extreme== the most extreme value encountered so
                        //     far or extreme== forbidden value if no values have
                        //     yet been encountered.
extreme = some "forbidden" value;
```

```
while (...) {
    ...
    if (extreme== forbidden value || current value is more
                                        extreme than extreme)
        extreme = current value
    ...
}
```

We apply this as follows to finding the largest integer read from a `BufferedReader` in a case where we know that all input is nonnegative:

```
int     largest;    // Largest int read so far or -1 if no ints have been read.
int     x;
largest = -1;
String  line;
line = br.readLine();
while (line!=null) {
    x = Integer.parseInt(line);
    if (largest == -1 || x>largest)
        largest = x;
    line = br.readLine();
}
System.out.println("Largest integer is " + largest);
```

That's because when `largest==-1`, `x`, (which is by assumption nonnegative), is greater than `largest`, that is, `x>largest`.

9.6.7 Loop Pattern: Extremes When We Know the Data Set Is Not Empty

Sometimes we know with assurance that the set of objects or data under consideration is not empty. When we search for an extreme under those circumstances, we can simplify the definition of our variables and our code considerably. For example, if we know we have a nonempty group of objects, our original definition of `extreme`

```
SomeType    extreme;    // extreme== a reference to the object that is most
                        //     extreme among the set of objects encountered so
                        //     far or that is null if no objects have been
                        //     considered.
```

can be changed as follows:

```
SomeType    extreme;    // extreme== a reference to the object that is most
                        //     extreme among the set of objects encountered
                        //     so far.
```

This definition states that `extreme` *from the beginning* is a reference to one of the objects under consideration. The only way to accommodate that requirement is to initialize `extreme` to refer to the first object under consideration, which by virtue of being the first is also the most extreme encountered so far. We illustrate this pattern by returning to the example of printing the longest `String` in a nonempty `Vector` of references to `String` objects, v:

```
//  v is known to contain at least one element.
Enumeration    e = v.elements();
String  s;
String  longest;                        // The longest String encountered so far.
longest  = (String) e.nextElement();  // The first string is always the
                                        //    longest up to that point.
while (e.hasMoreElements()) {
    s = (String) e.nextElement();
    if (s.length()>longest.length())
        longest = s;
}
System.out.println("Longest String is ".concat(longest));
```

Besides simplifying the definition, this guarantee of nonemptiness simplifies the condition in the loop: There is no need to check to see whether `longest` is `null`—we know it is not.

Because a `null` value does not enter the picture here, the code for primitive data types follows an identical pattern. We illustrate it by printing the largest integer read from a `BufferedReader br`. The simplifications are even more substantial—the `foundExtreme boolean` variable is eliminated entirely:

```
int      largest;
int      x;
String line;
largest  =  Integer.parseInt(br.readLine());
line  =  br.readLine();
while (line!=null) {
    x  =  Integer.parseInt(line);
    if (x>largest)
        largest = x;
    line = br.readLine();
}
System.out.println("Largest integer is " + largest);
```

EXERCISES

1. Write a `static` method that receives the name of a file and an integer *N* as arguments. The method returns a `Vector` of the first *N* `Strings` read from the file. If the file has fewer than *N* `Strings`, the `Vector` contains all the `Strings` it does have.

2. Write a `static` method that receives an integer N as argument and returns the sum of the first N cubes: $1^3 + 2^3 + 3^3 + \cdots + N^3$.

3. Write a `static` method that receives a file name as an argument. Assume that the file consists solely of integers. The method returns the product of the smallest and largest integers in the file.

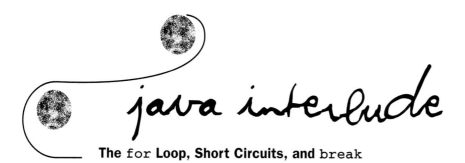

The `for` Loop, Short Circuits, and `break` and `continue`

THE `for` LOOP

In recognition of the frequency of counting loops, Java provides the `for` statement as an alternative to the `while` statement. In its simplest and most widely used form, a `for` statement is

```
for (initialization assignment; loop condition; increment)
    body
```

The *initialization assignment* is carried out once before the loop condition is tested, at the beginning of execution of the `for`—its purpose is to initialize the counter in the loop. The *loop condition* and *body* play the same role as in the `while` statement. The increment is an increment of the counter and is executed each time *after* the body is executed but before the loop condition is tested.

The `for` statement can be understood in terms of a `while` statement:

```
initialization assignment;
while (loop condition) {
    body
    increment;
}
```

We rewrite the header method code using a `for` statement as follows:

```
int     lines;      // lines== the number of lines read and printed so far.
int     header;     // header== the number of lines available from input.
```

```
header  =  Integer.parseInt(br.readLine());
for  (lines=0; lines!=header; lines++)
    System.out.println(br.readLine());
```

The `for` statement is actually much more flexible than this example shows and its use is not confined to counting loops. In general, its form is

```
for  (initialization;  loop condition;  step)
    body
```

The *initialization* does not have to be a single assignment to a counter. Several assignments may be supplied by separating them with commas:

```
for (i=0, sum=0; i<100; i++)     // Compute the sum from 0 to 100.
    sum += i;
```

Similarly, the *step* does not have to be a single increment—it too can be a comma-separated sequence of statements:

```
for (i=0, powOf2=1; i<10; i++, powOf2*=2)   // Print table of powers
    System.out.println("2 to the "          //    of 2.
        +i+" is "+powOf2);
```

SHORT-CIRCUITING

Java evaluates compound conditions in a strict left-to-right order. In addition, it evaluates only as much of the condition as necessary to arrive at the `boolean` result. Consider the following condition:

```
atBat!=0  &&  hits/atBat>0.300
```

Java evaluates `atBat!=0` first. If it is false, there is no need in going further because the `&&` must be `false` if the first operand is `false`. If `atBat!=0` is `true`, Java will go further and evaluate `hits/atBat>0.300`. Notice that the first condition guarantees that a division by 0, which is a fatal error, will not be performed.

Conditions involving the `||` operator are evaluated similarly. Consider the following condition:

```
person.age()>=17  ||  person.accompaniedByAdult()
```

Java evaluates `person.age()>=17` first. If it is true, there is no need in going further because the `||` must be `true` if the first operand is `true`. If `person.age()>=17` is `false`, Java will go further and evaluate `person.accompaniedByAdult()`.

This way of evaluating compound conditions is called **short-circuiting.**

We took advantage of short-circuiting when we searched for an extreme object:

```
if (longest==null || s.length()>longest.length())
```

This condition is safe to execute only because the first clause, `longest==null`, is tested first. If the clause is true, that is, if `longest` is **null,** the second clause is not tested at all. If this were not the case and both clauses were always tested, when `longest` was **null**, the second clause, which uses `longest` as a reference, would be in error for sending a message to a null reference.

THE `break` AND `continue` STATEMENTS

The **break statement** consists of a single keyword, `break`:

```
break;
```

When Java encounters this statement in a loop body, the loop is immediately terminated. The following loop terminates either when the loop condition is tested and `k` equals 5 or when end of file is reached, causing `s` to be assigned `null`:

```
int      k=0;
while  (k!=5) {
     String s = infile.readLine();
     if (s==null)
          break;
     process s
     k++;
}
// k==5 or s==null
```

Although there may be some occasions when using the `break` statement is justified, we caution beginning and intermediate programmers not to employ it. Its use leads to two problems. First, when there is more than one exit from the loop, the code becomes more complex and harder to analyze. The reader of the above loop has to mentally construct an *or* termination condition implicitly. If the loop had been written as

```
int      k=0;
String s = infile.readLine();
while (!(k==5 || s==null)) {
     process s
     k++;
     s = infile.readLine();
}
```

the reader could see the termination condition explicitly: `(k==5 ||` `s==null)`.

Secondly, programmers who rely on using the `break` statement often gloss over the step of determining the `while` condition. We have seen, however, that this step, although not hard, is an essential part of the design process.

Java also provides a **continue statement**, consisting of the single keyword, `continue`:

```
continue;
```

When Java encounters this statement in a loop, the remaining part of the loop body is skipped for this cycle. If the loop is a `for` statement, the increment is carried out, and then the condition is retested. In a `while` statement, there is no increment in the loop header, and so the condition is retested immediately after the `continue`:

```
for (i=0; i<100; i++) {
    if (i%2==1)
        continue;
    if (!veryComplicatedCondition(i))
        continue;
    process i
}
```

In the loop above, `i` is processed only if it is even and if the `veryComplicatedCondition` is true for `i`. The loop could have been written equivalently as follows:

```
for (i=0; i<100; i++) {
    if (i%2==0 && veryComplicatedCondition(i)) {
        process i
    }
}
```

The advantage of `continue` is that it can reduce levels of nesting and indentation within a loop body. Its danger is that the conditions for executing the rest of the loop body are not explicit—they must be inferred by the programmer reading the different conditions that result in `continue` statements.

The `continue` statement can be downright dangerous, particularly when used in a `while` statement. Consider the following loop:

```
String s = keybd.readLine();
while (s!=null) {
    if (!someCondition1(s))
        continue;
    if (!someCondition2(s))
        continue;
```

```
    process s
    s = keybd.readLine();
}
```

The intent here is that s should be processed only when some-Condition1 and someCondition2 are true. However, by using the continue statement, the entire loop body is skipped, including the read of the next String! Thus, s is never changed, and the loop is an infinite loop.

We therefore strongly advise beginners and intermediate programmers not to use the continue statement. Instead, work with explicit conditionals in the loop body.

The break and continue statements can be the inadvertent source of serious bugs. For example, a considerable portion of the long distance network of a major long distance provider went down in 1990 as a result of software error stemming from improper use of the break statement.

1. Rewrite all the loops in the exercises in Section 9.2, using the for statement in place of the while statement.

EXERCISES

9.7   A Loop Design Strategy: Refining an Imperfect Solution

Many computing problems may be solved by starting with an imperfect provisional solution and then improving (or refining) it. We call this *successive refinement*. This approach requires the following three capabilities:

- The ability to *construct an initial* provisional, albeit imperfect, solution
- The ability to take a provisional solution and *improve* it, thus yielding a new provisional solution that is, in some way, closer to an actual solution of the given problem
- The ability to *determine* whether a given provisional solution is actually a solution of the problem, that is, an ability to know when the job is done

We use the term *provisional solution* broadly. A provisional solution could be a very crude approximation or an extremely incomplete result—usually it is not close at all to the true solution. For example, if our goal was to compute the square root of a number x, a provisional solution might be the number x itself—certainly close to the solution if x is close to 0 or 1 but very crude if x is large.

To make our discussion of successive refinement concrete, we consider the problem of calculating the non-negative square root of a real number x. The three capabilities mentioned above may be developed in any order. For the square root, we start with the third one first.

How does one determine whether a double value stored, say, in y is the square root of a double value stored, say, in x? We might be tempted to write the condition

```
y*y == x
```

as our measure of success, but given the peculiarities of floating point arithmetic, it is more practical to ask not whether y*y equals x but rather to ask whether y*y is very close to x—remember, when floating point arithmetic is used, approximations are usually inevitable and, provided they are good enough, always acceptable. By writing

```
Math.abs(y*y-x) <= p
```

we can determine whether y*y is within a distance of p from x. If p is quite small (for example, 1.0e-10), we know that y is a close, perhaps a sufficiently close, approximation of the square root of x. The value of p determines the precision of our assessment.

A helper method that checks whether one value, y, is within a given precision the square root of x, is

```
private boolean closeEnough(double x, double y,
                    double precision) {
    return Math.abs(y*y-x) <= precision;
}
```

So we now have a method that tells us *when our job is done*, that is, whether our (square root) problem has been solved. Now we turn to improvement: Given a provisional solution that is not "good enough," how can we improve it? We base the method of improvement on an algorithm attributed to the great seventeenth century scientist Isaac Newton.

The essence of the algorithm lies in the observation that if you approximate the square root of x as y and if y is too big, that is, it is greater than the true square root of x, x/y will be smaller than the true square root. Likewise, if y is too small, x/y will be greater than the true square root. Furthermore, if you take the average of your approximation y and x/y

$$(y + x/y) / 2$$

you will get a number that is a closer approximation of the square root of x than either y or x/y. This is illustrated in Figure 9.1. For example, suppose we seek the square root of 100 and we approximate it as 20. With y as 20 and x as 100, we calculate

$$(20 + 100/20) / 2$$

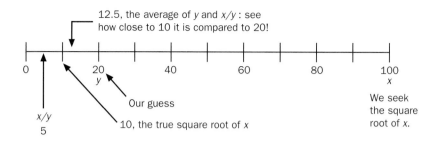

FIGURE 9.1   **Finding a square root using Newton's algorithm.**

which is 12.5—much closer to the true square root of 100 than 20. What we have, then, is a means for taking one approximation and producing a better one.

A helper method that uses this to improve a provisional solution to the square root of x is

```
private double improveSolution(double y, double x) {
    return (y+x/y) / 2.0;
}
```

We thus have our second capability: We can *improve our provisional solution* to the square root of x. Finally, we need to start somewhere, to come up with an *initial provisional solution* to the square root of x. It need not be a good one, because we know we can improve it. Any positive value here will do and so we may start with x itself.

In general, given these capabilities, it is often possible to solve the problem with iteration. Let's work through the general case with our loop-constructing approach and then apply it to our square root problem.

Informal Procedure   We start with our provisional solution and improve it. As long as our provisional solution is not good enough, we keep improving it. When it *is* good enough, the job is done and we stop.

Choosing and Defining Variables   We are talking in generalities now, and so we can't describe specific variables—each particular problem will have its own set of variables to represent a provisional solution (in the square root problem, a single variable, y, is all that is required). For purposes of discussion, let's have one variable, s, here that represents the provisional solution to our problem:

   SomeType s;   // Provisional solution to the problem at hand

Skeleton of the Code   Given our expectation of using iteration, we have

```
SomeType s;     // Provisional solution to the problem at hand
while (condition)
        body
```

The while Condition   Our informal procedure tells us that our job is complete when the solution is good enough:

```
while (condition)
        body
// closeEnough(s)
```

So the negation of this is our loop condition:

```
while (!closeEnough(s))
        body
// closeEnough(s)
```

Initialization   Because s is used in the while condition, it must first be initialized. Our first required capability, the ability to start with a provisional solution, allows us to do this:

```
s = provisional solution
while (!closeEnough(s))
        body
// closeEnough(s)
```

Guaranteeing Termination   According to our informal procedure, we repeatedly improve the provisional solution in hopes of reaching a solution that is good enough:

```
s = provisional solution
while (!closeEnough(s))
    s = improveSolution(s);
// closeEnough(s)
```

It is correct, however, to ask whether continually improving a solution is enough to guarantee termination. In some cases, it will not be. To take a silly but illustrative example, suppose that our goal was for s to reach the value 2, starting from 1.0. If we added successively 0.1, 0.01, 0.001, 0.0001, and so on, with each addition s gets closer to 2, but it never reaches that value. The question of whether the improvement necessarily leads to termination must always be examined carefully.

9.7.1   Finding the Square Root

Following this discussion, we write our square root method:

```
// squareRoot returns square root of x within the given precision.
private double squareRoot(double x, double precision) {
```

```
    double y;
    y = x;
    while (!closeEnough(x, y, precision))
        y = (y+x/y) / 2.0;
    return y;
}
```

By the nature of the `while` statement, there is no question that if `squareRoot` returns, it will return a value that equals the square root of *x* within the given precision. It is thanks to Isaac Newton that we know that our method of improvement leads to a sequence of approximations that converges to the square root of *x* and hence that the `while` loop will indeed terminate.

9.7.2   A Broader View

Actually all the loops we have encountered in this and the preceding chapter may be viewed in this light. Each of these loops in a sense takes a provisional solution to a problem and incrementally improves it. Consider, for example, the code that multiplies by repeated addition:

```
private int multiply(int x, int y) {
        int count,    // count== the number of additions done.
            result;   // result==0+x+x+···+x (count times), that is,
                      //    result==x*count.
        count = 0;
        result = 0;
        while (count!=y) {
            result += x;
            count++;
        }
        // count==y, result==x*y
        return result;
}
```

Our task is to make `result` equal `x*y`. In terms of the successive refinement,

- The provisional solution is 0.
- The way we improve our provisional solution is to add `x`.
- We test whether `count!=y` to determine whether our provisional solution is the actual solution to the problem.

The first two of these are straightforward, but how does testing `count!=y` show whether our provisional solution is the correct solution or not? The answer lies in the meaning of `count` and `result`—information that is provided in the comments associated with their definition and that is implicit in the code that was developed: `result==x*count`. Given that information, of course `count!=y` is a measure of whether the job has been done. The central role played by this fact of our design, `result==x*count`, underscores the importance of thinking carefully about the meaning of one's variables and expressing those meanings, with an equality if possible, in a comment.

1. The criterion for y being a satisfactory approximation is

   ```
   Math.abs(y*y-x) <= precision
   ```

   for some value of precision. Suppose precision is 0.000001. Can you think of a number for which this is a very poor criterion? Suppose the criterion was

   ```
   Math.abs(y*y-x) <= 1.0
   ```

   Can you think of a number for which this is a very poor criterion? Can you think of a number for which this criterion is quite reasonable?

2. (A challenge) Come up with a better criterion for a satisfactory approximation.

9.8   The Radio Station's Play Schedule

We close this chapter by returning to a couple of examples from WOLD in Chapter 8, allowing us to view iteration again in the context of class development as well as to encounter some new iteration problems.

9.8.1   Statement of the Problem

Its initial experience with a computerized system proves so successful, WOLD decides to computerize its afternoon show whose gimmick is the playing of commercial-free segments. Prior to air time, the DJ creates a file of the songs she wishes to play during the coming broadcast. The file is taken from the song library file whose entries have now been expanded to include song durations. The application is to prompt the DJ for the length of the commercial-free segment. The song list is then read and a printout is produced of sequences of songs whose total length is no less than the length of the commercial-free segment.

This example will be analyzed in our standard fashion.

Determining the Primary Objects   As before, the primary class is `SongLibrary`.

Determining the Desired Behavior   Now, however, there is no need for a `lookUp` method. Instead, we want the `SongLibrary` to make the list of commercial-free segments for the DJ, writing to standard output the names of the songs and their artists. So, the following methods are required:

- SongLibrary (constructor)
- makeSegments

Defining the Interface   As before, the constructor will have a file name as an argument (specifying the file where the song information is stored). We want to specify the desired minimum length of the music segments, so `makeSegments` will need an integer argument. We also want to pass it a `PrintStream` reference so that the `SongLibrary` can write the list to targets other than standard output. Because `makeSegments`' job is to write out a list of songs organized as segments, it need not return anything, and its return type is `void`. The interface then is

```
class SongLibrary {
    SongLibrary(String songFileName) {...}
    void makeSegments(int minLength, PrintStream ps) {...}
}
```

The use of this class can be illustrated with the application we are interested in:

```
class CommercialFree {
    public static void main(String[] args) throws Exception {
        String          songLibraryName;
        int             minSegmentLength;
        BufferedReader  br = new BufferedReader(
                              new InputStreamReader(
                                System.in));
        System.out.print("Name of song library: ");
        System.out.flush();
        songLibraryName = br.readLine();
        System.out.print("Minimum segment length: ");
        System.out.flush();
        minSegmentLength = Integer.parseInt(br.readLine());

        SongLibrary s = new SongLibrary(songLibraryName);
        s.makeSegments(minSegmentLength, System.out);
    }
}
```

Defining the Instance Variables   Following our second, more efficient, implementation of `SongLibrary` in the Chapter 8, we will maintain a `Vector` of `Song` objects:

```
class SongLibrary {
    SongLibrary(String songFileName) {...}
```

```
        void makeSegments(int minLength, PrintStream ps) {...}
        // Instance variables
        private Vector songColl;
    }
```

Implementing the Methods   The constructor is identical to that of Chapter 8.

```
public SongLibrary(String songFileName) throws Exception {
    songColl = new Vector();
    BufferedReader br =
            new BufferedReader(
                new InputStreamReader(new
                            FileInputStream(songFileName)));
    Song song = Song.read(br);
    while (song!=null) {
        songColl.addElement(song);
        song = Song.read(br);
    }
}
```

The makeSegments method will need to traverse the Vector of Song objects, querying these objects about their playing times. This need suggests that our Song class will need to provide a method called getPlayingTime. We leave this and the other resulting modifications to the Song class as an exercise and turn our attention to the implementation of makeSegments.

Implementing makeSegments   Recognizing that this method requires us to process many objects, we build an iterative solution using our usual approach.

Informal Procedure   Before computerizing, the DJ figured out the commercial-free segments the old-fashioned way: pencil and paper, that is, she drew lines between songs to mark segment boundaries. How did she know when to draw a line? As she worked her way through her song list, she always kept in mind how long the current segment was so far. Each time she passed over a song, she added the duration of the song to the duration of the segment she was working on. As soon as the segment went past the "limit," she drew the line (after the song that pushed the segment past the limit—remember WOLD guarantees a *minimum* of X commercial-free minutes). Our programs can't draw lines in the middle of files, but we can utilize the DJ's informal procedure this way: Our method models her inclusion of a song by printing it out, and it models her drawing a line by printing out "---- End of segment ----".

Choosing and Defining Variables   In the informal procedure the DJ is aware of three items at any given time: the limit on segment duration, the length (so far) of the current segment, and the next song to add to the segment (including its playing time, title, and any other properties.). The limit is given to the method as an argument and will be declared among the parameters. So, only two variables need to be declared:

```
int      currentSegmentLength;    // Duration of the current segment
Song     song;                    // Next song to add to segment
```

Skeleton of the Code   We sketch out the method:

```
public void makeSegments(int segmentLimit,
                         PrintStream ps) {
    int     segmentLength;     // Duration of the current segment
    Song song;                 // Next song to add to segment
    ...
    while (condition)
        body
    ...
}
```

The while Condition   According to plan, we want to create segments of all the songs in the list. Therefore, we are not done until the list is exhausted. Because our Song objects are stored in a Vector, we expect to access them using an Enumeration object reference, which we can call songList. In that case, the list of songs will be exhausted exactly when songList.has-MoreElements() is false. Hence we write

```
while (!songList.hasMoreElements())
    body
```

When there are no more songs, there is nothing to add to the current segment—it ends there. We might be tempted to unconditionally print an end-of-segment line at that point, but we ought to remember that the current segment might be empty, that is, the last song might have been the final song in a segment. We would look pretty silly having an empty segment, so we need to print an end-of-segment line only if the current segment is not empty:

```
while (!songList.hasMoreElements())
    body
if (segmentLength>0)
    ps.println("---- End of segment ----");
```

Initialization   To guarantee that the loop condition has a meaningful value, we must initialize the Enumeration reference songList before the while statement. Furthermore, we must add it to our list of declarations:

```
Enumeration     songList;      // List of songs remaining to be considered
songList = songColl.elements();
```

Guaranteeing Termination   To guarantee that the `while` loop eventually terminates (that is, that `songList.hasMoreElements` eventually returns false), we must get the next song in the `Enumeration` in the loop body. Our code skeleton now becomes

```
public void makeSegments(int segmentLimit,
                              PrintStream ps) {
    int     segmentLength=0;    // Duration of the current segment
    Song    song;               // Next song to add to segment
    Enumeration    songList;    // List of songs remaining to be considered
    songList = songColl.elements();
    while (songList.hasMoreElements()) {
        ...
        song = (Song) songList.nextElement();
        ...
    }
    if (segmentLength>0)
        ps.println("—— End of segment ——");
}
```

Guaranteeing termination ⟶ (points to `song = (Song) songList.nextElement();`)

Completing the Loop Body   Each time, upon entering the loop body, we can be certain that `songList` has more elements and hence that the `song` we extract using the `nextElement` method is the next song to add to the segment. *After* extracting this song, our task is to add it to the segment, take into account the increase in segment length, and then check to see if the duration of the segment has now exceeded the limit. When that happens, the current segment ends and a new one begins. Adding the song to the segment is a matter of first printing it out:

```
ps.println(song.toString());
```

Then we change `segmentLength` to reflect the playing time of the newly added song:

```
segmentLength += song.getPlayTime();
```

To check to see if the segment length exceeds the limit, we use a conditional:

```
if (segmentLength>segmentLimit))    // End this segment; start new one.
```

To end the current segment, we need to print the end-of-segment line:

```
ps.println("---- End of segment ----");
```

To start a new segment, we don't need do anything except set the duration of the new segment to 0:

```
segmentLength = 0;
```

Thus, the loop body is

```
song = (Song) songList.nextElement();      ◄──────── Guaranteeing termination
ps.println(song.toString());
segmentLength += song.getPlayTime();
if (segmentLength>segmentLimit)      // End this segment; start new one.
    ps.println("---- End of segment ----");
    segmentLength = 0;
}
```

Our method is nearly complete now:

```
public void makeSegments(int segmentLimit,
                         PrintStream ps) {
    int       segmentLength=0;   // Duration of the current segment
    Song      song;              // Next song to add to segment
    Enumeration    songList;     // List of songs remaining to be considered
    songList = songColl.elements();
    while (songList.hasMoreElements()) {
        song = (Song) songList.nextElement();  ◄──────── Guaranteeing termination
        ps.println(song.toString());
        segmentLength += song.getPlayTime();
        if (segmentLength>segmentLimit) { // End this segment; start
                                          //    new one.
            ps.println("---- End of segment ----");
            segmentLength = 0;
        }
    }
    if (segmentLength>0)
        ps.println("---- End of segment ----");
}
```

Initialization (Again)   Having added loop body code, we have introduced a variable that must be assigned meaningful values prior to the loop. Identifying this variable and the required initialization is left as an exercise.

9.8.2   Management Looks at the Bottom Line

After several months of running guaranteed commercial-free music segments, management decides that its advertising revenues are unacceptably low. The DJ's boss tells her that in making her segment boundaries, she has to make sure that there is a commercial at least every N minutes, for some value of N. In other words, the segments now have a maximum length that they can't exceed. Naturally the DJ, for her listeners' sake, seeks to make the segments as close to the maximum as possible. These changes lead to a different loop structure in the makeSegments method.

Informal Procedure   When she used pencil and paper, the DJ manually drew lines between songs to mark segment boundaries. How did she know when to draw a line? As she worked her way through her song list, she kept in mind the length of the current segment. Before adding a song to the segment, she checked to see whether the song's duration would make the current segment exceed management's limit. If it would not exceed the limit, she added the song to the segment; if it would exceed the limit, she drew the segment boundary before the song and considered the song to be the beginning of a new segment.

The development of a solution remains the same until we need to complete the loop body:

```
public void makeSegments(int segmentLimit,
                         PrintStream ps) {
    int      segmentLength=0;     // Duration of the current segment
    Song     song;                // Next song to add to segment
    Enumeration   songList;       // List of songs remaining to be considered
    songList = songColl.elements();
    while (songList.hasMoreElements()) {
        ...
        song = (Song) songList.nextElement();
        ...
    }
    if (segmentLength>0)
        ps.println("---- End of segment ----");
}
```

Guaranteeing termination ——————▶ `song = (Song) songList.nextElement();`

Completing the Loop Body   Where the current problem differs from the guaranteed music marathon is that before adding a song to the segment

```
segmentLength += song.getPlayTime();
ps.println(song.toString());
```

we must first check to see if the addition would exceed the limit—in which case the current segment is ended and a new segment is started:

```
if (segmentLength+song.getPlayTime() > segmentLimit) {
    ps.println("---- End of segment ----");
    segmentLength = 0;
}
```

Thus, the loop body is

Guaranteeing termination ——▶
```
song = (Song) songList.nextElement();
if (segmentLength+song.getPlayTime() > segmentLimit)  {
    ps.println("---- End of segment ----");
```

```
        segmentLength = 0;
    }
    segmentLength += song.getPlayTime();
    ps.println(song.toString());
```

Initialization (Again) The additional required initialization is the same as that of the previous version of this problem.

EXERCISES

1. Complete the first version of `makeSegments` by identifying the variable in the loop that needs initialization and adding the needed initialization.

2. Write a method that receives two `BufferedReader` references as arguments. The first refers to a file containing truck capacities. This file consists of many lines, each consisting of a single integer that corresponds to the capacity (in pounds) of a different truck. The second argument refers to a file containing weights of shipping containers. In this file, too, each weight is an integer on a line by itself. Assuming that the containers must be loaded in the order that they appear in the second file, and assuming that the trucks are dispatched in the order given by the first file, the method returns the number of trucks required to ship all the containers.   •

SUMMARY

Although familiarity with common patterns of loops in programs is helpful, a methodical approach to loop construction is an essential tool for the programmer. We advocate that a programmer start by considering an informal solution to a problem requiring a loop and then follow these steps:

- Identify the needed variables and write down precise definitions of their meaning.
- Make an overall sketch of the `while` statement and its context (the method it appears in).
- Determine the loop condition by taking the negation of the condition that should be true when the loop terminates.
- Write code before the loop to make sure any variables used in the loop condition are properly initialized.
- Write code in the loop body that guarantees termination—that is, that guarantees that the loop condition eventually will be false.

- Complete the loop body by adding code that maintains the consistent meaning of the variables.
- Write additional initialization code as needed.

In each step, particularly the last four, insight from the informal solution can and should be used.

STUDY AID: TERMINOLOGY REVIEW

accumulator   A variable that holds a partial sum, product, or analog for another binary operation besides + or *.

break statement   A statement that forces immediate termination of a loop.

continue statement   A statement that forces Java to skip the remainder of the loop body in the current iteration.

counter   A variable that keeps count of something.

counting loop   A loop whose termination is based on executing a certain number of times.

extreme   A value in a set that is no greater or no less than all the other elements.

header   An integer that indicates how much data follows in a set of input.

iteration   The repeated execution of a section of code until some condition is satisfied.

loop condition   The condition that controls the `while` statement's execution.

short-circuiting   Ending the evaluation of a condition without evaluating all its clauses as soon as the value of the condition is determined.

QUESTIONS FOR REVIEW

1. What can we be sure is the case when a `while` statement terminates?

2. Is the definition of n violated at some point in the code below? Is this a problem? Explain.

```
int     n=0;       // Number of stars printed out
while   (n!=5)  {
    System.out.print("*");
```

```
        n++;
    }
```

3. What loop pattern does the `SongLibrary` constructor of Section 9.

FURTHER EXERCISES

1. Consider the fragment of code below. Unfortunately, some coffee spilled on some it and it can't be seen. Can you tell what will be printed out even though some code is covered by coffee? (Assume that the loop does terminate.)

```
int      i, j;
i = 19;
j = 3;
while (i!=7)            coffee stain!
        i += j;


    }
System.out.println(i);
```

Threads

Introducing Threads   Consider the chefs working in the kitchen for a large restaurant. Each of them has a recipe and is following it while the others do the same. The chefs don't wait for each other to finish a task—they are all working simultaneously. If the restaurant is quite large, there may be times when more than one chef is following the same recipe—for different customers.

Now consider a football team. When play starts, each member is following a set of instructions, given by the coach or the captain. We see that when there is more than one task to carry out at a time, it is commonplace to have several people working, each following the instructions to handle a single task.

The same is true in programming. Let's start with a definition: a *thread* is the process of carrying out a set of instructions one at a time. Using this term in the above examples, we might see that each chef or football player is a separate thread carrying out his or her own set of instructions. These examples involve multiple threads, more than one chef or player. In contrast, the programs that we have written and worked with in the non-GUI parts of this book have all consisted of a single thread. This has worked out because they only had to perform a single task at a time.

However, programs are often required to carry out more than one task at the same time. For example, a multimedia application might need to perform the following tasks simultaneously:

- Play background music
- Display a sequence of images
- Scroll text that explains the images

This application might employ three threads—one for each of these tasks.

As another example of an application that benefits from more than one thread, consider a Web browser such as Netscape's Navigator. Suppose you are using Navigator and you click on a link to load in a new page. While Navigator is finding the source of the new page and establishing a connection, you can still scroll through the old page, type a new URL in the locator bar, or click the stop button to abort the new page. Navigator here is carrying out at least two tasks at once:

- Network input/output—accessing the new page
- Responding to controls (the Stop button, the Scroll Bar, and so on)

Now consider the applet shown in Figure 9.2, which consists of a `Canvas` and a single `Button`. Initially, the `Button`'s label is "start." When the user clicks the `Button` the label changes to "stop," the applet's `paint` method is invoked, and an alternating sequence of red and green rectangles is drawn on the `Canvas`.

The button changes to stop and an alternating sequence of red and green rectangles is drawn.

When the user clicks the button again, the label should change to start and the `paint` method should cease to draw:

```
import java.awt.*;
import java.awt.event.*;
```

FIGURE 9.2   The `RedGreen` applet after the start button has been clicked. The button changes to "stop" and an alternating sequence of red and green rectangles is drawn.

```
import java.applet.*;

public class RedGreen extends Applet
                       implements ActionListener{
    public void init() {
        setLayout(new BorderLayout(2,2));
        b = new Button("start");
        b.addActionListener(this);
        c = new Canvas();
        add("West",b);
        add("East",c);
        c.setSize(100,50);
    }

    public void paint(Graphics g) {
        Graphics gc = c.getGraphics();
        while (keepGoing) {
            gc.setColor(new Color(200,50,50));
            gc.fillRect(5,5,90,40);
            gc.setColor(new Color(50,200,50));
            gc.fillRect(5,5,90,40);
        }
    }

    public void actionPerformed(ActionEvent ae) {
        String s = ae.getActionCommand();
        if (s.equals("start"))
            handleStart();
        else if (s.equals("stop"))
            handleStop();
    }

    private void handleStart() {
        keepGoing = true;
        b.setLabel("stop");
    }

    private void handleStop() {
        keepGoing = false;
        b.setLabel("start");
    }
    private Button  b;
    private Canvas  c;
    private boolean keepGoing=false;
}
```

If we run this applet and click the start button, the paint method is invoked and a sequence of red and green rectangles is rapidly drawn. However, clicking the stop button elicits no response. The applet does not work properly.

The problem here is that the applet is written as a single thread—only one sequence of instructions is being executed at a time. Once `paint` is entered and its `while` loop starts executing, there is no chance for `actionPerformed` to execute and therefore no way that `keepGoing` can be made false again—the loop executes forever.

In this example there really are two tasks that must be carried out concurrently:

- Drawing the rectangles on the `Canvas`
- Responding to the user's actions

Building the applet to use two threads instead of one is a good way to address this.

Introducing the `Thread` Class   Java provides a class, called `Thread`, that models threads and allows us to build applications and applets in which more than one thread is at work. Using this class, we can create `Thread` objects that are associated with a particular piece of code that we want to execute as a thread—simultaneously with other threads. In the multimedia example, we might have one `Thread` object that executes the code to play music, a second `Thread` object that executes the code to display a sequence of images, and a third `Thread` object that executes the code that scrolls text. Each `Thread` object will execute its code at the same time as the other `Thread` objects and therefore carry out its task simultaneously.

Simultaneity and Concurrency

Simultaneity—literally carrying out instructions from different codes at exactly the same time—is not possible on most desktops at this time. Instead, the Java Interpreter, which implements the Java Virtual Machine, repeatedly cycles through the codes, doing a bit of work on each thread before going to the next. At this level there is only one thread, which is carrying out the code of the various `Thread` objects in the application. Thus, we can use `Thread`s to design our application as if they were multiple, simultaneously executing codes, and the Java Interpreter does all the work of making these codes execute not simultaneously but concurrently—running in an interwoven fashion, overlapped in time. If implemented correctly, the concurrent execution of these codes can be made to appear as if it were simultaneous execution.

Interweaving code is done quite differently from one desktop machine to the next. As a result, applications using `Thread`s on these machines may vary considerably in their time-dependent behavior.

The availability of Threads considerably expands the opportunities available to the programmer. Without Threads, our code carries out a single task at a time. It is like a band that consists of a single musician, say a bass player, just playing a bass line. With Threads, our program can carry out multiple tasks simultaneously (or at least concurrently). It's as if the one-player band can now acquire a drummer, a rhythm and lead guitarist, a saxophonist, and several vocalists.

The Thread class provides several methods that allow Thread objects to be controlled:

- start—starts the execution of the Thread. Until this method is invoked, the Thread may exist as an object, but the code it is associated with—the code that we want to execute simultaneously—has not yet started executing.
- suspend—asks the Thread to suspend the execution of its code until the resume method is invoked.
- resume—asks the Thread to continue executing code that has been suspended
- stop—asks the Thread to permanently cease execution of its code. Once stopped, a Thread cannot be started again.

Here is a simple example of a non-GUI application that creates two Threads and starts them executing:

```
class DoNothingThreadExample {
    public static void main(String[] a) {
        Thread t1 = new Thread();
        Thread t2 = new Thread();
        t1.start();
        t2.start();
    }
}
```

If you run this program, nothing happens—the program terminates almost immediately. That's because the code that a Thread object executes by default is empty—so it completes immediately and does nothing. To make a Thread object that does something useful, we need to extend the Thread class in a way that is similar to our extension of the Applet class:

```
class simpleCounter extends Thread {
    rest of the definition
}
```

We then provide it with a method called run with the following prototype:

```
public void run()
```

It is the run method that defines the code that the Thread object executes simultaneously.

A Non-GUI `Thread` Example   In this example, the code our `Thread` executes just prints out integers, starting from 0, incremented by a quantity given in the constructor:

```
class CountingThread extends Thread {
    public CountingThread(int x) {
        this.x = x;
    }
    public void run() {
        int    i=0;
        while (i<15) {
            System.out.println(i);
                i+=x;
        }
    }
    private    int              x;
}
```

The code below creates two `CountingThread` objects, with different increments (2 and 3), and starts each object executing:

```
class CountingThreadExample {
    public static void main(String a[]) {
        CountingThread  t1 = new CountingThread(2);
        CountingThread t2 = new CountingThread(3);
        t1.start();
        t2.start();
    }
}
```

The output of the program on a typical desktop computer depends on the way the Java Interpreter interweaves the two executing `Thread`s. The Java rules give it quite a bit of leeway in this regard. In fact, a likely output is

```
0
2
4
6
8
10
12
14
0
3
6
9
12
```

There is no interweaving at all. The rules of the Java interpreter require that if an executing `Thread` object becomes temporarily unable to proceed (for example, it is waiting for input or is temporarily suspended), any `Thread` that is able to execute will then do so.

We can force our `Thread` objects to become temporarily unable to proceed by making them *sleep*—that is, suspend their own execution for a time that we specify. The Java code that does this is

```
try {
    sleep(35);     Suspend my execution for 35 milliseconds.
} catch(Exception e) {}
```

The extra syntax here (`try...catch`) is unfortunate but necessary. Its meaning, which we can ignore for now, will be made clear in Chapter 14.

Using this feature to suspend execution for 1 millisecond after each increment of i, we rewrite the `run` method of `CountingThread` as follows:

```
public void run() {
    int    i=0;
    while (i<15) {
        System.out.println(i);
        i+=x;
        try {
            sleep(1);
        } catch(Exception e) {}
    }
}
```

Executing the program now, the output is

```
0
0
2
3
4
6
6
9
8
12
10
12
14
```

and the interweaving is apparent.

The `RedGreen` Applet with Threads   Let's use our thread technology to fix the `RedGreen` applet that we considered earlier. As we pointed out, there are two tasks:

- Drawing the rectangles on the `Canvas`
- Responding to the user's actions

If we make a separate thread for drawing that runs concurrently with the applet itself, the applet will be free to respond properly to button clicks. To do this, we define another class, a `RedGreenThread` class, extended from `Thread`. Its `run` method will contain code that is similar to that of the earlier applet's `paint` method. However, we will make the loop condition always `true` so that the thread never terminates as long as the applet is running. We also add a 50-millisecond `sleep` to the loop to improve the appearance of the alternating colors. Our first draft of this class is as follows:

```
class RedGreenThread extends Thread {
    RedGreenThread(Canvas c) {
        this.c = c;
    }
    public void run() {
        Graphics gc = c.getGraphics();
        while (true) {
            gc.setColor(new Color(200,50,50));
            gc.fillRect(5,5,90,40);
            try {
                sleep(50);
            } catch(Exception e) {}
            gc.setColor(new Color(50,200,50));
            gc.fillRect(5,5,90,40);
            try {
                sleep(50);
            } catch(Exception e) {}
        }
    }
    private Canvas c;
}
```

The applet will create the `Canvas` and add it to its display. It will have to pass a reference to it to the `RedGreenThread` constructor so that the run method can display rectangles on it.

We need to provide a way for the applet to suspend and resume execution of this thread. The `Thread` class provides `resume` and `suspend` methods. However, for security reasons, applets are not allowed to directly suspend, resume, or stop other threads (you wouldn't want to download some stranger's applet onto your machine and have it start suspending other threads on your browser, would you?). We can, however, provide our own version of these methods. They can set a `boolean` instance variable, `amRunning`, to `true` or `false`, and we can use this variable to control whether any painting actually gets done:

```
class RedGreenThread extends Thread {
    RedGreenThread(Canvas c) {
        this.c = c;
    }
```

```
public void run() {
    Graphics gc = c.getGraphics();
    amRunning = true;
    while (true)
        if (amRunning) {

            gc.setColor(new Color(200,50,50));
            gc.fillRect(5,5,90,40);
            try {
                sleep(50);
            } catch(Exception e) {}
            gc.setColor(new Color(50,200,50));
            gc.fillRect(5,5,90,40);
            try {
                sleep(50);
            } catch(Exception e) {}
        }
}

public void mySuspend() {
    amRunning=false;
}

public void myResume() {
    amRunning=true;
}

private Canvas c;
private boolean amRunning=false;
}
```

The RedGreen applet can then be rewritten using this class. The paint method is no longer needed because the red and green squares are constantly being redrawn by the run method in our thread. When the start button is clicked, the button's label is changed to stop, and the thread is created and started. When the stop button is clicked, the label is changed to resume, and the thread is suspended. When the resume button is clicked, the thread is resumed and the button label changed back to stop. (See Figure 9.3.) The actions for resume and stop now are taken in terms of the RedGreenThread:

```
import java.awt.event.*;
import java.applet.*;

public class RedGreen extends Applet
                        implements ActionListener{
    public void init() {
        setLayout(new BorderLayout(2,2));
        b = new Button("start");
```

FIGURE 9.3
Threaded version of
`RedGreen`. Using a
separate thread for
painting allows the
applet user to start,
stop, and resume the
alternation of red and
green images.

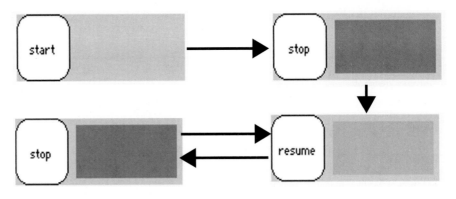

```
        b.addActionListener(this);
        c = new Canvas();
        add("West",b);
        add("East",c);
        c.setSize(100,50);
    }

    public void actionPerformed(ActionEvent ae) {
        String s = ae.getActionCommand();
        if (s.equals("start"))
            handleStart();
        else if (s.equals("resume"))
            handleResume();
        else if (s.equals("stop"))
            handleStop();
    }

    private void handleStart() {
        b.setLabel("stop");
        rgt = new RedGreenThread(c);
        rgt.start();
    }

    private void handleResume() {
        b.setLabel("stop");
        rgt.myResume();
    }

    private void handleStop() {
        b.setLabel("resume");
        rgt.mySuspend();
    }

    private Button          b;
    private Canvas          c;
```

```
        private RedGreenThread  rgt=null;
}
```

Note that in the course of using this applet, many `RedGreenThread` threads may be created, one for each time the start button is clicked.

Multiple Clocks: A More Elaborate Example We close this supplement with one more example of a thread-based applet. The applet shown in Figure 9.4, displays two digital clocks, each with its own start/stop button. One clock displays eastern standard time (EST), the other Greenwich mean time (GMT).

The architecture of this applet is essentially identical to the threaded `RedGreen` applet above. There are two classes, `ClockApplet` and `ClockAppletThread`. For each clock, the `ClockApplet`'s init method creates a `Button` for control and a `Label` for display. The `init` method goes through the usual gyrations to place these components properly. In addition, it sets the applet up as a listener for action events associated with the `Buttons`. The `actionPerformed` method of the `ClockApplet` determines the event that occurred and invokes the `handleStart` or `handleStop` helper method accordingly, passing an `int` argument to indicate which clock the event was associated with. These methods relabel the relevant `Button` so that start becomes stop, stop becomes resume, and resume becomes stop. In addition, the `handleStart` method creates and starts a `ClockThread` method, associating it with the appropriate `Label` and giving it a `String` indicating the time zone (GMT or EST). The `handleStop` method simply invokes the `mySuspend` method of the appropriate `ClockThread` object. The `handleResume` method invokes the `myResume` method. All this is analogous to the `RedGreen` applet that we studied above.

The `ClockAppletThread`'s constructor stores its parameter values, a reference to the `Label` for the clock and a `String` representing the time zone, in its instance variables. The `run`, `mySuspend`, and `myResume` methods and the `boolean` instance variable `amRunning` all play the same roles that they did in the `RedGreenThread` above.

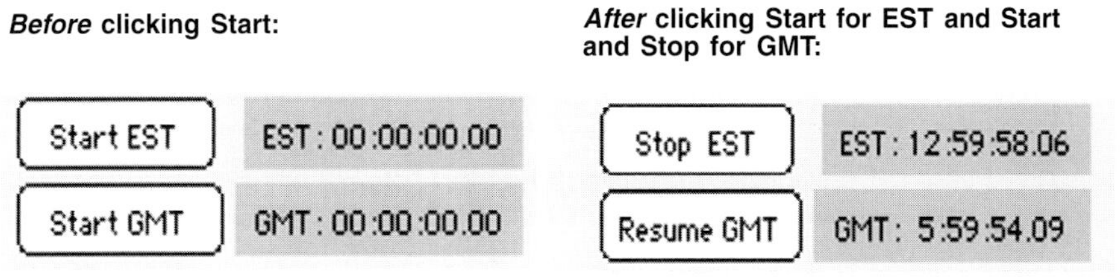

Before clicking Start:

After clicking Start for EST and Start and Stop for GMT:

FIGURE 9.4   A multiple clock applet. This applet displays time in two time zones: EST and GMT. Each clock has its own start and stop buttons. Once started, the time is updated constantly and displayed in hours/minutes/seconds and hundredths of seconds.

The actual work done by the `run` method is repeated invocations of the helper method `oneTick`, which models a single tick of the clock. This method makes use of the `GregorianCalendar` class that Java provides to model time and date in the context of the Gregorian calendar, the calendar used by most of the western countries and indeed by much of the world. A `GregorianCalendar` object represents a single moment in time. Its constructor requires an `int` that represents the time zone of interest. Rather than make programmers remember which `int` represents which time zone, Java provides a `TimeZone` class that offers a static method called `getTimeZone`. This method takes an easy-to-remember `String` (like "EST" or "PST") and returns the correct integer representation. Once created, the `GregorianCalendar` object can be sent messages to extract the hours, minutes, and seconds that are associated with its particular moment.

The remainder of `oneTick` builds the needed display `String` for the time using the integers extracted from the `GregorianCalendar` object. To handle the case of single-digit hours, minutes, and seconds it uses the `leadingDigit` helper method.

The Complete Applet   Here is the complete code for the `ClockApplet`:

```java
import java.util.*;
import java.awt.*;
import java.awt.event.*;
import java.applet.*;

public class ClockApplet extends Applet
                         implements ActionListener {

    public void init() {
        Color backgroundColor = new Color(200,255,255);
        setLayout(new FlowLayout(
                    FlowLayout.CENTER,4,1));
        clock1 = new Label("EST: 00:00:00.00",
                        Label.CENTER);
        clock2 = new Label("GMT: 00:00:00.00",
                        Label.CENTER);
        clock1Button = new Button(start1ButtonCommand);
        clock1Button.addActionListener(this);
        clock2Button = new Button(start2ButtonCommand);
        clock2Button.addActionListener(this);
        clock1Panel = new Panel();
        clock1Panel.setLayout(new BorderLayout(2,2));
        clock2Panel = new Panel();
        clock2Panel.setLayout(new BorderLayout(2,2));
        clock1Panel.add("West",clock1Button);
        clock1Panel.add("East",clock1);
        clock2Panel.add("West",clock2Button);
```

```
    clock2Panel.add("East",clock2);
      mainPanel = new Panel();
      mainPanel.setLayout(new BorderLayout(2,2));
      mainPanel.add("North",clock1Panel);
      mainPanel.add("South",clock2Panel);
      add(mainPanel);
      setBackground(backgroundColor);
   }

   public void actionPerformed(ActionEvent ae) {
      String whichButton = ae.getActionCommand();
      if (whichButton.equals(start1ButtonCommand))
         handleStart(1);
      else if (whichButton.
              equals(resume1ButtonCommand))
         handleResume(1);
      else if (whichButton.equals(stop1ButtonCommand))
         handleStop(1);
      else if (whichButton.
              equals(start2ButtonCommand))
         handleStart(2);
      else if (whichButton.
              equals(resume2ButtonCommand))
         handleResume(2);
      else if (whichButton.equals(stop2ButtonCommand))
         handleStop(2);
   }

   private void handleStart(int n) {
      if (n==1) {
         clock1Button.setLabel(stop1ButtonCommand);
         clockTicker1 = new
                    ClockThread(clock1,"EST");
         clockTicker1.start();
      } else if (n==2) {
         clock2Button.setLabel(stop2ButtonCommand);
         clockTicker2 = new
                    ClockThread(clock2,"GMT");
         clockTicker2.start();
      }
   }

   private void handleResume(int n) {
      if (n==1) {
         clock1Button.setLabel(stop1ButtonCommand);
         clockTicker1.myResume();
      } else if (n==2) {
         clock2Button.setLabel(stop2ButtonCommand);
         clockTicker2.myResume();
```

```
            }
        }

        private void handleStop(int n) {
            if (n==1) {
                clock1Button.setLabel(resume1ButtonCommand);
                clockTicker1.mySuspend();
            } else if (n==2) {
                clock2Button.setLabel(resume2ButtonCommand);
                clockTicker2.mySuspend();
            }
        }

        private     Panel     clock1Panel, clock2Panel,
                                          mainPanel;
        private     Button    clock1Button, clock2Button;
        private     String    start1ButtonCommand=
                                          "Start EST",
                              resume1ButtonCommand=
                                          "Resume EST",
                              stop1ButtonCommand=
                                          "Stop EST",
                              start2ButtonCommand=
                                          "Start GMT",
                              resume2ButtonCommand=
                                          "Resume GMT",
                              stop2ButtonCommand=
                                          "Stop GMT";
        private     Label     clock1, clock2;
        private     ClockThread    clockTicker1,clockTicker2;
}

class ClockThread extends Thread {
    ClockThread(Label theLabel, String timeZone) {
        this.clock = theLabel;
        this.timeZone = timeZone;
    }

    public void run() {
        amRunning = true;
        while (true)
            if (amRunning) {
                oneTick();
                try {
                    this.sleep(20);
                } catch (Exception e) {;}
            }
    }

    public void mySuspend() {
```

```
            amRunning = false;
        }

        public void myResume() {
            amRunning = true;
        }

        private void oneTick() {
            GregorianCalendar gc =
                        new GregorianCalendar(TimeZone.
                                        getTimeZone(timeZone));
            int     h = gc.get(Calendar.HOUR);
            int     m = gc.get(Calendar.MINUTE);
            int     s = gc.get(Calendar.SECOND);
            int     ms= gc.get(Calendar.MILLISECOND);
            String  hms = leadingDigit(h," ")+":" +
                        leadingDigit(m,"0")+":" +
                        leadingDigit(s,"0")+"." +
                        leadingDigit(ms/10,"0");
            clock.setText(hms);
    }

    private String leadingDigit(int n, String leader) {
        if (n<10)
            return leader+n;
        return ""+n;
    }

    private Label   clock;
    private boolean amRunning;
    private String  timeZone;
}
```

chapter 10

Organizing Objects

10.1   Indexing

A `Vector` does more than maintain a collection of references to objects—it maintains them in a particular order. The first element added to the `Vector` is in position 0, the next element added is in position 1, the next is in position 2, and so forth. As you can see in Figure 10.1, the positions are numbered, starting with 0. Numbering positions this way is called *indexing*. An **index** is an integer used to indicate the position of an element in a collection such as a `Vector`.

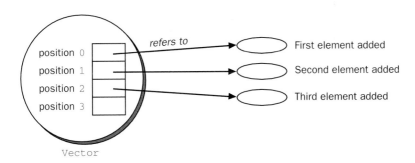

FIGURE 10.1   **Positions in a `Vector`.** The elements of a `Vector` object are maintained in indexed positions, starting from 0. Each element is a reference to an object.

To use the reference stored in a particular position, we use the `Vector`'s `elementAt` method, which takes an index as an argument:

```
v.elementAt(2)
```

This code returns the reference stored in position 2 of `Vector` v. Because positions are numbered from 0, this is the third reference stored in v. Thus, the code fragment

```
Vector v = new Vector();
v.addElement("What'll");
v.addElement("you do");
v.addElement("when you");
v.addElement("get lonely?");
String s = (String) v.elementAt(2);
System.out.println(s);
```

> Remember: The elements in a Vector are references to Objects; they must be cast to their actual type when used.

prints "when you." (See Figure 10.2.)

As elements are added to a `Vector`, the `Vector` object keeps count of the number of positions occupied and will provide that information through the `size` method:

```
System.out.println(v.size());
```

the above prints out the number of elements in `Vector` v. In the example above, this value would be 4. Note that the size of the `Vector` is always one more than the index of its last position. This relationship is a consequence of

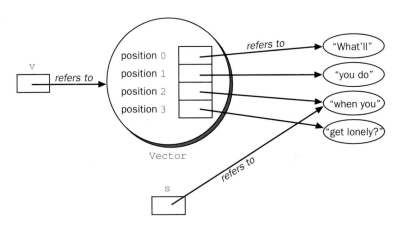

FIGURE 10.2 A `Vector` of `Strings`. After the assignment
`s = (String) v.elementAt(2);`
s refers to the same `String` object as position 2 of v.

the first position being numbered 0. Thus, the index of the last position of a
`Vector v` is given by

```
v.size()-1
```

(You might also think of it this way: If there is only one element, the last position is 0 even though the number of positions is 1.)

Example   **Finding Median Income.** Suppose we had a file, `incomes`, that contained the family income of every student in a college who receives financial aid. Each family's income appears on a line by itself. Assume that the file is sorted in increasing order and that we wish to find the median income in order to verify that financial aid is indeed going to those who need it most.

To make things simple, let's assume that each family income is unique (no two students have the same family income) and that there is an odd number of students. In that case, the median is that income in the set such that half the other incomes are larger and half are smaller. (So, for the set of numbers {13,500, 15,000, 18,000, 25,400, 31,600} the median is 18,000 because two values are above and two values below 18,000).

If we read all the lines from the file and store them in a `Vector v`, using the read/process loop pattern, we can calculate the index of the element containing the median:

```
v.size()/2
```

We can then use this value, with `elementAt`, to access and print the median:

```
System.out.println(v.elementAt(v.size()/2));
```

A complete program for printing the median income is:

```
class FindMedian {
    public static void main(String[] a) throws Exception {
        BufferedReader f = new BufferedReader(
                    new InputStreamReader(
                        new FileInputStream("incomes")));
        Vector v = new Vector();
        String s;
        s = f.readLine();
        while (s!=null) {
            v.addElement(s);
            s = f.readLine();
        }
        System.out.println(v.elementAt(v.size()/2));
    }
}
```

1. Rewrite FindMedian, and relax the assumption that there is an odd number of values. Instead, when the number of values is even, let the median be the average of the two middle-most values. (So, for {12, 21, 27, 42} the median would be 24, the average of 21 and 27.)

2. Given a Vector v with three elements, each a reference to a String, write code that will print every one of the six permutations of the three Strings.

10.2   The Limitations of Enumerations

When we traverse the elements of a Vector by creating an Enumeration, we have no control over the order of elements given to us by successive invocations of nextElement. The order is determined by the implementor of the Vector class. This order may not always suit our needs.

For example, suppose we wanted to read in a file (via standard input) and write its lines in reverse order to standard output. (See Figure 10.3.) We can read each line as a String and add it to a Vector:

```
class ReverseLines {
    public static void main(String[] a) throws Exception {
        BufferedReader f = new BufferedReader(
                        new InputStreamReader(System.in));
        Vector          v = new Vector();
        String          line;
        line = f.readLine();
        while (line != null) {
            v.addElement(line);
            line = f.readLine();
        }
        ...
```

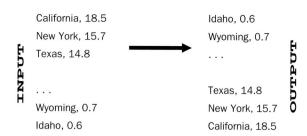

FIGURE 10.3   Reversing the lines in a file.

But if we use an `Enumeration` to extract the elements, we have no guarantee that they will come out in reverse order:

```
    ...
    Enumeration e = v.elements();                        These three lines
    while (e.hasMoreElements())                          won't print in
        System.out.println(e.nextElement());            reverse—we need to
                                                         replace them.
  }
}
```

In fact, it is extremely unlikely that the lines will be printed in reverse order.

We can resolve this problem by using indexing and the `elementAt` method to construct a loop that writes the elements of a `Vector` v to standard output in any order that we choose, in this case reverse.

Informal Procedure   To print the elements of a `Vector` in reverse order, we first print the element in the last position (given by `v.size()-1`), then the one in the second to last position, and so on, until we print out the first element of the `Vector` at position 0. At that point, having printed all of the elements out, we stop.

Choosing and Defining Variables   We need to keep track of the position we are up to. Position is given by an index, so we will need an integer variable. We must be very precise here. Should this integer denote the next position to print or should it denote the position printed most recently? Either meaning is fine so long as we are consistent. We will choose the first one:

```
int k;  // k== the index of the next position in the Vector to print.
```

According to our informal procedure, if k is the *next* position to print, all the positions after k, starting with `v.size()-1`, then `v.size()-2`, and on *down* to k+1, must already have been printed. This observation is worth adding as a comment to the declaration because it gives further information about the meaning of k. We might further remark that, according to our informal procedure, if k is the *next* position to print, then all the positions that remain to be printed are k, k-1, and on *down* to 0:

```
int k;  // k== the index of the next position in the Vector to print.
        // Positions v.size()-1, v.size()-2, ..., k+1 have already been printed.
        // Positions k, k-1, ..., 0 remain to be printed.
```

The first comment describes the next step of the task that is to be performed, the second describes the work that has already been performed, and the third describes the work that remains.

When working with variables that hold the index of a position in a `Vector`, it is helpful to use a diagram such as the one in Figure 10.4.

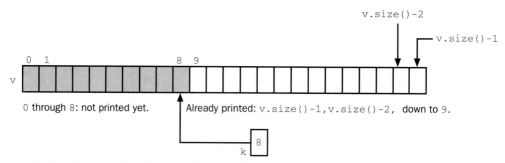

FIGURE 10.4   Visualizing the meaning of an index to a `Vector`. The vector is logically divided into two regions: (1) k, k-1, down to 0 where the elements have not yet been printed (shaded) and (2) `v.size()-1, v.size()-2`, down to k+1, where they have been printed (unshaded).

10.2.1   The `while` Condition

We are finished when all the `Vector` elements have been printed, that is, when positions

            `v.size()-1, v.size()-2, ..., 0`

have been printed. Our understanding of k is that positions

            `v.size()-1, v.size()-2, ..., k+1`

have been printed. These expressions are identical when k is -1. So, when k is -1, k+1 is 0 and we are done. To guarantee that k equals -1 when the loop terminates, our loop condition is `k!=-1`:

```
int k;  // k== the index of the next position in the Vector to print.
        // Positions v.size()-1, v.size()-2, ..., k+1 have already been printed.
        // Positions k, k-1, ..., 0 remain to be printed.
    ...
while (k != -1)
        body
        // k== -1 and therefore v.size()-1, v.size()-2, ..., 0 have already been
        //    printed. (see Figure 10.5.)
```

Initialization   The definition of k indicates that it is the index of the next position to print. Our informal procedure tells us that at the outset this must be `v.size()-1`:

            `k = v.size()-1;`

Guaranteeing Termination   Decrementing k by 1 in the loop body guarantees that eventually k will fall to -1:

```
int k;      // k== the index of the next position in the Vector to print.
            // Positions v.size()-1, v.size()-2, ..., k+1 have already been printed.
            // positions k, k-1, ..., 0 remain to be printed.
```

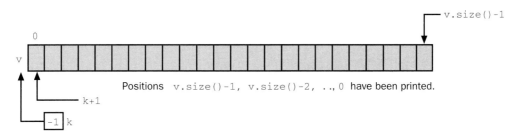

FIGURE 10.5   Visualizing the completion of printing. The task is complete when all the elements of the `Vector` have been printed in reverse, that is, when `k` equals −1 (and `k+1` equals 0).

```
k = v.size()-1;
while (k != -1) {
    body
    --k;
}
// k== -1 and therefore v.size()-1, v.size()-2, ..., 0 have already been printed.
```

Completing the Loop Body   Decrementing `k` means that what was position `k` is now position `k+1`; in order for this to be justified, that position must have been printed out before the decrement:

```
System.out.println(v.elementAt(k));
```

Copying the code from the beginning of this section, our completed code is as follows:

```
class ReverseLines {
    public static void main(String[] a) throws Exception {
        BufferedReader in = new BufferedReader(
                        new InputStreamReader(System.in));
        Vector          v = new Vector();
        String          line;
        line = f.readLine();
        while (line != null) {
            v.addElement(line);
            line = f.readLine();
        }
        int k;     // k== the index of the next position in the Vector to print.
                   // Positions v.size()-1, v.size()-2, ..., k+1 have already been
                   //    printed.
                   // Positions k, k-1, ..., 0 remain to be printed
        k = v.size()-1;
        while (k != -1) {
            System.out.println(v.elementAt(k));
            --k;
        }
```

```
            //  k== −1 and therefore v.size()−1, v.size()−2, ..., 0 have already
            //          been printed.
        }
    }
```

10.2.2   Discussion

In order to print the elements of a `Vector` in reverse of the order in which they were added, we needed to access every element in a `Vector` without using an `Enumeration`. The use of an index and `Vector`'s `elementAt` method allow us to do this. We will refer to this loop pattern as *downward index traversal*.

Why then use `Enumerations` at all? The answer is that very often the order of the elements is irrelevant and the simple loop pattern of `Enumeration`,

```
while (e.hasMoreElements()) {
    o = e.next();
    // process o
}
```

is far less error-prone than the loop we constructed above, careful though we were. A forgotten decrement, a miscalculated loop termination value (0 instead of −1), and the loop is incorrect.

EXERCISES

1. Given a `Vector` v of references to `String` objects, write a loop that prints the `String`s to standard output, one to a line, starting from position 0 but skipping the odd positions (indexes 1, 3, 5, ...).

2. You have two files, `names` and `numbers`. The `names` file has 20 names, one to a line. The `numbers` file has 20 integers, each between 1 and 20 inclusive, one to a line. Write a program that reads from these files and writes to standard output the names in the order given by the `numbers` file. That is, if the first line in `numbers` is 7, the seventh name is printed first. If the second line in `numbers` is 4, the fourth name is printed second, and so on.
   •

10.3   Searching

People spend much of their lives searching for keys, for a parking spot, for a biology lab section that is not closed and that doesn't meet on Friday afternoon, and so on. Programs spend even more time searching for a bank record corresponding to a customer number, for an inventory record corresponding to a part number, for the web page that a client browser has requested, and so on. Often the objects that programs search for are stored in collections such as `Vector`s.

The predicate method `contains` in the `Set` class from Chapter 8 used an `Enumeration` to search a `Vector`. That method returned `true` if the element was found. However, we often need to know more than whether the element is present. For example, we might want its index in the `Vector` so that we could use `elementAt` to access the element itself. Let's write a method, `search`, that receives a `String` parameter and searches for it in a `Vector`, v, that contains references to `String`s. The method returns the index of the `String` if it finds the `String` in the `Vector` and returns −1 otherwise. We choose −1 to represent "not found" because a negative integer cannot possibly be a legitimate index—any other negative integer would work as well. The prototype for `search` is as follows:

```
private int search(String s) {    // Returns the index of a match to s in v
    ...                           //    or −1 if there is no match.
}
```

As we did in `contains`, we will need to examine many elements from the `Vector`, and so we turn to our standard approach to loop design to construct this code.

Informal Procedure   We must check every element in the `Vector` until we find a match or until there are no more elements to check. One way to do this methodically is to check the element in position 0, then the element in position 1, then 2, and so on. By proceeding from 0 and going up, checking every position as we go, we will eventually get to each position—we won't miss any.

Choosing and Defining Variables   We need to keep track of our current position and so we need an integer variable to hold this index. As in the downward index traversal, we must be precise here. Should this integer denote the next position to check or the position checked most recently? Either meaning is fine, so long as we are consistent. We will choose the first one:

```
int k;       // k== the index of the next position in the Vector to check.
```

According to our informal procedure, if k is the next position to check, all the positions before k, that is, 0, ..., k-1, must already have been checked. We add this observation as an additional comment. (See Figure 10.6.)

```
int k;       // k== the index of the next position in the Vector to check.
             // No match has been found in positions 0 through k−1.
```

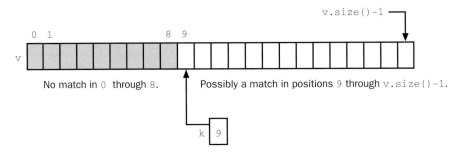

FIGURE 10.6   The meaning of the index in searching a `Vector`. The vector is logically divided into two regions by `k`: (1) 0 through `k-1`, where no match has been found (shaded) and (2) `k` through `v.size()-1`, where a match may yet by found (unshaded).

Skeleton of the Code   We write:

```
private int search(String s) {    // Returns the index of a match to s in
                                  //    v or −1 if there is no match

    int k;                        // k== the index of the next position in
                                  //    the Vector to check.
                                  // No match has been found in
                                  //    positions 0 through k−1.

    ...
    while (condition)
        body
    ...
}
```

The `while` Condition   We are finished when the object in the next position to check matches the parameter *or* when there are no more positions to check. The object in the next position is given by

```
v.elementAt(k)
```

To see if this object and the parameter object, `s`, are equal we may write

```
s.equals(v.elementAt(k))
```

If this condition is true, we have found a match to the parameter and are finished—we can return `true`.

On the other hand, if

```
k==v.size()
```

we are confident that no match exists. That's because the definition of `k` tells us that there is no match in positions 0, `...`, `k-1`; with `k==v.size()`, no

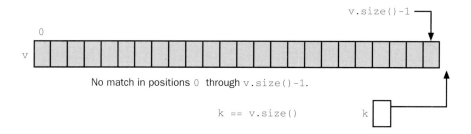

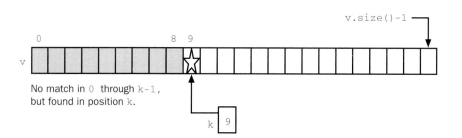

FIGURE 10.7 When the search is complete. (Top) The search is complete when we see that the object has no match in the Vector *or* (bottom) the object's match in the Vector has been found in position k.

match has been found in positions 0, ..., v.size()-1—no match anywhere in the Vector. Thus, we are finished when

```
// k==v.size() || s.equals(v.elementAt(k))
```

(See Figure 10.7.)

We plan to test k==v.size() first because v.elementAt(k) is illegal if k==v.size(). By testing k's value first we make sure—thanks to short-circuiting—that s.equals(v.elementAt(k)) will not be evaluated when k==v.size().

To guarantee that this is true when the loop terminates, the loop condition is

```
!(k==v.size() || s.equals(v.elementAt(k)))
```

Our code now is

```
private int search(String s) {      // Returns the index of a match to s in
                                    //    v or −1 if there is no match.
        int k;                      // k== the index of the next position in
                                    //    the Vector to check.
                                    // No match has been found in
                                    //    positions 0 through k−1.

        ...
```

```
        while (!(k==v.size() || s.equals(v.elementAt(k))))
            body
        // k==v.size() || s.equals(v.elementAt(k))
}
```

Before continuing our development, let's make sure that we can easily complete the method once it is known that

```
k==v.size() OR s.equals(v.elementAt(k))
```

In fact, we can. One or the other of the above conditions is `true`—they can't be both `true` because if `k` is equal to `v.size()`, it is the index of the position after the last valid position of the `Vector` and there is no element at that position—in that case we should return −1. If `k` is not equal to `v.size()`, we know that the second clause in the *OR* is true and `k` must be the index of the match we found—in that case we should return `k`:

```
if (k==v.size())
    return -1;
else
    return k;
```

Initialization   The definition of `k` indicates that it is the index of the next position to check. Our informal procedure tells us that this must be 0:

```
k = 0;
```

Guaranteeing Termination   By incrementing `k` by 1 in the loop body, we know that eventually `k` will equal `v.size()` or that we will find a match to `s` in position `k`.

```
private int search(String s) { // Returns the index of a match to s in v
                               //     or −1 if there is no match.
    int k;                     // k== the index of the next position in
                               //     the vector to check.
                               // No match has been found in positions
                               //     0 through k−1.
    k = 0;
    while (!(k==v.size() || s.equals(v.elementAt(k))))
        k++;
    // k==v.size || s.equals(v.elementAt(k))
    if (k==v.size())
        return -1;
    else
        return k;
}
```

Completing the Loop Body   Usually, this step is taken because the code that guarantees termination (k++ here) causes a momentary violation of the definition of one of our variables. Here, however, this violation does not occur because the loop condition itself has already ascertained that position k does not match the parameter and so incrementing k is safe—it will not violate the claim that no match has been found in positions 0 through k-1. Remarkably, perhaps, the loop is already complete. Because we added no new code, there is no need for additional initializations, and the method above is complete.

Discussion   The loop in our new search method starts in position 0 and accesses elements of the Vector from lower to higher index. The order we consider the elements in the Vector is now in our control, not the control of an Enumeration. The search method gives us the index of the element, unlike the contains method, which merely indicated whether the element was present or not. The search algorithm used here is called the **sequential search** because the elements are searched in the sequence in which they are stored in the Vector.

EXERCISES

1. Rewrite the search method so that it starts its search at the end of the Vector and searches backward toward position 0. In doing this, start from scratch, following the approach to loop construction that we have been following. Do not try to use the above search method as a starting point and then just modify it here and there. That path is error-prone.

2. Write a predicate method, vcontains, that receives two arguments: a String and a Vector of Strings. The method returns true if the first argument matches one of the elements of the Vector; otherwise it returns false.

3. Write a method, vsearch, that receives two arguments: Each is a Vector of Strings. The method returns the index of a String in the first Vector that matches an element of the second Vector. Use the vcontains method you wrote in the previous exercise to help you.   •

10.4   Self-Organizing Vectors

Suppose that most of the items in a Vector are rarely searched for and that most of the time we are looking for just a small subset of the items in the Vector. We might call this small group of times the "frequently requested items."

This request pattern is not unusual. For example, a phone-order application might have an `inStock` object that contains a `Vector` of `Strings` that represent items that are in stock. To tell an operator whether a customer's order item is available, the application invokes the `search` method, passing the order item as an argument. Although the number of in-stock items might be large (say around 2000), 90 percent of the time customers order from the 100 most commonly requested items—just 5 percent of the items in the `Vector`.

If we can store these frequently requested items near the front of the `Vector`, we can greatly speed up the sequential search. With no special arrangement, a sequential search through a `Vector` of 2000 elements requires 1000 iterations on the average. But if the 100 most frequently searched for items are among the first 200 elements in the `Vector` they can be found, on the average, with just 100 iterations, speeding up the search by a factor of 10.

The first step in storing the frequently requested items near the front of the `Vector` is to identify them. A useful insight here is this: When `search` finds a match to s, that is, when

```
s.equals(v.elementAt(k))
```

is `true`, the element at position k (the match) is likely to be a reference to one of the frequently requested items. These elements should be moved up within the `Vector`. But to where precisely and how can this be done? (See Figure 10.8.)

10.4.1 `move-to-front`: A Reordering Algorithm

One approach is to move the element found in position k to the very beginning of the `Vector`. This moves requires two steps:

- Insert (squeeze in) a copy of the element in front of position 0—the copy becomes the new position 0; the old position 0 will now be called position 1. All succeeding positions are renumbered similarly.

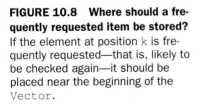

FIGURE 10.8 Where should a frequently requested item be stored?
If the element at position k is frequently requested—that is, likely to be checked again—it should be placed near the beginning of the Vector.

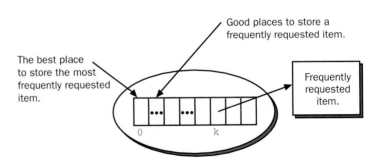

Good places to store a frequently requested item.

The best place to store the most frequently requested item.

Frequently requested item.

- Delete the original element that was found in position k—but be careful! That position is now called k+1 because we squeezed an new position in just before.

The Vector class provides methods for each step. The following does the squeeze:

```
v.insertElementAt(v.elementAt(k),0);
```

The first argument specifies the reference we want squeezed in and the second argument (0 in this case) specifies what we want it squeezed in front of. The following does the delete:

```
v.removeElementAt(k+1);  // k+1 because the insert caused a renumbering.
```

We can write a small helper method that carries out these two actions:

```
private void moveToFront(Vector v, int k) {
    v.insertElementAt(v.elementAt(k),0);
    v.removeElementAt(k+1);
}
```

and use this method to rewrite our search method:

```
private int search(String s) {          // Returns the index of a match to s in
                                        //    v or -1 if there is no match.
    int k;                              // k== the index of the next position in
                                        //    the vector to check.
                                        // No match has been found in
                                        //    positions 0 through k-1.
    k = 0;
    while (!(k==v.size() || s.equals(v.elementAt(k))))
        k++;
    // k==v.size() || s.equals(v.elementAt(k))
    if (k==v.size())
        return -1;
    else {
        moveToFront(v,k);               // Found a match at position k, so
                                        //    move it to the front.
        return 0;
    }
}
```

We only make a move if we have found a match—that is why we make sure it is not equal to v.size() before carrying out the move.

To visualize the effect of this strategy, let's suppose that we have 10 elements, A, B, C, D, E, F, G, H, I, and J, stored in that order in a Vector initially. Suppose the frequently requested items are D, G, and I with A and E occurring occasionally. Let's suppose the lookup sequence is DDGI DIID GADI EDGG. The following table shows the order of the Vector for each lookup and the number of positions checked before a match was found (for both move-to-front and with no reordering):

	Move-to-Front		No Reordering	
Item Sought	Vector	Number of positions checked	Vector	Number of positions checked
D	ABCDEFGHIJ	4	ABCDEFGHIJ	4
D	DABCEFGHIJ	1	ABCDEFGHIJ	4
G	DABCEFGHIJ	7	ABCDEFGHIJ	7
I	GDABCEFHIJ	9	ABCDEFGHIJ	9
D	IGDABCEFHJ	3	ABCDEFGHIJ	4
I	DIGABCEFHJ	2	ABCDEFGHIJ	9
I	IDGABCEFHJ	1	ABCDEFGHIJ	9
D	IDGABCEFHJ	2	ABCDEFGHIJ	4
G	DIGABCEFHJ	3	ABCDEFGHIJ	7
A	GDIABCEFHJ	4	ABCDEFGHIJ	1
D	AGDIBCEFHJ	3	ABCDEFGHIJ	4
I	DAGIBCEFHJ	3	ABCDEFGHIJ	9
E	DAGIBCEFHJ	7	ABCDEFGHIJ	5
D	EDAGIBCFHJ	2	ABCDEFGHIJ	4
G	DEAGIBCFHJ	4	ABCDEFGHIJ	7
G	GDEAIBCFHJ	1	ABCDEFGHIJ	7
TOTAL		56		94

The **move-to-front** approach involves considerably less position checking. In a large set, involving hundreds or thousands of positions, the results would be far more dramatic. There is, however, a hidden cost, which we will discuss in the Java Interlude below.

A vector whose order is changed as its elements are accessed is called a **self-organizing vector**. A self-organizing vector that moves its elements to the front when they are accessed is said to use the move-to-front strategy.

10.4.2   Behavior Versus Implementation

Although we have changed the `search` method to make it potentially more efficient, we have not changed its external behavior in the least—this change is strictly an internal one. Although a first course properly concentrates on the issues of program organization and behavior, much of computer science research and development is devoted to finding ways to make implementations more efficient. Often at the core of such endeavors is finding better ways to organize the data within a program (called *data structuring*). So it is no coincidence that it is in this chapter, where we acquire the ability to reorder objects, that we start exploring this other dimension of the field.

10.4.3 Transpose

One drawback of the move-to-front scheme is that on occasion a relatively infrequent element gets accessed and is moved to the front. The scheme overreacts in that sense. One alternative is to react less, much less, by just having the frequently requested item change places, that is, transpose it with the element ahead of it. So we replace the `moveToFront` helper method with the `transpose` helper method:

```
private void transpose(Vector  v,  int  k)  {
    if  (k!=0)  {
        v.insertElementAt(v.elementAt(k),k-1);◄——————— Position k−1 instead of position 0
        v.removeElementAt(k+1);
    }
}
```

Position `k-1` is the index of the element ahead of the one at position `k`. By inserting a copy of the element at position `k` ahead of position `k-1` and then deleting the original at what is now position `k+1` (it used to be `k`), we have made elements `k-1` and `k` swap places. Considering the same sequence as before:

	Transpose		No Reordering	
Item Sought	Vector	Number of positions checked	Vector	Number of positions checked
D	ABCDEFGHIJ	4	ABCDEFGHIJ	4
D	ABDCEFGHIJ	3	ABCDEFGHIJ	4
G	ADBCEFGHIJ	7	ABCDEFGHIJ	7
I	ADBCEGFHIJ	9	ABCDEFGHIJ	9
D	ADBCEGFIHJ	2	ABCDEFGHIJ	4
I	DABCEGFIHJ	8	ABCDEFGHIJ	9
I	DABCEGIFHJ	7	ABCDEFGHIJ	9
D	DABCEIGFHJ	1	ABCDEFGHIJ	4
G	DABCEIGFHJ	6	ABCDEFGHIJ	7
A	DABCEIGFHJ	2	ABCDEFGHIJ	1
D	ADBCEIGFHJ	2	ABCDEFGHIJ	4
I	DABCEIGFHJ	6	ABCDEFGHIJ	9
E	DABCIEGFHJ	6	ABCDEFGHIJ	5

	Transpose		No Reordering	
Item Sought	Vector	Number of positions checked	Vector	Number of positions checked
D	DABCEIGFHJ	1	ABCDEFGHIJ	4
G	DABCEIGFHJ	7	ABCDEFGHIJ	7
G	DABCEGIFHJ	6	ABCDEFGHIJ	7
TOTAL		71		94

This sequence suggests that move-to-front is superior to transpose, but we must not let ourselves be deceived by one comparison. It does take a longer time for the frequently requested items to move up to the front in the `transpose` strategy, but once they get there, the less frequently accessed items can do very little to displace them.

10.4.4   Move-Halfway-Up

One of the most enjoyable things in computer science is to try to think of better ways of doing the same thing—that is, looking for better implementations of the same behavior. Looking at move-to-front and transpose, we can make the following observations:

- Move-to-front gets frequently requested items to the front part of the `Vector` quickly but overreacts to occasionally referenced items, pushing them inappropriately to the front as well.
- Transpose doesn't let occasionally referenced items do much damage but is slow to get the frequently requested items to the front—they can advance only one position at a time.

Can we have it both ways? One attempt to get the benefit of both approaches without much drawback is to move the frequently requested item not by 1 and not all the way to the front but halfway. We can use the following helper method in place of `moveToFront` or `transpose`:

```
private void moveHalfwayUp(Vector v, int k) {
    if (k!=0) {
        v.insertElementAt(v.elementAt(k),k/2);
        v.removeElementAt(k+1);
    }
}
```

Position k/2, instead of position 0 or k−1. k/2 is halfway closer to the front.

Considering the same sequence as before:

	Move-to-Front		No Reordering	
Item Sought	Vector	Number of positions checked	Vector	Number of positions checked
D	ABCDEFGHIJ	4	ABCDEFGHIJ	4
D	ADBCEFGHIJ	2	ABCDEFGHIJ	4
G	DABCEFGHIJ	7	ABCDEFGHIJ	7
I	DABGCEFHIJ	9	ABCDEFGHIJ	9
D	DABGICEFHJ	1	ABCDEFGHIJ	4
I	DABGICEFHJ	5	ABCDEFGHIJ	9
I	DAIBGCEFHJ	3	ABCDEFGHIJ	9
D	DIABGCEFHJ	1	ABCDEFGHIJ	4
G	DIABGCEFHJ	5	ABCDEFGHIJ	7
A	DIGABCEFHJ	4	ABCDEFGHIJ	1
D	DAIGBCEFHJ	1	ABCDEFGHIJ	4
I	DAIGBCEFHJ	3	ABCDEFGHIJ	9
E	DIAGBCEFHJ	7	ABCDEFGHIJ	5
D	DIAEGBCFHJ	1	ABCDEFGHIJ	4
G	DIAEGBCFHJ	5	ABCDEFGHIJ	7
G	DIGAEBCFHJ	3	ABCDEFGHIJ	7
TOTAL		64		94

Move-halfway-up does not beat the move-to-front, because the latter always has the advantage at the outset because of its long moves forward. Note that of the three methods, only move-halfway-up left the three frequently requested letters here, D, G, and I, in the front of the `Vector`—this bodes well for additional item lookups.

1. What line in `search` must be changed if we replace `moveToFront` with `moveHalfwayUp` or `transpose`? What changes must be made?

2. Write the `search` method using the following rule: the item is moved up by one-tenth the size of the `Vector` itself, or if the item is too close to the front to be moved so far, just up to the front itself. So in a `Vector` of 1000 elements, elements 100 through 999 are moved up 100 positions, while elements 0 through 99 are moved to position 0.

3. Create your own rule.

The Methods of Vector and Their Efficiency

A SUMMARY OF THE METHODS OF THE Vector CLASS

When we first encountered the Vector class in Chapter 8, we used only two of its methods: addElement and elements. Now that we understand indexing, we can make use of the following methods:

- size()—returns an the number of elements in the Vector. Its value is 1 more than the index of the last element in the Vector.
- elementAt(int n)—returns an Object reference that is stored in position n of the Vector. The reference must be cast to the correct reference type in order to use it. This method allows us to access any element in a Vector given its index.
- insertElementAt(Object o, int n)—inserts the reference o just before the element whose index is n. This method allows us to insert elements in a Vector anywhere we choose, not just at the end.
- removeElementAt(int n)—removes the element whose index is n.

THE COSTS OF SQUEEZING IN AND DELETING ELEMENTS

Until now, we have not questioned the efficiency of methods, such as insertElementAt or nextElement, of Java's predefined classes. However, now that we are beginning to look at the efficiency of our own methods, we can't ignore this issue.

For example, our move-to-front approach in search seems to be a great improvement over the original implementation. But it includes an invocation of insertElementAt and removeElementAt. What if those methods were so slow that any gains that resulted from finding our match early were offset by the delay caused by using those methods?

As it turns out, the most common implementation of a Vector is reminiscent of a long row of movie theater seats. If seats 0 through 2 are occupied (from left to right) by Groucho, Chico, and Zeppo, respectively, and we want to insert Harpo to the left of Groucho, Zeppo has to move to seat 3, Chico to

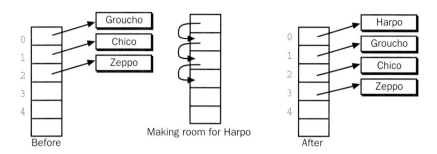

FIGURE 10.9   Squeezing in an element at position 0. The execution of `v.insertElementAt("Harpo",0)` places the reference to Harpo at position 0 and moves all the other elements down one position.

seat 2, and Groucho to seat 1 so that Harpo can sit down on seat 0. When we use `insertElementAt` to squeeze in an element before position 2, all the elements in position 2 and thereafter must move down one position. (See Figure 10.9.) If the `Vector` is long, there are many elements to move and the `insertElementAt` takes a long time.

Deleting an element using `removeElementAt` incurs a similar cost. If the element at position 5 is deleted, the element at position 6 takes its place, and the element at position 7 is moved to position 6, and so on. Again, if the `Vector` is long, there are a lot of elements to move and `removeElementAt` takes a long time.

To make move-to-front and transpose work efficiently, we will have to find better ways of implementing them.

THE `setElementAt` METHOD

The `setElementAt` method assigns an element to a particular position in a `Vector` without causing any other elements to move. This method is truly an assignment: Whatever reference was originally in that position is gone, just as in an assignment statement:

setElementAt	**Assignment**
`v.setElementAt("Monet",3);`	`s = "Monet";`
// Position 3 of v refers to "Monet".	// s refers to "Monet".
`v.setElementAt("Picasso",3);`	`s = "Picasso";`
// Now position 3 of v refers to // "Picasso";	// Now s refers to "Picasso";
// the reference to "Monet" is gone.	// the reference to "Monet" is gone.

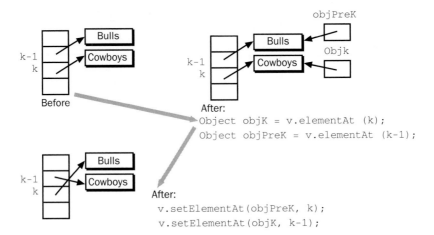

FIGURE 10.10 Exchanging elements at positions k and k-1. Initially, element k-1 is a reference to the `String` "Bulls" and element k is a reference to the `String` "Cowboys." Using the `elementAt` method of the `Vector` class we can exchange these elements. First we use the `elementAt` method save the two references that are to be exchanged; then we use the `setElementAt` method to assign them to their new transposed positions.

TRANSPOSING USING `setElementAt`

We can use this `setElementAt` method to carry out the transpose, the exchange of positions of two elements, in a very efficient way. To exchange the element in position k with the previous position we write (see Figure 10.10):

```
private void transpose(Vector  v,  int  k)  {
    if  (k!=0)  {
        Object  objK = v.elementAt(k);
        Object  objPreK = v.elementAt(k-1);
        v.setElementAt(objPreK,k);
        v.setElementAt(objK,k-1);
    }
}
```

EXERCISES

1. In the four lines of code that carry out the `transpose` above, eliminate the need for the `objPreK` reference variable by combining the second and third lines into a single line.

2. Write a loop that uses `setElementAt` to accomplish the same result as

```
insertElementAt(s,0);
```

3. Implement a helper method, `exchangeElements`,

   ```
   private void  exchangeElements(Vector v, int k, int j)
   ```

   that exchanges the elements in positions `k` and `j` in `Vector v` (much as `transpose` exchanges the elements in positions `k` and `k-1`). Use `transpose` as your model and note that `j` plays the role of `k-1`. Implement `exchangeElements` in the style of both the version of transpose that is given above and the version you wrote in Exercise 1, above.

4. Write a third version of `transpose` that uses the exchange method you wrote in Exercise 3, above.

5. (A challenge) Implement a method,

   ```
   private void moveToFront(Vector v, int k)
   ```

   that uses a loop and `setElementAt` to move the element in position `k` to position 0 and move the elements in positions `0, ..., k-1` to positions `1, ..., k`. •

10.5 Finding the Index of an Extreme

Section 9.6 presented several loop patterns for finding extremes. In those examples, our goal was to obtain an extreme value. Suppose, however, we have a `Vector`, `v`, of `String`s and we want a method that returns the *index* of the "smallest" `String`—smallest in the sense of the alphabetical order, for example, elephant is smaller than mouse:

```
int  getSmallest(Vector  v)  {
    if  (v==null  ||  v.size()==0)
        return  -1;
    ... rest of the method goes here ...
}
```

We adopt the same convention that we used in `search` earlier in this chapter: we return −1 if no extreme can be found—either because the `Vector` doesn't exist or it has no elements.

10.5.1 Informal Procedure

To complete the method, we examine elements in successive positions, remembering the index of the smallest one encountered so far. We start at position 1, with the element in position 0 considered the smallest—so far. We stop when all positions have been examined.

10.5.2 Choosing and Defining Variables

We need two integer variables—one to store the index of the next element to examine and the other to hold the index of the smallest element that we know of.

```
int      k;       // Index of next element to examine; all elements at positions
                  //    less than k have been examined already.
int      small;   // Index of smallest element that we know of
```

10.5.3 The `while` Condition

We stop when we have examined all the elements, that is, when `k==v.size())`:

```
while  (k!=v.size())  {
    ...
}
//  k==v.size()
```

At this point, `small` is the index of the smallest element in the `Vector` and can be returned:

```
return  small;
```

10.5.4 Initializing Variables

Before the loop, we write

```
k    =  1;
small    =  0;
```

Although we never actually examined the element at position 0, when k is 1 and only one position (0) is in question, that position contains the smallest (and for that matter the largest) element. Hence, we set `small` to 0.

10.5.5 Guaranteeing Termination

In the loop body, we write

```
k++;
```

10.5.6 Completing the Loop Body

To preserve the meaning of `small`, before incrementing k we must compare the `String` at position k with the smallest one encountered so far:

```
String  current   =   (String)  v.elementAt(k);
String  smallest  =   (String)  v.elementAt(small);
```

```
if  (current.compareTo(smallest)<0)
    small  =  k;
```

Putting all the pieces together, we have

```
//  Returns the index of the smallest element in v or −1 if none exist
int  getSmallest(Vector  v)  {
    if  (v==null  ||  v.size()==0)
        return -1;
    int    k;         // Index of next element to examine; all elements at
                      //    positions less than k have been examined already.
    int    small;     // Index of smallest element examined so far
    k  =  1;
    small  =  0;
    while  (k!=v.size())  {
        String current  =  (String)  v.elementAt(k);
        String smallest  =  (String)  v.elementAt(small);
        if  (current.compareTo(smallest)<0)
            small  =  k;
        k++;
    }
    //  k==v.size()
    return small;
}
```

EXERCISES

1. Modify the getSmallest method so that it receives an additional parameter, k, an int, and make it return the index of the smallest element from element k (of v) on (or −1 if none exists).

2. What must be changed in getSmallest to transform it to getLargest—a method that returns the largest element in a Vector?

3. Write a method getSecondSmallest that returns the index of the second smallest element or, if none exists, −1.   •

10.6   Binary Search

We have seen that changing the order in which Strings are stored in Vectors can make it easier to find them. We saw this in connection with a Vector containing a set of frequently requested items. However, we often have a Vector in which each element is as likely as the next one to be requested. In that case, transpose and move-to-front would be of little use—we would have to try a different approach.

When collections are sorted, a search can be quite efficient. Searching for a name in a phone book of 100,000 entries is feasible, whereas searching for a phone number is not because the phone book is sorted by name, not by phone number.

Suppose the `Strings` in our `Vector` had been added in alphabetical order:

```
v.addElement("manlius");
v.addElement("marlboro");
v.addElement("melville");
v.addElement("midwood");
...
```

How can we rewrite our search method to take advantage of this? Think of how people search for a listing in a phone book. We may use intuition to guide the search. For example, if the name is Whitman, we start near the end of the book. What is most important is that as we search, we divide the phone book into three parts:

- The portion of the book that the search has been narrowed down to
- The portion of the book before that
- The portion of the book after that

For example, in a search for Whitman, at one point we might have a finger on a page that starts with Van Dyke and another finger on a page that starts with Wolsey. Whitman could not appear in the pages before Van Dyke or in the pages after Wolsey, but it might appear in between.

The search proceeds by taking a look at a page roughly in the middle of the "might be" zone. In the search for Whitman, we might find Webster between Van Dyke and Wolsey. Because Whitman comes after Webster, we narrow down the "might be" zone to between Webster and to Wolsey. (See Figure 10.11.) The search continues until the "might be" zone has been narrowed to a single page.

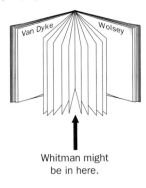

Whitman might be in here.

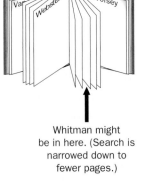

Whitman might be in here. (Search is narrowed down to fewer pages.)

FIGURE 10.11 Searching a phone book for a name. (Left) Locate an initial zone. Then (right), pick a page in the middle of where Whitman might be and use that page to narrow down the search.

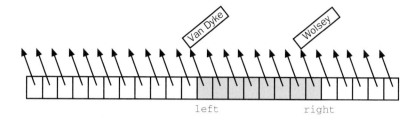

FIGURE 10.12   Searching a sorted `Vector` for a `String`. If it is anywhere, Whitman is in the shaded region, between left and right.

Guided by this intuition, let's construct a loop to carry out a search for a `String s` in a `Vector`.

Informal Procedure   Just as the phone book search in Figure 10.11 depended on two pages that defined the part of the book where the name might be found, so will our search through the `Vector` depend on two positions between which the `String` we are searching for might be found. For the sake of discussion, let's call these positions *left* and *right*. (See Figure 10.12.)

At each step we will look in the middle between left and right. If the `String` in the middle position comes before `s`, the middle position becomes the new left position. If the `String` in the middle position comes after `s`, the middle position becomes the new right position. (See Figure 10.13.) We repeat this procedure until we have narrowed the search down to a single position, at which point we stop and just check that position for a match to `s`.

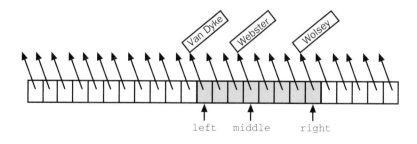

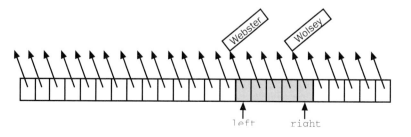

FIGURE 10.13   Narrowing down the search. (Top) Because Whitman comes after Webster, the middle becomes the new left. (Bottom) The part of the `Vector` that we still must search through is narrowed down.

Choosing and Defining Variables   We need integer variables to keep track of left and right. As always, precision in their meaning is essential. Does the middle region, where a match to s might be, include left? Does it include right? We may be guided by sketches we made in the diagrams that outlined our informal procedure, but we are not bound by them. Any decision on the precise meaning for left and right is fine, so long as we stick to that decision as we develop our code. We will choose the following definition:

```
int     left, right;   // If the String is anywhere, it's in positions left
                       //     through right−1.
                       // The String is not in a position before left.
                       // The String is not in a position after right−1.
```

This choice differs from the above diagrams in that it excludes position right from the middle (shaded) region, which now only goes as far as right-1. We revise our diagram to match our choice. (See Figure 10.14.)

We could just as easily have defined the middle to include right. Our choice—and this is not much more than a matter of whim—was made because the size method of Vector is the index of the position after the last position in the Vector. By analogy, right here is the index of the position after the last position in the middle region.

Our informal procedure tells us that we keep shrinking the middle region until we have narrowed it down to a single element. So left must never equal or exceed right, and we add the following comment:

```
// left<right
```

The while Condition   We stop when we have narrowed the search down to a single element. We will be down to a single element when left and right-1 are the same element, that is when

```
left==right-1
```

So our loop so far is

```
while (left!=right-1) {
    ...
```

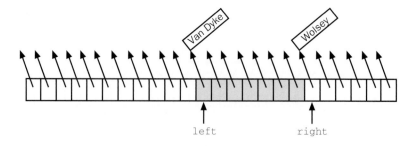

FIGURE 10.14   Searching a sorted Vector for a String (revised). If it is anywhere, Whitman is in the shaded region, from left up to but not including right.

FIGURE 10.15   Searching a `Vector` of size 1.
When the `Vector` has a size of 1, the termination condition, `left==right-1`, is immediately `true`.

left   right

```
}
// left==right-1
```

When the loop terminates, the only position that might match `s` is `left`. So the method can, at that point, test the element at this position:

```
if (s.equals(v.elementAt(left)))
    return  left;
else
    return  -1;
```

Note that when there is only one element in the `Vector`, the loop condition is `false` from the outset and the loop body will not be executed, as shown in Figure 10.15.

Initialization   At the outset, the match to `s` could be anywhere in the `Vector`, from position 0 to position `v.size()-1`. Consistency with the definitions of our variables, `left` and `right` calls for

```
left = 0;
right = v.size();
```

These assignments make it true that the match to `s` could be anywhere from `left` (0) to `right-1` (`v.size()-1`).

There is one special case we must check. If the `Vector` is empty, that is, if its size is 0, the above assignments violate our requirement that `left<right` always. In this case, however, we know that there is no match to `s`. We therefore precede these assignments with the following code:

```
if  (v.size()==0)  {
    process case of element not found
}
```

Guaranteeing Termination   We must make sure that, as we are guided by our informal procedure, the distance between `left` and `right` shrinks (that is, we narrow down the search region) but that `left` and `right` never meet or cross (`left<right`). We must also guarantee that the element for which we search is never before `left` or after `right-1`. That is,

- `right-left` must be smaller each time around the loop.
- `left<right` always.

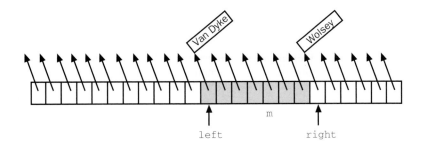

FIGURE 10.16 Finding the middle of the search area. m is the index of the location.

- The value we seek is between `left` and `right-1`, or it is nowhere to be found.

Our informal procedure asks us to find the element midway between `left` and `right`. We can think of that as the position that is the "average" of `left` and `right` (See Figure 10.16):

```
m  =  (left+right)/2;
```

We need to compare s, the `String` we search for, with the `String` at position m:

```
String sm  =  (String)  v.elementAt(m);
```

Comparing sm to s will provide us with valuable information about where the element we're searching for might be. We make use of this information to modify `left` or `right` or possibly both to narrow down the search range.

If s should come after sm, `left` moves to the middle (see Figure 10.17):

```
if  (sm.compareTo(s)<0)
    left  =  m;
```

If s comes before sm, `right` moves to the middle:

```
else  if  (sm.compareTo(s)>0)
    right  =  m;
```

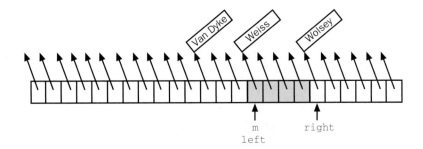

FIGURE 10.17 Narrowing down the search. Because Whitman comes after Weiss, our search area is narrowed down.

and if s and sm are equal, we've found a match and we can set the left and right so that the range has been reduced to a single element:

```
else  {
    left  =  m;
    right  =  m+1;
}
```

The code that we write, influenced by our informal procedure, is as follows:

```
while  (left!=right-1)  {
    m  =  (left+right)/2;
    String sm  =  (String)  v.elementAt(m);
    if  (sm.compareTo(s)<0)
        left  =  m;                 // Move left to the middle.
    else  if  (sm.compareTo(s)>0)
        right  =  m;                // Move right to the middle.
    else  {
        left  =  m;
        right  =  m+1;
    }
}
```

We must make sure that this code guarantees that right-left decreases each time around the loop but that left<right always. To do this, we have to look closely at the value of m in relation to the values of left and right.

For the moment, assume that left<right is true when the loop condition is evaluated. Then when we start executing the loop, we know that left<right-1, because

- We are, for the moment, assuming that left<right was true when we evaluated the loop condition, and it still will be true in that case.
- The loop condition, left!=right-1 must be true in order to execute the loop body.

If left<right-1, we have left<right-1<right: There is at least one value between left and right. In that case, m, which is assigned (left+right)/2 will take on one of these intermediate values. (See Figure 10.18.) So m will be greater than left and less than right:

```
left < m < right
```

The only way that the loop body ever changes left or right is by assigning one of them m. However, because left<m<right, left cannot be assigned a value as big as right and right can't be assigned a value as small as left. At the end of the loop body, left is still less than right.

Of course, the conclusion that left<right at the end of the loop body's execution depends on the assumption that left<right going in. Fortunately, our code initializes left and right so that at the outset left<right. And

We start by assuming that `left < right`.
So the closest `left` and `right` can be is shown.

However, if the loop condition is true
then `left! = right -1`.

`m` is assigned `(left + right) / 2`, which
will be the index of one of the elements
between `left` and `right`.

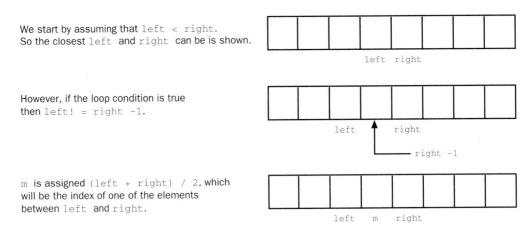

FIGURE 10.18   **The relationships between `left`, `right`, and `m`.**

we see that once `left<right` is `true`, this relationship won't vary as the loop is executed. Because the loop preserves this relationship and because we start out with that relationship we can be confident that `left<right` throughout the execution of the loop.

Because `left<m<right`, we also see that each time the loop body is executed, the search range, `left` through `right-1`, is narrowed down. That's because we either assign `m` to `left`, making `left` greater, or we assign `m` to `right`, making `right` smaller.

Completing the Loop Body   We have not violated any of the definitions of the variables, and so there is nothing more to add to the loop. The loop is complete and the method is

```
private boolean bsearch(String s) { // Returns true if and only if s
                                    //   equals one of the Strings in v
    int    left, right;
                // If the String is anywhere, it is in positions left through right−1.
                // The String is not in a position before left.
                // The String is not in a position after right−1.

    left = 0;
    right = v.size();
    while (left!=right-1)  {
        int m  =  (right+left)/2;
        String sm  =  (String)  v.elementAt(m);
        if  (sm.compareTo(s)<0)
            left  =  m;           // Move left to the middle.
        else  if  (sm.compareTo(s)>0)
```

```
        right  =  m;        // Move right to the middle.
      else  {
        left  =  m;
        right  =  m+1;
      }
    }
    return s.equals(v.elementAt(left));
  }
```

10.6.1   Binary Search: What's in a Name?

Suppose the `Vector` we are searching has 4000 elements. Initially, `left` is 0 and `right`, 4000, and the range of elements to consider is 4000. However, the first time around the loop, m has the value 2000 and either `left` or `right` assumes this value, leaving a range of just 2000 elements to consider. Suppose after the first pass that `left` is 2000 and `right` still is 4000. In the second pass, m will be 3000 and the range of elements to consider is reduced to 1000. In each pass through the loop body, the range to consider is cut in two. The algorithm's name, **binary search,** comes from this cutting-in-two characteristic.

10.6.2   Efficiency

Starting with a value N, how many times can you divide by 2 before reaching 1? Consider 4000:

$$4000 \rightarrow 2000 \rightarrow 1000 \rightarrow 500 \rightarrow 250 \rightarrow 125 \rightarrow 62 \rightarrow 31 \rightarrow 15 \rightarrow 7 \rightarrow 3 \rightarrow 1$$

Just 11. Imagine! To find out whether a particular `String` is stored among 4000 others requires just 11 executions of the loop body. In contrast, the `search` method of Section 10.3 requires 4000 executions of its loop body to discover that a particular `String` is not in the `Vector`, and on the average it requires 2000 executions to find a `String` that is there. Thus, 2000 versus 11 is a staggering ratio: about 180. Thus, a binary search executes its loop body 180 times less than the sequential search in this case. Of course, the loop body in the binary search is longer than the one in `search` and may take more time. But even if the loop body of the binary search is 4 times as slow (which it isn't) as that of `search`, it will run 180/4 = 45 times faster than `search`.

How does a speed factor of 45 translate into hardware prices? At the time of writing this text, 300-MHz Pentium Pro machines are just appearing on the market. Their cost is in the neighborhood of $4000. They are roughly 45 times faster than 33-MHz 386 machines that now can be had for about $250. So a $250 machine running a binary search is approximately the equivalent of a $4000 machine running `search` for data in this quantity.

The point of this comparison is to illustrate the profound impact that software has on a system. A good algorithm can be far more important to the efficiency of a system than the latest, most expensive hardware.

In mathematics, there is a function called log-base-2 that is written

$$\log_2$$

It equals the number of times its argument can be divided by 2 before reaching 1. So if the Vector's size is N, the binary search requires **$\log_2 N$** passes through the loop. In contrast, the sequential search of Section 10.3 requires $N/2$ passes through the loop on the average to find a String that is there and N passes to discover that a String is not present in the Vector.

The table below compares $\log_2 N$ and $N/2$ for different values of N:

N	$\log_2 N$	$N/2$	$(N/2)/\log_2 N$
100	7	50	7
500	9	250	27
1,000	10	500	50
5,000	13	2,500	192
10,000	14	5,000	357

The last column shows how many times greater $N/2$ is than $\log_2 N$. As is evident, the significance of using binary search becomes greater as the size of the Vector increases. In going from 5000 to 10,000 elements, although the cost of a sequential search doubles, the cost of a binary search increases by a small fraction, 1/13.

EXERCISES

1. The binary search loop in the binary search method can be sped up slightly if we assign m+1 to left and m-1 to right. Would these assignments violate the requirement that left<right? Use the inequality

   ```
   left < left+1 <= m <= right-1 < right
   ```

   to guide your answer and rewrite the method with the improvements that don't violate the requirement that left<right.

2. In our development of the binary search we made the following definitions of left and right:

   ```
   int     left, right;
                   // If the String is anywhere, it is in positions left through right−1.
                   // The String is not in a position before left.
                   // The String is not in a position after right−1.
   ```

Redevelop the binary search from scratch, using the following definitions
of `left` and `right`:

```
int     left, right;
                    // If the String is anywhere, it is in positions left through right
                    // The String is not in a position before left.
                    // The String is not in a position after right.
```

(`right-1` has been replaced by `right`.)

10.7   Sorting

The binary search is a powerful, efficient search algorithm, but it requires that
the `Vector` be sorted. What if the data that are read in and added to the `Vec-`
`tor` are not sorted? In that case, we need to sort the `Vector` ourselves. That
means that we have to rearrange the references in the `Vector`. This task is
similar to the self-organizing list, except that here the order is determined not
by item "popularity" but by the alphabet.

A `Vector` that is sorted has the following properties that we will make
use of:

- First, given any two integers, j and k, where $j<k$ and where both identify
  positions of elements within the `Vector`, the element at position j will
  be less than or equal to the element at position k.
- Phrased more formally, if we have integers j and k where
  $0<j<k<v.size()$, `v.elementAt(j)` is less than or equal to `v.ele-`
  `mentAt(k)`.
- Any element that appears before position k is less than or equal to any
  element that appears after position k.

There are dozens of sorting algorithms—we will use one of the simplest,
the **selection sort.** The basic idea of this sort is given in the informal procedure discussed below.

Informal Procedure   Given a `Vector` v of n elements, we take the following
steps:

- Put the correct element in position 0: Find the position of the smallest of
  the n elements in positions 0 through $n-1$ and exchange the element in
  that position with the element in position 0. (At that point, position 0 is
  taken care of—it has the smallest of the elements.)
- Put the correct element in position 1: Find the position of the smallest of
  the $n-1$ remaining elements in positions 1 through $n-1$ and exchange the
  element in that position with the element in position 1. (At that point,

positions 0 and 1 are taken care of and contain, in sorted order, the two smallest elements.)

- Put the correct element in position 2: Find the position of the smallest of the $n-2$ remaining elements in positions 2 through $n-1$ and exchange the element in that position with the element in position 2. (At that point, positions 0, 1, and 2 are taken care of and contain, in sorted order, the three smallest elements.)

- Continue doing this until position $n-2$ has been given the correct element. At that point position $n-1$ must contain the largest element because all the smaller ones were placed in positions 0, $\ldots$, $n-2$.

Figure 10.19 shows the changes a `Vector` of names undergoes as a result of this procedure.

Choosing and Defining Variables   We need to keep track of the position we are up to, and so we will need an integer variable, which we will call `k`. The position that `k` refers to divides the `Vector` into two regions:

```
private int k;   // k== the index of the next position in the Vector to take care of.
                 // All elements to the left of k are less than or equal to the
                 //    elements at k or to the right of k.
                 // All elements to the left of k are in ascending order.
```

For convenience, we also have a variable, `n`, which we will set to the size of the `Vector`:

```
int n=v.size();        // n== number of elements in the Vector.
```

Skeleton of the Code   We write

```
private void sort(Vector  v)   { // On return, the elements of v are
                                 //     sorted in ascending order.
        int k;              // k== the index of the next position in the Vector to
                            //    take care of.
                            // All elements to the left of k are less than or equal
                            //    to the elements at k or to the right of k.
                            // All elements to the left of k are in ascending order.
        int n=v.size(); // n== number of elements in the Vector.
        ...
        while (condition)
            body
        ...
}
```

(See Figure 10.20.)

Starting with an unsorted
`Vector` of `Strings`:

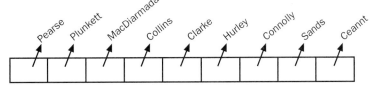

`0` is the next position to fill.
Move smallest
`String` to `0`.

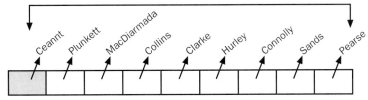

`1` is the next position to
fill. Move next smallest
`String` to `1`.

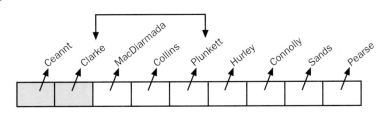

`2` is the next position to
fill. Move next smallest
`String` to `2`.

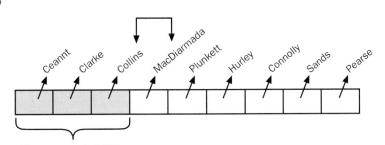

These are sorted AND
are all smaller than the
remaining elements (unshaded).

FIGURE 10.19 The state of a `Vector` after three steps in the selection sort. The shaded elements are those that have been sorted. Each step extends this group by one element.

FIGURE 10.20 The significance of the index in the simple selection sort. All the elements of lower index than k (shaded boxes) are sorted and are less than or equal to the elements at position k or beyond (unshaded).

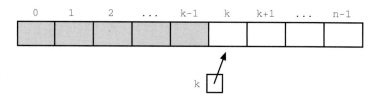

The `while` Condition We are finished when the object in the next position to take care of is the last one, $n-1$.

```
while  (k!=n-1)
    body
// k==n-1 and therefore elements 0, ..., n−2 are sorted; but because these
// elements are also less than the element in position n−1 (the last element), the
// entire Vector is sorted.
```

Initialization The definition of k indicates that it is the index of the next position to take care of. Our informal procedure tells us that this must be 0:

```
k = 0;
```

Guaranteeing Termination By incrementing k by 1 in the loop body, we know that eventually k will equal $n-1$.

Completing the Loop Body Before we increment k, however, we must make sure that position k is given the smallest of the elements in positions k, ..., n-1. Finding the smallest elements in a subportion of a `Vector` is a task by itself. We will use a helper method, `getSmallest`, that is a slight modification of the `getSmallest` method we wrote in Section 10.5 (see Exercise 1 of Section 10.5). This method will return the index of the smallest element of v from position k forward:

```
int   j = getSmallest(v,k);
```

This is in contrast to the version in Section 10.5 that returns the index of the smallest element from position 0 forward.

Once we have that index, we can use the `exchange` method (see Section 10.5, Exercise 3) to swap elements j and k:

```
private void  exchange(Vector  v,  int  k,  int  j)  {
    Object  obk = v.elementAt(k);
    v.setElementAt(v.elementAt(j),k);
    v.setElementAt(obk,j);
}
```

The sort method then becomes

```
private void sort(Vector  v) {   // On return, the elements of v are
                                 //    sorted in ascending order.
        int k;            // k== the index of the next position in the Vector
                          //    to take care of.
                          // All elements to the left of k are less than or
                          //    equal to the elements at k or to the right of k.
                          // All elements to the left of k are in ascending
                          //    order.
        int n=v.size(); // n== number of elements in the Vector.
        k = 0;
        while  (k!=n-1)  {
            int     j  =  getSmallest(v,k);
            exchange(v,k,j);
            k++;
        }
        // k==n-1 and therefore elements 0, ..., n-2 are sorted; but because
        //    these elements are also less than the element in position n-1 (the
        //    last element), the entire Vector is sorted.
}
```

10.7.1 The Modified getSmallest Method

The original method searched for the smallest method from position 0 forward. So k now plays the role of 0 and k+1, the role of 1; that is, at the outset, the smallest element we know of is at position k and the next position to examine is k+1:

```
//  Returns the index of the smallest element in v or -1 if none exist
private int getSmallest(Vector  v,  int  k)  {
    if  (v==null  ||  v.size()==k)
        return  -1;
    int     i;       // Index of next element to examine; all elements at positions
                     //    less than k have been examined already.
    int     small;  // Index of smallest element examined so far
    i  =  k+1;
    small  =  k;
    while  (i!=v.size())  {
        String current  =  (String)  v.elementAt(i);
        String  smallest  =  (String)  v.elementAt(small);
        if  (current.compareTo(smallest)<0)
            small  =  i;
        i++;
    }
    // i==v.size()
    return small;
}
```

10.7.2   Efficiency

A quick look at the `sort` method tells us that n-1 steps are carried out. However, these steps include the invocation of the `getSmallest` method. This method searches positions k through $n-1$ for the smallest element. To do that, every one of the k through $n-1$ positions must be checked—$n-k$ positions in all. When k is small, this is a big number, close to n; when k is large, that is, close to $n-1$, this is a small number.

Over the course of the sort, k ranges from 0 to $n-2$. So the number of elements checked in search of the smallest is shown in the following table:

When k is	Number checked is
0	n
1	$n-1$
2	$n-2$
...	...
$n-4$	4
$n-3$	3
$n-2$	2

How big is $2+3+4+...+(n-2)+(n-1)+(n)$? The answer is $(n)(n+1)/2-1$ (see Section 10.6, Exercise 2). If n is large, this value is approximately $n2/2$. (For example, suppose n is 2000. Then $n2/2$ is 2,000,000 and $(n)(n+1)/2-1$ is $(2000)(2001)/2-1$, which is 2,000,999. The difference between 2,000,999 and 2,000,000 is 999, which out of 2,000,000 is less than 1 percent.)

This analysis shows that the number of steps needed to carry out this sort is proportional to n^2 where n is the number of elements in the collection. This is a terrible state of affairs. Suppose the collection doubles in size. In place of n we have $2n$; and $(2n)^2$ equals $4n^2$—4 times the cost of sorting the original collection.

Although we would anticipate that doubling the size of our collection could easily double the time it takes to sort it, quadrupling the time for sorting seems quite unfair and prohibitive. Fortunately there are more efficient, although more complicated, sorting algorithms that are much faster than the one presented here.

EXERCISES

1. Write the definition for the following method

```
private int getSmallest(Vector v, int k)
```

that receives a `Vector` of `String`s and returns the index of the smallest (alphabetically) `String` among those stored in `v[k]` through the end of the `Vector`.

2. Show that $1+2+3+\cdots+(n-2)+(n-1)+(n)$ equals $(n)(n+1)/2$. Use this trick: Assume that n is even and pair 1 with n, 2 with $n-1$, 3 with $n-2$, and so forth. What is the sum of each of these pairs? How many pairs are there? What is the total? Now address the case where n is odd. Leave out n and pair 1 with $n-1$, 2 with $n-2$, 3 with $n-3$, and so forth. What is the sum of each pair? How many pairs are there? Taking into account n, what is the total? •

10.8 Introducing Arrays

An **array** is a language feature that uses indexing to support collections of data. An array shares some characteristics with a `Vector`:

- It consists of one or more positions.
- Each position is indexed by an integer.
- The first position's index is 0.
- It must be created with the `new` operation.
- It is an object.
- It is referenced using a reference variable.

There are also many differences between the two:

- An array is not a class. It is not defined in a class library. It is built into the language itself.
- There are no "array methods" to work with arrays or their elements; instead, special symbols are provided by the language that allow us to access array elements.
- An array has a *field*, called `length`, that indicates the number of elements of the array—in contrast to a `Vector`, which uses a *method*, `size`, to provide this information.
- Array elements can hold primitive data such as integer values as well as references to objects.
- The type of the elements of an array must be specified in the array's declaration. Everything stored in its elements must be of that type.
- Arrays can't grow—once an array has been created, it has a fixed numbed of elements.

10.8.1   Declaring and Creating Arrays

To declare an array reference variable, you write the type of data each element will hold, followed by an empty pair of square brackets and then the name of the reference variable:

```
int[]        lottoNumbers;   // This can refer to an array whose elements are
                             //     all ints.
String []    winners;        // This can refer to an array whose elements are
                             //     all references to String objects.
Employee [] personnel;       // This can refer to an array whose elements are
                             //     all references to Employee objects.
```

Of course, you have been seeing such declarations since Chapter 1: the parameter to `main` in a stand-alone application is `String[] a`. These declarations don't create arrays—just variables that can refer to them.

To create an array you use the `new` operator, followed by the element type and a pair of square brackets enclosing an integer that specifies the number of elements the array will have. For example, the following code creates an array of six elements, each of which may be assigned an integer value:

```
new  int[6]
```

As in the creation of any object, if we don't save the reference to the new object, we won't be able to do anything, so we normally would write something like the following:

```
lottoNumbers  =  new  int[6];
```

Now `lottoNumbers` refers to this six-element array. (See Figure 10.21.)

First we declare an array reference variable. Then we create an array of 6 integers, and make the variable refer to the new array.

The expression

```
arrayRefVariable.length
```

yields the **size** of the array that the array reference variable refers to. There are no parentheses after `length`: It is not a method.

So, the value of

```
lottoNumbers.length
```

FIGURE 10.21 Creating an array of integers. First we declare an array reference variable. Then we create an array of six integers and make the variable refer to the new array.

After executing

```
int[] lottoNumbers;
lottoNumbers = new int[6];
```

is 6, given the assignment above. As in the case of Vectors and the result of the size method, the value yielded by length is not a valid position—it is 1 more than the index of the last position in the array.

10.8.2   Array Elements

To set the element in position k of array z to a particular value we write

```
z[k]  =  value ;
```

The value assigned must match the type the array was declared to have. To use the value of the element in position k of array z we simply write

```
z[k]
```

as in

```
int  x  =  3*z[k];
int  y  =  z[k];
```

This square bracket element selection is analogous to the elementAt method of Vectors.

Array elements, lottoNumbers[3], winners[2], and z[k], for example, are very much like variables. They can be assigned values, and by using them in an expression, these values are retrieved. In fact, sometimes arrays are called indexed variables.

EXAMPLE   **Reading and Printing 100 Integers in Reverse Order.**
As an illustration of all this, let's use an array to write the following tiny program: Read in a list of 100 integers, one to a line, and print the list in reverse, again, one integer to a line. The logic is identical to that of the Vector reversal code in Section 10.2.

```
import  java.lang.*;
import  java.io.*;
class  ReverseIntegers  {
    public  static  void  main(String[]  a)
                        throws Exception {
        BufferedReader kb  =  new  BufferedReader(
                    new InputStreamReader(System.in));
        int[]  z = new int[100];
        int    i=0;   // Next position to fill; all positions before position i
                      //    have been filled.
        while  (i!=100)  {
           z[i]  =  Integer.parseInt(kb.readLine());
           i++;
        }
        int k=99;     // k== the index of the next position in the array to print.
                      // positions 99, 98, ..., k+1 have already been printed.
                      // positions k, k−1, ..., 0 remain to be printed.
```

```
            while (k!=-1) {
               System.out.println(z[k]);
               --k;
            }
         }
```

1. Declare x to be an array reference variable for an array of String
    references. Create such an array with the dimension 3. Initialize each
    element in the array by reading in a line from the keyboard.

10.9   Vectors **and Arrays**

In this section we compare arrays and Vectors and look at how code using
Vectors can be converted to code using arrays.

10.9.1   Arrays or Vectors?

Arrays offer three advantages over Vectors:

*   You can store primitive data values (such as int) in arrays.
*   Their elements can be accessed without sending a message, so code using
    an array will be somewhat faster than code using a Vector. However, the
    speed difference is nothing like the difference between binary and sequen-
    tial search—binary search using a Vector will be much, much faster than
    a sequential search using an array.
*   Arrays, because they are typed, offer a kind of checking at compile-time
    that Vectors don't. If you have a Vector that is intended to store refer-
    ences to Name objects, Java does not prevent you from mistakenly storing
    a String or Song reference because Vector elements can be assigned
    any reference to an object. But Java will give you a compile-time error if
    you try storing one of those references into an array that is declared to
    hold Name references. You might not like getting the error message, but at
    least it allows you to catch your mistake early.

On the other hand, arrays have the following disadvantages when compared to Vectors:

*   Arrays are fixed in size and will not grow.
*   Arrays do not offer the rich set of operations that the methods of the Vec-
    tor class offer—for example, insertElementAt.

Table 10.1 summarizes the differences between arrays and Vectors.

TABLE 10.1 **Differences between arrays and** `Vectors`

	Array a	`Vector` **v**
Element type	established by declaration of a	reference to object
Element referenced by	a[*index*]	v.elementAt(index)
Element assigned by	a[*index*] = *value*	v.setElementAt(value)
Number of elements	a.length	v.size()
Can store primitive data types?	yes	no
Can grow dynamically?	no	yes
Defined by	the Java language	the Java class library

10.9.2 From `Vectors` to Arrays

Much code written using `Vectors` can be converted to code using arrays. The first step is to eliminate all method invocations other than `size`, `elementAt`, and `setElementAt`. Doing this may require replacing methods such as `insertElementAt` with loops that use `setElementAt`. The second step is to replace `size` with the `.length` array notation and the `elementAt` and `setElementAt` methods with the square bracket index notation.

For example, here is the sequential search for a `Vector`:

```
private boolean search(String s) { // Returns true if and only if s
                                   //    equals one of the Strings in v.
        int k;                     // k== the index of the next position in
                                   //    the Vector to check.
                                   // No match has been found in positions 0
                                   //    through k−1.
    k = 0;
    while (k!=v.size() && !s.equals(v.elementAt(k)))
       k++;
    // k==v.size || s.equals(v.elementAt(k))
    return k!=v.size();
}
```

Below is the equivalent code for an array:

```
private boolean search(String s) { // Returns true if and only if s
                                   //    equals one of the Strings in v.
        int k;                     // k== the index of the next position in
                                   //    the array to check.
                                   // No match has been found in positions
                                   //    0 through k−1.
    k = 0;
```

```
        while (k!=v.length && !s.equals(v[k]))
            k++;
        //  k==v.length || s.equals(v[k])
        return k!=v.length;
    }
```

Code involving some of the more powerful `Vector` methods, such as `insertElementAt`, requires more work to convert.

EXERCISES

1. Rewrite the binary search method using an array. (That is, assume a sorted array of `String`s is passed to the method, along with a `String` parameter to look for.)

2. Define a method called `insertElementAt` that receives three arguments: an array of `int`s, an index, and an `int` value. The method returns an array that is the result of inserting the `int` value into the original array just before the position given by the index. For example, given the elements 34, 19, 41, and 72, an index 2, and an `int` value 86, the array returned would contain 34, 19, 86, 41, and 72. Note the similarity to `Vector`'s `insertElementAt`. (Hint: If the array is already full, you can always create a larger array, fill it with the appropriate values, and return it.) •

10.10 Command-Line Arguments

Throughout this text we have been declaring, as a parameter to the `static main` method of application classes, an array of `String` references:

```
public static void main(String[] arg)
```

The `arg` parameter is an array of `String`s corresponding to what are known as the **command-line arguments** of the application. These are `String` values that are supplied when a program is invoked. For example, in the invocation

```
java program grant sherman sheridan
```

the command-line arguments are `grant`, `sherman`, and `sheridan`. So the `arg` array's values become

```
arg[0] is "grant"
arg[1] is "sherman"
arg[2] is "sheridan"
```

In a command-line environment, this is a very convenient way to allow the user to provide basic information to an application or utility program.

A common use of command-line arguments is to specify a file name. As an example, consider the following program, which copies lines from one file to another:

```
import  java.io.*;

class  CopyFile  {
    public  static  void  main(String[]  a)
                              throws  Exception  {
        BufferedReader  in  =  new  BufferedReader(
                              new  InputStreamReader(
                                new  FileInputStream(
                                  new  File(a[0])))));

        PrintStream  out  =  new  PrintStream(
                              new  FileOutputStream(
                                new  File(a[1])));

        String  s  =  in.readLine();
        while  (s!=null)  {
           out.println(s);
           s  =  in.readLine();
        }
    }
}
```

EXERCISES

1. Write a program that gets a single command-line argument that specifies a file name; the program prints the contents of that file sorted in ascending order.

2. Write a program that receives one or more command-line arguments, each one the name of a file. The program prints the name of each file followed first line of the file. (Hint: Don't forget the .length feature.) •

10.11 Strings and Indices

Much of what we have learned in this chapter is applicable to String objects. That is because a String is a sequence of characters whose position in the sequence can be identified with an integer. Like arrays and Vectors, Strings are indexed starting from 0.

The String class provides a charAt method which, in analogy with Vector's elementAt, returns the character located at a particular index in a String object:

```
char  c  =  "abcdefg".charAt(3);
```

It assigns the char value d to the char variable c. The char primitive data type allows the representation of over 64,000 different characters including the western alphabet, numerals, and punctuation marks, as well as character sets from all around the world (Han, Arabic, Cyrillic, Greek, Hebrew, Katakana, Tamil, Ethiopic, Braille, and Cherokee, to name a few).

Suppose for the sake of illustration that we wished to determine whether String s1 is a prefix of String s2. We could use indexing and charAt to construct a loop as discussed below:

Informal Procedure   Start with position 0 of both Strings. Advance position by position in both Strings, stopping only when a position is found where the characters in the two Strings differ or when there are no more positions in s1 or s2. If at that point there are no more positions in s1, s1 is a prefix of s2; otherwise it is not.

Choosing and Defining the Variables   We need an int variable to represent the position—because we are always interested in the same position in both Strings, we can use the same int variable as an index for both Strings.

```
int      k;        // Position k is the next one to check; the Strings match in all
                   //     positions before k.
```

The while Condition   Our informal procedure tells us that upon ceasing to advance, the following must be the case:

```
//    k==s1.length() || k==s2.length() || s1.charAt(k)==s2.charAt(k)
```

The loop condition is the negation of this:

```
while  (!(k==s1.length()  ||  k==s2.length()  ||
            s1.charAt(k)==s2.charAt(k)))  {
    ...
}
```

Initialization   At the outset, the next position to check is 0:

```
k  =  0;
```

Guaranteeing Termination   To ensure that k eventually indexes a position with different characters or goes beyond the last position of s1, we increment k in the loop body:

```
k++;
```

Completing the Loop Body   As in the case of the sequential search, no further code is required. The increment of k is consistent with its definition because we increment it only after the loop condition has shown us that the characters in position k are equal—so when k increases, we can be assured that all the positions before the new, larger value of k match.

The completed code follows:

```
int      k;          // Position k is the next one to check; the Strings match in all
                     //    positions before k.
k  =  0;
while  (k!=s1.length()  &&  k!=s2.length()  &&
           s1.charAt(k)==s2.charAt(k))
     k++;
boolean  s1IsAPrefix  =  k==s1.length();
```

You may recognize this loop as being practically of the same form as the sequential search of a Vector or an array. This is no accident—it results from the fact that all three of these are indexed collections.

Because the String class provides a rich set of methods for String processing, the need for the kind of indexed loops such as the one above is somewhat diminished. For example, the startsWith method does the same prefix determination that our code above did. The code above can be replaced by

```
boolean  s1IsAPrefix  =  s2.startsWith(s1);
```

EXERCISES

1. Write a method that receives two Strings as arguments and returns the number of positions that have the same characters.

2. (A challenge) Write a method that receives two Strings as arguments and returns the largest String that is a substring of both arguments. •

10.12 The Game of Life: Two-Dimensional Arrays

In this section we look at some more sophisticated uses of indexing as we develop a program that plays the Game of Life.

10.12.1 The Rules of the Game

The Game of Life is not a game at all but a model of a population of idealized living things that interact with each other and their environment. At the heart of the model is a grid of squares representing "the world." (See Figure 10.22.)

In each square there may at most one life form. At the outset of execution, some squares are made to contain life and others not. (See Figure 10.23.)

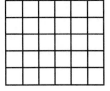

FIGURE 10.22   The Game of Life's world. The Game of Life is "played" on a grid of squares, such as this one. The grid usually consists of many more squares.

FIGURE 10.23   Starting the Game of Life. Initially, some squares are assigned to hold life (shaded) and others are not.

Execution consists of a sequence of generations, each one of which is a world derived in some way from the previous one. (See Figure 10.24.)

The presence of life in a square in the next generation depends on its immediate environment in the current generation. This environment consists of the square's neighbors—those squares with which it shares a side or a corner. (See Figure 10.25.) A square will contain life in the next generation if and only if 2 or 3 of its neighbors contained life in this generation. The game terminates when there is no life in the environment any more. (See Figure 10.26.)

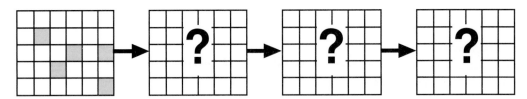

FIGURE 10.24   Executing the Game of Life. As the game is played, a sequence of worlds, each derived from the previous, is generated.

FIGURE 10.25   The environment of a square. The environment of a square consists of those neighbors with which it shares a side or a corner.

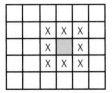

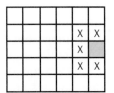

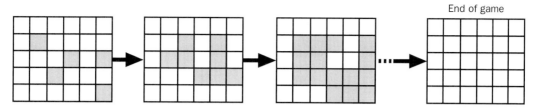

FIGURE 10.26   Following the rules of the Game of Life. Life may spread or be depleted depending on the environment. The game ends when there is no more life.

We will now design a class that plays the Game of Life. This example introduces two-dimensional arrays and the concept of separating the display from the calculation.

Statement of the Problem   Create an object that models the Game of Life by choosing an initial distribution of life and then carrying out the game from one generation to the next, following the game's rules. Provide a display of the generations as they are produced.

Scenario   We want the Game of Life object to carry out and display successive generations, pausing before each new generation so we can look at the display. Here we are working just with `System.out`, so the display is necessarily primitive. The object should choose the initial configuration at random, assigning life to each square with a certain probability. However, we should control both the size of the world and the value of the probability of starting off with life in a given square. Thus we should be able to make requests such as the following:

- Play the Game of Life.
- Use a 15 by 15 grid.
- Use a 10 percent probability of a square having life in it initially.

We could then watch it advance from generation to generation.

Finding the Primary Object   We will introduce a `Life` class. Another noun, however, also appeared in the statement of the problem and the scenario: *display*. We will develop a separate class, `LifeDisplay`, for handling that.

Determining the Behavior   Our problem statement provides us with the necessary behavior:

- `Life` (constructor)—set up the game, that is, determine the initial spread of life in the world.
- `doGenerations`—play the game from generation to generation.

Determining the Interface   The above behavior translates neatly into methods. Once the game is set up, no additional information is needed, so only the constructor requires arguments. It will have to be given the size of the environment as well as the initial probability of putting life into a given square—both these items are needed to set up the game. These considerations lead to the following interface:

```
class Life {
    public Life(int size, double probabilityOfLife) {...}
                                            // Set up the world
    public void doGenerations() {...}       // Play the game
}
```

We have already planned to handle the display of the generations using an object of a separate class, `LifeDisplay`. This object could be created by the `Life` object itself, or it could be created outside the `Life` object and passed to one of `Life`'s methods. The second alternative is appealing because it limits the responsibility of `Life` to playing the game—the responsibility for setting up the display lies outside the `Life` object, for example, in a `main` method.

If we take this alternative, however, we must provide a means for the `Life` object to be notified of this `LifeDisplay` object—we choose, somewhat arbitrarily at this point, to add a third parameter to the constructor to accomplish this. Our revised interface is:

```
class Life {
    public Life(LifeDisplay lifeDisplay, int size,
            double probabilityOfLife) {...}   // Set up the world
    public void doGenerations() {...}         // Play the game
}
```

Defining the Instance Variables   Each generation of the world is determined by the previous one. We need to represent the set of squares in the world in some way and maintain it as an instance variable because the first generation is created by the constructor and will have to be available to `doGenerations`.

A square itself is quite simple—it either has life or it does not. We can represent a square using a `boolean`, with the understanding that `true` means life and `false` means no life.

We know how to represent more than one thing—we need a collection. Because the things we are representing are primitive data types (`boolean`s) we will use an array, not a `Vector`.

If our world was one-dimensional, that is, if our world consisted of a single row of squares (see Figure 10.27), we could represent it simply as an array of `boolean`s:

```
private boolean[]        world;    // Good for a one-dimensional world
```

A one-dimensional world: just a row of squares

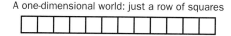

FIGURE 10.27   A one-dimensional world. Such a world could be represented by an array of `boolean: boolean[] world;`.

However, the world consists of many rows. Again, we know how to represent many things. If each row is an array of `boolean`s, the world is an array of arrays of `boolean`s:

```
private boolean [][]  world;    // Good for a two-dimensional world
```

Multidimensional Arrays   The above declaration can be read as follows: *The identifier* `world` *is declared as an array of arrays of type* `boolean`. Instead of each element of `world` being a primitive type or a reference to an individual object of some class, each element is itself an array that has `boolean` as *its* element type. The identifier `world` represents a reference variable to an array, whose elements are referred to as `world[0]`, `world[1]`, and so on. In the arrays we have encountered so far, these elements contained either primitive data values, such as `int`, or references to objects of some class. In our `world` array, the elements are themselves references to arrays of `boolean`. Thus `world[0]` is a reference to an array, `world[1]` is a reference to an array, and so on. The elements of the `world[0]` array, as in any other array, begin with subscript 0, and are referred to as `world[0][0]`, `world[0][1]`, and so on. (See Figure 10.28.) Although the abundance of brackets may be somewhat confusing, the concept is a straightforward consequence of our notion of an array.

An array of arrays is often called a *two-dimensional* array, or *matrix*. One could also have three-dimensional arrays, four-dimensional, and so on. There

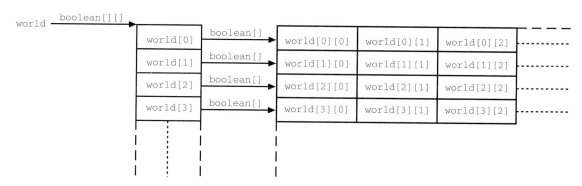

FIGURE 10.28   An array of arrays of booleans.

is nothing mysterious about them—the dimension is nothing more than the number of subscripts used to access an individual element.

Working with such an array is not much different from working with a one-dimensional array: The subscripts for each dimension begin at 0. To access an individual element of the array, a subscript must be supplied for each dimension:

```
int i = 2, j = 1;
System.out.print(a[i][j]);   // Prints a[2][1]
```

Creating a multidimensional array is analogous to a standard (one-dimensional) array, with the addition of having to specify the size of both subscripts. To create a `world` array whose first dimension (the rows in the figure) is of size 10, and whose second dimension (the columns) is of size 20, we write

```
boolean  [][]  world  =  new  boolean[10][20];
```

(You can also allocate the individual `world[i]` arrays, but we will not explore that capability.)

Iterating through a multidimensional array is an extension of the technique used for the single dimensional case—for each dimension, a loop is used to iterate through that dimension. These loops are nested to provide a full iteration of the array. For example, the following code iterates through the array `a` allocated above:

Iterates through a ⟶
Iterates through a[i] ⟶
don't forget a[i] is also an array ⟶

```
for (int i = 0; i < a.size; i++)
    for (int j; j < a[i].size; j++)
        a[i][j] = 0;
```

The Other Instance Variables   We need to keep track of the `LifeDisplay` object, given to the constructor and used by `doGenerations`:

```
private LifeDisplay    lifeDisplay;
```

We also find it convenient to define constant values representing the lower and upper bounds of the required number of neighbors for making life in a square:

```
static final int   MinNeighbors = 2, MaxNeighbors = 3;
```

Implementing the Methods   The constructor first saves the `LifeDisplay` reference in an instance variable and creates the `world` array, using the `size` parameter to determine the size of both dimensions:

```
public Life(LifeDisplay lifeDisplay, int size,
                    double probabilityOfLife) {
    this.lifeDisplay = lifeDisplay;
    world = new boolean[size][size];
```

Its next task is to give the elements of world their initial values. The statement of the problem requires us to do this randomly; that is, each element has a certain probability of containing life at the outset. This probability is given by the `probabilityOfLife` parameter, a number between 0 and 1. Zero means no chance of life, 1 means certainty, 0.5 means a 50 percent chance of life, and so on.

To model randomness, the `Math` class provides a static method called `random` that returns a `double` value between 0 and 1. Successive invocations to `random` yield a sequence of different numbers that appear to be random and independent of each other. In a given invocation, each value between 0 and 1 is as likely as the next to be returned. We can use this method to take an action a certain percentage of the time at random. For example, if we wanted to print out "this is your lucky day" at random 15 percent of the time (that is, with probability 0.15), we could write the following:

```
if (Math.random()<0.15)
    System.out.println("this is your lucky day");
```

This approach works because all values from 0 to 1 are equally likely to be returned by a `Math.random` invocation, and 15 percent of those values are from 0 to 0.15.

Applying this to the constructor's task, the constructor will have to execute, for each square, that is, for each element in the `world` array, the following code:

```
if (Math.random()<probabilityOfLife)
    set world element to true
else
    set world element to false
```

After a moment of reflection, we could write the equivalent

> set world element to the truth value of
> Math.random() < probabilityOfLife

To apply this to every element, we adapt the nested for loops shown above to our `world` array:

```
for (int i = 0; i < world.size; i++)          Iterates through a
    for (int j; j < world[i].size; j++)       Iterates through world[i]—it too is an array.
        world[i][j] = Math.random() < probabilityOfLife;
```

This loop pattern will be used repeatedly through the methods of this class.

The complete constructor is as follows:

```
public Life(LifeDisplay lifeDisplay, int size,
                double probabilityOfLife) {
    this.lifeDisplay = lifeDisplay;
```

```
    world = new boolean[size][size];
    for (int i = 0; i < world.length; i++)
        for (int j = 0; j < world[i].length; j++)
            world[i][j] = Math.random() < probabilityOfLife;
}
```

The doGenerations method displays the initial world and then, as long
as there is still life in the world, produces a new generation, which is then displayed. Display is accomplished by sending a message to the DisplayLife
object (that's what it's there for). We can call the method invoked by this message displayWorld. It will need access to our world instance variable in
order to know where life is and isn't.

To determine whether there is life, we can use a helper predicate method,
lifeIsExtinct, and to produce the next generation we'll use another
helper method, nextGeneration. The doGenerations method then is as
follows:

```
public void doGenerations() throws Exception {
    lifeDisplay.displayWorld(world);
    while (!lifeIsExtinct()) {
        nextGeneration();
        lifeDisplay.displayWorld(world);
    }
}
```

The lifeIsExtinct method uses our world-traversal loop to test each
world element. As soon as we find an element that is true, that is, that contains life, we know that life is not extinct and we can return false. If we complete the loop without returning false, no life has been found and we return
true. Note that this is essentially the same search loop pattern that we
encountered in Chapter 8. The method's code is as follows:

```
private boolean lifeIsExtinct() {
    for (int i = 0; i < world.length; i++)
        for (int j = 0; j < world[i].length; j++)
            if (world[i][j])
                return false;
    return true;
}
```

The nextGeneration method determines the life pattern of the world
in the next generation. It does this square by square. As it does so, it must store
its results somewhere—but not in the world array. That's because the world
array represents the current generation—it must not be modified until it is no
longer needed. Therefore we make use of a local array of booleans, new-
World:

```
boolean[][]   newWorld =
                new boolean[world.length][world.length];
```

Its elements (representing squares of the next generation's world) are given values by traversing over each position and counting the number of living squares there are in its immediate environment, according to the rules of the game. We use a helper method, `livingNeighbors`, to do the actual count. The decision for life in the next generation for a square in row `i` and column `j` can be written as

```
if (livingNeighbors(i, j) >= MinNeighbors &&
    livingNeighbors(i, j) <= MaxNeighbors)
        newWorld[i][j] = true;
else
    newWorld[i][j] = false;
```

Again, however, when we have an `if` statement to assign `true` or `false` to a `boolean`, we can rewrite it as a single assignment of the `if` condition to the variable as follows:

```
newWorld[i][j] = livingNeighbors(i, j) >= MinNeighbors
                        &&
                 livingNeighbors(i, j) <= MaxNeighbors;
```

Once the loop that applies this to all positions of `newWorld` completes, we can assign the `newWorld`'s reference to its array object to `world`:

```
world = newWorld;
```

Our method is as follows:

```
private void nextGeneration() {
    boolean[][]    newWorld =
               new boolean[world.length][world.length];
    for (int i = 0; i < world.length; i++)
        for (int j = 0; j < world[i].length; j++)
            newWorld[i][j] =
                    livingNeighbors(i, j) >= MinNeighbors
                            &&
                    livingNeighbors(i, j) <= MaxNeighbors;
    world = newWorld;
}
```

To help us write the `livingNeighbors` method, which must examine several squares for life, we write a predicate helper method, `isAlive`, that tells us whether a particular position has life. Naively, we might write

```
private boolean isAlive(int i, int j) {
    if (world[i][j])
        return true;
    else
        return false;
}
```

or the more elegant, but still naive code:

```
private boolean isAlive(int i, int j) {
    return world[i][j];
}
```

However, this does not take into account the possibility that i and j are beyond the range of world. If they are beyond that range, i, j does not refer to a square that is alive, and so we amend our method with additional requirements for liveness:

```
private boolean isAlive(int i, int j) {
    if (i >= 0 && i < world.length &&
            j >= 0 && j < world[i].length && world[i][j])
        return true;
    else
        return false;
}
```

Using isAlive makes it easier to write livingNeighbors. We just have to invoke isAlive for each neighbor, and where it returns true, we increment a count. Figure 10.29 shows us the indices that mark the neighbors of square i, j:.

Using Figure 10.29, the complete livingNeighbors method is

```
private int livingNeighbors(int i, int j) {
    int result = 0;
    if (isAlive(i-1, j-1)) result++;
    if (isAlive(i-1, j)) result++;
    if (isAlive(i-1, j+1)) result++;
    if (isAlive(i, j-1)) result++;
    if (isAlive(i, j+1)) result++;
    if (isAlive(i+1, j-1)) result++;
    if (isAlive(i+1, j)) result++;
    if (isAlive(i+1, j+1)) result++;
    return result;
}
```

The complete definition of the Life class is as follows:

```
class Life {
    public Life(LifeDisplay lifeDisplay, int size,
                        double probabilityOfLife) {
        this.lifeDisplay = lifeDisplay;
        world = new boolean[size][size];
        for (int i = 0; i < world.length; i++)
            for (int j = 0; j < world[i].length; j++)
                world[i][j] = Math.random()
                                    <probabilityOfLife;
    }
```

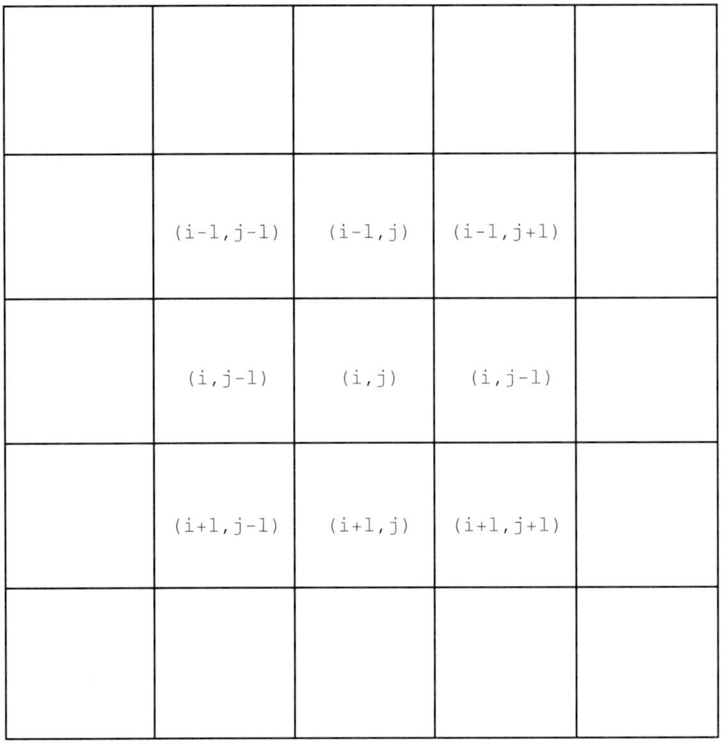

	(i-1,j-1)	(i-1,j)	(i-1,j+1)	
	(i,j-1)	(i,j)	(i,j-1)	
	(i+1,j-1)	(i+1,j)	(i+1,j+1)	

FIGURE 10.29 The indices of the neighbors of position i,j.
The grid shows the indices of the various neighbors of the element at position (i,j). If the element at position (i,j) is at the edge of world, some of these neighbors don't exist and their indices will not be in the range of the array.

```
public void doGenerations() throws Exception {
    lifeDisplay.displayWorld(world);
    while (!lifeIsExtinct()) {
        nextGeneration();
        lifeDisplay.displayWorld(world);
    }
}

private boolean lifeIsExtinct() {
    for (int i = 0; i < world.length; i++)
        for (int j = 0; j < world[i].length; j++)
            if (world[i][j])
                return false;
    return true;
}

private void nextGeneration() {
    boolean[][]    newWorld =
            new boolean[world.length][world.length];
    for (int i = 0; i < world.length; i++)
```

```
                    for (int j = 0; j < world[i].length; j++)
                        newWorld[i][j] = livingNeighbors(i, j) >=
                                                    MinNeighbors
                                        &&
                                    livingNeighbors(i, j) <=
                                                MaxNeighbors;
                world = newWorld;
            }

        private int livingNeighbors(int i, int j) {
            int result = 0;
            if (isAlive(i-1, j-1)) result++;
            if (isAlive(i-1, j)) result++;
            if (isAlive(i-1, j+1)) result++;
            if (isAlive(i, j-1)) result++;
            if (isAlive(i, j+1)) result++;
            if (isAlive(i+1, j-1)) result++;
            if (isAlive(i+1, j)) result++;
            if (isAlive(i+1, j+1)) result++;
            return result;
        }

        private boolean isAlive(int i, int j) {
            if (i >= 0 && i < world.length &&
                    j >= 0 && j < world[i].length &&
                                        world[i][j])
                return true;
            else
                return false;
        }

        private boolean [][] world;    // Good for a two-dimensional world
        private LifeDisplay lifeDisplay;
        private static final int MinNeighbors = 2,
                                MaxNeighbors = 3;
    }
```

10.12.2 The `LifeDisplay` Class

From the implementation of `Life`, we see that this class must provide a `displayWorld` method that is passed a two-dimensional array of `booleans` as an argument. The scenario used for the `Life` class tells us a bit about what this method should do: pause, waiting for a sign from the user to proceed, and the print a representation of the `world` array to system.out. A quick sketch of the `displayWorld` method that reflects this is as follows:

```
public void displayWorld(boolean[][] world)
                                    throws Exception {
    pause();
```

draw representation of world on standard output
```
}
```

Here we are using a helper method, `pause`, to wait for the user. We can have it just print out a message and wait for the user to hit the ENTER key:

```
private void pause() throws Exception {
    System.out.print("Hit return to continue ... ");
    System.out.flush();
    keybd.readLine();
}
```

We assume the availability here of a variable `keybd` that refers to a `Buff-eredReader` associated with the keyboard. We will therefore need an instance variable, `keybd`, whose value is assigned by the constructor.

The specifications for this class are not very constraining, so we have a certain amount of leeway. Let's display squares with life in them as asterisks and display squares with no life as blanks. A helper method, `drawSquare`, can be written to display a single square—its argument is the `boolean` value that represents the square in the program:

```
private void drawSquare(boolean s) {
    if (s)
        System.out.print("*");
    else
        System.out.print(" ");
}
```

To display the whole world we need to traverse each square and apply this method. The usual traversal is

```
for (int i = 0; i < world.length; i++)
    for (int j = 0; j < world[i].length; j++)
        drawSquare(world[i][j]);
```

However, this code prints all squares on the same line. We need to make sure that after each row has been printed, we go to a new line. The inner loop, which is the loop body of the outer loop, prints a row. So we modify the nested loops as follows:

```
for (int i = 0; i < world.length; i++) {
    for (int j = 0; j < world[i].length; j++)
        drawSquare(world[i][j]);
    System.out.println("");
}
```

This code is acceptable, but it does not show the borders of the world. Let's draw a horizontal line above and below the world and insert a vertical bar (|) at the beginning and end of each line to give the effect of vertical line borders on the sides of the world. Our complete `displayWorld` method then is as follows:

```
public void displayWorld(boolean[][] world)
                                       throws Exception {
    pause();
    drawLine(world.length+2);
    for (int i = 0; i < world.length; i++) {
        System.out.print("|");
        for (int j = 0; j < world[i].length; j++)
            drawSquare(world[i][j]);
        System.out.println("|");
    }
    drawLine(world.length+2);
}
```

Here we have made use of the following helper method, `drawLine`:

```
private void drawLine(int n) {
    for (int i = 0; i < n; i++)
        System.out.print("-");
    System.out.println();
}
```

The only requirement placed on the constructor comes from `pause`'s need for an available `BufferedReader`. So we let out constructor create this object and store a reference to it in the instance variable `keybd`. Our completed `LifeDisplay` class is as follows:

```
class LifeDisplay {
    public LifeDisplay() {
        keybd = new BufferedReader(
                      new InputStreamReader(System.in));
    }

    public void displayWorld(boolean[][] world)
                                       throws Exception {
        pause();
        drawLine(world.length+2);
        for (int i = 0; i < world.length; i++) {
            System.out.print("|");
            for (int j = 0; j < world[i].length; j++)
                drawSquare(world[i][j]);
            System.out.println("|");
        }
        drawLine(world.length+2);
    }

    private void drawLine(int n) {
        for (int i = 0; i < n; i++)
            System.out.print("-");
```

```
            System.out.println();
        }

    private void drawSquare(boolean s) {
        if (s)
            System.out.print("*");
        else
            System.out.print(" ");
    }

    private void pause() throws Exception {
        System.out.print("Hit return to continue ... ");
        System.out.flush();
        keybd.readLine();
    }
    private BufferedReader keybd;

}
```

EXERCISES

1. Why is 2 added to `world.length` in the argument to `drawLine` in the completed `LifeDisplay` class above?

2. Write a program that creates a `LifeDisplay` object and a `Life` object and displays the Game of Life on the screen.

3. Modify the `Life` class so that it can be constructed with different values of `MinNeighbors` and `MaxNeighbors`; write a program that experiments with these.

SUMMARY

Collections such as `Vector`s and arrays do more than maintain a group of objects or data—they maintain them in a particular order and permit the programmer to directly access individual elements according to their position in the collection. For example, in a sorted collection of data, the median element can be accessed by computing the middle position. An integer that represents a position is called an index.

The positions of both `Vector`s and arrays are numbered, or *indexed*, starting from 0. As a result, the last index in a `Vector` or array is 1 less than the total number of elements in the collection. Thus if there are eight elements, the positions are numbered from 0 through 7.

The most important application of indexing is efficient searching. By putting into the programmer's hands the order in which elements are checked in the course of a search, indexing allows a programmer to move through and rearrange the elements of a `Vector` or an array in a way that makes searching efficient.

STUDY AID: TERMINOLOGY REVIEW

array   A programming language feature that provides an indexed collection of data values.

binary search   An algorithm for efficiently searching a sorted collection by repeatedly dividing the region where the item might be found in half and reducing consideration to one half or the other.

command-line arguments   A set of `String` values that are supplied to a program when it is invoked

dimension   The number of indices required to access an element in an array.

index   An integer that denotes a position in an ordered collection.

$\log_2 N$ The number of times one can start with N and successively divide by 2 before reaching 1. The $\log_2$ is the inverse of exponentiation with 2 as the base: If 2^x is N, $\log_2 N$ is x.

move-to-front   A strategy for organizing a collection in which every time an item is requested, it is moved to the beginning of the collection on the assumption that it is likely to be asked for again.

search   An algorithm for finding a particular item that is stored in a collection of related values or objects.

self-organizing `vector`   An approach to searching where the order of elements in the `vector` is changed as information is learned about which elements are frequently accessed.

selection sort   An algorithm for sorting where one successively selects progressively ascending elements of a collection.

sequential search   An algorithm for searching an indexed collection, checking the elements in the same sequence that they are stored in the collection.

transpose   A strategy for organizing a collection where every time an item is requested, it is moved up one position, exchanging position with the item in front of it.

QUESTIONS FOR REVIEW

1. What determines the order of elements in a `Vector`?

2. How can the order of elements in a `Vector` be changed?

3. What determines the order of elements in an `Enumeration`?

4. What determines whether an `Enumeration` should be used to access the elements of a collection?

5. When would you use a sort and binary search instead of a self-organizing `Vector` and sequential search?

6. Why can't the `exchange` method in Section 10.5, Exercise 3, be used to implement the `moveToFront` method?

7. What are the similarities between arrays and `Vector`s?

8. What are the differences between arrays and `Vector`s?

9. When would you use an array instead of a `Vector`?

10. How can you access command-line arguments given on the command line that invoked the Java program?

FURTHER EXERCISES

1. Write a method, `vrotate`, that receives a `Vector` reference. The method rotates the elements in the `Vector` forward. That is, if there are N elements in the `Vector`, the elements in positions 0 through $N-2$ are moved to positions 1 through $N-1$ and the element in position $N-1$ is moved to position 0.

2. Write a method, `arotate`, that receives an array of `int`s. It carries out the same kind of rotate operation that is described in Section 10.13, Exercise 1.

3. Write a `search` method for an array that uses the *transpose* self-organizing approach.

4. Write a `search` method for an array that uses the move-to-front self-organizing approach. Be careful not to lose any elements.

5. Write a program that gets two command-line arguments, each naming a file. The program writes all the lines in the second file that appear in the first.

6. Modify the Game of Life so that the environment of a cell consists not just of the squares sharing its corners and sides but also of the squares sharing the corners and sides of those squares. Experiment to find reasonable `MinNeighbors` and `MaxNeighbors` values (instead of 2 and 3).

GUI *supplement*

The Game of Life Applet

In this supplement we design and implement a graphical version of the non-GUI Game of Life we developed earlier in this chapter.

The Game of Life Applet Design   Our Game of Life applet, `LifeApplet`, presents a canvas on which the Game of Life world is painted and the following four buttons for controlling the game:

- Start/resume—Initially labeled start, this button starts the game. Once started, the button's label is changed to resume—if the game is paused, the resume button allows it to continue.
- Pause—The pause button suspends the game until another button is pushed.
- Reset—The reset button ends the current game and starts a new one.
- Stop—The stop button halts any further execution of the game; once the stop button is pushed, the game cannot resume or be restarted.

In addition, instead of initializing life randomly in the world, as we did in our non-GUI version, we will start the game with a small square area of solid life, centered in the middle of the world. (See Figure 10.30). This will lead to symmetrical patterns such the one in Figure 10.31.

The Architecture of the Game of Life Applet   If we use `ClockApplet` from Chapter 9 as a model, transforming the non-GUI Game of Life to an applet does not involve a great deal of work. There are three classes in this model:

- An extended `Thread` class that does the *calculation*
- An extended `Canvas` class that does the *display*
- An extended `Applet` class that provides the *controls*

Our extended `Thread` class, `LifeThread`, will contain most of the methods and code of the `Life` class, along with the same methods that

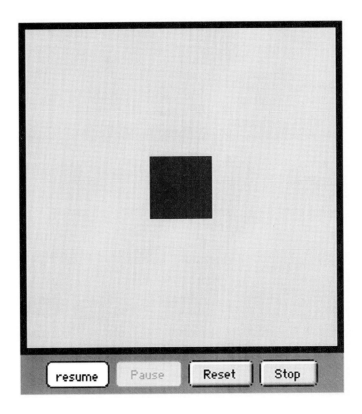

FIGURE 10.30 **The initial world in the Game of Life applet.**

`ClockThread` provided for thread control: `ourResume` and `ourSuspend`. We will have to provide, in addition, an `ourStop` method to support the stop and reset buttons' functions. The thread that this class defines will compute the generations in the Game of Life.

Our extended `Canvas` class, `LifeDisplay`, plays the same role that `LifeDisplay` played in the non-GUI implementation earlier in this chapter—and it provides the same interface. Its main difference is that instead of printing asterisks to `System.out`, it provides a `paint` method that fills in rectangles in a `Graphics` object.

Our extended `Applet` class, `LifeApplet`, creates the `LifeDisplay` object and the buttons, places them, and then handles the button action events. It responds to these events by creating, starting, suspending, resuming, and altogether stopping `LifeThread objects`.

The `LifeApplet` Class The `init` method creates the `LifeDisplay`. The reference to this extended `Canvas` is saved in an instance variable. This way, when the start button is pressed later, the `handleStart` method can pass the `LifeDisplay` reference to the `LifeThread` constructor when

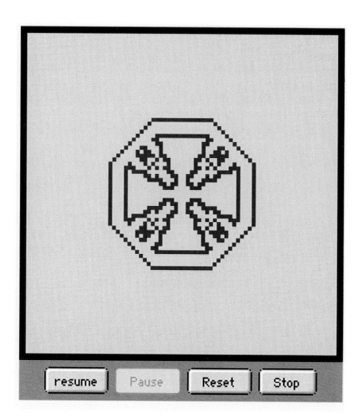

FIGURE 10.31 An early pattern in the Game of Life applet.

creating a new Game of Life. The `init` method also creates four buttons, `startButton`, `pauseButton`, `resetButton`, and `stopButton`. The `init` method sets up the applet as an `ActionListener` for these buttons, and it adds the four buttons to a `Panel` managed by `FlowLayout` so that within this `Panel` the buttons appear in a row from left to right. The applet itself uses `BorderLayout` and places the `Panel` of buttons at the "south" and the `LifeDisplay` canvas in the center. References to these `Buttons` must also be stored in instance variables because most of the `LifeApplet`'s methods use them.

At different times, certain buttons are inappropriate to use. For example, before the game has started, it does not make sense to push the pause, reset, or stop buttons. Once started and running, it does not make sense to push the resume button. The `Button` class provides a method, `setEnabled`, that allows the program to control the availability of a button. Sending a `false` argument makes the button unresponsive to clicks and sending a `true` argument does the opposite. Accordingly, the `init` method closes with several invocations of this method.

As usual, the applet provides an `actionPerformed` method, which simply determines which button was clicked and invokes the appropriate method. The methods it invokes, `handleStart`, `handlePause`, `handleReset`, and `handleStop`, are similar to those in `ClockApplet`. Except that it creates a new `LifeThread` object, the `handleStart` method is typical:

```
private void handleStart() {
    lifeThread = new LifeThread(lifeDisplay, 80);   // Create new LifeThread.
    lifeThread.start();                             // Start the new LifeThread
                                                    //   by sending it a start message.

    startButton.setEnabled(false);
    pauseButton.setEnabled(true);                   // Enable/disable buttons as
    resetButton.setEnabled(true);                   //   appropriate.
    stopButton.setEnabled(true);
}
```

Each handle method accomplishes its mission by sending a message to a `LifeThread` object and/or creating and starting such an object. Because there is only one Game of Life, that is one `LifeThread` object (as opposed to two clocks), these methods are somewhat simpler than the methods in the `ClockApplet`—they don't have to determine which `LifeThread` to work with. Most of the buttons have an unchanging label, so their handle methods don't have to invoke `setLabel`. They all send `setEnabled` messages to the `Button`s, passing `true` as an argument to enable the button and passing `false` to disable it. For example, `handlePause` disables the pause button (because the thread is now suspended) and enables the start button, which by now has been changed to reset.

The `handlePause` method here corresponds to the `ClockApplet`'s `handleStop` method. The `handleStop` method here allows us to completely shut down the thread, something we did not do in the `ClockApplet`. It accomplishes this by sending an `ourStop` message to the existing `LifeThread` and then creating and starting a new `LifeThread`. Figure 10.32 illustrates the role of the applet's methods in responding to button clicks.

The current `LifeThread` object also is sent messages in all of the handle methods, so it too must be referenced by an instance variable.

The code for the `LifeApplet` is as follows:

```
import java.awt.*;
import java.awt.event.*;
import java.applet.*;

public class LifeApplet extends Applet implements
ActionListener{
    public void init() {
        setLayout(new BorderLayout());
        lifeDisplay = new LifeDisplay();
```

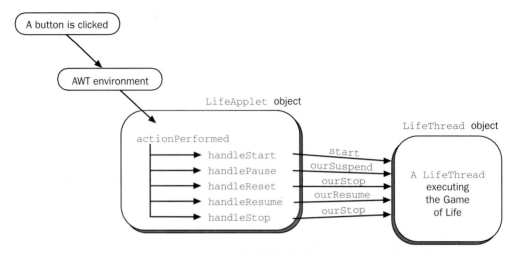

FIGURE 10.32 **How the Game of Life applet responds to buttons.** The handle-Start method also creates the LifeThread object before sending it a start message. After sending an ourStop message to stop the current LifeThread, the handleReset method invokes handleStart to start up a new LifeThread.

```
add("Center", lifeDisplay);
Panel p = new Panel();
add("South", p);
startButton = new Button("Start");
startButton.addActionListener(this);
p.add(startButton);
startButton.setEnabled(true);
pauseButton = new Button("Pause");
pauseButton.addActionListener(this);
p.add(pauseButton);
pauseButton.setEnabled(false);
resetButton = new Button("Reset");
resetButton.addActionListener(this);
p.add(resetButton);
resetButton.setEnabled(false);
stopButton = new Button("Stop");
stopButton.addActionListener(this);
p.add(stopButton);
setBackground(new Color(255, 20, 90));
startButton.setEnabled(true);
pauseButton.setEnabled(false);
resetButton.setEnabled(false);
stopButton.setEnabled(false);
startButton = new Button("Start");
startButton.addActionListener(this);
```

```
        p.add(startButton);
        startButton.setEnabled(true);
        pauseButton = new Button("Pause");
        pauseButton.addActionListener(this);
        p.add(pauseButton);
        pauseButton.setEnabled(false);
        resetButton = new Button("Reset");
        resetButton.addActionListener(this);
        p.add(resetButton);
        resetButton.setEnabled(false);
        stopButton = new Button("Stop");
        stopButton.addActionListener(this);
        p.add(stopButton);
        setBackground(new Color(255, 20, 90));
        startButton.setEnabled(true);
        pauseButton.setEnabled(false);
        resetButton.setEnabled(false);
        stopButton.setEnabled(false);
    }

    public void actionPerformed(ActionEvent ae) {
        String whichButton = ae.getActionCommand();
        if (whichButton.equals("Start"))
            handleStart();
        else if (whichButton.equals("resume"))
            handleResume();
        else if (whichButton.equals("Pause"))
            handlePause();
        else if (whichButton.equals("Reset"))
            handleReset();
        else if (whichButton.equals("Stop"))
            handleStop();
    }

    private void handleStart() {
        startButton.setLabel("resume");
        lifeThread = new LifeThread(lifeDisplay, 80);
        lifeThread.start();
        startButton.setEnabled(false);
        pauseButton.setEnabled(true);
        resetButton.setEnabled(true);
        stopButton.setEnabled(true);
    }

    private void handleResume() {
        lifeThread.ourResume();
        startButton.setEnabled(false);
        pauseButton.setEnabled(true);
        resetButton.setEnabled(true);
```

```
                        stopButton.setEnabled(true);
                   }

              private void handlePause() {
                   lifeThread.ourSuspend();
                   startButton.setEnabled(true);
                   pauseButton.setEnabled(false);
                   resetButton.setEnabled(true);
                   stopButton.setEnabled(true);
              }

              private void handleReset() {
                   lifeThread.ourStop();
                   handleStart();
              }

              private void handleStop() {
                   lifeThread.ourStop();
                   startButton.setEnabled(false);
                   pauseButton.setEnabled(false);
                   resetButton.setEnabled(false);
                   stopButton.setEnabled(false);
              }

              private LifeDisplay      lifeDisplay;
              private LifeThread       lifeThread;
              private Button           startButton, pauseButton,
                                              resetButton, stopButton;

         }
```

The `LifeDisplay` Class

This class is a close analog of the `LifeDisplay` class from the non-GUI Game of Life. It provides a constructor and `displayWorld` method with the same prototypes as the non-GUI version. To carry out the different printing tasks, the `displayWorld` method makes use of the following helper methods:

- `paintBackground`—draws a yellowish rectangle to serve as the background. Because we have a border, this rectangle is offset from the edge of the canvas by 5 pixels on all sides—its height and length therefore are 10 pixel less than those of the canvas:

```
g.fillRect(5,5,this.getSize().width-10,
     this.getSize().height-10);
```

- `paint1Square`—draws a single square from the Game of Life. If the square contains life, it is filled with dark blue.
- `paintWorld`—uses the usual pair of nested loops to traverse all the elements of `world`, invoking `paint1Square` for each of them.

Each of these methods requires a reference to the `Graphics` object associated with the `Canvas` class in order to draw, so `displayWorld` invokes `get-Graphics` and passes the result to each method.

Several of the methods make use of the `getSize` method. This is a method that all components (including `Applets` and `Canvases`) have. It returns a `Dimension` object, which carries the height and width dimensions of the object on the screen. These values are accessed by directly referring to the `Dimension`'s instance variables, `height` and `width`. Thus the following expression yields the height of whatever component is executing:

```
this.getSize().height
```

We are able to access `height` and `width` because, although they are instance variables, they are declared `public` instead of `private`. In our own class definitions, we avoid this practice. This is not, by the way, your first encounter with public variables. Throughout this text, we have been using `out`, which, like `err` and `in`, is a public variable of the `System` class.

As in the case of the non-GUI version, `displayWorld` is invoked directly by the Game of Life code that produces each new generation. However, in a GUI context we must also provide a `paint` method to display the `Canvas`. That's because in a GUI environment the display can be covered by other screen objects (other windows for example) and then uncovered, or the window it's in can be sized down and then sized back up. The AWT environment will invoke the `paint` method of the `Canvas` to display itself again. The default `paint` method of `Canvas` does nothing. Unless we provide a `paint` method, there won't be any redisplay. This would not be so terrible when the Game of Life is running—in that case, `displayWorld` would be called soon enough and the screen would be displayed properly. But if the game was paused, we would miss part or all of the picture until it was restarted again and the next generation displayed. Figure 10.33 shows the role of the various drawing methods in displaying the world of the Game of Life.

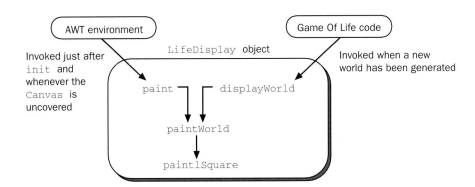

FIGURE 10.33
How the world gets displayed.

In order to display the Game of Life world, both `displayWorld` and `paint` need access to the two-dimensional array that represents it. As in the non-GUI version, `displayWorld` is passed a reference to this array as an argument. However, `paint` is invoked by the AWT environment, which has no knowledge of the nature of our applet, other than the fact that components have standard methods such `paint`. So `paint` cannot be passed a reference to this array. Therefore, our version of `LifeDisplay` needs an instance variable, `world`, set by `displayWorld` from its `world` argument to reference the array. This allows our implementation of the `paint` method to access this information.

Besides invoking `paint` whenever a formerly hidden part of the `Canvas` becomes exposed on the screen, the AWT invokes `paint` when it displays the `Canvas` and the other components of the applet, just after the `init` method completes. This is well before `displayWorld` is invoked. The fact that `paint` is invoked before `displayWorld` has the following consequences:

- `paint` must check to see if the `world` instance variable is still `null` before painting; `world` will be `null` until `displayWorld` has been invoked and gives it a value.
- `paint` must draw the border if it is to be there from the beginning; so `paint` also makes use of the `paintBorder` method, which draws a border consisting of four black rectangles of along the sides of the `Canvas`:

```
g.setColor(new Color(0,0,0));
g.fillRect(0,0,this.getSize().width,5);
g.fillRect(0,this.getSize().height-
5,this.getSize().width,5);
g.fillRect(0,0,5,this.getSize().height);
g.fillRect(this.getSize().width-
5,0,5,this.getSize().height);
```

Because the border never changes and is displayed at the outset by `paint`, `displayWorld` does not have to invoke `paintBorder`. The only time the border would need to be displayed again is if part of it was covered and then uncovered. In those circumstances, the AWT environment will invoke `paint`, which invokes `paintBorder`.

The code for the `LifeDisplay` class is as follows:

```
class LifeDisplay extends Canvas {
    LifeDisplay() {
        setBackground(new Color(0,210,90));
    }

    public void displayWorld(boolean [][] world) {
        this.world = world;
        Graphics g = this.getGraphics();
        paintBackground(g);
```

```
        paintWorld(g);
    }

    public void update(Graphics g) {
        paintBorder(g);
        paintBackground(g);
        paintWorld(g);
    }

    private void paintBackground(Graphics g) {
        g.setColor(new Color(240,210,0));
        g.fillRect(5,5,this.getSize().
                        width-10,this.getSize().height-10);
    }

    private void paintBorder(Graphics g) {
        g.setColor(new Color(0,0,0));
        g.fillRect(0,0,this.getSize().width,5);
        g.fillRect(0,this.getSize().
                        height-5,this.getSize().width,5);
        g.fillRect(0,0,5,this.getSize().height);
        g.fillRect(this.getSize().
                        width-5,0,5,this.getSize().height);
    }

    private void paintWorld(Graphics g) {
        g.setColor(new Color(30,20,120));
        if (world != null)
            for (int i = 0; i < world.length; i++)
                for (int j = 0; j < world[i].length; j++)
                    paint1Square(g,i,j);
    }

    private void paint1Square(Graphics g, int i, int j) {
        if (world[i][j])
            g.fillRect(5+i*CellWidth, 5+j*CellWidth,
                    CellWidth, CellWidth);
    }

    private boolean[][]      world = null;
    private static final int CellWidth = 3;
}
```

The LifeThread Class   This class is based on the Life class from the non-GUI version with the addition of those methods needed to make this class a Thread. First, let's note the methods that are identical to those of the non-GUI version:

- lifeIsExtinct
- nextGeneration

- livingNeighbors
- isAlive

The constructor has been changed only in the way that it initializes the `world` array. Rather than traversing every element in the array, it traverses only a square of elements at the center, the dimension of which is one-fifth that of the entire world. This is accomplished using the following nested pair of loops:

```
for (int i = world.length*4/10; i < world.length*6/10; i++)
    for (int j = world.length*4/10; j < world[i].length*6/
                                                      10; j++)
```

Here, `world.length*4/10` replaces `0` as the starting point, and `world.length*6/10` replaces `world.length` as the terminating value. Every element in that central square initially contains life:

```
world[i][j] = true;
```

The `run` method of any `Thread` defines the code that is executed once a start message has been sent to the `Thread` object. Here the `run` method is based on the `doGenerations` method from the `Life` class, with some extra thread-related code thrown in. In the following listing, the original code is shown in boldface:

```
public void run() {
    amRunning = true;
    amStopped = false;
    lifeDisplay.displayWorld(world);
    while (!amStopped && !lifeIsExtinct()) {
        try {
            Thread.sleep(25);
        } catch (Exception e)
        if (!amStopped && amRunning)
            nextGeneration();
        if (!amStopped && amRunning)
            lifeDisplay.displayWorld(world);
    }

}
```

There are two modifications to the original `doGenerations` method:

- A 25-millisecond delay is inserted into the loop body using `Thread`'s static `sleep` method.
- The boolean variables `amRunning` and `amStopped` are used to control the activity of the thread.

The `amRunning` variable plays exactly the same role as it does in the `ClockThread` of Chapter 9—when `false`, the loop in `run` is reduced to repeated sleeps. The `amStopped` variable is initially `false`. When it becomes `true`, the loop terminates. Both of these variables are set by the `ourSuspend`, `ourResume`, and `ourStop` methods, giving the `LifeApplet` the needed ability to control this thread.

Note that although the chief purpose of `amStopped` is to force the `while` loop to terminate, we also use it in the `if` statements that invoke `nextGeneration` and `displayWorld` if `amRunning` is true. This way the thread can respond to an `ourStop` message as soon as possible. This is also why two separate but identical `if` statements appear in the loop: It is possible that while `nextGeneration` is executing, `amRunning` becomes `false` or `amStopped` becomes `true`, in which case we want to cease displaying as soon as possible—by checking these `booleans` again before invoking `displayWorld`.

The complete code for the `LifeThread` class is as follows:

```
class LifeThread extends Thread {

    public LifeThread(LifeDisplay lifeDisplay, int size) {
        this.lifeDisplay = lifeDisplay;
        world = new boolean[size][size];
        for (int i = world.length*4/10; i <
            world.length*6/10; i++)
            for (int j = world.length*4/10; j <
                world[i].length*6/10; j++)
            world[i][j] = true;
    }

    public void run() { // was doGenerations
        amRunning = true;
        amStopped = false;
        lifeDisplay.displayWorld(world);
        while (!amStopped && !lifeIsExtinct()) {
            try {
                Thread.sleep(25);
            } catch (Exception e) {}
            if (!amStopped && amRunning)
                nextGeneration();
            if (!amStopped && amRunning)
                lifeDisplay.displayWorld(world);
        }
    }

    public void ourStop() {
        amStopped = true;
    }

    public void ourSuspend() {
        amRunning = false;
```

```
        }

        public void ourResume() {
            amRunning = true;
        }

        private boolean lifeIsExtinct() {
            for (int i = 0; i < world.length; i++)
                for (int j = 0; j < world[i].length; j++)
                    if (world[i][j])
                        return false;
            return true;
        }

        private void nextGeneration() {
            boolean[][]     newWorld =
                      new boolean[world.length][world.length];
            for (int i = 0; i < world.length; i++)
                for (int j = 0; j < world[i].length; j++) {
                    int x = livingNeighbors(i, j);
                    newWorld[i][j] = MinNeighbors <= x
                                      &&  x <= MaxNeighbors;
                }
            world = newWorld;
        }

        private int livingNeighbors(int i, int j) {
            int result = 0;
            if (isAlive(i-1, j-1)) result++;
            if (isAlive(i-1, j)) result++;
            if (isAlive(i-1, j+1)) result++;
            if (isAlive(i, j-1)) result++;
            if (isAlive(i, j+1)) result++;
            if (isAlive(i+1, j-1)) result++;
            if (isAlive(i+1, j)) result++;
            if (isAlive(i+1, j+1)) result++;
            return result;
        }

        private boolean isAlive(int i, int j) {
            if (i >= 0 && i < world.length &&
                    j >= 0 && j < world[i].length &&
                    world[i][j])
                return true;
            else
                return false;
        }

        private boolean amRunning, amStopped;
        private boolean[][] world;
```

```
      private LifeDisplay lifeDisplay;
      private static final int MinNeighbors = 2,
                               MaxNeighbors = 3;
}
```

The `Threads` **and Threads**   Where there is execution, there is a thread. All code executes as part of some thread. The `Thread` class provides a static method, `currentThread`, that returns a reference to a `Thread` object that is currently executing (the one that invokes `currentThread`). We can use the `getName` method of the `Thread` class to get the unique name of the currently executing thread. The following program uses this to illustrate the fact that there is always a thread executing:

```
class  Sample  {
   public  static  void  main(String[]  a)  {
      System.out.println(Thread.currentThread().getName());
   }
}
```

The output of this program is the word *main*, the name of the thread executing this program. From this little experiment we make the following observations:

- A thread does not only execute the code that is defined in a `Thread` class—here, for example, the main thread is executing the `main` method in the `Sample` class
- When our programs run, there may be threads that we did not create and are not defined by any `Thread` class of ours.

When our `LifeApplet` executes, there are at first two threads present:

- The main applet thread—it loads the applet, invokes `init`, and then invokes `start`.
- The AWT-environment thread—this thread runs AWT code that detects events associated with the user (button clicks, typing in text fields, and so on) and determines when our applet or parts of it need to be redrawn (for example, when another window that covered our applet is moved and exposes part or all of the applet). This thread invokes `action-Performed`, `paint`, and other applet methods as needed.

These two threads are present when any applet executes, including the first one we wrote in Chapter 3. These threads, like the main thread that was revealed by the `Sample` class above, are not created by our code or defined by a `Thread` class that we wrote. They are "given" to us by the execution environment.

When the `LifeApplet` executes, there may be additional threads executing, as our code creates new threads to execute the Game of Life.

Creating a thread involves two steps:

- Creating a `Thread` object
- Sending a `start` message to the `Thread` object

There is a difference between a `Thread` (an object) and a thread (an independent execution of code). When we create a `Thread` object, using the `new` operator, we have not yet created a new thread—just a new object. It is not until we send the `Thread` object a `start` message that a new *thread* is actually created.

The code executed by the threads we create is defined by but not limited to the `run` method of the `Thread` class we define. This run method invokes other methods with in its own class and in other classes as well. The `displayWorld` method in our `DisplayLife` class is executed by the `LifeThread` threads that we create in response to the start and reset buttons.

Figure 10.34 shows the methods of the three classes we defined in making the `LifeApplet` and the threads that execute them. Note that there are some methods that are executed by more than one thread, `paintWorld`, for example.

Repaint, Paint, Update, and Drawing Things Directly   The AWT environment thread takes responsibility for drawing all components (such as `Buttons` and `Canvas`es) that are added to a `Container`. This includes `Applet` objects because they are components and they too are added to a `Container`—the browser window. The AWT thread does this by invoking the `paint` method of each such component. Every component is responsible for providing a `paint` method that draws itself on the `Graphics` object that the AWT thread passes to the method.

For components whose appearance does not rapidly change—like `Buttons` and `Labels`—it is sufficient to simply provide a `paint` method. When such methods do need to redraw themselves, they usually just invoke the `repaint` method. This method tells the AWT environment that the component needs to be updated. As a result, the AWT method will eventually invoke the component's `update` method, which in turn invokes the component's `paint` method.

We could have taken this approach in `LifeDisplay`, by replacing our `displayWorld` method,

```
public void displayWorld(boolean [][] world) {
    this.world = world;
    Graphics g = this.getGraphics();
    paintBackground(g);
    paintWorld(g);
}
```

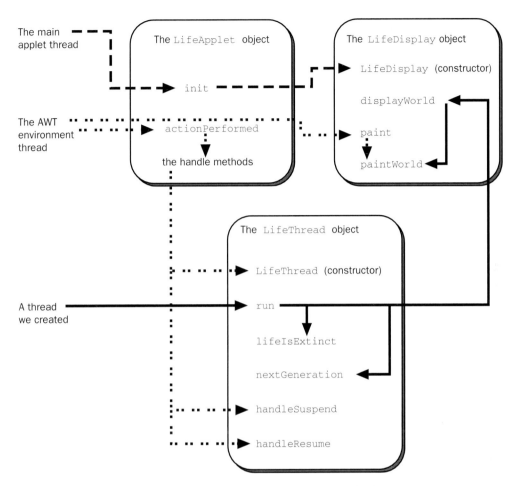

FIGURE 10.34   The threads of the `LifeApplet` and the methods they execute.
Not all the methods of every class are shown here.

with the simpler

```
public void displayWorld(boolean [][] world) {
    this.world = world;
    repaint();
}
```

Had we done this, the redrawing of the world would not have been carried out by the current `LifeThread` (remember, `LifeThread` executes
`displayWorld`). Instead, the AWT environment thread would eventually
invoke `LifeDisplay`'s `update` method.

We didn't write an update and repaint method because when we create a class by extending another class, as we did in LifeDisplay (and LifeThread and LifeApplet), we inherit the methods of the other class. In this case, update and repaint are examples of those methods.

Using repaint here is inappropriate, however. That's because the Game of Life world is rapidly changing. The AWT environment is not always in a hurry to do updates. By the time it invoked update and paint, the world could have changed, and we would miss some of the generations. Worse, while paint is drawing the world, the world could have changed, resulting in a picture that is partly one generation, partly the next generation—ugly and inconsistent. Finally, while we wait for the AWT to get around to invoking update, the LifeThread could have made multiple invocations to displayWorld and therefore to repaint. Many invocations of update would then be scheduled. As a result, when we paused or stopped the Game, we would observe many redrawings of the same world.

This is all a consequence of the fact that our Canvas here is being rapidly recomputed. If it changed only once every few hundred milliseconds, we could use repaint in displayWorld and leave all the painting to paint.

chapter 11

Recursion

11.1 Introduction

Imagine that you are at a big family or friends' reunion. Dinner is over and the sink is filled with a stack of dishes that seems a mile high. You walk by the kitchen at an inopportune moment and someone possessing a certain amount of authority tells you to *do the dishes.*

So what do you do? You might take the *lazy* approach:

- Wash one dish.
- Find the nearest person and, with all the authority you can muster, tell him or her to *do the dishes.*

You duck out of there as quickly as possible, but perhaps the person you passed the job to follows the same lazy approach you did:

- Wash one dish.
- Find the nearest person and, with all the authority you can muster, tell him or her to *do the dishes.*

Of course the newest "victim" can follow this same procedure—as can all succeeding dishwashers. This procedure might work out rather nicely—no one ends up having to do the whole sinkload—provided that each person called on can recognize an empty sink when it finally appears, in which case the lucky soul neither washes a dish nor gets someone else to do the rest of the job. Taking this into account, we amend the lazy approach as follows.

To do the dishes:

- If the sink is empty, then there is nothing to do.
- If it is not empty, then
  - Wash one dish.
  - Find the nearest person and, with all the authority one can muster, tell him or her to *do the dishes.*

The lazy approach contains a reference to itself (to do the dishes, we tell someone else to do the dishes). To guarantee that this approach does not become an endless passing of the buck, *each person does some of the work, and so the job given to the next person is somewhat smaller.*

Because the job gets smaller each time, eventually it is completed and the chain of getting another person to do the rest of the work can be broken.

A procedure that does part of a task and then gets the rest done by referring to itself is called **recursive procedure** and the execution of such a procedure is called **recursion**. The procedure to do the dishes is recursive because one of its steps includes "do the dishes"—a reference to itself.

EXERCISES

1. Suppose you have a stack of 500 advertisement flyers that must be stuffed into 500 envelopes for mailing. Take the lazy approach and describe a recursive procedure for carrying this out. Assume you have at least 499 friendly coworkers willing to lend a small helping hand.

2. Suppose you have two stacks of index cards, each with a name written on it. The stacks are not sorted. Your task is to write up a list of the names that appear in both stacks. Take the lazy approach and describe a recursive procedure for carrying out this task.

11.2   Example: Exponentiation

Recursion is not only an easy way to get out of doing a lot of dishes but also an easy and powerful way of tackling many difficult computing problems. Rather than starting our exploration of recursion using these difficult problems, we'll start with easier ones—problems for which iteration is well-suited and recursion not needed. We do this because it is easier to learn a new tool using easy problems than hard ones. We'll look at some more challenging problems later in this chapter. Therefore, let's start with a simple example.

Suppose we need a helper method that receives two `int` parameters, `x` and `y`, and returns an integer value, `x` raised to the power of `y`:

x^y

An outline of the method is:

```
private int power(int x, int y) {      // y>=0 returns x**y
    ...
}
```

(When we don't have superscripts available, the notation `x**y` is widely used to represent x^y.)

The definition of exponentiation is

$$x^y = 1*x*x*\cdots*x \text{ (}y\text{ times)}$$

In English, we say that x raised to the power of y equals 1 multiplied by x, y times.

To use recursion to write this method we start by imagining that we have to do the process ourselves by hand (without a calculator). It seems like quite a bit of work, especially if y is large. Let's take the lazy approach and get someone else to do most of the work. We have to compute x^y, but if we could get an assistant to compute x^{y-1}, all we would have to do is multiply the assistant's result by y.

Of course, our assistant might get an assistant to compute x^{y-2} and so on by following the same procedure. And what is this procedure exactly? If we take into account that each assistant should check for the easy case of x^0, where the result is 1, the procedure could be stated as follows.

To compute the power of x to the y

- If y is 0 then there are no multiplications to do, and the result is 1.
- If y is greater than 0, then
  - Tell an assistant *to compute the power of x to the y-1*.
  - The result is x times the assistant's result.

So, using the procedure to compute 4^3, we hire an assistant (A) to compute 4^2, who hires an assistant (B) to compute 4^1, who hires an assistant (C) to compute 4^0. The last assistant recognizes that y is 0, and so the result is 1. So B's result is $4*1$ (==4), and so A's result is $4*4$ (==16), and so our result is $4*16$ or 64, which is indeed 4^3. See Figure 11.1.

This procedure is recursive because it includes a reference to itself and it is valid for the following reasons:

- The procedure gives the assistant a smaller problem to compute.
- The procedure provides a way to check whether there is no more work to be done.

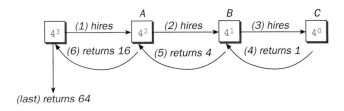

FIGURE 11.1 Recursion in exponentiation. To compute 4^3, we must compute 4^2. To compute 4^2 we must compute 4^1. To compute 4^1 we must compute 4^0.

To express this procedure in a Java method is straightforward:

> If y is 0 then there are no multiplications to do and the result is 1.

> Else (if y is greater than 0), tell an assistant to compute x to the y−1 power. The result is x times the assistant's result.

```
if (y==0)
    return 1;
else {
    assistantResult = power(x,y-1);
    return x*assistantResult;
}
```

Adding the required declaration, the power method is:

```
private int power(int x, int y) {      // y>=0, returns x**y
    int     assistantResult;
    if  (y==0)
        return 1;
    else {
        assistantResult = power(x,y-1);
        return x*assistantResult;
    }
}
```

11.2.1 The Recursive Call

The power method invokes itself:

```
private int power(int x, int y) {     // y>=0 returns x**y
    ...
        assistantResult = power(x,y-1);
    ...
}
```

An invocation of a method from within that method is a **recursive call**. A recursive call is legal in Java and it corresponds to the passing of the job on to an assistant. The arguments that are passed to a method determine the task it must perform. The arguments in a recursive call must define a task that is smaller or easier than the task given to the caller. Note that the caller must calculate x^y, but the recursive call involves an easier task, x^{y-1}.

11.2.2 Termination

The power method has a conditional return that does not involve a recursive call:

```
private int power(int x, int y) {     // y>=0 returns x**y
    if  (y==0)
        return 1;
    ...
    }
}
```

This code corresponds to checking whether there is a need to hire another assistant. This **termination step** is essential in any viable recursive procedure. It checks the task to see if it can be carried out without resort to recursion. If so, it terminates the recursion, that is, it prevents further recursive calls from being made. The termination code must appear before the recursive call—otherwise the recursive call would be repeatedly invoked and the termination code would never be reached.

EXERCISES

1. Write a recursive method that receives two nonnegative integer arguments and returns their product. The method does not use the * operator. Instead, it relies on the fact that $x*y = x + x + \cdots + x$ (where there are y terms in the sum). Here are some hints:

   - Think of the sum as the equivalent $0+x+x+\cdots+x$.
   - If you could hire an assistant to help you, what would you have the assistant do so that you would have to do only one addition?
   - For what value of y would it be silly to hire an assistant?

2. Write a recursive method that receives a nonnegative integer argument, n, and prints n hyphens, all on the same line.

11.3 How to Design a Recursive Method

In order to design a recursive solution to a problem, you must find a way to do the following:

- Use a solution to a smaller or easier version of the problem to arrive at the solution to your problem.
  - This step leads to the recursive call.
  - Usually laziness can be an inspiration at this step.
- Know when the problem is small enough to solve directly.
  - This step leads to the termination code.
  - Laziness can help here too. Ask, What is the easiest version of the problem to solve?

In the exponentiation example of Section 11.2 we applied this approach.

- We multiplied x^{y-1}, an easier exponentiation problem than x^y, by x to get our result.
- We were able to solve x^0 directly.

Let's apply this approach to some more examples.

11.3.1 Reading Data to Construct a Collection of `Employee` Objects

Let's write a helper method that receives a `BufferedReader` object and a `Vector` as arguments. Its task is to read all the `Employees` from the `BufferedReader` and add them to the `Vector`.

```
private void getEmployees(BufferedReader br, Vector v)
```

Step 1: Getting Lazy. With a long stream of data to read, we take inspiration from the dishwasher. We read just one `Employee` object from `br` and add it to `v`,

```
Employee e = Employee.read(br);
v.addElement(e);
```

We then let someone else (our recursive call) process the rest of the input, which is now slightly smaller because we have read and processed one `Employee`. So our recursive call will be

```
getEmployees(br,v);
```

The arguments don't seem to make the problem smaller, but `br` refers to a `BufferedReader` that has one less `Employee` in it.

Step 2: Knowing When to Quit. When is the task so small that we can solve it directly? That's easy! We can quit when there is no more input and the `Employee.read` method returns `null`, there is nothing to add to `v`, so there is no need to have someone else process the rest of the input. Our termination code is as follows:

```
if (e==null)
    return;
```

The termination code must come after the attempt to read but before we add to `v` or make the recursive call. The following is the completed method.

```
private void getEmployees(BufferedReader br, Vector v)
    Employee e = Employee.read(br);
    if (e==null)
        return;
```

```
        v.addElement(e);
        getEmployees(br,v);
}
```

11.3.2   Searching a Collection for the Employee with the Highest Pay

Let's write a helper method that receives an `Enumeration` object for a group of employees and returns a reference to the `Employee` object that has the highest pay or returns `null` if the `Enumeration` is empty:

```
private Employee  getHighestPaid(Enumeration  e)
```

Step 1: Getting Lazy.   We don't want to look at all the `Employee` objects and make comparisons. We could, however, take just one `Employee` object from the `Enumeration` and let someone else find the highest paid of those left:

```
Employee  oneEmployee,  highestOfThoseLeft;
emp  =  (Employee)  e.nextElement();
highestOfThoseLeft  =  getHighestPaid(e);
```

The argument doesn't seem to define a smaller task, but the `Enumeration e` has gotten smaller because we removed `emp` from it—e may in fact now be empty.

We now find out who has the higher pay: `emp` or `highestOf-ThoseLeft`. If `highestOfThoseLeft` is `null`, there is no contest. Otherwise, we have to compare its pay rate with that of `emp`.

```
if  (highestOfThoseLeft==null
          || highestOfThoseLeft.getPay() < emp.getPay())
      return  emp;
else
      return  highestOfThoseLeft;
```

Step 2: Knowing When to Quit.   The easiest form of this task is when the `Enumeration` has no more elements, in which case the only thing to do is return `null`. Our termination code is:

```
if  (!e.hasMoreElements())
    return null;
```

This check for termination must be placed before we attempt to remove an element from e, so the completed method is as follows:

```
private Employee  getHighestPaid(Enumeration  e) {
    if  (!e.hasMoreElements())
        return null;
```

```
Employee   emp,   highestOfThoseLeft;
emp  =  (Employee)  e.nextElement();
highestOfThoseLeft  =  getHighestPaid(e);
if (highestOfThoseLeft==null
       || highestOfThoseLeft.getPay() < emp.getPay())
    return  emp;
else
    return  highestOfThoseLeft;
}
```

11.3.3   Two Recursion Patterns

We have encountered four recursion examples, counting our dishwasher. Two patterns emerge, shown in Figure 11.2.

Pattern 1 is simple. We solve the problem by handling a small part of it and making a recursive call to solve the rest. This is the way `getEmployees` and the dishwasher worked. In pattern 2, a smaller version of the problem is passed in the recursive call and the resulting solution is used to solve the problem at hand. This is the way `power` and `getHighestPaid` worked.

EXERCISES

1. Consider the methods you wrote in the exercises in the previous section. (If you have not written them, do so now!) Which of the patterns of Figure 11.2 characterizes each of them?

2. Write a recursive method that receives two nonnegative integer arguments, x and y, and returns their sum, $x+y$. The method is not allowed to use the $+$ or $-$ operators, but it may use ++ and --. *Hint:* Note that $x+y$ is equal to $x + 1 + 1 + \cdots + 1$ (where there are y 1's in the sum).

```
method (problem)          {
    if (problem is very easy)
        solve it and return
    solve part of the problem,
        leaving a smaller problem
    method (smaller problem);

}
```
Pattern 1

```
method (problem)          {
    if (problem is very easy)
        return solution to easy problem
    solution to smaller problem=method (smaller problem);
    solve problem, using solution to smaller problem
    return solution
}
```
Pattern 2

FIGURE 11.2   Two patterns of simple recursion.

11.4   Recursive Methods: Under the Hood

We have yet to meet the student who is not curious to know how recursion works, that is, how it is possible for a method to invoke itself. We explain that in this section with a stern warning:

> Understanding how recursion actually works is of little help in using it to solve problems. To use recursion **to solve problems, use the lazy approach** given in the previous section.

Remember what happens when a method is invoked:

- A message is sent to a receiving object; the sender of the message suspends execution.
- The receiver gets the message and arranges for the correct method to execute.
- The receiver *creates* the local variables of the method (parameters and other local variables).
- The parameters get the values from the arguments.
- The method executes.
- The method completes and destroys the local variables of the method; any return value replaces the expression that sent the message.
- The sender of the message resumes execution.

In order for this to work, every time a method is invoked, the system allocates a new piece of memory for the method to store the following:

- The local variables that it creates
- The parameters it uses
- The location in the code of the sender of the message

Such pieces of memory are called activation records. An **activation record** is a block of memory holding the parameters and local variables of a method, along with the return address of the invoker of the method.

Let's look again at the `power` method.

```
private int power(int x, int y) {     // y>=0 returns x**y
    if  (y==0)
        return 1;
    else {
        int    assistantResult;
        assistantResult = power(x,y-1);   method power, line 5
        return  x*assistantResult;
    }
}
```

and let's assume that it is invoked by method `f` as follows:

Sender: whoever invoked f   Activation record for f(. . .)

Sender: method f, line N

| X | 3 | Y | 2 | assistantResult | |

Activation record for power(3,2)
(the current activation record)

FIGURE 11.3   **A stack of activation records after invoking power(3,2).** After invoking power(3,2), the activation record for power(3,2) is on top of the stack.

```
void  f(...) {
    ...
    int  q  =  power(3,2);    method f, line N
    ...
}
```

Thus, the power method is first invoked as power(3,2). Consider the structure of memory once power starts executing. There is an activation record for f, the sender of the message, and there is an activation record for power as well. See Figure 11.3.

When the recursive call, power(x,y-1), is made in line 5, a message is sent to same object that is executing power(3,2), telling it to execute power(3,1). So the object takes the following steps:

- It suspends its execution of power(3,2).
- It sends the power(3,1) message to itself.
- It receives the power(3,1) message.
- It creates a new activation record with x==3, y==1, and
  sender: method power, line 5.
- It starts executing the power method from the beginning.

The resulting structure of memory is shown in Figure 11.4.

Now there are two activation records for power—one for the invocation by f, the other for the recursive invocation by power itself. The contents of the two activation records are different and reflect this distinction.

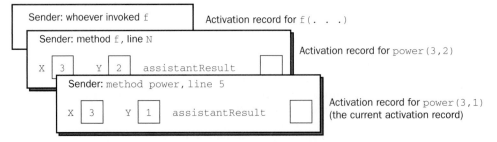

Sender: whoever invoked f   Activation record for f(. . .)

Sender: method f, line N

| X | 3 | Y | 2 | assistantResult | |

Activation record for power(3,2)

Sender: method power, line 5

| X | 3 | Y | 1 | assistantResult | |

Activation record for power(3,1)
(the current activation record)

FIGURE 11.4   **A stack of activation records after invoking power(3,1).** Now the activation record for power(3,1) is on top of the stack.

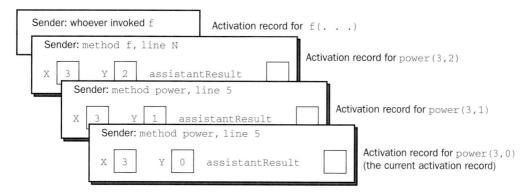

FIGURE 11.5   A stack of activation records after invoking `power(3,0)`. Now the activation record for `power(3,0)` is on top of the stack.

There are two x, two y, and two `assistantResult` variables now that belong to the different activation records. Only the most recent activation record, the **current activation record**, is used. So when `power` refers to x, there is never any ambiguity; the reference is always to the x in the current activation record.

As execution continues, `power`, discovering that y, which now equals 1, is not equal to 0, makes another recursive invocation: `power(3,0)`. So the object takes the following steps:

- It suspends its execution of `power(3,1)`.
- It sends the `power(3,0)` message to itself.
- It receives the `power(3,0)` message.
- It creates a new activation record with x==3, y==0, and `sender: method power, line 5`.
- It starts executing the `power` method from the beginning.

and the resulting structure of memory is shown in Figure 11.5.

The `power` method starts executing now for the third time—it has yet to return. However, this time, the y in the current activation record is 0, so the test y==0 succeeds. The method then executes

```
return 1;
```

The `return` statement does each of the following:

- It evaluates the return value (in this case 1).
- It destroys the current activation record.
- It replaces the expression that invoked the method with the return value.
- It resumes execution of the sender.

The resulting structure of memory is shown in Figure 11.6.

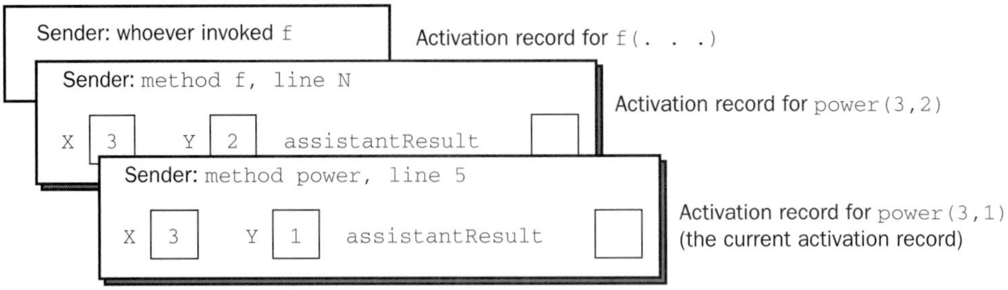

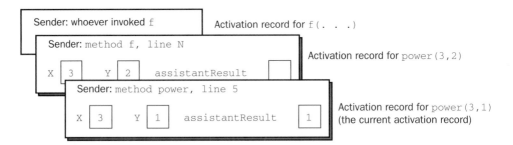

FIGURE 11.6 **A stack of activation records after return from `power(3,0)`.** The activation record for `power(3,0)` has been discarded, leaving the activation record for `power(3,1)` at the top of the stack once more.

and the `power(3,1)` resumes executing on line 5:

```
assistantResult  =  1;
```

The value returned by `power(3,0)`, 1, replaces `power(3,0)` in the execution. See Figure 11.7.

Power now executes

```
return  x*assistantResult;
```

which does the following steps:

- It evaluates the return value (in this case, 3).
- It destroys the current activation record.
- It replaces the expression that invoked the method with the return value.
- It and resumes execution of the sender.

These steps lead to the state shown in Figure 11.8.

FIGURE 11.7 **A stack of activation records: `assistantResults` gets the return value.** The return value of `power(3,0)` is stored in a local variable of the activation record of `power(3,1)`, at the top of the stack.

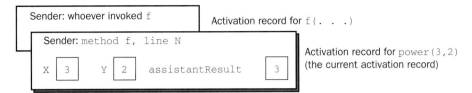

FIGURE 11.8   A stack of activation records after return from `power(3,1)`. The activation record for `power(3,1)` has been discarded, leaving the activation record for `power(3,2)` at the top of the stack once more. The return value of `power(3,1)` is stored in a local variable of the activation record of `power(3,2)`.

Finally, the original invocation of `power`, `power(3,2)`, resumes and executes

```
return  x*assistantResult;
```

At this point, `assistantResult` is 3 and so 9 (the correct evaluation of 3^2) is returned to `f`, which resumes its execution. Its activation record is once again the current activation record. See Figure 11.9.

As you can see, the implementation of recursion, that is, what's "under the hood," is quite involved. Keep the following important guideline in mind as you work:

Thinking about the implementation when you are designing a recursive method will distract you from the real task; instead, focus on finding a procedure that contributes a little to the solution and has an "assistant" do the rest by carrying out the same procedure.

In other words, we've shown you how recursion actually is implemented; now let's forget it and go back to the business of designing recursive solutions to problems.

```
┌─────────────────────────────────┐   Activation record for f(. . .)
│                                 │   (the current activation record)
│    Sender: whoever invoked f    │
│                                 │
└─────────────────────────────────┘
```

FIGURE 11.9   A stack of activation records after return from `power(3,2)`. When the first invocation completes, there are no activation records of the recursive procedure still on the stack.

11.5 Recursion with `Vectors`, Arrays, and `Strings`

Recursion is often fruitfully applied to collections, particularly ones with indices such as `Vectors`, arrays, and `Strings`. Typically, the original task involves the entire collection. The smaller versions of the task passed to an "assistant" usually involve a subsection of the collection. One can specify a subsection of a collection with the following three arguments (see Figure 11.10):

- A reference to the collection itself
- The index of the first position in the subsection
- The first position after the subsection or the number of elements in the subsection

The third argument can be omitted if it is assumed that the subcollection goes to the end of the original collection itself. Thus, recursive methods for a collection will have the first two or all three arguments as well as any additional ones needed for the particular task.

EXAMPLE **Reading Integers from a `BufferedReader` into an Array.** The helper method will require a reference to a `BufferedReader` as well as the other arguments, and we will have it return the number of elements it has read:

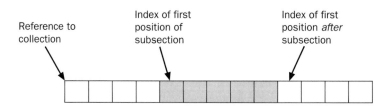

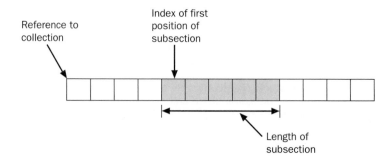

FIGURE 11.10 Two ways of specifying a subsection of a collection. Subsections of a collection can be specified by starting point and ending point (top) or starting point and length (bottom) of the subcollection.

```
//    Read integers (one per line) from br and store in a[first], ..., a[beyond−1];
//    Read until end of file or until no more elements are available.
//    Return the number of integers read and stored.
private int  readIntArray(int[]  a,   int   first,
                          int  beyond, BufferedReader  br)  {

}
```

Step 1: Getting Lazy.   The laziest thing we can do is to read a single integer and store it in the first element of the subcollection. Then we can give our assistant a slightly smaller subcollection to work on:

```
String  s  =  br.readLine();
a[first]  =  Integer.parseInt(s);
return  1+readIntArray(a,first+1,beyond,br);
```

The assistant tells us how many integers it read. So we add 1 to that number, because we also read in one integer, and we return the sum to our invoker. We give the assistant exactly the same arguments given to us, except that first becomes first+1, reflecting the fact that we have stored a value in a[first].

Step 2: Knowing When to Quit.   There are two situations that require us to quit: when the array is full, that is, first is up to beyond (first==beyond) and when there are no more data (s==null).

The test for the array being full must be done *before* we invoke readLine. If we did it afterward, our method would be reading data and then not doing anything with them (and hence losing data) in the event that the array is full.

On the other hand, the test for end of data must be done after readLine has been invoked. The only way we can tell if the data have ended is to see if readLine's return value is null. In both cases we return without reading integers and so we return 0. The method then is as follows:

```
//    Read integers (one per line) from br and store in a[first], ..., a[beyond−1];
//    Read until end of file or until no more elements are available.
//    Return the number of integers read and stored.
private int  readIntArray(int[]  a,   int   first, int   beyond,
                          BufferedReader  br)  throws Exception {
        if  (first==beyond)
           return  0;
        String  s  =  br.readLine();
        if  (s==null)
           return  0;
        a[first]  =  Integer.parseInt(s);
        return 1+readIntArray(a,first+1,beyond,br);
}
```

and would be invoked as:

```
int[]   x   =   new int[50];
int     count;
count   =   readIntArray(x,0,x.length,br);
```

We can now note that `beyond` never changes—it is always the length of the array. We may therefore leave it out as a parameter and replace it with `a.length` in the `readIntArray` method body:

```
//    Read integers (one per line) from br and store in a[first], ..., a[a.length−1];
//    Read until end of file or until no more elements are available.
//    Return the number of integers read and stored.
private int   readIntArray(int[]   a,   int   first,
                         BufferedReader br) throws Exception {
      if  (first==a.length)
         return  0;
      String  s  =  br.readLine();
      if  (s==null)
         return  0;
      a[first]  =  Integer.parseInt(s);
      return  1+readIntArray(a,first+1,a.length,br);
}
```

● EXAMPLE   Binary Search, Again. The method requires the item we are looking for and three arguments that specify the part of the `Vector` we are searching:

```
//    Returns true if s is among v[first], ..., v[beyond−1]
private boolean  bsearch(String s, Vector  v,
                         int  first,  int  beyond)  {
}
```

As in Chapter 10, we pick the middle element and by comparing it with `s`, determine which half of `v[first], ..., v[beyond-1]` `s` might be found.

Step 1: Getting Lazy.   Taking the lazy approach, however, we do hardly more work than that. After we identify the half to search, we get our assistant to do the rest, returning whatever the assistant returns to us.
First find the middle element:

```
int  m  =  (first+beyond)/2;
String sm  =  (String)  v.elementAt(m);
```

If the middle is less than what we search for, the assistant should search after position `m` (from `m+1` on):

```
if  (sm.compareTo(s)<0)
     return  bsearch(s,v,m+1,beyond);
```

If the middle is more than what we search for, then position m could be considered "beyond" where the item may be found and the assistant should search from position `first` up to m:

```
if  (sm.compareTo(s)>0)
    return  bsearch(s,v,first,m);
```

Step 2: Knowing When to Quit.   When is the task so small that we can solve it directly? As usual, that's pretty easy! When there are no elements at all to look for, that is, when `first==beyond` or `first>beyond` we know the item won't be found, so we can return `false`. On the other hand, if the element we are looking for matches the one in the middle, we can return `true`— it's been found.

The check to see whether `first>=beyond` should be done first because it is meaningless to compute the middle if there is nothing there. We don't need to directly check the middle element for a match. If the `compareTo` invocations do not yield <0 or >0, then we know we have a match and can just return `true`.

```
//   Returns true if s is among v[first], ..., v[beyond−1]
private boolean  bsearch(String s, Vector   v,
                                   int  first,  int  beyond)  {
        if  (first>=beyond)
          return  false;
        int  m  =  (first+beyond)/2;
        String sm  =  (String)  v.elementAt(m);
        if  (sm.compareTo(s)<0)
          return  bsearch(s,v,m+1,beyond);
        if  (sm.compareTo(s)>0)
          return  bsearch(s,v,first,m);
        return  true;
}
```

EXERCISES

1. Write a recursive method that receives an array of `int`s and initializes each element to 0.

2. Write a recursive method that receives two `String`s and determines whether the first is a substring of the second.

11.6 Permutations

In the game of Scrabble, each player has a rack of seven tiles, each with a letter on it. In each move the player uses the letters to make a word on a board. There is a premium for using all seven letters. A program playing Scrabble might search for seven-letter words by checking every permutation of its letters, that is, every possible ordering of the seven letters, and look each one up in a dictionary. A method to help it do this is:

```
public static Vector getWords(Set dictionary,
                              String letters)
```

The method is passed a `Set` (see Chapter 8) of words that we call `dictionary` and a `String` of seven letters that we call `letters`. It returns a `Vector` of `Strings`. Each of these `Strings` corresponds to a word in the dictionary `Set` and is a permutation (see Exercise 1 in Chapter 2's section on Using String Methods) of the seven letters in the `letters` `String`.

Given a set of letters, say, A B C D E F G, how could we construct a permutation? At the outset, our permutation is empty, and we have no letters in it. Our situation is:

```
permutation:            letters  left: A B C D E F G
```

We could start by choosing a letter, say D, to be add to the permutation:

```
permutation:   D        letters  left: A B C E F G
```

Then we could choose another letter, say B:

```
permutation:   DB       letters  left: A C E F G
```

And then another, say F:

```
permutation:   DBF      letters  left: A C E G
```

And so it would go until the permutation contained seven letters and there were no letters left:

```
permutation:   DBFAEGC  letters  left:
```

The problem is to methodically generate all permutations.

Step 1: Getting Lazy.   Suppose we viewed our job as the following:

- We are given a `string`, p, and a group of letters.
- Find all the strings that consist of the `String` p concatenated with a permutation of the letters in the group.

If our string was the empty string, then this job would simply amount to finding all the permutations of the letters in the group. Now we can find a role for some assistants.

Keeping track of permutations is hard, but choosing letters is easy. Let's follow this procedure:

- Pick one of the letters and give the following to an assistant:
  - A `string` consisting of p concatenated with the letter we picked

- A new set of letters consisting of our letters minus the one we appended to `p`
- The assistant carries out this same procedure, of course.
- Then we do the same for all the other letters.

Step 2: Knowing When to Quit. When there are no more letters left, the `String` p is a complete permutation of the original letters. At that point we need to see if it is actually a word, and if it is, we need to add it to our `Vector`. Either way, we return.

From this informal outline, we see that our recursive method, which we shall call `permutations`, needs four parameters:

- The `Vector` to which a word should be added.
- The dictionary that we use to check if a permutation is a word or not.
- The `String` p that has been constructed so far.
- The set of letters still available for choosing.

Because the `String` class offers so many convenient methods for manipulating a sequence of characters, we will use `String` objects for the last two. Our method then is:

```
private static void permutations(Vector v, Set dict,
                                 String p, String letters)
```

and `getWords` can be implemented with it:

```
static Vector getWords(Set dictionary, String letters)  {
    Vector  v  =  new  Vector();
    permutations(v,dictionary,"",letters);
}
```

Now we must turn steps 1 and 2 above into code to implement `permutations`. Step 2 is easy:

```
private static void permutations(Vector v, Set dict,
                                 String perm, String letters){
    if  (letters.length()==0)  {
        if  (dict.contains(p))
            v.addElement(p);
        return;
    }
```

Step 1 is more difficult. We have to set up an assistant for each one of the characters in the `letters`:

```
int      i;
i  =  0;
while   (i<letters.length())  {
```

```
        String newPermutation  =   The permutation we have with
                                        the ith letter added
        String  newLetters  =   The letters we have with
                                        the ith letter deleted
        permutations(v,dict,newPermutation,newLetters);
        i++;
    }
```

Adding the `ith` letter to `perm` is just a matter of appending the substring of the `ith` character in the letters:

```
p + letters.substring(i,i+1)
```

and creating a `String` with all the characters in letters but the `ith` one is a matter of joining the substring of characters before `i` with the substring of characters after `i`:

```
letters.substring(0,i) + letters.substring(i+1)
```

The finished method is:

```
private static void permutations(Vector v, Set dict,
                                    String p, String letters){
    if  (letters.length()==0)  {
        if  (dict.contains(p))
            v.addElement(p);
        return;
    }
    int    i;
    i  =  0;
    while  (i<letters.length())  {
        String  newPermutation  =  p +
                            letters.substring(i,i+1);
        String  newLetters = letters.substring(0,i) +
                            letters.substring(i+1);
        permutations(v,dict,newPermutation,newLetters);
        i++;
    }
}
```

EXERCISES

1. Write a program that opens a file called `dictionary` that contains a list of words in English, one per line. The program creates a `Set` object containing the words in this file. The program then reads in a seven-letter "word" and uses the `getWords` and `permutations` methods to print out all the permutations of these seven letters that appear in the dictionary file.

2. Our `permutations` method does not guarantee that each "word" added to the `Vector` is unique. Under what circumstances would there be duplicate words? Modify the `permutations` method so that no word in the `Vector` appears more than once.

3. How many permutations are there of a set of two elements? Three? Four? Seven? Write and run a program that uses the `permutations` method for a set of seven elements. Time the program (a rough estimate should do). •

11.7   Towers of Hanoi

11.7.1   The Puzzle

The Towers of Hanoi is a puzzle that consists of three poles, or "towers," and seven disks, no two of which have the same size. Each disk has a hole in the center so that it a pole can go through it. The puzzle is to start with all the disks placed on tower 1, move them all to tower 3 with the following constraints:

- No disk can ever be on top of a disk that is smaller.
- Only one disk can be moved at a time.
- A disk must always be placed on a tower, never off to the side.
- Only the disk at the top of a tower can be moved, never a lower one.

Disks can be moved to tower 2, and may be moved back and forth off of towers 1 and 3 as needed. See Figure 11.11.

A solution to the puzzle consists of a sequence of directions that accomplishes the goal given the constraints. Here is an example of a solution.

- Move a disk from tower 1 to tower 3.
- Move a disk from tower 1 to tower 2.
- Move a disk from tower 3 to tower 2.
- Move a disk from tower 1 to tower 3.
- Continue . . .

Note that because only the top disk can be moved, we never have to specify which disk is moved from a tower, we just need to specify the source and target towers.

Our goal is to define a class whose objects can produce a solution to this puzzle.

This puzzle is relevant to the study of recursion because, like the permutation problem above, it is a good example of how recursion makes an

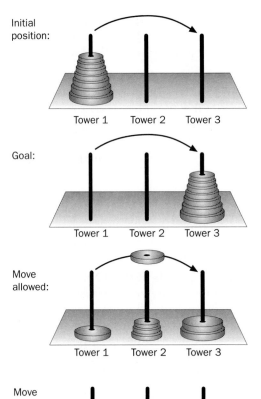

Initial position:

Tower 1 Tower 2 Tower 3

At the outset, all the disks are on tower 1. The largest disk is on the bottom, then the second largest, and so on.

Goal:

Tower 1 Tower 2 Tower 3

The goal is to move all the disks to tower 3, with the largest on the bottom, then the second largest, and so on.

Move allowed:

Tower 1 Tower 2 Tower 3

Only one disk may be moved at a time. It can never be put to the side. A larger disk can never be put on top of a smaller one.

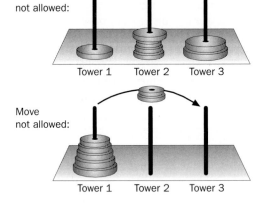

Move not allowed:

Tower 1 Tower 2 Tower 3

Move not allowed:

Tower 1 Tower 2 Tower 3

FIGURE 11.11 The Towers of Hanoi puzzle. The Towers of Hanoi puzzle requires the player to move all the disks from one pole to another, subject to several constraints.

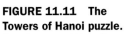

otherwise extremely difficult puzzle become relatively easy. Before taking the recursive approach, however, take some time to think about this puzzle yourself.

- Try solving it yourself. Use concrete objects, coins, tokens, dishes—whatever is available. Start with using only three objects, then try solving the puzzle with four, and work up to seven.
- Try writing code using one or more loops that would solve this puzzle. Be warned: It is extremely difficult, but worth trying anyway.
- Try thinking of a recursive procedure that solves this puzzle. (The procedure need not be in Java code; an informal one is fine).

11.7.2 Taking the Easy Way Out

A good strategy in recursive design is to let one's assistant do as much of the work as possible. Our problem is to move seven disks from one pole to the other. Let's imagine an assistant who could move six disks. For starters, we come up with the following procedure (see Figure 11.12):

To move seven disks from tower 1 to tower 3, using tower 2 as a holding tower:

- Step 1: Move six disks from tower 1 to tower 2 (the assistant).
- Step 2: Move the remaining disk from tower 1 to tower 3 (our contribution).
- Step 3: Move six disks from tower 2 to tower 3 (the assistant).

The following aspects of this procedure are worth noting:

- The task we give the assistant, though still challenging, is smaller than the task we have to do.
- We invoke the assistant before we do any work ourselves.
- We invoke the assistant twice.
- Tower 2 is used as a temporary holding tower for the six smaller disks until the largest one is moved to tower 3.
- This approach requires that initially, on towers 2 and 3, there are no disks smaller than any of the six disks being moved. If there were, the assistant would not necessarily be able to move the six disks.

For this to be an acceptable recursive procedure, the task we give the assistant must be of the same form as the task we give ourselves. In the above procedure, we move disks from 1 to 3, and the assistant moves disks from 1 to 2 and from 2 to 3. We are responsible for seven, our assistant is responsible for six. By changing the task statement, we put it into a form that is applicable to both ourselves and our assistant.

The new statement of the task is: Move n disks from the source tower to the target tower, using the other tower as a holding tower.

Initial
position:

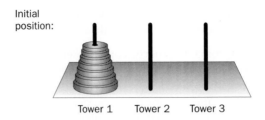

The assistant somehow
moves six disks from tower
1 to tower 2, one at a time
following the rules
of the puzzle.

After
step 1:

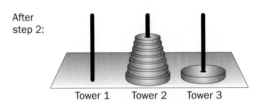

After
step 2:

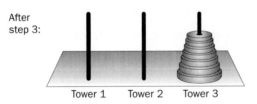

We can then move the
seventh disk from tower 1
to tower 3.

**FIGURE 11.12 Towards a
recursive solution of the
Towers of Hanoi puzzle.** To
work towards a recursive
solution, we imagine how to
make use of an assistant
who can move six disks.

After
step 3:

The assistant somehow
moves six disks from tower
2 to tower 3, one at a
time following the rules
of the puzzle.

The steps are as follows:

- Step 1: Move $n-1$ disks from *source* to *holding*.
- Step 2: Move 1 disk from *source* to *target*.
- Step 3: Move $n-1$ disks from *holding* to *target*.

We also have to know when to quit. That's easy: When n is 0, there are no disks to move and we don't have to do anything. Our procedure now becomes as follows:

- Move n disks from *source* to *target*:
- If n is 0 do nothing. Otherwise:
- Determine which tower is the *holding* tower: It's the one that is not *source* or *target* (a preliminary to steps 1–3).
- Step 1: Move $n-1$ disks from *source* to *holding*.

- Step 2: Move 1 disk from *source* to *target*.
- Step 3: Move $n-1$ disks from *holding* to *target*.

The solution to the Towers of Hanoi puzzle comes from using this procedure with *n* set to 7, *source* set to 1 and target *set* to 3.

At different points in the computation, the three towers switch their respective roles as *source, target,* and *holding.* For example, in the recursive invocation in step 1, *source* is still 1, but *target* is 2 and *holding* is 3. In step 3, *source* is now 2, *target* is 3, and *holding* is 1. See Figure 11.13.

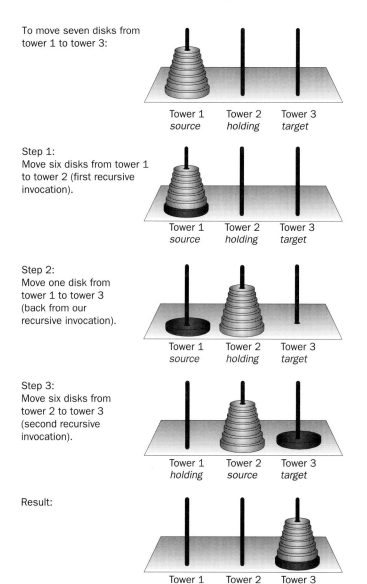

To move seven disks from tower 1 to tower 3:

Tower 1	Tower 2	Tower 3
source	*holding*	*target*

Step 1:
Move six disks from tower 1 to tower 2 (first recursive invocation).

Tower 1	Tower 2	Tower 3
source	*holding*	*target*

Step 2:
Move one disk from tower 1 to tower 3 (back from our recursive invocation).

Tower 1	Tower 2	Tower 3
source	*holding*	*target*

Step 3:
Move six disks from tower 2 to tower 3 (second recursive invocation).

Tower 1	Tower 2	Tower 3
holding	*source*	*target*

Result:

Tower 1	Tower 2	Tower 3

FIGURE 11.13 The changing roles of the towers. At different points in the computation, the three towers switch their respective roles as *source, target,* and *holding.*

We will now design a class that solves the Towers of Hanoi. You will see that the structure of this problem has much in common with the Game of Life in Chapter 10.

The point of this example is to introduce another example of solving a hard problem with recursion and reinforce the concept of separating display from calculation.

Statement of the Problem   Create an object that models the Towers of Hanoi and produces a solution by starting from the initial configuration and then generating a sequence of moves, consistent with the game's rules. Display each move and the resulting picture of the Towers.

Scenario   We want the `Towers` object to generate the moves. We also want to see these moves on a display. Because we are working with `System.out`, the display is primitive. Just printing the source and target of the move of a single disk and then representing the towers and their disks in some simple fashion is sufficient. As an extra feature, when we create the `Towers` object, we want to specify the number of disks it starts with. Thus we should be able to make requests such as the following:

- Set up a Tower with *n* disks and a display.
- Solve the puzzle, using the above information.

Finding the Primary Object   We will introduce a `Towers` class. Another noun, however, that also appeared in the statement of the problem and the scenario is "display." We will develop a separate class, `TowerDisplay`, for handling that.

Determining the Behavior   Our problem statement provides us with the necessary behavior:

- Tower (constructor)—Set up the puzzle
- Solve It—Figure out the moves and display them, along with the changes to the Towers as they are made

Determining the Interface   The above behavior translates neatly into methods. Once the game is set up, no additional information is needed, so only the constructor receives arguments: a reference to the `TowerDisplay` object that `Towers` will use to display its moves and the number of disks. Our interface is as follows:

```
class Towers  {
    public Towers(TowerDisplay td, int nDisks) {
```

```
        ...
    }
    public void solveIt()  {
        ...
    }
}
```

Defining the Instance Variables   The `solveIt` method will need the values of the constructor's parameters: the reference to the display object, and the number of disks. So these must be stored in instance variables:

```
private     int         nDisks;
private     TowerDisplay  td;
```

Are additional instance variables required? For example, do we need some sort of collection, perhaps three collections, to keep track of the disks that are on each tower?

Interestingly, solving the puzzle doesn't require that we maintain this information. The informal recursive procedure we developed above never needed to know where any particular disk was located.

Apparently then, we need no further instance variables. Our class skeleton is as follows:

```
class Towers  {
    public Towers(TowerDisplay td, int nDisks) {
        ...
    }
    public void solveIt() {
        ...
    }
    private     int         nDisks;
    private     TowerDisplay  td;
}
```

11.7.3   Implementing the Methods

The constructor must save the values of the parameters in the instance variables. In addition, at some point before the solution is generated, the `Life-Display` object will have to be told how many disks are to be used and where they are so that it can set up its model of the towers. The constructor should be able to send this object a `setup` message with this information. The constructor therefore is as follows:

```
public Towers(TowerDisplay td, int nDisks) {
    this.td = td;
    this.nDisks = nDisks;
    td.setup(nDisks,1);        // Starting with nDisks in tower 1
}
```

The informal recursive procedure we developed above can be coded as a recursive method. However, this method requires the same parameters as our procedure: number of disks, source tower, target tower:

```
void solveIt(int  nDisks,  int  source,  int  target)  {...}
```

The `Towers` interface calls for a different prototype for `solveIt`:

```
void solveIt() {...}
```

Apparently we need two versions of `solveIt`: one to serve as part of the interface, the other to get the job actually done by implementing our recursive procedure:

```
public void solveIt() {...}           // Invoked by the outside to display a
                                      //    solution
private void solveIt(int nDisks,  // Recursively generate a solution.
        int source, int target) {...}
```

Fortunately Java allows overloading.

To make sure that the job gets done when the public `solveIt` is invoked, we implement it as a single invocation of the private `solveIt` method:

```
public void solveIt() {
    solveIt(nDisks, 1, 3);
}
```

We start with `nDisks` at tower 1 and ask for them to be moved to tower 3. The implementation of the recursive `solveIt` follows from the informal recursive procedure. We check to see if there is no work to do:

```
if (nDisks<=0)
    return;
```

We figure out the tower that we use as the holding tower. That will require a few messy `if` statements, so we encapsulate that in a private helper method. This way we won't obscure the recursive structure of the `solveIt` method:

```
int    holdingTower = getholdingTower(source,target);
```

We solve the problem of moving $n-1$ disks from *source* to *holding* (generating all the moves to do that):

```
solveIt(nDisks-1,source,holdingTower);
```

We then move a disk from *source* to *target*. Because we are not maintaining the state of the towers here, all we need to do is inform the `TowerDisplay` object of this move:

```
td.displayMove(source,target);
```

Finally, we solve the problem of moving $n-1$ disks from *holding* to *target:*

```
solveIt(nDisks-1,holdingTower,target);
```

The completed method is as follows:

```
private void solveIt(int nDisks, int source, int target) {
    if (nDisks<=0)
        return;
    int     holdingTower = getholdingTower(source,target);
    solveIt(nDisks-1,source,holdingTower);
    td.displayMove(source,target);
    solveIt(nDisks-1,holdingTower,target);
}
```

To complete the class, we implement the `getholdingTower` method. It involves a straightforward though messy pair of `if` statements. The complete `Towers` class is as follows:

```
class Towers {
    public Towers(TowerDisplay td, int nDisks) {
        this.td = td;
        this.nDisks = nDisks;
        td.setup(nDisks,1);
    }

    public void solveIt() {
        solveIt(nDisks, 1, 3);
    }

    private void solveIt(int nDisks, int source,
                         int target) {
        if (nDisks<=0)
            return;
        int     holdingTower =
                        getholdingTower(source,target);
        solveIt(nDisks-1,source,holdingTower);
        td.displayMove(source,target);
        solveIt(nDisks-1,holdingTower,target);
    }

    private int getholdingTower(int source, int target) {
        if (source==2 && target==3 ||
            source==3 && target==2)
                return 1;
        if (source==1 && target==3 ||
            source==3 && target==1)
                return 2;
        return 3;
    }
```

```
        private     int              nDisks;
        private     TowerDisplay     td;
}
```

Implementing the `TowerDisplay` Class   The interface and behavior of the `TowerDisplay` class has been determined by the above discussion. It is as follows:

```
class TowerDisplay {
    public TowerDisplay() {...}
    public void setup(int nDisks, int source) {...}
    public void displayMove(int from, int to) {...}
}
```

The key issue to address here is how to represent the towers and their disks. If we choose to display the disks as single digit numbers (and thereby restrict this class's usefulness to representing at most nine disks) we can make use of `String` objects and their methods in a rather neat way. If we are doing the standard version of the puzzle, a tower holding all seven disks is represented and displayed by the `String "1234567"`. A tower with no disks is just the empty `String, ""`. Moving a disk from one tower to another is a matter of removing the last character of the `String` of one and concatenating it to the other. See Figure 11.14.

With this in mind, we choose to represent the towers with three `String`s. The `displayMove` method parameters will be either 1, 2, or 3, indicating which towers a disk is moved from and to. If we use an array of four elements to store our `String`s, we can use these integers to index the array and access the `String` representing the tower indicated by the parameter. So our instance variable is:

```
        private     String[]     tower;
```

Tower 1 is represented by `tower[1]`, tower 2 by `tower[2]`, tower 3 by `tower[3]`.

The `setup` method uses its parameters to initialize this array:

```
public void setup(int nDisks, int source) {
    if (nDisks>9)
        nDisks = 9;
    tower = new String[4];
    tower[1] = "";
    tower[2] = "";
    tower[3] = "";
    tower[source] = "123456789".substring(0,nDisks);
}
```

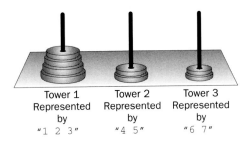

Each disk can be represented by a single digit. "1" represents the largest disk, "7" the smallest. A String of digits can represent the disks on a particular tower.

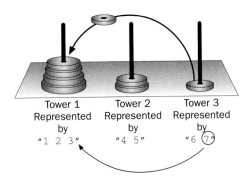

To represent the movement of a disk, we remove a digit from the String representing the tower of origin and place it at the end of the String representing the destination.

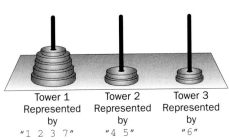

FIGURE 11.14 Representing the disks on towers with String objects. The towers can be represented by Strings and movement can be represented by changes to the Strings.

The displayMove method writes a description of the move to standard output and then modifies the Strings indexed by from and to so that the array of Strings reflects the move. See Figure 11.15.

It then writes out all three Strings to standard output. The code for displayMove is as follows:

```
public void displayMove(int from, int to) {
    System.out.println("MOVE from "+from+" to "+to);
    int fromLast = tower[from].length()-1;
    tower[to] = tower[to].concat(tower[from].
                                 substring(fromLast));
    tower[from] = tower[from].substring(0,fromLast);
```

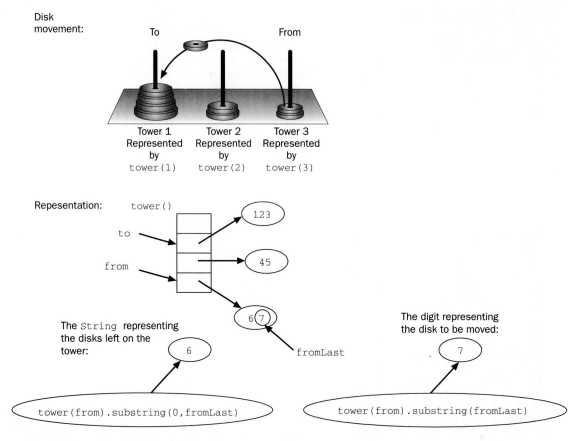

FIGURE 11.15 Manipulating Strings to model the movement of a disk. In removing a disk from a tower, we need an expression that represents the disk to be moved and another expression that represents the disks left on the tower.

```
System.out.println("    tower 1:"+tower[1]);
System.out.println("    tower 2:"+tower[2]);
System.out.println("    tower 3:"+tower[3]);
}
```

The full solution to the problem is as follows, with the addition of a main method to the Towers class so that it can be directly executed:

```
import  java.io.*;
import  java.util.*;

class Towers {
    public static void main(String[] a) {
        if (a.length!=1)
```

```
                 System.err.println(
                        "Usage: java Towers <number of disks> ");
            else {
                int nDisks = Integer.parseInt(a[0]);
                Towers    th = new Towers(new TowerDisplay(),
                                         nDisks);
                th.solveIt();
            }
    }

    public Towers(TowerDisplay td, int nDisks) {
        this.td = td;
        this.nDisks = nDisks;
        td.setup(nDisks,1);
    }

    public void solveIt() {
        solveIt(nDisks, 1, 3);
    }

    private void solveIt(int nDisks, int source,
                                            int target) {
        if (nDisks<=0)
            return;
        int    holdingTower =
                         getholdingTower(source,target);
        solveIt(nDisks-1,source,holdingTower);
        td.displayMove(source,target);
        solveIt(nDisks-1,holdingTower,target);
    }

    private int getholdingTower(int source, int target) {
        if (source==2 && target==3 ||
                source==3 && target==2)
                return 1;
        if (source==1 && target==3 ||
                source==3 && target==1)
                return 2;
        return 3;
    }
    private    int          nDisks;
    private    TowerDisplay  td;
}

class TowerDisplay {
    public TowerDisplay() {
    }
```

```
        public void setup(int nDisks, int source) {
            if (nDisks>9)
                nDisks = 9;
            tower = new String[4];
            tower[1] = "";
            tower[2] = "";
            tower[3] = "";
            tower[source] = "123456789".substring(0,nDisks);

        }

    public void displayMove(int from, int to) {
        System.out.println("MOVE from "+from+" to "+to);
        int fromLast = tower[from].length()-1;
        tower[to] = tower[to].concat(tower[from].
                                    substring(fromLast));
        tower[from] = tower[from].substring(0,fromLast);
        System.out.println("   tower 1:"+tower[1]);
        System.out.println("   tower 2:"+tower[2]);
        System.out.println("   tower 3:"+tower[3]);
    }

    private    String[]   tower;
}
```

EXERCISES

1. Implement a more general `TowerDisplay` class that is not limited to a maximum of nine disks. Do not, of course, change the interface of the class!

2. Try writing a different `Towers` class for the following variation of Towers of Hanoi. The disks on tower 1 are colored red and black, in alternating colors. In addition to the other rules of the game, no two disks of the same color can ever be placed one on top of the other.

3. If there is just one disk in the Towers of Hanoi, how many invocations of `solveIt` will there be? What if there are two disks? How about three disks? How about seven disks? n disks?

11.8   Recursion and Iteration

Recursion and iteration both result in the controlled repeated execution of a body of code—the method body in the case of recursion, and the loop body in the case of iteration. In both techniques, a terminating condition that ends the repeated execution is essential to the design.

Any iteration can be implemented with recursion. Consider the following general form for iteration:

```
while   (condition)        Using variables v1, v2, ..., vN and p1, p2, ..., pN
        body
```

where:

- {v1, v2, ..., vN} is the set of variables that appear in the condition and the body whose values will be needed after the loop terminates.
- {p1, p2, ..., pN} is the set of variables that appear in the condition and the body whose values will *not* be needed after the loop terminates.

The equivalent recursive solution is to declare {v1, v2, ..., vN} as instance variables and write the following method:

```
private void  recursiveWhile (declaration of parameters p1,
                                                  p2, ..., pN) {
     if   (!condition)
          return;
     body
     recursiveWhile(p1, p2, ..., pN);
}
```

The original loop is replaced by the following invocation:

```
recursiveWhile(p1, p2, ..., pN);
```

Each recursive invocation corresponds to another evaluation of the loop condition and execution of the loop body. Note that each loop body execution in the recursive equivalent requires its own activation record in memory.

As an example, let's consider the following method that returns the sum of the first *n* elements of an array of integers, x, that is declared as an instance variable:

```
class SomeClass {
    ...
    public int getSum(int n) {
        int i = 0;
        int sum = 0;
        while (i!=n) {
            sum += x[i];
            i++;
        }
        // sum == x[0] + x[1] + ... + x[n-1]
        return sum;
    }

    ...
    private int[] x;
}
```

The variables n and i are used in the loop but their values are not needed after the loop, so i and n become parameters to the recursive method. The variable sum is needed after the loop, so it becomes an instance variable. We replace the loop with an invocation of recursive method, recComputeSum, which we add to the class as a helper method. The implementation of rec-ComputeSum follows the pattern presented above:

```
class SomeClass {
    ...
    public int getSum(int n) {
        int i = 0;
        sum = 0;
        recComputeSum(i,n);             recursiveWhile (p1, p2)
        // sum == x[0] + x[1] + ... + x[n-1]
    }

    private void recComputeSum(int i, int n) {   recursiveWhile (p1, p2)
        if (!(i!=n))                             if (!condition)
            return;                                  return
        sum += x[i];                             body
        i++;                                     body
        recComputeSum(i,n);                      recursiveWhile (p1,p2);
    }
    ...
    private int    sum;                          v1, made an instance variable
    private int[]  x;
}
```

11.8.1 Performance

Recursion can, in principle, compute anything that iteration can compute and is comparable in speed to iteration. However, as the memory diagrams of Section 11.4 show, recursion can be demanding in memory. In general, the amount of memory required by a loop is independent of the number of times the loop body executes, but the "further down" we go in the recursion process, the more memory is needed to save all the previous activation records.

Memory demand is a peculiar kind of cost. As long as you have enough memory, using it has little impact on performance. However, once memory is exhausted, the cost of needing more is catastrophic—the program fails!

A recursive method that replaces a simple iteration that makes 50,000 loop cycles is a silly waste of space because the simple iteration is fine and 50,000 activation records have to be created and stored while the recursion proceeds. On the other hand, the recursive solution to the Towers of Hanoi never requires more than eight activation records at a time. Each recursive invocation decreases nDisks by 1 and returns if nDisks is 0. Of course, many more than eight activation records are created, but there are never more than eight at a time. This recursive method therefore uses very little memory.

Transforming recursion in general into iteration is much harder, as you will see if you try it for our Towers of Hanoi problem! It is possible, however, to do it using techniques for manipulating collections that you will learn later in your career.

Most computer scientists and programmers would regard the use of recursion in the simple kinds of problems that we examined in the beginning of the chapter as overkill. On the other hand, recursion can often be the easiest way to solve a problem, and it is usually much easier to verify the correctness of a recursive solution than an iterative one. Certainly, for problems such as generating permutations and the Towers of Hanoi recursion is the method of choice.

EXERCISES

1. Write a recursive method that is equivalent to the following loop:

```
int i=0,  sum=0;
while (i!=1000) {
    sum+=a[i];
    i++;
}
```

2. Consider the `permutations` method. What is the greatest number of activation records of `permutations` if it is invoked for a set of five elements?

SUMMARY

Recursion is a convenient yet powerful technique for designing methods. Both its convenience and power derive from the fact that the designer of a recursive method need only write code that does part of the task or makes the task smaller in some way. The remainder of the work is done by reapplying the same method to the smaller task—we have whimsically called this part of the process "giving the work to an assistant" in this chapter.

QUESTIONS FOR REVIEW

1. What is a recursive method?

2. In what sense is recursion a "lazy" approach?

3. What is the termination step? Why must it always be present?

4. What are the two key steps to take in designing a recursive solution?

5. Why does recursion require more memory than iteration? When is the increased memory requirement a problem? When is it not a problem?

6. What is an activation record?

STUDY AID: TERMINOLOGY REVIEW

activation record   A block of memory holding the parameters and local variables of a method, along with the return address of the invoker of the method.

current activation record   The most recently allocated activation record, which corresponds to the currently executing method.

recursive call   An invocation of a method from within that method.

recursive procedure   A procedure that carries out a part of a task and refers to itself to carry out the rest of the task.

recursion   The process of using a recursive procedure; the carrying out of a recursive call.

termination step   An essential step in any viable recursive procedure, in which the task is checked to see if it can be carried out without resort to recursion.

FURTHER EXERCISES

1. Write a recursive method that receives an array of integers and returns their sum.

2. Write a recursive method that returns the smallest value in a subsection of an array.

3. Write a method that prints out all possible 3×3 "magic squares." An $n \times n$ magic square is an $n \times n$ grid with the numbers 1 through n^2 placed in each square of the grid and where all the rows, columns, and diagonals add up to the same number. Below is one example

```
8  1  6
3  5  7
4  9  2
```

You can view any 3 × 3 magic square as a permutation of the integers 1 to 9. For example, the above square is 8 1 6 3 5 7 4 9 2. So, one strategy might be to generate all permutations of the integers 1 to 9 and test each one to see if it satisfies the requirements for a magic square. It would be a good idea to have a separate method do that part.)

#

Towers of Hanoi Applet

In this supplement we develop a graphical implementation of the Towers of Hanoi program.

The Towers of Hanoi Applet Design   Our Towers of Hanoi applet has much in common with the Game of Life. It presents a `Canvas` on which the moves are printed out and the configuration of the disks on the towers displayed. After displaying each move, there is a delay (see below) followed by a redrawing of the differently colored disks, to update the tower configuration. It also provides two buttons and two textfields for controlling the applet (see Figure 11.16):

* Start/restart button—Initially labeled "start," this button starts the solution of a puzzle. Once started, the button's label is changed to "restart." If the game is paused, the resume button allows the game to continue.

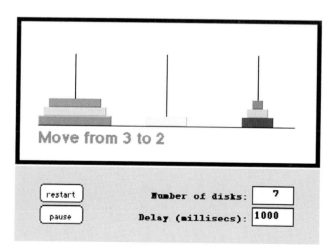

FIGURE 11.16   A moment in the execution of the Towers of Hanoi applet.

- Pause/resume button—Initially labeled "pause," this button suspends activity and changes its label to "resume." When the resume button is pressed, activity resumes and the button changes its label back to "pause."
- Number of disks textfield—Initially set at 7, this field determines the number of disks in the puzzle. The user can edit this number and by pressing the RETURN key to inform the applet that there is a new value. The new value will be used the next time the start/restart button is pressed.
- Delay (millisecs) textfield—Initially set at 1000, this field determines the number of milliseconds delay between steps in the display of the solution to the puzzle.

The Architecture of the Towers of Hanoi Applet   The class architecture of this applet is the same as that of the Game of Life. There are three classes in this model:

- An extended `Thread` class that does the *calculation*
- An extended `Canvas` class that does the *display*
- An extended `Applet` class that provides the *controls*

Our extended `Thread` class, `TowersOfHanoiThread`, contains the same methods and code of the `Towers` class, along with the usual methods for thread control: `ourResume`, `ourSuspend`, and `ourStop`.

Our extended `Canvas` class, `TowerDisplay`, plays the same role that the non-GUI `TowerDisplay` did earlier in this chapter, and it provides the same interface. Instead of writing moves to `System.out` and displaying towers as strings of digits written to `System.out`, it paints these onto a `Graphics` object.

Our extended `Applet` class, `TowerApplet`, creates the `TowerDisplay` object, the buttons, and the text fields. It places these controls and handles button and textfield action events. It responds to these events by creating, starting, suspending, resuming, and altogether stopping `TowerApplet` objects, and by notifying the `TowerDisplay` object of the new delay time value when the delay time has been changed.

The thread architecture of this applet is also the same as that of the Game of Life. There are three threads:

- The main applet thread, which executes `init` and the methods `init` invokes. Among these are the `TowerDisplay` constructor.
- The AWT-environment thread, which executes `actionPerformed` of `TowerApplet` and `paint` of `TowerDisplay` and the methods they invoke.
- The thread defined by the `run` method of the `TowerThread` class, which executes `solveIt` and the methods it invokes. This is the thread that does the actual work of solving the puzzle and displaying the moves of the solution.

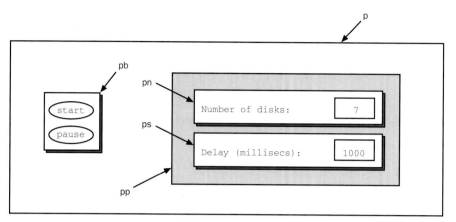

FIGURE 11.17 Use of Panels in the TowerApplet layout. The layout of the controls is organized using multiple nested panels: pb, pn, ps, pp, and p.

The TowerApplet Class The init method, though messy as ever, should be familiar by now. It creates the TowerDisplay, the Buttons, the Textfields and the Labels that label them. Various BorderLayout-using Panels are created to place the controls in a reasonable way (see Figure 11.17).

Likewise, the general idea of the implementation of actionPerformed and the various handle methods should be familiar to you. Although there are only two buttons, there are four handle methods associated with them. That's because both buttons operate with two different labels and each label signifies a different desired response. (Why have a different label otherwise?) The two textfields are handled differently. A change in the number of disks affects only the initial setup of a Towers of Hanoi puzzle, so the applet does not respond to those changes immediately. It just uses the value in that textfield when creating a TowerThread. On the other hand, any keyboard action causes the applet to read the number in the delay textfield and immediately send a setDelay message to the TowerDisplay object. That guarantees an immediate response to the user setting the delay. Figure 11.18 illustrates the role of the applet's methods in responding to button clicks.

The code for TowerApplet follows:

```
import java.util.*;
import java.awt.*;
import java.awt.event.*;
import java.applet.*;


public class TowerApplet extends Applet
                         implements ActionListener {
    public void init() {
        setBackground(new Color(200,255,255));
        this.setLayout(new BorderLayout(20,2));
        td = new TowerDisplay();
```

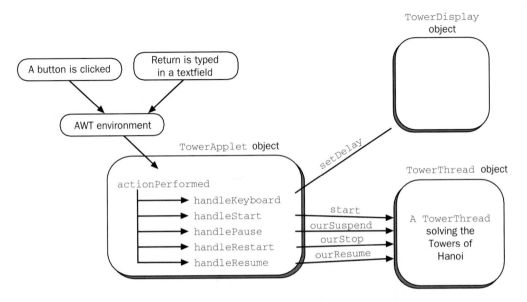

FIGURE 11.18 How the `TowerApplet` responds to buttons and textfields. The action-Performed method is invoked by the AWT environment in response to action events. This method handles the different action events that occur by invoking various helper methods that control the TowerThread or modify the display. The handleStart method also creates the *TowerThread* object before sending it a start message. After sending an ourStop message to stop the current TowerThread, the handleRestart method invokes handleStart to start up a new TowerThread.

```
add("Center",td);
startButton = new Button("start");
startButton.addActionListener(this);
pauseButton = new Button("pause");
pauseButton.addActionListener(this);
Panel pb = new Panel();
pb.setLayout(new BorderLayout(2,2));
pb.add("North",startButton);
pb.add("South",pauseButton);

numDisks = new TextField(" 7");
numDisks.setFont(new Font("Courier",Font.BOLD,10));
Label numDisksLabel = new Label(
                " Number of disks:",Label.RIGHT);
Label stepDelayLabel = new Label(
                "Delay (millisecs):",Label.RIGHT);
numDisksLabel.setFont(new
                Font("Courier",Font.BOLD,10));

stepDelayLabel.setFont(new
                Font("Courier",Font.BOLD,10));
```

```
        Panel pn = new Panel();
        pn.setLayout(new BorderLayout(2,2));
        pn.add("East",numDisks);
        pn.add("West",numDisksLabel);

        stepDelay = new TextField("1000");
        stepDelay.addActionListener(this);
        stepDelay.setFont(new
                         Font("Courier",Font.BOLD,10));
        Panel ps = new Panel();
        ps.setLayout(new BorderLayout(2,2));
        ps.add("East",stepDelay);
        ps.add("West",stepDelayLabel);

        Panel pp = new Panel();
        pp.setLayout(new BorderLayout(2,2));
        pp.add("North",pn);
        pp.add("South",ps);

        Panel p = new Panel();
        p.setLayout(new
                    FlowLayout(FlowLayout.CENTER,50,20));
        p.add(pb);
        p.add(pp);
        p.setBackground(new Color(255,200,200));

        add("South",p);

    }

    public void actionPerformed(ActionEvent ae) {
        String whichButton = ae.getActionCommand();
        if (whichButton.equals("start"))
           handleStart();
        else if (whichButton.equals("restart"))
           handleRestart();
        else if (whichButton.equals("pause"))
           handlePause();
        else if (whichButton.equals("resume"))
           handleResume();
        else
           handleKeyboard();
    }

    private void handleStart() {
        int nDisks =
              Integer.parseInt(numDisks.getText().trim());
        handleKeyboard();
```

```
                          towersTicker = new TowersOfHanoiThread(td, nDisks);
                          towersTicker.start();
                          startButton.setLabel("restart");
                          pauseButton.setLabel("pause");
                      }

                      private void handleRestart() {
                          towersTicker.ourStop();
                          handleStart();
                      }

                      private void handlePause() {
                          towersTicker.ourSuspend();
                          pauseButton.setLabel("resume");
                      }

                      private void handleResume() {
                          towersTicker.ourResume();
                          pauseButton.setLabel("pause");
                      }

                      private void handleKeyboard() {
                          int sDelay =
                                  Integer.parseInt(stepDelay.getText().trim());
                          td.setDelay(sDelay);
                      }

                      private   Button                  startButton,
                                                                pauseButton;
                      private   TextField               numDisks, stepDelay;
                      private   TowerDisplay            td;
                      private   TowersOfHanoiThread     towersTicker = null;
                      private   int                     source = 1;
                      private   int                     target = 3;
                  }
```

The `TowerDisplay` Class   This class is a close analog of the `Tower-Display` class from the non-GUI Towers of Hanoi. It provides the same services to the `TowerThread` that the non-GUI class provided the `Tower` class. It therefore provides a constructor, a `setup` method, and a `displayMove` method with the same prototypes as the non-GUI version.

At the same time `TowerDisplay` shares similarities with the `Life-Display` class from Chapter 10, it must draw graphical objects and provide a `paint` method for the AWT environment.

The `TowerDisplay` constructor creates an array of nine different `Color` objects so that the disks can be painted later with different colors.

The `setup` method computes a large set of locations on the `Canvas` to facilitate displaying the moves and the towers later.

The `displayMove` method does the actual display of the move and the towers. It draws a `String` that indicates the move to be made. It pauses for the user-specified delay time and then invokes `paint` to draw the towers. The reason `paint` doesn't handle the display of the move but just the display of the towers is that it is also invoked by the AWT environment, which has no idea about the current move. There may, in fact, not be a current move. Figure 11.19 illustrates the role the `TowerDisplay` methods have in displaying the moves and towers.

The `TowerDisplay` class here uses the same array of four `String`s technique that the non-GUI TowerDisplay class used to maintain its internal picture of the state of the three towers.

The `setup` Method   The `setup` method starts with the same code used in its non-GUI counterpart to initialize the tower model. It then calculates the sizes and positions of the various graphical elements in the display, for use in the `paint` and `displayMove` methods. These variables containing these quantities and their relation to the graphical display are shown in Figures 11.20 and 11.21. At the end of the method, `paint` is invoked to display the towers before the solution is generated. After `paint` returns, delay is invoked so that the display will persist for a bit before being changed.

The size and position values calculated by `setup` cannot be determined in advance and made into constants, that is, final variables. This is because the display is affected by the number of disks.

The basic drawing layout strategy is to divide the width of the `Canvas` and subdivided it into three regions for displaying towers, with each region separated from each other or the border by the same amount of space. The lengths of the four intertower regions add up to the size of one of the tower regions. This scheme is shown in Figure 11.22.

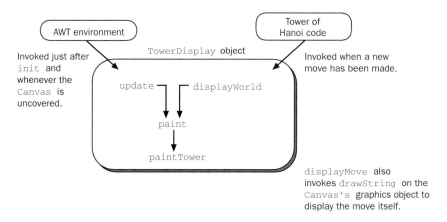

FIGURE 11.19   How the move and towers get displayed.

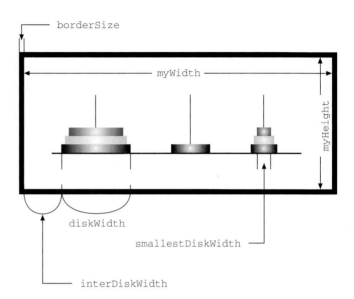

**FIGURE 11.20
The principal
size and position
variables of
TowerDisplay
(I).** Achieving an
appealing display
requires careful
planning in
advance. Here we
show the basic
sizes of the graphi-
cal objects in the
display.

The width and height of the area available for display is calculated by subtracting twice the borderSize from the actual width of the Canvas and
storing the result in myWidth:

```
myWidth  = this.getSize().width-borderSize;
myHeight = this.getSize().height - 2*borderSize;
```

This width is divided by 4 to reflect the division of the Canvas into three
tower regions and a set of intertower regions whose combined width is the

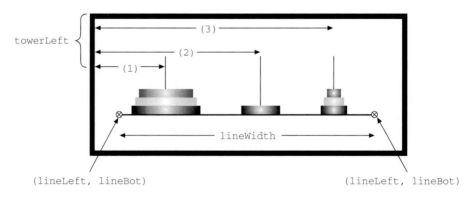

FIGURE 11.21   The principal size and position variables of TowerDisplay (II).
Here we show the positions of the baseline's end points and the horizontal positions of
the three towers, towerLeft[1], towerLeft[2], towerLeft[3].

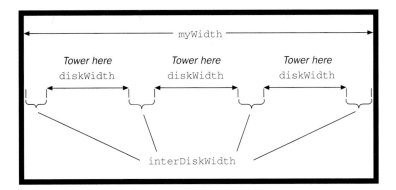

FIGURE 11.22 Partitioning the width of the `Canvas.` The maximum disk width—the width of each tower—is calculated from the width of the applet. The spaces separating the towers from each other and from the borders are the same and add up to one disk width.

same as a tower region. This quantity is divided by the number of disks to yield the width of the smallest disk:

```
smallestDiskWidth = (myWidth/4)/nDisks;
```

Multiplying this by the number of disks yields the width of the largest disk:

```
diskWidth = nDisks * smallestDiskWidth;
```

The width of the largest disk is also the width of the tower region. Our strategy calls for each of the four intertower distances to be one-fourth this size:

```
interDiskWidth = diskWidth/4;
```

Regardless of the number of disks our problem has, we choose the height of each disk to be 10:

```
diskHeight = 10;
```

We want the towers to extend one disk height past the top disk, even when all the disks are stacked on the same tower. So the height of the tower is:

```
towerHeight = (nDisks+1) * diskHeight;
```

The left and right positions of the base line for the towers are then calculated. The line is inset one `interDiskWidth` past the border:

```
lineLeft = borderSize + interDiskWidth;
```

Vertically it is positioned so that the poles of the towers (whose height is `towerHeight`) are centered:

```
lineBot  = myHeight - (myHeight-towerHeight)/2;
```

(Remember: Position 0 is at the top of the `Canvas`, and `myHeight` marks the bottom.) This scheme is shown in Figure 11.23.

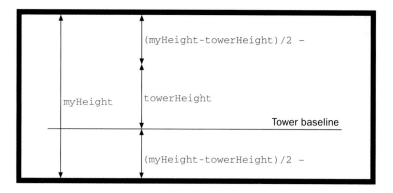

FIGURE 11.23 Partitioning the height of the Canvas. Here we show the calculation of the tower baseline and the vertical positions of the bases of the towers. It is calculated so that the towers are centered vertically in the display.

The width of the line is just enough to hold three towers and two intertower distances. The right position of the line is just the left plus the width:

```
lineWidth = 3*diskWidth + 2*interDiskWidth;
lineRight = lineLeft+lineWidth;
```

Finally, we allocate an array to store the horizontal coordinates of each tower, taking into account their widths and the intertower distances between them:

```
towerLeft = new int[4];
towerLeft[1] = lineLeft + diskWidth/2;
towerLeft[2] = towerLeft[1] + diskWidth/2
                            + interDiskWidth + diskWidth/2;
towerLeft[3] = towerLeft[2] + diskWidth/2
                            + interDiskWidth + diskWidth/2;
```

The displayMove and paint Methods The displayMove method is invoked from the TowerThread. In order to do any drawing, it first has to access the Graphics object associated with the TowerDisplay:

```
Graphics g = this.getGraphics();
```

It then gets the integer representing the disk to be moved by accessing the last character of the tower specified by the from parameter and uses that digit to determine the color to display the move in. This color will be the same as that of the disk that is being moved, making it easier for the observer to correlate the printed moves with the graphical moves of the disks:

```
int fromLast = tower[from].length()-1;
Color    c = getDiskColor(from,fromLast);
```

Once this information has been obtained, the `Strings` modeling the towers are updated, as they were in the non-GUI version:

```
tower[to] =
        tower[to].concat(tower[from].substring(fromLast));
tower[from] = tower[from].substring(0,fromLast);
```

In order to clear any residual display of a previous move, `paintLower-Background` is invoked:

```
paintLowerBackground(g);
```

`paintLowerBackground` just fills a white rectangle over the area below the tower base line, the area where the moves are printed out. The color is then set along with a nice clear font, and the move itself is drawn, with a starting position directly below the left end of the tower baseline and halfway between the baseline and the bottom of the display:

```
g.setColor(c);
g.setFont(new Font("Helvetica",Font.BOLD,18));
g.drawString("Move from "+from+" to "+to, lineLeft,
                myHeight - (myHeight-towerHeight)/4);
```

Once the move is drawn, we delay, letting the user anticipate the change in the towers displayed by `paint`. The delay, `sdelay`, is set by the `setDelay` method that is invoked by the `handleKeyboard` method of the `TowerApplet`.

```
delay(sdelay);
paint(g);
```

After displaying the towers, there is another, shorter display before returning to the `solveIt` method of the `TowerThread`.

```
delay(sdelay/3);
```

The `paint` method itself invokes `paintBackground` to clear the background of the towers with a white rectangle, redraws the borders by invoking `paintBorders`, draws the tower baseline using the `drawLine` method and then invokes `paintTower` for each of the towers. The `paintTower` method iterates over each digit in the `String` representing a tower, and uses that digit to determine the color and size of a disk to draw. The coordinates of each disk are determined using the variables whose values were given in the `setup` method.

The Complete `TowerDisplay` Class   The code for the `TowerDisplay` class is as follows:

```
class TowerDisplay extends Canvas {
    public TowerDisplay() {
```

```
        c = new Color[10];
        c[0] = new Color(255,0,0);
        c[1] = new Color(0,255,0);
        c[2] = new Color(0,0,255);
        c[3] = new Color(255,255,0);
        c[4] = new Color(255,0,255);
        c[5] = new Color(0,255,255);
        c[6] = new Color(44,150,44);
        c[7] = new Color(44,44,150);
        c[8] = new Color(150,150,44);
        c[9] = new Color(150,44,150);
    }

    public void setup(int nDisks, int source) {
        if (nDisks>9)
            nDisks = 9;
        tower = new String[4];
        tower[1] = "123456789".substring(0,nDisks);
        tower[2] = "";
        tower[3] = "";
        this.nDisks = nDisks;
        myWidth = this.getSize().width - 2*borderSize;
        myHeight = this.getSize().height - 2*borderSize;
        smallestDiskWidth = (myWidth/4) / nDisks;
        diskWidth = nDisks*smallestDiskWidth;
        interDiskWidth = diskWidth/4;
            diskHeight = 10;
            towerHeight = (nDisks+1) * diskHeight;
            lineLeft = borderSize + interDiskWidth;
            lineBot  = myHeight - (myHeight-
                                    towerHeight)/2;
            lineWidth = 3*diskWidth + 2*interDiskWidth;
            lineRight = lineLeft+lineWidth;
            towerLeft = new int[4];
            towerLeft[1] = lineLeft + diskWidth/2;
            towerLeft[2] = towerLeft[1] + diskWidth/2
                        + interDiskWidth + diskWidth/2;
            towerLeft[3] = towerLeft[2] + diskWidth/2
                        + interDiskWidth + diskWidth/2;

            paint(this.getGraphics());
            delay(1000);
        }

    public void setDelay(int d) {
        sdelay = d;
    }

    public void displayMove(int from, int to) {
        Graphics g = this.getGraphics();
```

```
            int fromLast = tower[from].length()-1;
            Color   c = getDiskColor(from,fromLast);
            tower[to] = tower[to].concat(tower[from].
                                    substring(fromLast));
            tower[from] = tower[from].
                                    substring(0,fromLast);
            paintLowerBackground(g);
            g.setColor(c);
            g.setFont(new
                        Font("Helvetica",Font.BOLD,18));
            g.drawString("Move from "+from+" to "+to,
                        lineLeft,myHeight - (myHeight-
                        towerHeight)/4);

    delay(sdelay);
    paint(g);
    delay(sdelay/3);
}

public void update(Graphics g) {
    paint(g);
}

public void paint(Graphics g) {
    paintBackground(g);
    paintBorder(g);
    g.setColor(new Color(0,0,0));
    if (tower==null)
        return;
    g.drawLine(lineLeft,lineBot,lineRight,lineBot);
    paintTower(g,1);
    paintTower(g,2);
    paintTower(g,3);
}

private void paintTower(Graphics g, int whichTower) {
    int j;
    String s = tower[whichTower];
    g.setColor(new Color(0,0,0));
    g.drawLine(towerLeft[whichTower],lineBot,
            towerLeft[whichTower],lineBot-towerHeight);
    for (int i=0;i<s.length();i++) {
        j = nDisks - Integer.parseInt(s.substring(i,
                                    i+1));
                g.setColor(getDiskColor(whichTower,i));
                int  jWidth = (1+j)*smallestDiskWidth;
                int  jLeft = towerLeft[whichTower] -
                                        jWidth/2;
```

```
                    int   jBot = lineBot - diskHeight -
                                       i*diskHeight;
                    g.fill3DRect(jLeft, jBot, jWidth,
                                      diskHeight, true);
            }
    }

    private void paintLowerBackground(Graphics g) {
            g.setColor(new Color(255,255,255));
            g.fillRect(lineLeft-2, lineBot+4,
                    lineWidth+4,(myHeight-towerHeight)/4);
    }

    private void paintBackground(Graphics g) {
            g.setColor(new Color(255,255,255));
            g.fillRect(5,5,this.getSize().width-
                            10,this.getSize().height-10);
    }

    private void paintBorder(Graphics g) {
            g.setColor(new Color(0,0,0));
            g.fillRect(0,0,this.getSize().
                            width,borderSize);
            g.fillRect(0,this.getSize().height-
                            borderSize,
                            this.getSize().width,borderSize);
            g.fillRect(0,0,borderSize,this.
                            getSize().height);
            g.fillRect(this.getSize().width-
                            borderSize,0, borderSize,this.
                            getSize().height);
    }

    private Color getDiskColor(int whichTower, int n) {
            String s = tower[whichTower];
            int j = nDisks -
                        Integer.parseInt(s.substring(n,n+1));
            return c[j%10];
    }

    private void delay(int n) {
        try {
            Thread.sleep(n);
        } catch(Exception e) {}
    }

    private final   int     borderSize = 5;
    private     int         sdelay=100;
    private     int         nDisks;
    private     String[]    tower = null;
```

```
        private     Color[]     c;
        private     int         myHeight;
        private     int         myWidth;
        private     int         diskWidth;
        private     int         smallestDiskWidth;
        private     int         interDiskWidth;
        private     int         diskHeight;
        private     int         towerHeight;
        private     int         lineBot;
        private     int         lineLeft;
        private     int         lineRight;
        private     int         lineWidth;
        private     int[ ]      towerLeft;
    }
```

The `TowerThread` Class   This class is based on the `Towers` class from the non-GUI version with the addition of those methods needed to make this class a `Thread`. The constructor and the `getHoldingTower` methods are identical in both classes, as is the meaning of the instance variables `nDisks` and `td`.

The usual thread-control methods, `ourSuspend`, `ourResume`, and `our-Stop` and the instance variables they manipulate, `amRunning` and `am-Stopped`, are provided. Their meaning and operation is the same as in the `LifeThread` class from Chapter 9.

The `run` method—required by a `Thread` class—replaces and plays the role of the public `solveIt` method in the non-GUI version of Towers. It sets the `boolean` thread-control variables to their proper initial values and invokes the private recursive `solveIt` method.

The `solveIt` method here is identical to its non-GUI counterpart, except that before invoking the display of a move, the following code is executed:

```
if (amStopped)
    return;
while (!amRunning)
    delay(80);
```

This code allows an appropriate and rapid response to changes in the thread-control variables `amStopped` and `amRunning`. As long as `amRunning` is false, we repeatedly invoke the `delay` method, which happens to be identical to the `delay` method in the `TowerDisplay` class.

The complete code for the `TowerThread` class is as follows:

```
class TowersOfHanoiThread extends Thread {
    public TowersOfHanoiThread(TowerDisplay td,
                                            int nDisks) {
        this.td = td;
```

```
            this.nDisks = nDisks;
            td.setup(nDisks,1);
        }

    public void run() {
        amRunning = true;
        amStopped = false;
        solveIt(nDisks, 1, 3);
    }

    public void ourSuspend() { amRunning = false;}
    public void ourResume()  { amRunning = true;}
    public void ourStop()    { amStopped = true;}

    private void delay(int n) {
        try {
            Thread.sleep(n);
        } catch(Exception e) {}
    }

    private void solveIt(int nDisks, int source,
                                            int target) {
        if (nDisks<=0)
            return;
        int holdingTower = getholdingTower(source,target);

        solveIt(nDisks-1,source,holdingTower);

        if (amStopped)
            return;
        while (!amRunning)
            delay(80);
        td.displayMove(source,target);

        solveIt(nDisks-1,holdingTower,target);
    }

    private int getholdingTower(int source, int target) {
        if (source==2 && target==3 ||
            source==3 && target==2)
                return 1;
        if (source==1 && target==3 ||
            source==3 && target==1)
                return 2;
        return 3;
    }

    private boolean       amRunning, amStopped;
    private int           nDisks;
    private TowerDisplay  td;
}
```

chapter 12

Examples

12.1 Introduction

With the conclusion of Chapter 11, you have encountered most of the language features and programming techniques that are covered in this book. Now it is time to apply these features to some nontrivial applications. These examples are not merely a review of the earlier material. They introduce some new programming concepts and apply the techniques that we have introduced earlier to problems of a larger and more complex scale.

12.2 The LOGO Turtle

LOGO is a programming language developed in the 1970s as part of an effort to introduce basic programming concepts at the elementary school level. The LOGO language revolves around the concept of a "turtle" moving about on a surface. The turtle has a pen on its underside, which can be raised or lowered to allow it to draw a line as it moves. The surface that the lines are drawn on is called the turtle's *world*. LOGO statements are commands to the turtle: turn left, move forward some distance, raise the pen, and so on. In addition, several basic programming constructs such as conditionals and looping are provided to allow more complex shapes (such as squares) to be conveniently drawn. The result is an environment that is both motivating and encouraging to a young would-be programmer, providing instant positive feedback in the form of the interesting shapes that could be drawn.

Our next example develops a very simple turtle object modeled after this language.

Statement of the Problem   Create an object that models the turtle of the LOGO language. The commands that the turtle should respond to are: turn left or right, move forward some distance, and raise or lower the pen.

Scenario   We will provide the various commands as methods. An application could then create a turtle object and control it through invocations of the methods:

```
Turtle t = new Turtle(40);   the world should be 40 × 40 units
t.penUp();
t.move(5);
t.left();
t.move(5);
t.penDown();
for (int i = 0; i < 4; i++) {
    t.move(10);
    t.left();
}
```

We do not propose conditional or loop capabilities because we can use Java features such as the loop in this code fragment.

The turtle output might be a display of the world on `System.out` that uses some character to represent the pen line. See Figure 12.1.

Finding the Primary Object   This is a straightforward task. We are trying to model the LOGO turtle. We will introduce a `Turtle` class. We use the simple output described above.

```
* * * * * * * * * *
*                 *
*                 *
*                 *
*                 * * * * * * * * * *
*
*
*
```

FIGURE 12.1   A textual display of the turtle's world. The pen mark generated by the turtle at a position is represented by an *.

Determining the Behavior   The behavior required by our problem statement is as follows:

- `Turtle` (constructor)
- `left` (turn left)
- `right` (turn right)
- `move` (move forward)
- `penUp` (lift pen—subsequent moves do not draw lines)
- `penDown` (lower pen—subsequent moves do draw lines)

Output Behavior.   The simplest output is to print the turtle's world on `System.out`. Unfortunately, we don't have full control over movement on that device. We can't move up a line or to the left because output to `System.out` models that of a typewriter—strictly left-to-right, up-to-down. We often refer to such devices as TTY devices. (TTY stands for teletype, meaning a computer-linked typewriter.)

Therefore, because the `Turtle` cannot display each move as it occurs, our class will provide a method that displays the turtle's world in its entirety. We thus have an additional behavior:

- `display` the turtle's world

Determining the Interface   The above behavior translates neatly into methods. Only the `move` method requires additional information—the distance the turtle is supposed to move. In addition, to make things interesting, we will allow the user to specify the size of the turtle's world as an argument to the constructor (we'll assume the world is square):

```
class Turtle {
    Turtle(int size) {...}          // Creates turtle in a world of the size
                                     //    given by "size"
    void move(int distance) {...}    // Move distance squares in the
                                     //    current direction.
    void penUp() {...}               // Raises drawing pen
    void penDown() {...}             // Lowers drawing pen
    void left() {...}                // Turn left.
    void right() {...}               // Turn right.
    void display() {...}             // Display turtle's world
}
```

Defining the Instance Variables   The `display` method will need information that represents the turtle's world. This information will be needed by each invocation of `display` and may be modified by `move`. We therefore need an instance variable that represents the turtle's world. We can employ the same technique used in the Game of Life in Chapter 10—a two-dimensional array.

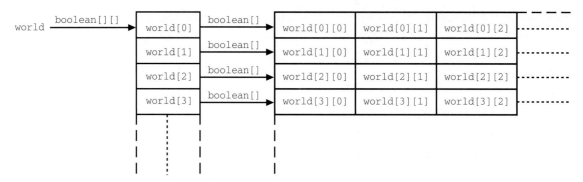

FIGURE 12.2 The turtle world as a two dimensional `boolean` array. The rows and columns of the turtle's world are represented as a two-dimensional array. Each element represents one position.

Because each position of the turtle's world is either blank or has been drawn on, we choose `boolean` to be the element type. (See Figure 12.2):

```
boolean [][] world;
```

We have to keep track of whether the pen is raised or lowered and we have to remember the turtle's current position, represented by a pair of subscript values for the `world` array:

```
boolean penLowered;
int x, y; // x is horizontal position (first subscript), y is vertical (second subscript).
```

We also need to keep track of the direction the turtle is facing. We choose to speak of the turtle facing north, east, south, or west (as shown in Figure 12.3).

We could represent the current direction as a `String`: `"North"`, `"East"`, `"South"`, `"West"`. The problem with this approach is that it requires remembering the exact strings, for example, `"North"` vs. `"north."`

FIGURE 12.3 The turtle's position and direction. The turtle occupies one of the world positions. It may face one of the four compass directions; that direction becomes its direction of movement.

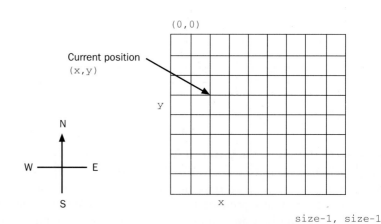

Furthermore, this representation precludes using a `switch` based upon the direction, an approach we will show to be useful.

Instead, we represent the direction using an integer, for example, 0 for north, 1 for east, and so on. To avoid having to remember which value represents which direction, we use integer constants:

```
private int direction;
private static final int NORTH=0, EAST=1, SOUTH=2, WEST=3;
```

This approach allows us to perform a `switch` based upon the direction. In addition, mistakes in the spelling of the directions, for example, `North` rather than `NORTH`, will generate an *Undeclared identifier* compiler error.

Implementing the Methods   The constructor creates the world, and it initializes a starting position, direction, and pen position. We choose to place the turtle initially in the center of the world facing north with the pen down.

```
public Turtle(int size) {
    world = new boolean[size][size];
    int i, j;
    for (i = 0; i < size; i++)
        for (j = 0; j < size; j++)
            world[i][j] = false;        ◄───   Iterate through the world array,
    direction = NORTH;                          setting each square to false.
    x = size / 2;
    y = size / 2;
}
```

The `world`, `x`, and `y` instance variables depend upon the value of the `size` argument supplied to the constructor and thus must be initialized there. The `penLowered` variable, however, is always initialized to `true`, and this initialization may therefore be performed at the point of declaration as follows:

```
class Turtle {
    ...
    // Instance variables
    private boolean penLowered = true;
    ...
}
```

The `penUp` and `penDown` methods modify the pen position to the appropriate value:

```
public void penUp() {      // Raises drawing pen
    penLowered = false;
}
public void penDown() {    // Lowers drawing pen
    penLowered = true;
}
```

Turning to the left or right causes a change to the current direction. We take the straightforward, though somewhat lengthy approach of listing all the possible cases and explicitly setting the new direction based upon the current direction:

```java
public void left() { // Turns left
    switch (direction) {
        case NORTH:
            direction = WEST; break;
        case WEST:
            direction = SOUTH; break;
        case SOUTH:
            direction = EAST; break;
        case EAST:
            direction = NORTH; break;
    }
}
public void right() { // Turns right
    switch (direction) {
        case NORTH:
            direction = EAST; break;
        case EAST:
            direction = SOUTH; break;
        case SOUTH:
            direction = WEST; break;
        case WEST:
            direction = NORTH; break;
    }
}
```

The `display` method iterates through the array row by row, printing the contents of the elements as shown in Figure 12.4:

```java
public void display() { // Displays turtle's world on System.out
    int i, j;
    for (i = 0; i < world.length; i++) {
        for (j = 0; j < world.length; j++)
            if (world[i][j])
                System.out.print("*");
            else
                System.out.print(" ");
        System.out.println();
    }
}
```

The `move` method performs the following three tasks:

- Calculates the starting and end positions of the line to be drawn.
- Draws the line, if the pen is down.
- Updates the state of the `Turtle` object.

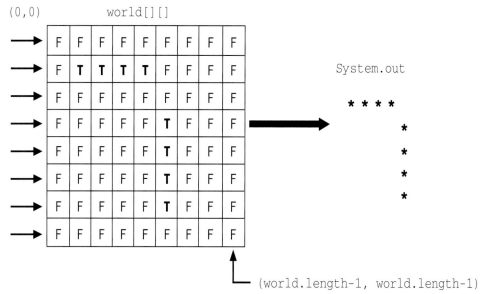

FIGURE 12.4 Displaying the turtle's world. Each of the turtle's rows is displayed as a line of text (using * and blanks) on System.out as a result of invoking the display() method.

To draw, we will rely on a helper method, draw, that is passed the starting and end positions of the line to be drawn:

```
private void draw(int startX, int startY, int destX,
                  int destY)
```

To calculate these positions we save the indices of the starting position in two int variables, startX and startY. We calculate the indices of the end position and place their values directly into this.x and this.y, thereby updating the state:

```
public void move(int distance) {
    int startX = this.x,
        startY = this.y;
    Calculate new values of this.x and this.y.
    if (penDown)
        draw(startX,startY,this.x,this.y);
}
```

The details of the calculation of the end points depend on the direction of movement. Because we only allow the turtle to face one of the four primary compass directions, only one coordinate varies as we move forward. The rules for moving in the various directions are as follows (see Figure 12.5):

- North—y coordinate decreases as we move forward; edge is encountered when $y == 0$.

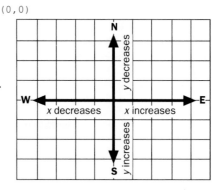

FIGURE 12.5
Coordinate changes corresponding to movement in the various directions. Either the *x* or the *y* coordinate changes with movement in a particular direction; the other coordinate remains fixed.

- East—*x* coordinate increases as we move forward; edge is encountered when x == world.length-1.
- South—*y* coordinate increases as we move forward; edge is encountered when y == world.length-1.
- West—*x* coordinate decreases as we move forward; edge is encountered when x == 0.

We will handle each direction as a separate case:

```
switch(this.direction) {
    case NORTH:
            Handle northward move.
            break;
    case EAST:
            Handle eastward move.
            break;
    case SOUTH:
            Handle southward move.
            break;
    case WEST:
            Handle westward move.
            break;
}
```

We will develop the eastward movement; the other directions are similar. When the turtle moves eastward, the *x* coordinate increases, while the *y* coordinate remains constant; see Figure 12.6.

The diagram shows that if we disregard the edge of the world, our destination square's x coordinate could be calculated this way:

```
this.x = this.x + distance;
```

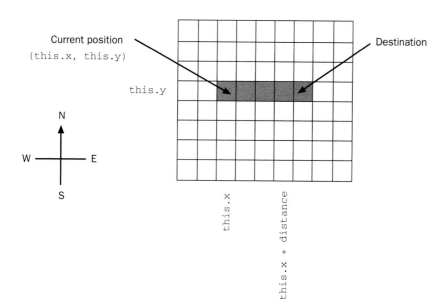

FIGURE 12.6 The squares visited during an eastward movement (edge ignored). If we ignore the edge of the world, moving `dis-tance` squares in the eastward direction takes us to square `this.x + distance`. The result of performing a `move(4)` is shown.

However, we must take the edge of the world into consideration and stop at the edge if we reach it. Our rules tell us that the edge of the world, when we are heading east, is encountered when x is equal to `world.length-1`. Therefore, when calculating the x coordinate of the destination square, we can go no further than the end of the world (Figure 12.6), and we therefore revise the assignment of `this.x` to:

```
this.x = Math.min(x + distance, world.length-1);
```

Here the (static) method `Math.min` returns the smaller of its two values.

The other directions are analogous, the only changes being the subscript being changed (y for north/south, x for east/west), the manner in which the subscript is changed (increment for south/east, decrement for north/west), and the test for the edge of the world. The resulting method is:

```
// Move distance squares in the current direction.
public void move(int distance) {
    int startX=this.x,
        startY=this.y;

    switch (direction) {
        case NORTH:
            this.y = Math.max(this.y - distance, 0);
            break;
        case SOUTH:
```

```
                this.y = Math.min(this.y + distance,
                                      world.length-1);
                break;
            case WEST:
                this.x = Math.max(this.x - distance, 0);
                break;
            case EAST:
                this.x = Math.min(this.x + distance,
                                      world.length-1);
                break;
        }
        if (penLowered)
            draw(startX, startY, this.x, this.y);
    }
```

All that is left is the implementation of our `draw` method. Based on the current direction we use a simple `for` loop to drop a mark in each intervening position:

```
    private void draw(int startX, int startY, int destX,
                                    int destY) {
        switch (direction) {
            case NORTH:
                for (int i = startY; i >= destY; i--)
                    world[destX][i] = true;
                break;
            case SOUTH:
                for (int i = startY; i <= destY; i++)
                    world[destX][i] = true;
                break;
            case WEST:
                for (int i = startX; i >= destX; i--)
                    world[i][destY] = true;
                break;
            case EAST:
                for (int i = startX; i <= destX; i++)
                    world[i][destY] = true;
                break;
        }
    }
```

12.2.1   The Complete Implementation

Putting the pieces together, the complete implementation of the `Turtle` class is as follows:

```
    import java.io.*;

    class Turtle {
```

```
// Creates turtle in a world "size"-by-"size" squares
public Turtle(int size) {
    world = new boolean[size][size];
    int i, j;
    for (i = 0; i < size; i++)
        for (j = 0; j < size; j++)
            world[i][j] = false;
    direction = NORTH;
    x = size / 2;
    y = size / 2;
}

// Move distance squares in the current direction.
public void move(int distance) {
    int startX = this.x,
        startY = this.y;

    switch (direction) {
        case NORTH:
            this.y = Math.max(this.y - distance, 0);
            break;
        case SOUTH:
            this.y = Math.min(this.y + distance,
                            world.length-1);
            break;
        case WEST:
            this.x = Math.max(this.x - distance, 0);
            break;
        case EAST:
            this.x = Math.min(this.x + distance,
                            world.length-1);
            break;
    }
    if (penLowered)
        draw(startX, startY, this.x, this.y);
}

private void draw(int startX, int startY, int destX,
                int destY) {
    switch (direction) {
        case NORTH:
            for (int i = startY; i >= destY; i--)
                world[destX][i] = true;
            break;
        case SOUTH:
            for (int i = startY; i <= destY; i++)
                world[destX][i] = true;
            break;
        case WEST:
```

```
                            for (int i = startX; i >= destX; i--)
                                world[i][destY] = true;
                            break;
                    case EAST:
                            for (int i = startX; i <= destX; i++)
                                world[i][destY] = true;
                            break;
                }
            }

            // Raises drawing pen
            public void penUp() {
                penLowered = false;
            }

            // Lowers drawing pen
            public void penDown() {
                penLowered = true;
            }

            // Turns left
            public void left() {
                switch (direction) {
                    case NORTH:
                        direction = WEST; break;
                    case WEST:
                        direction = SOUTH; break;
                    case SOUTH:
                        direction = EAST; break;
                    case EAST:
                        direction = NORTH; break;
                }
            }

            // Turns right
            public void right() {
                switch (direction) {
                    case NORTH:
                        direction = EAST; break;
                    case EAST:
                        direction = SOUTH; break;
                    case SOUTH:
                        direction = WEST; break;
                    case WEST:
                        direction = NORTH; break;
                }
            }
```

```
public void display() { // Displays turtle's world on System.out
    int i, j;
    for (i = 0; i < world.length; i++) {
        for (j = 0; j < world.length; j++)
            if (world[i][j])
                System.out.print("*");
            else
                System.out.print(" ");
        System.out.println();
    }
}

// Instance variables
private boolean [][] world;
private int x, y;
private int direction;
private boolean penLowered = true;

// Static variables
private static final int NORTH=0, EAST=1, SOUTH=2,
                         WEST=3;

public static void main(String [] args) {
    Turtle t = new Turtle(40);
    t.penUp();
    t.move(5);
    t.left();
    t.move(5);
    t.penDown();
    for (int i = 0; i < 4; i++) {
        t.move(10);
        t.left();
    }
    t.display();
}
}
```

EXERCISES

1. Change the Turtle class so that the Turtle's world does not have to be square but can be any rectangle.

2. Add an overloaded constructor that accepts no arguments and creates a world of some default size.

3. Add an overloaded move method that accepts no arguments. Instead the turtle is to be moved forward by the same distance as the most recent move method. Does this new condition require a change to the internal state of the class? Why is this method useful?

4. Rewrite the `left` and `right` methods so that they do not use a conditional. (Hint: Take advantage of the `int` representation of the direction instance variable.)

5. Our implementation treated the world as flat and we "clipped" the turtle's movement at the edge. Implement a "round" world, one without edges. That is, when the turtle reaches an edge, it simply continues to the opposite side.

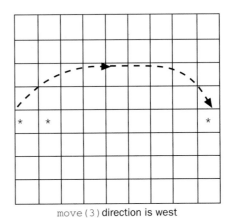

move(3) direction is west

6. Define a class called `Smiley` whose objects, when constructed, creates a `Turtle` object and use it to create a smiling face. The turtle display should then be followed by the message *Have a nice day!!* Thus:

```
Smiley sm = new Smiley();
```

produces the following output:

12.3 Web Site Maintenance

World Wide Web sites are ever-changing. Web pages come into and go out of existence. As a result, it is not too long before a person surfing the Web encounters the frustrating message "404 Not Found." This message indicates that the Web address given does not exist.

To minimize this problem, web site managers sometimes take on the role of surveyor. They check all the pages in their site for bad links—links to non-existent web pages. A survey consists of a list of the site's web pages, and any bad links that they have.

Typically, the URLs of the pages in a web site are characterized by a common substring. (See Chapter 3.) For example, the URLs of the pages in Your State University's chemistry department's web site might all contain the string `www.chem.ysu.edu` or perhaps `www.ysu.edu/chemistry` as in the following:

http://www.ysu.edu/chemistry/index.html
http://www.ysu.edu/chemistry/faculty.html
http://www.ysu.edu/chemistry/students.html
http://www.ysu.edu/chemistry/courses/undergrad.html
http://www.ysu.edu/chemistry/courses/graduate.html

and so on.

In conducting a survey for bad links, site managers usually restrict themselves to one site, their own, and start their search from a single URL, that of the top-level web page in the site (see Figure 12.7). Automating this activity is quite desirable, especially for large, complex sites.

Analyze the Problem Yourself First   Before going further in this section, take a few moments to consider how you would manually survey a site for web pages with bad links, starting from a given URL. Then consider what directions you would give to a friend as to how to accomplish this task.

In this example we develops a simple web surveyor program.

Statement of the Problem   Model a surveyor of a web site. A surveyor gets an URL and provides a list of web pages that are accessible from that URL and that may contain bad links. For simplicity, we will consider only URLs that end in ".html" or ".htm". Associated with each web page is a list of bad links that the page contains. It does not simply list the bad links because the site manager needs to know which pages have the bad links so they can be fixed.

In addition to the URL, the surveyor is provided with a site string—a string that defines the site being surveyed. The surveyor examines only those web pages whose URL contains the site string as a substring. This string confines the surveyor to just a small part of the Web, for example, to just the URLs that contain `www.awl.com`.

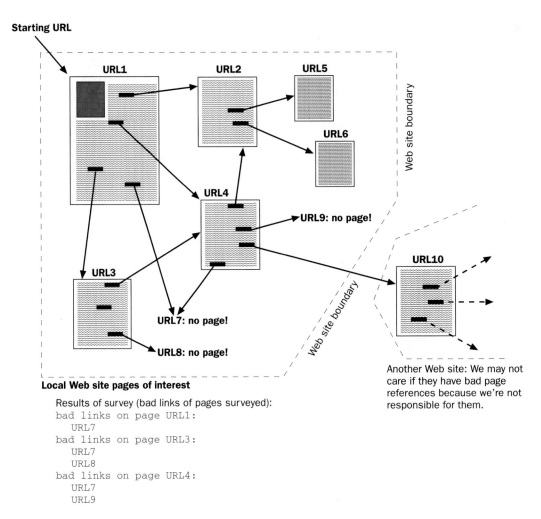

Starting URL

Local Web site pages of interest

Results of survey (bad links of pages surveyed):
```
bad links on page URL1:
   URL7
bad links on page URL3:
   URL7
   URL8
bad links on page URL4:
   URL7
   URL9
```

FIGURE 12.7 Surveying a web site for pages with links to bad URLs. A surveyor starts with an initial URL and examines all the pages in a given site that are reachable from that URL. The site is defined by a common *site string* that all the URLs in the site contain. In the example shown, URLs 1–9 are part of one site and contain some common site string. URL 10 is on a different site and presumably does not contain this string. The surveyor examines the links within the web pages of URLs 1–6. To verify that the link to URL10 within the URL4 web page is valid, the surveyor accesses URL10, but does not examine the links in that page because that page is not part of the site.

Scenario   The web administrator types

```
java Survey http://www.awl.com/cp/ awl.com/cp/
```

and sees a list of all pages accessible from `http://www.awl.com/cp/`, whose URL contains the string `awl.com/cp/` and that contain bad links. The bad links should be listed with each page. For example:

```
bad links on page http://www.awl.com/cp/disc.html:
    http://www.awl.com/cp/obsolete.html
    http://www.awl.com/cp/part1.html
bad links on page http://www.awl.com/cp/comingSoon.html
    http://www.awl.com/cp/javaPlusPlus.html
```

This output indicates that two pages, `http://www.awl.com/cp/disc.html` and `http://www.awl.com/cp/comingSoon.html`, contain bad links. The bad links themselves are listed under the URLs for these pages.

12.3.1   Finding the Primary Object

The essence of the statement of the problem can be reduced to: "surveyor provides list." The `WebSurveyor` then is our primary object. We also see that the `WebSurveyor` provides a list of web pages. A list is a collection of some sort and the things in the list—web pages—are subsidiary objects. Later we will develop a class, `WebPage` to model them.

12.3.2   Determining the Behavior of `WebSurveyor`

The `WebSurveyor` behavior is simple:

* `WebSurveyor` (constructor).
* `getPages`.

12.3.3   Determining the Interface of `WebSurveyor`

The constructor gets the URL of the top-level web page to search from as well as the site string that must be a part of every web page we examine. The only other method in the interface is `getPages`, which needs no arguments and provides a list. We choose to use the `Set` class developed at the end of Chapter 8 to model the list. So, `getPages` returns a `Set` object and we have the following interface:

```
class WebSurveyor {
    WebSurveyor(String startingUrl,
                String siteString) {...}
    Set getPages() {...}
}
```

12.3.4 Defining the Instance Variables of `WebSurveyor`

The purpose of the `WebSurveyor` is to provide a set of pages. We choose to create this set in the constructor, and so we need to maintain that set between the invocation of the constructor and invocations of `getPages`. Accordingly, we declare the following instance variable:

```
private Set wpList;    // Set of existing web pages whose URLs contain the
                       //      siteString and that are reachable from the initial
                       //      URL given to WebSurveyor
```

We also must avoid getting stuck in a loop between two pages. Suppose page A has a link to page B and page B has a link to page A. We must not survey one, then the other, then the first one again, and so forth. To prevent that situation, we need to maintain a set of URLs that have already been surveyed, using the following instance variable:

```
private Set urlList;    // Set of URLs—good or bad—that have already
                        //      been surveyed
```

In summary, we need two sets that serve different purposes. One set, `wpList`, maintains information about existing web pages that may contain bad links. The other set, `urlList`, remembers all the URLs—good or bad—that we've looked at. The `wpList` will therefore never be larger than the `urlList`. See Figure 12.8.

12.3.5 Implementing the Methods of `WebSurveyor`

The constructor starts by initializing the two instance variables to empty sets as follows:

```
public  WebSurveyor(String  startingUrl,
                         String  siteString)  {
    wpList  =  new  Set();
    urlList  =  new  Set();
```

The first parameter of the constructor contains the starting URL, a `String`. If it does not contain the site string as a substring, there is nothing

FIGURE 12.8 The state maintained by WebSurveyor. The `WebSurveyor` state consists of two sets.

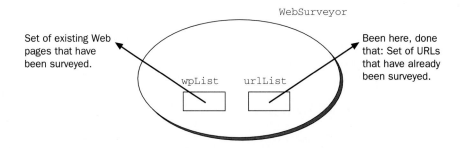

more to do—the set of pages should remain empty. To check for this condition, we write the following conditional:

```
if  (startingUrl.indexOf(siteString)  ==  -1)
    return;
```

The `indexOf` method of the `String` class returns the index of the first place where the argument appears as a substring. If the argument is not a substring, -1 is returned. We will use this technique repeatedly in testing whether one string contains a particular substring.

If `startingUrl` does contain `siteString` as a substring, then it represents a web page that we add to our set of web pages. We use the following statements:

```
WebPage  wp  =  new  WebPage(startingUrl);
wpList.addElement(wp);
```

Here we introduce the class, `WebPage`, that we anticipated earlier. Although we don't know with certainty the arguments its constructor will require, it is likely that it will need at least the URL that identifies the web page itself. Once it has been constructed, we add it to our set of web pages, `wpList`.

Because we have now surveyed the web page by constructing its corresponding `WebPage` object, we add its URL to the set of URLs already surveyed. We use the following statement:

```
urlList.addElement(startingUrl);
```

Now, how do we find all the other web pages? It's a rather complicated business. We have to look at a link on our first page and get the web page to which it refers. Then we have to look at a link on that web page. Or should we come back to look at other links on our first page? How can we keep track of all this?

A Recursive Procedure for Traversing Web Pages A good rule to remember is: When the going gets tough, get someone else to do most of the work. We therefore turn to recursion, which we introduced in Chapter 11. Now the task can be restated: Given a `WebPage` object, the site string, and a list of URLs already surveyed, find all the URLs reachable, directly or indirectly, from our `WebPage` and add their corresponding `WebPages` to `wpList`.

We can carry out this task with a recursive procedure. We ask our `WebPage` object for the set of links (URLs) it contains. For each URL that contains the site string and that is not yet on `urlList`, we do the following:

- Add the URL to `urlList`.
- Make up a new `WebPage` object to model the URL's web page.
- If the web page for the URL actually exists,
  - add the new `WebPage` object to `wpList`.
  - carry out this task for the new web page by *recursively applying this procedure to the new WebPage object.*

As more sites are visited, the number of URLs on the `urlList` will grow. By excluding the URLs on `urlList`, we guarantee that each recursive invocation has a smaller task than its "master." That's because, as the `urlList` grows, the number of sites that are eligible to visit decreases. Eventually, all eligible sites will have been visited. When that happens, no new `WebPage` objects can be created and no new recursive invocations will be made. The recursion will then terminate.

We need a helper method to implement this recursive procedure. The method is given the `WebPage` object and `siteString`. The `wpList` that it will be adding `WebPage` objects to and the `urlList` that it will be checking (and adding to) are accessible as instance variables. The method is `void` because its purpose is to add to `wpList` and `urlList`, not to return any particular value. Its prototype, therefore, is as follows:

```
private void  survey(WebPage  wp,  String  siteString)  {
```

Before implementing `survey`, let's complete the `WebSurveyor` constructor by invoking this method:

```
//    Initialize a WebSurveyor object capable of giving a set of WebPages reachable from
//            startingUrl, all on the site defined by siteString.

public WebSurveyor(String startingUrl,  String siteString)
                                        throws IOException {
    wpList  =  new Set();
    urlList  =  new Set();
    if  (startingUrl.indexOf(siteString)  ==  -1)
        return;
    WebPage  wp  =  new WebPage(startingUrl);
    wpList.addElement(wp);
    urlList.addElement(startingUrl);
    survey(wp,siteString);
}
```

Examine web page of starting URL.
Add to set of examined pages.
Been there, done that.
Examine all its descendant
    web pages in site.

Implementing the Recursive Procedure Writing `survey` is a matter of turning our informal recursive procedure into code. We get a set of links from our `WebPage` object with the following statement:

```
Set  links  =  wp.getLinks();
```

Next, we use an `Enumeration` and a simple loop to examine every URL on the page. We process only the ones that contain `siteString` as a substring and that are not already on the `urlList`:

```
Enumeration  e  =  links.elements();
while  (e.hasMoreElements())  {
    String  url  =  (String)  e.nextElement();
    if  (url.indexOf(siteString)!=-1 &&
        !urlList.contains(url))  {
```

> *process url*
>   }
> }

For those eligible URLs that are new, we add them to `urlList` and create a new `WebPage` object for the URL using the following code:

```
urlList.addElement(url);
WebPage  wp2  =  new  WebPage(url);
```

If the web page is not "bad" (that is, it actually exists), we add the object to `wpList` and recursively invoke `survey` to handle the new page:

```
if (!wp2.isBad()) {
    wpList.addElement(wp2);
    survey(wp2,siteString);
}
```

The completed survey method is:

```
//  Examine the web pages of the site defined by siteString and reachable from the web
//       page wp.
private void survey(WebPage wp, String siteString)
                        throws IOException {
    Set links = wp.getLinks();
    Enumeration e = links.elements();
    while (e.hasMoreElements()) {
        String url = (String) e.nextElement();
        if  (url.indexOf(siteString)!=-1 &&
                !urlList.contains(url))  {
            WebPage wp2 = new WebPage(url);
            urlList.addElement(url);
            if (!wp2.isBad()) {
                wpList.addElement(wp2);
                survey(wp2,siteString);
            }
        }
    }
}
```

Annotations:
- Get the direct descendants of this page (its links).
- For each link (URL) on this page
- If on sit and not yet seen, examine it
- we've seen it
- if it exists
- Add to set of examined pages, and survey its descendants.

The `getPages` method simply returns `wpList`. The complete implementation for the `WebSurveyor` class is shown below. We have added a `main` method that creates a `WebSurveyor` object, gets the set of pages reachable from the initial URL, and then sends each page the message

```
wp.getBadLinks();
```

to get the set of bad links on that page. If this `Set` is not empty, a static helper method—`showBad`—is invoked to print the URL of the web page. This URL is

obtained from the `WebPage` with a `getURL` message along with a list of the
bad links.

```java
import java.io.*;
import java.util.*;
import java.net.*;

public class WebSurveyor {

    // Initialize a WebSurveyor object capable of giving a set of WebPages reachable
    //       from startingUrl, all on the site defined by siteString.
    public WebSurveyor(String startingUrl,
                       String siteString) throws IOException {
        wpList  =  new  Set();
        urlList  =  new  Set();
        if  (startingUrl.indexOf(siteString)  ==  -1)
            return;
        WebPage wp = new WebPage(startingUrl);
        wpList.addElement(wp);
        urlList.addElement(startingUrl);
        survey(wp,siteString);
    }

    // Examine the web pages of the site defined by siteString and reachable from the
    //       web page wp.
    private void survey(WebPage wp, String siteString)
                                       throws IOException {
        Set links = wp.getLinks();
        Enumeration e = links.elements();
        while (e.hasMoreElements()) {
            String url = (String) e.nextElement();
            if (url.indexOf(siteString)!=-1 &&
                    !urlList.contains(url)) {
                WebPage wp2 = new WebPage(url);
                urlList.addElement(url);
                if (!wp2.isBad()) {
                    wpList.addElement(wp2);
                    survey(wp2,siteString);
                }
            }
        }
    }

    public Set getPages() {
        return wpList;
    }

    private Set wpList; // Set of existing web pages whose URLs contain
                        //    the siteString and that are reachable
                        //    from the initial URL given to WebSurveyor.
```

Margin annotations:

- Examine web page of starting URL.
- Add to set of examined pages.
- Been there, done that.
- Examine all its descendant web pages in site.
- Get the direct descendants of this page (its links).
- For each link (URL) on this page
- If on site and not yet seen,
- examine it.
- We've seen it (been there).
- If it exists,
- add to set of
- examined pages
- and survey its
- descendants.

```
        private Set urlList; // Set of URLs—good or bad—that have already
                            //           been surveyed
        private static  void  showBad(WebPage  wp,
                                      Set  badset)  {
            System.out.println("\nBad pages of "+
                           wp.getURL()+":");
            Enumeration ebad = badset.elements();
            while (ebad.hasMoreElements())
               System.out.println(ebad.nextElement());
        }

        public static void main(String[] args)  throws
                                            IOException {
            String startingUrl = args[0];
            String siteString = args[1];
            WebSurveyor ws =
                    new WebSurveyor(startingUrl,siteString);
            Set pset = ws.getPages();
            Enumeration e = pset.elements();
            while (e.hasMoreElements()) {
               WebPage wp = (WebPage) e.nextElement();
               Set badset = wp.getBadLinks();
               if (!badset.isEmpty())
                   showBad(wp,badset);
            }
            System.exit(0);
        }
    }
```

> Get the pages from this site. For each page:

> If it has bad links, show 'em.

We now define the `WebPage` class that `WebSurveyor` has used.

Determining the Behavior of `WebPage`   In   the   development   of   `Web-Surveyor`, we modeled a web page using a `WebPage` class with the following behavior:

- `WebPage` (constructor)
- `getLinks` (used by the `survey` method of `WebSurveyor`).
- `getBadLinks` (used by the `main` method of `WebSurveyor`).
- `isBad` (used by the `survey` method of `WebSurveyor`).
- `getURL` (used by the `showBad` method of `WebSurveyor`).

Determining the Interface of `WebPage`   As we implemented the `WebSurveyor` class we developed, provisionally, the following interface for `WebPage`:

```
class WebPage {
    WebPage(String url) {...}
    Set getLinks() {...}
```

```
        Set getBadLinks() {...}
        boolean isBad() {...}
        String getURL() {...}
}
```

Defining the Instance Variables of `WebPage`   From the constructor's interface and the presence of a `getURL` method, it is obvious that `WebPage` needs to maintain the URL of the web page it models:

```
String url;   // URL of this web page
```

Implementing the Methods of `WebPage`   The constructor must initialize its instance variable as follows:

```
WebPage(String url) {
    this.url = url;
}
```

Do we need it do more? We have methods such as `getLinks` that deliver part of the web page's content, so we might consider reading the actual web page in advance and preparing that information. However, web pages are dynamic. Anything we read now may become out of date later. We will let all the other methods—other than `getURL`—rely on obtaining current information by directly reading the web page. Therefore, our constructor is complete as it stands.

The `getURL` method, of course, is a "piece of cake":

```
String getURL() {
    return url;
}
```

The `getLinks` method must read from the actual Web page and pick up just the links that are HTTP references (that is, the links that refer to another web page). For example, suppose the surveyor is examining a (small) Web page whose HTML content is as follows:

```
<HTML>
    <HEAD>  <TITLE>  My  Kids  </TITLE>  </HEAD>
<BODY>
    <A  HREF="joanna.html">Joanna</A>  <BR>
    <A  HREF="alena.html">Alena</A>  <BR>
    <A  HREF="http:www.stateu.edu/students/kera.html">
            Kera</A>  <BR>
    <A  HREF="mailto:david@isp.com">Questions?  Email
            me!</A>  <BR>
</BODY>
</HTML>
```

The information that the `getLinks` method needs from this page consists of the following `Strings`:

```
joanna.html
alena.html
http:www.stateu.edu/students/kera.html
```

It does not need the rest of the HTML.

Therefore, from the point of view of `getLinks`, a web page consists not of lines of HTML but rather of hypertext references (we'll call them HREFs) that are explicitly or implicitly references to HTTP links as distinct from mailto, telnet, news, ftp, or other links that are often found in web pages. We will call this kind of HREF an "HTTP HREF."

To model this view of a web page, we will define a class called `HttpReader`. Our `getLinks` method will create an `HttpReader` object, passing its constructor the URL of the particular web page it is modeling. Then it will send `readLine` messages to get back successive HTTP HREFs. See Figures 12.9 and 12.10.

We will require even more service from the `HttpReader`. The fact is, strings such as `alena.html` are only a convenient shorthand for a complete URL. If such a link appears on a Web page whose URL is `http://www.myisp.com/arnow/family/kids.html` then the full URL that

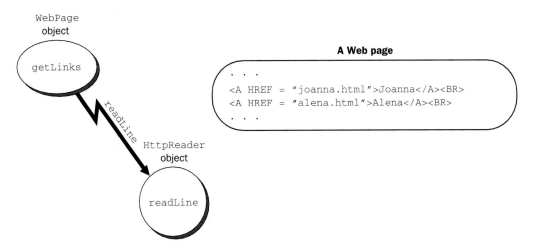

FIGURE 12.9 A `WebPage` object and its `HttpReader`: Requesting links. To examine the links in a web page, a `WebPage` object can send `readLine` messages to an `HttpReader` object.

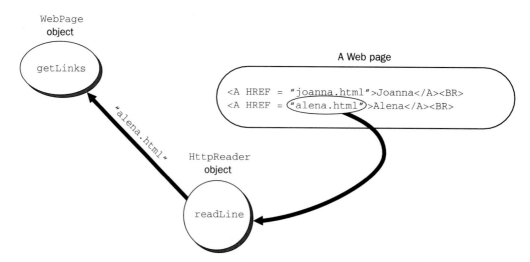

FIGURE 12.10   What `HttpReader` returns. In response to a `readLine` message, the `HttpReader` returns the next HTTP HREF found in the web page.

`joanna.html` represents is `http://www.myisp.com/arnow/family/alena.html`. We will require that `HttpReader` return the HTTP HREFs that it finds in full URL format.

This organization greatly simplifies the task of writing `getLinks`. The `getLinks` method does the following:

- Creates a new `Set`, `links`.
- Creates an `HttpReader` based on the URL of the `webPage`.
- Uses a read/process loop to get all the HTTP URLs from the `HttpReader` until end of data. Each of these URLs is added to the `links`.
- Returns the `links` `Set`.

The following code implements this last task:

```
//    Return a set of all the HTTP HREFs in this web page.
public Set getLinks() throws IOException {
    Set    links = new Set();
    HttpReader hr = new HttpReader(url);
    String link = hr.readLine();
    while (link!=null) {
        links.addElement(link);
        link = hr.readLine();
    }
    return links;
}
```

Create an HttpReader based on our URL.
Read all the HTTP HREFs
and add them to the links set.

The implementation of `getBadLinks` is the same, except that we add only bad URLs to the `links` local variable. A helper method, `isBad`, simplifies this method as follows:

```
//   Return a set of all the HTTP HREFs in this web page that are bad links.
public Set getBadLinks() throws IOException {
    Set links = new Set();
    HttpReader hr = new HttpReader(url);
    String link = hr.readLine();
    while (link!=null) {
        if (isBad(link))    Only add bad URLs.
            links.addElement(link);
        link = hr.readLine();
    }
    return links;
}
```

Web servers inform their clients of a bad link by returning a *response code* (an integer) that is greater than or equal to 300 when an HTTP connection is made to the link. Java's `HttpURLConnection` class models such a connection. We get a reference to an `HttpURLConnection` object by sending an `openConnection` message to an `URL` object. To get the response code, we then send a `getResponseCode` message to the `HttpURLConnection`. We therefore can write our `isBad` method as follows:

```
private boolean isBad(String url) throws IOException {
    URL u = new URL(url);
    HttpURLConnection uC = (HttpURLConnection)
                            u.openConnection();
    int responseCode = uC.getResponseCode();
    return responseCode>=300;
}
```

One serious inadequacy that we can't address until the end of Chapter 14 is the fact that our program will crash if the URL is bad because the host does not exist. We will fix this problem in Chapter 14. Despite this flaw, our program as it stands is useful. Most URLs are bad because the filename gets out of date, not because of an incorrect host name.

The only remaining method to implement is the `isBad` public method that is part of the `WebPage` interface. It has no argument, because it pertains to the URL of the `WebPage` object itself. The method is easily implemented using the helper method `isBad`:

```
public boolean isBad() throws IOException {
    return isBad(this.url);
}
```

The complete class, along with a simple test driver (`main`), is:

```
class WebPage {

    public WebPage(String url) {
        this.url = url;
    }
    public boolean isBad() throws IOException {
        return isBad(this.url);
    }

    //    Return a set of all the HTTP HREFs in this web page.
    public Set getLinks() throws IOException {
        Set     links = new Set();
        HttpReader hr = new HttpReader(url);
        String link = hr.readLine();
        while (link!=null) {
            links.addElement(link);
            link = hr.readLine();
        }
        return links;
    }

    //    Return a set of all the HTTP HREFs in this web page that are bad links.
    public Set getBadLinks() throws IOException {
        Set links = new Set();
        HttpReader hr = new HttpReader(url);
        String link = hr.readLine();
        while (link!=null) {
            if (isBad(link))
                links.addElement(link);
            link = hr.readLine();
        }
        return links;
    }

    public String getURL() {
        return url;
    }

    private boolean isBad(String url) throws IOException {
        WebReader wr = new WebReader(url);
        URL u = new URL(url);
        HttpURLConnection uC =
            (HttpURLConnection) u.openConnection();
        int responseCode = uC.getResponseCode();
        return responseCode>=300;
    }
```

Create an HttpReader based on our URL.
Read all the HTTP HREFs
 and add them to the links set.

Only bad URLs get added to links.

Create a WebReader based on this URL

```
    private String url;

    public static void main(String[] a) {
        WebPage     wp = new WebPage(a[0]);     Create a WebPage object.
        Set         links = wp.getLinks();      Get the page's links.
        Enumeration e = links.elements();
        while (e.hasMoreElements())             Print them all out.
            System.out.println(wp.getURL()+
                    " has this link: "+
                    e.nextElement());
    }
}
```

We now turn to the implementation of `WebReader` and `HttpReader`.
`WebReader` is simpler; it just returns lines (the kind of `Strings` that `Buff`-
`eredReader` objects return in `readLine` messages) from a web page. We'll
start with it first.

12.3.6   The `WebReader` Class

The `WebReader`'s constructor uses the URL it receives to construct a `Buff`-
`eredReader`, which is associated with an `InputStream` that brings data
from the web page. Using the `BufferedReader`, the `WebReader`'s constructor can read individual lines from the web page source. The code in the constructor that does this is straight out of the last section of Chapter 3. The
`BufferedReader` is maintained as an instance variable so that `readLine`
can use it to read and return a single line:

```
class WebReader {
    public WebReader(String url) throws IOException {
        URL u = new URL(url);
        InputStream ins = u.openStream();
        InputStreamReader isr = new InputStreamReader(ins);
        br = new BufferedReader(isr);
    }

    public  String readLine() throws IOException {
        return br.readLine();
    }

    private BufferedReader br;
}
```

The `HttpReader` has to extract the HTTP HREFs, and this turns out to be quite a messy task! It requires the following steps:

- Open a network connection and read lines from it. (This is the only easy step. We can use a `WebReader` to help us.)
- Recognize HTML tags, which may be on a single line or may span many lines.
- Pick up the references found in the tags, that is, examine only what is in the quotes in HREF="...".
- Transform the reference into a complete URL. References may just be pathnames and may leave out the protocol (HTTP by default), the hostname of the computer, and the port number. (The port number is usually left out; by default the port number for HTTP is 80.)
- Select only those references that are HTTP (web page) references to URLs that end in ".htm" or ".html".

To make it more challenging, remember that tags are not case sensitive, so HREF is the same as href, which is the same as HreF, and so on.

When we attempt to implement these steps in a single class, let alone a single method, we are faced with terribly complex, hard-to-develop, and hard-to-maintain code. Furthermore, such an implementation ignores the fact that each of the above steps represents a different model of a web page. The first views the web page as a collection of lines of text (the `WebReader` model), the second as a collection of tags, the third as a collection of HREFs, the fourth as a collection of complete URLs corresponding to these references, and the last as a collection of HTTP-only references.

Each of these models can be represented by a distinct class whose chief behavior is provided by a `readLine` method that returns the basic element of the model. Thus we have:

Class name	readLine returns (basic element)	Model of web page
WebReader	Line of text from web page	Collection of lines
TagReader	HTML tag, with angle brackets stripped off	Collection of tags
HrefReader	HREF argument, with double quotes removed	Collection of HREFs
LinkReader	Complete URL	Collection of HREFs that are complete URLs
HttpReader	Just HTTP URLs	Collection of HTTP HREFs that are complete URLs

This list of classes suggests a layered approach to implementing `HttpReader`. Instead of using a `WebReader` to get lines of text from a `WebPage`, it can use a `LinkReader` that will return complete URLs of HREFs. Then `HttpReader` only has to check whether these `String`s are HTTP HREFs or some other kind. `LinkReader` in turn can use an `HrefReader` to return `String`s that are HREFs of any kind. Then `LinkReader` only has to turn them into complete URLs. `HrefReader` can use a `TagReader` to return successive tags. `HrefReader` won't have the responsibility of looking for angle brackets and worrying whether a tag extends over several lines. That responsibility belongs to `TagReader`. `HrefReader` only has to look inside the tags and pick out the HREFs.

You may recognize our approach here as similar to the approach that Java takes to input (see Chapter 3): A `FileInputStream` class provides access to a file, an `InputStreamReader` provides a stream of bytes, and a `BufferedReader` provides line by line reads.

We now turn to this set of classes used to read web pages: `HttpReader`, `LinkReader`, `HrefReader`, and `TagReader` (see Figure 12.11). Each of these classes has the same interface:

- Constructor (URL as argument)
- `readLine` (no argument, returns a `String`)

They differ in the kind of `String` that `readLine` returns (line from web page source, versus tag, versus link, and so on).

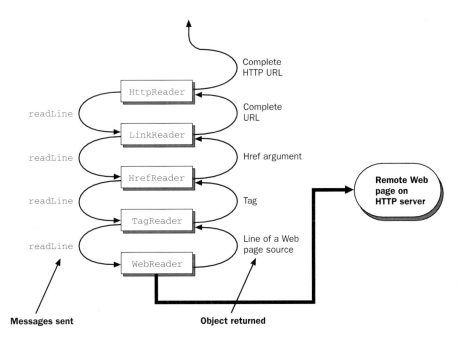

FIGURE 12.11   The classes used to read URLs. It is convenient to use the composition of several classes to read URLs from a web page.

We start with `HttpReader` and work our way down to `TagReader`. The `HttpReader` class provides a `readLine` method that returns the successive HTTP links embedded in web pages. Our design calls for it to use a `LinkReader`, which returns successive URLs (in complete form) from a web page. So the constructor of `HttpReader` needs to create a `LinkReader` object associated with the web page specified by its URL argument. The `readLine` method will, each time invoked, read URLs from the `LinkReader` until end of data or until an HTTP URL that ends with ".htm" or ".html" is found.

The class is quite similar in structure to `WebReader`. Its only instance variable is a reference to the `LinkReader` it is using. For convenience we use two helper methods, `isHTML` and `isSuffix`, which we also implement here.

```
class HttpReader {
    public  HttpReader(String urlString) throws IOException {
        lr = new LinkReader(urlString);
    }

    //   Return the next HTTP HREF in complete URL form.
    public  String readLine() throws IOException {
        String  line = lr.readLine();
        while (line != null &&
            !(line.toUpperCase().indexOf("HTTP:") == 1
            || isHTML(line)))
            line = lr.readLine();
        return line;
    }

    private static boolean isSuffix(String s, String suffix) {
        return s.lastIndexOf(suffix)==
                                s.length()-suffix.length();
    }

    private static boolean isHTML(String url) {
        return isSuffix(url, ".html") || isSuffix(url, ".htm");
    }

    private LinkReader lr;
}
```

> Keep reading HREFs until no more data or an HTTP HREF is found.

12.3.7 The `LinkReader` Class

The job of the `LinkReader` class is to get URLs that are incomplete and transform them into complete ones. The `LinkReader` returns successive full URLs that are embedded as references (links) in a web page. It employs an `HrefReader` much as `HttpReader` uses the `LinkReader`. The `HrefReader`'s `readLine` method will return successive links. These links are not necessarily in the following full URL form:

```
protocol://hostname:portnumber/pathname
```

The pathname may be as simple as a filename:

```
info.html
```

or as complex as a long sequence of directories (or folders) with a filename at the end, as in the following:

```
schoolOfScience/biology/faculty/fullTime/crick.html
```

In general, when a link in a web page leaves out some of the components of an URL, it is understood that they will be taken from the URL of the web page in which the link appears.

For example, the web page whose URL is

```
http://www.xyz.edu/~mary/paper1.html
```

might have a link that contains only the filename `bib.html`. The missing components, including the directory in which the filename appears will be taken from the complete URL just shown. The full URL for `bib.html` becomes

```
http://www.xyz.edu/~mary/bib.html.
```

Pathnames in URLs can use the notation "`..`" to refer to the parent directory of the web page in which they appear. For example, the link `../part-Time/watson.html`" in

```
http://www.abc.edu/schoolOfScience/biology/faculty/
       fullTime/crick.html
```

becomes:

```
http://www.abc.edu/schoolOfScience/biology/faculty/
       partTime/watson.html
```

The `..` refers to and is replaced by the directory `schoolOfScience/biology/faculty/`.

For that reason, the `LinkReader` constructor not only creates an `Href-Reader`, which it uses to read links, but also creates an `URL` object, using one of Java's predefined classes. The `URL` object makes parsing the URL string a snap, and the constructor picks up the protocol, host, port, and pathname of the web page (the resource or file). The messiest part of the constructor is determining from the absolute pathname the `String`s that are the directory and parent directory names. These are used by `readLine` to form complete URLs from links that are just filename or that start with "`..`".

The constructor makes use of the `lastIndexOf` method of the `String` class. It is the same as the `indexOf` method except that it starts looking from the end of the `String` rather than the beginning.

```
class LinkReader {
    public LinkReader(String urlString) throws IOException {
        hr = new HrefReader(urlString);
        url = new URL(urlString);
        host = url.getHost();
        resource = url.getFile();  This is the pathname for this URL.
        directory = null;
        parentDirectory = null;
        int   k = resource.lastIndexOf("/");
```

<table>
<tr><td>

k marks the last /.
The directory goes up to the last /.

Now k marks the second to last /.

</td><td>

```
if (k!=-1) {
    directory = resource.substring(0,k);
    k = directory.lastIndexOf("/");
    if (k!=-1) {
        parentDirectory = resource.substring(0,k);
        parentDirectory = parentDirectory.concat("/");
    }
    directory = directory.concat("/");
}
port = url.getPort();
protocol = url.getProtocol();
}
    ...
}
```

</td></tr>
</table>

The readLine method invokes the readLine method of the Href-Reader to get a reference. No loop is needed because HrefReader's readLine will only return a reference or null to signify end of data.

Once a String is obtained from the HrefReader, it is a matter of determining what URL parts, if any, are missing and then adding the necessary default parts to the String and returning the full URL.

```
class LinkReader {
    ...
    public String readLine() throws IOException {
        String   link;
        link = hr.readLine();
        if (link==null)
            return null;

        int k = link.indexOf("://");
        if (k!=-1)
            if (link.substring(k+3).indexOf("/")==-1)
                return link+"/";
            else
                return link;

        k = link.indexOf(":");
        if (k!=-1 && link.substring(0,k).indexOf(".")==-1)
            return link;

        if (link.length()>=2 &&
                            link.substring(0,2).equals(".."))
            return protocol
                + "://"
                + host + parentDirectory
                + link.substring(3);
```

of form: prot://host•••
of form: prot://host

of form: prot://host/•••

check for mailto:, telnet: and so on

reference to resource in parent directory?

```
    if (link.length()>=1 && link.substring(0,1).
                                      equals("/"))
        return protocol +
                 "://" + host + link;
    return protocol + "://" + host + directory + link;
}
```
full path reference to resource on same host?

assume reference to resource in same directory

```
private HrefReader hr;          // The HrefReader to read HREFs from
private URL        url;         // The URL of this page
private String     host,        // The host portion of this URL
                   resource,    // The resource portion of this URL
                   protocol,    // The protocol portion of this URL
                   directory,   // The resource's directory
                   parentDirectory;   // The directory of the
                                      //    resource's directory
private int        port;        // The port number of this URL
}
```

The complete LinkReader class is as follows:

```
class LinkReader {

    public LinkReader(String urlString) throws IOException {
        hr = new HrefReader(urlString);
        url = new URL(urlString);
        host = url.getHost();
        resource = url.getFile();      This is the pathname for this URL.
        directory = null;
        parentDirectory = null;
        int k = resource.lastIndexOf("/");
        if (k!=-1) {                              k marks the last /.
            directory = resource.substring(0,k);  The directory goes up to the last /.
            k = directory.lastIndexOf("/");       Now k marks the second to last /.
            if (k!=-1) {
                parentDirectory = resource.substring(0,k);
                parentDirectory =
                            parentDirectory.concat("/");
            }
            directory = directory.concat("/");
        }
        port = url.getPort();
        protocol = url.getProtocol();
    }

    public String readLine() throws IOException {
        Stringlink;
        link = hr.readLine();
        if (link==null)
            return null;
```

of form: prot://host•••
of form: prot://host

of form: prot://host/•••

```
                              int k = link.indexOf("://");
                              if (k!=-1)
                                  if (link.substring(k+3).indexOf("/")==-1)
                                      return link+"/";
                                  else
                                      return link;
```

check for mailto:, telnet: and so on

```
                              k = link.indexOf(":");
                              if (k!=-1 && link.substring(0,k).indexOf(".")==
                                  -1)
                                  return link;
```

reference to resource in
parent directory?

```
                              if (link.length()>=2 &&
                                              link. substring(0,2).equals(".."))
                                  return protocol
                                      + "://"
                                      + host + parentDirectory
                                      + link.substring(3);
```

full path reference to resource
on same host?

```
                              if (link.length()>=1 &&
                                              link. substring(0,1).equals("/"))
                                  return protocol
                                      + "://" + host + link;
```

assume reference to resource
in same directory

```
                          return protocol
                                          + ": //" + host + directory + link;
                      }

      private HrefReader hr;           // The HrefReader to read HREFs from
      private URL        url;          // The URL of this page
      private String     host,         // The host portion of this URL
                         resource,     // The resource portion of this URL
                         protocol,     // The protocol portion of this URL
                         directory,    // The resource's directory
                         parentDirectory;     // The directory of the
                                              //   resource's directory
      private int        port;         // The port number of this URL
  }
```

12.3.8 The `HrefReader` class

The `HrefReader` returns successive URLs that are embedded as references (links) in a web page. It employs a `TagReader` in a by-now-familiar manner. The `TagReader`'s `readLine` method will return any HTML tag, not necessarily those containing an HREF. Therefore, the `readLine` method here loops,

repeatedly sending `readLine` messages to the `TagReader` until it returns
`null` (signifying end of data) or a tag that contains an HREF.

Once a tag with an HREF has been found in `readLine`, it is a matter of
trimming off the quotes and any other text other than the actual embedded
reference.

To aid with the trimming, two helper methods are employed, `trimFrom`
and `trimUpThrough`. The first finds the position of a substring in a `String`
and trims that substring and all the characters that follow it. The other does
the same task but at the other end: It trims all the characters from the beginning up to and including the substring. When these methods are used with a
single quote and a double quote as the substrings, the `readLine` method is
greatly simplified.

```
class HrefReader {

    public HrefReader(String url) throws IOException {
        tr = new TagReader(url);
    }

    // return index of HREF href HrEf and so on in s
    private int hrefIndex(String s) {
        return s.toUpperCase().indexOf("HREF");
    }

    // return the largest prefix of s that does not contain x— with spaces trimmed
    private String trimFrom(String s, String x) {
        int k = s.indexOf(x);
        if (k!=-1)
            return s.substring(0,k).trim();
        else
            return s.trim();
    }

    // return the largest suffix of s that does not contain x— with spaces trimmed
    private String trimUpThrough(String s, String x) {
        int k = s.indexOf(x);
        if (k!=-1)
            return s.substring(k+x.length()).trim();
        else
            return s.trim();
    }

    public String readLine() throws IOException {
        String   tag;
        tag = tr.readLine();
        while (tag!=null && hrefIndex(tag)==-1) // get a tag with an HREF in it
            tag = tr.readLine();
        if (tag==null)
            return null;
```

```
                              int   k = hrefIndex(tag);
eliminate chars before HREF   tag = tag.substring(k+1).trim();

eliminate chars through 1st = tag = trimUpThrough(tag,"=");
eliminate chars from 1st      tag = trimFrom(tag," ");
    embedded space

eliminate chars before and    if (tag.indexOf("\"")!=-1) {
    after double quotes (including ")   tag = trimUpThrough(tag,"\"");
                                  tag = trimFrom(tag,"\"");
                              }

eliminate chars before and    if (tag.indexOf("'")!=-1) {
    after single quotes (including ')   tag = trimUpThrough(tag,"'");
                                  tag = trimFrom(tag,"'");
                              }
                              tag = trimFrom(tag,"#");
                              return trimFrom(tag,"?");
                          }

                          private TagReader tr;   // The TagReader to read tags from
                      }
```

12.3.9 The `TagReader` Class

The last of our classes in this example is `TagReader`. The class it uses to
obtain input is `WebReader`, which we have already implemented. There is an
interesting twist to `TagReader`. Unlike the other classes we have seen, which
needed only to maintain information that was determined by the constructor
(typically just a reference to some "Reader" object), a `TagReader` object must
maintain the unprocessed portions of lines that it reads. The reason is that the
`TagReader`'s `readLine` is expected to return one tag only, whereas the
actual lines of a web page, returned by `WebReader`'s `readLine`, may contain
multiple tags.

The logic of `readLine` is straightforward: Keep reading lines until one
has the beginning of a tag or until the end of data has been reached:

```
while (line!=null && line.indexOf("<")==-1)
    line = wr.readLine();
```

Then, we need to make sure we have an end of a tag in line. We keep reading lines and append them to our `String` as long as necessary. (We first are
careful to ignore any > that appears before the first <):

```
int k = line.indexOf(">");
if (k!=-1 && k<line.indexOf("<"))
    line = line.substring(k+1);
String nextLine = wr.readLine();
```

```
while (nextLine!=null && line.indexOf(">")==-1) {
    line = line.concat(nextLine);
    nextLine = wr.readLine();
}
```

Once we know we have a tag, we find its boundaries, create a `String` consisting just of the tag, adjust the line so that it consists of only the characters after the tag, and return the tag:

```
int tagStart = line.indexOf("<");
int tagEnd = line.indexOf(">");
if (tagStart<0 || tagEnd<0 || tagStart>tagEnd)
    System.err.println("Bad angle brackets: "+line);
    String tag = line.substring(tagStart+1,tagEnd);
    line = line.substring(tagEnd+1);
    return tag;
```

The complete class implementation is as follows:

```
class TagReader {

    public TagReader(String url) throws IOException {
        wr = new WebReader(url);
        line = null;
    }

    public String readLine() throws IOException {
        if (line==null)                                    // Search for a line from the web page
            line = wr.readLine();                          // that has a < in it— a tag beginning
        while (line!=null && line.indexOf("<")==-1)
            line = wr.readLine();
        if (line==null)

            return null;
        int k = line.indexOf(">");                         // Search for a > — a tag end
        if (k!=-1 && k<line.indexOf("<"))
            line = line.substring(k+1);
        String nextLine = wr.readLine();
        while (nextLine!=null && line.indexOf(">")==-1) {   // Keep concatenating lines until >
            line = line.concat(nextLine);                   // is found
            nextLine = wr.readLine();
        }
        if (nextLine!=null)
            line = line.concat(nextLine);
        if (line.indexOf(">")==-1)
            return null;

        int tagStart = line.indexOf("<");                   // Get the positions of < and >
        int tagEnd   = line.indexOf(">");
        if (tagStart<0 || tagEnd<0 || tagStart>tagEnd)      // Check positions
```

```
                        System.err.println("Bad angle brackets: "+line);
                        String tag = line.substring(tagStart+1,tagEnd);
                        line = line.substring(tagEnd+1);
                        return tag;
                }

        private String    line;     // The unprocessed part of the most recent
                                    //    line read from wr
        private WebReader wr;       // The WebReader to read lines from
    }
```

Isolate tag
line is what remains
  after the tag

12.3.10 The Complete `WebSurveyor` Application

The complete `WebSurveyor` application follows:

```
import java.io.*;
import java.util.*;
import java.net.*;

public class WebSurveyor {

        // Initialize a WebSurveyor object capable of giving a set of WebPages reachable
        //          from startingUrl all on the site defined by siteString
        public WebSurveyor(String startingUrl,
                        String siteString) throws IOException {
            wpList = new Set();
            urlList = new Set();
            if (startingUrl.indexOf(siteString) == -1)
                return;
            WebPage wp = new WebPage(startingUrl);
            wpList.addElement(wp);
            urlList.addElement(startingUrl);
            survey(wp,siteString);

        }

        // Examine the web pages of the site defined by siteString and reachable from the
        //      web page wp
        private void survey(WebPage wp, String siteString)
                                            throws IOException {
            Set links = wp.getLinks();
            Enumeration e = links.elements();
            while (e.hasMoreElements()) {
                String url = (String) e.nextElement();
                if (url.indexOf(siteString)!=-1
                        && !urlList.contains(url)) {
                    WebPage wp2 = new WebPage(url);
                    urlList.addElement(url);
                    if (!wp2.isBad()) {
```

examine web page of starting URL
add to set of examined pages
been there, done that
examine all its descendant
  web pages in site

get the direct descendants
of this page (its links)
for each link (URL) on this page

if on site and not yet seen...

examine it
we've seen it (been there)
if it exists...

```
                    wpList.addElement(wp2);
                    survey(wp2,siteString);
                }
            }
        }
    }

    Set getPages() {
        return wpList;
    }

    private Set wpList;    // set of existing web pages whose URLs contain
                           //    the siteString and that are reachable from
                           //    the initial URL given to WebSurveyor
    private Set urlList;   // set of URLs— good or bad— that have already
                           //    been surveyed

    private static void showBad(WebPage wp, Set badset) {
        System.out.println("\nBad pages of "+wp.getURL()+":");
        Enumeration ebad = badset.elements();
        while (ebad.hasMoreElements())
            System.out.println(ebad.nextElement());
    }

    public static void main(String[] args)
                                        throws IOException {
        String startingUrl = args[0];
        String siteString = args[1];
        WebSurveyor ws = new
                      WebSurveyor(startingUrl,siteString);
        Set pset = ws.getPages();
        Enumeration e = pset.elements();
        while (e.hasMoreElements()) {
            WebPage wp = (WebPage) e.nextElement();
            Set badset = wp.getBadLinks();
            if (!badset.isEmpty())
                showBad(wp,badset);
        }
        System.exit(0);
    }
}

class WebPage {

    public WebPage(String url) {
        this.url = url;
    }

    public boolean isBad() throws IOException {
        return isBad(this.url);
    }
```

The annotations at the right of the code read:

- add to set of examined pages and survey its descendants
- Get the pages from this site / For each page:
- if it has bad links show 'em

```
                              //  return a set of all the HTTP HREFs in this web page
                              public Set getLinks() throws IOException {
                                  Set       links = new Set();
create an HttpReader based on our url    HttpReader hr = new HttpReader(url);
read all the HTTP HREFS                  String       link = hr.readLine();
and add them to the links set            while (link!=null) {
                                      links.addElement(link);
                                      link = hr.readLine();
                                  }
                                  return links;
                              }

                              //  return a set of all the HTTP HREFs in this web page that are bad links
                              public Set getBadLinks() throws IOException {
                                  Set    links = new Set();
                                  HttpReader hr = new HttpReader(url);
                                  String  link = hr.readLine();
                                  while (link!=null) {
only add bad URLs get added to links        if (isBad(link))
                                          links.addElement(link);
                                      link = hr.readLine();
                                  }
                                  return links;
                              }

                              public String getURL() {
                                  return url;
                              }

                              private boolean isBad(String url) throws IOException {
                                  URL u = new URL(url);
                                  HttpURLConnection uC =
                                              (HttpURLConnection) u.openConnection();
                                  int responseCode = uC.getResponseCode();
                                  return responseCode>=300;
                              }

                              private String url;

                              public static void main(String[] a) {
create a WebPage object           WebPage  wp = new WebPage(a[0]);
get the page's links              Set       links = wp.getLinks();
                                  Enumeration  e = links.elements();
print them all out                while (e.hasMoreElements())
                                      System.out.println(wp.getURL()+
                                              " has this link: "+
                                              e.nextElement());
                                  }
                              }

                              class WebReader {
                                  public WebReader(String url) throws IOException {
                                      URL            u = new URL(url);
```

```
            InputStream ins = u.openStream();
            InputStreamReader   isr = new InputStreamReader(ins);
            br = new BufferedReader(isr);
        }

    public String readLine() throws IOException {
        return br.readLine();
    }

    private BufferedReader br;
}

class HttpReader {
    public HttpReader(String urlString) throws IOException {
        lr = new LinkReader(urlString);
    }

    //  return the next HTTP HREF in complete URL form
    public String readLine() throws IOException {
        String line = lr.readLine();
        while (line!=null &&
            ! (line.toUpperCase().indexOf("HTTP:")==1       keep reading HREFs
            || isHTML(line)))                                until no more data or
            line = lr.readLine();                            an HTTP HREF is found
        return line;
    }

    private static boolean isSuffix(String s, String suffix) {
            return s.lastIndexOf(suffix)==
                                s.length()-suffix.length();
    }
    private static boolean isHTML(String url) {
            return isSuffix(url, ".html")
                                || isSuffix(url, ".htm");
    }

    private LinkReader lr;
}

class LinkReader {
    public LinkReader(String urlString) throws IOException {
        hr = new HrefReader(urlString);
        url = new URL(urlString);
        host = url.getHost();
        resource = url.getFile();                this is the pathname for this url
        directory = null;
        parentDirectory = null;
        int   k = resource.lastIndexOf("/");
        if (k!=-1) {                             k marks the last /
            directory = resource.substring(0,k); the directory goes up to the last /
            k = directory.lastIndexOf("/");
            if (k!=-1) {                         now k marks the second to last /
                parentDirectory = resource.substring(0,k);
                parentDirectory = parentDirectory.concat("/");
            }
```

```
                        directory = directory.concat("/");
                    }
                    port = url.getPort();
                    protocol = url.getProtocol();
                }

            public String readLine() throws IOException {
                String    link;
                link = hr.readLine();
                if (link==null)
                    return null;

                int k = link.indexOf("://");
                if (k!=-1)
                    if (link.substring(k+3).indexOf("/")==-1)
                        return link+"/";
                    else
                        return link;

                k = link.indexOf(":");
                if (k!=-1 && link.substring(0,k).indexOf(".")==-1)
                    return link;

                if (link.length()>=2 &&
                                link.substring(0,2).equals(".."))
                    return protocol
                            + "://"
                        + host + parentDirectory +
                            link.substring(3);

                if (link.length()>=1 && link.substring(0,1).
                                                equals("/"))
                    return protocol
                            + "://" + host + link;

                return protocol + "://" + host + directory + link;
            }

            private HrefReader hr;           // The HrefReader to read HREFs from
            private URL        url;          // The URL of this page
            private String     host,         // The host portion of this URL
                               resource,     // The resource portion of this URL
                               protocol,     // The protocol portion of this URL
                               directory,    // The resource's directory
                               parentDirectory; // The directory of the
                                                //   resource's directory
            private int        port;         // The port number of this URL
        }

        class HrefReader {
```

of form: prot://host•••
of form: prot://host

of form: prot://host/•••

check for mailto:, telnet: and so on

reference to resource in
parent directory?

full path reference to resource
on same host?

assume reference to resource
in same directory

```
public HrefReader(String url) throws IOException {
   tr = new TagReader(url);
}

//  return index of HREF href HrEf and so on in s
private int hrefIndex(String s) {
   return s.toUpperCase().indexOf("HREF");
}

//  return the largest prefix of s that does not contain x— with spaces trimmed
private String trimFrom(String s, String x) {
   int k = s.indexOf(x);
   if (k!=-1)
      return s.substring(0,k).trim();
   else
      return s.trim();
}

//  return the largest suffix of s that does not contain x— with spaces trimmed
private String trimUpThrough(String s, String x) {
   int k = s.indexOf(x);
   if (k!=-1)
      return s.substring(k+x.length()).trim();
   else
      return s.trim();
}

public String readLine() throws IOException {
   String   tag;
   tag = tr.readLine();
   while (tag!=null && hrefIndex(tag)==-1)   get a tag with an HREF in it
      tag = tr.readLine();
   if (tag==null)
      return null;

   int   k = hrefIndex(tag);
   tag = tag.substring(k+1).trim();          eliminate chars before HREF
   tag = trimUpThrough(tag,"=");             eliminate chars through 1st =
   tag = trimFrom(tag," ");                  eliminate chars from 1st embedded space

   if (tag.indexOf("\"")!=-1) {              eliminate chars before and
      tag = trimUpThrough(tag,"\"");         after double quotes (including ")
      tag = trimFrom(tag,"\"");
   }

   if (tag.indexOf("'")!=-1) {               eliminate chars before and
      tag = trimUpThrough(tag,"'");          after single quotes (including ')
      tag = trimFrom(tag,"'");
   }
```

```
                        tag = trimFrom(tag,"#");
                        return trimFrom(tag,"?");
                }

                private TagReader tr;              // The TagReader to read tags from
        }

        class TagReader {
                public TagReader(String url) throws IOException {
                        wr = new WebReader(url);
                        line = null;
                }

                public String readLine() throws IOException {
                        if (line==null)
                                line = wr.readLine();
                        while (line!=null && line.indexOf("<")==-1)
                                line = wr.readLine();
                        if (line==null)
                                return null;

                        int k = line.indexOf(">");
                        if (k!=-1 && k<line.indexOf("<"))
                                line = line.substring(k+1);
                        String nextLine = wr.readLine();
                        while (nextLine!=null && line.indexOf(">")==-1) {
                                line = line.concat(nextLine);
                                nextLine = wr.readLine();
                        }
                        if (nextLine!=null)
                                line = line.concat(nextLine);
                        if (line.indexOf(">")==-1)
                                return null;

                        int   tagStart = line.indexOf("<");
                        int   tagEnd   = line.indexOf(">");
                        if (tagStart<0 || tagEnd<0 || tagStart>tagEnd)
                                System.err.println("Bad angle brackets: "+line);
                        String      tag = line.substring(tagStart+1,tagEnd);
                        line = line.substring(tagEnd+1);
                        return tag;
                }

                private String line;       // The unprocessed part of the most recent line
                                           //    read from wr
                private WebReader wr;      // The WebReader to read lines from
        }
```

Search for a line from the web page that has a < in it— a tag beginning

Search for a > — a tag end

Keep concatenating lines until > is found

Get the positions of < and >

Check positions

Isolate tag
line is what remains
after the tag

12.4 The Game of Mancala

Mancala is an ancient African board game that has enjoyed a recent revival. It is a two-player game with fairly simple rules that allow for some interesting tactical and strategic play. A typical game takes from 5 to 15 minutes.

12.4.1 The Rules of Mancala

Mancala is played with a wooden board and stones, often brightly colored. The board contains two opposing rows of six *pits*, bordered by a larger pit at each end, known as a *mancala*. The pits along the bottom of the board together with the mancala to the right belong to one player, whom we shall call player 0; the pits along the top together with the left mancala belong to player 1. (See Figure 12.12.)

The game can be described in terms of its initial board setup; the basic movement of the players; and the ways in which an extra turn is gained, stones are captured, and the game terminates:

- **Initial board setup**—Each pit on the board is filled with four stones. The mancalas are empty. (See Figure 12.13.)
- **Basic movement**—Players alternate picking up the contents of one of their playing pits and moving in a counterclockwise direction, dropping one stone in each pit, including their own mancala. No stone is dropped in the opposing player's mancala. For example, given the board position in Figure 12.14, if player 1 moves, the resulting board is illustrated in Figure 12.15.
- **Getting an extra turn**—If the last stone is dropped into the moving player's mancala, that player gets to move again. Continuing play from the board position of Figure 12.15, player 0 now moves, choosing the indicated pit. The result is the position shown in Figure 12.16.

Player 1

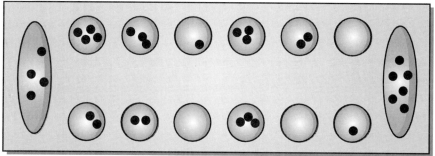

Player 0

FIGURE 12.12 A typical Mancala board with a game in progress. The six pits on the top along with the large mancala on the left belong to player 1. The other pits and mancala belong to player 0.

FIGURE 12.13 The board set up for play. At the beginning of the game each playing pit contains four stones and the mancalas are empty.

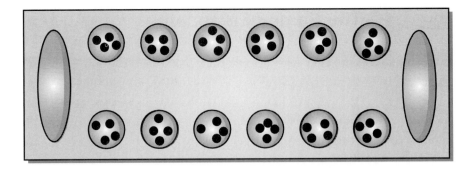

FIGURE 12.14 A sample board position, illustrating the rules of movement. It is now player 1's move. In this illustration, player 1 selects the pit marked with an X.

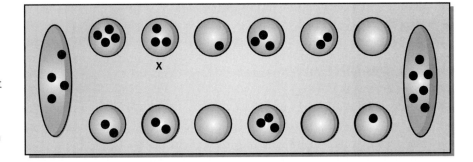

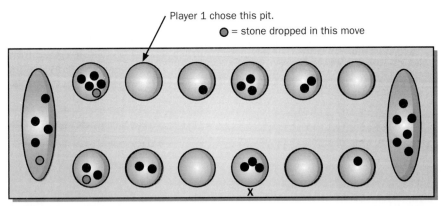

FIGURE 12.15 Basic movement. Player 1 takes the stones from one of her pits and, moving counterclockwise, drops them one at a time into pits. Although a stone is dropped into the moving player's mancala (as seen here), the opposing player's mancala would be skipped. Now it is player 0's move. Player 0 selects the pit marked with an X.

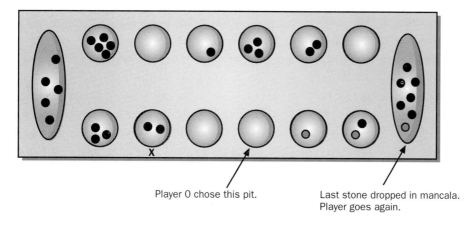

Player 0 chose this pit.

Last stone dropped in mancala.
Player goes again.

⬤ = stone dropped in this move

**FIGURE 12.16
Getting an extra
turn.** If the last
stone is dropped
into one's own
manacala, that
player gets to move
again. Player 0
therefore goes
again, this time
selecting the pit
marked X.

- **Capturing stones**—If the last stone is dropped into an empty playing pit
  belonging to the moving player, any stones in the opposing playing pit of
  the other player are moved to the moving player's mancala. Continuing
  play from Figure 12.16, player 0 moves again. The result is the position of
  Figure 12.17.

Stones captured from this pit

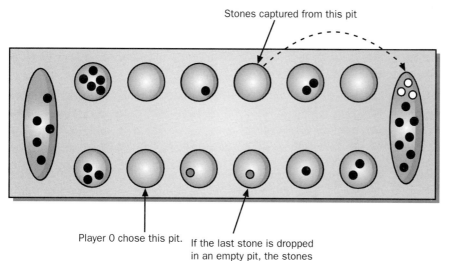

Player 0 chose this pit.

If the last stone is dropped
in an empty pit, the stones
are captured.

**FIGURE 12.17 Cap-
turing stones.** If the
last stone is dropped
into an empty pit
belonging to the mov-
ing player, any
stones in the oppos-
ing player's pit are
captured and placed
into the moving
player's mancala.

⬤ = stone dropped in this move

◯ = stone captured

Player 1 moves.

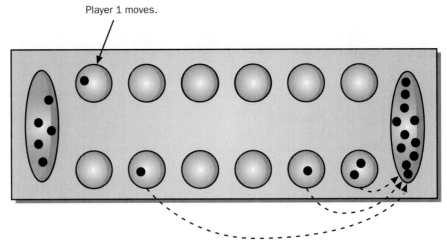

FIGURE 12.18 Ending the game. When one player has no stones left, the game is over. Any stones remaining in the opposing player's pits are moved into that player's mancala, the stones counted, and the winner announced.

After the move, Player 1 has no more stones, so the stones remaining in Player 0's pits are moved into Player 0's mancala. The game is over.

- **Ending the game**—When no stones are left in one player's playing pits, the game is over. Any stones left in the opposing player's pits are placed into that player's mancala. In Figure 12.18, player 1 is about to move her last stone into her mancala, after which her playing pits are all empty. The stones remaining in player 0's pits are then moved into his mancala. The stones in the player's mancalas are now counted, and the player with the most stones is the winner.

12.4.2 A Mancala-Playing Program

In the rest of this section we develop a program that plays the game of Mancala.

Statement of the Problem   Implement the game of Mancala.

Scenario   To describe the moves in a board game—either for the purpose of recording the game or to input a move into a computer—some form of notation is needed.

We will identify our players by their numbers: 0 and 1. We label the pits by their distance from the player's mancala (see Figure 12.19).

If we use this notation, a mancala may be identified by the player to which it belongs and a pit by the player and pit number. Making a move in Mancala boils down to selecting a pit to move from. After that is done, the rest of the move is completely determined. Therefore, a player may specify a move

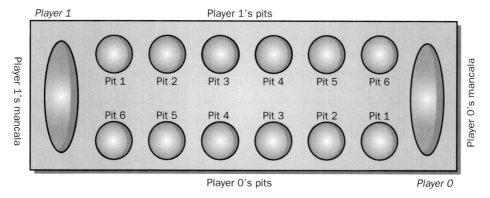

FIGURE 12.19   A pit numbering scheme. In order to identify the pits, we assign each a number corresponding to its distance from the associated player's mancala.

by identifying the pit. That, together with the player's number, is sufficient to specify the move.

Our implementation uses `System.out` and therefore displays the board in the textual manner displayed in Figure 12.20. A graphical display similar to the diagrams above is developed in the GUI supplement to the chapter.

We will not bother displaying the pit numbers because it would require an extra two lines that would clutter up the `System.out` display.

Finding the Primary Objects   One of the reasons games make such good examples for an object-oriented language is the concrete nature of the objects. In Mancala, we have the board, pits, stones, and players, and we expect to have classes corresponding to each of these:

- `Player` class
- `MancalaBoard` class

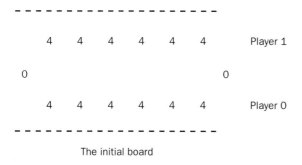

The initial board

FIGURE 12.20   A textual representation of the Mancala board. The board is represented by a display of the number of stones in each pit and mancala.

- `Pit` class
- `Stone` class

The primary objects seem to be the players and the board. Pits and stones are part of the board and are thus subsidiary to it.

Defining the Behavior—An Overview   The `Player` class models a real-life player. In contrast, the `MancalaBoard` models an inanimate object that possesses no real behavior. In real life, the board is a passive object. The players make their moves upon it, but the board itself does nothing. Similarly, the pit is another real-life object that possesses no behavior of its own.

Associated with these inanimate objects is information that must be maintained. However, it is not obvious which class has the responsibility for this information. For example, what class keeps track of the number of stones in each pit? As a player moves from pit to pit dropping stones, what class determines the next pit to drop a stone in? How do the players know whose turn it is? What class is responsible for counting the stones and declaring the winner at the end of the game?

It is possible to design a version of our game in which the only class with real behavior is the player class, so that behavior in the game corresponds to the truly active objects in real life. However, this approach places the entire burden of the game's implementation—maintaining the board, determining who goes next, when to end, and so on—on this class. Rather than using this approach, we instead provide the other objects with some degree of behavior. In this approach, player objects don't have to deal with all aspects of the game. If we assign useful behavior to the various objects, the individual classes become simpler to design and implement, and so does the entire application.

For example, while a pit in real life possesses no behavior, we can create a `Pit` class that models an "intelligent" pit. Appropriate methods (behavior) for this class would include adding stones, returning the number of stones in the pit, and removing the stones from the pit.

This is really not as strange as it seems. In fact, we encountered this concept of assigning intelligent behavior to inanimate objects back in Chapter 2 when we first looked at `String`s and their methods. We introduced the notion of *smart and helpful objects* that are provided useful behavior to make it easier for users to work with them. While in real life one would not speak of requesting a string to reveal its length, having a `length` method in class `String` places the responsibility of maintaining that information squarely where it logically belongs, in the implementation of the `String` object.

Viewed in this manner, behavior is *not* assigned on the basis of what occurs in the analogous real-world situation; it also depends upon which class is best suited to be responsible for maintaining that behavior. It is for this reason that object-oriented programming is often called **responsibility-driven programming.** Much of the design of an application hinges upon determining a proper distribution of responsibility among the various classes in the system. Once responsibility for some form of behavior has been delegated to a class, users of that class should be able to rely upon that behavior, while at the same time ignoring its implementation. The appropriate model is then not necessarily the one that most closely mirrors the real-world application, but rather the one in which responsibility has been assigned so that the resulting software system is the most understandable.

A useful technique to aid in the design of intelligent models of normally inanimate objects is to imagine an automated version of the application. In our case, imagine an electronic Mancala game you might buy in an electronics boutique at the mall. Such a game might consist of the basic board, augmented with some controlling buttons as seen in Figure 12.21.

In this scenario, the board is no longer a passive object, but possesses some degree of behavior. The move buttons light up to indicate that it is the human player's turn to move. While it is the player that selects the move, it is the electronic board that actually carries it out, making the necessary changes to the pits and mancalas according to the rules of the game. If the player gets to move again, the buttons remain lit. At the end of the game, the stones are emptied into the appropriate mancala and the proper winner light lit.

The usefulness of thinking of the game in this manner is that the electronic version is also a model that must address many of the same issues as our software solution. Working with such a concrete model often helps us construct our software model.

A Controlling Class   The electronic Mancala board has a number of responsibilities: it carries out the actual moves, keeps track of the pits and mancalas, determines whose turn it is, determines when the game is over, and announces the winner. These responsibilities roughly fall into two basic categories: board maintenance and refereeing, or controlling the flow of the game:

- Board maintenance
    - Carrying out moves
    - Keeping track of pits

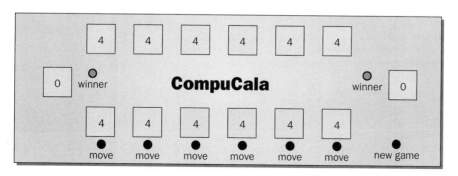

FIGURE 12.21   An electronic version of Mancala. Imagining an automated version of Mancala aids us in creating our own software model.

- Referee (game control)
  - Determining whose turn it is
  - Determining the winner
  - Keeping track of the players

The first of these categories corresponds to the `MancalaBoard` class that we introduced earlier. The second category defines the responsibilities of an additional class that we need: a controlling class that we call `MancalaGame`. Our initial set of classes then becomes

- `MancalaGame` class
- `Player` class
- `MancalaBoard` class
- `Pit` class
- `Stone` class

We now proceed to develop the classes.

Defining the Behavior of Class `MancalaGame`   Our controlling class's behavior controls the play of the game: the move-by-move action, determining the end of the game, and the winner. We will have a single method, `play`, which we invoke to begin game play and terminate when the game is over.

- `MancalaGame`—constructor
- `play`—begin game play

Defining the Interface of Class `MancalaGame`   Let us provide some sample usage code. We decide to allow any combination of human and computer players. Furthermore, we identify human players with their names:

<table>
<tr><td>Arrow (player 0) vs
computer (player 1)</td><td>

```
MancalaGame game =
         new MancalaGame("Arrow", null);
game.play();      ◄——— Play the game.
```

</td></tr>
</table>

We need to provide the names of the players, to the `MancalaGame` constructor. We adopt the convention that a `null` argument indicates the corresponding player is to be the computer. Thus:

<table>
<tr><td>Two human players—
Arrow vs. Weiss</td><td>

```
MancalaGame game1 =
         new MancalaGame("Arrow", "Weiss");
```

</td></tr>
<tr><td>Arrow (player 0) vs.
computer (player 1)</td><td>

```
MancalaGame game2 =
         new MancalaGame("Arrow", null);
```

</td></tr>
<tr><td>Computer (player 0) vs.
Arrow (player 1)</td><td>

```
MancalaGame game3 =
         new MancalaGame(null, "Arrow");
```

</td></tr>
</table>

```
MancalaGame game4 =
        new MancalaGame(null, null);  Computer vs. computer
```

Because the game is keeping track of the players and board, no additional information need be provided to the `play` method. The code is therefore as follows:

```
class MancalaGame {
    public MancalaGame(String player0Name,
                       String player1Name)
    public void play();
    ...
}
```

Defining the Instance Variables of Class `MancalaGame` A Mancala game consists of a board and two players. We use a `MancalaBoard` variable and an array of two `Player` objects. To keep track of the player who is currently moving, we introduce an `int` variable, `currentPlayer`, whose value alternates between 0 and 1 and represents the index of the current player in our `players` array:

```
class MancalaGame {
    ...
    private MancalaBoard board;
    private Player [] players;
    private int currentPlayer;
}
```

Implementing the Methods of Class `MancalaGame` The constructor must create the board and the `Player` array, and must initialize `currentPlayer`. (We choose player 0 as the one to make the first move.) It must also create two `Player` objects, providing these with their names and player number:

```
public MancalaGame(String name0, String name1) {
    board = new MancalaBoard();  ◀——— Creates board
    board.setUpForPlay();        ◀——— Fills up the board with stones
    players = new Player[2];
    players[0] = new Player(name0, 0);
    players[1] = new Player(name1, 1);
    currentPlayer = 0;
}
```

The `play` method provides the basic move-by-move behavior: deciding who moves next, sending a message to the appropriate player to make a move, checking if the game is over, and end-of-game processing.

The basic move-by-move play consists of getting the next move from the current player. We accomplish this task by sending a message to the current player object, passing it the board so that it can make its decision. The selected pit number is returned as the chosen move:

```
int pitNum = players[currentPlayer].selectAMove(board);
```

The `board` object is then sent a `doTheMove` message to carry out the selected move. Whether the current player goes again is an outcome of the move, so the board's `doTheMove` method returns a `boolean` value indicating whether the current player goes again. If not, we switch to the other player, as shown:

```
boolean goAgain = board.doTheMove(currentPlayer, pitNum);
if (!goAgain)                         If the current player does not go again,
    if (currentPlayer == 0)           switch to the other player.
        currentPlayer = 1;
    else
        currentPlayer = 0;
```

As usual, in the course of developing our primary object's class, `Mancal-aGame`, we are setting up the required behavior for our subsidiary classes, `Player` and `MancalaBoard`.

The movement of the players is repeated until the game is over, a situation determined by the board's configuration (no stones remaining in one of the player's mancalas), and thus it is the responsibility of the `MancalaBoard` class. It must provide a `gameOver` predicate method to indicate when the game is over. The resulting move-by-move play is:

```
while (!board.gameOver()) {
    int move = players[currentPlayer].makeAMove(board);
    boolean goAgain = board.doTheMove(currentPlayer, move);
    if (!goAgain)                         If the current player does not go again,
        if (currentPlayer == 0)           switch to the other player.
            currentPlayer = 1;
        else
            currentPlayer = 0;
}
```

Once the game is over, any remaining stones are emptied into the proper mancala. This action, again, is accomplished by sending a message to the board object:

```
board.emptyStonesIntoMancalas();
```

Finally, the stones in the mancalas are counted and the winner declared. We require a `MancalaBoard` method, `stonesInMancala`, that returns the number of stones in the mancala of the specified player.

```
if (board.stonesInMancala(0) > board.stonesInMancala(1))
    System.out.println(players[0].getName()+" wins");
```

```
else if (board.stonesInMancala(0) <
        board.stonesInMancala(1))
    System.out.println(players[1].getName()+" wins");
else
    System.out.println("Tie");
```

During the course of the game, we must display the state of the game to the human player. We do this through a helper method, `display`. This method is not part of the specified external behavior of the class—it will only be invoked from within the `play` method. This display method is different from the `display` method of the `Turtle` class of the last example; there the user of the `Turtle` class decided when to display the turtle's world. After we have incorporated the `display` method and a couple of other descriptive messages, the complete `play` method becomes:

```
public void play() throws IOException {
    display();                                    Display initial board
    while (!board.gameOver()) {
        int pitNum =
                players[currentPlayer].selectAMove(board);   The player chooses the move.
        boolean goAgain = board.doTheMove(currentPlayer,
                                    pitNum);       ◄── It is then carried out by the
                                                       board.
        System.out.println("Player " + currentPlayer +
                        " moved from " + pitNum);
        display();      Display the resulting board.
        if (!goAgain)  ◄───────────────  If the current player does not go again,
            if (currentPlayer == 0)      switch to the other player.
                currentPlayer = 1;
            else
                currentPlayer = 0;
        else
            System.out.println("Player " + currentPlayer +
                            " goes again");
    }
    board.emptyStonesIntoMancalas();     Game is over—have board
                                         empty stones,

    display();                           display final board,
    if (board.stonesInMancala(0) >
            board.stonesInMancala(1))
        System.out.println(players[0].getName()+" wins");   announce winner.
    else if (board.stonesInMancala(0) <
            board.stonesInMancala(1))
        System.out.println(players[1].getName()+" wins");
    else
        System.out.println("Tie");
}
```

The `display` method displays the state of the game: the current state of the board, the player's information, and an identification of the current player. Although the method is somewhat detailed, its primary concern is a proper formatting of the textual version of the board presented in the scenario. Because the board display makes the first and greatest impression, it is important to get its appearance correct. However, if you want to see the rest of the development of the game and don't want to get bogged down in formatting issues, you can skip the next subsection and come back to it later.

Formatting the Board Display The display consists of a mancala line displaying the contents of the two mancalas, and two pit lines, one per player. Each pit line displays the contents of the player's pits and the player's number and name. An arrow acts as a turn indicator, showing whose turn it is. A top and bottom border separate our board display from any other output. (Figure 12.22).

The primary formatting challenge is the proper spacing of the mancala line, in particular making sure player 0's mancala is properly positioned *beyond* the pit line entries. We accomplish this by building a filler string as we output the first pit line. Every time we output a pit, we append a spacer to the filler line. This way, when we are ready to output the mancala line, the appropriate spacing has been set up.

The only other interesting item is that we must display player 0's pits *in reverse.* The pits are numbered by their distance from the mancala, so the first of player 0's pits that should be printed is pit 6.

We introduce a second helper method, `displayPlayer`, to handle the player information. We also require another `MancalaBoard` method,

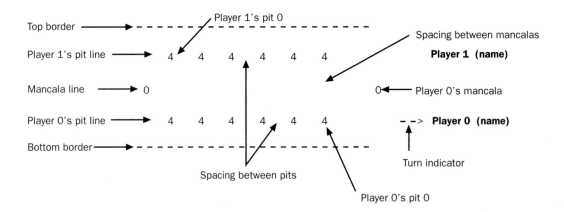

FIGURE 12.22 **The elements of the board.** To help us format the board, we analyze the relationships between the various display elements.

stonesInPits, that returns the number of stones in the specified pit of the specified player.

Here is the code to handle the board display:

```
private void display() {
    String mancalaLineFiller = "";       // Used to properly separate
                                         //     the mancala line
    System.out.println("----------------------");   Top border


    //  Player 1's pit line
    System.out.print(" ");                        // Space past mancala entry.
    for (int i = 1; i <= board.playingPits; i++) {
        System.out.print(board.stonesInPit(1, i) + " ");    Print pits contents +
                                                            pit spacing.

        mancalaLineFiller += " ";      Build mancala
                                       spacing string.
    }
    displayPlayer(1);    Player 1 info

    //  Mancala line
    System.out.print(board.stonesInMancala(1) + " ");     Print player 1's manacala
                                                          and spacing.

    System.out.print(mancalaLineFiller);                  Spaces past pit entries
    System.out.println(board.stonesInMancala(0));         Print player 0's
                                                          mancala.

    //  Player 0's pit line
    System.out.print("    ");
    for (int i = board.playingPits; i >= 1; i--)
                                                  Print player 0's pits in
                                                  reverse!

        System.out.print(board.stonesInPit(0, i) + " ");    Print pit's contents and
                                                            spacing.

    displayPlayer(0);    Player 0 info
    System.out.println("----------------------");   Bottom border

}

private void displayPlayer(int playerNum) {
    if (currentPlayer == playerNum)
                                                    If it this player's turn,
                                                    display turn indicator
        System.out.print("       -->");
    else
        System.out.print("          ");
                                                  or display equal number
                                                  spaces otherwise.


    System.out.println("Player " + playerNum + "( " +      player info
                  players[playerNum].getName() + ")");
}
```

turn indicator

This completes our implementation of the `MancalaGame` controlling class. The full class listing is presented, along with the rest of the application at the very end of the example.

12.4.3   The Player Class

Defining the Behavior of Class `Player`   The `Player` class is responsible for selecting moves. We have already seen that selecting a move is different from actually making one. The former involves examining the possible moves and making an intelligent decision based on strategy; the latter merely modifies the board in consequence of the decision—no strategy is required. Although the player could be responsible for both selecting and making the move, we introduced the `MancalaBoard` class whose responsibility is the maintenance of the board and also carrying out the actual moves.

The `MancalaGame` class displays the players' names as part of the board display and naming the winner. Even though the `MancalaGame` class could keep track of the player's names, that information is more properly maintained in the `Player` class and supplied when requested. The resulting behavior of `Player` is as follows:

- constructor
- getName
- selectAMove

Defining the Interface of Class `Player`   As we will be maintaining the player's name, we pass that information to the constructor. This name is what is returned in response to a `getName` method invocation.

When selecting a move, the player must be able to examine the board, which is therefore passed as an argument. The return value of `selectAMove` is the pit number that the player has chosen for the move:

```
class Player {
    public Player(String name) {...}
    public String getName() {...}
    public int selectAMove(MancalaBoard board) {...}
    ...
}
```

Defining the Instance Variables of Class `Player`   A `Player` object maintains the name passed to the constructor.

```
class Player {
    ...
    // Instance variables
```

```
        private String name;  // null for computer player
}
```

The board need not be maintained. Its current state is passed as an argument to the `selectAMove` method.

Implementing the Methods of Class `Player` The constructor assigns the passed name to the corresponding instance variable:

```
public Player(String name,  int  playerNum) {
    this.name = name;
}
```

Method `getName` is a straightforward query method. If the supplied name was `null`, the `String "Computer"` is returned:

```
public String getName() {
    if (name != null)
        return name;
    else
        return "Computer";
}
```

The `selectAMove` method requires the player to return the number of the selected pit. If the player is human, a prompt is displayed, and the pit number input from the keyboard and returned:

```
if (name != null) {                         // Human player, not the computer
        BufferedReader br =
           new BufferedReader(new
                     InputStreamReader(System.in));
        System.out.print("Enter a pit to move from: ");
        System.out.flush();
        int pitNum = Integer.parseInt(br.readLine());   read the move
}
```

Otherwise, we must calculate a move. We could simply choose the first nonempty pit; however, this would not result in a very interesting game. Instead, we will try to apply some rules to determine a good move. A rule used by an application to aid in the making of a seemingly intelligent decision is known in computer game-playing as a **heuristic.** By setting up a rich enough set of rules we can provide a program with what seems to be intelligence.

The first step in constructing a heuristic is to determine what constitutes a "good" move. In the long term, a good move is one that leads to a win, no matter what the other player does (that is, actually a best move). It is conceivably possible to look far enough ahead in the game to obtain this kind of information, but this strategy is quite time-consuming. A discussion of this approach is beyond the scope of this book.

If we don't follow a move's consequences all the way to the end of a game, how do we tell if it is a good one? One way is to assign a numerical value to the state of the game—in our case, the board—so that the higher the value, the better the position. The value we will use is the number of stones in the player's mancala; after all, the player with the most stones wins.

We focus only on the effect of the current player's move. We try each possible move and examine the result. There are several possible results to a move (in increasing order of desirability):

- No stones are added to our mancala. This occurs when there are insufficient stones to reach our mancala and no capture is possible. This move is the worst choice for our heuristic. (Note that a more sophisticated heuristic might use this move, for example, if our next move could perform a large capture.)
- One stone is added to our mancala because we reach it but we continue on to the opposing player's side. The opposing player now gets to move.
- The last stone is dropped into our mancala. Again, we obtain only a single additional stone. However, we get to move again, so we rank this higher than the previous move.
- Multiple stones are added to our mancala. This result occurs when we manage to capture one of our opponent's pits. The more stones the better.

By considering the best move to be the one that adds the most stones to our mancala, we automatically choose any move that captures the opponents stones.

We proceed by trying out each possible move.

```
for (int pitNum = 1; pitNum <= board.playingPits; pitNum++) {
    Try the move resulting from selecting pitNum.
}
```

To try a move without disturbing the actual board, we make a copy of the board. This introduces the need for a makeACopy method in the Mancala-Board class.

```
MancalaBoard testBoard = board.makeACopy()   Make a copy of the board.
```

We pass our attempted move to the copied MancalaBoard object and examine the result. If our mancala accumulated more stones as a result of this move than any other so far, this move becomes our best one. This strategy is a variation of our *finding extremes* pattern. If this move allows us to go again, we keep track of that as well, in case there is no capturing move (for example, as might occur at the very beginning of the game).

In order to send the `doTheMove` message to the `board` object, and also to get the number of stones in our mancala, we need to know our player number. We could obtain this information by having it passed to `selectThe-Move` as an argument by the invoking method (`play` in class `MancalaGame`, which does know the player numbers). However, using an argument similar to the one which caused us to maintain the name, we decide to maintain the player number as well, which results in an additional instance variable, `playerNum` for the `Player` class. Here is the next part of our `selectAMove` method:

```
boolean goAgain = testBoard.doTheMove(playerNum, pitNum);
```
Try the move on the board copy.

```
if (goAgain)
    repeatMove = pitNum;
```
If move allows us to go again remember it.

```
int newStones = testBoard.stonesInMancala(playerNum) -

             board.stonesInMancala(playerNum);
if (newStones > maxNewStones) {
    maxNewStones = newStones;
    bestMove = pitNum;
}
```
See how many stones this move added to our mancala.

More stones than so far?
Remember how many and the move.

When all moves have been tried, we choose the best one. Again, the one that performs a multistone capture is best; second best is a move that allows the player to go again. In the absence of either of these cases, we simply choose the last move tried that added 1 (or at worst 0) stones to the mancala. Our choice is then returned as our move.

By initializing `maxNewStones` to -1, we guarantee that even if no move reaches the mancala or causes a "go again," a best move is still chosen. That is because, at the very minimum, the number of stones added to a mancala is 0; this number will cause that move to be selected as the best move so far, if `maxNewStones` has the value -1.

```
int bestMove = -1;
int repeatMove = -1;
int maxNewStones = -1;
```
No best move initially.
No go again move.
No move has added stones to the mancala.

```
// Trying the possible moves
for (int pitNum = 1; pitNum <= board.playingPits;
     pitNum++) {
    if (board.stonesInPit(playerNum, pitNum) != 0) {
```
Only nonempty pits may be moved from.

```
        MancalaBoard testBoard = board.makeACopy();
```
Make a copy of the board.

```
        boolean goAgain = testBoard.doTheMove(playerNum,
                                     pitNum);
```
Try the move on the board copy.

```
    if (goAgain)
        repeatMove = pitNum;
    int newStones =
```
If move allows us to go again, remember it.

See how many stones this move added to our mancala.

```
            testBoard.stonesInMancala(playerNum) -
            board.stonesInMancala(playerNum);

    if (newStones > maxNewStones) {
        maxNewStones = newStones;
        bestMove = pitNum;

    }
  }
}
```
More stones than so far? Remember how many. Remember the move.

```
// Tried all possibilities, return the best one
if (maxNewStones > 1)
```
maxNewStones > 1 means a multistone capture occurred

```
    return bestMove;
else if (repeatMove != -1)
```
Barring that, use a "go again".

```
    return repeatMove;
else
    return bestMove;
```
1 or possibly 0 stones added; oh well!

The complete implementation of selectAMove follows. The throws IOException is necessary because we are performing data input in the non-computer player logic:

```
public int selectAMove(MancalaBoard board)
                                throws IOException {
    if (name != null) {
```
Real player, not the computer

```
        DataInputStream ds = new
                    DataInputStream(System.in);
        System.out.print("Enter a pit to move from: ");
        System.out.flush();
```
Read the move
```
        int pitNum = Integer.parseInt(ds.readLine());
        return pitNum;
    }

    // Computer player—need to determine best move
    int bestMove = -1;
    int repeatMove = -1;
    int maxNewStones = -1;
```
No best move initially
No go again move.
No move has added stones to the mancala.

```
    // Trying the possible moves
    for (int pitNum = 1; pitNum <= board.playingPits;
        pitNum++) {
```
Only nonempty pits may be moved from
```
        if (board.stonesInPit(playerNum, pitNum) != 0) {
```
Make a copy of the board.
```
            MancalaBoard testBoard = board.makeACopy();
```

```
        boolean goAgain = testBoard.doTheMove(playerNum,
                                     pitNum);
    if (goAgain)
        repeatMove = pitNum;
    int newStones =
            testBoard.stonesInMancala(playerNum) -
            board.stonesInMancala(playerNum);

    if (newStones > maxNewStones) {

        maxNewStones = newStones;

        bestMove = pitNum;

    }
   }
  }

// Tried all possibilities, return the best one
if (maxNewStones > 1)

    return bestMove;
else if (repeatMove != -1)
    return repeatMove;
else
    return bestMove;
}
```

Try the move on the board copy.

If move allows us to go again, remember it.

See how many stones this move added to our mancala.

More stones than so far?

Remember how many and the move.

maxNewStones > 1 means a multistone capture occurred.

Barring that, use a "go again".

1 or possibly 0 stones added; oh well!

The full class implementation, including the `Player` constructor, modified to include the `playerNum` instance variable is presented at the end of the example.

12.4.4 The Mancala Board Class

Defining the Behavior of Class `MancalaBoard` The behavior required of the `MancalaBoard` class arose as a result of implementing the `Mancala-Game` and `Player` classes, as often occurs when a class models an intelligent version of an inanimate object. Since the primary purpose of supplying a class with intelligence is to relieve the other classes of the burden of maintaining it, its behavior is to a large degree dictated by what those other classes would do with the object.

Reviewing our requirements of this class, we come up with the following necessary behavior:

- Constructor
- `gameOver`

- doTheMove
- stonesInPit
- stonesInMancala
- makeACopy

Defining the Interface of Class `MancalaBoard`   A Mancala board is a fixed entity and requires no arguments be passed it for creation. The `gameOver` method returns a `boolean` indicating when one of the players has no stones left in his or her pit.

The `stonesInPit` and `stonesInMancala` each return an `int` corresponding to the number of stones. The first of these requires both a player and pit number to fully identify the pit; the second only requires a player number.

Finally, the `doTheMove` method accepts a selected pit and performs the actual move. Again, the pit must be identified by a player and pit number. The method modifies the receiving object (the board) and returns whether the current player goes again. That is, it returns `true` in the case in which the last stones land in that player's mancala. The resulting interface is

```
class MancalaBoard
    public MancalaBoard() {...}
    public int stonesInMancala(int playerNum) {...}
    public int stonesInPit(int playerNum, int pitNum) {...}
    public MancalaBoard makeACopy() {...}
    public boolean doTheMove(int currentPlayerNum,
                    int chosenPitNum) {...}
    public boolean gameOver() {...}
    public void emptyStonesIntoMancalas() {...}
    ...
}
```

Defining the Instance Variables of Class `MancalaBoard`   The board needs to keep track of the two set of pits as well as the two mancalas. Besides keeping track of the individual pits and their contents, the `MancalaBoard` class must also reflect the *geometry* of the board, that is, the relationship of the pits and mancalas to each other. The geometry includes: the order in which the pits follow each other, which mancala belongs to which player, and so on.

Although the players identify the pits by two values—the player number and the pit number—we will find it easier to simply give each pit a unique number on the board. We start with player 0's mancala, assigning it pit number 0 and assigning sequential numbers in a clockwise fashion (see Figure 12.23). In this scheme, both pits and mancalas are grouped together. We will refer to this as the *internal* numbering scheme because the user does not see it—it is used only within the `MancalaBoard` class to make the board manipulation easier.

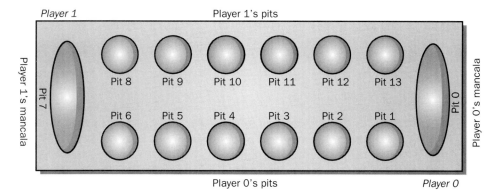

FIGURE 12.23   A second (internal pit-numbering scheme). The pit-numbering scheme introduced in the context of the `MancalaGame` class provided an easy means for the players to identify pits and mancalas. This new scheme reflects the internal board structure and makes it easy for us to implement the various `MancalaBoard` methods.

Our internal numbering assignment is not arbitrary; it reflects the geometry of the pits and simplifies calculation of various board properties such as which player a mancala belongs to and which pits are opposite each other. We will need this information in our implementation of the `doTheMove` method. Our scheme also aids us in the basic movement of moving from pit to pit dropping stones.

One consequence of using a different numbering scheme from the one viewed by the users of this class (classes `Player` and `MancalaGame`) is that we must be able to translate back and forth from one numbering system to the other.

We introduce an array of pits as the instance variable for the class. We also introduce two constants reflecting the number of playing pits per player, as well as the total number of pits on the board; these will prove useful in our calculations:

```
class MancalaBoard {
    ...
    public Pit [] pits;
    public static final int
        playingPits=6,
        totalPits = 2*(playingPits+1);   // Two players, each having
                                         //   one mancala and
                                         //   playing pits
}
```

Notice, by the way, that our decision also implies that we intend to treat pits and mancalas as members of the same class, `Pit`.

Implementing the Methods of Class `MancalaBoard` The constructor creates the `Pit` array and its elements:

```
public MancalaBoard() {
    pits = new Pit[totalPits];
    for (int pitNum = 0; pitNum < totalPits; pitNum++)
        pits[pitNum] = new Pit();
}
```

The `setUpForPlay` method places four stones in each of the playing pits. We use a helper method, `isAMancala`, which we shall write, to avoid putting stones into the mancalas:

```
public void setUpForPlay() {
    for (int pitNum = 0; pitNum < totalPits; pitNum++)
        if (!isAMancala(pitNum))
            pits[pitNum].addStones(4);
}
```

You might object and say that this initialization is properly performed in the `MancalaBoard` constructor, and you would have a legitimate point. However, we have designed the constructor to create a board with *empty* pits to allow for the `makeACopy` method, which we implement next. We therefore break up the creation of the actual board and the filling of the pits with their initial four stones into two methods.

The `makeACopy` method creates and returns a new `MancalaBoard` object whose pits' contents are identical to those of the receiving object. The implementation introduces the need for a `getStones` method for class `Pit`.

```
public MancalaBoard makeACopy() {
    MancalaBoard newBoard = new MancalaBoard();
    for (int pitNum = 0; pitNum < totalPits; pitNum++)
        newBoard.pits[pitNum].addStones(
            this.pits[pitNum].getStones());
    return newBoard;
}
```

Copy stones from pit of original board to corresponding pit of new board ⟶

Had we placed stones in the pits within the constructor, we would have had to remove them from the new board prior to copying the contents of the receiver's pits.

To implement the methods `stonesInMancala` and `stonesInPit` (which accept the user's pit numbering system), we have to be able to translate those into our internal scheme. We introduce a helper method, `getPitNum`, for this purpose. The method first determines the starting point of the specified player's pits: 0 for player 0, 7 for player 1. This is accomplished by the expression:

```
playerNum * (playingPits+1)      0-> 0, 1 -> 7
```

(Recall that the constant `playingPits` corresponds to the pits only. The mancala adds one more.) The proper pit is then `pitNum` distant from the starting point (because that's how we defined the user's pit number):

```
private int getPitNum(int playerNum, int pitNum) {
    return playerNum * (playingPits+1) + pitNum;
}
```

We could use conditionals to perform this transformation, but by using a well-thought-out internal representation we are able to reduce the geometry of the board to a simple arithmetic expression.

There are several other useful helper methods that deal with the pit/mancala/player relationships of the board. We will refer to these methods as they are needed and implement them after we have finished coding the methods comprising the external behavior.

Given our `getPitNum` method, the method `stonesInPit` becomes:

```
public int stonesInPit(int playerNum, int pitNum) {
    return pits[getPitNum(playerNum, pitNum)].getStones();
}
```

The `stonesInMancala` method, which requires only a player number as an argument, uses another helper method, `getMancala`, which returns the pit number of the player's mancala:

```
public int stonesInMancala(int playerNum) {
    return pits[getMancala(playerNum)].getStones();
}
```

Performing the Move The `doTheMove` method accepts a pit specification of player number and player pit number and carries out the move modifying the receiving `MancalaBoard` object. The first thing we do is transform the user's pit specification to our internal numbering scheme and remove the stones from the corresponding pit:

```
int pitNum = getPitNum(currentPlayerNum, chosenPitNum);
int stones = pits[pitNum].removeStones();
```

We then begin dropping these stones into pits. The movement is counter-clockwise, so the pit numbers are descending as we go from pit to pit (see the board diagram). The pits form a circle for the purposes of our movement, so when we get down to pit 0 (player 0's mancala), the next pit is 13 (player 1's pit 6). The code to accomplish this pit-to-pit (circular) movement is as follows:

```
pitNum--;
if (pitNum < 0)
    pitNum = totalPits - 1;
```
If pitNum was 0, it's now −1, in which case set back to highest pit number.

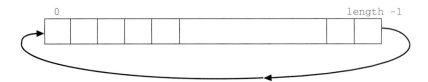

FIGURE 12.24 Working with an array in a circular manner. We can treat an array as a circular structure by returning to the first element after we have reached the last.

This sort of logic occurs quite often when we wish to treat an array as a circular object. When we reach the end, we then continue at the beginning, as shown in Figure 12.24.

We move from pit to pit in this manner, dropping stones in each pit except for the opposing player's mancala. In order to test this condition, we introduce another helper method, `otherPlayerNum`. Given one player's number, `otherPlayerNum` returns the opposing player's number.

> Drop a stone but only if the pit is not the other player's mancala.

```
if (pitNum != getMancala(otherPlayerNum(currentPlayerNum))) {
    pits[pitNum].addStones(1);
    stones--;
}
```

The dropping of stones continues as long as we have stones left:

```
while (stones != 0) {
    pitNum--;
    if (pitNum < 0)
        pitNum = totalPits - 1;

    // Drop a stone but only if the pit is not the other player's mancala.
    if (pitNum !=
            getMancala(otherPlayerNum(currentPlayerNum))) {
        pits[pitNum].addStones(1);
        stones--;
    }
}
```

Once we have finished, we check the final pit in which we dropped a stone. If it is our mancala, the current player gets to go again, and we return `true` as the value of our method.

```
if (pitNum == getMancala(currentPlayerNum))
    return true;
```

Otherwise, we will return `false`; but first we must check if a stone capture has occurred. If the final stone was dropped into an empty pit belonging to the current player, all the stones in the opposite pit of the other player are moved to the current player's mancala. We use a helper method, `ownerOf`, which returns the player number of a specified pit. To determine whether the pit had been empty (prior to dropping the stone in), we test whether there is now exactly one stone in it. To remove the stones from the opposite pit of the other player, we introduce the helper method, `oppositePitNum`, which accepts a pit number and returns the (internal) number of the opposing pit:

```
if (ownerOf(pitNum) == currentPlayerNum &&
        pits[pitNum].getStones() == 1) {
    stones = pits[oppositePitNum(pitNum)].removeStones();
    pits[getMancala(currentPlayerNum)].addStones(stones);
}
return false;
```

> The pit corresponding to pitNum belongs to the current player and contains one stone (therefore previously empty)

The full implementation of the method is as follows:

```
boolean doTheMove(int currentPlayerNum, int chosenPitNum) {
    int pitNum = getPitNum(currentPlayerNum, chosenPitNum);
    int stones = pits[pitNum].removeStones();
    while (stones != 0) {
        pitNum--;
        if (pitNum < 0)
            pitNum = totalPits - 1;
        if (pitNum !=
                getMancala(otherPlayerNum(currentPlayerNum))) {
            pits[pitNum].addStones(1);
            stones--;
        }
    }
    if (pitNum == getMancala(currentPlayerNum))
        return true;
    if (ownerOf(pitNum) == currentPlayerNum &&
            pits[pitNum].getStones() == 1) {
        stones =
                pits[oppositePitNum(pitNum)].removeStones();
        pits[getMancala(currentPlayerNum)].
                addStones(stones);
    }
    return false;
}
```

> Drop a stone, but only if the pit is not the other player's mancala.

> The pit corresponding to pitNum belongs to the current player and contains one stone (therefore previously empty)

The gameOver predicate returns true if one player's pits are all empty. We accomplish this by adding up the stones for each player and testing the result against 0.

```
public boolean gameOver() {
    for (int player = 0; player < 2; player++) {     Test each player.
        int stones = 0;
        for (int pitNum = 1; pitNum <=
                playingPits; pitNum++)
            stones +=
                pits[getPitNum(player, pitNum)].getStones();
        if (stones == 0)     No stones?—game over.
            return true;
    }
    return false;          Both player's have stones—play continues.
}
```

Finally, the emptyStonesIntoMancalas takes any stones in either player's pits and places them into that player's mancala. This method is invoked when the game is over and when only one player has stones remaining in the playing pits. However, it is simpler to write the code so that the pits of both players are emptied—the player whose pits are already empty will not be affected:

```
public void emptyStonesIntoMancalas() {
    for (int player = 0; player < 2; player++)
        for (int pitNum = 0; pitNum <=
                        playingPits; pitNum++) {
            int stones =
             pits[getPitNum(player, pitNum)].removeStones();
            pits[getMancala(player)].addStones(stones);
        }
}
```

The Helper Methods   We now turn to implementing the various helper methods. From the diagram displaying the internal pit number scheme, we see that the mancalas are at 0 and 7 for players 0 and 1, respectively. We can use an expression analogous to the ones we used in getPitNum to transform the player number into the pit number for the corresponding mancala:

```
private int getMancala(int playerNum) {
    return playerNum * (playingPits+1);     0 for player 0, 7 for
                                            player 1
}
```

To determine whether a pit is a mancala simply means testing the pit number against 0 or 7. This test may be performed in a single expression using the `%` (remainder) function:

```
private boolean isAMancala(int pitNum) {
    return pitNum % (playingPits+1) == 0;    true for 0 and 7
}
```

Pits 0 through 6 belong to player 0, while pits 7 through 13 belong to player 1. We can test for those ranges by dividing the pit number by the total pits per player (including the mancala—that's where the +1 comes in):

```
private int ownerOf(int pitNum) {       0 for 0..6
    return pitNum / (playingPits+1);    1 for 7..13
}
```

Examining the board diagram, we see that the numbers of pits that lie opposite each other add up to 14. Thus pit 6 is opposite pit 8, pit 1 is opposite 13, and so on. (This works only for the playing pits and not for the mancalas, but we have no need to find the pit opposite a mancala). This observation directly leads to the following implementation of the `oppositePitNum` method:

```
private int oppositePitNum(int pitNum) {
    return totalPits - pitNum;
}
```

Finally, the `otherPlayerNum` method simply examines the supplied player number and returns the opposing player's number as its value:

```
private int otherPlayerNum(int playerNum) {
    if (playerNum == 0)
        return 1;
    else
        return 0;
}
```

We could have used an arithmetic expression to do this in a single step. We leave that as an exercise.

While most of our helper methods work with pits, we do not place them in the `Pit` class. We make this choice because they actually deal with the geometry of the pit relationships. Pits know of nothing other than the stones within them; in particular, they have no knowledge of their neighboring or opposing pits. That information is the responsibility of the board, and that is why these helper methods properly belong to the `MancalaBoard` class.

12.4.5 The Pit Class

Defining the Behavior of Class `Pit`   Our implementation of the `Mancala-Board` provided us with the required behavior of the `Pit` class:

- Constructor
- `addStones`
- `removeStones`
- `isEmpty`
- `getStones`

Defining the Interface of Class `Pit`   Similarly, we obtain the interface from the requirements of the `MancalaBoard` class.

```
class Pit {
    public Pit() {...}
    public int getStones() {...}
    public void addStones(int stones) {...}
    public boolean isEmpty() {...}
    public int removeStones() {...}
    ...
}
```

Defining the Instance Variables of Class `Pit`   All a pit needs to keep track of is the number of stones contained within it:

```
class Pit {
    ...
    private int stones;
}
```

Implementing the Methods of Class `Pit`   We will provide two constructors: One creates an empty pit, the second is passed an argument corresponding to the stones initially in the pit.

```
public Pit() {this.stones = 0;}
```

The `getStones`, `addStones`, and `isEmpty` methods are straightforward:

```
public int getStones() {return stones;}
public void addStones(int stones) {this.stones += stones;}
public boolean isEmpty() {return stones == 0;}
```

The method `removeStones` returns the number of stones in the pit, after emptying it:

```
public int removeStones() {
    int stones = this.stones;
```

Remember the number of stones in the pit and empty it.

```
            this.stones = 0;
            return stones;
    }
```

"Class" Stone The stones have no behavior. All that is required is to know how many stones are in a pit or mancala, and this information can be maintained by an integer variable representing the number of stones. We, therefore, have no need for a Stone class.

12.4.6 The Complete Implementation

Here is the full implementation of the Mancala game. The final set of classes are: MancalaGame, MancalaBoard, Pit, and Player.

```
import  java.io.*;

class  MancalaGame  {
    MancalaGame(String  name0,  String  name1)  {
        board  =  new MancalaBoard();
        board.setUpForPlay();

        players  =  new Player[2];
        players[0]  =  new Player(name0,  0);
        players[1]  =  new Player(name1,  1);
        currentPlayer  =  0;
    }

    public  void play()  throws  IOException  {
        displayBoard();
        while  (!board.gameOver())  {
            int  pitNum =
                  players[currentPlayer].selectAMove(board);

            boolean  goAgain  =
                  board.doTheMove(currentPlayer, pitNum);

            System.out.println("Player  "  +  currentPlayer  +
                        "  moved  from  "  +  pitNum);
            displayBoard();

            if  (!goAgain)
                if  (currentPlayer  ==  0)
                    currentPlayer  =  1;
                else
                    currentPlayer  =  0;
            else
                System.out.println("Player  "  +
                        currentPlayer  +  "  goes  again");
```

The player chooses the move.

which is then carried out by the board

If the current player does not go again, switch to the other player.

```
        }
        board.emptyStonesIntoMancalas();
```
Game is over—have board empty stones,

```
        displayBoard();
```
display final board,

```
        if (board.stonesInMancala(0) >
            board.stonesInMancala(1))
            System.out.println(players[0].getName()+" wins");
        else if (board.stonesInMancala(0) <
                board.stonesInMancala(1))
```
announce winner.

```
            System.out.println(players[1].getName()+" wins");
        else
            System.out.println("Tie");
    }

    private void displayBoard() {
        String mancalaLineFiller = "";      // Used to properly
                                            //    space the
                                            //    mancala line
```
Top border
```
        System.out.println("----------------------");
```

```
        // Player 1's pit line
        System.out.print("         ");
```
space past mancala entry
```
        for (int i = 1; i <=
                        board.playingPits; i++) {
```
Print pit's contents and pit spacing.
```
            System.out.print(board.stonesInPit(1, i) +
                    "     ");
```
Build mancala spacing string.
```
            mancalaLineFiller += "        ";
```

```
        }
        displayPlayer(1);
```
Player 1 info

```
        // Mancala line
```
Print player 1's manacala and spacing.
```
        System.out.print(board.stonesInMancala(1) +
                "     ");
```
Space past pit entries.
```
        System.out.print(mancalaLineFiller);
```
Print player 0's mancala.
```
        System.out.println(board.stonesInMancala(0));
```

```
        // Player 0's pit line
        System.out.print("         ");
        for (int i = board.playingPits;
            i >= 1; i--)
```
Print pit's contents and spacing.
```
            System.out.print(board.stonesInPit(0, i) +
                    "     ");
        displayPlayer(0);
```
Player 0 info
Bottom border
```
        System.out.println("----------------------");
```

```
    }

    private void displayPlayer(int playerNum) {
        // Turn indicator
        if (currentPlayer == playerNum)
            System.out.print("               -->");

        else
            System.out.print("                  ");


        // player info
        System.out.println("Player " + playerNum +
                "( " +
                players[playerNum].getName() + ")");
    }

    public static void main(String [] args) throws
                         IOException {
        MancalaGame game =
                     new MancalaGame("Weiss", null);
        game.play();
    }

    int currentPlayer = 0;
    MancalaBoard board;
    Player [] players;
}

class MancalaBoard {
    MancalaBoard() {
        pits = new Pit[totalPits];
        for (int pitNum = 0; pitNum < totalPits;
            pitNum++)
          pits[pitNum] = new Pit();
    }

    public void setUpForPlay() {
        for (int pitNum = 0; pitNum < totalPits;
            pitNum++)
          if (!isAMancala(pitNum))
            pits[pitNum].addStones(4);
    }

    public int stonesInMancala(int playerNum) {
       return pits[getMancala(playerNum)].getStones();
    }

    public int stonesInPit(int playerNum, int pitNum) {
       return pits[getPitNum(playerNum,
                           pitNum)].getStones();
```

If it this player's turn, display turn indicator.

```
    }

    private int getPitNum(int playerNum, int pitNum) {
        return playerNum * (playingPits+1) + pitNum;
    }

    private int getMancala(int playerNum) {
        return playerNum * (playingPits+1);
    }

    private boolean isAMancala(int pitNum) {
        return pitNum % (playingPits+1) == 0;
    }

    public MancalaBoard makeACopy() {
        MancalaBoard newBoard = new MancalaBoard();
        for (int pitNum = 0; pitNum < totalPits;
                pitNum++)
            newBoard.pits[pitNum].addStones(this.
                                pits[pitNum].getStones());
        return newBoard;
    }

    public boolean doTheMove(int currentPlayerNum,
                            int chosenPitNum) {
        int pitNum = getPitNum(currentPlayerNum,
                            chosenPitNum);
        int stones = pits[pitNum].removeStones();
        while (stones != 0) {
            pitNum--;
            if (pitNum < 0)
                pitNum = totalPits - 1;
            if (pitNum !=
                    getMancala(otherPlayerNum(
                            currentPlayerNum))) {
                pits[pitNum].addStones(1);
                stones--;
            }
        }

        if (pitNum == getMancala(currentPlayerNum))
            return true;
        if (ownerOf(pitNum) == currentPlayerNum &&
                pits[pitNum].getStones() == 1) {
            stones = pits[oppositePitNum(pitNum)].
                                        removeStones();
            pits[getMancala(currentPlayerNum)].
                                addStones(stones);
        }
        return false;
    }
```

```
private  int  ownerOf(int  pitNum)  {
      return  pitNum  /  (playingPits+1);
}

private  int  oppositePitNum(int  pitNum)  {
   return  totalPits  -  pitNum;
}

private  int  otherPlayerNum(int  playerNum)  {
   if  (playerNum  ==  0)
      return  1;
   else
      return  0;
}

public  boolean  gameOver()  {
   for  (int  player  =  0;  player  <  2;  player++)  {
      int  stones  =  0;
      for  (int  pitNum  =  1;  pitNum  <=  playingPits;
            pitNum++)
         stones  +=
            pits[getPitNum(player, pitNum)].getStones();
      if  (stones  ==  0)
            return  true;
   }
      return  false;
}

public  void  emptyStonesIntoMancalas()  {
  for  (int  player  =  0;  player  <  2;  player++)
    for  (int  pitNum  =  0;  pitNum  <=
                        playingPits;  pitNum++)  {
       int  stones  =
          pits[getPitNum(player, pitNum)].removeStones();
       pits[getMancala(player)].addStones(stones);
    }
}

private Pit  []  pits;
public static  final  int  playingPits=6,
                        totalPits  =  2*(playingPits+1);
}

class  Pit  {
   public Pit()  {this.stones  =  0;}

   public  int  getStones()  {return  stones;}
   public  void  addStones(int  stones)
      {this.stones  +=  stones;}
```

```java
      public  boolean  isEmpty()  {return  stones  ==  0;}
      public  int  removeStones()  {
         int  stones  =  this.stones;
         this.stones  =  0;
         return  stones;
      }
         int  stones;
      }

      class  Player  {
         public Player(String  name,  int  playerNum)  {
            this.name  =  name;
            this.playerNum  =  playerNum;
         }

         public  String  getName()  {
            if  (name  !=  null)
               return  name;
            else
               return  "Computer";
         }

         public  int  getPlayerNum()  {
            return  this.playerNum;
         }

         public  int  selectAMove(MancalaBoard board)    throws
                               IOException  {
            if  (name  !=  null)  {
               BufferedReader  br  =
                  new  BufferedReader(new
                            InputStreamReader(System.in));
               System.out.print("Enter  a  pit  to  move
                         from:  ");
               System.out.flush();
```

Read the move.
```java
               int  pitNum  =  Integer.parseInt(br.readLine());

               return  pitNum;
            }
```

```java
            //  Computer player–need to determine best move
            int  bestMove  =  -1;
            int  repeatMove  =  -1;
            int  maxNewStones  =  -1;
```

No best move initially
No go again move.
Mo move has added stones
to the mancala.

```java
            //  Trying the possible moves
            for  (int  pitNum  =  1;  pitNum  <=
                  board.playingPits;  pitNum++)  {
```

```
      if  (board.stonesInPit(playerNum,
          pitNum)  !=  0)  {

          MancalaBoard  testBoard  =  board.makeACopy();

          boolean  goAgain  =
                     testBoard.doTheMove(playerNum,
                     pitNum);
          if  (goAgain)

              repeatMove  =  pitNum;
          int  newStones  =
              testBoard.stonesInMancala(playerNum) -
              board.stonesInMancala(playerNum);

          if  (newStones  >  maxNewStones)  {

              maxNewStones = newStones;
              bestMove  =  pitNum;
          }
       }
    }

    // Tried all possibilities, return the best one
    if  (maxNewStones  >  1)

       return  bestMove;
    else  if  (repeatMove  !=  -1)

       return  repeatMove;
    else
       return  bestMove;
  }

  private String  name;
  private int  playerNum;
}
```

Only nonempty pits may be moved from

Make a copy of the board

Try the move on the board copy.

If move allows us to go again, remember the move.

See how many stones this move added to our mancala.

More stones than so far?

Remember how many and the move.

maxNewStones > 1 means a multistone capture occurred.

Barring that, use a "go again".

1 or possibly 0 stones added; oh well!

EXERCISES

1. Modify the player class so that it chooses "go again" moves over stone captures. Which heuristic is better; that is, which leads to a more challenging game? Try a player that only chooses stone captures.

2. There is a subtle bug in the display method of class `MancalaGame`. See if you can discover it. (Hint: What happens when there are more than nine stones in a pit or mancala?) Challenge: Can you fix it?

3. Rewrite the helper methods that use arithmetic expressions to calculate the board geometry by using conditionals instead. Which version do you find more readable?

4. See if you can redesign the mancala game without the `MancalaGame` controlling object.

SUMMARY

This chapter has presented three examples in order to give you a glimpse of the applications that can be constructed using the programming tools you already possess. The complexity of these examples greatly exceeds that of previous ones. That is because they are solutions to real problems, not merely illustrations of one programming technique or another. You should not, however, be discouraged. Instead, take heart from the following points:

- As you increase your familiarity with Java and programming, what seems complicated today will seem more manageable tomorrow.
- The ability to define different classes to take responsibility for different aspects of a problem will minimize additional increases in complexity as you take on new and increasingly challenging problems.

STUDY AID: TERMINOLOGY REVIEW

heuristic   A rule used by an application to aid in the making of a seemingly intelligent decision.

responsibility-driven programming   A perspective on class design, in particular, the assignment of behavior in which the burden of maintaining an object lies as much as possible with the object's class. This approach makes it easier for other objects to work with that object.

QUESTIONS FOR REVIEW

1. What is a controlling object? How does it aid in class design?

FURTHER EXERCISES

1. Using Mancala as a guide, implement the game of tic-tac-toe. A reasonable heuristic is to count the number of rows, columns, and diagonals the player controls. A player controls a row, column, or diagonal if it contains no entries of the opposing player, as shown in the accompanying diagram—the more the better.)

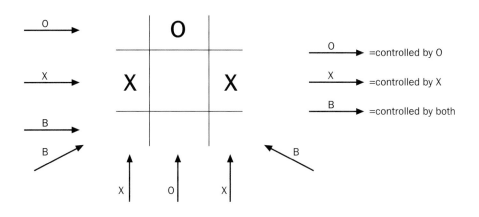

GUI *supplement*

A Graphical Interface for the Game of Mancala

Like the other examples in this chapter, we have chosen a nontrivial application for our GUI example—creating an applet that plays Mancala. As in several of the earlier GUI Supplements, the actual computation, in this case the game play, is already written; what we must provide is a graphical display and user interface. The techniques presented in this supplement include the drawing of a graphic image of a complexity greater than any we've seen until now, and the processing of mouse movements.

At the beginning of this chapter we noted that these examples were not trivial in nature. The applet program presented here is especially challenging. Graphics programs that do anything interesting are fairly complex, and a reasonable familiarity with analytic geometry and trigonometry is essential.

Although we can offer tips and advice, writing such a program is not an easy task. On the other hand, there is a tremendous sense of satisfaction in writing a graphical application. Furthermore, it is usually obvious when you make a mistake—the image is wrong, or the mouse doesn't respond as expected.

To analyze this application, we will break it up into various pieces and attack them separately.

An Overview   Presenting the user with a graphical representation of the game means both displaying the game in a graphical manner as well as providing a mechanism for the user to input a move, preferably by using the mouse. These issues are largely independent of those encountered when we implemented the game's logic earlier in the chapter. As we will see, the `MancalaBoard` and `Pit` classes are unchanged, as they have nothing to do with the user interface. On the other hand, the `MancalaGame` class, which was responsible for the display of the board, will be replaced by a applet that does the same action, only graphically. Those portions of the `MancalaGame` class that did not deal with output are largely duplicated in our new applet class. Finally, the `Player` class must be slightly modified to remove the logic that reads the human player's moves from the keyboard.

The Graphical Interface   Our proposed display is in Figure 12.25. There is no question that this representation is easier and more pleasing to play with than the textual representation presented previously. In addition to the board, there are a pair of buttons for moves and a list box that will display the moves made so far.

For the sake of simplicity, the human player will always be player 0 (and will therefore go first), and the computer will be player 1.

FIGURE 12.25 Our Mancala applet's display. Our game display consists of a Mancala board, complete with pits, mancalas, and stones, together with a pair of buttons for moves and a list box for recording the moves of the game.

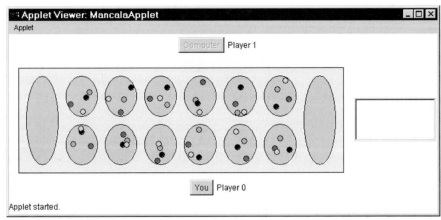

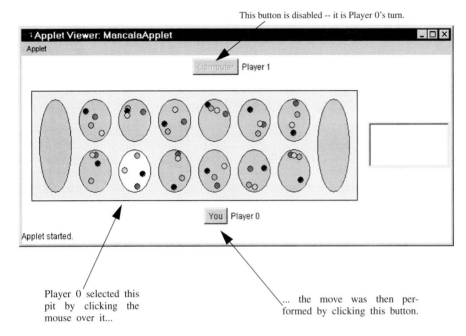

This button is disabled -- it is Player 0's turn.

Player 0 selected this pit by clicking the mouse over it...

... the move was then performed by clicking this button.

FIGURE 12.26 The user interface— entering moves. Only the button belonging to the player making the next move is enabled—the other player's button is disabled. The human player is able to select his move by clicking the mouse over a pit.

Textually or graphically, there are two aspects to interfacing with the user: input and output. The board diagram represents the second of these; to allow input from the user, we choose a combination of button-clicking and positioning of the mouse on the board. Player 0 may select a move by clicking the mouse while it is positioned over the desired pit, then clicking the You button (see Figure 12.26).

Note that the move is obtained from the graphic interface. In particular, we will *not* be using the keyboard input logic in the selectAMove of the Player class, and that logic should be removed from the Player class.

Once the move is performed (by invoking the doTheMove method of class MancalaBoard), the board is redisplayed. If player 1 is to move now, the You button is disabled (which is indicated by the text being grayed out) and the Computer button enabled. (See Figure 12.27.)

The process repeats until the game is over. The winner is then announced in the list box.

There are other possible designs for obtaining user input. We selected this one because it is within our current ability, is relatively simple, and fairly elegant.

The MancalaApplet Class Our text version of the Mancala game had a controlling class, MancalaGame, which was responsible for supervising the flow of the moves as well as the display of the board. We will replace that class

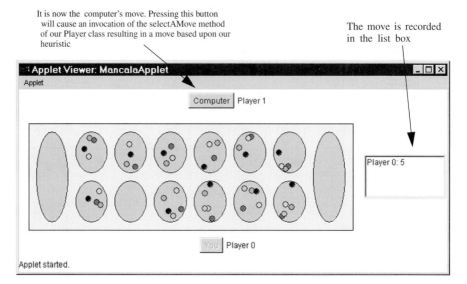

It is now the computer's move. Pressing this button will cause an invocation of the selectAMove method of our Player class resulting in a move based upon our heuristic

The move is recorded in the list box

FIGURE 12.27 The user interface— recording the moves. When it is the computer's turn to move, the Computer button is enabled, and the human player's button disabled. Previous moves are recorded in the list box.

with a class, `MancalaApplet`, that has similar responsibilities, except that it will model our graphical interface.

Supervising the Play Since the `MancalaApplet` is replacing the `MancalaGame` class, it must also assume the refereeing responsibility of maintaining the board and players and controlling the action. Part of our applet's `init` method thus looks quite similar to the constructor of the `MancalaGame` class. We also have a similar set of instance variables:

```
public class MancalaApplet extends Applet {
    public void init() {
        board = new MancalaBoard();
        board.setUpForPlay();

        players = new Player[2];   // Players
        players[0] = new Player("", 0);   No names in applet
        players[1] = new Player(null, 1)  Computer
        currentPlayer = 0;
        ...
    }
    ...

    // Game stuff
    private MancalaBoard board;
    private Player [] players;
```

```
        private int currentPlayer;
        ...
}
```

Laying out the Applet   Looking at our proposed applet, we see it consists of the following graphical components (see Figure 12.28):

- Two move buttons
- Two labels
- A list box
- A canvas upon which we will draw a series of graphic shapes representing the board. We will employ a `BorderLayout` to obtain the buttons above and below the board and list box.

The `North`, `South`, and `Center` will each be composed of a `Panel` to allow the placement within those areas of several components. For `North` and `South`, these are the `Button` and `Label` for the two players; the `Center` `Panel` will contain a `Canvas` and `List` component. We also register our applet as an `ActionListener` for the two buttons:

```
        public class MancalaApplet extends Applet
                        implements ActionListener {
        public void init() {
            board = new MancalaBoard();
```

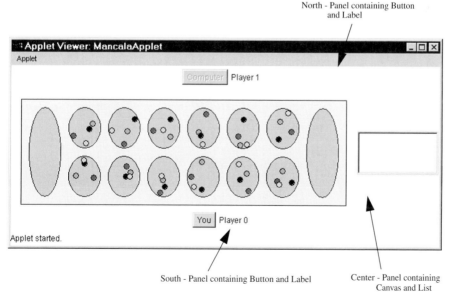

North - Panel containing Button and Label

South - Panel containing Button and Label

Center - Panel containing Canvas and List

FIGURE 12.28   The various panels laid out on our applet. We use the `BorderLayout` layout manager to divide the applet's window into `North`, `Center`, and `South` areas. A panel is placed in each of those areas, and the appropriate components added to the panels.

```
        board.setUpForPlay();

        players = new Player[2];
        players[0] = new Player("", 0);

        players[1] = new Player(null, 1);
        currentPlayer = 0;

        // Set up display.
        setLayout(new BorderLayout());

        Panel p = new Panel();                          Top (North)
        add("North", p);
        moveButton[1] = new Button("Computer");
        moveButton[1].addActionListener(this);          Handle own
                                                        buttons.
        moveButton[1].setEnabled(false);
        p.add(moveButton[1]);
        p.add(new Label("Player 1"));

        p = new Panel();                                Center
        add("Center", p);
        canvas = new MancalaCanvas(board);
        p.add(canvas);
        moveList = new List();
        p.add(moveList);

        p = new Panel();                                Bottom
        add("South", p);
        moveButton[0] = new Button("You");
        moveButton[0].addActionListener(this);          Handle own
                                                        buttons.
        p.add(moveButton[0]);
        p.add(new Label("Player 0"));
    }
    ...

    // Game stuff
    private MancalaBoard board;
    private Player [] players;
    private int currentPlayer;

    // Display stuff
    private MancalaCanvas canvas;
    private Button [] moveButton = new Button[2];
    private List moveList;
}
```

The MancalaCanvas class will be responsible for displaying the board. We supply its constructor with a reference to our MancalaBoard object so that it will be able to obtain the number of stones in the pits and mancalas.

The `MancalaCanvas` Class Our `MancalaCanvas` class will handle the graphical display of the board. The shapes used in the drawing of the board and their functions are as follows:

- Rectangles—for the board
- Ovals—for the pits and mancalas
- Circles—for the stones

Since this class is responsible for the board display, we will also have it handle the user's selection of a pit. We introduce an instance variable, which keeps track of the pit chosen by the player:

```
private int chosenPit;
```

Rectangles and Ovals Rectangles are drawn by invoking the `drawRect` method of the `Graphics` class. The prototype of this method is:

```
public void drawRect(int x, int y, int width, int height)
```

The `x` and `y` parameters specify the coordinates of the upper-left corner of the rectangle (see Figure 12.29).

We would also like to be able to fill these shapes with a color. Using the `setBackground` method is inappropriate because it sets the background of an entire component. Because the shapes are not components, this method would result in the entire canvas's background being set to the color. Instead, we fill a rectangle using the method, `fillRect`, with similar prototype:

```
public void fillRect(int x, int y, int width, int height)
```

The rectangle will be filled with the color most recently sent to the `Graphics` object using the `setColor` method.

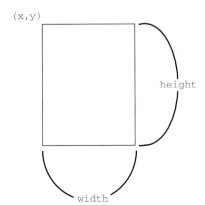

FIGURE 12.29 The parameters for drawing a rectangle. A rectangle is described by supplying the position of its upper-left corner, its width, and its height.

Ovals, or ellipses, are drawn and filled using the drawOval and fill-Oval methods, respectively:

```
public void drawOval(int x, int y, int width, int height)
public void fillOval(int x, int y, int width, int height)
```

In this case, the x and y parameters correspond to the upper-left corner of the enclosing, or *defining* rectangle (see Figure 12.30).

Parameterizing the Various Parts of the Board We could try to simply paint the board in a hit-or-miss fashion. Alternatively, we could exactly plot the size and position of each rectangle, oval, and circle on graph paper. The first of these approaches would be inefficient; the second requires too much effort. With a little bit of thought, we can reduce our effort substantially and produce a well-formatted board in little time. Our approach also has the advantage that we will be able to make the board larger or smaller with almost no effort. The idea is to relate all the various shapes and spacings on the board:

- Pits are six times as wide as stones.
- A pit is one-and-one-quarter times as high as it is wide.
- The space between pits is one-quarter their width.
- Mancalas are the same width as pits.
- The height of a mancala is twice the height of a pit plus a pit spacing.
- The border between the pits and the edge of the board is the same as the space between pits.
- The width of the board is twice the border, plus the width of the six pits and their spacings, plus the width of two mancalas, plus one more spacing.
- The height of the board is twice the border plus the height of the mancala.

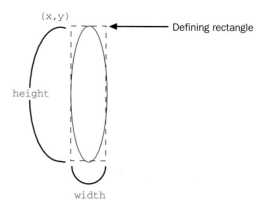

FIGURE 12.30   The parameters for drawing an oval. An oval may be thought of as being contained within a defining rectangle. Describing the oval involves describing the defining rectangle, that is, supplying the position of the upper-left corner, the width, and the height of that rectangle.

Some of these relationships were arbitrary and based upon an aesthetic sense of balance (such as the spacing between pits being one-quarter their width). Others were dictated by the board (for example, the board height being twice the border plus the mancala height). This approach is often known as *parameterizing the relationships*. By making the various values dependent upon one another, we can make a few simple changes and the effect ripples through our entire display.

The above relationships may be expressed as constants in our `Mancala-Canvas` class. We arbitrarily choose the width of our stone to be 8 and everything else follows:

```
private static final int
    StoneWidth = 8,
    StoneHeight = StoneWidth,
    StoneRadius = StoneWidth / 2,
    PitWidth = StoneWidth * 6,
    PitSpacing = PitWidth / 4,
    FullPitWidth = PitWidth + PitSpacing,
    PitHeight = (int)(PitWidth * 1.25),
    PitXRadius = PitWidth / 2,
    PitYRadius = PitHeight / 2,
    MancalaWidth = PitWidth,
    FullMancalaWidth = MancalaWidth + PitSpacing,
    MancalaHeight = 2 * PitHeight + PitSpacing,
    MancalaXRadius = MancalaWidth / 2,
    MancalaYRadius = MancalaHeight / 2,
    BoardBorder = PitSpacing,
    BoardWidth = 2 * BoardBorder +
                    FullMancalaWidth + 6 * FullPitWidth +
                    MancalaWidth,
    BoardHeight = MancalaHeight + 2 * BoardBorder,
    CanvasBorder = BoardBorder,
    CanvasWidth = BoardWidth + 2 * CanvasBorder,
    CanvasHeight = BoardHeight + 2 * CanvasBorder;
```

We have added several additional constants that will prove useful, such as including `FullPitWidth`, which represents the width of the pit plus a pit spacing. We also have some `Radius` constants that are nothing more than the widths and heights divided in half. We have two values each for the pits and mancalas since they are ovals. Finally, we also introduce some space between the edge of the board and the edge of the canvas. Without this space, the list box would be placed too close to the board. The board display parameters are indicated in the diagram of Figure 12.31.

As we will see in the next section, establishing these relationships greatly simplifies the job of drawing the board. In addition, if the board does not seem balanced, we can easily play with the various relationships to improve it. (For example, we can change the ratio of the pit height to its width.) Finally,

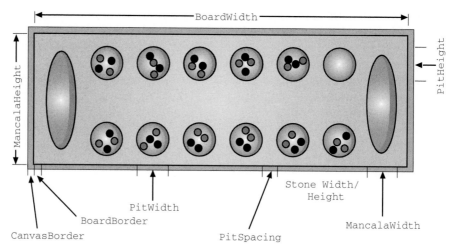

FIGURE 12.31 The various parameters used in displaying the board. Assigning constants to the various parts of the display simplifies the task of painting the board.

by simply modifying the stone width we can immediately reduce or enlarge the entire board. Thus, if our first board display is too small, we can easily make it larger.

Defining the Colors   In addition to the size and position constants, we also have several color constants:

```
private static final Color
ChosenPitColor = Color.white,
StoneColor[] = {
    Color.red, Color.green,
    Color.black, Color.orange,
    Color.cyan, Color.yellow
},
BoardColor = new Color(255, 234, 203),
PitColor = new Color(204, 187, 163);
```

ChosenPitColor represents the color we will use to fill the inside of the pit the player had chosen with the mouse. StoneColor is an array of several colors that we will use for our brightly colored stones. BoardColor and PitColor represent the colors of the board surface and pit interiors, respectively. We create custom colors using the Color constructor, which accepts an RGB specification. (The standard color constants provided by the Color class didn't provide us with the colors we wanted for painting the board and pits.)

Painting the Canvas   Our MancalaCanvas object, when requested to paint itself, must draw the current state of the board. We draw the board, by first filling the board's rectangle with our chosen board color, then resetting to the original color and drawing the actual board rectangle. We need both actions:

Filling gives us the interior color and drawing gives us a sharp (black) edge. The position and dimensions of the board rectangle are easy, given our relationship constants. (The coordinates begin with (0,0) at the upper-left corner of the canvas).

Once the board's rectangle is done, we print the mancala and pits, using a pair of helper methods, `paintMancala` and `paintPit`. These methods are passed the `Graphics` object passed into `paint` because they too will need it to do their own drawing. They are also supplied with the player number and pit number (for `paintPit`) so the method can determine where to place the mancala or pit. Finally, the number of stones, which is obtained from querying the `MancalaBoard` object, is passed to these helper methods.

```
public void paint(Graphics g) {

    // Paint board.
    Color c = g.getColor();              get and hold onto current color
    g.setColor(BoardColor);
    g.fillRect(CanvasBorder, CanvasBorder, BoardWidth,
            BoardHeight);
    g.setColor(c);                       Restore original color
    g.drawRect(CanvasBorder, CanvasBorder, BoardWidth,
            BoardHeight);

    // The pits, mancalas, and stones
    for (int playerNum = 0; playerNum < 2; playerNum++) {
        paintMancala(g, playerNum,
                board.stonesInMancala(playerNum));
        for (int pitNum = 0; pitNum < board.playingPits;
                pitNum++)
            paintPit(g, playerNum, pitNum,
                board.stonesInPit(playerNum, pitNum+1));
    }
}
```

Painting the Mancalas Using the `paintMancala` Method As with painting the board, our relationships are invaluable here as well as we paint the mancalas. We space vertically by the sum of the canvas and board borders. We space horizontally by that amount as well for player 1's mancala. For player 0, we must position ourselves beyond player 1's mancala and six pits, together with their spacings.

Once the mancala has been painted, we use yet another helper method to fill it with the proper number of stones. That method receives the `Graphics` object: the position and dimensions of the mancala to be filled and the number of stones. Here is the resulting method:

```
private void paintMancala(Graphics g, int playerNum,
                    int stones) {
```

```
int x = CanvasBorder + BoardBorder;   // Fixed horiz. spacing
int y = CanvasBorder + BoardBorder;   // Fixed vert. spacing
if (playerNum == 0)   // 0's mancala on right
    x += FullMancalaWidth +
        board.playingPits * FullPitWidth;   // Skip past pits.

// Set color and draw mancala.
Color c = g.getColor();
g.setColor(PitColor);
g.fillOval(x, y, MancalaWidth, MancalaHeight);
g.setColor(c);
g.drawOval(x, y, MancalaWidth, MancalaHeight);

paintStones(g, x, y, MancalaXRadius, MancalaYRadius,
            stones);
}
```

Painting the Pits   Painting the pits is similar to painting the mancalas, with the addition of a pit number passed as an argument.

We determine how many pits must be skipped to get to our desired position, remembering that player 0's pits are displayed in reverse and at the bottom of the board (see Figure 12.32). We then set our color. If the pit to be painted is the one that was chosen, we use the ChosenPitColor; otherwise, we choose just the plain PitColor. After our oval is drawn, we paint the stones, as with the mancala:

```
private void paintPit(Graphics g, int playerNum,
                      int pitNum, int stones) {

    // Determine pit's location.
    int pitsToSkip;
    if (playerNum == 0)   // 0's pits are displayed in reverse (5 ... 0)
```

FIGURE 12.32   The pit-numbering system. The pits are numbered by their distance from the corresponding player's mancala—the bottom pits thus displayed in reverse order because they are associated with the mancala on the right.

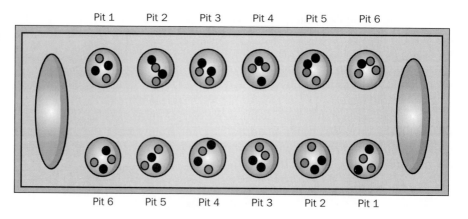

Pit 1   Pit 2   Pit 3   Pit 4   Pit 5   Pit 6

Pit 6   Pit 5   Pit 4   Pit 3   Pit 2   Pit 1

```
                pitsToSkip = MancalaBoard.playingPits - 1 -
                                pitNum;
        else
            pitsToSkip = pitNum;

        int x = CanvasBorder + BoardBorder +
                FullMancalaWidth +                  // Fixed horiz. spacing
                pitsToSkip * FullPitWidth;    // Skips  preceding
                                              //     pits

        int y = CanvasBorder + BoardBorder;  // Fixed vert. spacing
        if (playerNum == 0)        // 0's pits are on bottom
            y += MancalaHeight - PitHeight;   // Spaces to bottom
                                              //     row

    //  Select color and draw the pit.
    Color c = g.getColor();
    if (playerNum == 0 && pitNum == chosenPit)
        g.setColor(ChosenPitColor);
    else
        g.setColor(PitColor);
    g.fillOval(x, y, PitWidth, PitHeight);
    g.setColor(c);
    g.drawOval(x, y, PitWidth, PitHeight);
    paintStones(g, x, y, PitXRadius, PitYRadius, stones);
}
```

Painting the Stones in the `paintStones` Method   The `paintStones`
method receives a `Graphics` object for drawing, the position and dimensions of the oval (mancala or pit) in which to paint the stones, and the number of stones to be painted. We would like the stones to appear as if they were
dropped into the pits. We would also like to use different colors for the stones
and to make sure the stones are not too close to each other.

The basic idea is as follows: We generate a random position for the stone
that lies completely within the specified oval. We then check that it doesn't lie
too close to any other stone already placed in the oval. If it does, we try
another position. Once the stone is placed, we remember its position and continue on to the next stone.

Accomplishing this positioning requires a little bit more sophistication
than painting the mancalas or pits. Here is where the geometry really begins to
enter the picture. We are given an oval with the position and dimensions
shown in Figure 12.33.

We want to place a stone so that it lies completely within the oval. We
therefore wish to position stones so that their centers lie no farther away than
the inner oval shown in Figure 12.34.

The equation for an oval (centered at the origin) is:

$(x * height)^2 + (y * width)^2 = (width * height)^2$

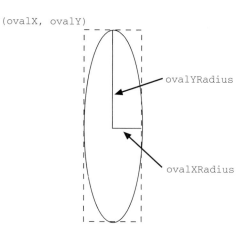

(ovalX, ovalY)

ovalYRadius

ovalXRadius

FIGURE 12.33 The parameters of the pit within which the stones are to be painted. When we are painting stones, we are supplied with the dimension of the oval corresponding to the pit or mancala within which they are to be drawn. These parameters consist of the position and size of the enclosing rectangle.

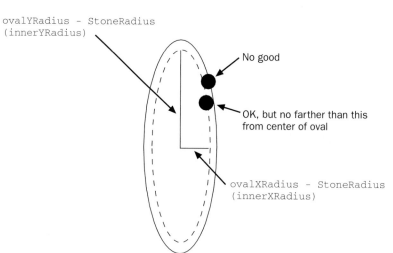

ovalYRadius - StoneRadius
(innerYRadius)

No good

OK, but no farther than this
from center of oval

ovalXRadius - StoneRadius
(innerXRadius)

FIGURE 12.34 Making sure the stone lies within the pit. To ensure the painted stone lies wholly within the boundary of the pit, we imagine a smaller (concentric) oval one-half of a stone's radius inside the boundary. Any stone whose center is on or within the inner oval will lie completely within the pit.

If we assume for the moment a center of (0,0), the above inner oval therefore has the equation:

$$(x*innerYRadius)^2 + (y*innerXRadius)^2 = (innerXRadius*innerYRadius)^2$$

To generate random positions satisfying the above equation, we will first generate a random value for y in the range –*innerYRadius*...*innerYRadius* (the negative values lying on one side of the center, the positive on the other). This represents the maximum range y may assume and still lie within the inner

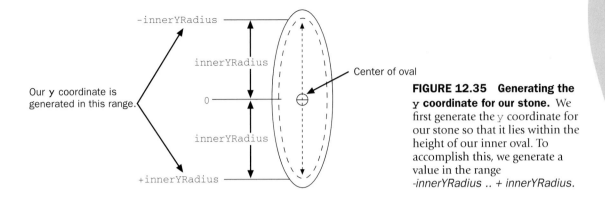

FIGURE 12.35   Generating the y coordinate for our stone. We first generate the y coordinate for our stone so that it lies within the height of our inner oval. To accomplish this, we generate a value in the range -innerYRadius .. + innerYRadius.

oval (see Figure 12.35). We generate such a value using the static `random` method of class `Math`:

```
static double random()
```

This method returns a value in the range `0.0...1.0`. To transform this into an integer value of our required range, we can write:

```
(int)(Math.random() * 2*innerYRadius) - innerYRadius;
```

Generate a random value in the range 0 ... 2*innerYRadius

```
possibleCenterY = (int)(Math.random() * 2*innerYRadius);
```

scale the value to -innerYRadius ... innerYRadius.

```
possibleCenterY -= innerYRadius;
```

By multiplying the returned random value by 2*innerYRadius in the first statement, possibleCenterY is assigned a value in the range 0...2*innerYRadius. Subtracting innerYRadius then leaves us in the desired range: -innerY-Radius...innerYRadius.

Once the y value of our stone's center is fixed we can plug it into our equation for the inner oval and solve for x:

$$x = \sqrt{innerXRadius^2 - (y^2 innerXRadius^2)/(innerYRadius^2)}$$

The above equation represents the farthest distance the stones can lie from the center of the oval. Thus, we are actually looking for any x values *up to* the above value, that is, x satisfying the following condition:

$$|x| \leq \sqrt{innerXRadius^2 - (y^2 innerXRadius^2)/(innerYRadius^2)}$$

As with y, the positive values satisfying this equation will lie to one side of the center of the oval, the negatives on the other (see Figure 12.36).

We now have a position for a stone whose center lies within the inner oval and thus the stone lies entirely within the original oval. However, we don't

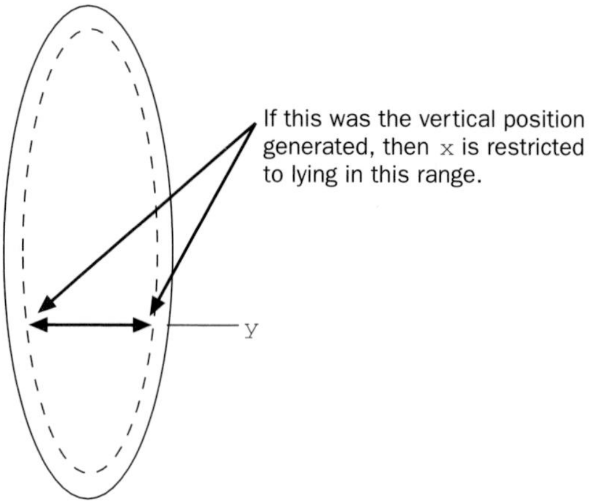

If this was the vertical position generated, then x is restricted to lying in this range.

FIGURE 12.36 Generating the x coordinate for our stone. Once y has been determined, x is restricted to the area shown. This range can be determined from the equation for the inner oval.

want stones to overlap *too* much. We thus use a pair of arrays to keep track of all stones placed so far in the oval. If the new position is too close, and if, for example, it overlaps more than half another stone, we reject the position and generate another. Once we have a valid position for the center of our stone, we save its position in our arrays. In order to draw the stone, we select a color from our StoneColor array, using cycling logic similar to that used in moving around the MancalaBoard pit array in a circular fashion. Finally, we obtain the upper-left corner of the defining rectangle and draw the stone.

```java
    private void paintStones(Graphics g,
                    int ovalX, int ovalY,    // Upper-left corner of def rect
                    int ovalXRadius, int ovalYRadius,
                    int stones) {

        int ovalCenterX = ovalX + ovalXRadius;
        int ovalCenterY = ovalY + ovalYRadius;

        // x radius (width) and y radius (height) of inner oval
        int innerXRadius = ovalXRadius - StoneRadius;
        int innerYRadius = ovalYRadius - StoneRadius;

        // Their squares—needed for the various calculations
        int innerXRadiusSq = (int)Math.pow(innerXRadius, 2);
        int innerYRadiusSq = (int)Math.pow(innerYRadius, 2);

        // Used to keep track of centers of stones already positioned
        int [] stoneCenterX = new int[stones];
        int [] stoneCenterY = new int[stones];

        for (int s = 0; s < stones; s++) {
            boolean done = false;
        int possibleCenterX = 0;  // Java forces us to initialize.
```

```
int possibleCenterY=0;  // Java forces us to initialize.

// Generate possible stone centers until we get a good one.
while (!done) {
    done = true;   // Assume we'll find a point this time through loop.

    // Generate a candidate for the y coordinate of our stone's center.

    // Generate a random value in the range 0 ... 2*innerRadius
    possibleCenterY = (int)(Math.random() *
                        2*innerYRadius);
    //    and scale the value to –innerYRadius ... innerYRadius.
    possibleCenterY -= innerYRadius;

    // Now that y is fixed, generate a candidate for x within the bounds set
    //    by our choice for y.

    // Solve the equation of the oval for x (y is known)
    int maxCenterX =
        (int)Math.sqrt(innerXRadiusSq -
            (innerXRadiusSq * Math.pow(
            possibleCenterY,2) /  innerYRadiusSq));

    // We have maximum value for x; now generate value in range 0 ...
    //    2*maxCenterX.
    possibleCenterX = (int)(Math.random() *
                        2*maxCenterX);

    // Scale to –maxCenterX ... maxCenterX;
    possibleCenterX -= maxCenterX;

    // Now check that we're not too close to any other stone position.
    for (int i = 0; i < s; i++) {

        // if our candidate position is too close to another stone, discard it
        //     and try again.
        if (distance(possibleCenterX,
            possibleCenterY, stoneCenterX[i],
            stoneCenterY[i]) < StoneRadius)
          done = false;  // Forces us back into the while (!done) loop
    }
}

// The variable done has remained true—We have obtained a new stone
//     position with center possibleCenterX, possibleCenterY—remember it.
stoneCenterX[s] = possibleCenterX;
stoneCenterY[s] = possibleCenterY;

// Determine upper left edge of def rect by subtracting
//     stone's radius from its center's x/y coordinates.
int definingX = ovalCenterX + (possibleCenterX -
```

```
                                     StoneRadius);
              int definingY = ovalCenterY + (possibleCenterY -
                                     StoneRadius);

        //  Select color and draw the stone.
        Color c = g.getColor();
        g.setColor(StoneColor[s % StoneColor.length]);
                                              // Cycle through colors.
        g.fillOval(definingX, definingY, StoneWidth,
                   StoneWidth);
        g.setColor(c);
        g.drawOval(definingX, definingY, StoneWidth,
                   StoneWidth);
    }
  }
```

The static Math class method pow(x,y) returns x^y. The distance helper method returns the distance between the pair of passed x,y coordinates, using the standard equation for distance:

$$\sqrt{(x2 - x1)^2 + (y2 - y1)^2}$$

```
private int distance(int x1, int y1, int x2, int y2) {
    return (int)Math.sqrt(Math.pow(x2-x1, 2) +
                          Math.pow(y2-y1, 2));
}
```

The `.html`-Specified Applet Size   The only value we have no control over from within the applet is the size of the applet itself. We may resize an applet only if we are running within the applet viewer supplied with the Java development tools. Browsers running an applet do not allow the applet to resize itself—it would ruin the rest of the page.

The size of the applet is specified in the `.html` file, and in our case was the result of trial and error, until we achieved a balanced look.

Handling Pit Selection   The MancalaCanvas class is also responsible for capturing the user's pit selection. The button clicks are handled by the MancalaApplet class—another distribution of responsibility. The ManacalaApplet managed the layout of the components, so it should take care of the buttons. The MancalaCanvas is managing the board display, so it should be responsible for detecting mouse movement over the pits.

The task of determining whether the mouse has been clicked over one of the pits is actually easier than it sounds. The trick is to determine that the mouse's position at the time of the click lies within the pit's boundaries, a feat analogous to what we did when painting the stones.

We have seen that button clicks are handled by a class serving as an ActionListener. When a button is clicked, the listener is notified through the invocation of its `actionPerformed` method, passing an `ActionEvent` object as the argument. In a similar fashion, mouse clicks are handled by a class serving as a `MouseListener`. When the mouse is clicked, the listener is notified through the invocation of its `MouseClicked` method, which is passed a `MouseEvent` object as the argument.

In order to handle the pit selection, our `MancalaCanvas` object registers itself as its own `MouseListener` within its constructor:

```
addMouseListener(this);   In MancalaCanvas constructor
```

The only event associated with buttons is clicking them. Therefore, an `ActionListener` object need only supply a single method, `action-Performed`, which handles that single kind of event. In contrast, the mouse can generate several events: entering or exiting a component's area of the screen, holding down, or releasing the mouse, and clicking. In order to serve as a `MouseListener`, an object must therefore must provide several methods: `mousePressed`, `mouseReleased`, `mouseEntered`, `mouseExited`, and `mouseClicked`. As we are only interested in `mouseClicked`, we code the other four with empty bodies—no action will be taken for any of those events:

```
public void mousePressed(MouseEvent e) {}
public void mouseReleased(MouseEvent e) {}
public void mouseEntered(MouseEvent e) {}
public void mouseExited(MouseEvent e) {}
```

When the `mouseClicked` method is invoked as a result of the user clicking the mouse, the `MouseEvent` object passed as an argument contains information specific to that event. In particular, the x and y coordinates of the mouse at the time of the click may be obtained through invoking the `getX` and `getY` methods of the `MouseEvent` class. These coordinates can be used to determine if the mouse was clicked inside the boundaries of any of the pits. We use a helper method `liesInsidePit`; it accepts an x,y coordinate and a pit number and returns whether the coordinate lies within that pit for player 0. If the click did indeed occur within one of the pits, we keep track of that pit in `chosenPit`. Finally, we indicate that we wish to repaint the canvas. When the `paintPit` method is invoked, it will highlight the newly chosen pit.

```
public void mouseClicked(MouseEvent me) {
    int x = me.getX(),     Get the coordinates of the click
    y = me.getY();         from the MouseEvent object.

    // Go through each of 0's (human's) pits and check if mouse was
    //    clicked within its boundaries
    for (int pitNum = 0; pitNum < board.playingPits;
        pitNum++)
        if (liesInsidePit(x, y, pitNum)) {
            chosenPit = pitNum;   // Will cause pit to be highlighted.
```

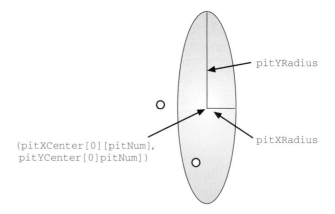

FIGURE 12.37 Determining whether a point lies within a pit. We can use the equation of the oval to determine whether a point lies inside or outside of the pit. We determine the distance of the point from the center and whether it lies beyond the boundary point of the oval.

```
            repaint();        Redisplay to show choice.
        }
    }
```

We only bother with player 0 because that is the human player. Player 1 uses our player class's `selectAMove` heuristic to choose its move.

The `liesInsidePit` helper method uses the equation for an oval to determine whether the passed *x,y* point lies within the specified pit (see Figure 12.37).

Rather than constantly recalculating the center point of each pit, we maintain them in a pair of array instance variables, `pitXCenter`, and `pitY-Center`, which are initialized in the `MancalaCanvas` constructor. For the sake of readability, we break up the equation of the oval into an `xterm`, a `yterm`, and an `edgeterm`.

```java
private boolean liesInsidePit(int x, int y, int pitNum) {
        double xTerm = Math.pow((x -
                pitXCenter[0][pitNum]) * PitYRadius, 2);
        double yTerm = Math.pow((y -
                pitYCenter[0][pitNum]) * PitXRadius, 2)
        double edgeTerm = Math.pow(PitYRadius *
                PitXRadius, 2);
        return xTerm + yTerm <= edgeTerm;
    }
```

Controlling the Moves The user selecting a pit does not cause a move to occur. Thus, the user can initially change her mind and select a different pit. It is only after the move button is pressed that the move is carried out. Similarly, when it is the computer's turn to move, we invoke the `selectAMove` method only after the computer's move button has been pressed.

We process the button clicks in the `actionPerformed` method of the `MancalaApplet` class. Depending upon which button is clicked, we either use the chosen pit, which we obtain from the `MancalaCanvas` object via a `getChosenPit` method, or we invoke the `selectAMove` method of the (computer) `Player` object. In either case, we record the move in the list box, disable/enable the buttons based upon who goes next, and reset the chosen pit, causing the highlighted pit to revert to normal color. If the game is over after the move, the winner is announced in the list box.

As items are added to a `List` component, they may become too numerous to remain visible within the list box. When this occurs, `List` adds a vertical scroll bar, allowing the user to move through the list. However, the `List` remains at its current position, so that we have to keep scrolling to see the newly added items. To avoid this situation, we invoke the `makeVisible` method of the `List` class, which accepts an index of the item of the `List` that is to become visible. By passing as an argument to that function the index of the last item (which we obtain using the `getItemCount` methods, also of the `List` class), we guarantee that the end of the list will be displayed. Here is the final code for our `actionPerformed` method:

```java
public void actionPerformed(ActionEvent ae) {
    int theMove = 0;
    if (currentPlayer == 0) {          Human player
        theMove = canvas.getChosenPit() + 1;
        if (theMove == 0) ◄─────── No move selected,
            return ;                    ignore button click
    }
    else                               Computer player
        theMove = players[1].selectAMove(board);

    moveList.addItem("Player " + currentPlayer + ": " +
                        theMove);

    // Determine next player and enable/disable buttons accordingly.
    if (!board.doTheMove(currentPlayer, theMove))
        currentPlayer = Math.abs(currentPlayer-1);
    moveButton[currentPlayer].setEnabled(true);
    moveButton[Math.abs(currentPlayer-
                        1)].setEnabled(false);

    canvas.resetChosenPit();           Clear human player's pit choice.

    if (board.gameOver()) {
        int stonesOf0 = board.stonesInMancala(0);
        int stonesOf1 = board.stonesInMancala(1);
        if (stonesOf0 > stonesOf1)
            moveList.addItem("Player 0 wins");
```

```
                        else if (stonesOf1 > stonesOf0)
                            moveList.addItem("Player 1 wins");
                        else
                            moveList.addItem("Tie");
                    }
                    moveList.makeVisible(moveList.getItemCount()-1);
            }
```

Putting it all Together   Here's the entire applet:

```
import java.awt.*;
import java.awt.event.*;
import java.applet.*;

public class MancalaApplet extends Applet
                            implements ActionListener {
    public void init() {                        // Set up game for play.
        board = new MancalaBoard();    // Creates board and initializes
                                       //      it for play.
        board.setUpForPlay();

        players = new Player[2];    // Players
        players[0] = new Player("", 0);      // No names used in
                                             //     applet
        players[1] = new Player(null, 1);    // Computer
        currentPlayer = 0;

        // Set up display.

        setLayout(new BorderLayout());

        Panel p = new Panel();                          Top
        add("North", p);
        moveButton[1] = new Button("Computer");
        moveButton[1].addActionListener(this);          Handle own
                                                        buttons.
        moveButton[1].setEnabled(false);
        p.add(moveButton[1]);
        p.add(new Label("Player 1"));

        p = new Panel();                                Center
        add("Center", p);
        canvas = new MancalaCanvas(board);
        p.add(canvas);
        moveList = new List();
        p.add(moveList);

        p = new Panel();                                Bottom
        add("South", p);
        moveButton[0] = new Button("You");
        moveButton[0].addActionListener(this);          Handle own
                                                        buttons.
```

```
        p.add(moveButton[0]);
        p.add(new Label("Player 0"));
    }

    public void actionPerformed(ActionEvent ae) {

        int theMove = 0;
        if (currentPlayer == 0) {                  // Human player
            theMove = canvas.getChosenPit() + 1;
            if (theMove == 0)
                return ;
        }
        else   // Computer player
            theMove = players[1].selectAMove(board);
        moveList.addItem("Player " + currentPlayer +
                        ": " + theMove);

        // Determine next player and enable/disable buttons accordingly.
        if (!board.doTheMove(currentPlayer, theMove))
        currentPlayer = Math.abs(currentPlayer-1);
        moveButton[currentPlayer].setEnabled(true);
        moveButton[Math.abs(currentPlayer-
                        1)].setEnabled(false);

        canvas.resetChosenPit();   // Clear human player's pit
                                   //    choice.

        if (board.gameOver()) {   // Determine winner
            int stonesOf0 = board.stonesInMancala(0);
            int stonesOf1 = board.stonesInMancala(1);
            if (stonesOf0 > stonesOf1)  // and announce winner.
                moveList.addItem("Player 0 wins");
            else if (stonesOf1 > stonesOf0)
                moveList.addItem("Player 1 wins");
            else
                moveList.addItem("Tie");
        }
        moveList.makeVisible(moveList.getItemCount()-1);
}


// Game stuff
private MancalaBoard board;
private Player [] players;
private int currentPlayer;

// Display stuff
private MancalaCanvas canvas;
private Button [] moveButton = new Button[2];
private List moveList;
}
```

```
class MancalaCanvas extends Canvas
                              implements MouseListener {
    public MancalaCanvas(MancalaBoard board) {
        this.board = board;

        setSize(CanvasWidth, CanvasHeight);
        addMouseListener(this);
```

We'll handle our own mouse events.

```
        // Determine and save centers of the playing pits (for paintStones).

        pitXCenter = new int[2][MancalaBoard.playingPits];
        pitYCenter = new int[2][MancalaBoard.playingPits];

        for (int playerNum = 0; playerNum < 2; playerNum++) {
            for (pitNum = 0; pitNum < MancalaBoard.payingPits;
                    pitNum++) {
```

Fixed horiz spacing

```
                int x = CanvasBorder + BoardBorder +
                        FullMancalaWidth +
```

skips preceeding pits

```
                        ((board.playingPits - 1) - pitNum) *
                        FullPitWidth;
```

Fixed vert spacing
0's pits are on bottom.
Space downwards.

```
                int y = CanvasBorder + BoardBorder;
                if (playerNum == 0)
                    y += MancalaHeight - PitHeight;

                // We now have left/top edge of pits—space by a radius to get center.

                pitXCenter[playerNum][pitNum] = x + PitXRadius;
                pitYCenter[playerNum][pitNum] = y + PitYRadius;
            }
        }
    }

    public void paint(Graphics g) {

        // Paint board.
        Color c = g.getColor();
        g.setColor(BoardColor);
        g.fillRect(CanvasBorder, CanvasBorder, BoardWidth,
                BoardHeight);
        g.setColor(c);
        g.drawRect(CanvasBorder, CanvasBorder, BoardWidth,
                BoardHeight);

        // The pits, mancalas, and stones
        for (int playerNum = 0; playerNum < 2; playerNum++) {
            paintMancala(g, playerNum,
                        board.stonesInMancala(playerNum));
            for (int pitNum = 0; pitNum < board.playingPits;
                        pitNum++)
                paintPit(g, playerNum, pitNum,
```

```
                            board.stonesInPit(playerNum,
                        pitNum+1));
        }
    }

    private void paintMancala(Graphics g, int playerNum,
                             int stones) {
        int x = CanvasBorder + BoardBorder;   // Fixed horiz. spacing
        int y = CanvasBorder + BoardBorder;   // Fixed vert. spacing
            if (playerNum == 0)                // 0's mancala on right
                x += FullMancalaWidth +
                    board.playingPits * FullPitWidth;   // Skip past
                                                        //  pits.

            // Set color and draw mancala.
            Color c = g.getColor();
            g.setColor(PitColor);
            g.fillOval(x, y, MancalaWidth, MancalaHeight);
            g.setColor(c);
            g.drawOval(x, y, MancalaWidth, MancalaHeight);
            paintStones(g, x, y, MancalaXRadius,
                        MancalaYRadius, stones);
        }

    private void paintPit(Graphics g, int playerNum,
                         int pitNum, int stones) {

            // Determine pit's location.
            int pitsToSkip;
            if (playerNum == 0)
                pitsToSkip = MancalaBoard.playingPits - 1 -
                            pitNum;
            else                    // 1's pits are displayed 0 .. 5
                pitsToSkip = pitNum;

            int x = CanvasBorder + BoardBorder +
                    FullMancalaWidth +              // Fixed horiz. spacing
                    pitsToSkip * FullPitWidth;      // Skips preceding
                                                    //    pits
            int y = CanvasBorder + BoardBorder;     // Fixed vert.
                                                    //    spacing
            if (playerNum == 0)    // 0's pits are on bottom.
                y += MancalaHeight - PitHeight;     // Spaces to bottom
                                                    //    row

            // Select color and draw the pit.
            Color c = g.getColor();
            if (playerNum == 0 && pitNum == chosenPit)
                g.setColor(ChosenPitColor);
```

```
            else
                g.setColor(PitColor);
            g.fillOval(x, y, PitWidth, PitHeight);
            g.setColor(c);
            g.drawOval(x, y, PitWidth, PitHeight);

            paintStones(g, x, y, PitXRadius, PitYRadius,
                        stones);
    }

    private void paintStones(Graphics g,
                int ovalX, int ovalY,    // Upper-left corner of def rect.
                int ovalXRadius, int ovalYRadius,
                int stones) {

        int ovalCenterX = ovalX + ovalXRadius;
        int ovalCenterY = ovalY + ovalYRadius;

        // x radius (width) and y radius (height) of inner oval
        int innerXRadius = ovalXRadius - StoneRadius;
        int innerYRadius = ovalYRadius - StoneRadius;

        // Their squares—needed for the various calculations
        int innerXRadiusSq = (int)Math.pow(innerXRadius,
                                    2);
        int innerYRadiusSq = (int)Math.pow(innerYRadius,
                                    2);

        // Used to keep track of centers of stones already positioned
        int [] stoneCenterX = new int[stones];
        int [] stoneCenterY = new int[stones];

        for (int s = 0; s < stones; s++) {
            boolean done = false;
            int possibleCenterX=0; // Java forces us to initialize.
            int possibleCenterY=0; // Java forces us to initialize.

            // Generate possible stone centers until we get a good one.
            while (!done) {
                done = true;   // Assume we'll find a point this time through
                               //    loop.

                // Generate a candidate for the y coordinate of our stone's center.

                // Generate a random value in the range 0 .. 2*innerRadius
                possibleCenterY = (int)(Math.random() *
                                    2*innerYRadius);
                //      and scale the value to –innerYRadius ... innerYRadius.
                possibleCenterY -= innerYRadius;

                // Now that y is fixed, generate a candidate for x within the
                //      bounds set by our choice for y.
```

```
        // Solve the equation of the oval for x (y is known).
        int maxCenterX =
            (int)Math.sqrt(innerXRadiusSq -
                (innerXRadiusSq *
                 Math.pow(possibleCenterY, 2) /
                 innerYRadiusSq));

        // We have maximum value for x; now generate value in range 0 ...
        //     2*maxCenterX.
        possibleCenterX = (int)(Math.random() *
                            2*maxCenterX);

        // Scale to –maxCenterX ... maxCenterX;
        possibleCenterX -= maxCenterX;

        // Now check that we're not too close to any other stone position.
        for (int i = 0; i < s; i++) {
            // If our candidate position is too close to another stone, discard it
            //     and try again.
            if (distance(possibleCenterX, possibleCenterY,
                    stoneCenterX[i], stoneCenterY[i]) <
                    StoneRadius)
                done = false; // Forces us back into the while (!done) loop
        }
    }

    // The variable done has remained true—We have obtained a new stone
    //     position with center possibleCenterX, possibleCenterY—remember it.
    stoneCenterX[s] = possibleCenterX;
    stoneCenterY[s] = possibleCenterY;

    // Determine upper-left edge of def rect by subtracting
    //     stone's radius from its center's x/y coordinates.
    int definingX = ovalCenterX + (possibleCenterX -
                    StoneRadius);
    int definingY = ovalCenterY + (possibleCenterY -
                    StoneRadius);

    // Select color and draw the stone.
    Color c = g.getColor();
    g.setColor(StoneColor[s % StoneColor.length]);
                                        // cycle through colors
    g.fillOval(definingX, definingY, StoneWidth,
            StoneWidth);
    g.setColor(c);
    g.drawOval(definingX, definingY, StoneWidth,
            StoneWidth);
    }
}

public void mouseClicked(MouseEvent me) {
```

```
        int x = me.getX(),
        y = me.getY();

        // Go through each of O's (human's) pits and check if mouse was
        //     clicked within its boundaries
        for (int pitNum = 0; pitNum < board.playingPits;
            pitNum++)
            if (liesInsidePit(x, y, pitNum)) {
                chosenPit = pitNum;   // Will cause pit to be highlighted.
                repaint();
            }
    }

    // Empty methods—not responding to these events
    public void mousePressed(MouseEvent e) {}
    public void mouseReleased(MouseEvent e) {}
    public void mouseEntered(MouseEvent e) {}
    public void mouseExited(MouseEvent e) {}
    public int getChosenPit() {
        return chosenPit;
    }

    public void resetChosenPit() {
        chosenPit = -1;
        repaint();
    }

    // Calculates standard distance between two points.
    private int distance(int x1, int y1, int x2, int y2) {
        return (int)Math.sqrt(Math.pow(x2-x1, 2) +
                Math.pow(y2-y1, 2));
    }

    // Plugs x and y into equation of oval and determines if the point lies within the edge.
    private boolean liesInsidePit(int x, int y, int pitNum) {
        double xTerm = Math.pow((x -
                        pitXCenter[0][pitNum]) * PitYRadius, 2);
        double yTerm = Math.pow((y -
                        pitYCenter[0][pitNum]) * PitXRadius, 2);
        double edgeTerm = Math.pow(PitYRadius * PitXRadius, 2);
        return xTerm + yTerm <= edgeTerm;
    }

    // Game stuff
    private MancalaBoard board;

    // Display stuff
    private int chosenPit = -1;
    private int pitXCenter[][];
    private int pitYCenter[][];
```

```
    private static final int
        StoneWidth = 8,
        StoneHeight = StoneWidth,
        StoneRadius = StoneWidth / 2,
        PitWidth = StoneWidth * 6,
        PitSpacing = PitWidth / 4,
        FullPitWidth = PitWidth + PitSpacing,
        PitHeight = (int)(PitWidth * 1.25),
        PitXRadius = PitWidth / 2,
        PitYRadius = PitHeight / 2,
        MancalaWidth = PitWidth,
        FullMancalaWidth = MancalaWidth + PitSpacing,
        MancalaHeight = 2 * PitHeight + PitSpacing,
        MancalaXRadius = MancalaWidth / 2,
        MancalaYRadius = MancalaHeight / 2,
        BoardBorder = PitSpacing,
        BoardWidth = 2 * BoardBorder +
                    FullMancalaWidth
                    MancalaBoard.playingPits *
                    FullPitWidth + MancalaWidth,
        BoardHeight = MancalaHeight + 2 * BoardBorder,
        CanvasBorder = BoardBorder,
        CanvasWidth = BoardWidth + 2 * CanvasBorder,
        CanvasHeight = BoardHeight + 2 * CanvasBorder;

    private static final Color
        ChosenPitColor = Color.white,
        StoneColor[] = {
            Color.red, Color.green,
            Color.black, Color.orange,
            Color.cyan, Color.yellow
        },
        BoardColor = new Color(255, 234, 203),
        PitColor = new Color(204, 187, 163);
}
```

GUI Summary   As we promised, this was a nontrivial GUI example. Don't be discouraged if you had trouble following some of the graphics analysis. Many issues had to be addressed, all in the context of solving a single problem. This leads us to the moral of this example, and in a sense of the entire chapter:

Programming is not trivial.

For all its seeming complexity, this last example is typical of all but the simplest graphical applications. The applications covered in a first semester programming course are not at all indicative of the sort of real applications you might encounter as a commercial programmer. Their main purpose is to teach you the basics in a simple, controlled manner. But when it comes time to do some real stuff, you're going to have to get down and dirty, just as we did here. That leads us to the second moral:

Use whatever means at your disposal to make your job easier.

That means using any techniques that simplify the analysis or coding of an application, whether it is a class design technique, an approach to loop design, tips on analyzing graphic images, and so on. Throughout the text we have attempted to stress clear-cut techniques of this sort. You will learn many others as you progress.

chapter 13

Extending Class Behavior

13.1 Introduction

Until now, we started from scratch in defining every class in the sense that we explicitly defined every method and instance variable of the class. This approach did not build on previous effort. We want the ability, however, to start from an existing class and add behavior and state to it, thereby defining a new class. Thus, the new class would be an extension of the original.

13.1.1 Building a Better `BufferedReader`

The `BufferedReader` class provides a base set of behavior for reading `String`s. Whenever we read a value, either from the keyboard or a disk file, we must first create a `BufferedReader` object. In Chapter 3 we showed how to do this, and we explained why several intermediate objects such as `FileInputStream` and `InputStreamReader` must be created in the process.

After we have a `BufferedReader`, we can invoke the `readLine` method to read a line of text. To read an integer, however, we must first read the line, using `readLine`, and then convert the returned `String` to an `int` value, using `Integer.parseInt`.

In both of these situations—creating the `BufferedReader` object and reading integers—all we are really interested in is the final product: a `BufferedReader` object and a `int` value. The intermediate steps are just a necessary annoyance.

We thus wish to transform those intermediate steps required to create the `BufferedReader` object or read an integer into behavior that can be invoked by a user; that is, we wish to turn them into methods. One possible solution is to add these methods to the existing class. For various reasons, this solution may not be appropriate:

- The class may have been rigorously tested. Adding even a single line of code (not to speak of entire methods) changes the behavior of the class and will require a full retesting of the class. Programmers often make the error of assuming that the change they are making "could not possibly affect the rest of the class." Confidence in the modified class can only result from testing that is as rigorous as the testing that was originally performed.
- Others may be using this class and not want the additional behavior, either because of performance costs or increased complexity.
- It may not be possible or advisable to modify the class. For example, modifying a Java predefined class is definitely not a recommended action. Any mistakes can affect all of your programs in strange and mysterious ways. Furthermore, the sources of the class definitions are not always available. You may be supplied with the *.class* file (the output of the Java compiler), rather than the *.java* file (the actual source text). Our example is such a case; we cannot modify the `BufferedReader` class.

In general, modifying an existing class, especially one you did not create, requires a full understanding of the class's implementation, and such an understanding may not be possible or practical.

Object-oriented languages such as Java provide a very powerful mechanism for the extension of class behavior. In fact, this mechanism, known as inheritance, is considered one of the crucial elements required for a language to be called object-oriented.

███ 13.2 ███ Extending Classes—Inheritance I

Class behavior may be extended through a process known as **inheritance.** In the following class definition:

```
class BetterBR extends BufferedReader {
    ...
}
```

the keyword `extends` is followed by the class name `BufferedReader`. This defines `BetterBR` as a class that automatically inherits all the methods and instance variables of the `BufferedReader` class; that is, objects of class `BetterBR` possess all methods and instance variables of class `Buffered-Reader`.

This means that before writing even a single line of code, we have defined a new class, `BetterBR`, that contains a full set of behavior—the behavior inherited from `BufferedReader`.

We say that `BufferedReader` is the **superclass** of `BetterBR`, and `Bet-terBr` is a **subclass** of `BufferedReader`.

After the `BetterBR` class has been defined, we can use it like any other class. We can create objects of the class and invoke methods upon them. In the case of a subclass, objects of the class have available to them all the methods defined in the superclass:

```
BetterBr bbr = new BetterBR(...);   We'll talk about the constructor later.
String s = bbr.readLine();          A method inherited from BufferedReader
```

A subclass is everything the superclass is. In our example, the `BetterBR` subclass contains all the behavior of the `BufferedReader` superclass.

If a subclass were to provide only the methods inherited from its super-class, there would be no point to the inheritance. For example, the `BetterBR` class would provide us with no behavior beyond that of the original `BufferedReader` class. However, by defining additional instance variables and methods in the subclass, we introduce new behavior, unique to the sub-class:

```
class BetterBR extends BufferedReader {
    ...
    int readint() {...}          Method unique to BetterBR
    ...
    instance variables unique to BetterBR
    ...
}
```

Now, given the `BetterBR` reference variable `bbr` declared above, we can invoke the new methods with code such as the following:

```
int i = bbr.readint();           A BetterBR method
```

Now let's develop a `BetterBR` class that contains the additional behavior we spoke of above.

13.3   A Better `BufferedReader`

The following example provides an introduction to the process of inheritance.

13.3.1   Statement of the Problem

Create a more convenient `BufferedReader` class that possesses the following behavior:

- All the behavior of class `BufferedReader`, in particular the `readLine` method
- The ability to create a reader object associated with a file specifying the file name only. If no file name is specified, we create a reader associated with `System.in`.
- A method that provides direct reading of `int` values

13.3.2   Scenario

The following is a sample scenario of using this class.

Just the filename. The constructor takes care of everything else. ⟶

Inherited ⟶

New method ⟶

```
BetterBR    bbr = new BetterBR("data13");
String name = bbr.readLine();
int sales1 = bbr.readint();
int sales2 = bbr.readint();
System.out.println("Total sales for " +name +
                   " = "+sales1+sales2);
```

13.3.3   Finding the Primary Object

Our problem statement provides us with the primary object, namely a smart `BufferedReader` class. We'll name the class `BetterBR` and have it inherit from `BufferedReader`:

```
class BetterBR extends BufferedReader {
    ...
}
```

13.3.4   Determining the Behavior

Our desired behavior is also obtained from the problem statement as follows:

- `BetterBR` (constructor)
- `readint`—Read an integer, returning it as an int.
- All the behavior of the `BufferedReader` class. (We get that automatically through the inheritance process.)

13.3.5   Defining the Interface

We wish to be able to create a `BetterBR` object by specifying simply a file name. Alternatively, if we specify nothing, we want the input source to be `System.in`. We therefore overload our constructor:

```
BetterBR(String fileName) {...}
BetterBR() {...}
```

Our `readint` method requires no arguments and should return as its result an `int` corresponding to the integer value read in:

```
int readint() {...}
```

This code completes the interface of the methods introduced by the `BetterBR` class. Again, in addition to these methods, we inherit all the functionality of the `BufferedReader` class.

13.3.6   Defining the Instance Variables

Defining class `BetterBR` by extending class `BufferedReader` means that all of `BufferedReader`'s instance variables and methods are inherited and thus become part of any `BetterBR` object. Remember—a `BetterBR` object is a `BufferedReader` object. We can think of no new state information for our extended behavior. However, we may have to introduce instance variables as we implement our new methods.

13.3.7   Implementing the Methods

None of the behavior being implemented is unfamiliar to us. We have been creating `BufferedReader` objects from file names or `System.in` since Chapter 3, and reading in `int` values since Chapter 5. What is new here is the packaging of this behavior into a subclass's methods.

The Constructors   The job of a constructor is to provide a valid initial state for the newly created object. Because a `BetterBR` object is a `BufferedReader` object, we must make sure that this `BufferedReader` object is properly initialized. Normally, the invocation of the `BufferedReader` constructor is performed automatically when a user of the class creates a `BufferedReader` object:

```
BufferedReader br;
br = new BufferedReader(new InputStreamReader(System.in));
```

The constructor for
BufferedReader
is invoked.

In our situation the user is not directly creating a `BufferedReader` object. Instead, it is being created automatically as part of the creation of a `BetterBR` object:

```
BetterBR bbr = new BetterBR();
```
<— BufferedReader object created as part of this object

The `BetterBR` constructor is invoked because we are creating a `BetterBR` object; however, there is no invocation of the `BufferedReader` constructor. It therefore becomes the responsibility of the `BetterBR` constructor to invoke the `BufferedReader` constructor as follows:

```
public BetterBR() throws IOException {
    super(new InputStreamReader(System.in));
}
```
Another sort of invocation of BufferedReader's constructor

The first action taken by the `BetterBr` constructor is to invoke the constructor of its superclass, `BufferedReader`, providing any necessary arguments, in this case the `InputStreamReader` object created from `System.in`. Rather than invoking the constructor in the usual way, that is, through `BufferedReader(new InputStreamReader(System.in))`, a different invocation is used. When a superclass's constructor is invoked from a subclass's constructor, the keyword `super` is substituted for the name of the superclass. This usage emphasizes the inheritance relationship between the subclass and its superclass.

Following the invocation of the superclass's constructor, the subclass constructor performs any initialization specific to the subclass. As we have no state information new to our subclass, no further initialization is necessary.

The second `BetterBR` constructor accepts a file name that is used to construct the object. The sequence of steps is as follows:

- Create a `File` object from the name.
- Create a `FileInputStream` from the `File` object.
- Create an `InputStreamReader` object from the `FileInputStream` object.
- Create a `BufferedReader` object from the `InputStreamReader` object.

Our constructor therefore is

```
BetterBR(String fileName) throws IOException {
    super(new InputStreamReader(
            new FileInputStream(new File(fileName))));
}
```

Again, no further initialization is required beyond the invocation of the `BufferedReader` superclass's constructor.

The `readint` Method We read in a line with the `readLine` method and then use `Integer.parseInt` to convert the line into an `int`. Here is the code:

```
int readint() throws IOException {
    String line;
    line = readLine();
    return Integer.parseInt(line);
}
```

Turning this behavior into a method, however, introduces the problem of how to handle the end of file condition. Until now, we could test whether the value returned by the `readLine` method was equal to `null`. If it was, there were no more data to read, and no `int` was produced. How does the `readint` method indicate this situation to the caller? That is, what value could it return to indicate that no number was read? We cannot return `null` as we do for methods that read in objects—`null` is not a valid `int` value! Values like -1 or even `-999999` are not really special; they could legitimately appear as numeric data.

One solution to this problem will be presented in Chapter 14. For the moment, we leave the responsibility of detecting the end of numeric input to the caller of `readint`. The `main` method of the full class implementation in the next section illustrates how this responsibility can be assumed by the caller.

13.3.8 The Full Class Implementation

Here is the complete code for the `BetterBR` class. The sample code in the `main` method creates a `BetterBr` object associated with the file `data13`, whose contents follow the class definition. The `main` method then reads integers until a negative value is read, after which it simply reads lines until the end of the file is encountered. Here, `main`—the caller of `readint`—uses a negative number to signal the end of the numeric input.

```
import java.io.*;

class BetterBR extends BufferedReader {
    public BetterBR() throws IOException {
        super(new InputStreamReader(System.in));
    }

    public BetterBR(String fileName) throws IOException {
        super(new InputStreamReader(
            new FileInputStream(new File(fileName))));
    }
```

```
public int readint() throws IOException {
    String line;
    line = readLine();
    return Integer.parseInt(line);
}

public static void main(String[] arg) throws IOException {
    int i;
    String s;
    BetterBR bbr = new BetterBR("junk");
    i = bbr.readint();
    while (i >= 0) {           ←─────────  Positive numbers only—a negative
        System.out.println("i = "+i);       value signals the end of the input.
        i = bbr.readint();
    }
    s = bbr.readLine();
    while (s != null) {        ←─────────  Read in strings
        System.out.println("s = "+s);       until end of file
        s = bbr.readLine();
    }
}
}
```

Contents of the `data13` File   Here are the contents of the `data13` file:

```
3
5
237
-1
A line
Line #2
This is the last line
```

EXERCISES

1. Modify the `readint` method so that an integer may be placed anywhere on the line. (Hint: Look at the `trim` method of class `String`.)

2. Modify the `readint` method so that blank lines are ignored.

3. In the `main` method, what would happen if the file `date13` did not have a negative value at the end of the numeric section? That is, what if the `-1` in the file was omitted?

4. Add a `readdouble` method to the `BetterBR` class that reads in and returns a `double` value using the technique presented in Section 5.8. •

13.4   Adding State to the Subclass— Accessing the Superclass's State

The `BetterBR` class extended its `BufferedReader` superclass through the addition of methods only. These methods performed their tasks by invoking the superclass's own methods and using local variables. The new class required no state of its own nor any knowledge of the superclass's state.

The extension of behavior, however, usually requires that the subclass introduce some additional instance variables of its own in order to maintain the state associated with the new behavior. For example, in the next section, we will develop an extended `Name` class, based upon the class introduced in Section 4.8. The extended state will add a middle name to the information maintained by the original `Name` class and this new information will be maintained in the subclass.

```
class ExtendedName extends Name {
    ...
    // Instance variables
    private String middleName;   Introduced by ExtendedName
}
```

Furthermore, in order for a subclass to implement its additional behavior, it often needs to access the state of the superclass. While the methods provided by the superclass provide "packaged" behavior suitable for a user, the methods may not (and usually do not) supply access to the underlying instance variables directly—access often required by the subclass. Again, looking ahead, our extended `Name` class will require access to the title and first and last name of the superclass if it wishes to create a `String` composed of title, first. middle, and last name.

As matters stand, however, the subclass is unable to access the instance variables of its superclass because we have been declaring them `private`. To solve this problem, Java possesses an additional access keyword, `protected`, which is similar to `private` except that access is provided to subclasses as well as to the class itself. Thus, given the following pair of class definitions:

```
class Name {
    ...
    // Instance variables
    protected String last;
}

class ExtendedName extends Name {
    ...
}
```

the methods of the `ExtendedName` class have access to the `last` instance variable of class `Name`, because it has been declared `protected`.

▮ 13.5 ▮   Revisiting the `Name` Class—Adding Additional State

We now develop a class that introduces additional state information as well as new methods. This example shows a subclass that adds state (instance variables) of its own.

13.5.1   Statement of the Problem

Extend the `Name` class developed in Section 4.8 so that it supports a middle name. In addition to the behavior provided by the `Name` class, the new class should provide methods to return the middle initial and a formal name consisting of title, first, middle, and last names.

13.5.2   Finding the Primary Object

As with our previous example, our problem statement provides us with our primary object—an extended name class that we call `ExtendedName`.

13.5.3   Determining the Behavior

Our desired behavior is also obtained from the problem statement as follows:

- `ExtendedName` (constructor)
- `middleInitial`—Returns middle initial
- `formalName`—Returns title followed by first, middle, and last name
- All the behavior of the `Name` class. (We get that automatically through the inheritance process.)

13.5.4   Defining the Interface

Our original `Name` constructor required two arguments: the first and last names. These must be supplied to our `ExtendedName` constructor so that the `Name` constructor (invoked as `super(...)` in `ExtendedName` constructor) can be passed these values. In addition, we must supply the middle name to our `ExtendedName` constructor:

```
ExtendedName(String firstName, String middleName,
             String lastName) {...}
```

It is also possible that someone has no middle name, so we overload the constructor to allow the user to specify a first and last name only:

```
ExtendedName(String firstName, String lastName) {...}
```

The getFormalName method, like the other get... methods inherited from the Name class, requires no arguments and returns a String object. Our completed interface is

```
class ExtendedName extends Name {
    public ExtendedName(String firstName, String
                          middleName, String lastName) {...}
    public ExtendedName(String firstName,
                          String lastName) {...}
    public String getFormalName() {...}
    // Instance variables
    ...
}
```

This completes the interface of the methods introduced by the Extend-edName class. Again, in addition to these methods, we automatically acquire, through inheritance, all the functionality of the Name class.

13.5.5 Defining the Instance Variables

We need to maintain the middle name in our class, so we introduce an instance variable, middleName. This instance variable is present *only* at the subclass level—objects of type Name do not possess such a value. However, ExtendedName objects do inherit the lastName, firstName, and title instance variables from their superclass. In order to allow the methods of ExtendedName to access these variables, we must change their access to protected. Here are the two classes:

```
class Name {
    // Methods
    ...
    // Instance variables
    protected String firstName, lastName, title;
}

class ExtendedName extends Name {
    // Methods
    ...
    // Instance variables
    String middleName;
}
```

13.5.6 Implementing the Methods

In addition to invoking the Name constructor, the constructor for Extended-Name must also initialize its own middleName instance variable. Initialization is done after the superclass constructor invocation:

```
public ExtendedName(String firstName, String middleName,
                      String lastName) {
```

```
        super(firstName, lastName);
        this.middleName = middleName;
    }
```

The second constructor, which accepts just a first and last name, initializes the middle name to the empty string:

```
public ExtendedName(String firstName, String lastName) {
    super(firstName, lastName);
    this.middleName = "";
}
```

The `getMiddleInitial` method checks whether there is a middle name and returns the first initial; otherwise, the (somewhat conventional) string `NMI`, short for "No Middle Initial," is returned.

```
public String getMiddleInitial() {
    if (!middleName.equals(""))
        return middleName.substring(0, 1);
    else
        return "NMI";
}
```

The `getFormalName` method simply returns the concatenation of the title, first, middle, and last names. Declaring the `Name` class's instance variables `protected` allows `getFormalName` to access those variables.

```
public String getFormalName() {
    return title + " " + firstName + " " + middleName +
                " " + lastName;
}
```

13.5.7 The Complete Class

Here is the completed `ExtendedName` class together with the `Name` class, which has been modified so that its instance variables are now declared `protected`. Note that we have declared the `middleName` instance variable of the `ExtendedName` class to be `private`.

The sample code in the `main` method of the `ExtendedName` class creates a pair of `ExtendedName` objects, one with a middle name, the other without. It then invokes both `ExtendedName` methods, `getMiddleInitial` and `getFormalName`, as well as the `getLastFirst` method defined in the `Name` class.

```
class ExtendedName extends Name {
    public ExtendedName(String firstName, String
                        middleName, String lastName) {
        super(firstName, lastName);
        this.middleName = middleName;
    }
```

```java
    public ExtendedName(String firstName,
                        String lastName) {
        super(firstName, lastName);
        this.middleName = "";
    }

    public String getMiddleInitial() {
        if (!middleName.equals(""))
            return middleName.substring(0, 1);
        else
            return "NMI";
    }

    public String getFormalName() {
        return title + " " + firstName + " " + middleName
                     + " " + lastName;
    }

    public static void main(String [] args) {
        ExtendedName en = new ExtendedName("Anna",
                                      "Louise", "Strong");
        System.out.println(en.getMiddleInitial());
        System.out.println(en.getFormalName());
        System.out.println(en.getLastFirst());
        en = new ExtendedName("Gerald", "Weiss");
        System.out.println(en.getMiddleInitial());
        System.out.println(en.getFormalName());
        System.out.println(en.getLastFirst());
    }

    private String middleName;    the middle name of
}                                 an ExtendedName

class Name{
    public Name(String first, String last){
        firstName = first;
        lastName = last;
        title = "";
    }

    public String getInitials(){
        String s;
        s = firstName.substring(0,1);
        s = s.concat(".");
        s = s.concat(lastName.substring(0,1));
        s = s.concat(".");
        return s;
    }

    public String getLastFirst(){
        return lastName.concat(",").concat(firstName);
    }
```

```
public String getFirstLast(){
    return title.concat("").
              concat(firstName).
                  concat("").concat(lastName);
}

public void setTitle(String newTitle){
    title = newTitle;
}

protected String firstName;    Refers to the first name of this Name
protected String lastName;     Refers to the last name of this Name
protected String title;        Refers to the title part of this Name
}
```

EXERCISES

1. Extend the Name class to create a new class, SuffixedName, that provides for a suffix, for example, M.D., Esq., Ph.D., and so on. Introduce a method that prints out a name with the suffix.

2. Have the SuffixedName class of Exercise 1 extend the ExtendedName class rather than the Name class. Do any issues arise?

3. Why did we bother returning NMI for the return value of getMiddleInitial if there is no middle name? What would happen if we did not perform the check for a middle name in that method? Can you think of a better value to return?

4. There are some subtle output mistakes in the ExtendedName class. Apply the testing techniques of Chapter 7 to uncover and fix them.

java interlude

Inheritance

BASIC MECHANICS AND TERMINOLOGY

If we use our ExtendedName class as an illustration, the class definition:

```
class ExtendedName extends Name {
    ...
}
```

causes the class `ExtendedName` to inherit all of the `Name` class's instance variables and methods.

We say that `ExtendedName` **extends** `Name`. Thus, `ExtendedName` is a **subclass** of `Name`, and `Name` is a **superclass** of `ExtendedName`. In addition to the inherited items, `ExtendedName` may define its own instance variables and methods.

Creating an `ExtendedName` object such as

```
ExtendedName en = new ExtendedName("David", "Moss",
                                   "Arnow");
```

causes a *single* object to be created. This object consists of the `Name` superclass object augmented with the instance variables and methods of the `ExtendedName` subclass (see Figure 13.1). All `Name`-defined methods may be directly invoked upon the object, in addition to those methods defined specifically for a `ExtendedName`:

```
en.getLastFirst();        Invokes a Name-defined method
en.getMiddleInitial();    Invokes an ExtendedName defined method
```

Within the `ExtendedName`'s methods, the methods and instance variables defined by the `Name` superclass may be referred to using either `this` as the receiver or no receiver at all, exactly as would be done for `Name` objects. Thus, our `getFormalName` method can refer to the `title` instance variable either as `title` or `this.title`.

CONSTRUCTORS

Until now, we explicitly created each object by invoking the `new` operator, passing the appropriate arguments to the object's constructor:

```
Employee e = new Employee("Zvi Weiss", 23);
Song s = new Song("Daniel", "Elton John");
```

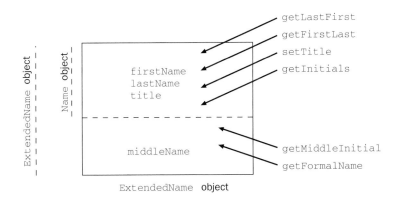

ExtendedName object

FIGURE 13.1 The anatomy of a subclass object. An `ExtendedName` subclass object can be thought of as consisting of the `Name` superclass object augmented with the instance variables and methods introduced in the `Extended-Name` class. The methods defined in the `Name` superclass can only refer to those instance variables in the superclass, because they know nothing of the subclass's state.

In the presence of inheritance, matters become slightly more complicated. Suppose we create an `ExtendedName` object:

```
Extended en = new ExtendedName("John", "Fitzgerald",
                                "Kennedy");
```

Although a *single* object is created, in some sense that object is composed of a pair of *nested* parts: a `Name` object within an `ExtendedName` object, the latter consisting only of methods and instance variables defined within the `ExtendedName` class. Although both portions require proper initialization, it is only the `ExtendedName` constructor that is explicitly invoked during the creation. It thus becomes the responsibility of the `ExtendedName` constructor to ensure that the constructor of the embedded `Name` object is invoked. It does this without an invocation of the `new` operator because the `Name` object is already created as part of the `new ExtendedName` invocation. Therefore, Java introduces a new syntax to allow a subclass to invoke the constructor of its superclass with the proper arguments. The invocation emphasizes the sub/superclass relationship of the two classes:

```
super(arguments to the superclass's constructor);
```

We usually get the arguments to `super` from the arguments to the subclass's *own* constructor, as we did with the `firstName` and `lastName` arguments to the `ExtendedName` constructor.

The invocation of the superclass's constructor must be the first action of the subclass's constructor:

```
public ExtendedName(String firstName, String middleName,
                    String lastName) {
    super(firstName, lastName);          This must be invoked first.
    this.middleName = middleName;
}
```

To invoke a superclass constructor that accepts no arguments we just write the following:

```
super();    Invoking the superclass's constructor
            without arguments.
```

Alternatively, we can omit such an invocation without arguments entirely, in which case it is performed automatically for us.

INHERITANCE AND THE *IS-A* RELATIONSHIP

We created the `ExtendedName` class by extending the `Name` class in order to provide additional behavior. The `ExtendedName` class, however, still retains all the methods and instance variables of the `Name` class (in addition to its own) and we say that any object of class `ExtendedName` **is-a** `Name` object.

The term *is-a* relationship is widely used to denote the subclass/superclass relationship. An `ExtendedName` object may therefore be freely used as a `Name` object. For example, the following code creates an `ExtendedName` and assigns it to a `Name` reference variable. This assignment is legal because `Name` reference variables may contain references to `Name` objects, and an `ExtendedName` object is a `Name` object:

```
Name n = new ExtendedName("Yocheved", "Chaya", "Weiss");
```

This illustrates a very important and powerful aspect of inheritance: *the ability to use an object of a subclass anywhere a superclass object is allowed.*

As another example, an array declared to contain an element type of `Name` objects may contain `ExtendedName` objects as well:

```
Name[] na = new Name[10];
na[0] = new Name("George", "Washington");        No surprises here
na[1] = new ExtendedName("George",
                "Washington", "Carver");     ExtendedNames are Names too!
```

Code that was written even before the class `ExtendedName` was defined can still properly operate on objects of that class. However, in the context of a `Name` reference variable context, `ExtendedName` objects can only behave as the more restricted `Name` objects. For example:

```
Name n = new ExtendedName("Wolfgang", "Amadaeus",
                "Mozart");
n.getInitials();          OK, Name objects can return initials.
n.getFormalName();        Wrong!! We are acting as a Name now.
                          No such method in Name.
```

Fortunately, the above mistake is caught by the compiler.

THE `protected` KEYWORD

In addition to `public`, which permits all classes to access a method or instance variable, and `private`, which restricts access to members of the class only, Java provides the keyword `protected` to permit access by subclasses but not other classes. This keyword allows a subclass to provide extended behavior that requires access to the instance variables of its superclass.

There are two basic problems with the use of `protected`. First, the designer of a class is assumed to have foreknowledge of two possible eventualities:

- There may eventually be a subclass defined extending this class.
- The subclass will require access to the state (instance variable) of this class.

Although this information may be available under certain circumstances, we cannot be sure that this information is available in general. There is a school of thought that recommends that *all* instance variables be declared `protected` to allow for eventual subclass definition.

The second problem associated with the use of `protected` is one of responsibility and integrity of state. If we view a class as being the sole entity responsible for its behavior, then it is not clear that even subclasses should have access to its internal state. Once a subclass is able to access the instance variables of its superclass, the superclass can no longer guarantee that its state is always correct. No matter how much the superclass's own methods are tested, the variables can be corrupted by the methods of the subclass. That is why the "all protected" school is a small minority. In fact, there is another school of thought that frowns on *any* use of `protected`.

INHERITANCE VERSUS COMPOSITION

Defining an `ExtendedName` class as inheriting from a `Name` object is completely different from defining a class that contains a reference to a `Name` object as an instance variable:

```
class Name2 {
    // Methods
    public Name2(String firstName, String middleName,
                      String lastName) {...}
    public String getMiddleInitial() {...}
    public getFormalName() {...}
    // Instance variables
    private Name n;
    private String middleName;
}
```

This code shows the type of construction we have been using all along. It declares a reference variable of one class as an instance variable of a second class. This is the *has-a* relationship we spoke of in Section 6.3. In the above class definition, the class `Name2` *has-a* `Name` object as part of its state.

Building classes in this way is called **composition** because the class is *composed* of instance variables that are objects of other classes. Again, the `Name2` class is composed of a `Name` object, as well as a `String` object.

In this case, the `Name2` does not inherit the methods and instance variables of the `Name` object. When it is created, only a *reference* to a `Name` object is created (see Figure 13.2). An actual `Name` object must be created as a separate step, usually within the constructor:

```
Name2(String firstName, String middleName, String lastName) {
    n = new Name(firstName, lastName);
    this.middleName = middleName;
}
```

same as this.n ➝

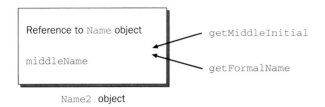

FIGURE 13.2   Using composition to define a new class. With composition, an object of the existing class is used as an instance variable of the new class.

In addition, the only methods directly available to the object are those defined in the new `Name2` class. The original `Name` class methods are not inherited and cannot be invoked upon an `Name2` object:

```
Name2 n2 = new Name2("Louisa", "May", "Alcott");
n2.getMiddleInitial();     Ok, getMiddleInitial defined for Name2.
n2.getLastFirst();         Error—no such method for Name2
```

Finally, when composition is used, the `protected` keyword does not buy us anything. That access is only granted to subclasses, not classes that incorporate the object as an instance variable.

INHERITANCE OR COMPOSITION?

Inheritance and composition each have their applications; one is not necessarily superior to the other. The thing to remember is that inheritance models an *is-a* relationship whereas composition models a *has-a* relationship. Given an existing class, X, and the need for a related new class, Y, the following guidelines can help you to decide whether to use composition or inheritance.

- If *all* the methods of the original class X should be methods of the new class Y, then use inheritance.
- If *some* of the methods of the original class X make no sense as methods of the new class Y, use composition.
- If it feels right to say that "a Y is an X" (as in "a part-timer is an employee"), then use inheritance.
- If it feels right to way that "a Y has an X" (as in "an employee has a name"), then use composition.

Furthermore, when you are deciding on inheritance vs. composition, in Java a class may have only one superclass; that is, it may inherit from one class only. On the other hand, a class may contain instance variables of many classes. Thus, composition is not restricted to an object of a single class. It often turns out that a particular class uses both techniques: inheriting from one class and using composition for several others.

A COMMON MISTAKE

Programmers new to inheritance often forget that the instance variables of the extended class (`Name` in our case) are *automatically inherited*. A

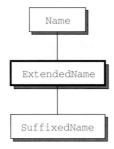

FIGURE 13.3   A subclass with its own subclass. The subclass `ExtendedName` can itself be extended. It then becomes a superclass to the new subclass `SuffixedName`.

common mistake is to repeat the declarations of these variables in the inheriting class:

```
class ExtendedName extends Name {
    // Methods
    ...
    // Instance variables
    String title, lastName, firstName;    INCORRECT!!! These are already
                                          inherited from Name!

    String middleName;    This is the only instance variable that should
                          be explicitly defined by ExtendedName.
}
```

What's even worse, the Java compiler will not complain about this situation. The result is that you have introduced a new set of instance variables, unique to `ExtendedName` objects, which are identically named to those of `Name`.

CLASS HIERARCHIES

There is no reason why subclasses cannot themselves be extended. We might decide at some later date to extend the behavior of our `ExtendedName` to provide even more behavior (see Exercise 2 of Section 13.5 and Figure 13.3):

```
class SuffixedName extends ExtendedName {
    ...
}
```

It's also possible to have two *different* classes inherit from the same class (see Figure 13.4):

```
class SuffixedName extends Name {
    ...
}
```

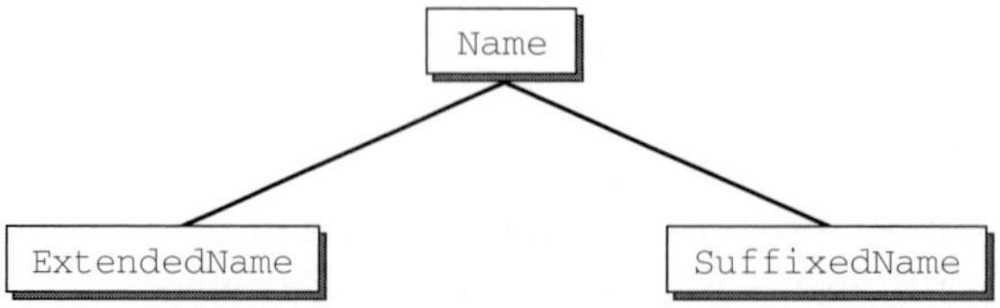

FIGURE 13.4   A superclass with two subclasses. A class can be extended by more than one class.

The resulting class relationship is called a **class hierarchy** and is illustrated graphically using a structure known as a **class hierarchy tree**. Figures 13.3 and 13.4 are both examples of a hierarchy tree. This tree can extend to multiple levels.

THE `Object` CLASS

We can now finally provide a full explanation of the `Object` class with which we became acquainted back in Chapter 7.

Every class in Java, with one exception, must be a subclass of some other class. The resulting class hierarchy is what we call the **Java class hierarchy**. The one exception is the class that resides at the top, or **root** position of the hierarchy. In Java, the `Object` class occupies this distinguished position in the class hierarchy (see Figure 13.5). This means that all classes in Java have `Object` as a superclass (though usually with several classes intervening).

Before we reached this chapter our class definitions did not contain the `extends` clause. Whenever this clause is omitted, the class is assumed to inherit directly from the `Object` class:

```
class MyClass {   Same as "class MyClass extends Object"
    ...
}
```

13.6   Overriding Methods

The behavior of the `ExtendedName` class was a strict extension of the `Name` class. `ExtendedName` added new behavior only; there was no modification of the original `Name` behavior.

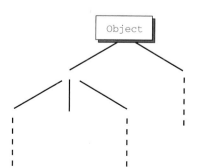

FIGURE 13.5   The root of the Java class hierarchy. Class `Object` is the root of the Java hierarchy tree. All classes inherit, directly or indirectly, from this `Object` class.

With a little thought, however, we can uncover a discrepancy in the behavior of `ExtendedName`, in particular in the behavior of the `getInitials` method inherited from the `Name` class. This method returns a `String` corresponding to the first and last initials of the `Name` object. With the introduction of the `ExtendedName` class, however, the `getInitials` method should properly return all three initials—first, middle, and last. What we must do is modify the behavior of the `getInitials` method for `ExtendedName` objects. However, we don't wish to modify the behavior of the `getInitials` method for `Name` objects—in fact, we can't because they have no middle name in their state.

What we must do in this situation is *replace* the original `getInitials` method with one defined in `ExtendedName` that incorporates a middle initial. In order for this replacement to work, the `getInitials` method that we will define in `ExtendedName` must match the signature of the original `getInitials` of `Name`. We write it as follows:

```
class ExtendedName extends Name {
    ...
    public String getInitials() {
        return firstName.substring(0,1)+"."+
            getMiddleInitial()+"."+lastName.substring(0,1);
    }
    ...
}
```

This technique of redefining a method in a class further down the hierarchy is known as **overriding**. Overriding refers to the act of reimplementing a method in a subclass with the same signature of a method in the superclass. In effect, we are circumventing the superclass's original method. In our situation, invoking the `getInitials` method on an `ExtendedName` object causes the new method, defined in `ExtendedName`, to be invoked.

EXERCISES

1. Extend the `Employee` class of Chapter 6 to create a `TaxableEmployee` class. In addition to the information associated with an `Employee`, a `TaxableEmployee` has a `double` that is a tax rate. Override the `calcPay` method so that the return value reflects the amount earned after tax.

2. Think about it: If we override a method of a superclass, are we *really* able to say that the *is-a* relationship holds?

Polymorphism

THE MECHANICS OF OVERRIDING

Let us consider a simplified but useful way to understand how overriding works. During execution, when a message is passed to an object, the message is compared against the object's class's own message signatures (name plus argument list). If a match is found, the corresponding method is invoked. If not, the message is compared against the prototypes of the superclass's messages. The process repeats until a match is encountered. A match is guaranteed because the Java compiler will issue a compile-time error if a message is invoked upon an object that does not have the message name defined either within itself or some superclass.

Let us apply this to the context of `Name` and `ExtendedName` objects. Suppose we have the following declarations:

```
Name n = new Name("Shlomo","Weiss");
ExtendedName en = new ExtendedName("William","Tecumseh",
                                   "Sherman");
```

Let us invoke a `getInitials` method on each of these objects and examine the effect.

First we invoke the method on the `Name` object:

```
String initials = n.getInitials();  Invokes the getInitials method in Name
```

The Java interpreter looks up the `getInitials` method, with no arguments, in class `Name` (which is the object upon which the method was invoked) and finds that such a method exists. That method is therefore invoked.

Now let us invoke this method on the `ExtendedName` object:

```
initials = en.getInitials();        Invokes the getInitials method in ExtendedName
```

The interpreter again finds a matching method immediately, this time in the `ExtendedName` class and that is the one that is then invoked.

Compare this second call to the following invocation:

```
String s = en.getLastFirst();
```
Invokes the getLastFirst method in Name

This time the Java interpreter looks up the `getLastFirst` method in class `ExtendedName` and does not find any such method. The interpreter then moves up to `ExtendedName`'s superclass, `Name`, where it finds a matching `getLastFirst` method and invokes it.

POLYMORPHISM

It gets even better than that! Given the following declaration:

An ExtendedName object referenced by a Name variable

```
Name n = new ExtendedName("Thomas","Alva","Edison");
```

Again, this code is perfectly legal because *a subclass object may be used wherever an object of its superclass is allowed.* Because an `ExtendedName` *is-a* `Name`, it may be assigned to a `Name` reference variable. Now here's where the fun begins. Invoking the `getInitials` method on n:

Invokes the getInitials method in ExtendedName!

```
n.getInitials();
```

causes the interpreter to begin searching for a matching method *in the object upon which the method was invoked*—the receiver. Now n may be a `Name` reference variable, but the object it references is a `ExtendedName` (see Figure 13.6). This means that the class in which the method matching begins is `ExtendedName`, and the method invoked is the `getInitials` method defined in that class.

This leads to the following important rule:

> When invoking overridden methods, the type of the actual object is what counts, not the type of the reference variable. Method matching thus begins in the object's class, not the class of the reference variable.

This means that invoking the *same* method on the *same* reference variable will invoke *different* methods depending upon the object being referred to:

```
Name n = new Name("James","Michener");
String s = n.getInitials();
```
Invokes getInitials defined in Name

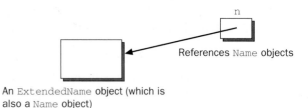

FIGURE 13.6   A `Name` reference variable referencing an `ExtendedName` object.

An `ExtendedName` object (which is also a `Name` object)

```
n = new ExtendedName("James","Clerk","Maxwell");
s = n.getInitials();     Invokes getInitials defined in ExtendedName
```

All of the above hinges on our ability to override methods. As we have said, the search for the matching method is performed by the Java interpreter and is thus performed at run time. The ability to override methods coupled with the run-time determination of which method to invoke means that different objects (even when using the same reference variable) can respond to the same message in different ways. This capability is known as **polymorphism** (literally "many forms") because the same message can evoke different behavior depending upon the receiver. Polymorphism is a feature of object-oriented languages in which the exact method to be invoked is determined at run time by the class of the receiving object.

Another example of polymorphism is the familiar toString method. This method is defined in the Object class with the intention that it be subsequently overridden by subclasses. The purpose of toString is to construct a String representation of an object, usually for the purpose of printing:

```
Enumeration e = v.elements();
while (e.hasMoreElements())
    System.out.println((e.nextElement()).toString());     Invokes the toString method
                                                           of the element's class
```

The method toString returns a String representation of an object. This method was introduced in Chapter 8 as being available to all objects, as it was defined in class Object. Furthermore, any class could rewrite that method to provide its own behavior for that method, providing the exact same signature as the one defined in class Object.

During execution, sending the message toString() to an object causes the Java interpreter to check whether the object's class possesses such a method, and if so, it invokes that method. If the method is not found in that class, the immediate superclass is checked. This process repeats itself until a class is found with a toString method. If no class defined its own toString method, eventually the Object class will be encountered and its toString method (which returns as its value a not-very-descriptive string).

OVERRIDING VERSUS OVERLOADING

Overriding differs from overloading in that overriding requires signatures to be identical whereas overloading requires signatures to be different. From a usage point of view, the two have completely different applications. Overloading allows the programmer to use the same name for two distinct methods. The invoker of the method implicitly specifies which method is being invoked by the argument list passed in the message, which is then compared against the prototypes of the various candidate methods until a match is found. The determination of which is the correct method is performed at compile time (by the Java compiler).

In contrast, overriding provides the programmer with the ability to redefine the behavior of a particular method in a subclass. When overriding methods are employed, the method invoked is determined at run time in the manner described above.

13.7   Factoring out Common Behavior— Inheritance II

The inheritance encountered by the beginning Java programmer is usually of the form presented in the previous sections. An existing class provides a base of behavior and the programmer extends it to provide additional behavior. In our examples, we extended the existing `Name` class to create an `ExtendedName` class and the Java predefined `BufferedReader` class to create a `BetterBR` class.

This ability to build upon previous effort provides unprecedented power to the relative beginner. For example, Java provides a powerful graphical interface class called `Applet`. This class can be extended by a novice who provides only the specifics of the application at hand—the sophisticated window management is automatically inherited.

There is another common use for inheritance, one that arises during the design of applications involving numerous related classes. Because the beginner does not usually encounter such applications (entry-level positions usually do not involve large-scale design), this form of inheritance is seen less often. It is, however, a critical part of understanding class hierarchies in an object-oriented system, and we therefore provide an introduction to it.

As our example, let us assume we are designing an inventory system for a camera store that is to track the various items in the warehouse. Different categories of items require different information be maintained. For example, we might have the following categories and information:

- Lenses will possess a focal length and may or may not zoom.
- Film must remain cool and thus there is a recommended storage temperature, as well as a film speed and number of exposures.
- Cameras may or may not come with a lens, and have a maximum shutter speed and body color.

In addition, all inventory items must contain the following information:

- A description of the item
- An inventory identification number

- The quantity on hand
- The price of the item

Each information element associated with an inventory item can be maintained as an instance variable. Our example has three distinct categories of items: lens, film, camera, and we will define three corresponding classes, `Lens`, `Film`, and `Camera`.

It makes little sense to lump them all into the same class because that class would have to maintain the union of *all* the instance variables for all three types of items.

Here is a brief sketch of the proposed classes. We will not be developing a full application using these classes, so we ignore the constructor details as well as the methods that are specific to the different classes.

```
class Lens {
    public Lens(...) {...}  Constructor
    public String getDescription() {return description;};
    public int getQuantityOnHand() {return quantityOnHand;}
    public int getPrice() {return price;}
    ...
    methods specific to Lens
    ...
    private String description;
    private int inventoryNumber;
    private int quantityOnHand;
    private int price;
    private boolean isZoom;
    private double focalLength;
}

class Film {
    public Film(...) {...} Constructor
    public String getDescription() {return description;};
    public int getQuantityOnHand() {return quantityOnHand;}
    public int getPrice() {return price;}
    ...
    methods specific to Film
    ...
    private String description;
    private int inventoryNumber;
    private int quantityOnHand;
    private int price;
    private int recommendedTemp;
    private int numberOfExposures;
}

class Camera {
    public Camera(...) {...} Constructor
```

```
    public String getDescription() {return description;};
    public int getQuantityOnHand() {return quantityOnHand;}
    public int getPrice() {return price;}
    ...
    methods specific to Camera
    ...
    private String description;
    private int inventoryNumber;
    private int quantityOnHand;
    private int price;
    private boolean hasLens;
    private int maxShutterSpeed;
    private String bodyColor;
}
```

While the three classes do model the three separate types of inventory items, there is a significant amount of repetition regarding their common elements: `description`, `inventoryNumber`, `quantityOnHand`, and `price`. This repetition is reflected in both instance variables and methods operating on those variables. If an additional piece of information is to be maintained for all inventory items, we must add another instance variable, together with any associated methods to *all three classes*. In short, all three classes are required to model behavior common to all inventory items, and it seems a waste of effort to have each of them accomplish this individually.

Each of the three classes is actually modeling two related, but distinct concepts: a general inventory item as well as the specific sort of item: lens, film, and camera. This is where inheritance can help. We create a superclass, `InventoryItem`, which models the behavior of a generic inventory item:

```
class InventoryItem {
    // Methods
    InventoryItem(...) {...} Constructor
    String getDescription() {return description;};
    int getQuantityOnHand() {return quantityOnHand;}
    int getPrice() {return price;}
    ...
    // Instance variables
    String description;
    int inventoryNumber;
    int quantityOnHand;
    int price;
}
```

This class knows nothing of specific items; it is responsible solely for behavior common to all inventory items. Any modifications to the behavior of all inventory items need be maintained by this class only.

We can now define three subclasses that extend the `InventoryItem` class:

```
class Lens extends InventoryItem {
```

```
    Lens(...) {...}  Constructor
    ...
    methods specific to Lens
    ...
    //  Instance variables
    boolean isZoom;
    double focalLength;
}
class Film extends InventoryItem {
    Film(...) {...}  Constructor
    ...
    methods specific to Film
    ...
    //  Instance variables
    int recommendedTemp;
    int numberOfExposures;
}
class Camera extends InventoryItem {
    Camera(...) {...}  Constructor
    ...
    methods specific to Camera
    ...
    //  Instance variables
    boolean hasLens;
    int maxShutterSpeed;
    String bodyColor;
}
```

These three classes model the specifics of the individual types of items.
The general behavior of inventory items is inherited from the `Inventory-
Item` class.

What we have done here is to recognize that our original classes were
abstracting two sets of behavior, one of which was common to all of them. We
then factored that common behavior out to a common superclass.

We haven't introduced anything new here—all we have done is shown a
different use of inheritance. Our original motivation for using inheritance was
to take advantage of existing class behavior when creating new classes. What
we have done here is to use inheritance to factor out common behavior when
we are designing logically related classes. In both cases, we are trying to share
as much code as possible.

As with any subclass/superclass, the *is-a* relationship holds between the
`Lens`, `Film`, and `Camera` subclasses and the `InventoryItem` superclass. A
reference variable of type `InventoryItem` may reference an object of any of
the three classes:

```
InventoryItem ii;
ii = new Lens(...);  .        OK—Lens objects are InventoryItem objects
```

```
ii = new Film(...);        OK—Film objects are InventoryItem objects.
ii = new Camera(...);      OK—Camera objects are InventoryItem objects.
```

As we have already seen, the *is-a* relationship allows for some fairly powerful programming capabilities. Consider the following array declaration and initialization:

```
InventoryItem[] invarr = new InventoryItem[3];
invarr[0] = new Lens(...);
invarr[1] = new Film(...);
invarr[2] = new Camera(...);
```

We can now iterate through the array and print out the element's description and quantity on hand:

```
for (int i = 0; i < invarr.length; i++)
    System.out.println(invarr[i].getDescription() + ": "+
        invarr[i].getQuantityOnHand() + " available");
```

13.8 Abstract Methods and Classes

Let's take a closer look at the array code presented at the end of the last section:

```
InventoryItem[] invarr = new InventoryItem[3];
invarr[0] = new Lens(...);
invarr[1] = new Film(...);
invarr[2] = new Camera(...);
for (int i = 0; i < invarr.length; i++)
    System.out.println(invarr[i].getDescription() + ": "+
        invarr[i].getQuantityOnHand() + " available");
```

This code prints out only the information that is available in the `InventoryItem` superclass. This is because in the context of the `InventoryItem` array, `invarr`, the various items are viewed as `InventoryItems` and not as objects of the individual subclasses.

Suppose we wanted to be able to go through the array and print out detailed information for the individual objects: the temperature, the number of exposures of `Film` objects, the focal length and zoom capability of a `Lens` object, and so on.

To accomplish this task, we need to do the following:

- Define a method called `print` in each of the subclasses `Lens`, `Film`, and `Camera`.

- In order to invoke these `print` methods polymorphically using an `InventoryItem` reference variable, a `print` method must be defined in the `InventoryItem` class.
- The `print` methods of the subclasses, therefore override the `InventoryItem`'s `print` method.

We thus require `print` methods in both the subclasses and the super-class:

```
class InventoryItem {
    ...
    void print() {...}
    ...
}

class Lens extends InventoryItem {
    ...
    void print() {...}    Overrides print of InventoryItem
                          and prints Lens-specific data.
    ...
}

class Film extends InventoryItem {
    ...
    void print() {...}    Overrides print of InventoryItem
                          and prints Film-specific data.
    ...
}

class Camera extends InventoryItem {
    ...
    void print() {...}    Overrides print of InventoryItem
                          and prints Camera-specific data.
    ...
}
```

Note, however, that the `print` method in the superclass exists only so that it can be overridden. It cannot by itself provide any behavior specific to the individual classes. So, in actuality, we really don't want to implement the `print` method in the `InventoryItem` class. It is the responsibility of each subclass to provide an overridden method customized to itself. What we really want is to specify the existence of such a `print` method, but require that it be overridden by a subclass.

Java provides this capability through the use of the `abstract` keyword in the method header. Declaring a method to be `abstract` announces that the class recognizes the existence of the method, *but its implementation is left to the subclass.* No method body is supplied; instead, the method header is followed by a semicolon. An **abstract method** is thus a method that is declared with the keyword abstract. It has no method body and must be overridden by a subclass.

```
abstract void print();
```

Because no implementation exists for the `print` method in class `InventoryItem`, it makes no sense to be able to create an object of that class—its behavior is incompletely specified. A class that contains one or more abstract methods is an **abstract class,** and the Java compiler requires that you indicate it in the definition of the class with the keyword `abstract`.

With `print` an abstract method, our `InventoryItem` class becomes:

```
abstract class InventoryItem {
    ...
    abstract void print();   No method body for an abstract method
    ...
}
```

Because you can't create objects that are instances of an abstract class, the following code is in error:

```
InventoryItem inv = new InventoryItem(...);   Incorrect—will generate
                                              a compiler error!
```

You may, however, declare reference variables whose type is of an abstract class:

```
InventoryItem inv;   OK, not creating InventoryItem object
```

However, because no `InventoryItem` objects can exist, such a variable can only reference objects belonging to subclasses. This is another consequence of the *is-a* relationship.

```
inv = new Lens(...);   OK—a Lens is an InventoryItem too
```

Suppose we are given our abstract `print` method and let us assume it has been implemented in the `Lens`, `Film`, and `Camera` subclasses. We can then write the printing iteration code for our array:

```
for (int i = 0; i < invarr.length; i++)
    invarr[i].print();
```

The above code exploits both the *is-a* relationship and polymorphism. The *is-a* relationship allows us to store the subclass objects in a superclass array. Polymorphism ensures that the actual `print` method invoked is determined at run time by the type of the receiver object, the object referred to by `invarr[i]`. When i equals 0, the object referenced by `invarr[i]` is a `Lens`, and thus the `print` method defined in the `Lens` class is invoked. When i equals 1, the `Film` class `print` method is invoked. And, finally, when i equals 2, the `Camera` class `print` method is invoked.

13.9 Specifying Common Behavior— Interfaces

Abstract methods allow us to state in a superclass that a particular method must exist and may be invoked on a reference variable belonging to the superclass. The actual implementation of the method remains the responsibility of the subclasses. In essence, we are requiring that all subclasses implement behavior that is only being specified (not implemented) in the superclass.

There is a constraining element to working with abstract methods: the superclass/subclass relationship. When the superclass declares an abstract method, the requirement that the method be implemented applies only to its subclasses—no other class in the hierarchy is required to implement that method.

There are times, however, when we wish to impose the requirement that certain behavior be adhered to for objects that have no direct relationship to each other in the hierarchy. An example that we have already encountered is the Enumeration. Enumerations model iteration behavior through some collection—Vector, Set, and so on. The various Enumerations we define have no relationship to each other; rather they are more closely tied to the collection objects they enumerate over. What Enumerations *should* have in common is the ability to get the next element, nextElement, and test for termination, hasMoreElements. We can't provide a *single* implementation for these because the implementation really depends upon the type of collection we intend to enumerate over. Nonetheless, we would like to require that any candidate Enumeration object provides these methods. In other words, we are specifying a set of abstract methods that must be implemented by any class wishing to call itself an Enumeration. We could write this as:

```
abstract class Enumeration {
    abstract Object nextElement();
    abstract boolean hasMoreElements();
}
```

A class implementing these methods would not be inheriting anything because there are no instance variables or implemented methods. The relationship would thus be quite different than the usual subclass/superclass one. There is no extension of existing behavior. This relationship is one of *conforming to a specified set of behaviors,* namely the abstract methods in the class.

Remember, however, Java allows a class to have only one superclass. If we defined a class to be an extension of the above Enumeration class, we would be wasting the one superclass from which we would like to inherit all sorts of useful behavior. We would be wasting our choice on a class that provides no behavior but just forces us to implement two methods.

Rather than extend an abstract class that contains only abstract methods, Java allows us to define a nonclass type that consists only of abstract methods.

Such a type is called an **interface.** An interface corresponding to the above abstract class is as follows:

```
interface Enumeration {
    Object nextElement();
    boolean hasMoreElements();
}
```

A class can be declared to implement the set of methods specified in an interface by adding the keyword `implements` followed by the name of the interface:

```
class VectorEnumeration implements Enumeration {
    ...
}
```

The above declaration states that the `VectorEnumeration` class guarantees that it will implement every method declared in the `Enumeration` interface. That is, we are guaranteed that there will be a pair of methods, `nextElement` and `hasMoreElements`, inside the class as follows:

```
class VectorEnumeration implements Enumeration {
    VectorEnumeration(...) {...}    Whatever the constructor does
    Object nextElement() {
        Here we would implement getting the next element for the Vector
    }
    boolean hasMoreElements() {
        Here we would implement the test for termination
    }
}
```

The commitment of a class to implement the methods of an interface does not prevent the class from inheriting from a superclass. One could write

```
class VectorEnumeration extends OtherClass implements
            Enumeration {
    ...
}
```

Interfaces do not reside in the class hierarchy—they are not classes. They inherit nothing and possess nothing to inherit. Classes do not extend interfaces because there is no implemented behavior to extend. Rather we say they **implement** the interface.

We can declare the type of a reference variable to be an interface. We have already seen this whenever we declared an `Enumeration` reference variable:

```
Enumeration e;
```

This declaration is similar to the declaration of a reference variable whose type is that of an abstract class. Even though there are no objects of the interface itself, the reference variable may be used to refer to an object of any class implementing the interface.

Furthermore, while the relationship between an interface and the class that implements it is not one of subclass/superclass, it is still an *is-a* relationship. Any object of a class that implements an interface is considered an object of the interface as well and therefore may be assigned to a reference variable of the interface type:

```
VectorEnumeration ve = new VectorEnumeration(...);
Enumeration e = ve;
```

Java's usage of the `interface` and `implements` keywords in this context corresponds nicely with the way we have used those terms until now. An interface is merely the specification of some behavior. That specification must then be implemented in order for a user to evoke the behavior.

We conclude this chapter with one last example that defines an interface.

13.10   A Generic Sorting Method

Recall the selection sort of Chapter 10:

```
void sort(Vector v) { // On return, the elements of v are sorted in
                      //    ascending order.
        int k; // k==the index of the next position in the Vector to take care of.
               // All elements to the left of k are less than or equal to the
               //    elements at k or to the right of k.
               // All elements to the left of k are in ascending order.
        int n=v.size(); // n==number of elements in the Vector
        k = 0;
        while (k!=n-1) {
            int     j = getSmallest(v,k);
            exchange(v,k,j);
            k++;
        }
        // k==n-1 and therefore elements v[0]...v[n-2] are sorted; but since these
        //    elements are also less than the element in v[n-1] (the last element),
        //    the entire Vector is sorted.
}

// Returns the index of the smallest element in v or -1 if none exist
int getSmallest(Vector v, int k) {
    if (v==null || v.size()==k)
        return -1;
```

```
    int    i;      // Index of next element to examine; all elements at positions
                   //    less than k have been examined already
    int    small;  // Index of smallest element examined so far
    i = k+1;
    small = 0;
    while (i!=v.size()) {
        String current = (String) v.elementAt(i);
        String smallest = (String) v.elementAt(small);
        if (current.compareTo(smallest)<0)
            small = i;
        i++;
    }
    // i==v.size()
    return small;
}
```

This sort was constrained to work on a `Vector` of `String`s only. This restriction stems from the code in the `getSmallest` method

```
if (current.compareTo(smallest)<0)
        smallest = current;
```

which compares the current `String` element against the smallest `String` encountered to that point. The `sort` method itself is oblivious to the element type of the `Vector`.

We could not use this pair of methods to sort `int`s because the elements of a `Vector` must be objects, whereas `int` is a primitive data type. We could, however, use the `Integer` wrapper class. Its primary purpose is to allow integer-valued collections. We would then have to modify the `getSmallest` method. The variables `current` and `smallest` need to be redeclared as `Integer`s. We must also cast the extracted elements to `Integer`. Finally, the comparison operation must be changed. We use the `intValue` method of the `Integer` class, which returns the integer value of the object as `int`. Here is the resulting method:

```
// Returns the index of the smallest element in v or −1 if none exists
int getSmallest(Vector v, int k) {
    if (v==null || v.size()==k)
        return -1;
    int    i;      // Index of next element to examine; all elements at positions
                   //    less than k have been examined already.
    int    small;  // Index of smallest element examined so far
    i = k+1;
    small = 0;
    while (i!=v.size()) {
        Integer current = (Integer) v.elementAt(i);
        Integer smallest = (Integer) v.elementAt(small);
        if (current.intValue() < smallest.intValue()<0)
            small = i;
```

```
        i++;
    }
    // i==v.size()
    return small;
}
```

Now suppose we wish to sort a `Vector` whose elements are of some other class, say, our old friend `Name` of Chapter 4. The variables and casts must change and we must have a method that compares two `Name` objects, allowing us to determine which was the smaller of the two.

The problem with this scheme is that every time we wish to sort a `Vector` with a different element type, we must either modify `getSmallest` or make a copy of it. (Overloading doesn't help here because the signature will always be the same, and you'd have to come up with a different name for each copy.)

The answer to our problem is to introduce an interface; let's call it `Sortable`. The purpose of an interface is to provide a specification of required behavior. The behavior we require of an object that is sortable is that it possesses a method that allows it to be compared against another sortable object. Calling that method `lessThan`, we get:

```
interface Sortable {
    boolean lessThan(Sortable s); // Returns true if receiver < s
}
```

All we are doing is requiring that a sortable object provide a `lessThan` method; the implementation of that method is the responsibility of the implementing class. Thus a `lessThan` for `Strings` would use `comparesTo`, for `Integers`, a comparison using `intValue`, and so on. Our `getSmallest` then becomes the following:

```
//  Returns the index of the smallest element in v or −1 if none exists
int getSmallest(Vector v, int k) {
    if (v==null || v.size()==k)
        return -1;
    int    i;        // Index of next element to examine; all elements at
                     //    positions less than k have been examined already.
    int    small;    // Index of smallest element examined so far
    i = k+1;
    small = 0;
    while (i!=v.size()) {
        Sortable current = (Sortable) v.elementAt(i);
        Sortable smallest = (Sortable) v.elementAt(small);
        if (current.lessThan(smallest))
            small = i;
        i++;
    }
    // i==v.size()
```

```
        return small;
    }
```

This method will correctly sort any `Vector` whose elements are `Sort-able`, that is, objects of a class implementing that interface.

Before we finish, let us define a class `MyInteger` that implements the `Sortable` interface for integer values. The constructor stores its argument in the `int` instance variable. The `lessThan` method casts its argument to a `MyInteger`. (Implementing the methods of an interface is like overriding. The signature of `lessThan` in the implementing class must match the signature of the interface's `lessThan`, that is, the parameter must be declared a `Sortable`.) The `lessThan` method then compares the `MyInteger` value to the receiver.

```
class MyInteger implements Sortable {
    public MyInteger(int val) {this.val = val;}
    boolean lessThan(Sortable s) {
        MyInteger mi = (MyInteger)s;
        return this.val < mi.val;
    }
    private int val;
}
```

EXERCISES

1. Define a class that implements `lessThan` for `String` objects.

2. Define a class that implements `lessThan` for `Name` objects. What is a reasonable meaning for one `Name` to be less than another?

●

SUMMARY

Inheritance provides a mechanism to extend the behavior of an existing class. A new class may be defined that inherits all the methods and instance variables of the existing class. In addition, the new subclass may provide additional behavior through the introduction of its own methods and instance variables. Using inheritance, classes with immensely rich behavior can be quickly and easily defined by extending existing classes that provide the bulk of that behavior—the programmer need only add the behavior specific to the application at hand.

In addition to extending behavior, a subclass must often modify the existing behavior of its superclass. This often occurs because additional state information introduced at the subclass level requires a change in the subclass's behavior. A subclass may override a method of its superclass by redefining that method, making sure that the method's signature matches that of the original method in the superclass. When the method is invoked on objects of the subclass, it is the new, overriding method that is invoked.

Inheritance is a reflection of an *is-a* relationship between the subclass and the superclass. This means that any object of the subclass is also an object of the superclass. An object of the subclass may thus be used anywhere the superclass's objects can be used. In particular, references to objects of the subclass may be assigned to superclass reference variables. Invoking an overridden method on a subclass object referenced through a superclass variable causes the subclass's overriding method to be invoked. This mechanism is known as polymorphism and allows different objects to behave in their own different and appropriate ways, even when referenced through the same object.

Inheritance also allows the class designer to move behavior common to several related classes into a superclass. This helps avoid code redundancy and often provides for a more realistic modeling of behavior.

If a method is to be invoked through a superclass variable, the method must be known to the superclass. Often, however, the behavior is dependent upon the particular subclass and thus the implementation of the method can only be completed at the subclass level. Abstract methods allow the designer to specify that a method with a particular signature must be defined by any extending subclass. A class containing one or more abstract methods is known as an abstract class. No instance of an abstract class may be created as the class's behavior is incomplete.

If all the methods of a class are abstract, there is nothing to inherit. Rather than wasting a class's one superclass on such a class, an interface is defined instead, consisting solely of the method specifications. Classes implement interfaces, that is, they provide the bodies of the specified methods. Unlike inheritance, which allows a class to have only one superclass, a class may implement many interfaces.

Table 13.1 provides a roadmap to the various examples in this chapter. Each of the sample classes is presented along with the section in which the class is developed and the features illustrated by the example.

TABLE 13.1   A guide to Chapter 13 examples and features

Class	Section	Feature illustrated
BetterBR	A Better BufferedReader	Inheritance—behavior extension
ExtendedName	Revisiting the Name Class	Inheritance—additional state
InventoryItem	Factoring out Common Behavior Inheritance II (Section 13.7)	Inheritance—common behavior
Enumeration	Specifying Common Behavior—Interfaces	Interface
Sortable	A Generic Sorting Method	Interface

STUDY AID: TERMINOLOGY REVIEW

abstract class A class that contains at least one abstract method.

abstract method A method declared but not implemented by a superclass. It is the responsibility of a subclass to implement the method.

class hierarchy The structure resulting from the subclass/superclass relationships of a set of classes.

class hierarchy tree A graphical depiction of a class hierarchy. Each class is displayed below its superclass and above its subclasses.

composition A technique in which a class is defined using instance variables that are references to objects of other classes.

implements The guarantee that a class makes that it will provide the methods specified in an interface.

inheritance A technique in object-oriented languages in which one class assumes all the methods and instance variables of another class as its own. The inheriting class may also provide its own additional behavior.

interface An abstract class containing only abstract methods.

is-a The relationship between subclass and superclass. An object of a subclass *is-a* object of the superclass and may be used wherever an object of the superclass may be used.

Java class hierarchy The class hierarchy composed of Java's classes.

overriding The act of reimplementing a method in a subclass with the *exact* same signature of a method in the superclass.

polymorphism A feature of object-oriented languages in which the exact method to be invoked is determined at run time by the class of the receiving object.

root The class at the top of a class hierarchy. The root has no superclass.

subclass A class that inherits from some other class.

superclass A class that is inherited from.

QUESTIONS FOR REVIEW

1. How is inheritance specified in Java?

2. What is a class hierarchy?

3. What is the root of the Java class hierarchy?

4. Does every class in Java have a superclass? a subclass?

5. How is an interface specified in Java? How does a class implement an interface in Java?

6. What is the difference between overriding and overloading? Which is done at compile time? at run time?

7. Can you create a object whose type is an abstract class? an interface?

8. Can you declare a reference variable whose type is an abstract class? an interface?

9. How does an interface differ from an abstract class?

FURTHER EXERCISES

1. Extend the `Turtle` class developed in Chapter 12 to provide a method `move(x,y)` that raises the pen and moves to the given coordinates. What changes must be made to the `Turtle` superclass to permit this movement?

2. Extend the `Turtle` class to allow a character to be specified for the pen-mark instead of `"*"`.

3. Extend the Game of Life example of Chapter 11 so that the edges wrap around. That is, a cell at the edge of the world has as its neighbors the cells on the opposite side of the world.

Exploring the AWT Portion of the Java Class Hierarchy

In this GUI Supplement, we're going to do something a little bit different. Rather than presenting yet another applet that introduces a new graphic technique or component, we're going to explore the AWT (abstract window toolkit) portion of the Java class hierarchy, focusing on the inheritance and interface issues.

The AWT Hierarchy—A Brief Overview If you recall, when we introduced the `BufferedReader` class in Chapter 3, we pointed out that the various intermediate classes used in the creation of a `BufferedReader` model different ways of looking at an input source. In the same way, the different layers in the Java class hierarchy model the different roles that objects play. For example, consider the following portion of the hierarchy corresponding to a text area component:

```
class  Object
    class  Component
        class  TextComponent
            class  TextArea
```

A text area is a graphic component that allows the user to enter and edit multiple lines of text.

The above hierarchy indicates the following:

- A text area is first of all an object and thus inherits behavior from `Object` class, which models *all* objects in the system. For example, we can store references to a text area in a `Vector`, as we can do with any object.
- A text area is a graphic component and therefore it also inherits behavior from the `Component` class, which models graphic components in the AWT. For example, a text area may be moved—a behavior associated with all components.
- A text area is a text component and therefore it also inherits behavior from the `TextComponent` class, which models a graphic component that allows text editing. For example, the text area may change the text cursor—a behavior common to all text components.
- Finally, a text area is an area containing text and whose specific behavior is provided by the `TextArea` class that models behavior specific to the text area itself. For example, a text area may be created with a scroll bar— behavior that is specific to a multiline text component.

This layering of classes and behavior is an application of using inheritance to factor common behavior out to a superclass. Each class in a hierarchy models behavior common to all classes below it. By placing that behavior into a single class—the superclass—we are placing the responsibility for that behavior in exactly one place. Inheritance then allows each subclass requiring the behavior to possess it.

The Interfaces Interfaces are not part of the class hierarchy. However, they can form hierarchies of their own. One interface can extend another interface using the same sort of syntax for class extension (inheritance). For example, the following code declares the `ActionListener` interface to be an extension of the `EventListener` interface:

```
interface  ActionListener  extends  EventListener  {
    Method specifications unique to ActionListener
}
```

This code states that the `ActionListener` is a specification of all the methods that are specified by the `EventListener` interface. It is also a specification of any new methods introduced in `ActionListener`. Any class that implements `ActionListener` must therefore implement all the methods of the `EventListener` interface as well. Interface extension allows us to add a new set of method requirements to an existing one.

Methods That Query or Modify Behavior   The classes in the AWT maintain different properties associated with the interface: component size, color, font, and so on. Many of these properties are made accessible to the user of the class through *get/set* methods, that is, methods that allow the user to query (*get*) or modify (*set*) the value of a property. These methods usually travel in get/set pairs.

A Very Brief Look at Packages   The Java predefined class hierarchy consists of several hundred classes and interfaces—and that's not counting any classes you may write. To maintain some order among this huge collection, Java provides a mechanism that logically groups related classes—the package. The packages provided by Java along with some of their related classes include:

- `java.applet`—Applet-related classes: `Applet`
- `java.awt`—AWT-related classes: `Button`, `Checkbox`, `Color`
- `java.awt.event`—Event-related classes: `ActionEvent`, `MouseEvent`
- `java.io`—Input/output-related classes: `BufferedReader`, `File`
- `java.lang`—Java language-related classes: `String`, `Integer`, `Object`
- package `java.math`—Math-related classes: `BigInteger`
- package `java.net`—Network-related classes: `URL`, `URLConnection`
- `java.text`—Text-related classes: `DateFormat`, `DecimalFormat`
- `java.util`—Utility and collection classes: `Date`, `Vector`

There are several other packages predefined by Java, but their description is beyond the scope of this book.

We will not go into any detail here regarding the creation or use of packages beyond noting that when we used `import`, we were effectively informing the compiler of the identities of the packages whose classes we were using.

The full name of a class is actually the class name with the package name as a prefix. Thus, the text area hierarchy could have been written:

```
class  java.lang.Object
    class  java.awt.Component
        java.awt.class  TextComponent
            java.awt.class  TextArea
```

Note that it is possible to define a class in one package that inherits from a class in a different package.

The Graphical Components   Here is the portion of the hierarchy modeling the various graphical components. The classes in bold are the ones we discuss.

```
class  java.lang.Object
    class  java.awt.Component
        class  java.awt.Button
        class  java.awt.Canvas
        class  java.awt.Checkbox
        class java.awt.Choice
        class  java.awt.Container
            class  java.awt.Panel
                class  java.applet.Applet
            class  java.awt.ScrollPane
            class  java.awt.Window
                class  java.awt.Dialog
                    class j ava.awt.FileDialog
                class  java.awt.Frame
            class  java.awt.Label
            class  java.awt.List
            class  java.awt.Scrollbar
            class  java.awt.TextComponent
                class  java.awt.TextArea
                class  java.awt.TextField
```

Class `Component` is the superclass for all graphic component classes, the classes that model windows, buttons, list boxes, and so on. The `Component` class models behavior common to all graphic components. Methods defined in this class deal with properties such as visibility, size, colors, and font. A `paint` method is provided. It is invoked when the component must be repainted when the component is reopened after being minimized, when the component is exposed after being hidden by another window, or when an object sends a `repaint` message to the component. The `paint` method is usually overridden by the subclass to provide component-specific behavior.

The `Component` class also provides methods for registering a listener of various component-related events: hiding, showing, moving, or resizing a component. Other events specific to particular component subclass are registered by using methods defined in that component's class.

By virtue of being in the superclass of every component, the above methods are inherited by every component class, providing a rich base set of behavior.

Component Subclasses   Each of the subclasses of `Component` models a specific graphical component, and therefore provides behavior specific to that component. We now very briefly describe some of the more commonly used component classes and their behavior.

The `Button` class models a clickable command button. The class provides methods to modify/query the button's label, as well as a method that allows an object to register as a listener of button clicks.

The `Canvas` class models a surface upon which to draw graphic shapes, such as circles, lines, and text. A primary purpose of the component is to isolate the drawn items from other graphical components. This class primarily serves as a superclass to programmer-defined classes that override the `paint` method to draw application-specific information on the canvas.

The `Checkbox` class models a check box that can be selected or deselected. Several `Checkbox` objects can be used together with the `CheckBox-Group` class to provide a set of mutually exclusive boxes: clicking one deselects the previous clicked box. Methods are provided to select/deselect the box, access the box's text label, register event listeners, and obtain information about the related `CheckboxGroup` object.

Class `Container` is the superclass for all classes that model components that may contain other components: for example, windows and panels. The methods provided therefore focus on the relationship between a container and its embedded components: specification of layout managers, addition and removal of components, and registration of container-related events. In addition, the `paint` method is overridden so that it contains code to invoke the `paint` method of the container's components.

The `Panel` class provides the most basic of container functionality. It essentially does nothing more than inherit its methods from its superclass. Its main purpose is to provide a convenient mechanism to break up a larger container into groups of components, each in its own panel, that can be laid out independently of the rest of the container.

The `Applet` class models an applet—a program that executes while embedded within a browser. It inherits from `Panel` all the basic container behavior so that components may be added to the applet, providing a graphical interface. Methods defined at the `Applet` level include those that deal with the program perspective of this class: initialization code to be performed when the applet is initially loaded and when it begins execution.

Class `Window` provides the basic functionality of a window residing on the desktop. Its methods deal with displaying the window, moving the window to the front or back of its desktop position—that is whether the window is below or above all other windows residing at the same location—and registration of window-related events.

The `Dialog` class models the behavior of a window whose purpose is to accept user input. Often this input is required before the program can proceed, in which case we want no other user activity to be allowed in any other window of the program until the user has completed the dialog window. In such a situation, we say the dialog is *modal*. If the user can perform action in another window, it is *nonmodal*. The methods of the `Dialog` class include testing and setting modality as well as manipulating the text in the title bar of the window.

In Java, a *frame* is a window with a title bar; various control elements to minimize, maximize, and close the window; and possibly a menu bar across the top. The `Frame` class models the behavior of a frame. The methods deal with manipulating the title and menu bar as well as event registration.

In an applet, an `Applet` object is the top-level container. Stand-alone applications, that is, programs with a main method, can also use a graphical user interface. The top-level container in that case is a programmer-defined subclass of the `Frame` class. The constructor of this subclass typically contains the code that would appear in an applet's `init` method.

The `Label` class models a component consisting of text that is displayed but cannot be edited by the user. Methods include obtaining or setting this text.

The `List` class provides the functionality of a box displaying a list of items from which one or more selections may be made. Scroll bars are automatically added to the list as it grows beyond the number of items displayable in the box. Methods include manipulating and selecting the list items, specifying whether multiple items may be selected, and list-specific event registration.

The `TextComponent` class is the superclass for editable text components. Its methods provide manipulation of the text, positioning of the text cursor, controlling whether the text may be modified, selecting portions of the text, and text-specific event registration. The `TextArea` component class extends `TextComponent` to model a multiline text field, and thus supplies methods dealing with scrollbars. The `TextField` class restricts the text component to a single line.

The Event Classes   Here is the event portion of the hierarchy. The occurrence of an event within the AWT environment causes the system to create an object in this hierarchy whose state contains information specific to the event. Thus, moving the mouse causes the AWT environment to create a

`MouseEvent` object with information regarding the mouse move, for example, the position of the mouse.

```
class   java.util.EventObject
    class   java.awt.AWTEvent
        class   java.awt.event.ActionEvent
        class   java.awt.event.AdjustmentEvent
        class   java.awt.event.ComponentEvent
            class   java.awt.event.ContainerEvent
            class   java.awt.event.FocusEvent
            class   java.awt.event.InputEvent
                class   java.awt.event.KeyEvent
                class   java.awt.event.MouseEvent
            class   java.awt.event.PaintEvent
            class   java.awt.event.WindowEvent
        class   java.awt.event.ItemEvent
        class   java.awt.event.TextEvent
```

The `Event` class is the superclass of the event portion of the hierarchy and as such models the behavior common to *all* events. Its primary method, `getSource`, returns the object, known as the *event source*, that generated the event.

The `AWTEvent` class is the superclass for all AWT-related events; these are the only ones we are examining. The method of interest is `getID`, which returns an integer identifying the sort of event that occurred. These integer values usually are declared as constants in the specific event subclass.

The `ActionEvent` class models an action event specified by the user, for example, a button click. Its methods provide access to what is known as the *command name* associated with the event. In the case of a button click, the command name is the text of the button. Any special keys, for example, the `Alt` or `Ctrl` keys, held down during the click may also be obtained through the `getModifiers` method.

The `AdjustmentEvent` class maintains information about events generated by components that can be adjusted, most notably scrollbars. The methods include querying the type of adjustment and the current value. For example, a scrollbar can generate a small or large motion, depending upon where the bar is clicked.

The `ComponentEvent` class deals with component-related events. The events associated with this class include hiding, moving, or resizing the component.

Events associated with the `ContainerEvent` class include the addition or removal of a component in the container.

The `FocusEvent` class maintains the information associated with a component gaining the *focus*. That is, the component becomes the active element of the interface. The two basic events are gaining and losing the focus.

The `InputEvent` class is the superclass of events involving user input. Methods include the ability to test whether special keys such as `Alt` or `Ctrl`—known as *modifiers*—were held down at the time of the event.

The `KeyEvent` class extends the behavior of its `InputEvent` superclass by adding behavior specific to keyboard input. The methods include querying for the key that was pressed generating this event. Constants are defined in this class corresponding to the various function keys, allowing the user to refer to these keys.

The `MouseEvent` class is the other subclass of `InputEvent`; it maintains the state of a mouse-generated event. Event types include clicking, dragging, moving, pressing, and releasing the mouse. Associated with the event and accessible through methods are the coordinates of the mouse position, and the number of clicks causing the event (for example, single versus double click).

The `WindowEvent` class maintains window-related events: closing, minimizing, and restoring a window.

The `ItemEvent` handles events generated by making a selection, for example, from a list box. The events of interest are selecting and deselecting.

The `TextEvent` class models an event generated through the manipulation of text. The single event type defined in this class is the text-changed event. The associated text can be obtained through the methods of the component generating the event.

The Listener Interfaces   In order to handle an event generated by a component object, an object must register itself as a *listener* of the component object. It accomplishes this by invoking the listener registration method of the component object. The method name is of the form set*EventType*`Listener` or add*EventType*`Listener`. In addition, the class of the listener object must support a standard set of methods to handle the events when they occur. The listener class is usually already a subclass of some superclass that provides it with the bulk of its nonevent-related behavior. Therefore, the listener method-set is specified as an interface that the listener object must implement.

We've said that interfaces can form their own hierarchies representing increasing sets of required methods. Here is the interface hierarchy corresponding to listeners. The root of the hierarchy is the `EventListener` interface. The indentation reflects the hierarchy of the interfaces.

```
interface  java.util.EventListener
    interface  java.awt.event.ActionListener
    interface  java.awt.event.AdjustmentListener
    interface  java.awt.event.ComponentListener
    interface  java.awt.event.ContainerListener
    interface  java.awt.event.FocusListener
    interface  java.awt.event.KeyListener
    interface  java.awt.event.MouseListener
```

```
interface   java.awt.event.MouseMotionListener
interface   java.awt.event.TextListener
interface   java.awt.event.WindowListener
```

Each listener interface specifies one or more event-handling methods that must be provided by an implementing class. These event-handling methods accept as an argument an object of an event class corresponding to the listener type, for example, an `ActionEvent` for the `ActionListener` methods. These methods are invoked when the corresponding event occurs. Thus, the `actionPerformed` method of the `ActionListener` interface is invoked when an action event—a button click, for example—occurs. This invocation is performed by the AWT environment, which is also responsible for creating and initializing the associated event object.

The `ActionListener` interface requires an implementing class to provide a single method `actionPerformed` that accepts an `ActionEvent` object as its single argument. The class implementing this method can use the argument to obtain information regarding the event in order to process it.

The `AdjustmentListener` interface requires that one method, `adjustmentValueChanged`, be implemented. Its accepts an `AdjustmentEvent` object as its argument.

The `ComponentListener` interface has four required methods corresponding to the hiding, displaying, resizing, and moving a component. Each of these methods accepts a `ComponentEvent` argument.

The `ContainerListener` requires two event-handling methods corresponding to adding interface and removing an embedded component. The methods accept a `ContainerEvent` argument.

The `FocusListener` interface specifies two methods: gaining and losing the focus. They accept a `FocusEvent` argument.

An `ItemEvent` is associated with a component from which a selection may be made. The `ItemListener` interface requires that a single method be implemented. This method is invoked when some change has been made regarding the selection, for example, if the user has changed the highlighted selection in the list box. The method accepts an `ItemEvent` as its argument.

The `KeyListener` interface requires three methods to be implemented corresponding to pressing, releasing, or the combined press-and-release of a key, called *typing a key* (a combination of the other two). The methods accept a `KeyEvent` as their argument.

The `MouseListener` interface contains method specifications corresponding to all mouse-related events except mouse movement. The methods correspond to pressing, releasing, clicking (similar to the typing of the `KeyListener` in that it involves a press/release event pair occurrence), as well as the mouse entering or exiting the boundaries of a component. The methods accept a `MouseEvent` as argument.

The `MouseMotionListener` interface handles mouse movement. Moving the mouse is handled through a separate mechanism because of the large number of mouse movement events generated and the consequent effect upon performance. There are two events associated with mouse movement— simple movement, and dragging a component. Each is specified in a separate method that accepts a `MouseEvent` as its argument.

The `TextListener` interface specifies a single method corresponding to the event occurring when a text-related event occurs. The method accepts a `TextEvent` as its argument.

The `WindowListener` interface specifies a number of methods corresponding to window-related events: minimizing, restoring, closing, opening, and so on. Each accepts a `WindowEvent` as its argument.

The Adapter Classes   Although many of the listener interfaces specify only a single method, several of them require that multiple methods be provided by an implementing class. It is often the case that an application is only interested in handling one or two of these event types and thus only wishes to provide the methods corresponding to these. However, neglecting to implement the remaining methods will cause a compile-time error to the effect that the interface is incompletely specified. To reduce the burden upon a class implementing an interface with multiple methods, Java provides a set of classes, known as the *adapter* classes, which provide empty method bodies for each of the methods specified in a listener interface. For example, the `Component-Adapter` class, which implements the `ComponentListener` interface, appears this way:

```
class ComponentAdapter implements ComponentListener {
    public void componentResized(ComponentEvent e) {}
    public void componentMoved(ComponentEvent e) {}
    public void componentShown(ComponentEvent e) {}
    public void componentHidden(ComponentEvent e) {}
}
```

A class that is intended to be a `ComponentListener` without implementing all of the required methods can then inherit from the `Component-Adapter` class and override only those methods it is interested in. For example, the following class wishes only to handle the resize event:

```
class MyComponentListenerClass extends ComponentAdaptor {
    public void componentResized(ComponentEvent e) {
        code to handle the resize event
    }
}
```

The remaining (empty) event-handling methods are inherited from the `ComponentAdapter` superclass.

One word of caution when using adapter classes—they are inherited, thus preventing the subclass from inheriting behavior from any other class. Because the behavior inherited from the adapter class consists of empty method bodies, their usefulness is limited.

GUI *supplement 2*

Swing

Introduction   Up to now, our GUI supplements have used the AWT—the Abstract Window Toolkit—Java's basic graphic user interface. It is important to remember that the AWT is not part of the Java language proper, but rather a package of classes that is provided as part of the 'predefined' Java environment. It is thus possible to substitute a new graphical user interface package for the AWT, by developing a different set of classes for handling a GUI. In fact, the Java Development Kit version 1.2, also known as Java 2, provides exactly that—a replacement for the AWT. This replacement, known as **Swing**, offers many enhancements over the AWT: a much broader choice of controls, a more polished appearance, and in general a greater degree of programmer control over the appearance and operation of the interface. Each of the basic AWT controls such as `Button` or `TextField` has a Swing counterpart, making it fairly easy to move from an AWT-based GUI to one that is Swing-based. In addition, there are a number of controls that are new to Swing and that provide the programmer with a very rich and powerful set of tools for GUI development.

   In this Supplement, we examine some of the new features introduced in Swing:

- The *look-and-feel* facility
- Swing's improved component hierarchy
- One or two of the new controls and features

   This supplement, however, is not just about a better GUI package. In the context of this chapter—inheritance, polymorphism, and the brief look at the AWT hierarchy—the most interesting thing about Swing is that there's no new Java, just a new set of classes. As Java matured, its designers decided to produce a more powerful GUI, but to do so they didn't make changes to the language or even the AWT—instead they wrote a new set of classes—the Swing package. As we will see, the new package uses behavior of AWT such as layout managers and events. Far from throwing out or even ignoring the AWT, Swing's designers incorporated whatever useful behavior they could from the AWT. In several places they extended existing AWT classes or implemented AWT interfaces, thus reducing the amount of code that had to be written and tested. If the AWT is a superb example of designing a class hierarchy that takes advantage of inheritance and polymorphism, Swing is the perfect example of exploiting and extending behavior and proof that object-orientation is an invaluable design and programming approach. We will continue to emphasize this point throughout the supplement.

We first present the basic mechanics of writing a Swing-based applet and then we'll explore some of the enhancements.

A Simple Swing-Based Applet Coding simple Swing-based applets is not that much different than coding applets using AWT—Swing was designed that way to ease the transition.

Let us start with a very simple applet that displays a button and changes the button's text when clicked. We will code it in both AWT and Swing and compare the differences. We'll look at the code (what we have to be concerned about) and at what the user sees (which is the ultimate point of having a different interface). Here is the AWT-based version:

```
import java.awt.*;        // AWT classes ...
import java.awt.event.*;  //... and events
import java.applet.*;     // Applet-related classes

public class PushApplet extends Applet implements
                                          ActionListener {
    public void init() {
        theButton = new Button("Push Me!");
        add(theButton);

        theButton.addActionListener(this);
    }

    public void actionPerformed(ActionEvent e) {
        theButton.setLabel("Ouch!");
    }

    Button theButton;
}
```

Here is the applet in action before clicking (Figure 13.7) and after clicking (Figure 13.8):

FIGURE 13.7
Before clicking

FIGURE 13.8
After clicking

Now let's take a look at the Swing-based version. For this and many applets, much of the coding is the same as for the AWT-based version. Event handling, layout management, and the logic specific to the applet are the same. There are differences, but many of them are straightforward, requiring little in the way of actual design of logic changes. Here are the principal differences:

- The basic Swing classes and, in particular, the components (buttons, text boxes, and so forth) are imported from the package `javax.swing`. The name `javax` indicates that the package is a Java *extension*, that is, a package of classes that has been added to the predefined Java class environment, which is known as the *core*. This exact distinction is not important to us—what is important is to remember that the Swing's package name begins with `javax`, not `java`.

- For each of the AWT components, buttons, text fields, lists, and so on, there is a corresponding Swing component. The name of the Swing component is the same as its AWT counterpart, prefixed with a 'J'. Thus we have JButton, JTextField, and so on. There is also a Swing-based applet class, `JApplet`, that should be used whenever Swing components are employed.

- In AWT, components may be placed directly upon the `Applet`'s surface, using the `add` method. In Swing, the JApplet does not act as a container for its components. Rather, the JApplet contains a single `Container` object, known as the *content pane*, and it is the content pane upon which all of the `JApplet`'s components are placed, again using the `add` method. A reference to the content pane can be obtained from the `JApplet` via the `getContentPane` method.

- The default layout manager for the `JApplet`'s content pane is `Border-Layout`, whereas `Applet`'s default layout manager is `FlowLayout`. Therefore, if we wish to lay out components on the content pane in the same way as they are laid out on the applet, we must set the content pane's layout manager to `FlowLayout`.

`JApplet` extends the `Applet` class and therefore inherits all standard applet behavior. The JApplet class need only add new behavior specific to Swing, in particular to the presence of the new Swing components.

The superclass of Swing components is the JComponent class, which itself derives from the standard AWT Container class and thus from the AWT Component class as well. This means that all Swing components inherit all AWT component behaviors including the ability to set foreground and background colors, generate events, and so on.

Taking into account the above differences, we have the following Swing code for our applet. We've highlighted the Swing-related changes.

```
import java.awt.*;        // Still use some AWT classes
import java.awt.event.*; //   (Container) and events
                         //   (ActionEvent)
```

```
import javax.swing.*;      // For Swing components and
                          //    JApplet

public class PushJApplet extends JApplet implements
                                        ActionListener {
    public void init() {
        Container contentPane = getContentPane();
        contentPane.setLayout(new FlowLayout());
        theButton = new JButton("Push Me!");
        contentPane.add(theButton);

        theButton.addActionListener(this);
    }

    public void actionPerformed(ActionEvent e) {
        theButton.setText("Ouch!");
    }

    JButton theButton;
}
```

As you can see, the code modifications are relatively simple. This makes it easy for a programmer to make the initial transition from AWT to Swing simply by making the above changes. More advanced Swing-specific features can then be introduced as desired.

Here is the output of the Swing-based applet before clicking (Figure 13.9) and after clicking (Figure 13.10):

FIGURE 13.9   **FIGURE 13.10**
Before clicking   **After clicking**

The applet looks quite similar to the AWT one, the primary differences being the background color and the appearance of the button. Such differences give the user interface its *look and feel*. This change in appearance is one of the prominent features of Swing, and is discussed in the next section.

Look and Feel (L&F) If you've ever worked on more than one type of machine, for example on a PC and a Macintosh, you may have noticed that the graphical components look somewhat different. A button is recognizable as a button, but its exact appearance will usually differ from one system to the next. For example, here is what a button looks like in two of the more common graphical environments, Microsoft Windows (Figure 13.11) and Motif, a Unix-based interface (Figure 13.12):

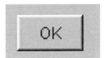

FIGURE 13.11
A Window-style
Button

FIGURE 13.12
A Motif-Style
Button

Although they both look like buttons, there is a distinctive difference between the two. In fact, with a bit of experience on both systems, it is fairly easy to look at a display and say which system is running— Windows or Motif, or some other. Each interface is said to have its own distinctive *look and feel*, or L&F for short. We also refer to the look and feel as the *user interface*.

Java is designed to be cross-platform, and so it has a bit of an 'identity' problem when it comes to GUI: Which look and feel should it use? The AWT took the approach of using the look and feel of the machine it is running on, what the Java documentation speaks of as the *native*, or *system*, look and feel. Thus an applet running on a Windows platform looked like Windows, one running on a Mac looked like a Mac, and so on. The native look and feel is accomplished by using the graphic components of the native system: a `But-ton` is displayed using a Windows button when running on Windows. While this solves the identity problem, it doesn't provide a uniform look to the applet as one moved from one platform to another.

Swing provides *pluggable look and feel*, that is, the ability for the programmer to choose a particular look and feel. There are several look and feels distributed with the JDK:

- The Java look and feel (JLF). This is the default and is meant to be cross-platform, giving the interface a uniform appearance regardless of platform. This look and feel is also called the *cross-platform look and feel*. The actual name of this look and feel is *Metal* because the surface and components have a metallic appearance.
- The Windows look and feel
- The Motif look and feel

When we introduced canvases, we explained that what distinguishes a component from simple graphic shapes such as lines, ovals, or text is the association of a component with a class and its ability to generate events. The actual appearance of the component on the display, however, is itself nothing more than a series of graphic shapes. The display of a button, for example, is nothing more than a rectangle (the border of the button), some text (the label), and some shading in a contrasting color (giving the button its 3D appearance). It is *not* a real button. Changing the set of graphic shapes associated with a component can thus change its appearance.

A particular look and feel is implemented by first designing the appearance of the various components. A graphic artist rather than a programmer would typically be responsible for this task. The components are designed around some uniform theme, just like the characters of a single font. Once the 'look' of the components has been designed, the programmer implements that design by coding the logic to paint the component shapes.

The above technique is not restricted to the JDK-supplied look and feels. We can produce our own look and feel by coding the painting of our components. Although this is not terribly difficult, it does get somewhat involved and is beyond the scope of our present discussion.

Instead, let us develop a Swing-based applet that will demonstrate some typical components using the look and feels provided by Java. The applet provides a four-button interface, allowing the user to choose among the various look and feels. Initially, the applet is displayed using the default L&F, as shown in Figure 13.13:

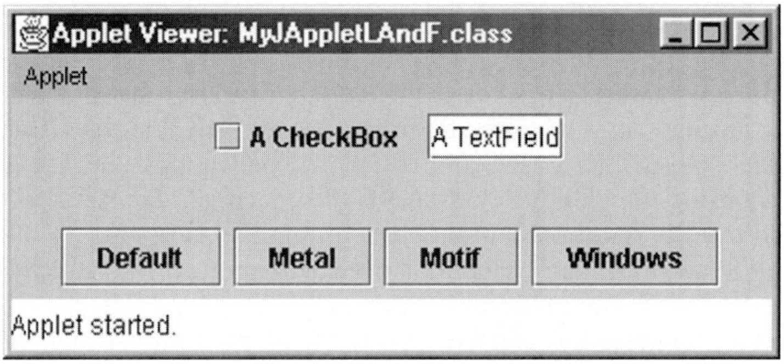

FIGURE 13.13   **The default (Metal) cross-platform look and feel.**

Three classes are of importance when working with look and feel:

- The abstract superclass `LookAndFeel` models the notion of look and feel. Subclasses of this class implement particular look and feels: Windows, JLF, and so on.
- The `UIManagerClass` is responsible for maintaining the current look and feel of the applet. The behavior of this class includes:
  - Retrieving the current L&F (`getLookAndFeel`)
  - Changing the L&F (`setLookAndFeel`)
  - Retrieving a reference to a `LookAndFeel` instance corresponding to the native L&F (`getSystemLookAndFeel`)
- The `SwingUtilities` class contains useful Swing-related utility methods that don't quite belong anywhere else. In particular, `SwingUtilities` contains the `updateComponentTreeUI` method that causes a component to update its current look and feel.

Changing an applet's L&F involves finding a subclass of `LookAndFeel` that provides the desired L&F (or creating a new one), invoking `setLookAndFeel`, and finally, invoking `updateComponentTreeUI`.

```java
import javax.swing.*;
import java.awt.*;
import java.awt.event.*;

// Different 'look-and-feel' packages
import com.sun.java.swing.plaf.windows.*;
import com.sun.java.swing.plaf.motif.*;
import javax.swing.plaf.metal.*;

public class MyJAppletLAndF extends JApplet implements
                                        ActionListener {
    public void init() {
        Container contentPane = getContentPane();

        defaultLookAndFeel =
                    UIManager.getLookAndFeel();

        defaultButton = new JButton("Default");
        metalButton = new JButton("Metal");
        motifButton = new JButton("Motif");
        windowsButton = new JButton("Windows");

        // Create panel of sample components, some
        // with borders
        JPanel components = new JPanel();
        JCheckBox checkBox = new JCheckBox(
                            "A CheckBox");
        components.add(checkBox);
        JTextField textField = new JTextField(
                            "A TextField");
        components.add(textField);

        // Create panel of buttons
        JPanel buttons = new JPanel();
        buttons.add(defaultButton);
        buttons.add(metalButton);
        buttons.add(motifButton);
        buttons.add(windowsButton);

        // Add the panels to the content pane
        contentPane.add("North", components);
        contentPane.add("South", buttons);

        // Register with the buttons as a Listener
        defaultButton.addActionListener(this);
        metalButton.addActionListener(this);
        motifButton.addActionListener(this);
        windowsButton.addActionListener(this);
    }
```

```
public void actionPerformed(ActionEvent ev) {
    try {
        if (ev.getSource() == motifButton)
            UIManager.setLookAndFeel(
                    new MotifLookAndFeel());
        else if (ev.getSource() ==
                                windowsButton)
            UIManager.setLookAndFeel(
                    new WindowsLookAndFeel());
        else if (ev.getSource() ==
                                defaultButton)
            UIManager.setLookAndFeel(
                    defaultLookAndFeel);
        else
            UIManager.setLookAndFeel(
                    new MetalLookAndFeel());
        SwingUtilities.updateComponentTreeUI
                                (this);
        validate();
    } catch (UnsupportedLookAndFeelException e) {
        System.out.println("
            UnsupportedLookAndFeelException");
    }
}

LookAndFeel defaultLookAndFeel;
JButton defaultButton, metalButton, motifButton,
        windowsButton;
}
```

The basic logic of the applet is straightforward. When a button is clicked, the corresponding L&F is set and the componets updated by invoking `Swing-Utilities.updateComponentTreeUI(this)`. This causes the applet and all the components within it to change their L&F. During applet initialization, we obtain the current (default) L&F and save it in an instance variable for use if the user clicks the `Default` button.

Here is the applet using the Motif look and feel (Figure 13.14) and the Windows look and feel (Figure 13.15):

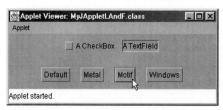

FIGURE 13.14 The Motif look and feel

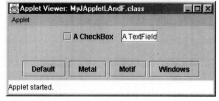

FIGURE 13.15 The Windows look and feel

Swing's Enhanced Controls   While pluggable look and feel provides great flexibility in the appearance of the interface, Swing's most popular feature is probably its introduction of numerous additional controls as well as its enhancements to the AWT controls. We now present a small applet that demonstrates some of these features. Though relatively simple to code, the applet contains a quite sophisticated control—the tabbed pane.

Despite larger displays and increased screen resolutions, screen 'real estate' is always at a premium. It always seems that no matter how big our screen is, we seem to always manage to fill it, and even want more. If the components of our interface require a window larger than our screen, we could always ad scroll bars; however, it's awkward to be constantly scrolling through the window trying to find a particular component. One solution adopted by many graphic interfaces such as Motif and Windows 95 is to use a *tabbed pane* (see Figure 13.16). Windows may be added as separate tabs to the pane; clicking a tab exposes the associated window.

FIGURE 13.16   A tabbed pane

Our applet contains a tabbed pane of two tabs: one with a pair of buttons, the other a single line text field and a multiline text area. Each button contains a small picture, or *icon*, in addition to the button's text. The multiline text area has a border containing a title, while the single-line text field has a slightly thicker, colored border. Finally, pausing the cursor over the text field causes a small help box, known as a *tool tip*, to appear. We won't bother responding to the buttons, we're just interested in displaying the various controls. Figures 13.17 and 13.18 show some displays of the applet.

One of the new control classes introduced with Swing is the `TabbedPane`. Components—usually panels—may be added with the `addTab` method. The complexity of the tab switching and the exposing of the correct window is all

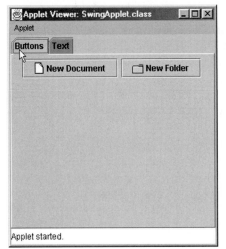

FIGURE 13.17   The Buttons tab exposed

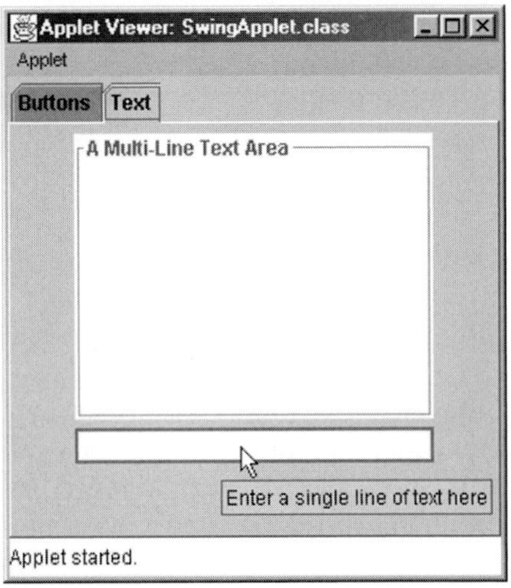

FIGURE 13.18   The Text tab exposed and a visible tool tip

handled by the code in the `TabbedPane` class. The applet programmer does not have to do anything.

Although the behavior of the tabbed pane is somewhat complex, it is completely implemented by the `TabbedPane` class. A few wisely chosen public methods are all the programmer using the control requires in order to work with it. This is the big advantage of interface versus implementation—the user works with the former and is protected from the litter by use of `private` and `protected` access control.

In the AWT, only `Window`, `Frame`, `Panel`, `Applet`, and a few other classes were derived from `Container`. Controls such as `Button` or `TextField` derived directly from `Component` and thus were not subclasses of `Container`, and could not have other components added to them. While the inability to add a component to a button may at first not seem very restrictive, it does prevent us from adding a picture to the button's surface.

Swing's hierarchy removes this and other related restrictions. `JComponent`, the superclass of all Swing components extends the AWT `Container` class, and therefore all Swing components can act as a GUI container.

The `JButton`, method `setIcon`, is used to place the icon on the button's surface. Although the programmer could do this directly with the `add` method, `setIcon` makes sure the icon does not interfere with the button's text. Our applet uses two icons present in the JDK, primarily to ensure that it runs correctly on any installation.

The structure of a system's class hierarchy can have far-reaching, and sometimes unexpected, consequences. The AWT's restriction on which components are containers can impact upon a totally unrelated feature. The larger a software problem, the more important the need to carefully design its class structure.

We're also adding some borders to our controls—Swing allows us to specify a border for any component. Adding a border to, say, a button in AWT is possible, but somewhat cumbersome. Swing, on the other hand, abstracts the job of maintaining a border into an `AbstractBorder` superclass. There are several subclasses of `AbstractBorder`: `LineBorder`, and `TitledBorder` are two. `LineBorder` models a simple line border with a color and border width, while `TitledBorder` allows for a border with a text heading. A programmer can create instances of these border classes and associate them with components, using the `setBorder` method. Similarly, using the `setToolTipText` method, a programmer can associate with any Swing component a piece of text to act as a tool tip.

All Swing components derive from the `JComponent` class. The `setBorder` and `setToolTipText` methods are defined at the `JComponent` level and therefore are inherited by all Swing components.

Having all border classes derive from a single superclass, `AbstractBorder`, allows all Swing components to treat all border objects in the same way and with the same methods.

As before, the applet is surprisingly simple, given its relative sophistication. Its basic logic is also quite similar to an AWT applet's, the primary difference being the use of Swing rather than AWT components. Components are declared, created, and added to various GUI containers. The applet code follows.

```java
import java.awt.*;
import java.awt.event.*;
import javax.swing.*;
import javax.swing.border.*;

// Accesses two predefined icons
import javax.swing.plaf.metal.MetalIconFactory.*;

public class SwingApplet extends JApplet {
    public void init() {

        JTabbedPane tp = new JTabbedPane();
        getContentPane().add("Center", tp);

        JPanel buttons = new JPanel(); // Create the button
                                       // panel
        tp.addTab("Buttons", buttons); // Add it as a new tab
```

```
        // Add buttons to the button tab
        JButton b1 = new JButton("New Document");
        b1.setIcon(new FileIcon16());// Add icon
        buttons.add(b1);
        JButton b2 = new JButton("New Folder");
        b2.setIcon(new FolderIcon16());// Add icon
        buttons.add(b2);

        // Add text components to the text tab
        JPanel texts = new JPanel();
        tp.addTab("Text", texts);
        JTextArea textArea = new JTextArea(10, 20);
        textArea.setBorder(new TitledBorder(
                                "A Multiline Text Area"));
        texts.add(textArea);
        JTextField textField = new JTextField(20);
        // Add a red border of thickness 2
        textField.setBorder(new LineBorder(Color.red, 2));

        // Add a tool tip to the text field
        textField.setToolTipText(
                        "Enter a single line of text here");
        texts.add(textField);
    }
}
```

With all the increased sophistication of the Swing GUI, all that is really new here is the behavior of the Swing classes. While the new controls are much more powerful than those of the AWT, working with them is not much different. Components are still laid out, colored, and sized, and event handlers written. The beauty of object-oriented programming lies with the objects' assuming responsibility for their own actions and allowing their user to concentrate on the important part—composing, combining, and extending them into applications.

chapter 14

Exceptions

14.1 Expect the Unexpected

Imagine the following code, which might appear in an inventory program:

```
int    numberInStock = Integer.parseInt(br.readLine());
```

We expect that all is well with the input source represented by the `Buff-eredReader` object referenced by `br` and that eventually it will produce a line containing a number. We generally don't expect the following to occur:

- The `BufferedReader` object represents a file on a floppy disk that has been erroneously ejected from the computer by the user.
- The `BufferedReader` object represents a network connection that has suddenly failed because a leaky pipe suddenly ruined one of the campus routers.
- The `BufferedReader` object represents a file on a hard disk that has just failed.

We don't expect circumstances such as these unless we are professional programmers, that is. Professional programmers must learn to *expect the unexpected*.

The unexpected does not consist only of physical interferences such as those mentioned above. When we write

```
int    numberInStock = Integer.parseInt(br.readLine());
```

we are expecting that a number will appear in the input at this point. Consider, however, the following possibilities:

- What if the data entry operator types a "w" instead of a "2" by mistake?
- What if the operator had been distracted while typing and had accidentally held the 3 key down too long, adding twenty-two 3's to the end of the number?

The context in which software executes is not as predictable as we would like. Good software is designed to take this into account. In this chapter we examine the mechanism that Java provides to handle unexpected circumstances.

EXERCISES

1. Return to the `Employee` example of Chapter 6. What unexpected circumstances could occur in its various methods?

2. Return to the `WWWWH` example program at the end of Chapter 3. What unexpected circumstances could arise in executing that program?　　•

14.2　Encountering the Unexpected

Responding to the unexpected is as much a part of the required behavior of our "smart and helpful" objects as dealing with the expected. Behavior, as we know, is implemented in methods. But what can methods do when they encounter the unexpected?

Let's consider a method from the `Integer` class that we've been using since Chapter 5, `parseInt`. Its argument is a `String`—hopefully one that is a well-formed decimal representation of an integer. But what if it's not? What should `parseInt` do, for example, if its argument is `"eggplant"`?

One thing `parseInt` cannot do is correct the error—it has no way of knowing what the argument should have been. Nor could `parseInt` query the user for the correct argument with code such as the following:

```
System.err.print("Hi, parseInt here. I have a +
                bad non-numeric argument");
System.err.print(... argument goes here ...);
System.err.print("Please type in the proper value: ");
... = ...readLine();        Read new String from keyboard.
```

First, there may not be any available user. The invocation of `parseInt` may be in a program that is processing files or carrying out network operations. Second, it is impossible for `parseInt` to let a user know the context in which this problem has occurred because `parseInt` doesn't know whether it is converting a pay-rate value, an hours-worked value, a number-of-dependents value, and so on. There may be hundreds of places in the program where integers are read in. That being the case, how could the user possibly know the correct value to type in?

In sum, *it is not the responsibility of `parseInt` to correct or even identify the ultimate source of the error.* The argument came from its invoker, so the responsibility therefore rests on the invoker of `parseInt`. Thus, `parseInt` must inform its invoker that a problem has occurred. How can that be done?

Normally, information from a method is communicated to its invoker by a return value. Perhaps an unexpected situation could be communicated via a return value that the invoker could test. But the unexpected does not occur "normally." The designer of `parseInt` could not specify that if the method encounters an error it will return a `String` "bad number format" because `parseInt`'s prototype demands that it always return an `int`. Nor could the designer arrange for some special `int` value like `-999` to be returned in the event of an error. What if the `String` argument was `-999`—how could the resulting integer be distinguished from an error?

14.2.1 Throwing `Exceptions`

To allow methods to respond to the unexpected, Java provides an alternate means of terminating the execution of a method. This is accomplished with the `throw` statement

```
throw reference
```

where the reference is to an object of a subclass of the class `Exception`—a class that represents unexpected situations. (We will discuss `Exception` classes in the Java Interlude later in this chapter). The `throw` statement usually takes on the following form:

```
throw new Exception-Class(String-Argument);
```

where *Exception-class* is a subclass of Exception.

When a method executes the `throw` statement, we say that it *throws an exception.*

Picture the chain of method invocations that leads to the invocation of a particular method. The first method that executes is `main`. It invokes a method that in turn invokes a method, and so on until the method that encounters the unexpected situation is invoked (see Figure 14.1).

Throwing an `Exception` causes the executing method to terminate immediately. However, the `throw` statement does not return a value, nor does the sender resume execution from the point where the invocation occurred. Instead, the thrown `Exception` passes through each invocation along the

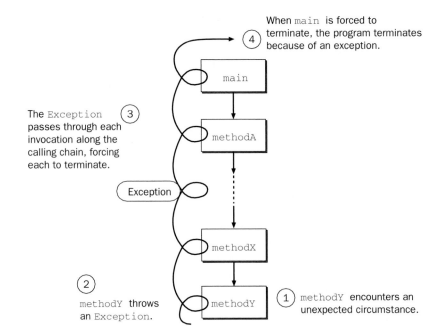

When `main` is forced to terminate, the program terminates because of an exception.

The `Exception` passes through each invocation along the calling chain, forcing each to terminate.

Exception

methodY throws an `Exception`.

methodY encounters an unexpected circumstance.

FIGURE 14.1   A chain of method invocations leading to an unexpected circumstance. The main `method` invoked `methodA`, which invoked another method, which eventually invoked `methodX`, which invoked `method-Y`. Now `methodY` encounters an unexpected situation–what happens?

chain, forcing each invoked method to terminate. To each method along the way, it appears as if the method it had invoked had thrown the `Exception`. In fact, we say that each method along the way throws the `Exception`. Eventually this cascades all the way back to the `main` method that started the program's execution, at which point the program terminates.

Thus the statement

`throw` *reference-to-Exception-object*

causes the program to terminate. You might think of it as an escape hatch. Java systems typically respond to such an outcome by displaying on standard output or a window the `Exception` being thrown, followed by the names of the methods that terminated their execution by throwing an `Exception`. The following is an example of this display:

```
SomeException
        at TryThrow.method2(TryThrow.java:18)
        at TryThrow.method1(TryThrow.java:15)
        at TryThrow.main(TryThrow.java:12)
```

You might recognize this as the same output generated by the `Thread.dumpStack` method introduced in Chapter 7 section 4.

The above output is typical and serves as text representation of the invocation chain that led to `method2`. It shows that in line 12 of `TryThrow.java`, the `main` method invoked `method1`, and in line 15 of `TryThrow.java`, `method1` invoked `method2`. In line 18 of `TryThrow.java`, `method2` threw a `SomeException` object. This terminated `method2`, `method1`, and `main`.

EXAMPLE **parseInt.** The `parseInt` method contains a statement similar to

```
throw new NumberFormatException(String-Argument);
```

This creates a new `NumberFormatException` object and throws the reference to this object. `NumberFormatException` is a subclass of `Exception`.

14.2.2 The `throws` Clause

The verb "throw" is not altogether unfamiliar to you—you have undoubtedly noticed that Java often requires that we include a `throws` clause in the header of a method declaration. For example,

```
public static void main(String[] a) throws Exception {
```

We can now (finally!) explain this requirement: Any method that might throw an `Exception` must acknowledge it in its declaration with a `throws` clause. A `throws` **clause** consists of the keyword `throws` and a list of subclasses of Exception that could be thrown by the method. This requirement applies not only to methods that contain a `throws` statement but to methods that may throw an `Exception` because they invoke other method's `throws` `Exceptions`.

EXERCISES

1. Write a method that receives a nonnegative integer as an argument and returns `true` if the integer is a perfect square and returns `false` otherwise. The method, `isPerfectSquare`, should throw an `Exception` if the argument is negative. Test this method using both acceptable and unacceptable values as arguments.

2. Write a method that receives an array of nonnegative integers as an argument and returns `true` if every integer in the array is a perfect square and returns `false` otherwise. The method, `areAllPerfectSquares`, repeatedly invokes `isPerfectSquare` (see Exercise 1). Test this method using both acceptable and unacceptable values in the elements of the array argument. •

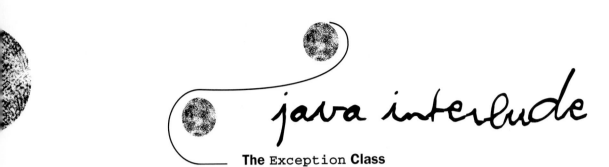

The Exception Class

The reference that appears in a throws statement must refer to an object of the Exception class. Because of the rules of inheritance, any object that is an instance of a subclass of the Exception class is also an Exception object.

Why have different Exception classes? These classes allow us to make distinctions between the different kinds of unexpected situations that arise. For example, the requirement for throws clauses forces programmers to be more aware of the possibility of unexpected situations. If every throws clause simply had Exception, the programmer would not receive or convey specific information as to what type of exception could arise. Writing

```
... throws  IOException
```

uses the IOException class, which models problems that pertain to an I/O operation. However, writing

```
throws  FileNotFoundException,  RemoteException
```

uses subclasses of IOException that model even more specific unexpected circumstances.

LABELING EXCEPTIONS

One Exception constructor takes as an argument a String that is printed out when the invocation chain is displayed. This allows the thrower of the Exception to label the Exception in order to convey additional information:

```
throw new FileNotFoundException("log file is always " +
                                "necessary");
```

CHECKED EXCEPTIONS VERSUS RUNTIME EXCEPTIONS

The Java class library defines a RuntimeException class that is an extension of Exception. Going further down the hierarchy, Exception subclasses like `NullPointerException`, `IOException`, `NumberFormatException`, and so on are defined as extensions to `RuntimeException`. Unlike other `Exception`s, the compiler does not require that any of these be mentioned in a `throws` clause. The reason is that these exceptions generally represent coding errors. Because such errors could occur anywhere, *every* method would have to mention `RunTimeException` in its declaration. Thus no distinctive information would be provided and so the `throws` requirement is waived.

Exceptions that must be mentioned in a `throws` clause are called **checked Exceptions** because the compiler checks that the `throws` clauses match any `throws` statements or `throws` clauses of other methods invoked.

EXERCISES

1. Modify the method you wrote in Exercise 1 of the previous section so that the `Exception` thrown is labeled with an explanatory `String`.

2. Define a new class, `NegativeIntegerException`, that is an extension of the `Exception` class. Modify the `isPerfectSquare` method so that it throws a `NegativeIntegerException` instead of simply throwing an `Exception`.

14.3 Handling the Unexpected

By default, the `throws` statement launches a chain of method terminations, beginning with the method executing the `throws` statement and ending with the `main` method of the program, and terminating the program itself. This is often too harsh a way of handling an unexpected situation. Often it is possible for the program to respond to the unexpected and recover. How can a method respond to an `Exception` thrown by another method that it invokes?

Java provides a way for methods to *catch* any `Exception` that is thrown their way by methods that they invoke. Catching an `Exception` means breaking the cascade of `Exception`-throwing that leads to the termination of the program. Instead, the method catching the `Exception` regains control and can then—hopefully—handle the situation in a less extreme way than abrupt program termination.

To catch an `Exception`, the statements containing invocations of `Exception`-throwing methods must be surrounded by braces and preceded with the keyword `try`:

```
try {
    someObject.someMethod();
}
```

Following this is the keyword `catch` and a parenthesized declaration of a reference variable that will refer to the thrown `Exception` object:

```
try {
    someObject.someMethod();
} catch (Exception e)
```

After that comes a group of statements surrounded by braces. If an exception is thrown, these statements will be executed when the `Exception` object reaches this method:

```
try {
    someObject.someMethod();
} catch (Exception e) {
    statements that are executed if and only if an exception
    is thrown by the code within the try
}
```

The code that appears in the braces that follow the keyword `try` is called the *try part*; we also say that this code is surrounded by a *try-catch*. The code that appears after the catch is called the *catch part*.

EXAMPLE **Improved Error Messages.** Let us take a simple example. Suppose we have a `Movie` class that has a static method `readMovie`. This method is passed a `BufferedReader` and returns a `Movie` object. It is expected to read the name of the movie and the number of minutes of playing time from the `BufferedReader`, pass these values (`String` reference and `int`) to the `Movie` constructor, and return the resulting `Movie` reference. If end of file is reached, a `null` reference is returned.

Ignoring the unexpected, we have:

```
static Movie readMovie(BufferedReader br)
                            throws IOException {
    String name;
    int    playingTime;
    Movie  newMovie;

    name = br.readLine();
    if (name==null)
        return null;
    playingTime = Integer.parseInt(br.readLine());
    newMovie = new Movie(name,playingTime);
    return newMovie;
}
```

Recognizing the possibility of data error in the integer input, we note that it is possible for `parseInt` to throw an `NumberFormatException`.

We don't want the program to terminate without some explanation for the user.

We therefore enclose the statement that invokes `parseInt` within a `try` and catch any `NumberFormatException` that it throws:

```
static Movie readMovie(BufferedReader br)
                        throws IOException {
    String name;
    int    playingTime;
    Movie  newMovie;

    name = br.readLine();
    if (name==null)
        return null;
    try {
        playingTime = Integer.parseInt(br.readLine());
    } catch (NumberFormatException e) {
        System.err.println("Bad playingTime format for "
                            +name);
        throw e;
    }
    newMovie = new Movie(name,playingTime);
    return newMovie;
}
```

After writing out a meaningful error message to the user, we rethrow the `Exception` and let it continue to take its course. We do this because we have not fully handled the error.

EXAMPLE   Recovering from an Error. Now let's consider a more involved example. It might not be reasonable to allow a single error in the data to terminate an entire run. Rather, we would like to display a warning message, skip the erroneous data, go on and read the next movie entry, and process it. We write:

```
static Movie readMovie(BufferedReader br)
                        throws IOException {
    String name;
    int    playingTime;
    Movie  newMovie;

    name = br.readLine();
    if (name==null)
        return null;
    try {
        playingTime = Integer.parseInt(br.readLine());
    } catch (NumberFormatException e) {    // Skip this movie; do
                                           //    next one.
```

```
System.err.print("Bad playing time data for "+name);
System.err.println(" -- movie skipped");
name = br.readLine();
if (name==null)
    return null;
playingTime = Integer.parseInt(br.readLine());
newMovie = new Movie(name,playingTime);
return newMovie;
```

This code is executed if parseInt throws a NumberFormatException.

```
    }
```

```
newMovie = new Movie(name,playingTime);
return newMovie;
```

This code is executed if parseInt does not throw a NumberFormatException.

```
}
```

Can you see the problem here? The code that skips the movie with bad input and goes onto the next movie also calls `parseInt` and faces the same possibility of bad input. If there were two instances of bad data in a row, the program would terminate.

Let's take a step back from this code. What we really want to do is keep trying to get some good movie data. This may conceivably (though hopefully not!) take many reads. A loop is needed, therefore, one that ends either when there are no more data (`name` is `null`) or when good data (`String` and `int`) have been successfully read. To keep track of the second condition, we will use a `boolean` variable, `gotGoodData`.

At this point we have:

```
boolean gotGoodData;        // True if and only if both name and playingTime
                            //    have valid data
...
while (name!=null && !gotGoodData)) {
     ...
}
```

After the loop, we can check `name` and either return `null` or a new `Movie` based on the good data we have:

```
if (name==null)
    return null;
else
    return new Movie(name,playingTime);
```

We must initialize `name` before the loop. Because we don't yet have a good value for `playingTime`, `gotGoodData` is initialized to `false`. Our method at this point is as follows:

```
static Movie readMovie(BufferedReader br)
                        throws IOException {
    String name;
```

```
int     playingTime;
boolean gotGoodData;  // True if and only if both name and playingTime
                      //     have valid data
Movie   newMovie;

name = br.readLine();
gotGoodData = false;
while (!(name==null || gotGoodData)) {
    ...
}
if (name==null)
    return null;
else
    return new Movie(name,playingTime);
}
```

The loop's termination is guaranteed by trying to complete the reading of the movie input data:

```
try {
    playingTime = Integer.parseInt(br.readLine());
} catch (NumberFormatException e) { // Skip this movie; do next one.
    ... exception handling code goes here ...
}
```

If `parseInt` throws an `Exception`, we warn the user, set `gotGood-Data` to `false` and read in the name of the next movie in the input. The body of the catch part then is as follows:

```
System.err.print("Bad playing time data for "+name);
System.err.println("--movie skipped");
gotGoodData = false;
name = br.readLine();
```

The definition of `gotGoodData` requires that it be true when the movie data are good, that is, when no `Exception` was thrown. We therefore, rather optimistically, set `gotGoodData` to be true before trying to read `playing-Time`. If the attempt to read `playingTime` fails, then catching the `Exception` will set `gotGoodData` back to `false`.

The completed method is:

```
static Movie readMovie(BufferedReader br)
                       throws IOException {
    String name;
    int     playingTime;
    boolean gotGoodData;  // True if and only if both name and playingTime
                          //     have valid data
    Movie   newMovie;
```

```
        name = br.readLine();
        gotGoodData = false;
        while (!(name==null || gotGoodData)) {
            gotGoodData = true;  // Optimistic! but if an Exception
                                 //    is thrown, it will be set to false.

            try {
                playingTime = Integer.parseInt(br.readLine());
            } catch (NumberFormatException e) { // Skip this movie; do
                                                //    next one.
                System.err.print("Bad playing time data for "
                                +name);
                System.err.println(" -- movie skipped");
                gotGoodData = false;
                name = br.readLine();
            }
        }
        if (name==null)
            return null;
        else
            return new Movie(name,playingTime);
    }
```

EXERCISE

1. Rewrite the `Truck.read` method from Chapter 5 so that it can recover from input errors. •

14.4   Responsibility for the Unexpected

In object-oriented programming, each object takes "responsibility" for its behavior. Handling unexpected circumstances is often part of the behavior we desire from our "smart and helpful" objects.

For example, imagine the following group of objects:

- The `NetHeadlineScanner` object. Models a network headline service. A `NetHeadlineScanner` object continuously displays headlines containing certain keywords. These headlines are obtained from a `NetHeadlines` object.
- The `NetHeadlines` object. Obtains continual headline news from any one of several alternative sources. Such an object is implemented using a `NetReader`.

- The NetReader object. Reads continuously updated information from a source on the network. The NetReader in turn may be implemented using a BufferedReader.
- The BufferedReader object. Constructed from an InputStream delivered by a connected Socket object. Socket is a Java predefined class that models low-level network connections.

Thus, the NetHeadlineScanner object invokes a readLine method of the NetHeadline class, which in turn invokes a readLine method of the NetReader class, which in turn invokes BufferedReader's readLine method.

The "unexpected" in this case is the current news source going down, that is, suddenly becoming unavailable, while it is being accessed. Which classes should take responsibility for this occurrence? What should their behavior be?

One way to approach this question is to note where the Exception is generated and then consider the objects along the invocation chain, considering which object is in a position—in terms of the scope of its responsibility—to do something about the exception. Let's try that here:

BufferedReader.readLine throws the Exception, so we can hardly expect it to catch it. But why does it throw the Exception? Why couldn't it handle the network data source going down? It could not simply because a BufferedReader is itself an idealized data source and has no knowledge of whether it is providing data from a network, a file, or a keyboard. It can only know that there has been an abnormal interruption of data (as distinct from an end-of-file). It can only throw up its hands—and throw an Exception.

What about NetReader? The description above tells us that the NetReader object knows that it is reading from the network location of its source. But getting data from that particular source is the entire behavior of a given NetReader object. If data from that source are now not available, the NetReader object too can only throw up its hands—and rethrow the Exception generated by BufferReader.

What about NetHeadlines? According to the description, a NetHeadlines object knows about several alternative news sources on the network. Therefore, the NetHeadlines object could conceivably respond to the situation by catching the Exception, selecting a different network address, creating a different NetReader object based on that address, and continuing as before—the NetHeadlineScanner need never know that this happened.

Let's still consider NetHeadlineScanner. Perhaps it would do as well or better than NetHeadlines in handling this Exception. That, however, turns out not to be the case. The NetHeadlineScanner takes a source of headlines for granted. Its responsibility is the selection of headlines based on keywords.

FIGURE 14.2 Where should an exception be caught? The exception pictured here is thrown in BufferedReader's readLine method, but it can only be handled in the readLine method of NetHeadlines. So it is caught in that method.

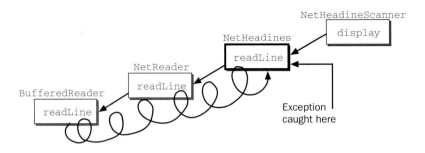

Thus, we see that the place that ought to deal with the Exception is the readLine method of NetHeadlines (see Figure 14.2).

14.5 Exceptions Are Not Always Errors

In this chapter we have adopted Java's rather optimistic view that errors are exceptions. However, the Exception mechanism is a flexible and powerful mechanism and its use goes beyond handling errors.

As an example, let's write a simple program that gets an URL as its single command-line argument and prints the evaluation "good" or "bad", depending on whether the URL is the address of a web page that exists and is accessible to us.

To do this, we make use of the integer *response codes* that web servers send when web clients (like browsers) make connections to them. Response codes of 300 or greater signify some kind of error in the URL. For example, 404 means the resource does not exist. The HttpURLConnection class in the java.net package models HTTP connections to web resources that are specified by URLs. We can create such an object by sending an openConnection message to a URL object. Once we have an HttpURLConnection object, we can send it a getResponseCode message to get the response code resulting from an attempt to connect to the URL. Testing the resulting integer allows us to determine whether the URL is good or bad:

```
import java.net.*;
import java.io.*;
class CheckURL {
    public static void main(String[] a)
                        throws Exception {
        URL u = new URL(a[0]);
        HttpURLConnection uC =
```

```
              (HttpURLConnection) u.openConnection();
        int responseCode = uC.getResponseCode();
         System.out.println(responseCode);
        if (responseCode>=300)
                System.out.println("bad");
        else
                System.out.println("good");
    }
}
```

Unfortunately, our program will print out "bad" or "good" only if it actually can make a connection to an HTTP server. If the machine address part of the URL doesn't exist or if that machine is not an HTTP server, the program will throw an Exception instead of printing "bad". This is not an error however—merely a result of a bad URL. So we solve this problem by enclosing all the statements in the method in a try clause and printing the appropriate message if an Exception occurs:

```
import java.net.*;
import java.io.*;
class CheckURL {
    public static void main(String[] a) {
        try {
            URL u = new URL(a[0]);
            HttpURLConnection uC =
                (HttpURLConnection) u.openConnection();
             int responseCode = uC.getResponseCode();
             System.out.println(responseCode);
            if (responseCode>=300)
                    System.out.println("bad");
            else
                    System.out.println("good");
        } catch (Exception e) {
            System.out.println("bad");
        }
    }
}
```

14.5.1 The `WebSurveyor` Revisited

We can apply this lesson to the WebSurveyor example from Chapter 12. Like the program above, the WebSurveyor identified bad web page references successfully as long as the host part of the URL was good and reachable. Otherwise, the program would terminate with an Exception such as:

```
java.net.UnknownHostException:
                    nothinglikethisanwhere.ugh.com
```

```
    at java.net.InetAddress.getAllByName0(InetAddress.java)
    at java.net.InetAddress.getByName(InetAddress.java)
    at java.net.Socket.<init>(Socket.java:89)
    at sun.net.NetworkClient.doConnect(NetworkClient.java:54)
    at sun.net.www.http.HttpClient.openServer
                                    (HttpClient.java:259)
    at sun.net.www.http.HttpClient.openServer
                                    (HttpClient.java:324)
    at sun.net.www.http.HttpClient.<init>
                                    (HttpClient.java:203)
    at sun.net.www.http.HttpClient.<init>
                                    (HttpClient.java:211)
    at sun.net.www.http.HttpClient.New(HttpClient.java:222)
    at sun.net.www.protocol.http.HttpURLConnection.connect
                                    (HttpURLConnection.java:318)
    at ...http.HttpURLConnection.getInputStream
                                    (HttpURLConnection.java:399)
    at java.net.HttpURLConnection.getResponseCode
                                    (HttpURLConnection.java:143)
        at WebPage.isBad(WebSurveyor.java:119)
        at WebPage.getBadLinks(WebSurveyor.java:105)
        at WebSurveyor.main(WebSurveyor.java:69)
```

The listing of the invocation chain tells exactly where the Exception is thrown:

```
class WebPage {
    ...
    private boolean isBad(String url) throws Exception {
            URL u = new URL(url);
            HttpURLConnection uC =
                (HttpURLConnection) u.openConnection();
            int responseCode = uC.getResponseCode();
            return responseCode>=300;
    }
    ...
}
```

The Exception is thrown, understandably, when a bad host name appears in the URL. After all, if the host does not exist or can't be contacted, there is no way one can get a response code from that machine. What can we do?

As we did in the previous section, we have to travel up the chain of invocation to find a class whose responsibility encompasses this "unexpected" situation. Fortunately, this time we don't have to look very far. The purpose of the isBad method is to find out whether a URL is bad or not. Clearly, when HttpURLConnection's getResponseCode throws an Exception because of a bad host name, the URL is bad.

Accordingly, we have to rewrite the `isBad` method to catch `Exceptions` thrown by `HttpURLConnection`. When such an `Exception` is caught, `isBad` should return true because the URL is bad:

```
private boolean isBad(String url) {
    try {
        URL u = new URL(url);
        HttpURLConnection uC =
                (HttpURLConnection) u.openConnection();
        int responseCode = uC.getResponseCode();
        return responseCode>=300;
    } catch (Exception e) {
        return true;
    }
}
```

This use of `Exception` catching illustrates an important point. Although most of the discussion of `Exceptions` in this chapter was in the context of errors, not all `Exceptions` are errors. Here, for example, the purpose of the program is to find bad URLs lurking in a set of web pages. Finding them is hardly an error. Yet we use the `Exception` mechanism quite conveniently here to identify them.

For that matter, the `Exceptions` here are not particularly unexpected either.

SUMMARY

How an object handles unexpected circumstances is as much a part of its behavior as how it responds to messages in normal situations. Java provides a class, `Exception`, that models unexpected situations. Along with this class, Java provides the `throw` statement, a mechanism for abruptly changing the flow of control. When a method encounters a situation that it cannot handle in the normal way, it may create and throw an `Exception` object. The `throw` statement transfers control to the first enclosing `try-catch` statement for that particular `Exception`. If none is found in the current method, the method terminates, throwing the same `Exception` and the search for a `try-catch` continues in the invoking method. This process will continue all the way up the chain of invocation until a matching `try-catch` is found. If none is found, the `main` method itself throws the `Exception` and the program terminates.

STUDY AID: TERMINOLOGY REVIEW

checked `Exception` An `Exception` that, if thrown by a method, must appear in the methods `throws` clause; so-called because the Java compiler checks for its presence in the clause.

invocation chain The sequence of method invocations starting with `main` that leads to and includes the invocation of the currently executing method.

Exception An object that represents an unexpected circumstance or an out-of-the-ordinary situation.

runtime `Exception` An `Exception` that reflects a programming error that typically can occur "anywhere" and ought to occur "nowhere" in the code and therefore is not required to be in the `throws` clause.

Throwable The parent class from which `Exception` is derived.

throws clause A clause in a method declaration that identifies all the checked exceptions the method might throw.

QUESTIONS FOR REVIEW

1. What happens when an `Exception` is thrown?

2. Why isn't the normal return mechanism sufficient for handling out of the ordinary situations?

3. How can a method handle `Exceptions` thrown by methods it invokes?

4. What is a checked `Exception`? Give an example of an `Exception` that is not a checked `Exception`.

5. How can a method attach additional information to an `Exception` that it throws?

6. Why have different `Exception` classes that are extensions of `Exception`?

FURTHER EXERCISES

1. Reconsider the `Time` class from Chapter 6. Define a `TimeException` class and rewrite the methods of the `Time` class to throw a `Time-Exception` when their arguments violate the assumptions (require-

ments) of the methods. For example, the `Time` constructor assumed that its third argument was `"am"` or `"pm"`. Verify this argument now and if the argument is neither of these two, throw a `TimeException`. Make this analysis and carry out this rewrite for each of the `Time` methods.

Clients and Servers

One of the reasons for the increasing interest in Java is its delivery mechanism. Java applets do not reach their users on diskettes or CD-ROMs in shrink-wrapped software. Nor are they downloaded once from some network source to be used over and over again. Instead, they are embedded within a web page and downloaded anew with each loading of the web page. Java applets are not only on the Internet but are creatures of the Internet as well.

In this final supplement, we will explore further some of the technology underpinning the Internet and therefore this aspect of Java.

Internet Communication

Communication on the Internet is the transfer of data from one machine to another. This encompasses downloading of web pages and applets, as well as email, remote logins, chat rooms, and all other Internet applications. Communication is accomplished by breaking up the data to be transferred into small pieces called *packets* and transferring these packets. The sending machine is almost never directly connected to the receiving machine, so these packets actually are transferred from one machine to another on the Internet until they arrive at their destination. The machines involved in the process must have specialized routing software that enables them to transfer the data packets. These machines are called *routers* and are usually dedicated to this purpose. Every machine on the Internet must be on a local area network with at least one router—and every router must be connected to at least one other router so that there can be a path of routers between any two machines. See Figure 14.3.

Unfortunately, the transfer of packets is unreliable—packets can get lost on the way. Not only are the communication connections unreliable but the routers and the receiving machine themselves have limited memory. If packets

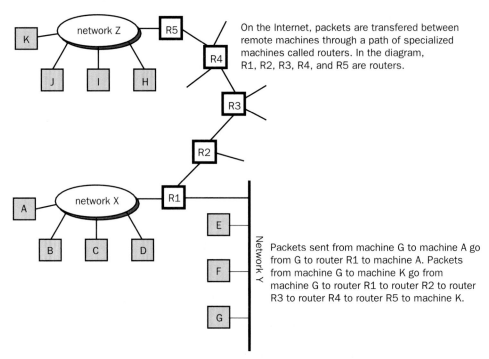

On the Internet, packets are transfered between remote machines through a path of specialized machines called routers. In the diagram, R1, R2, R3, R4, and R5 are routers.

Packets sent from machine G to machine A go from G to router R1 to machine A. Packets from machine G to machine K go from machine G to router R1 to router R2 to router R3 to router R4 to router R5 to machine K.

FIGURE 14.3   Routing packets on the Internet.

arrive faster than they can be processed, there may not be enough memory to hold them and some packets will be lost.

This underlying reality of Internet communication—individual packets unreliably moved through many intermediate machines—is a very poor facility for most Internet applications. From the application's point of view, a better facility would be a reliable, direct connection between two programs on different machines, allowing a stream of data in both directions. All machines on the Internet run software that uses the actual Internet communication facility, called Internet Protocol or IP, to provide this better facility, called Transmission Control Protocol or TCP, for applications (see Figure 14.4). Together these facilities are referred to as TCP/IP.

Sockets   A TCP connection between two programs in many ways is like a phone connection. Data can move reliably and continuously in both directions simultaneously. Furthermore, before communication can take place a connection has to be made—one party must call the other. Finally, both parties need something besides the connection. In phone connections, both parties need a telephone—a device that allows some one to hear and speak on a phone line. In TCP connections, the programs need objects of the `Socket`

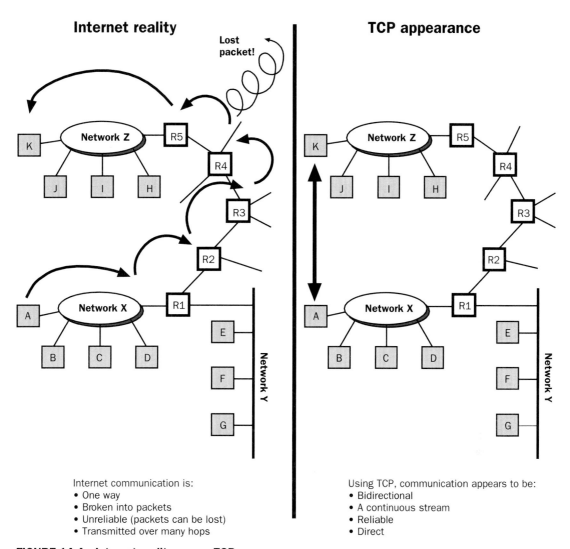

FIGURE 14.4   Internet reality versus TCP appearance.

class—objects that model telephones in that they allow programs to communicate across a connection.

The Socket class models a disposable telephone. A Socket object is created for making a single TCP connection. In fact, the arguments to the constructor are the machine being contacted and the port number to which the answering program will be responding. (You can think of the port number as analogous to an extension in a large phone system. For example, the following code creates a `Socket` that makes a TCP connection to the web server at www.yahoo.com:

```
new  Socket("www.yahoo.com",80);
```
80 is the standard port number for web servers.

The `Socket` class provides `getInputStream` and `getOutputStream` methods from whose return values `BufferedReader` objects and `PrintStream` objects can be constructed. These objects use the TCP connection as their input source or output target.

A `TCPconnection` Class   We can use Java's predefined `Socket` class to develop a class, `TCPConnection`, that models a TCP connection. Later we can use `TCPConnection` objects to build simple Internet application classes.

The behavior of a `TCPconnection` is straightforward:

- Create a connection to a particular machine and port.
- Read a line in the form of a `String` from the connection.
- Write a line in `String` form to the connection.

The interface of the class then is as follows:

```
class TCPClient {
    public TCPConnection(String hostname,
                         int portnumber) {}
    public String readLine() {}
    public void println(String s) {}
}
```

The repeated calls to `readLine` and `println` require that references to a `BufferedReader` object and a `PrintStream` object be maintained as instance variables:

```
private BufferedReader   br;
private PrintStream      ps;
```

The `BufferedReader` and `PrintStream` objects must be associated with the actual TCP connection, so that, for example, a read from the `BufferedReader` involves reading data from the TCP connection itself.

Given these instance variables, the implementation of `readLine` and `println` is as follows:

```
public String readLine() throws Exception {
    return br.readLine();
}
public void println(String s) {
    ps.println(s);
}
```

It is the responsibility of the constructor to initialize the instance variables. To do this, it creates a socket using the address and portnumber given, and then sends it `getInputStream` and `getOutputStream` messages to get `InputStream` and `OutputStream` objects from which a `Buffered-edReader` and `PrintStream` are constructed. The complete class definition is as follows:

```java
import java.net.*;
import java.io.*;

class TCPConnection {
    public TCPConnection(String hostname, int portnumber)
                                            throws Exception {
        Socket s = new Socket(hostname,portnumber);
        br = new BufferedReader(
            new InputStreamReader(
                s.getInputStream()));
        ps = new PrintStream(s.getOutputStream());
    }

    public String readLine() throws Exception {
        String s;
        try {
            s = br.readLine();
        } catch (IOException ioe) {
            System.err.println("TCP input failure: network "
                            + "error");
            throw new Exception("Input Failure: Network "
                            + "I/O Error");
        }
        return s;
    }

    public void println(String s) {
        ps.println(s);
    }

    private BufferedReader  br;
    private PrintStream     ps;
}
```

We can write the following simple, though limited, test program for this class. It creates a `TCPconnection` object to model a connection to a well-known web server, sends a two-line HTTP request on the connection, and then reads from the connection:

```java
import java.net.*;
import java.io.*;
class TestTCPConnection {
```

```
public  static  void  main(String[]  a)
                              throws  Exception  {
    TCPConnection  tc =
            new TCPConnection("www.yahoo.com",80);
    tc.println("GET "+"/"+" HTTP/1.0\n");
    String  s  =  tc.readLine();
    while  (s!=null)  {
        System.out.println(s);
        s = tc.readLine();
    }
}
```

Note the \n—we're sending two lines, the second of which is blank.

Client-Server Computing

Sockets and TCP connections allow programs to communicate across the Internet, but they don't determine any particular style of communication or relationship between the programs. There is a widely used design approach for Internet applications—called the *client-server model*—that does just that, however. In the client-server model, an application consists of one program running as server—a program that provides a service—and another program running as a client—a program that requests a service.

To accomplish its mission, a client takes the following steps:

- It creates a `Socket` object with the machine address and appropriate port number of the server. (There are standards that determine what port number to use for what service. For example, the standard port number for the Web is 80.)
- It sends a message to the server on the TCP connection that is associated with the `Socket`.
- It waits for a response from the server, indicating a need for more information, indicating that the requested action has been performed, or providing the data requested.

Depending on the application, the conversation between client and server may be more elaborate, with variations of the last two steps being repeated several times.

The client-server model works very nicely for the Internet because the most common Internet applications involve users either seeking data from some source (for example, web browsing or receiving email) or seeking to transfer data to some place (sending email for example). Thus, a web browser is a client. It accomplishes its task by repeatedly (for each new URL) creating `Socket` objects that make TCP connections to successive web servers, sending these servers requests for data, and receiving the responses and displaying them.

Client-Server Protocols Each client-server application has its own rules (or protocol) governing the conversation between client and server. So the web clients and servers use one protocol called Hyper-Text Transport Protocol or HTTP. Email clients and servers use a different protocol, called Simple Mail Transfer Protocol or SMTP. The protocols are fairly elaborate and a detailed discussion is beyond the scope of this text. However, let's listen in on a few client-server conversations and infer a few of the rules in these protocols so that we can experiment with a few client and server programs of our own.

Example: A Web Client-Server Exchange When a web client just wants an HTML file to display, all it has to do is make a TCP connection to the appropriate web server and send two lines of text:

- The first line starts with the word GET, then has the name of the file sought, and finally indicates the name of the protocol (just so the server really knows it is talking the same language).
- The second line is blank. The blank line indicates the end of the request to the server.

In fact, our test program for the TCPconnection class sent these two lines. Here is a hypothetical exchange between a web client and server:

```
client:GET  /~arnow/answers/answer15.html HTTP/1.0
client:                              Blank line signifies tend of client request
server:HTTP/1.0  200  Document  follows
server:Date:  Thu,  13  Nov  1997  23:26:47  GMT
server:Server:  NCSA/1.5.2
server:Last-modified:  Mon,  13  Oct  1997  01:18:38  GMT
server:Content-type:  text/html
server:Content-length:  110
server:                Blank line signifies that the HTML content follows
server:<HTML>
server:<HEAD>
server:<TITLE>Answer  to  Question  15</TITLE>
server:</HEAD>
server:
server:<BODY>
server:Answer  to  question  15:  YES
server:</BODY>
server:</HTML>
```

Information about the server and the data sent in the transmission

The contents of the file requested.

At that point the server breaks of the connection.

Example: Email Client-Server Exchange Email protocol, SMTP, is downright chatty compared to the Web's HTTP. In SMTP, the server starts, with a brief introduction of itself—its internet address—and the protocol it is using. Here, as in all its messages, the SMTP server's message starts with a number code. The email client responds with `EHLO` (an anagram of a misspelled "HELLO") and its machine address. The mail server answers with a lengthy list of information about its configuration.

At this point the niceties (often called "handshaking") end and the client gets down to business. It sends a `MAIL From:` line and a `RCPT To:` line. These lines indicate who the sender and recipient are. To each, the server merely responds that the information is `ok`.

The email client then sends a `DATA` line followed by the contents of the email. A period by itself in a line indicates the end of the mail contents. Finally, the client sends a `QUIT` line and the server terminates the connection.

```
server:220 mailhost.mycollege.edu ESMTP
client:EHLO m3.mycollege.edu
server:250-mailhost.mycollege.edu Hello
       arnow@m3.mycollege.edu
       [146.245.37.30], pleased to meet you
server:250-EXPN
server:250-VERB
server:250-8BITMIME
server:250-SIZE
server:250-DSN
server:250-ONEX
server:250-ETRN
server:250-XUSR
server:250 HELP
client:MAIL From: <arnow@m3.mycollege.edu>
server:250 <arnow@m3.mycollege.edu>... Sender ok
client:RCPT To: <weiss>
server:250 <weiss>... Recipient ok
client:DATA
server:354 Enter mail, end with "." on a line by itself
client:I hope the students liked this book.
client:.
server:250 SAA05661 Message accepted for delivery
client:QUIT
server:221 mailhost.mycollege.edu closing connection
client:Connection closed by foreign host.
```

Introductions in conversation between client and server

Specifying sender

Specifying recipient

Content of email
Signifies end of email

Request termination of session

14.5.2 Some Simple Client Classes

In this subsection, we develop classes that model a web client and an email client. The `WebClient` object will model a web client's access of a single HTML file. A web client application could then repeatedly create `WebClient` objects as the user surfs from one HTML file to the next. The `MailClient` object will model an email client's sending of a single email. An email client application could then repeatedly create `MailClient` objects as the user sends different emails to various recipients.

The `WebClient` Class   The behavior that we desire from a `WebClient` is as follows:

- Create a `WebClient` based on a `hostname`, a `portnumber`, a `resource` (file) name; it should also be possible to leave out either the `portnumber` or the filename or both and have these replaced by appropriate default values (80 and /, respectively).
- Read lines of HTML from the page accessed by the `WebClient`.

The interface for the class is as follows:

```
class WebClient {
    public WebClient(String hostname, int portnumber,
                       String resource) {}
    public WebClient(String hostname, String resource) {}
    public WebClient(String hostname, int portnumber) {}
    public WebClient(String hostname) {}
    public String readLine()  {}
}
```

Web clients, like most Internet client applications, use a TCP connection to get data from their server. Repeated invocations of `readLine` will therefore require that `WebClient` maintain a `TCPConnection` object as an instance variable as follows:

```
private TCPConnection tc;
```

The `readLine` method is no more than the following wrapper to a `readLine` invocation using `tc`:

```
public String readLine()  {
    return tc.readLine();
}
```

The constructor's task is to create the `TCPConnection` and to make sure subsequent invocations of `readLine` will return the successive lines of the HTML file. The constructor thus carries out the following steps:

- Create the `TCPConnection`.
- Send the HTTP request for resource desired.
- Read up through and including the blank line that signifies that the HTML content follows.

The constructor with the full set of arguments can therefore be implemented as follows:

```
public WebClient(String hostname, int portnumber,
                   String resource)  throws Exception {
    tc = new TCPConnection(hostname, portnumber);
    tc.println("GET "+resource+" HTTP/1.0\n");
```

Create connection.
Send request.

```
                                String  s  =  tc.readLine();
                                while  (s!=null  &&  !s.equals(""))
                                    s  =  tc.readLine();
                        }
```

The remaining constructors can be implemented by invoking the above constructor, substituting default values when necessary:

```
public WebClient(String hostname, String resource)
                                        throws Exception {
    this(hostname,80,resource);
}
public WebClient(String hostname, int portnumber)
                                        throws Exception {
    this(hostname,portnumber,"/");
}
public WebClient(String hostname) throws Exception {
    this(hostname,80,"/");
}
```

The complete class, with a simple test driver, is as follows:

```
class WebClient {
    public WebClient(String hostname, int portnumber,
                        String resource) throws Exception {
        tc  =  new  TCPConnection(hostname,  portnumber);
        tc.println("GET  "+resource+"  HTTP/1.0\n");
        String  s  =  tc.readLine();
        while  (s!=null  &&  !s.equals(""))
            s  =  tc.readLine();
    }

    public WebClient(String hostname, String resource)
                                        throws Exception {
        this(hostname,80,resource);
    }

    public WebClient(String hostname, int portnumber)
                                        throws Exception {
        this(hostname,portnumber,"/");
    }

    public WebClient(String hostname) throws Exception {
        this(hostname,80,"/");
    }

    public String readLine() {
        return  tc.readLine();
    }

    private  TCPConnection tc;
```

```
public static void main(String[] a) throws Exception {    test driver
    if (a.length!=2)
        System.err.println("usage: java WebClient " +
                            "host resource");
    else {
        WebClient wc = new WebClient(a[0],80,a[1]);
        String          s = wc.readLine();
        while (s!=null) {
            System.out.println(s);
            s = wc.readLine();
        }
    }
}
}
```

The MailClient Class   The behavior that we desire from a MailClient is as follows:

- Create a MailClient based on the address of a recipient and a sender.
- Write a line of the email content to the MailClient with the expectation that it will send these to the recipient.
- Indicate the end of the message by sending a period and a QUIT.
- Find the status of our interaction with the server (success or failure).

The interface for the class, therefore, is as follows:

```
class MailClient {
    public MailClient(String toAddress, String
                        fromAddress) {}
    public void println(String s) {}
    public void close() throws Exception {}
    public boolean success() throws Exception {}
}
```

Like the web client, the mail client uses a TCP connection to send data and receive data from the server. Our implementation of MailClient will be illustrative, but crude. For example, it has the following requirements:

- The full email address of both sender and recipient must be specified.
- The hostname part of the recipient's address must be the address of the actual mail server used by the recipient's system. (Usually all that is required is the name of the network rather than that of the specific server.)

It has a similar structure to that of the WebClient. A TCPConnection object is maintained as an instance variable, allowing for an easy implementation of println and close as follows:

```
class  MailClient  {
    ...
```

```
        public void println(String  s) {
            tc.println(s);
        }

        public void close() {
            println("\n.\nQUIT");
        }
        private TCPConnection tc;
    }
```

The `success` method makes use of two facts:

- Every message from the mail server starts with a three-digit number.
- Error messages from the mail server always start with a number in the 500s.

So the `success` method just reads server responses from the TCP connection until it reaches end of file or it finds a 5 at the beginning of the line:

```
public boolean success() throws Exception {
    String  s  =  tc.readLine();
    while  (s!=null  &&  !s.substring(0,1).equals("5"))
        s  =  tc.readLine();
    return  s==null;
}
```

> null means no 5 was found; therefore, it was successful.

The `MailClient` constructor carries out the following steps:

- Create the `TCPConnection`.
- Send the SMTP information announcing identity, sender, and recipient.
- Send the `DATA` line indicating that the content of the email message is coming next.

Much of the work in the constructor involves extracting the sender's machine, the recipient's machine, and the recipient from the `to` and `from` addresses. The position of the "@" (as in *someone@somewhere.org*) is used to distinguish the user from the machine. We write the constructor as follows:

```
public MailClient(String to, String from)
                                    throws Exception {
    int     atInTo   =  to.indexOf("@");
    int     atInFrom =  from.indexOf("@");
    String  serverHost  =  to.substring(atInTo+1);
    String  senderHost  =  from.substring(atInFrom+1);
    String  recipient   =  to.substring(0,atInTo);
    tc = new TCPConnection(serverHost, 25);
    println("EHLO "+senderHost);
    println("MAIL From: <"+from+">");

    println("RCPT To: <"+recipient+">");
```

> Location of @ in to address
> Location of @ in from address
> Create connection.
> Identify our machine.
> Announce mail with sender's address.
> Specify recipient on mail server.

```
         println("DATA");                                    Content of email follows.
     }
```

The complete `MailClient` class, including a simple test driver, is as
follows:

```
class MailClient {
    public MailClient(String to, String from)
                                     throws Exception {
        int    atInTo   = to.indexOf("@");            Location of @ in to
                                                      address.

        int    atInFrom  = from.indexOf("@");         Location of @ in from
                                                      address

        String serverHost  = to.substring(atInTo+1);
        String senderHost  = from.substring(atInFrom+1);
        String recipient = to.substring(0,atInTo);
        tc = new TCPConnection(serverHost, 25);       Create connection.
        println("EHLO "+senderHost);                  Identify our machine.
        println("MAIL From: <"+from+">");             Announce mail with
                                                      sender's address.
        println("RCPT To: <"+to+">");                 Specific recipient on
                                                      mail server.
        println("DATA");                              Content of email follows.
    }

    public boolean success() throws Exception {
      String s  =  tc.readLine();
      while  (s!=null &&
              !s.substring(0,1).equals("5"))
          s = tc.readLine();
       return  s==null;                               null means no 5 was
                                                      found; therefore, it was
                                                      successful.

    }

    public void println(String s) {
       tc.println(s);
    }

    public void close() {
       println("\n.\nQUIT");
    }

    private TCPConnection tc;
    public static void main(String[] a)
                                     throws Exception {
       MailClient mc = new MailClient(a[0],a[1]);
       mc.println("Subject: test message!");
       mc.println("Just let me know if you received "
               + "this. Thanks!");
```

```
            mc.close();
            if (mc.success())
                System.out.println("mail success");
            else
            System.out.println("mail failure");
        }
    }
```

Handling Client Exceptions   In the classes we developed above, we have continued to take the approach we have followed throughout the book, that is, wherever a method might encounter an exception, we added the `throws Exception` clause to the method header. Now that we know more about exceptions in Java, we can take a more refined approach. We will consider the `TCPConnection` class, and leave the client classes as exercises.

One problem with our TCPConnection class is that its constructor gives up too easily. For example, the `Socket` constructor may throw an exception for several reasons. On the one hand, the `hostname` may be invalid. In that case, there is no possible recovery. On the other hand, the host machine being contacted may not be responding. That might be just because of transient network problems. Rather than throwing an exception, we might wish for more patient behavior—several retry attempts before giving up, for example.

To achieve this, we will define our own private method, `makeSocket`, for creating a `Socket`, and we will use this method in our `TCPConnection` constructor as follows:

```
public TCPConnection(String hostname, int portnumber)
                                        throws Exception {
    Socket   s=makeSocket(hostname,portnumber);
    br = new BufferedReader(
            new InputStreamReader(
                s.getInputStream()));
    ps = new PrintStream(s.getOutputStream());
}
```

The essence of the `makeSocket` method is the creation of a `Socket`:

```
Socket   s=null;
...
s  = new Socket(hostname, portnumber);
...
return  s;
```

However, the `Socket` constructor may throw an exception. We don't want to terminate in that case; instead, we want to examine the exception. If the exception reflects an improper `hostname`, we will issue a diagnostic to the user and give up, that is, rethrow the exception. If failure occurred for another reason, we will try again:

```
while  (...)  {
    try {
        s  = new Socket(hostname, portnumber);
    } catch (UnknownHostException uhe) {
        System.err.println("Cannot make TCP connection."+
                "Reason: Unknown Host: "+hostname);
        throw new TCPException("Connection Failure: "+
                            "Unknown Host");
    } catch (IOException ioe) {
        System.err.println("Connection failed "+
                "due to Network I/O Error: retrying ...");
    }
}
```

We don't want to keep trying forever, though. We will keep track of the number of attempts with a local variable, `attempts`, and we will declare an instance variable to define the maximum number of attempts to connect as follows:

```
private final int       maxAttempts=5;
```

Then, when the loop terminates we should either have our `Socket`, that is, `s` should no longer be `null`, or the `attempts` should equal `maxAttempts`. Our loop then is:

```
int     attempts = 0;
while (s==null && attempts<maxAttempts) {
    try {
        s = new Socket(hostname, portnumber);
    } catch (UnknownHostException uhe) {
        System.err.println("Cannot make TCP connection."+
                "Reason: Unknown Host: "+hostname);
        throw new TCPException("Connection Failure: "+
                            "Unknown Host");
    } catch (IOException ioe) {
        System.err.println("Connection failed "+
                "due to Network I/O Error: retrying ...");
    }
    attempts++;
}
```

When the loop terminates we check the value of `s` and either rethrow an `IOException` or return `s`. The revised implementation of `TCPConnection` is as follows:

```
import java.net.*;
import java.io.*;
```

```
class TCPConnection {
    public TCPConnection(String hostname, int portnumber)
                                        throws Exception {
        Socket   s = makeSocket(hostname,portnumber);
        br = new BufferedReader(
                new InputStreamReader(
                    s.getInputStream()));
        ps = new PrintStream(s.getOutputStream());
    }

    public String readLine() throws Exception {
        String  s;
        try {
            s = br.readLine();
        } catch (IOException ioe) {
            System.err.println("TCP input failure: "+
                            "network error");
            throw new Exception("Input Failure: "+
                            "Network I/O Error");
        }
        return s;
    }

    public void println(String s) {
        ps.println(s);
    }

    private Socket makeSocket(String hostname,
                        int portnumber) throws Exception {
        Socket s=null;
        int    attempts = 0;
        while (s==null && attempts<maxAttempts) {
            try {
                s  = new Socket(hostname, portnumber);
            } catch (UnknownHostException uhe) {
                System.err.println("Cannot make TCP "+
                    "connection."+"Reason: Unknown Host: "
                    +hostname);
                throw new TCPException("Connection "+
                            "Failure: Unknown Host");
            } catch (IOException ioe) {
                System.err.println("Connection failed "+
                    "due to Network I/O Error: retrying ...");
            }
            attempts++;
        }
        if  (s==null)
            throw new IOException("Connection Failure: "+
                            "Net I/O Errors");
```

```
        else
            return  s;
    }
    private final int      maxAttempts=5;
    private BufferedReader  br;
    private PrintStream      ps;
}

start of inserts
```

Insert A

Insert B
Insert C
Insert D

Insert E

appendix a

Glossary of Terms

abstract class—A class that contains at least one abstract method. (Chapter 13)

abstract method—A method declared but not implemented by a superclass. It is the responsibility of a subclass to implement the method. (Chapter 13)

Abstract Window Toolkit—A collection of Java classes that allows the programmer to create graphical user interfaces. (Chapter 3 GUI Supplement)

access control—The ability to allow or prevent access to a method or variable. (Chapter 4)

accumulator—A variable that holds a partial sum or product or the analog for another binary operation besides + or *. (Chapter 9)

activation record—A block of memory holding the parameters and local variables of a method, along with the return address of the invoker of the method. (Chapter 11)

adapter class—A class introduced to facilitate the implementation of an event listener. (Chapter 13 GUI Supplement)

all-paths testing—An approach to testing in which every possible sequence of statements is tested at least once. (Chapter 7)

applet life cycle—The phases an applet goes through from being initially loaded through its execution and subsequent termination. (Chapter 4 GUI Supplement)

argument—Information provided in a message in addition to the method-name and ultimately made available to the method via a parameter; one of the two ways that methods get needed information. (Chapters 2,4)

array—A programming language feature that provides an indexed collection of data values. (Chapter 10)

assignment—The association of a value with a variable. (Chapter 2)

automatic testing—An approach to testing in which the test suite verifies the correctness of the test results. (Chapter 7)

AWT—See Abstract Window Toolkit. (Chapter 3 GUI Supplement)

behavior—Any action that an object may take in response to a message. Similarly, any action that the object may take; any change it may undergo or any characteristic it may reveal. (Chapters 1, 2)

behavior—Any action that the object may take, any change it may undergo, or any characteristic it may reveal as a result of a method being invoked. (Chapter 4)

binary search—An algorithm for efficiently searching a sorted collection by repeatedly dividing the region where the item might be found in half and reducing consideration to one half or the other. (Chapter 10)

boolean—A primitive data type modeling true and false values. (Chapter 6)

boolean expression—An expression evaluating to a boolean value. (Chapter 6)

break statement—A statement that forces immediate termination of a loop. (Chapter 9)

buffer—A place to store information temporarily, prior to further processing. (Chapter 3)

bug—A run-time error in a program. (Chapter 7)

cascaded if/else—a sequence of if/else statements in which the else portion of one if statement consists of another if statement. (Chapter 6)

cascading—A technique in which the result of one method invocation is used as the receiver of a second method invocation. (Chapter 2)

character—A distinct elementary symbol, often corresponding to a single keyboard keystroke; letters, digits, punctuation marks, space, and tab are all examples of characters. (Chapter 1)

character generator—A portion of the display hardware responsible for the display of characters in text mode. (Chapter 5 GUI Supplement)

checked Exception—An Exception that, if possibly thrown by a method, must appear in the methods throws clause; so-called because the Java compiler checks for its presence in the clause. (Chapter 14)

class—A category of objects that share the same behavior. (Chapter 1)

class method—A method that is not associated with any particular object of a class but rather with the class itself. As a result, it can be invoked without reference to an object. Such a method is also called a static method. (Chapter 4)

client-server model—A program design approach in which one program, the server, provides a service to another program, the client, which is requesting that service. (Chapter 14 Net Supplement)

code—A section of text written in some programming language such as Java. (Chapter 1)

collection—A class or language construct that manages one or more objects. (Chapter 8)

command name—Text associated with an action event. (Chapter 13 GUI Supplement)

compiler—A program that translates code written in a high-level programming language into machine language. (Chapter 1)

composition—A technique in which the result of one method invocation is used as an argument in a second method invocation. (Chapter 2)

composition—A technique in which a class is defined using instance variables that are references to objects of other classes. (Chapter 13)

compound condition—A condition (boolean expression) containing one or more logical operators. (Chapter 6)

compound statement—One or more statements surrounded by braces that are thereby treated as a single statement. (Chapter 6)

computer network—A collection of computers, connected by wires, that can exchange data with each other. (Chapter 3)

concurrent threads—Two or more threads running at the same time or in an interweaved fashion. (Chapter 9 GUI Supplement)

conditional—A statement that allows selective execution of code depending upon some true or false condition. (Chapter 6)

constant—A variable whose value may not be changed after initialization. (Chapter 5)

constructor—A method that is invoked when an object is created. The name of the constructor method is the same as the corresponding class name. The purpose of the constructor is to guarantee a reasonable and consistent state at the time of object creation. (Chapters 3,4)

container—A graphic component, such as an applet, that can contain other graphic components. (Chapter 4 GUI Supplement)

continue statement—A statement that forces Java to skip the remainder of the loop body in the current iteration. (Chapter 9)

coordinates—The horizontal (x) and vertical (y) position of a pixel on a graphic mode display. (Chapter 5 GUI Supplement)

counter—A variable that keeps count of something else. (Chapter 9)

counting loop—A loop whose termination is based on executing a certain number of times. (Chapter 9)

current activation record—The most recently allocated activation record, which corresponds to the currently executing method. (Chapter 11)

dangling else—A problem occurring in a nested if statement, in which the single else is associated with the wrong if. (Chapter 6)

debugging—The process of finding and fixing bugs. (Chapter 7)

declaration—A Java statement which introduces a variable into a Java program. A declaration of a reference variable specifies the name (identifier) of the variable and the class of object to which it may refer. (Chapter 2)

default—A behavior or value that is used if no explicit behavior or value is provided. (Chapter 4)

device driver—Software used to communicate with a hardware device such as the monitor or printer. (Chapter 5 GUI Supplement)

dialog box—A window whose purpose is to receive input from the user. (Chapter 13 GUI Supplement)

dimension—The number of indices required to access an element in an array. (Chapter 10)

display parameterization—A technique in which the various graphic shapes of a display are related to each other so that modifications may be easily made. (Chapter 12 GUI Supplement)

double—A primitive data type that models high precision floating-point numbers. (Chapter 5)

elements—The individual objects contained within a collection. (Chapter 8)

end user—A person who is using a program, usually not the author of the code. (Chapter 3)

enumerate—List or go through all members of a collection. (Chapter 8)

event—An action occurring within the graphical interface, such as a button click, requiring attention from the program. (Chapter 6 GUI Supplement)

event source—The component that generated an event. (Chapter 6 GUI Supplement)

event-driven programming—A style of programming, usually associated with graphical interfaces, in which an interface is created and subsequent processing occurs as a result of events generated by the interface. (Chapter 6 GUI Supplement)

every-statement testing—An approach to testing in which every statement is tested at least once. (Chapter 7)

Exception—An object that represents an unexpected circumstance or an out-of-the-ordinary situation. (Chapter 14)

execute—To carry out instructions of program code. (Chapter 1)

expression—A sequence of operands and operators producing a value. (Chapter 5)

extreme—A value in a set that is no greater or no less than all the other elements (Chapter 9)

false—The literal of type boolean representing a false value. (Chapter 6)

file—A collection of information that has a name and that can be stored on a disk of a computer system. (Chapters 1,3)

fixed-width font—A font in which all characters are the same width. (Chapter 5 GUI Supplement)

float—A primitive data type that models floating-point numbers. (Chapter 5)

floating-point—Numbers of fixed precision that are associated with measurements and are used typically in scientific and engineering applications. (Chapter 5)

flush—The forced output of characters saved in a buffer. (Chapter 3)

font—A character style in which each character reflects the theme of that style. (Chapter 5 GUI Supplement)

font metrics—Information regarding the dimensions of a font. (Chapter 5 GUI Supplement)

font style—A variation on a font—bold, plain, or italic. (Chapter 5 GUI Supplement)

frame—A window with a title bar, optional menu, and control elements to minimize, maximize, and close the window. (Chapter 13 GUI Supplement)

gaining the focus—Becoming the currently active component. (Chapter 13 GUI Supplement)

graphical user interface—An interface that uses graphic elements such as buttons, menus, scrollable windows, and graphical drawings to communicate with end users. (Chapter 1 GUI Supplement)

graphics mode—A mode of screen or printer display in which the screen is broken into a grid of dots, allowing the display of graphic shapes. (Chapter 5 GUI Supplement)

GUI—See graphical user interface. (Chapter 1 GUI Supplement)

GUI component—A control, such as a button, that can be placed into an applet. (Chapter 4 GUI Supplement)

has-a—A relationship between an object and some value such that the value is part of the object's state. This is usually expressed in Java by the object possessing an instance variable corresponding to the value. (Chapter 6)

header—An integer that indicates how much data follow in a set of input (Chapter 9)

heuristic—A rule used by an application to aid in the making of seemingly intelligent decision. (Chapter 12)

HTML—See HyperText Markup Language. (Chapter 2 GUI Supplement)

HTTP—See HyperText Transport Protocol. (Chapter 14 Net Supplement)

hypertext—Text with embedded links allowing the information to be read in a nonlinear manner. (Chapter 2 GUI Supplement)

HyperText Transport Protocol—The protocol used by web servers and their clients. (Chapter 14 Net Supplement)

HyperText Markup Language—The set of rules that govern the construction and use of tags on a web page. (Chapter 2 GUI Supplement)

identifier—A sequence of characters that may be used as a name in a Java program. An identifier typically consists of an alphabetic character (A–Z, a–z) followed by zero or more alphanumeric characters (A–Z, a–z, 0–9). (Chapter 1)

if statement—The if statement conditionally executes a statement based upon the value of a boolean condition. The if part is executed if the condition is true, the else part, if present, is executed if the condition is false. (Chapter 6)

implement—Provide the code that realizes a design. (Chapter 4)

implementation—The specific code that realizes a class. (Chapter 4)

implements—The guarantee that a class makes to implementing the methods specified in an interface. (Chapter 13)

index—An integer that denotes a position in an ordered collection. (Chapter 10)

inheritance—A technique in object-oriented languages in which one class assumes all the methods and instance variables of another class as its own. The inheriting class may also provide its own additional behavior. (Chapter 13)

initialized—Given a first value. (Chapter 4)

input—Information from outside the program that is provided to the program. (Chapter 4)

instance—A particular object of a class. (Chapter 1)

instance variable—A variable that is declared within a class but outside of any method; its purpose is to store information needed by methods to be preserved in between invocations. Each object has its own set of instance variables that have their own unique values. It is these values that distinguish one object from another. The entire set of the instance variables of an object defines its state. (Chapter 4)

int—A primitive data type modeling whole numbers (integers). (Chapter 5)

interactive—An arrangement of bidirectional and alternating data flow between user and program. (Chapter 3)

interface—An abstract class containing only abstract methods. (Chapter 13)

interleaved execution—Two or more threads alternating execution. (Chapter 9 GUI Supplement)

Internet—A rapidly growing, very widely used global network of networks. (Chapter 3)

Internet address—A String, such as www.aw.com, that identifies a machine on the Internet. (Chapter 3)

Internet Protocol—A method of communication used by the Internet, in which information is moved unreliably through intermediate machines. (Chapter 14 Net Supplement)

interpreter—A program that directly carries out the statements of a high-level programming language. (Chapter 1)

invocation chain—The sequence of method invocations starting with main that lead to and include the invocation of the currently executing method. (Chapter 14)

IP—See Internet Protocol. (Chapter 14 Net Supplement)

is-a—The relationship between subclass and superclass. An object of a subclass *is-a* object of the superclass and may be used wherever an object of the superclass may be used. (Chapter 13)

iteration—The repeated execution of a section of code until some condition is satisfied. (Chapter 9)

Java—The name of one of the most recent and popular programming languages; also the one used in this text. (Chapter 1)

Java API—See Java Application Programming Interface. (Chapter 3 GUI Supplement)

Java applet—A Java program that is part of a web page and executes within a browser. (Chapter 2 GUI Supplement)

Java Application Programming Interface—A description of the classes and methods distributed with Java. (Chapter 3 GUI Supplement)

keyword—A word with a special, predefined meaning in Java language. (Chapter 1)

layout managers—A family of classes in the AWT that facilitate the placement of controls within a container component. (Chapter 4 GUI Supplement)

listener—A class that notifies a component that it wishes to be informed of events generated by that component. (Chapter 6 GUI Supplement)

literal—A value whose name is a literal representation of itself, e.g., 2. (Chapter 5)

local variable—A variable that is declared within a method; it exists only during the invocation of the method and is used as a temporary, convenient holder of information. (Chapter 4)

$\log_2 N$—The number of times one can start with N and successively divide by 2 before reaching 1. The $\log_2$ is the inverse of exponentiation, with 2 as the base: if $2x$ is N, then $\log_2 N$ is x. (Chapter 10)

logical operator—An operator that combines boolean expressions into larger boolean expressions. (Chapter 6)

long—A primitive data type modeling very large integers. (Chapter 5)

loop—A language construct that repeatedly executes a section of code. (Chapter 8)

loop condition—The condition that controls the while statement's execution (Chapter 9)

loop pattern—The code structure of a loop that is frequently used. (Chapter 8)

loop termination—The ending of a loop's execution, usually because a particular condition has become satisfied. (Chapter 9)

message—The mechanism by which a method is invoked. A message consists of a method name that identifies the behavior followed by a (possibly empty) argument list that provides further details. (Chapters 1,2)

method—A self-contained section of code belonging to a class that achieves a specific behavior for that class. A method consists of a return type, method-name, and parameter list, all of which form the method's signature, and the section of code that is called the body of the method. (Chapter 2,4)

method name—The identifier associated with a method. (Chapter 2)

modal dialog box—A dialog box, which when active prevents activity in any other window of the applet. (Chapter 13 GUI Supplement)

model—A representation of something. Models are usually simpler than the object they are representing; they only contain those aspects relevant to the user of the model. (Chapter 1)

modifiers—Special keys, such as the alt or ctrl keys, that may be held down in conjunction with other keys. (Chapter 13 GUI Supplement)

move-to-front—A strategy for organizing a collection where every time an item is requested, it is moved to the beginning of the collection on the assumption that it is likely to be asked for again. (Chapter 10)

multithreaded programming—Programs written with more than one thread executing at a time.

mutually exclusive check boxes—A group of check boxes for which only one may be chosen at any one time. (Chapter 8 GUI Supplement)

nested if/else—An `if/else` or `if` statement appearing as the true portion of another `if` or `if/else` statement. (Chapter 6)

network resource—A resource, usually a file, that is available to users on machines other than the one on which the file is stored. (Chapter 3)

nonmodal dialog box—A dialog box, which when active allows activity in other windows of the applet. (Chapter 13 GUI Supplement)

object—An entity in Java that models something; a member of a class. (Chapter 1)

operand—A value participating in an operation. (Chapter 5)

operation—An action in Java that results in a value. (Chapter 3)

operator—A symbol or keyword representing an operation (e.g., the identifier `new` represents the operation that creates an object). (Chapter 3)

output—Information that the program provides to the external world. (Chapter 4)

overloading—The practice of having a class provide different—though highly related—methods of the same name; the methods are distinguished by the types of arguments they receive. (Chapter 2)

overriding—The act of reimplementing a method in a subclass with the exact same signature of a method in the superclass. (Chapter 13)

packet—A small piece of data resulting from breaking up information for communication across a network. (Chapter 14 Net Supplement)

parameter—A variable that is declared in the parentheses of a method signature and whose purpose is to store the value of the corresponding argument; naturally, the type of the argument and the parameter must match in some sense. (Chapter 4)

picture element—See pixel. (Chapter 5 GUI Supplement)

pixel—A single dot of a graphic mode display. (Chapter 5 GUI Supplement)

point—A unit of measurement for a font's size—1 point equals 1/72 of an inch. (Chapter 5 GUI Supplement)

polymorphism—A feature of object-oriented languages in which the exact method to be invoked is determined at run-time by the class of the receiving object. (Chapter 13)

predicate—A method whose return value is boolean. (Chapter 6)

prepend—Place in front of, place before. (Chapter 4)

primitive data type—A data type provided as part of the language definition rather than through a class definition. No class or methods are associated with the data type. (Chapter 5)

private—A keyword modifier in a method definition or instance variable declaration that prevents access to a method or variable from any code outside the class. (Chapter 4)

program—A Java text that can be compiled and executed. (Chapter 1)

prompt—A String that is written to the screen to tell an end user what kind of input should be entered next. (Chapter 3)

proportional font—A font in which the width of the characters vary. (Chapter 5 GUI Supplement)

protocol—The set of rules governing the interaction between a client and a server. (Chapter 14 Net Supplement)

prototype—Part of a method definition that consists of return-type, method-name, and argument list in parentheses. (Chapters 2,4)

public—A keyword modifier in a method definition or instance variable declaration that allows access to a method or variable from any code outside the class. (Chapter 4)

receiver—An object that is the recipient of a message in response to which it therefore exhibits some behavior. (Chapter 1)

recursion—The process of using a recursive procedure; the carrying out of a recursive call. (Chapter 11)

recursive call—An invocation of a method from within that method. (Chapter 11)

recursive procedure—A procedure that carries out a part of a task and refers to itself to carry out the rest of the task. (Chapter 11)

reference—A value or expression that refers to an object, thereby allowing us to send messages to the object. (Chapters 1, 4)

reference variable—An identifier that may be assigned a reference to an object of a particular class. (Chapter 2)

relational operator—An operator that compares two values, producing a boolean expression as the result. (Chapter 6)

responsibility—The characteristic of being obligated to provide a certain behavior or carry out a certain task. (Chapter 4)

responsibility-driven programming—A perspective on class design, in particular the assignment of behavior, in which the burden of maintaining an object lies as much as possible with the object's class. This makes it easier for other objects to work with the object. (Chapter 12)

return—The action of the receiver of a message providing a value that is given to the sender; the value replaces the phrase that sent the message. (Chapter 2)

return value—The value given back to the sender by the receiver of a message. (Chapter 2)

return statement—A verb keyword that allows a method to terminate its own execution and allows the sender of the message to resume execution; additionally, the return statement allows the method to send some information back to the receiver. (Chapter 4)

return type—The first part of the prototype; it specifies what kind of information will be returned by the method. (Chapter 4)

router—A machine on a network that transfers (routes) packets. (Chapter 14 Net Supplement)

runtime Exception—An Exception that reflects a programming error that typically can occur "anywhere" and ought to occur "nowhere" in the code and therefore is not required to be in the throws clause. (Chapter 14)

sanity check—A test in a program that verifies what the programmer believes to be true at that point in the code. (Chapter 7)

search—An algorithm for finding a particular item that is stored in a collection of related values or objects. (Chapter 10)

selection sort—An algorithm for sorting where one successively selects progressively ascending elements of a collection. (Chapter 10)

self-organizing vector—An approach to searching where the order of elements in the vector is changed as it is learned which elements are frequently accessed. (Chapter 10)

sequential search—An algorithm for searching an indexed collection checking the elements in the same sequence that they are stored in the collection. (Chapter 10)

short-circuiting—Ending the evaluation of a condition without evaluating all its clauses as soon as the value of the condition can be determined. (Chapter 9)

signature—A method's name along with a description of its arguments. (Chapter 2)

Simple Mail Transfer Protocol—The protocol used by email servers and their clients. (Chapter 14 Net Supplement)

SMTP—See Simple Mail Transfer Protocol. (Chapter 14 Net Supplement)

socket—A communication endpoint—analogous to a telephone—that permits a program to communicate to another program across a network. (Chapter 14 Net Supplement)

state—The collection of values of the instance variables of an object at any given time. (Chapter 4)

statement—A sentence of the Java programming language. A statement represents an action to be carried out. (Chapter 1)

static final—The Java keywords used to declare a constant. (Chapter 5)

static method—See class method. (Chapter 4)

String constant—A sequence of characters embedded in double quotes, e.g, `"Hello"`. The constant is a reference to the `String` object consisting of the characters between the quotes in our case, the characters `Hello`. (Chapter 2)

subclass—A class that inherits from some other class. (Chapter 13)

superclass—A class that is inherited from. (Chapter 13)

switch statement—A multiway conditional. The switch allows selective execution of multiple cases based upon the value of an expression. (Chapter 6)

tag—A notation that controls the appearance of data on a web page. A tag consists of an open angle bracket, a tag word, additional tag-dependent information, and a close angle bracket.(Chapter 2 GUI Supplement)

tag word—The text in a tag that specifies how the tag controls the page's appearance. (Chapter 2 GUI Supplement)

TCP—See Transmission Control Protocol. (Chapter 14 Net Supplement)

TCP/IP—A collection of network communication protocols that includes TCP and IP. (Chapter 14 Net Supplement)

termination step—An essential step in any viable recursive procedure, where the task is checked to see if it can be carried out without resort to recursion. (Chapter 11)

test driver—A method (or collection of methods) whose purpose is to test the behavior of one or more classes. (Chapter 7)

text mode—A mode of screen or printer display in which each position can display a text character. (Chapter 5)

this—A pronoun keyword that refers to the current object; *this* allows for convenient reference to the object's instance variables, particularly when the parameters have the same name. (Chapter 4)

thread—The process of carrying out a set of instructions one at a time. (Chapter 9 GUI Supplement)

Throwable—The parent class from which Exception is derived. (Chapter 14)

throws clause—A clause in a method prototype that lists the Exception objects the method might throw. (Chapter 14)

Transmission Control Protocol—A reliable, conceptually direct communication between two machines that is coded on top of the Internet Protocol. (Chapter 14 Net Supplement)

transpose—A strategy for organizing a collection in which every time an item is requested, it is moved up one position, exchanging position with the item in front of it. (Chapter 10)

true—The literal of type boolean representing a true value. (Chapter 6)

typeface—The combination of a font, style, and size. (Chapter 5 GUI Supplement)

typing a key—The event generated by pressing then releasing a key. This is essentially the combination of two events: key press and key release. (Chapter 13 GUI Supplement)

URL—A unique identification of a network resource, including the Internet address of the machine on which the resource is stored, the file name of the resource, and the protocol (such as HyperText Transfer Protocol, or HTTP) that should be used to access the resource. (Chapter 3)

while statement—A particular loop construct in the Java language. (Chapter 8)

Three Java Environments

Introduction

This appendix illustrates how to create, compile, and execute Java programs. We will use the first program presented in Chapter 4 as an example:

```
import java.io.*;
class Program1 {
    public static void main(String arg[]) {
        System.out.println("Welcome To Java!");
    }
}
```

We present the development of this program for three operating systems: Unix, Windows 95/NT, and MacOS. We use the Java Development Kit (JDK) from Sun Microsystems for Unix and Windows for its simplicity and because you can download it without cost from the Java Web site at www.java-soft.com. There are several integrated development environments (IDEs) available for Windows. An IDE provides editing, compiling, and execution in a single program. If you are using one of these environments, please consult your instructor about its use.

At the time of this writing, Sun had not yet released a latest-version JDK for the Macintosh. We therefore show you how to develop a Java program using the popular Metrowerks development environment.

Unix

Step 1: Edit and save the program as a *.java* source file.   Type in the program using the Unix vi editor. From the Unix shell command line, type the following:

```
vi  Program1.java
```

In general, Java source files must have the same name as the class followed by the suffix *.java.* (If you prefer, you can use a different editor.)

Step 2: Compile the *.java* source file.   From the Unix shell command line, run the Java compiler by typing:

```
javac  Program1.java
```

Any errors are displayed by the compiler accompanied by their line numbers. For example, forgetting the semicolon in the fifth line of the program produces this output:

```
>  javac  Program1.java
Program1.java:5:  ';'  expected.
    System.out.println("Welcome  To  Java!")                    ^
1 error
>
```

Fix any errors and recompile. When the program is error-free, the compiler issues no error output:

```
>  javac  Program1.java
>
```

Step 3: Execute the *.class* file.   From the Unix shell command line, execute the program by typing the following:

```
java  Program1
```

Do *not* include the *.class* suffix. The output of the program is displayed on the screen as follows:

```
>  java  Program1
Welcome  To  Java!
>
```

Windows 95/NT

Step 1: Edit and save the program as a *.java* source file. Type in the program using the Windows notepad editor. From the Start Menu/Run dialog box, type the following:

```
notepad  path\Program1.java
```

The path is the directory in which you wish the source file to be created. For example, if you have a directory \Java\Programs on the C drive, you would type:

```
notepad  C:\Java\Programs\Program1.java
```

In general, Java source files must have the same name as the class followed by the suffix *.java.*

Step 2: Open a command prompt window and move to the proper directory. From the Start Menu/Programs popup menu, open a command prompt window. At the command prompt, change directories to the one containing the source file you have created. For example, using the directory example of step 1, type the following:

```
C:\>cd  C:\Java\Programs
```

Step 3: Compile the *.java* source file. Remaining in the command prompt window, run the Java compiler by typing:

```
javac  Program1.java
```

Any errors are displayed by the compiler accompanied by their line numbers. For example, forgetting the semicolon in the fifth line of the program produces the output:

```
C:Java\Programs\>  javac Program1.java
Program1.java:5:  ';'  expected.
   System.out.println("Welcome  To  Java!")                  ^
1 error
C:\Java\Programs>
```

Fix any errors and recompile. When the program is error-free, the compiler issues no error output:

```
C:\Java\Programs>  javac  Program1.java
C:\Java\Programs>
```

Step 3: Execute the *.class* file. From the command prompt shell command line, execute the program by typing:

```
java  Program1
```

Do *not* include the *.class* suffix. The output of the program is displayed on the screen:

```
C:\Java\Programs>  java  Program1
Welcome  To  Java!
C:\Java\Programs>
```

Macintosh: Metrowerks CodeWarrior

Step 1: Open up CodeWarrior IDE 2.1.

Step 2: Go to the File menu and select New Project.   A New Project dialog box appears. Make sure the Create Folder box is checked. If it is not checked, click on it to check it. See Figure B.1.

Step 3: Click on the triangle next to the word Java.   Five Java templates are displayed. See Figure B.2.

FIGURE B.1

Step 4: Select Java Application and click OK.   A dialog box will appear, asking you to choose a name for the project. The name should be the name of the class that contains your main method with an *.mcp* suffix. In the case of Program1 from Chapter 1, the project name should be Program1.mcp. See Figure B.3.

Step 5: Click on Save.   A project window will appear. See Figure B.4.

Step 6: Click on the triangle next to Sources. Then click on TrivialApplication.java as shown in Figure B.5.

Step 7: Go to the Project menu and choose Remove Selected Items.   The entry for TrivialApplication.java will disappear.

Step 8: Go to the File menu and choose New.   A   program   text   window named "untitled" appears. Type your program in this window. For the example from Chapter 1, type in the program given at the beginning of this appendix.

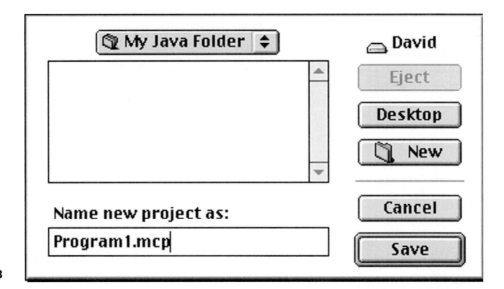

FIGURE B.3

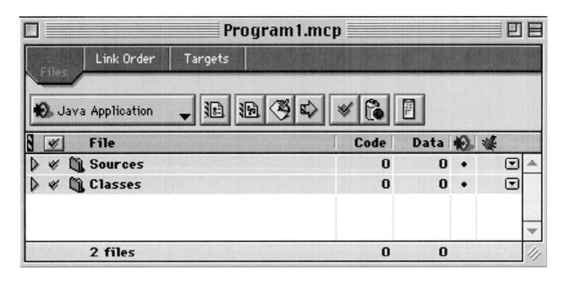

FIGURE B.4

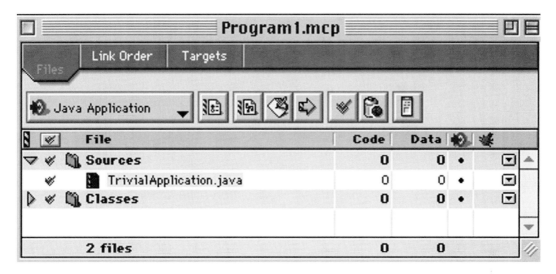

FIGURE B.5

Step 9: Go to the File menu and select Save As.   A file-save window appears.
See Figure B.6.

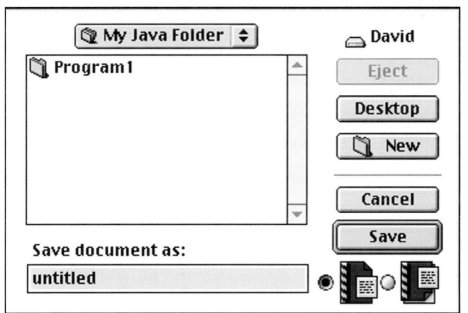

FIGURE B.6

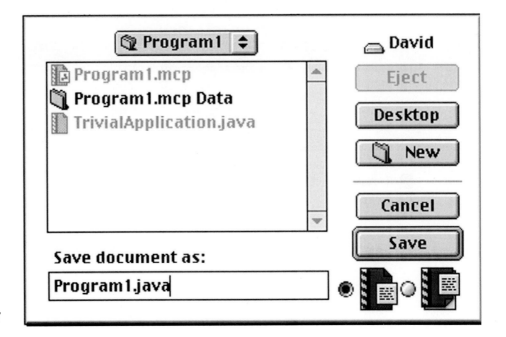

FIGURE B.7

Step 10: Give your program file a name.   It should be the name of the class (in this case Program1) followed by the suffix *.java*. (See Figure B.7.) Type Program1.java and double click the Program1 folder icon.

Step 11: Go to the Project menu and select Add Files.   The Add Files dialog box will appear. See Figure B.8.

Step 12: Select your newly created program file.   In the case of Chapter 1, select Program1.java. Click on Add and then click on Done.
    A dialog box will pop up—just click OK.

Step 13: Go to the Edit menu and select Java Application Settings (at the bottom).

Step 14: Select JavaTarget and then replace TrivialApplication with the name of your class (Program1, in the case of Chapter 1). (See Figure B.9.) Click on Save in the bottom right.   A message that you must "relink" will appear—click OK in response.

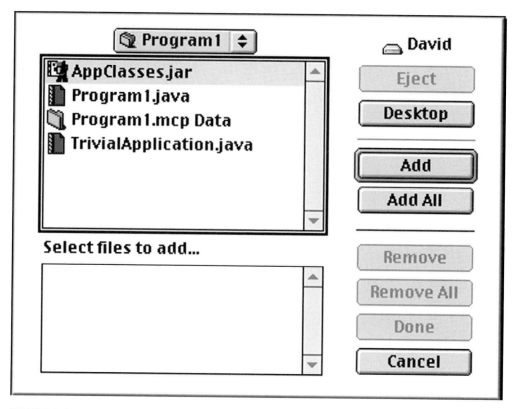

FIGURE B.8

Step 15: Close the Java Application Settings window. Go to the Project menu and Select Run.   A series of windows will appear, providing various fleeting messages. In the end, if you have typed in your program correctly, your program will run and produce its output in the Java Output window. See Figure B.10.

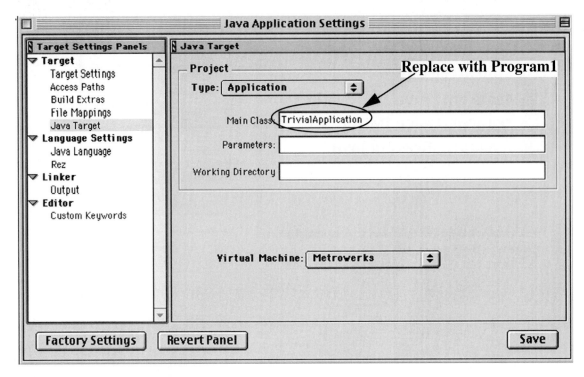

FIGURE B.9

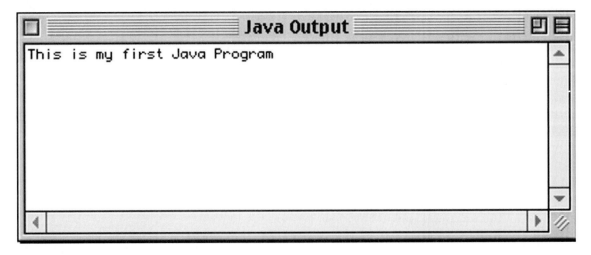

FIGURE B.10

Some of Java's Predefined Classes, Interfaces, Methods, and Constants

To the Instructor

This appendix is not meant to be a complete, precise, or comprehensive reference to the Java API. Instead, its purpose is to provide the student with an accessible reference to use when reviewing the examples and completing the exercises that appear in this text. We therefore restrict ourselves to the methods, variables, classes, and interfaces discussed in this book.

Introducing inheritance in Chapter 13 leaves us with something of a conundrum with regard to the presentation of inherited methods and the implicit upcasting of subclass objects to superclass reference variables. On the one hand, we have no way of explaining, for example, why a Button object may be passed to the add method of class Panel, which expects a Component parameter (or even what a Component object is). On the other hand, we do not wish to present the student with incorrect prototypes or other information. We choose a somewhat compromising approach. Parameters whose types are of superclasses not discussed (for example, the above Component parameter) are italicized and an informal explanation is given for them in the section of this appendix titled How To Use the Indexes. Thus, the student is made aware that something unusual is occurring and is given some understanding of the issue, while the correct prototype is still presented. Similarly, inherited methods are documented in the subclasses in whose context they are actually discussed in the text. For example, the above add method is documented in both the Applet and Panel class, although it is actually the same method in both classes. In both cases it is inherited from the Container superclass. To maintain correctness, a bracketed comment containing the actual class defining the method is included for the student who has already encountered inheritance.

This reference is thus graduated in the sense that it provides information of increasing precision and sophistication to the student as he or she progresses through the text. (On a lighter note, one might say this reference is polymorphic.)

Our second goal is to gently introduce the student to the world of API references. While the basic format of our index is similar to that of a standard API reference, the explanations and presentation have been geared toward the beginner. After completing this text and using this appendix, the student will, we hope, be ready to begin navigating the official Java API Reference, having seen all the basic elements of such documentation. Think of this as an API manual with training wheels.

To the Student

This appendix is designed to provide you with a central location in which all the Java predefined classes, methods, and variables used in this book are documented. As you progress through the text, you will become comfortable working with several classes in a program and will become familiar with many of the predefined classes and methods. Even experienced programmers, however, often must consult the documentation to verify a method's prototype or the name of a class. Such information is documented in an Application Programming Interface (API) reference manual. An API reference usually contains an index of the predefined classes explaining each class's purpose and behavior as well as listing the methods and variables defined by each class. Each method is presented with its prototype and with some explanation of the parameters, returns type, and general behavior of the method. In addition, a method index is often provided to allow the reader to quickly find the class in which a method is defined.

This appendix follows this same pattern. We first present an alphabetic index of those predefined methods and variables presented in the text, together with the prototype and the class in which the method is defined. We then document each of the predefined classes discussed in the text, explaining the class's use, and listing the methods and variables of that class. The explanation of each method is presented here as well.

An introductory section illustrates a typical entry in both the method and class index. That section also provides explanation of some issues that might prove somewhat confusing at the beginning.

Once you have worked with this appendix for a while, you might want to try your hand at an actual Java API reference manual. There are several books documenting the Java API; in addition, the JavaSoft web site at www.java-soft.com contains an online API reference manual.

How To Use the Indexes

The Method and Variable Index

A typical entry in the index is as follows:

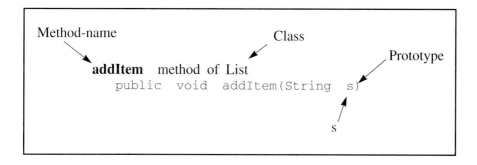

There are several possible variations. Bracketed text appearing after the class name indicates the method is inherited—a topic covered in Chapter 13. The bracketed text will then specify the actual class in which the method is defined. For example:

```
paint  method of Applet [defined in Container]
     public  void  paint(Graphics  g)
```

If you have not yet covered Chapter 13, you can simply ignore the brackets.

Finally, a parameter type might be italicized as follows:

add   method of Panel [defined in Container]
        public void add(*Component* c)

This indicates that one of several class types is acceptable for the parameter. A list of acceptable parameter types and the class types that may be used for each of them is discussed in the italicized parameters subsection below. Again, a precise explanation is presented in Chapter 13; until you get to that chapter, simply refer to the acceptable substitutions.

The Class and Interface Index

A typical entry in the index is as follows:

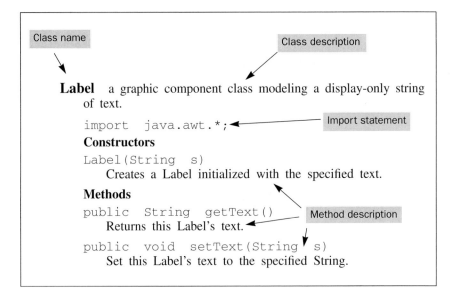

The class name and a brief description of the class are presented first, followed by the import statement required in order to use the class. If the class comes from java.lang, an import statement is unnecessary as the Java compiler always makes those classes available.

A list of constructors, methods, and/or variable prototypes and descriptions is then presented.

Italicized Parameters

Several methods have parameters that may be passed one of several class types. We indicate this situation by italicizing the types of these parameters. The following is a list of those types and the types that may be passed to them:

- *Component*—Button, Panel, CheckBox, Label, List, and any other graphic component.
- *Container*—Applet or Panel
- *InputStream*—FileInputStream or BufferedInputStream
- *OutputStream*—FileOutputStream
- *Reader*—InputStreamReader

See also Chapter 13.

Method and Variable Index

abs   method of Math

```
public  static  int  abs(int  i)
```

actionPerformed   method of ActionListener

```
public  void  actionPerformed(ActionEvent  ae)
```

add   method of Applet [defined in Container]

```
public  void  add(Component  c)
```

add   method of Panel [defined in Container]

```
public  void  add(Component  c)
```

add   method of Applet [defined in Container]

```
public  void  add(String  s,  Component  c)
```

add   method of Panel [defined in Container]

```
public  void  add(String  s,  Component  c)
```

addActionListener   method of Button

```
public  void  addActionListener(ActionListener  al)
```

addElement   method of Vector

```
public  void  addElement(Object  o)
```

addItem   method of List

```
public  void  addItem(String  s)
```

addItemListener method of List

```
public void addItemListener(ItemListener il)
```

addMouseListener method of Canvas [defined in Component]

```
public void addMouseListener(MouseListener ml)
```

black variable of Color

```
final static Color black
```

BOLD variable of Font

```
final static int BOLD
```

BorderLayout constructor of BorderLayout

```
BorderLayout()
```

BufferedInputStream constructor of BufferedInputStream

```
BufferedInputStream(InputStream is)
```

BufferedReader constructor of BufferedReader

```
BufferedReader(Reader rd)
```

Button constructor of Button

```
public Button(String label)
```

charAt method of class String

```
public char charAt(int i)
```

Checkbox constructor of Checkbox

```
Checkbox(String label)
```

CheckboxGroup constructor of CheckboxGroup

```
CheckboxGroup()
```

Color constructor of Color

```
Color(int red, int green, int blue)
```

compareTo method of String

```
public int compareTo(String label)
```

concat method of String

```
public String concat(String s)
```

cyan   method of Color

```
final  static  Color  cyan
```

delete   method of File

```
public  void  delete()
```

doubleValue   method of Double

```
public  double  doubleValue()
```

drawLine   method of Graphics

```
public  void  drawLine(int  x1,  int  y1,  int  x2,
                       int  y2)
```

drawOval   method of Graphics

```
public  void  drawOval(int  x,  int  y,  int  width,
                       int  height)
```

drawRect   method of Graphics

```
public  void  drawRect(int  x,  int  y,  int  width,
                       int  height)
```

drawString   method of Graphics

```
public  void  drawString(String  text.  int  x,
                         int  y)
```

dumpStack   method of Thread

```
public  static  void  dumpStack()
```

elementAt   method of Vector

```
public  Object  elementAt(int  i)
```

elements   method of Vector

```
public  Enumeration  elements()
```

equals   method of Object

```
public  boolean  equals(Object  o)
```

equals   method of String

```
public  boolean  equals(Object  o)
```

File   constructor of File

```
File(String  name)
```

FileInputStream constructor of FileInputStream

```
FileInputStream(File  f)
```

FileOutputStream constructor of FileOutputStream

```
FileOutputStream(File  f)
```

fillOval method of Graphics

```
public  void  fillOval(int  x,  int  y,  int  width,
                       int  height)
```

fillRect method of Graphics

```
public  void  fillRect(int  x,  int  y,  int  width,
                       int  height)
```

fill3DRect method of Graphics

```
public  void  fill3DRect(int  x,  int  y,  int  width,
                         int  height,  boolean  isRaised)
```

FlowLayout constructor of FlowLayout

```
FlowLayout()
```

flush method of PrintStream

```
public  void  flush()
```

Font constructor of Font

```
Font(String  font,  int  style,  int  size)
```

FontMetrics constructor of FontMetrics

```
FontMetrics(Font  f)
```

getActionCommand method of Button

```
public  String  getActionCommand()
```

getColor method of Graphics

```
public  Color  getColor()
```

getContent method of URLConnection

```
public  Object  getContent()
```

getFile method of URL

```
public  String  getFile()
```

getFont method of Graphics

```
public  Font  getFont()
```

getFontMetrics   method of Graphics

```
public   FontMetrics   getFontMetrics()
```

getHost   method of URL

```
public   String   getHost()
```

getInputStream   method of Socket

```
public   InputStream getInputStream()
                              throws   IOException
```

getItemCount   method of List

```
public   int   getItemCount()
```

getOutputStream   method of Socket

```
public   OutputStream   getOutputStream()
                              throws   IOException
```

getSelectedCheckbox   method of CheckboxGroup

```
public   Checkbox   getSelectedCheckbox()
```

getText   method of Label

```
public   String   getText()
```

getText   method of TextField [defined in TextComponent]

```
public   String   getText()
```

getURL   method of URLConnection

```
public   URL   getURL()
```

getX   method of MouseEvent

```
public   int   getX()
```

getY   method of MouseEvent

```
public   int   getY()
```

green   variable of Color

```
final   static   Color   green
```

hasMoreElements   method of Enumeration

```
public   boolean   hasMoreElements()
```

in   variable of System

```
public   final   static   InputStream   in
```

indexOf   method of String

```
public  int  indexOf(String)
```

init   method of Applet

```
public  void  init()
```

InputStreamReader   constructor of InputStreamReader

```
InputStreamReader(InputStream  in)
```

insertElementAt   method of Vector

```
public  void  insertElementAt(Object  o,  int  i)
```

Integer   constructor of Integer

```
Integer(int)
```

intValue   method of Integer

```
public  int  intValue()
```

ITALIC   variable of Font

```
final  static  int  ITALIC
```

Label   constructor of Label

```
Label(String  s)
```

List   constructor of List

```
List()
```

max   method of Math

```
public  static  int  max(int  i1,  int  i2)
```

min   method of Math

```
public  static  int  min(int  i1,  int  i2)
```

mouseClicked   method of MouseListener

```
public  void  mouseClicked(MouseEvent  me)
```

mouseEntered   method of MouseListener

```
public  void  mouseEntered(MouseEvent  me)
```

mouseExited   method of MouseListener

```
public  void  mouseExited(MouseEvent  me)
```

mousePressed   method of MouseListener

```
public   void   mousePressed(MouseEvent   me)
```

mouseReleased   method of MouseListener

```
public   void   mouseReleased(MouseEvent   me)
```

nextElement   method of Enumeration

```
public   Object   nextElement()
```

openConnection   method of URL

```
public   URLConnection   openConnection()
```

orange   variable of Color

```
final   static   Color   orange
```

out   variable of System

```
public   final   static   PrintStream   out
```

paint   method of Applet [defined in *Container*]

```
public   void   paint(Graphics   g)
```

paint   method of Canvas

```
public   void   paint(Graphics   g)
```

Panel   constructor of Panel

```
Panel()
```

parseInt   method of Integer

```
public   static   int   parseInt(String   s)
                    throws NumberFormatException
```

PLAIN   variable of Font

```
final   static   int   PLAIN
```

pow   method of Math

```
public   static   double   pow(double   d1,   double   d2)
```

print   method of PrintStream

```
public   void   print(double   d)
```

print   method of PrintStream

```
public   void   print(int   i)
```

print   method of PrintStream

```
public   void   print(String   s)
```

println   method of PrintStream

```
public   void   println(double)
```

println   method of PrintStream

```
public   void   println(int   i)
```

println   method of PrintStream

```
public   void   println(String   s)
```

PrintStream   constructor of PrintStream

```
PrintStream(OutputStream)
```

random   method of Math

```
public   static   double   random()
```

readLine   method of BufferedReader

```
public   String   readLine()   throws   IOException
```

red   variable of Color

```
final   static   Color   red
```

removeAll   method of List

```
public   void   removeAll()   -   method   of   List
```

removeElementAt   method of Vector

```
public   void   removeElementAt(int   i)
```

renameTo   method of File

```
public   boolean   renameTo(File   f)
```

repaint   method of Applet [defined in Component]

```
public   void   repaint()
```

repaint   method of Canvas [defined in Component]

```
public   void   repaint()
```

resize   method of Applet

```
public   void   resize(int   width,   int   height)
```

run   method of Thread

```
public  void  run()
```

setBackground   method of Applet [defined in Component]

```
public  void  setBackground(Color  c)
```

setBackground   method of Button [defined in Component]

```
public  void  setBackground(Color  c)
```

setBackground   method of Panel [defined in Component]

```
public  void  setBackground(Color  c)
```

setCheckboxGroup   method of Checkbox

```
public  void  setCheckboxGroup(CheckboxGroup  cbg)
```

setColor   method of Graphics

```
public  void  setColor(Color  c)
```

setElementAt   method of Vector

```
public  void  setElementAt(Object  o,  int  i)
```

setEnabled   method of Button [defined in Component]

```
public  void  setEnabled(boolean  b)
```

setFont   method of Graphics

```
public  void  setFont(Font  f)
```

setLabel   method of Button

```
public  void  setLabel(String  s)
```

setLayout   method of Applet

```
public  void  setLayout(LayoutManager  lm)
```

setLayout   method of Panel

```
public  void  setLayout(LayoutManager  lm)
```

setSelectedCheckbox   method of CheckboxGroup

```
public  void  setSelectedCheckbox(Checkbox  cb)
```

setSize   method of Canvas [defined in Component]

```
public  void  setSize(int  width,  int  height)
```

setText   method of Label

```
public   void   setText(String   s)
```

setText   method of TextField [defined in TextComponent]

```
public   void   setText(String   s)
```

sleep   method of Thread

```
public   static   void   sleep(long   delay)
```

sqrt   method of Math

```
public   static   double   sqrt(double)
```

start   method of Thread

```
public   void   start()
```

String   constructor of String

```
String()
```

String   constructor of String

```
String(String   s)
```

stringWidth   method of FontMetrics

```
public   int   stringWidth(String   s)
```

style   method of Font

```
public   int   style()
```

substring   method of String

```
public   String   substring(int   start,   int   end)
```

textField   constructor of TextField

```
TextField(int   i)
```

toLowerCase   method of String

```
public   String   toLowerCase()
```

toString   method of Object

```
public   String   toString()
```

toUpperCase   method of String

```
public   String   toUpperCase()
```

trim   method of String

```
public  String  trim()
```

valueOf   method of Double

```
public  static  Double  valueOf(String)
                 throws  NumberFormatException
```

Vector   constructor of Vector

```
Vector()
```

white   variable of Color

```
final  static  Color  white
```

yellow   variable of Color

```
final  static  Color  yellow
```

Class and Interface Index

ActionEvent—A class containing information about an action event. A Button component generates an action event when it is clicked.

```
import  java.awt.event.*;
```

Methods

```
public  String  getActionCommand()
```
   Returns the text corresponding to the command name of the event source Component generating this ActionEvent. The default command name value for a Button is its label.

ActionListener—The interface for classes wishing to listen to action events, for example a button click.

```
import  java.awt.event.*;
```

Methods

```
public  void  actionPerformed(ActionEvent  ae)
```
   Invoked by the AWT environment when the event source generates an event. This method is not invoked directly by the programmer.

Applet—A class modeling a program executing within a browser. The class is responsible both for supporting a graphic interface as well as the execution of the program. This class is usually extended to provide application-specific init and paint methods.

```
import  java.applet.*;
```

Methods

```
public void add(Component c)
```
Adds the specified *Component* to this Applet. Used when the layout manager is FlowLayout.

```
public void init()
```
Invoked by the AWT environment when this Applet is initially loaded. This method is not invoked directly by the programmer.

```
public void paint(Graphics g)
```
Invoked by the AWT environment when this Applet must be painted, for example, when initially displayed, after being moved, resized, uncovered, or maximized from an icon. This method is usually not called by the programmer.

```
public void repaint()
```
Notify the AWT environment that this Applet is to be repainted. This eventually results in the Canvas's paint method being invoked.

```
public void resize(int width, int height)
```
Requests that the Applet be resized. In the context of a browser, this request will usually be ignored; however, it may be fulfilled by the applet viewer.

```
public void setBackground(Color c)
```
Sets this Applet's background color to the specified color.

```
public void setLayout(LayoutManager lm)
```
Sets the layout manager responsible for the component layout of this Applet to the specified *LayoutManager*.

BorderLayout—A *LayoutManager* class; after it is constructed its only use for us is to specify it as the layout manager of a *Container* using the setLayout method. BorderLayout partitions the container surface into five areas: north, east, south, west, and center. When adding a component to the container (using the add method) one of "North", "East", "West", "South", and "Center" is passed to specify where to place the component.

```
    import java.awt.*;
```

Constructors

```
BorderLayout()
```

BufferedInputStream—An I/O class that models a stream of input that buffers characters, not releasing them to the program until a new line has been entered.

```
    import java.io.*;
```

Constructors

```
BufferedInputStream(InputStream is)
```

BufferedReader—An I/O class that models a stream of characters from a buffered, line-oriented input source.

```
import java.io.*;
```

Constructors

```
BufferedReader(Reader)
```

Methods

```
public String readLine() throws IOException
```
Returns a String containing the text of the next line read from this BufferedReader.

Button—A graphic component class that models the behavior of a clickable button.

```
import java.awt.*;
```

Constructors

```
public Button(String label)
```
Creates a Button object with the passed String as the label.

Methods

```
public void addActionListener(ActionListener al)
```
Registers the specified ActionListener to be notified of action events generated by this Button.

```
public void setEnabled(boolean b)
```
Enables this Button component if the specified boolean is true; otherwise the Button is disabled (cannot be clicked).

```
public void setBackground(Color c)
```
Sets this Button's background color to the specified color.

```
public void setLabel(String s)
```
Sets the label of the Button to the specified String.

Canvas—A graphic component class that models a drawing canvas. It serves to isolate graphic drawing from the graphic components of the interface. This class is usually extended to provide an application-specific paint method.

```
import java.awt.*;
```

Methods

```
public void addMouseListener(MouseListener ml)
```
Registers the specified MouseListener to be notified of mouse events generated by this Canvas.

```
public void paint(Graphics g)
```
Invoked by the AWT environment when this Canvas must be painted, for example, when initially displayed, after being moved, resized,

uncovered, or maximized from an icon. This method is usually not called by the programmer.

```
public void repaint()
```
Notify the AWT environment that this Canvas is to be repainted. This eventually results in the Canvas's paint method being invoked.

```
public void setSize(int width, int height)
```
Sets the size of this Canvas to the specified width and height.

Checkbox—A graphic component class that models the behavior of a check box that may be selected. Check boxes may be grouped using the CheckboxGroup class, providing mutually exclusive selection.

```
import java.awt.*;
```

Constructors

```
Checkbox(String)
```
Creates a Checkbox with the specified String as a label.

Methods

```
public void setCheckboxGroup(CheckboxGroup cbg)
```
Makes this Checkbox a member of the specified CheckboxGroup.

CheckboxGroup—A class providing mutually exclusive selection among a set of Checkboxes. Only one of the Checkboxes belonging to a CheckboxGroup may be selected at any one time.

```
import java.awt.*;
```

Constructors

```
CheckboxGroup()
```

Methods

```
public Checkbox getSelectedCheckbox()
```
Returns the currently selected Checkbox of this CheckboxGroup.

```
public void setSelectedCheckbox(Checkbox cb)
```
Sets the specified Checkbox as the currently selected check box of this CheckboxGroup.

Color—A class modeling colors used for graphical display. In addition to working with programmer-defined colors specified using an RGB (red/green/blue) value, color constants for a number of standard colors are provided by the class.

```
import java.awt.*;
```

Constructor

```
Color(int red, int green, int blue)
```
Creates a color based upon the specified red, green, and blue components. Each integer must be in the range 0...255—the lower the value, the less of the component is present in the resulting color.

Variables

```
final  static  Color  black
final  static  Color  cyan
final  static  Color  green
final  static  Color  orange
final  static  Color  red
final  static  Color  white
final  static  Color  yellow
```

Double—A wrapper class for the double primitive data type. This class allows double values to be inserted into collection objects such as Vectors, in addition to being a repository of double-related methods.

```
import  java.lang.*;//  Unnecessary
```

Methods

```
public  double  doubleValue()
```
Returns the double value contained in this Double object.

```
public  static  Double  valueOf(String)
   throws NumberFormatException
```
Returns a newly created Double initialized with the value obtained by the specified String to a double. If the String cannot be converted, for example, if it contains alphabetic characters, a run-time exception is generated.

Enumeration—An interface specifying the methods required to perform enumeration or traversal of a collection. The Enumeration object is usually created by invoking a method on the object to be traversed.

```
import  java.util.*;
```

Methods

```
public  boolean  hasMoreElements()
```
Returns true if this Enumeration contains more elements to be processed.

```
public  Object  nextElement()
```
Returns the next Object of this Enumeration.

Exception—Models an unexpected situation during execution of the program.

```
import  java.lang.*;//  Unnecessary
```

Constructor

```
Exception(String  label)
```
Creates an Exception object carrying the label as additional information.

File—An I/O class modeling a file on disk.

```
import  java.io.*;
```

Constructors

`File(String name)`
Creates a File object corresponding to the specified file name.

Methods

`public void delete()`
Deletes the disk file specified by this File.

`public boolean renameTo(File f)`
Renames the file associated with this File to the name associated with the specified File. Returns true if successful.

FileInputStream—An I/O class modeling a stream of data read from a disk file.

`import java.io.*;`

Constructors

`FileInputStream(File f)`

FileOutputStream—An I/O class modeling a stream of data written to a disk file.

`import java.io.*;`

Constructors

`FileOutputStream(File f)`

FlowLayout—A layout manager class; once constructed, its only use for us is to specify it as the layout manager of a *Container* using the setLayout method. FlowLayout is most commonly used to place Buttons on a Panel. The Buttons are added left-to-right, until the line is filled, at which point a second line of Buttons is begun. Each line is centered within the panel.

`import java.awt.*;`

Constructors

`FlowLayout()`

Font—A class modeling a typeface. A typeface is specified by a font, a style, and a size specified in points, or 1/72 of an inch.

`import java.io.*;`

Constructors

`Font(String font, int style, int size)`
Creates a Font with the specified font name, style, and size.

Methods

`public int style()`
Returns this Font's style (BOLD, PLAIN, ITALIC).

Variables

```
final   static   int   BOLD
final   static   int   ITALIC
final   static   int   PLAIN
```

FontMetrics—A class containing information concerning the dimensions of a Font within a Graphics context.

```
import   java.io.*;
```

Constructors

```
FontMetrics(Font   f)
```
   Creates a FontMetrics corresponding to the specified Font.

Methods

```
public   int   stringWidth(String   s)
```
   Returns the width of the specified String using the Font associated with this FontMetrics.

Graphics—A class modeling a graphic surface (context) such as a printer or screen window. This class maintains information required for graphical drawing, including color, font, and coordinates.

```
import   java.awt.*;
```

Methods

```
public   void   drawLine(int   x1,   int   y1,   int   x2,
                        int   y2)
```
   Draws a line, using this Graphics context, from the point specified by the first pair of parameters to the point specified by the second pair.

```
public   void   drawOval(int   x,   int   y,   int   width,
                        int   height)
```
   Draws an oval, using this Graphics context, with the specified width and height. The position of the oval is determined by its defining (enclosing) rectangle whose upper-left corner is specified by the first pair of coordinates.

```
public   void   drawRect(int   x,   int   y,   int   width,
                        int   height)
```
   Draws a rectangle, using this current Graphics context, with the specified width and height, and whose upper-left corner is specified by the first pair of coordinates.

```
public   void   drawString(String   text.   int   x,
                          int   y)
```
   Draws the specified String, using this Graphics context, at the position specified by the second and third parameters.

```
public void fillOval(int x, int y, int width,
                int height)
```
Fills an oval, using this current Graphics context, with the specified width and height. The position of the oval is determined by its defining (enclosing) rectangle whose upper-left corner is specified by the first pair of coordinates.

```
public void fillRect(int x, int y, int width,
                int height)
```
Fills a rectangle, using this current Graphics context, with the specified width and height, and whose upper-left corner is specified by the first pair of coordinates.

```
public void fill3DRect(int x, int y,
        int width,int height, boolean isRaised)
```
Fills a rectangle with 3D shading, using this current Graphics context, with the specified width and height, and whose upper-left corner is specified by the first pair of coordinates. The last parameter specifies whether the rectangle should appear raised or sunken.

```
public Color getColor()
```
Returns the current drawing Color of this Graphics context.

```
public Font getFont()
```
Returns the current Font of this Graphics context.

```
public FontMetrics getFontMetrics()
```
Returns the current FontMetrics of this Graphics context.

```
public void setColor(Color c)
```
Sets the current drawing Color of this Graphics context.

```
public void setFont(Font f)
```
Sets the current Font of this Graphics context.

Integer—A wrapper class for the int primitive data type. This class allows int values to be inserted into collection objects such as Vectors, in addition to being a repository of int-related methods.

```
import java.lang.*;// Unnecessary
```

Constructors

```
Integer(int)
```
Creates an Integer initialized with the specified int value.

Methods

```
public int intValue()
```
Returns the int value contained within this Integer.

```
public static int parseInt(String s)
    throws NumberFormatException
```
Returns the int value resulting from converting the specified String to an integer. If the String cannot be converted, for example, if it contains alphabetic characters, a run-time exception is generated.

Label—A graphic component class modeling a display-only string of text.

```
import java.awt.*;
```

Constructors

```
Label(String s)
```
Creates a Label initialized with the specified text.

Methods

```
public String getText()
```
Returns this Label's text.

```
public void setText(String s)
```
Set this Label's text to the specified String.

List—A graphic component class that models a list of scrollable values.
import java.awt.*;

Constructors

```
List()
```

Methods

```
public void addItem(String s)
```
Adds the specified String to the end of this List.

```
public void addItemListener(ItemListener il)
```
Registers the specified ItemListener to be notified of item events generated by this List.

```
public int getItemCount()
```
Returns the number of items contained in this List.

```
public void removeAll() - method of List
```
Removes all the items from this List component.

Math—A class containing various mathematical constants and static methods.

```
import java.lang.*;// Unnecessary
```

Methods

```
public static int abs(int i)
```
Returns the absolute value of the specified integer.

```
public static int max(int i1, int i2)
```
Returns the maximum of the two specified integer.

```
public static int min(int i1, int i2)
```
Returns the minimum of the two specified integers.

```
public static double pow(double d1, double d2)
```
Returns the first parameter raised to the power specified by the second parameter.

```
public static double random()
```
Returns a random number in the range 0.0...1.0.

```
public static double sqrt(double)
```
Returns the square root of the specified double.

MouseEvent—A class containing information about a mouse event.

```
import java.awt.event.*;
```

Methods

```
public int getX()
```
Returns the *x* (horizontal) coordinate of the position the mouse was at when this MouseEvent was generated.

```
public int getY()
```
Returns the *y* (vertical) coordinate of the position the mouse was at when this MouseEvent was generated.

MouseListener—The interface for classes wishing to listen to mouse events. A MouseListener registers itself with a *Component* through the addMouseListener method.

```
import java.awt.event.*;
```

Methods

```
public void mouseClicked(MouseEvent me)
```
Invoked by the AWT environment when the mouse is clicked (pressed and released) while within the boundaries of the event source *Component*. This method is not invoked directly by the programmer.

```
public void mouseEntered(MouseEvent me)
```
Invoked by the AWT environment when the mouse enters the boundaries of the event source *Component*. This method is not invoked directly by the programmer.

```
public void mouseExited(MouseEvent me)
```
Invoked by the AWT environment when the mouse exits the boundaries of the event source Component. This method is not invoked directly by the programmer.

```
public void mousePressed(MouseEvent me)
```
Invoked by the AWT environment when the mouse is pressed while within the boundaries of the event source *Component*. This method is not invoked directly by the programmer.

```
public void mouseReleased(MouseEvent me)
```
Invoked by the AWT environment when the mouse is released while within the boundaries of the event source *Component*. This method is not invoked directly by the programmer.

Object—A class modeling the common behavior of all objects. The root of the class hierarchy. Methods and variables in this class are common to all objects.

```
import java.lang.*;// Unnecessary
```

Methods

```
public boolean equals(Object o)
```
Returns true if the specified Object and this Object are the same object. This method is typically overridden by a subclass.

```
public String toString()
```
Produces a String representation of this Object consisting of the class name and a sequence number. This method is usually overridden by a subclass.

Panel—A container class, that is, a class that can have components added to it; Panels can be used together with FlowLayout to quickly create a collection of Buttons or other graphic components.

```
import java.awt.*;
```

Constructors

```
Panel()
```
Creates the Panel.

Methods

```
public void add(Component c)
```
Adds the specified *Component* to this Applet. Used when the layout manager is FlowLayout.

```
public void add(String s, Component c)
```
Adds the specified *Component* to this Container in the positionString: "North", "South", "East", "West", and "Center". Used when the layout manager is BorderLayout.

```
public void setBackground(Color c)
```
Sets this Panel's background color to the specified color.

```
public void setLayout(LayoutManager lm)
```
Sets the layout manager responsible for the component layout of this Panel to the specified *LayoutManager*.

PrintStream—A class that models an output target.

Constructor

```
PrintStream(OutputStream)
```

Methods

```
public void flush()
```
Forces any text remaining in this PrintStream's buffer to be written to the associated device or file.

```
public void print(double d)
public void print(int i)
public void print(String s)
```
Prints the parameter on this PrintStream.

```
public  void  println(double)
public  void  println(int  i)
public  void  print(String  s)
```
Prints the parameter on this PrintStream. Subsequent output will be printed on the next line.

Socket—A class that models a communication endpoint; think of it as a disposable telephone that is used for just one call and that helps to communicate with another program on another machine that is also using a socket.

Constructors
```
public  Socket(String  host,  int  port)
```
Creates a socket connected to the specified port on the specified host.

Methods
```
public  InputStream  getInputStream()
    throws  IOException
public  OutputStream  getOutputStream()
    throws  IOException
```

String—A class that models a sequence of characters. The first character is located at position 0 of the String. Strings are immutable, that is, they cannot be modified. Any transformations on the String such as taking the substring or converting lowercase to uppercase result in the creation of a new String object.

```
import  java.lang.*;//  Unnecessary
```

Constructors
```
String()
```
Creates a String initialized to the empty string.

```
String(String  s)
```
Creates a String initialized to the same sequence of characters as the specified String.

Methods
```
public  char  charAt(int  i)
```
Returns the character at the specified position of the String. Specifying a position out of range (less than 0 or greater than length( )−1) generates a run-time exception.

```
public  int  compareTo(String)
```
Performs a lexical (character-by-character) comparison of this String with the specified String. Returns a value less than 0 if this String is less than the passed String, returns 0 if they are equal, and returns a value greater than 0 if this String is greater than the passed String.

```
public  String  concat(String  s)
```
Returns a new String consisting of the specified String appended to the end of this String.

```
public  boolean  equals(Object  o)
```
Returns true if the specified Object is a String that lexically compares as equal to this String.

```
public  int  indexOf(String)
```
Returns the (first) position in this String at which the specified String occurs. If the specified String does not appear in this String, −1 is returned.

```
public  String  substring(int  start,  int  end)
```
Returns the substring of this String formed by taking the characters beginning at the specified start position and end at the character before the specified end position. If either position is out of range, a run-time exception is generated.

```
public  String  toLowerCase()
```
Returns a String corresponding to this String with all uppercase characters converted to lowercase.

```
public  String  toUpperCase()
```
Returns a String corresponding to this String with all lowercase characters converted to uppercase.

```
public  String  trim()
```
Returns a String consisting of this String with all leading and trailing spaces removed.

System—A class containing objects that are used systemwide.

```
import  java.lang.*;//  Unnecessary
```

Variables

```
public  final  static  InputStream  in
```
The standard input source corresponding to the keyboard by default.

```
public  final  static  PrintStream  out
```
The standard output target corresponding to the screen by default.

```
public  final  static  PrintStream  err
```
The standard error target corresponding to the screen by default.

TextField—A graphic component class modeling a string of text that may be edited by the user. It is used to allow textual data to be entered in a graphical interface.

```
import  java.awt.*;
```

Constructors

```
TextField(int  i)
```
Creates a TextField with the specified number of columns.

Methods

```
public  String  getText()
```
Returns this TextField's text.

```
public  void  setText(String  s)
```
Set this TextField's text to the specified String.

Thread—A class modeling the execution of a single instruction at a time. An executing Java program consists of at least one Thread. Creating one or more threads within a program results in several executions proceeding concurrently, a situation known as multithreaded programming. This class is usually extended to include an application-specific run method.

```
    import  java.lang.*;//  Unnecessary
```

Methods

```
public  static  void  dumpStack()
```
Prints the call chain of the current thread.

```
public  void  run()
```
Invoked by the Java interpreter after the operating system thread has been created as a result of the programmer invoking the start method. This method is not invoked directly by the programmer.

```
public  static  void  sleep(long  delay)
```
Causes the current thread to stop executing for the specified number of milliseconds

```
public  void  start()
```
Performs any necessary actions necessary for the start of execution of this Thread, then invokes this Thread's run method.

URL—A class that models an URL.

```
    import  java.next.*;
```

Constructors

```
public  URL(String  s)
```
Creates an URL from the specified String.

Methods

```
public  String  getFile()
```
Returns the "file" or resource part of the URL.

```
public  String  getHost()
```
Returns the machine or host name part of the URL.

```
public  String  getProtocol()
```
Returns the protocol name part of the URL.

```
public  URLConnection  openConnection()
```
Creates a TCP connection to the server for the URL, and returns an URLConnection object that models this connection.

URLConnection—A class that models a TCP connection to the server for an URL.

```
import  java.next.*;
```

Constructors

```
public  URLConnection(URL  u)
```
Creates a connection to the specified URL.

Methods

```
public  Object  getInputStream()
```
Returns an InputStream that models the input half of the TCP connection. This allows the program to read the input coming from the server at the other end of the connection.

Vector—A collection class that allows the insertion and removal of objects as well as general indexing. The first element of the Vector is at location 0, the last at size()−1.

```
import  java.util.*;
```

Constructors

```
Vector()
```

Methods

```
public  void  addElement(Object  o)
```
Adds the specified object to end of this Vector.

```
public  Object  elementAt(int  i)
```
Returns the Object contained in the specified position of this Vector. If the index is out of range, a run-time exception is generated.

```
public  Enumeration  elements()
```
Returns an Enumeration object corresponding to this Vector, allowing traversal.

```
public  void  insertElementAt(Object  o,  int  i)
```
Inserts the specified Object into this Vector at the position specified by the second parameter. The elements from that specified position to the end of this Vector are moved upward to the next position. If the specified position is out of range, a run-time exception is generated.

```
public  void  removeElementAt(int  i)
```
Removes the element at the specified position of this Vector. All elements from the next position until the end of this Vector are moved down one position. If the specified index is out of range, a run-time exception is generated.

```
public  void  setElementAt(Object  o,  int  i)
```
Replaces the element at the specified index with the specified Object. If the index is out of range a run-time exception is generated.

```
public  int  size()
```
Returns the number of elements in this Vector.

Exercises for Selected GUI Supplements

1. Write a small HTML file that sets up a web page that contains your name, centered and in boldface. The title of the page should be also be your name.

   CHAPTER 2

2. Write a Java program whose output is the complete HTML code that you created in the previous exercise.

3. Take all three versions of this chapter's applet and experiment with the arguments to all the methods. Try making beautiful and hideous colors, big bold print, and fine print suitable for disclaimers. Replace fillOval with the other geometric object drawing methods.

   CHAPTER 3

4. Write an applet that displays your first name in red 10-point Times Roman font and below displays your last name in orange 14-point Helvetica. (Hint: You will have to use drawString twice with different coordinates.)

CHAPTER 4

5. For each of the designs in the figure below, try to construct an applet that provides the indicated controls in the given layout:

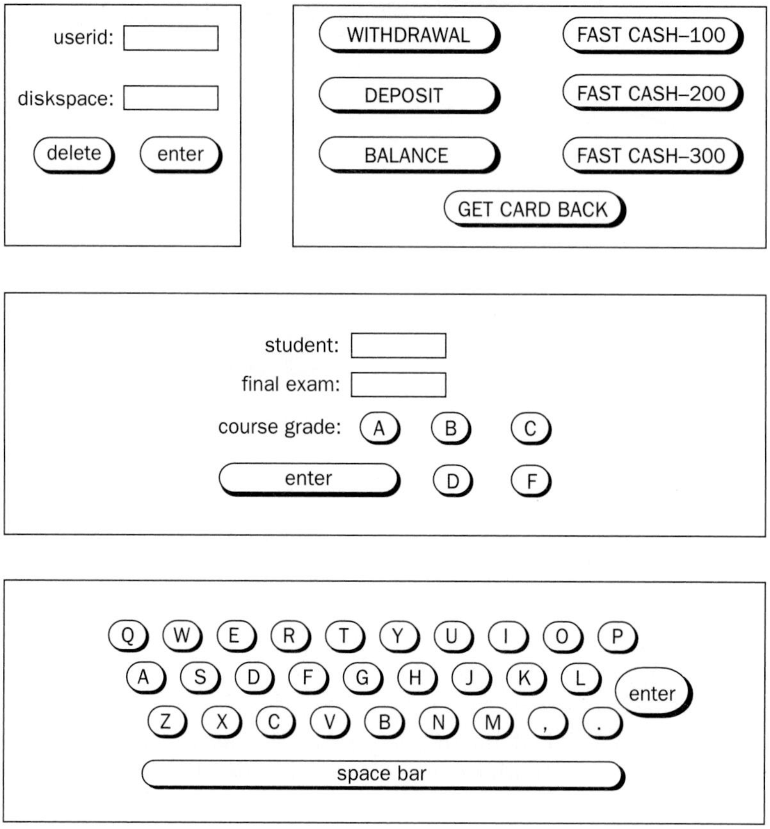

CHAPTER 5

6. Code the two versions (correct and incorrect) of the applet that combined text and buttons.

7. Write an applet that *right justifies* a line of text read in from a file. Right-justifying a string of text entails having the last character of the string flush against the right edge of the applet (or canvas). Start by using a constant value for the width of the applet and progress to obtaining the width of the applet from a method invocation. (Hint: For this last part, you will need to invoke the getSize method of class Applet (or Canvas) to determine the width of the applet. You will also have to investigate the fairly simple Dimension class.)

8. Repeat Exercise 7, but this time center the line of text between the left and right edges of the applet (or canvas).

9. Repeat Exercise 7, but this time center the line of text vertically as well as horizontally.

10. Implement an applet that performs the student average calculation of Exercise 2 of the Java Interlude on if statements in this chapter.

CHAPTER 6

11. Modify Exercise 10 so that the user can enter the cutoff points for the various marks.

12. Add a remainder function to the calculator applet.

13. Modify the calculator applet to allow a unary minus to be entered.

14. Modify the Set applet to include the complement and symmetric complement operations.

CHAPTER 8

15. Create an applet that displays a list of names in a list box.

16. Investigate selection from a list box. Selecting (double-clicking) an item from a list box generates an ActionEvent. Modify the applet of Exercise 15 to display the name selected by the user.

17. Modify the ClockApplet so that it displays the all the time zones of your country, as well as GMT.

CHAPTER 9

18. Modify the ClockApplet so that instead of using a Label for display it uses a Canvas and draws an analog clock (with hands). (In this case, don't bother displaying hundredths of a second!)

19. Modify the Game of Life applet so that cells change color the older they get. For example, newborns are blue; then after 10 generations, they turn green, then red, then yellow, and finally white.

CHAPTER 10

20. Write an applet that challenges the users' reflexes. Display a circle that is constantly changing color. When the circle is red, the users are supposed to click a button. If they succeed, they get a point. Display the score in a text field. To do this nicely, you may wish to investigate the Random class in java.util, which allows you to generate random integer values.

21. Based on your knowledge of how multiple threads execute, why might Exercise 20 not work quite as well as you might want?

CHAPTER 12

22. Implement tic-tac-toe as an applet using Mancala as a guide.

23. Implement the Logo turtle as an applet. Have a Canvas upon which the turtle moves, and buttons for the various commands. You will also need a Vector to remember all the moves the turtle has made. When the Canvas's paint function is called, you must redo all those moves.

CHAPTER 14

24. Revise the WebClient and MailClient classes so that they catch all exceptions and write appropriate diagnostics.

AWIO

Introduction

This appendix provides an alternative approach to that taken in Sections 3.4 through 3.9. In this appendix we introduce the AWIO package, a package of predefined Java classes written specially for this book. These classes allow the student to write programs that perform the same input and output that is discussed in Chapter 3 without having to learn the important lessons in object-oriented programming concepts and techniques developed in that chapter.

Using AWIO for Output

We create a new file, or overwrite an existing one in the same way in Java. Both require a pathway (or *stream*) for output from the program to provide the newly created or existing file with content.

The `AWPrinter` Class

The AWIO package provides a predefined class, similar to `PrintStream` for modeling a stream of output. This class is called **AWPrinter**. There are two constructors for `AWPrinter`— another example of overloading. One constructor has no arguments:

```
new AWPrinter()
```

This creates an `AWPrinter` object that has the same behavior as `System.out`: You can send it `println` and `print` messages and they will cause output to display on standard output (usually the monitor). For example

```
AWPrinter awout = new AWPrinter();
awout.println("Just like PrintStream!");
```

creates an `AWPrinter` object associated with standard output and displays the string "Just like PrintStream!".

The other constructor accepts a reference to a `String` object as its argument, as follows:

```
new AWPrinter(String)
```

This creates an `AWPrinter` object that also has the same `PrintStream`-like behavior as `System.out` except that the object is associated with a file on disk. You can still send it `println` and `print` messages but now these will cause output to be stored in the file named by the `String`. An example of this follows:

```
AWPrinter    awout = new AWPrinter("Simplicity");
```

This code opens the disk file `Simplicity` so that it can receive output; it creates the file if it doesn't already exist. The reference to the new `AWPrinter` object is returned and stored in `f`. As soon as the `AWPrinter` is constructed, the file is created if it did not exist before or its contents are removed if the file already exists. Now a statement such as

```
awout.println("You should still read Chapter 3 sometime!");
```

will store the string "`You  should  still  read  Chapter  3  some-time!`" in the disk file `Simplicity`.

EXAMPLE   **Maintaining a Backup of Screen Output.** Suppose we want our program to maintain a disk file copy (named "`backup`", say) of the screen output that it generates. Let's assume this is an improvement of `Program1`. We write the program as before but add the code needed to create a new file "`backup`" with an associated `AWPrinter`. Then, whatever we write to `System.out`, we also write to this `AWPrinter` object, as follows:

```
import java.io.*;
import AWIO.*;
```

```
class Program1Backup {
    public static void main(String arg[]) throws Exception {
        AWPrinter     backup;
        backup = new AWPrinter("backup");
        System.out.println("This is my first Java program");
        backup.println("This is my first Java program");
        System.out.println("... but it won't be my last.");
        backup.println("... but it won't be my last.");
    }
}
```

What can go wrong?

As our programs interact further with their computing environment—creating new files, for example—there are more opportunities for them to fail through no fault of their own. For example, the program above is perfectly correct, but if someone runs it in a directory where he or she doesn't have permission to create files, the program will fail. Java requires that the programmer acknowledge potential failures of this kind by adding the phrase `throws Exception` to the boilerplate, as we have done above. If the phrase is omitted, the compiler will issue an error. The phrase means that it is conceivable that an unrecoverable error might occur because of a problem in the computing environment and, as a result, the program might terminate abruptly. We learned more about this issue and Exceptions in general in Chapter 14.

See the exercises at the end of Section 3.4.

EXERCISES

Using AWIO for Keyboard Input

We have not yet considered how to use *input*—information coming from a keyboard or stored in a file—to create objects. We have been forced to place all information into the programs themselves. If we could get information, such as `String`s, from input, our programs could be more general. For example, instead of writing a program that changes a file's name from "`ford`" to "`lincoln`" by specifying the names, we could write a program that reads in two `String`s from the keyboard (what the user types) and treats them as the old and new names of a file that is renamed. We'll learn how to read input in this and the next two sections.

In the preceding section, we introduced a class, `AWPrinter`, that we used to write `String`s either to standard output or to a file. Here we introduce a class, **AWReader**, that we can use to read Strings either from the keyboard (standard input) or a file.

An AWReader object models a stream of input coming from a file or the keyboard. As is the case for AWPrinter, AWReader has two constructors—yet another example of overloading.

One constructor has no arguments:

```
new AWReader()
```

This creates an AWReader object that is associated with the keyboard, or, more generally, standard input. Let's store the resulting reference in a variable as follows:

```
AWReader keyb = new AWReader();
```

Once we have an AWReader object, we can use its ability to read in a line from some source of input and create a String object, whose characters are those that appeared in the input line. The method that models this behavior is called readLine. Because it creates an object, it returns a reference to that object, just as the String methods toUpperCase and substring return references to the new String objects that they create. Therefore, the following is a reference to the String:

```
keyb.readLine()
```

The String is returned by AWReader when it reads in the next line of input from the keyboard in response to the readLine message.

To use the String object that keyboard creates, we declare a String reference variable, as follows:

```
String       inputLine;      // Models a line of input
```

We use it to save the String reference that the AWReader returns, as follows:

```
inputLine = keyb.readLine();
```

Let's use these new tools to write a program that reads in a singular noun from the keyboard and displays its plural on the screen. We don't yet have the tools to come close to doing this correctly, so we will assume that merely adding the letter s to a word correctly results in the plural form (thereby ignoring words like fox and baby).

We write a comment defining the meaning of the program followed by the usual first two lines of boilerplate notation and then the above four pieces of code, as follows:

```
import java.io.*;
import AWIO.*;
/*
 * Program4: Displays the plural form of the word typed on
 *           the keyboard. Uses the naive and wrong(!)
```

```
 *           approach of just adding s.
 */
class Program4 {
   public static void main(String arg[]) throws Exception {
      AWReader       keyboard;   // Models a keyboard that
                                 // reads in lines as Strings
      String         inputLine; // Models a line of input.
      keyboard = new AWReader();
      inputLine = keyboard.readLine();
      //
      // Rest of the program goes here ...
      //
   }
}
```

All that remains is to arrange to display the String as intended. We will send a print (not a println) message to System.out with the word read from input as an argument. We send print instead of println because we want the s to appear on the same line as the word, not on the succeeding line. Then we will send a println message with s as an argument in order to display the s and complete the line, as follows:

```
System.out.print(inputLine);
System.out.println("s");
Here is the complete program:
import java.io.*;
/*
 * Program4: Displays the plural form of the word typed on
 *           the keyboard. Uses the naive and wrong(!)
 *           approach of just adding s.
 */
class Program4 {
   public static void main(String arg[]) throws Exception {
      AWReader       keyboard;   // Models a keyboard that
                                 // reads in lines as Strings.
      String         inputLine; // Models a line of
                                 // input.
      keyboard = new AWReader(isr);
      inputLine = keyboard.readLine();
      System.out.print(inputLine);
      System.out.println("s");
   }
}
```

See the exercises at the end of Section 3.6.

EXERCISES

Interactive Input/Output

Keyboards are only one source of input for programs. Other sources include data files on disk and even other programs that are running on the computer. We will explore all of these other sources as we proceed in this book.

One characteristic distinguishing keyboard input is that it directly involves a human being, often termed an **end-user** (of the program). In practice, end-users are almost never the authors of the programs that they use. Millions of people use WordPerfect; only a handful of them had a role in writing that program.

Because end-users (or users for short) are not the authors of the programs they use, they cannot be expected to automatically know what to type on the keyboard and when to type it. A program that expects input from a keyboard must, in order to be useful, provide that information to the users as it runs. It must display messages such as "`Please enter your PIN # now`" and "`Sorry, that choice is not correct — please make your selection again.`" These **prompts** tell the user what to type on the keyboard. The flow of data between users and programs is referred to as **interactive** input and output.

Consider `Program4` from the previous section. The program includes the following line:

```
inputLine = keyboard.readLine();
```

It expects the user to type in a word that is to be made plural. But how will the user know that this is expected of him or her? The `readLine` method waits silently for the user to type in a line—it cannot offer any guidance. The solution is to display a prompt, such as, "`Type in a word to be made plural, please`" just before the `readLine` message is sent to `keyboard`. We know how to display such a string to the user: We must send a `print` message to `System.out` prior to reading in the line, as follows:

```
System.out.println("Type in a word to be made plural, "
                   "please ");
inputLine = keyboard.readLine();
```

Unfortunately, the prompt might not be displayed until after the line is read in—defeating the whole purpose of having a prompt in the first place. The reason for this delay lies in the details of the behavior of `PrintStream`, the class that `System.out` is an instance of. (Using `AWPrinter` will not help because it is based on `PrintStream`.)

A `PrintStream` object receives `print` and `println` messages and will eventually display the `String`s requested. However, the key word here is *eventually*. `PrintStream` behaves much as you do when you write several letters for mailing. You do not write a letter, go off to the mailbox and mail it, and come home to write another. You write a batch (all you had planned to) and then mail them together, saving multiple trips to the mailbox.

PrintStream and AWPrinter take the same approach, and for similar reasons. It is costly (relatively speaking) in computer time to transfer a String from a program to an output device such as a screen. It is more efficient to do the transfer all at once or at least in large batches. So, Print-Stream collects the Strings it is to display in a holding area in memory. Such a holding area is called a **buffer.** PrintStream does not display the Strings in its buffer until the program completes or the buffer gets full. If the output is going to a file, this is fine—the file definitely does not mind waiting for its output from AWPrinter.

On the other hand, for issuing prompts, this approach is a disaster. It means that we could write a line of code that asks System.out (an instance of PrintStream) to display a String, but the String wouldn't be displayed until the program completes—after the user has typed in his or her input.

It turns out that most implementations of Java recognize this problem and arrange for output held in a System.out buffer to be displayed when keyboard input is requested. That's good, but not good enough. At the time of this writing, this approach is optional for implementations of Java and one might still encounter implementations in which System.out's buffer is not displayed.

There is a fix. AWPrinter and PrintStream provide another method, flush, which forces it to write out all the Strings in the buffer. The flush method requires no arguments. An example of its use is as follows:

```
System.out.flush();
```

This forces the PrintStream System.out to display all the messages it had been keeping in its buffer. To guarantee that the prompt appears right away, we must write the following:

```
System.out.println("Type in a word to be made plural, "
                    "please ");
System.out.flush();
inputLine = keyboard.readLine();
```

A general form for interactive input and output is as follows:

```
System.out.println(prompt goes here);
System.out.flush();
string reference variable = keyboard.readLine();
```

possibly compute something (using, for example, concatenation)

```
System.out.println(output string goes here);
```

There can be variations on this prompt-flush-compute-output paradigm. For example, the prompt may be generated by several println messages. The flush method only has to be invoked after the last of these and before the readLine method.

EXERCISES   See the exercises at the end of Section 3.7.

Using AWIO for Disk File Input

Obtaining input from a disk file is as easy as writing output to one. All you need to do is create an `AWReader` object with the name of the file as an argument to the constructor, as follows:

```
AWReader awin = new File("Americas.Most.Wanted");
```

The object that `awin` references is an `AWReader`, just like the one keyboard referenced earlier. We can send `readLine` messages to this object to read successive lines from the file, which we will print out, as follows:

```
String      line;
line = fileInput.readLine();
System.out.println(line);
line = fileInput.readLine();
System.out.println(line);
```

EXAMPLE   Making a copy of a file. Let's write a program that reads, interactively from the keyboard, the name of a file that contains two lines. The program creates a copy of the file whose name is the original name with `.copy` added to it. We write it using sections of code based on the various examples we have seen so far in this chapter. Here is the program:

```
import java.io.*;
class CopyFile {
    public static void main(String arg[]) throws Exception {
    AWReaderkeyboard;
    StringfileNameOrig;
    AWReaderrdrOrig;
    StringfileNameCopy;
    Strings;
    AWPrinter        awout;
    AWReader = new AWReader();
    System.out.print("name of file to copy: ");
    System.out.flush();
    fileNameOrig = keyboard.readLine();
    fileNameCopy = fileNameOrig.concat(".copy");
    rdrOrig = new AWReader();
    awout = new AWPrinter(fileNameCopy);
    s = rdrOrig.readLine();
    awout.println(s);
```

```
     s = rdrOrig.readLine();
     awout.println(s);
     }
 }
```

See the exercises at the end of Section 3.8.

Using AWIO in the Rest of the Book

This appendix has described the use of the AWIO package, a collection of classes that reduce the amount of code that must be typed for a program to do file output, keyboard input, and file input. This appendix serves, therefore, as a limited alternative to Sections 3.4 through 3.7.

In those places where input/output appears in examples in Chapters 4 through 14, the techniques of Chapter 3 are used, not the AWIO package. However, it is fairly straightforward to use the AWPrinter and AWReader classes as alternatives in those situations.

For example, throughout the text, BufferedReader objects are used to perform input. Wherever you see BufferedReader in the text, replace it with AWReader (both provide the same readln method). Similarly, wherever you see PrintStream, replace it with AWPrinter.

Furthermore, replace the creations of BufferedReader objects such as

```
     BufferedReader br = new BufferedReader(
                         new InputStreamReader(
                           new FileInputStream(
                             new File("SomeFileName"))));
```

with

```
     AWReader br = new AWReader("SomeFileName");
```

By not changing the name of the instance variable, br, you can use code such as

```
     br.readLine()
```

without modification.

Similarly, replace the creations of BufferedReader objects such as

```
     BufferedReader br = new BufferedReader(
                         new InputStreamReader(System.in));
```

with

```
AWReader br = new AWReader();
```

and creations of `PrintStream` objects such as

```
PrintStream ps = new PrintStream(
                     new FileOutputStream(
                       new File("SomeFileName")));
```

with

```
AWPrinter ps = new AWPrinter("SomeFileName");
```

Again, by not changing the names of the instance variables, you minimize the need for other changes.

Index

-- (decrement), 160
- (subtraction), 154

Symbols

!, 221
!=, 201
% (remainder operator), 154
&&, 220
* (multiplication), 154
*=, 158
+ (addition), 154
+ (String concatenation), 160
++ (increment), 160
+=, 158
.class file, 17
    for applets, 86
    from a class definition, 95
.java file, 17
    containing a class definition, 95
/ (division), 154
<, 201
<=, 201
==, 201
>, 201
>=, 201
{...}
    compound statement, 200
||, 220

Numerics

1916, 415
32-bit arithmetic, 164
64-bit arithmetic, 164
64-bit computer, 164

A

abs method, 162
abstract classes, methods— See
    inheritance.

abstract keyword, 657
Abstract Window Toolkit (AWT), 84
abstraction, 3
access control
    in class definitions, 106
accumulator, 339
ActionEvent class, 229, 673
ActionListener interface, 231
actionPerformed method, 229
activation record, 469–473
active content, 63
adapter class, 676
add method, 132
addElement method, 280
AdjustmentEvent class, 673
Alanis Morrisette, 118
ambiguity, 157
ambiguous expression, 157
and — See operator, logical.
Anna Livia Plurabelle, 118
applet, 83–85, 129–138
    add method, 132
    as a container class, 133
    as active content in a web page, 64
    buttons, 131
    class definitions, 130
    drawing and painting, 458–460
    embedding in a web page, 85
    extends, 130
    graphical user interface, 131
    init method, 131, 227
    initialization, 131
    interactivity, 130
    LayoutManagers, 133
    life cycle, 131
    paint method, 131, 458–460
    security limitations on threads, 370
    setLayout method, 133
    size of, 135
    threads, 369–377
    update method, 458
    validate method, 136